FIFTY YEARS (AND TWELVE)
OF CLASSICAL SCHOLARSHIP

FIFTY YEARS
(AND TWELVE)
of
CLASSICAL SCHOLARSHIP

Being *Fifty Years of Classical Scholarship*
Revised with Appendices

BASIL BLACKWELL · OXFORD
1968

First printed 1954
Second Edition 1968
631 10510 7

Printed by offset in Great Britain by
Alden & Mowbray Ltd
at the Alden Press, Oxford

CONTENTS

LIST OF ILLUSTRATIONS	viii
LIST OF ABBREVIATIONS	ix
PREFACE TO THE FIRST EDITION	xiii
PUBLISHER'S NOTE TO THE SECOND EDITION	xiv

I HOMER
    i Homer and the Analysts
    ii Homer and the Unitarians
    iii Homer as Oral Poetry
    By E. R. DODDS, D.LITT., Student of Christ Church and Emeritus Professor of Greek in the University of Oxford   1
    iv Homer and the Philologists
    By L. R. PALMER, Fellow of Worcester College and Professor of Comparative Philology in the University of Oxford   17
    v Homer and the Archaeologists
    By DOROTHEA GRAY, Fellow of St. Hugh's College, Oxford   24

II EARLY GREEK LYRIC POETRY
    By J. G. GRIFFITH, Fellow of Jesus College, Oxford   50

III GREEK TRAGEDY
    By T. B. L. WEBSTER, Professor of Greek in the University of London (University College)   88

IV GREEK COMEDY
    By K. J. DOVER, Professor of Greek in the University of St. Andrews   123

V THE GREEK PHILOSOPHERS
    By SIR DAVID ROSS, D.LITT., formerly Provost of Oriel College, Oxford; with supplement by D. J. ALLAN, Professor of Greek in the University of Glasgow   159

CONTENTS

VI THE GREEK HISTORIANS
By G. T. GRIFFITH, Fellow of Gonville and Caius College, Cambridge, and Laurence Reader in Ancient History in the University of Cambridge ... 182

VII GREEK ORATORS AND RHETORIC
By H. LL. HUDSON-WILLIAMS, Professor of Greek in the University of Newcastle upon Tyne ... 242

VIII HELLENISTIC POETRY
By the late E. A. BARBER, Rector of Exeter College, Oxford; with Appendix by G. GIANGRANDE, Reader in Classics at Birkbeck College, London ... 267

IX ROMAN DRAMA
By W. A. LAIDLAW, LITT.D., formerly Professor of Classics in the University of London (Queen Mary College); with Appendix on COMEDY by M. M. WILLCOCK, Professor of Classics in the University of Lancaster; and on TRAGEDY by MICHAEL COFFEY, Lecturer in Greek and Latin in the University of London (University College) ... 292

X LATE REPUBLICAN POETRY
i Lucretius
By the late C. BAILEY, D.LITT., Honorary Fellow of Balliol College, Oxford; with Appendix by D. E. W. WORMELL, Fellow of Trinity College, Dublin, and Professor of Latin ... 345

ii Catullus
By R. G. C. LEVENS, Fellow of Merton College, Oxford
... 357

XI THE AUGUSTAN POETS
By T. E. WRIGHT, formerly Professor of Humanity in the University of St. Andrews ... 387

CONTENTS

XII ROMAN ORATORY
By S. F. BONNER, Senior Lecturer in Latin and Greek in the University of Liverpool   416

XIII THE ROMAN HISTORIANS
By A. H. MCDONALD, Fellow of Clare College, Cambridge, and Lecturer in Ancient History in the University of Cambridge   465

XIV SILVER LATIN POETRY
By H. H. HUXLEY, Senior Lecturer in Latin in the University of Manchester; Visiting Associate Professor of Classics, Brown University, R.I., U.S.A.   496

ILLUSTRATIONS
(*Between pages 56 and 57*)

Plate I
'Phrynos-cup.' Black-figure vase in British Museum (B424)
Fig. 1(*a*) Birth of Athena
(*b*) Athena presenting Herakles to Zeus
From J. C. Hoppin, *Handbook of Black Figure Vases* (Paris, Champion, 1924)

Plate II
Fig. 2 Winged Geryon. Amphora in Paris (Cabinet des Médailles 202)
From A. Rumpf, *Chalkidische Vasen*, taf. VII (Berlin, de Gruyter, 1923)
Fig. 3 Herakles and the Chariot of the Sun. Scyphos in Taranto (7029)
From *Corpus Vasorum Antiquorum*, Italy, fasc. XVIII (Rome, Libreria dello Stato, 1943)

Plate III
Fig. 4 Herakles in the Cup of the Sun. Cup in Vatican
From E. Gerard, *Auserlesene Griechische Vasenbilder* (Berlin, G. Reimer, 1840-58)
Fig. 5 Anacreon and Revellers. Kylix in British Museum (E18)
From Schefold, *Bildnisse* (Basel, Benno Schwabe Verlag, 1943)

Plate IV
Fig. 6 Self-devotion of Croesus. Amphora by Myson-painter in Paris (Louvre G. 197)
From Furtwängler-Reichhold, *Griechische Vasenmalerei* (Munich, F. Bruckmann, 1904-32)

LIST OF ABBREVIATIONS

AA	Archäologischer Anzeiger
AAT	Atti della Accademia delle Scienze di Torino
AClass	Acta classica
A & R	Atene e Roma
AAWW	Anzeiger der Akademie der Wissenschaften in Wien
ABAW	Abhandlungen der bayerischen Akademie der Wissenschaften
ABSA	Annual of the British School at Athens
AC	L'Antiquité classique
AE	Ἀρχαιολογικὴ Ἐφημερίς
AFLC	Annali della Facoltà di Lettere . . . di Cagliari
AGG	Abhandlungen der Gesellschaft der Wissenschaft zu Göttingen
AGPh	Archiv für Geschichte der Philosophie
AGWG	= AGG
AHR	American Historical Review
AILC	Anales del Istituto de Literaturas Clásicas
AIV	Atti del (r.) Istituto Veneto di scienze, lettere e arti
AJA	American Journal of Archaeology
AJP, AJPh	} American Journal of Philology
ALL	Archiv für lateinische Lexicographie
APA	Abhandlungen der preussischen Akademie der Wissenschaft
ASNP	Annali della Scuola Normale Superiore di Pisa
Ath	Athenaeum
BAGB	Bulletin de l'Association Guillaume Budé
BCH	Bulletin de Correspondance hellénique
BICS	Bulletin of the Institute of Classical Studies of the University of London
BIE	Bulletin de l'Institut d'Égypte
BKT	Berliner Klassische Texte
BPh	Berliner Philologische Wochenschrift
BRL	Bulletin of the John Rylands Library
BSAA	Bulletin de la Société d'Archéologie d'Alexandrie
BSAF	Bulletin de la Société nationale des Antiquaires de France
BSAW	Berichte der sächsischen Akademie der Wissenschaft
BSC	Bollettino storico Catanese
BSG	Berichte der sächsischen Gesellschaft der Wissenschaft
CAH	Cambridge Ancient History
CE	Chronique d'Égypte
CHJ	Cambridge Historical Journal
CJ	Classical Journal
CS	Critica storica
CPh, ClPh	} Classical Philology
CQ	Classical Quarterly
CR	Classical Review
CRAI	Comptes rendus des séances de l'Académie des Inscriptions et Belles Lettres
CSSH	Comparative Studies in Society and History
C & M	Classica et Mediaevalia
CUP	Cambridge University Press
CW	Classical Weekly

LIST OF ABBREVIATIONS

EHR	English Historical Review
Er	Eranos
FA	Fasti archaeologici
F & F	Forschungen und Fortschritte (Berlin)
FGrH	F. Jacoby, Die Fragmente der griechischen Historiker
Gl	Glotta
G and R	Greece and Rome
GRBS	Greek, Roman and Byzantine Studies
HSCPh	} Harvard Studies in Classical Philology
HSPh	
HThR	Harvard Theological Review
HZ	Historische Zeitschrift
ILN	Illustrated London News
JAW	Jahresbericht über die Fortschritte der klassischen Altertumswissenschaft
JDAI	Jahrbuch des deutschen archäologischen Instituts
JHS	Journal of Hellenic Studies
JKPh	Jahrbuch für klassische Philologie
JNG	Jahrbuch für Numismatik und Geldgeschichte
JŒAI	Jahreshefte des österreichischen archäologischen Instituts in Wien
JPh	Journal of Philosophy
JRS	Journal of Roman Studies
JW	Journal of the Warburg Institute
Kl	Klio
LEC	Les Études classiques
MAL	Memorie della (r.) Accademia dei Lincei
MAT	Memorie della (r.) Accademia delle scienze di Torino
MB	Musée Belge
MDAI	Mitteilungen des deutschen archäologischen Instituts ((A) Athenische Abteilung: (R) Römische Abteilung)
MH	Museum Helveticum
Mn	Mnemosyne
NGG	Nachrichten von der Gesellschaft der Wissenschaft zu Göttingen
NJA	Neue Jahrbücher für das klassische Altertum
NJKlP	Neue Jahrbücher für klassische Philologie
NJW	Neue Jahrbücher für Wissenschaft und Jugendbildung
NRH	Nouvelle Revue historique de Droit français
OCT	Oxford Classical Text
OUP	Oxford University Press
Ox. Pap.	= P.Oxy
PAA	Πρακτικά τῆς ἐν ᾿Αθήναις ᾿Αρχαιολογικῆς ᾿Εταιρείας
PACA	Proceedings of the African Classical Association
PBA	Proceedings of the British Academy
PBSR	Papers of the British School at Rome
Phil	} Philologus
Ph	
PhQ	Philological Quarterly
PhilosQ	The Philosophical Quarterly
PhW	Philologische Wochenschrift
POxy	Oxyrhynchus Papyri
PrAPhA	Proceedings of the American Philosophical Association
PSI	Papiri della Società italiana
P-W (PW)	= RE

LIST OF ABBREVIATIONS

RA	Review archéologique
RAL	Rendiconti della (r.) Accademia dei Lincei
RBPh	Revue Belge de Philologie et d'Histoire
RCC	Revue des Cours et Conférences
RE	Pauly-Wissowa; Real-Encyclopädie der classischen Altertumswissenschaft
REA	Revue des études anciennes
REG	Revue des études grecques
REI	Revue des études Indo-européennes
REL	Revue des études latines
RFC / RFIC	Rivista di Filologia e d'Istruzione Classica
RhM / RhMus	Rheinisches Museum
RIL	Rendiconti del (r.) Istituto Lombardo di scienze et lettere
RLC	Rassegna italiana di Lingue e Letterature classiche
RP	Revue de Paris
RPh	Revue de Philologie
R Philos	Revue Philosophique
RSA	Rivista di Storia antica
RSI	Rivista Storica Italiana
SAWW	Sitzungsberichte der Akademie der Wissenschaft in Wien
SBA / SBAW	Sitzungsberichte der bayerischen Akademie der Wissenschaften
SCO	Studi Classici e Orientali
SHA / SHAW	Sitzungsberichte der Heidelberger Akademie der Wissenschaften
SIFC	Studi Italiani di Filologia Classica
SO	Symbolae Osloenses
SPAW	Sitzungsberichte der preussischen Akademie der Wissenschaften
SS / SSAC	Studi storici per l'antichità classica
SIFC	Studi Italiani di Filologica Classica
StudUrb	Studi Urbinati di Storia
TAPA / TAPhA	Transactions and Proceedings of the American Philological Association
UMS	University of Michigan Studies
VDPh	Verhandlung der Versammlung deutscher Philologen
WJA	Würzburger Jahrbücher für die Altertumswissenschaft
WS	Wiener Studien
YClS	Yale Classical Studies
YWCS	Year's Work in Classical Studies
ZDMG	Zeitschrift der Deutschen Morgenländischen Gesellschaft
ZRG	Zeitschrift für Rechtsgeschichte
ZVS	Zeitschrift für vergleichende Sprachforschung

PREFACE TO THE FIRST EDITION

IN April of this year the Classical Association held its Jubilee meeting; and the close of the half-century seems a fitting occasion for the publication of a book which sums up the advance made along the main lines of classical scholarship during that period. This advance has not been so rapid, and certainly not so spectacular, as has been that of, say physics; yet advance there has been, and that not only thanks to the discovery of new material but also because of what scholars hope is a sounder re-interpretation of the material they already have. As Anatole France once wrote, 'Chaque génération imagine à nouveau les chefs-d'œuvre antiques et leur communique de la sorte une immortalité mouvante.' It is just this *immortalité mouvante* that the contributors to the present volume now illustrate for the contemporary reader.

Brasenose College, MAURICE PLATNAUER
    Oxford.
  September 22nd, 1954

PUBLISHER'S NOTE TO THE SECOND EDITION

WITHIN a decade of its publication this book has become a rarity, and persistent demand encouraged the publisher to undertake a reprint. It was suggested that the opportunity might be taken to bring it up to date by inviting the original contributors to prepare appendices to their chapters. With a few exceptions they were able and willing to do so; other scholars have helped by furnishing appendices for the chapters of authors who have died since the book first appeared; and Professor Allan has provided a supplement to Sir David Ross's chapter on The Greek Philosophers.

June 1967

FIFTY YEARS (AND TWELVE)
OF CLASSICAL SCHOLARSHIP

CHAPTER I
HOMER
i. Homer and the Analysts
BY E. R. DODDS

IN the second volume of his *Geschichte des Altertums*, published in 1893, the great historian Eduard Meyer summed up the results achieved by the intensive study of the Homeric poems during the nineteenth century. It could, he said, be considered as scientifically proved that they were neither the work of an individual nor yet a conglomerate of 'lays', but the outcome of an activity of minstrel-poets which had extended over centuries; and he added that the stratification within each poem could be determined with an adequate measure of confidence. This was the general opinion of the time, in England as well as in Germany; the same verdict had been given, if in rather more cautious terms, by Sir Richard Jebb in his *Homer: an Introduction* (1887),[1] and by Walter Leaf in his *Companion to the Iliad* (1892). Unitarianism was not indeed dead (despite frequent announcements of its demise), but it was a heretical minority view, at least among professional scholars;[2] its chief public upholders were isolated figures like Andrew Lang[3] in England — a brilliant scholar who enjoyed amateur status — and Carl Rothe[4] in Germany. On the other hand, Lachmann's fantastic 'lay-theory' had been abandoned for good, although it continues to figure in the popular imagination (and in the books of some unitarians) as the typical outcome of Homeric analysis. With one possible exception, no serious analyst has maintained within living memory that the *Iliad* can be resolved into a conglomeration of short independent poems which an 'editor' has joined together by placing them end to end, as Dr. Lönnrot produced the Finnish pseudo-epic known as the *Kalevala*.[5] That both the Homeric poems have in their present form a carefully conceived design and a basic structural unity has long been recognized by analysts as well as unitarians: e.g. Jebb wrote that 'each of the poems forms an organic and artistic whole', while adding that certain parts 'appear to disturb the plan or to betray inferior workmanship'.[6] And on the whole the tendency of modern analysis has been to place increasing emphasis on the element of design at all stages in the assumed development of the poems; we hear much less of the 'bungling redactor', that *diabolus ex machina* whom early analysts invoked to explain every blemish that seemed to mar the faultless perfection of the 'genuine' Homeric poetry.

The view of the *Iliad* which held the field at the turn of the century, and is still today the most widely accepted alternative to unitarianism, maintains that its central subject was from the first the theme announced in the proem, the Wrath of Achilles, but that the poem has been gradually enlarged by the accretion of other material round this central nucleus. Such a view was naturally suggested by the peculiar structure of the *Iliad*, which has been described as 'a drama with retardations'; it was a natural guess that the drama formed a nucleus to which more and more retardations had in the course of time been added. Originally propounded in 1832 by one of the greatest of all Greek scholars, Gottfried Hermann, it had been developed and popularized in England by George Grote in the second volume of his *History of Greece* (1846-56). In the two generations which followed Grote it was accepted, in one form or another, by most of the leading German and English scholars — by Theodor Bergk, Wilhelm Christ, Eduard Meyer, Paul Cauer, Carl Robert, Erich Bethe, by Sir Richard Jebb, Walter Leaf, J. B. Bury, and Gilbert Murray, to name only a few. Later it was for a time eclipsed by the rival theory of Wilamowitz (see below) and by the sudden growth of unitarianism; but it has been revived in several recent analyses of the *Iliad* — in the admirable *Introduction à l'Iliade* by Mazon, Chantraine, and others (the analysis is Mazon's), and in two works by distinguished Swiss scholars, W. Theiler's essay 'Die Dichter der Ilias', and the *Kritisches Hypomnema zur Ilias* lately published by the veteran Peter Von der Mühll.[7] By most of these writers the author of the original Wrath-poem is identified, either firmly or tentatively, with the historical bearer of the personal name 'Homer'; the old view which saw in 'Homer' a mere personification of the genius of epic poetry, or the mythical eponymous ancestor of the Homeridae, has been generally (and rightly) abandoned.[8]

There is thus more agreement in principle among modern analysts than might be supposed by an unwary reader of unitarian polemics. But when it comes to defining the limits of the Wrath-poem, or determining the successive stages of the later expansion, agreement seems more remote today than it did fifty years ago. The *minimum* content of the Wrath-poem must have included at least the Quarrel of the Chiefs (Book I), the Greek defeat in Book XI, the Patrocleia (Book XVI, with the end of XV), and the death of Hector (Book XXII), together with connecting pieces which are no longer recoverable in their original form. But how much more it included remains, and seems likely to remain, a matter of dispute. Did it, for example, end with the dragging of Hector's body (Leaf)? Or with Andromache's lament at the close of Book XXII (Von der Mühll)? Or did it go on to tell of Achilles' own death, so often predicted in our *Iliad* (Robert, Wilamowitz)? Or did the tale of the Wrath always end as it does now, not with the death of Hector or of Achilles, but with the death of the Wrath itself and the ransoming of Hector's body (Mazon)? To many readers the last will seem the most reasonable assumption, despite the many signs which appear to indicate that the final book of the *Iliad* is in its present form relatively late work.[9] Again, is it certain that the original poem included no 'retardations' at all? The older analysts tended to assume this, apparently because they felt that 'Homer's' work must have had the sort of strict organic unity that Aristotle expected of a tragedy. But Homer had not had the advantage of reading Aristotle, and it may be that, like Shakespeare, he cared less about organic unity than about pleasing his audience. May he not, to that end, have included in his poem further battle-pieces which gratified the pride of Greek listeners by describing Achaean victories, and enabled traditional heroes like Diomede and Ajax to show their paces? Considerations of this kind account for the widely varying estimates of the length of the Wrath-poem, ranging between the extreme views of Bethe,[10] who cut it down to some 1500 lines, and of Mazon, who is willing to attribute to the original poet fourteen books of the present *Iliad* (Books I, XI to XVIII, and XX to XXIV). Such differences indicate the limited usefulness of the nucleus-theory, though they do not, of course, disprove its correctness. They were in fact foreseen by the founder of the German analytic school, F. A. Wolf, who wrote in a moment of pessimistic foresight 'forsitan ne probabiliter quidem demonstrari poterit, a quibus locis potissimum nova subtemina et limbi procedant'.[11]

There is hardly less disagreement about the 'stratification' of the expansions and the manner in which they were brought about. Leaf imagined a gradual process of growth, in which it was possible to distinguish two main strata: an earlier, consisting mainly of 'aristeiai' of different heroes, which had the effect of transforming the Wrath-poem into an *Iliad*, a general picture of the Trojan War; and a later, consisting of freely invented short poems, some of them of the highest quality, which reflects the humanity and the psychological interest of a later age. Bethe, on the other hand, postulated a second great individual poet (situated, rather unconvincingly, at Athens in the sixth century) who transformed the Wrath-poem at a single stroke into our *Iliad* by incorporating in it a large number of short pieces which had grown up round it in the interval. Others again, like Theiler, assume a much more complicated process of development, involving five or six different strata, but dispensing with the assumption of independent short poems. It is, however, untrue to suggest that *no* generally agreed conclusions have emerged. There are at least a few specific problems on which there is an approach to unanimity. For example, all analysts (and many unitarians) are agreed that the Doloneia (Book X) is a late addition to the poem.[12] It is, again, agreed by most analysts (and some unitarians) that the Embassy (Book IX), and the battle in Book VIII which was invented to lead up to it,[13] formed no part of the original Wrath-poem; and that certain subordinate figures — Nestor, Glaucus and Sarpedon, Aeneas — owe their prominence in the *Iliad* to later poets who introduced them to gratify local interests.

The nucleus-theory, in its traditional form, places its 'Homer' at the *beginning* of the long poetic development which produced our *Iliad*. To this it has been objected (*a*) that the language and style of the *Iliad*, even in its 'oldest' parts, is far from being 'primitive', but has a technical perfection which presupposes a long tradition of epic poetry; (*b*) that the matter of many parts of the *Iliad* seems to be saga-stuff, which presumably was current long before the tale of the Wrath was invented. To meet these and other difficulties, Wilamowitz devised the novel view which he presented in *Die Ilias und Homer* (Berlin, Weidmann, 1916). Wilamowitz's Homer comes in the *middle* of the development: living at Chios in the eighth century, he took over, combined, and in some cases remodelled, the work of various pre-Homeric poets; his own work was in turn enlarged, and in places remodelled, by a succession of post-Homeric poets. Homer's *Iliad*, according to Wilamowitz, included the main substance of Books I to VII, XI to XVII, and XXI to XXIII as far as the burial of Patroclus; the original ending is lost, and the connecting links between XVII and XXI largely obliterated by later work. But in most of this Homer was building on earlier compositions. Much of the detailed analysis fails to carry conviction: it is not easy to think that Hector's visit to Troy in Book VI is lifted from a pre-existent *Hectoreis*, and it is harder still to believe that an independent *Patrocleia* ever existed apart from the Wrath-poem. Nevertheless, *Die Ilias und Homer* is one of the great books on Homer. It is inspired throughout by a deep and true feeling for Homeric poetry, and is full of fresh and delicate observations on the many variations of style to be found in the *Iliad* — style-analysis being for Wilamowitz quite as important as structural analysis. It also marked an important advance in the understanding of the genesis of the poem. Its influence is apparent not only in the later analyses of Mazon and Von der Mühll, both of whom recognize that our *Iliad* incorporates much 'pre-Homeric' material, but in the recent work of continental unitarians on 'Homer's sources' (see below, §ii). It is not the least of Wilamowitz's services that he built in this way an undesigned bridge between the two warring schools.

Wilamowitz's date for Homer is also now widely accepted, by unitarians as well as analysts. Fifty years ago a much earlier dating was fashionable: Leaf, Jebb, Bury, Ridgeway, all dated back the older parts of the *Iliad* to the eleventh century or thereabouts. This was due in part to a misunderstanding of Homer's silence on such matters as the Dorian migration and the colonization of Asiatic Greece, in part to the discoveries of Schliemann and the recognition of 'Mycenaean' elements in Homer (see below, §v). But the evidence of the similes points clearly to Ionian authorship;[14] and it is now seen that both Homer's silences and the survival in the poems of Mycenaean elements can be explained by the conservatism of an epic tradition and, in particular, by the conservative influence of a formulaic diction. The archaeological evidence makes it difficult to maintain that anything resembling our *Iliad* existed much before the eighth century; and a *terminus ante quem* is furnished by Callinus' reference to Homer (as the author of a *Thebais!*), as well as by seventh-century allusions, imitations, and graphic representations (see below, §v) which seem to presuppose *an Iliad* (though not necessarily just the *Iliad* that we read today). But the dating of the various 'posthomerica' and 'antehomerica' incorporated in the *Iliad* still presents many unresolved problems.[15]

English writers since Leaf have contributed much less to the structural analysis of the *Iliad* than to the elucidation of its historical and cultural background. But this is perhaps the place to mention two well-known and justly admired books in English which approach the latter question, or group of questions, from the general standpoint of the analytical school — Gilbert Murray's *Rise of the Greek Epic* (Clar. Press, 1907, 4th ed., 1934), and Martin Nilsson's *Homer and Mycenae* (London, Methuen, 1933). Murray's book is nearing its half-century, and inevitably wears in places an old-fashioned air: certain of its hypotheses are outmoded and perhaps unlikely to return to favour, such as the theory which sees in a large number of Homeric heroes faded gods or 'year spirits'.[16] But it will, and should, continue to be read, not only for its characteristically vivid portrayal of the conditions of life in the Submycenaean Age, but more especially for its inquiry into the nature of 'traditional books' and its interpretation of the growth of the *Iliad* in the light of that inquiry (we now have reason to believe that the Homeric poems are in fact oral compositions, but many of the illuminating things that Murray has to say about the traditional book are equally applicable to an oral tradition). Nilsson's book is predominantly concerned with the historical and archaeological questions which are discussed below (§v); but it includes also sound and valuable chapters on the principles at issue between analysts and unitarians, on Homeric language and style, on the origin and transmission of epic poetry, and on Homeric mythology (a subject on which its author is probably the greatest living expert). There is no book on Homer which the present writer would more willingly place in the hands of the intelligent inquirer, whether sixth-form boy, undergraduate, or general reader, if only because its author has the rare virtue of not claiming that his arguments prove more than they do.

The *Odyssey* is a very different kind of poem from the *Iliad*,[17] and is thought by most analysts (and some unitarians) to have had a different authorship and a rather different history. Among other differences, it has a much closer structural unity and lends itself less easily to a theory of gradual accretion round a nucleus. Nevertheless it reveals some striking structural inconsistencies, and the range of variation in style is perhaps wider than in the *Iliad*. Many of the problems which it poses were already seen and stated by Kirchhoff (*Die homerische Odyssee und ihre Entstehung*, 1859); his observations were brilliantly exploited and developed, with much more feeling for the poetry and understanding of the historical background, in Wilamowitz's remarkable early book, *Homerische Untersuchungen* (1884; near the end of his long life he revised some of its conclusions in *Die Heimkehr des Odysseus*, 1927). In our own time, besides many minor critical contributions, important analyses of the *Odyssey* have been published by Bethe, Schwartz, Bérard, Von der Mühll, and two scholars of a younger generation, Friedrich Focke and Reinhold Merkelbach.[18] All these, save Bérard's, are in German; the only book in English which covers this line of country is W. J. Woodhouse's ingenious and charmingly written *Composition of Homer's Odyssey* (Clar. Press, 1930). Woodhouse's standpoint was unitarian: the author of our Odyssey was for him 'Homer'. But he utilized many of the discoveries of the German analysts as a means of getting back to what he regarded as 'Homer's sources'. His main originality lay in his recognition of the numerous folklore themes which are among the ingredients of the *Odyssey*.[19]

Limitations of space forbid any description of the results arrived at by individual analysts. While there is virtual unanimity on certain points, such as the lateness of Book XXIV[20] and of some parts of the Nekyia[21] (both already recognized by Aristarchus), there is, as might be expected, more divergence of opinion about the growth of the poem than there is among *Iliad*-analysts, most of whom have at least the nucleus-theory in common. But certain general probabilities may be said to have emerged from the long debate. (i) Whereas the *Iliad* grew out of a Wrath-poem, 'the *Odyssey*', as Von der Mühll has put it, 'was always an *Odyssey*'; from the first it told a connected tale of Odysseus' homeward voyage and his vengeance on the suitors. But there were different versions of the story, which have been combined in our poem but not quite perfectly harmonized.[22] There were longer and shorter accounts of the hero's wanderings, which freely borrowed incidents and motifs from older tales of travel, including the Argonaut-story.[23] And there were rival versions of the Vengeance, whose imperfect harmonization is responsible for a number of obscurities, in particular the curious behaviour ascribed to Penelope in Books XVIII and XIX.[24] (ii) The 'Telemachy' (i.e. approximately Books I to IV, with XV, XVI, and the beginning of XVII) formed no part of the older *Odyssey*. But it is very doubtful if it ever existed as an independent poem. On this point Focke seems to the present writer to have reason on his side (against the opinion of most of the earlier analysts[25]). The simplest view seems to be that the whole Telemachus sub-plot was invented by the same poet who gave the *Odyssey* its present shape by combining all the best features of the older versions and adding some further expansions in his own characteristic manner (e.g. the extra day which Odysseus is allowed to spend with the Phaeacians[26]). It has often been remarked, even by analysts,[27] that the *Odyssey* for all its discrepancies bears, much more than the *Iliad*, the impress of a single mind; also that it makes as a whole an impression of relative modernity. This is perhaps best explained by the assumption that the poem was enlarged and reconstructed in the seventh century[28] by a single poet, who allowed himself a much freer hand than any of those who made their contributions to the *Iliad*.

In conclusion, it may be suggested that what is most needed now is not further analyses of either poem, which at the present time would, one fears, have even less prospect of general acceptance than had their predecessors, but rather a careful review of the traditional analytic arguments and methods, in the light both of unitarian criticisms and of Milman Parry's proof that the poems are oral compositions.

ii. Homer and the Unitarians

BY E. R. DODDS

It is now more than thirty years since the old logical game of discovering inconsistencies in Homer was replaced in public esteem by the new and equally enjoyable aesthetic game of explaining them away. The exhilarating conviction that for several generations the best scholars in Europe had been playing the wrong game dawned on the public mind with surprising suddenness shortly after the First World War. It may be surmised that the reasons for so abrupt a change lay in part outside the field of Homeric scholarship. There is evidence[29] that in some quarters resentments left behind by the war were not without influence; Homeric analysis was in the main a German achievement, and the arrogance of some of its exponents was felt to be typical of the German mind. But the basic causes certainly lay deeper. Parallel changes occurred about the same time in New Testament criticism, where the confident claims of nineteenth-century analysts were similarly called in question; and in textual criticism proper, where the old arrogant disregard for manuscript tradition began to be replaced in many quarters by an almost superstitious reverence for it. And something not altogether dissimilar happened in philosophy, where the whole speculative structure reared by nineteenth-century idealism was swept away within a few years. All these developments can be regarded as necessary processes of disinfection — a cutting out of unsound wood. And in the case of Homer the reckless proliferation of hypotheses in the preceding half-century certainly called for a drastic pruning operation. But that was not all. The notion of a monolithic Homer, a supreme poetic genius whose work it was sacrilege to analyse, undoubtedly corresponded to certain tendencies of the time — a distrust of cold logic, a yearning to follow 'the dictates of the heart', and, more specifically, a widespread rejection of the intellectual approach to poetry.[30]

The unitarian reaction was thus to some extent a manifestation of the *Zeitgeist*. It was announced almost simultaneously by J. A. Scott in America, by Sheppard in England, and by Drerup in Germany. Drerup[31] was the most learned and systematic of the three; in particular, he adduced much interesting evidence from other early literatures (which, however, has seemed to analysts to prove the opposite of what Drerup thought it proved). Sheppard[32] represented the aesthetic wing: he contented himself with discovering 'patterns' in the *Iliad* which seemed to him to establish its unity of design and therefore its unity of authorship (but is not the inference from the former to the latter a question-begging *non sequitur*?). It was, however, Scott's book, *The Unity of Homer* (Berkeley, Univ. of California Press, 1921), which made the deepest impression, at least on the English-speaking public. A skilful if unscrupulous controversialist, he succeeded by a careful choice of examples in conveying the suggestion that the greatest scholars of Germany were not only pedants but fools. He devoted pages to *minutiae* such as the trivial oversight about Pylaemenes[33] — killed in *Iliad* Book V, resurrected in Book XIII to attend his father's funeral — which no modern analyst thinks important, while saying nothing at all about the Embassy problem, about the Διάπειρα problem, or about the apparent doublets in the *Odyssey*. The reader was left with the impression that the analysts' case was founded on trivialities.[34] The part of Scott's work which has been most generally accepted as important by scholars is the series of painstaking statistical arguments by which he tried to show that there are no significant linguistic differences between the two poems. He certainly revealed the inaccuracy of some earlier statistics; but it may be questioned whether in matters of vocabulary and grammar a statistical approach is the right one. The most significant differences, being qualitative, often escape the net of the statistician.[35]

A feature common to Scott, Drerup, and many later unitarians is their passionate insistence on Homer's 'originality'. This led Drerup into an extreme anti-historicism: everything in Homer was poetic invention, and most of it was his own invention. Certainly, the English historical school has been guilty at times of fantastic exaggerations through treating Homer, in Wilamowitz's phrase, 'as if he were a war-correspondent'. One of its members has even professed to know the exact date of Hector's death: it occurred on August 28th, 1185 B.C.![36] In the present writer's opinion it is permissible to doubt whether the debate about the identity of the Phaeacians, or even the debate about the identity of Homer's Ithaca, is a discussion about anything real. But it is much more difficult to doubt, with Drerup and Carpenter,[37] that the Trojan War took place (see below, §v). Scott did not go so far; but he put up a plausible case, which has recently been supported on different grounds by Schadewaldt and Wade-Gery,[38] for regarding Hector, and with him the whole Wrath-story, as a poetic invention. It must be said, however, that in the light of our present awareness of 'antehomerica' to equate 'poetic invention' with 'Homer's invention' is to beg a very large question. And in any case the unitarian emphasis on originality appears somewhat misplaced. As Nilsson has reminded us, 'ancient poets, and epic poets especially, did not think that the greatest possible independence of previous writers increases a poet's glory'.[39] Nor, for that matter, did Shakespeare.

The 'naive unitarians', of whom Scott, Drerup, and Sheppard are representative, held a fundamentalist faith in the integrity of the Homeric Scriptures; their religion forbade them to make any concession whatever to the infidel, although it compelled them at times to fall back on arguments as unconvincing as the worst efforts of the analysts. But the purity of the original faith soon declined. Old difficulties were rediscovered, heresies arose, and breaches appeared in the monolithic structure. In his *Homer: the Origins and the Transmission* (Clar. Press, 1924) T. W. Allen, the most learned and formidable of English unitarians, admitted in principle that the poems contain both 'posthomerica' and 'antehomerica'. With the Alexandrine scholars, he recognized that the end of the *Odyssey* is an 'interpolation'; he also held that Homer worked on the basis of a pre-existent verse chronicle, and that the Catalogue of Ships, which was certainly not composed for our *Iliad*, is the oldest piece of Greek verse we possess. On the last point his view appears to be substantially confirmed by recent research, and is accepted in principle by Bowra, Miss Lorimer and Wade-Gery.[40] But there is much in his book which cannot be accepted, in particular his opinion that Homer 'sang the language he spoke' (see p. 35, n. 19), and his extraordinary reliance on the Greco-Roman romances of Dictys and Dares as preserving an authentic tradition of the Trojan War.

Further bits of the monolith have been discarded by subsequent unitarians. Schadewaldt, Miss Lorimer, Wade-Gery, and recently Bowra have rejected the Doloneia; Miss Lorimer rejects also *Iliad* VIII (though *Iliad* IX must be Homer's, since its removal 'would lower the value of the poem'[41]), together with the Supplicatio in Book VI, the Shifting of the Arms in the *Odyssey*, and some other things. There has also been a revival of 'separatism': unitarian scholars like Reinhardt,[42] Miss Lorimer, and Wade-Gery have not concealed their opinion that there are two monoliths and not one. In short, 'naive' unitarianism is slowly[43] being replaced by a 'critical' unitarianism which does not despise analytical methods and is prepared to adopt some part of the analysts' conclusions. While the analysts have gradually advanced to a fuller appreciation of the over-all design, their opponents are moving from angry assertion of the design to a closer study of the sometimes jarring parts. One may even feel that between the more moderate spokesmen of the two schools the difference is now largely one of terminology: what the analysts call nuclei or prototypes, the unitarians call sources; what the analysts call expansions, the unitarians call interpolations. Nevertheless, the schizophrenia which has so long afflicted Homeric studies has not been completely overcome. Analysts and unitarians are slow to learn from each other, and sometimes give the impression of not having troubled to read each other's works.

Apart from general studies of the economy and cultural background of the poems, such as Bowra's well-known and very useful book, *Tradition and Design in the Iliad* (Clar. Press, 1930), or the more recent *Homère* of A. Severyns (3 small vols., Brussels, Office de Publicité, 1943-48), and from Wade-Gery's interesting but highly speculative attempt to establish the personality and date of Homer (*The Poet of the Iliad*, Cambridge Univ. Press, 1952), the main positive work of the unitarians in recent years has been directed towards the exploration of 'Homer's sources'. This is really the old analytic game in a new form, which is felt to be compatible with a proper recognition of the essential unity of each of the poems. One example, Woodhouse's book on the *Odyssey*, has already been mentioned. Others are Reinhardt's penetrating and original study of the sources of Odysseus' travels;[44] Kakridis' convincing proof that the Meleager-story in *Iliad* IX is abbreviated from an older poem on the Wrath of Meleager;[45] and the thesis recently developed by Pestalozzi, Howald and Schadewaldt,[46] according to which a whole series of motifs in the *Iliad* were borrowed from an older poem, the 'Cyclic' *Aethiopis* (or its predecessor), which recounted the slaying of Memnon by Achilles and Achilles' own death at the hands of Paris. As to this last contention, certain of the motifs in question do look as if they had been invented for the Memnon story, but others, like the Funeral Games and the avenging of a friend, may well have been drawn by both poets from a dateless traditional stock; and in an oral tradition it is perfectly possible for two poems which belonged to the repertory of the same reciters to have influenced each other reciprocally, and to have continued to influence each other over a long period.[47]

It may be thought, finally, that the unitarians, no less than their rivals, ought to re-examine the validity of some of their own arguments. They have let a salutary breath of fresh air into the stale den of the Homeric specialist; but as a recent critic has said, there is a real danger of their movement developing 'internal excesses rather distressingly like those which contributed so much to the collapse of the analysts'.[48] In particular, we should beware of importing modern psychological subtleties into Homer;[49] and should also remember that in poems designed for piecemeal oral recitation there is a limit to the amount of deliberate cross-reference ('Fernverbindung') which it is reasonable to postulate.[50]

iii. Homer as Oral Poetry

BY E. R. DODDS

We have still to consider what is perhaps the most important single discovery about Homer made during the past half-century, the decisive proof that the poems are oral compositions. This is mainly if not entirely[51] due to a gifted American scholar, Milman Parry. The essentials of his proof are contained in his Paris thesis, *L'épithète traditionelle chez Homère* (Paris, 'Les Belles Lettres', 1928); but the English reader can form a good idea of his work from the two long papers which he published in *Harvard Studies in Classical Philology*, vols. 41 (1930) and 43 (1932).[52] His argument was cumulative, but his main point was that the peculiar technique of the poems, with their recurrent epithets, recurrent formulaic phrases, recurrent descriptions of scenes and situations, must have been devised as a safeguard against a possible breakdown in improvisation. He showed, for example, that for each of 37 leading characters in the two poems the poet has a stock descriptive phrase of exactly the same length, extending from the caesura to the end of the line, and normally only one such phrase for each (on the principle of 'epic economy'). And he argued that the purpose of this provision lay in its enabling the poet to apply any statement he wishes to any of his characters without risk of metrical breakdown, provided he lets the statement end at the caesura; he has then only to select from stock the appropriate descriptive phrase to complete safely and simultaneously his line and his sentence. Parry supplied a negative check on this by showing that no such system of metrically controlled epithets is to be found in pen-poets like Apollonius Rhodius. On the other hand he showed (and it has been independently shown by the Chadwicks) that techniques broadly similar to Homer's, though less elaborate, have been developed for a similar purpose in the oral poetry of other societies.

That the Homeric poems are oral compositions is of course no new idea. It was put forward by Robert Wood in 1767, and developed (as regards the original state of the poems) by Wolf in 1795. But before Milman Parry it was open to any one to deny the assertion, and many scholars dismissed it as out of the question. This seems to be no longer possible; and some current theses, both analytic and unitarian, may need considerable readjustment in consequence. Parry unfortunately died young, before he had worked out the implications of his own discovery, and, strangely enough, these have not yet been adequately discussed. His work was received with hostility by the aesthetic school (this was not their notion of how great poetry is produced), and it appears to be still largely unknown in Central Europe;[53] its importance was recognized, however, by Nilsson,[54] and is today generally acknowledged by English and French scholars.

If the poems were composed without the use of writing, the question when they were first written down is of vital consequence. For if they passed through even a short period of oral transmission, it becomes impossible to claim that what we read today is the *ipsissima verba* of the individual poet Homer. Oral transmission can preserve the substance of a long poetic narrative, often with remarkable fidelity; but it would be a miracle if it preserved it *verbatim*. To escape this embarrassing conclusion, it has lately been suggested that Homer did indeed compose his poems orally, but subsequently wrote them down, having learned to write in the meantime.[55] It may be doubted whether this convenient explanation will win wide acceptance. For one thing, the separatists, who are now probably in the majority, will have to imagine two different oral poets at two different dates each acquiring in the nick of time the means of preserving his exact words for posterity. Even less probable is the view that Homer was a pen-poet using an inherited oral technique.[56] For it appears incredible that a pen-poet would fall into the unmetrical or strikingly inappropriate use of formulae which we find at times in the poems. As Parry pointed out,[57] these are the characteristic marks of oral composition. Further, devaluation of formulae by inappropriate use seems to be much commoner in the *Odyssey* than in the *Iliad*,[58] and is especially noticeable in parts which analysts consider late. This looks less like the carelessness of Homer misapplying his own formulae than like the carelessness of a later oral poet: it suggests that parts of the *Odyssey* date from a period of declining oral technique.

The art of writing was certainly known in the latter part of the eighth century. But it does not follow that the oral poets were literate — literacy seems to kill the oral technique, and some of them, like the author of the *Hymn to Apollo*,[59] were blind men — or that, if they were, they wrote down poems as long as the *Iliad*. One may ask, with Bethe,[60] whether such a feat was technically possible in the eighth century, and, with Carpenter,[61] whether either the poets or their audience had a sufficient motive for attempting it. As the latter puts it, 'in a community where oral literature flourishes, there must be some special occasion or incentive to justify the otherwise pointless expenditure of energy involved in manuscript notation'. Like Cauer, Wackernagel,[62] and others, he sees the special occasion in the institution of recitations at the Panathenaea, where the poems had to be recited ἐξ ὑποβολῆς, each rhapsode beginning where his predecessor left off. This would account for the legend of the Peisistratean recension, which 'assembled' the 'scattered' poems of Homer, hitherto orally preserved.[63] That legend, which had played a great part in the theories of Wolf and other early analysts, was for a time wholly discredited by the criticisms of Lehrs, Wilamowitz, and Allen.[64] But several recent writers[65] have urged that it contains at least a kernel of truth: we can accept it as fairly certain (a) that in the fourth-century dispute between Athenians and Megarians about interpolations in Homer both parties knew or believed that a written redaction of Homer had been made at Athens in the sixth century; (b) that at the time of the dispute no other redaction was available for comparison. Taken together these two facts may be held to support the assumption that the poems were first written down at Athens, though they plainly do not prove it.

Whatever be the truth about the 'Peisistratean recension', the supposition that the poems have passed through a period of oral transmission can be used to explain a number of their characteristics. It will account for the concertina-like structure of the *Iliad*: when time was no object, the oral poet could recite the poem at full length and perhaps insert (as oral reciters do[66]) fresh episodes of his own composition; when his audience was in a hurry, he could leave out anything up to two-thirds of it without making more structural changes than a skilled reciter could improvise, and he would still have 'sung the Wrath of Achilles'. It will also account for what looks like conflation of variants, as in the Diapeira, or duplication of incidents, as at several points in the *Odyssey*: the oral poet, piously anxious to preserve and utilize whatever seems to him best in the work of his predecessors, will at times fuse together features derived from different local versions, and at others duplicate an incident rather than sacrifice either version of it.[67] Again, it will explain the presence of a few seemingly seventh-century elements in a substantially eighth-century poem: such things as the allusions to hoplite equipment which appear sporadically in the *Iliad* (see §v) might well be thoughtlessly slipped in by a reciter in the course of improvisation, but are less easily understood as deliberate yet apparently motiveless 'interpolations' in a written text. And finally, it will explain why, while Hesiod's *Theogony* evidently presupposes Homer, the Homeric poems appear in places to imitate the *Theogony*; for we know that reciters transfer passages from one poem in their repertory to another, just as actors transfer lines from one play to another.

It seems clear that the comparative study of oral poetry — full of pitfalls as all comparative study is — must in future be a matter of serious concern to Homeric scholars. The material for it exists in abundance, particularly in the three stately volumes of the Chadwicks' great work, *The Growth of Literature* (Cambridge Univ. Press, 1932-40), and in Parry's still unpublished collections of Jugo-Slav oral poetry at Harvard. Some of the questions which it raises for the Homeric scholar are discussed in Bowra's new book, *Heroic Poetry* (London, Macmillan, 1952); but much remains to be done. It will also be necessary, if the view taken above is correct, to adjust many traditional positions and arguments to the consequences that flow from Parry's work. Obviously, on this view, 'naive' unitarianism will cease to be tenable (if it ever was); but scholars will also have to abandon finally the sort of 'naive' analysis which claims to recover older poems from the *Iliad* and the *Odyssey* by a process of simple subtraction,[68] since in oral transmission successive poets not only incorporate but as a rule remodel earlier work. Analysts, again, will have to be more cautious in using arguments from contradiction, since in this matter oral poetry is naturally more tolerant than are written compositions; but this principle of 'oral tolerance' has limits, which can only be settled, if at all, by comparative studies. So too with arguments from repetition. We know now that most of the recurrent elements are formulaic, and are drawn from an ancient traditional stock; every poet uses them as often as he needs them. But it will still be open to the analyst to point to cases where lines evidently composed for a specific situation are elsewhere misapplied to a different situation, and to ask whether the original poet is likely to have so misused his own invention. In these respects as in others the Homeric Question is far from being *chose jugée*.

iv. Homer and the Philologists

BY L. R. PALMER

The progress of philological research into the Homeric language may conveniently be reviewed in 1954, since 1953 saw the completion of the first full-scale grammar of the Homeric language[1] since Monro[2] and van Leeuwen.[3] While grammatical work is necessarily concerned largely with minutiae, a brief survey[4] must confine itself to generalities.

It has become increasingly clear that many of the forms presented in the manuscripts of Homer are orthographical errors which occurred early in the tradition. Meillet[1a] has summarized the problems of reconstituting the *Urtext* with his customary lucidity. False division of words is responsible for certain strange forms such as νήδυμος (B 2 and K 187), a metrically convenient form which was then generalized (e.g. ν 79). The adjective ὀκρυόεις had a similar origin (see below). Leumann[5] has given other instances of this phenomenon.

It is well known, too, that the original text of Homer did not distinguish between long and short ε and ο respectively. The transcription of ē and ō into the conventions of the reformed alphabet offered difficulties in the case of words no longer current in the spoken language: hence ΚΑΙΡΟΣΕΟΝ was rendered as καιροσέων instead of καιρουσσέων, ΘΕΟΜΕΝ as θείομεν instead of θήομεν, etc. Meillet also believed that double vowels in hiatus were written only singly in the original text. Thus κλέ(F)ε' ἀνδρῶν was written ΚΛΕΑΝΔΡΟΝ and this accounts for the

c

vulgate's κλέα ἀνδρῶν (I 187, 524) with its intolerable hiatus; we should read κλέε' ἀνδρῶν. Again, the genitive singular of σπέος was σπέεος, which being first written as ΣΠΕΟΣ was subsequently interpreted as σπείους to remove the apparent metrical irregularities. We can thus also account for the difficult contracted genitives such as εἰς Αἰόλου κλυτὰ δώματα κ 60, for which we should restore Αἰόλοο, originally written ΑΙΟΛΟ. Again, as Payne Knight saw, ὀκρυοέσσης in Z 344 is due to a false division of κακομηχάνοο κρυοέσσης. This hypothesis of a single writing of double vowels has been accepted by Chantraine and Schwyzer,[6] although the latter, like Kretschmer, points out that epigraphical confirmation is lacking for the orthographical convention.

Meillet also held that the orthographical distinction between ε and η, and ο and ω was later than the first written text of Homer. This is implied by the scholiast T on H 238 (on βῶν v. l. βοῦν). This hypothesis would account for phenomena such as θείομεν (for θήομεν written originally ΘΕΟΜΕΝ,) μαχήσασθαι (for μαχέσσασθαι written ΜΑΧΕΣ-) and the like. Both Schwyzer[7] and Chantraine[8] would reject this theory. The latter supposes that the poems were committed to writing in Ionia, where H was used (e.g. in Miletus) from the seventh century, and ω from the beginning of the sixth. Orthographic changes may have occurred during the transmission of the text in Ionia itself. How then are we to account for ἕως (before vowel) and εἵως (before consonant)? Metre demands the primitive Ionic ἧος or even the Aeolic ἆος. If the written tradition started in Ionia, where H was written from early times, at what stage and by what process did εἵως arise from ἧος? The explanation is easy if we assume early Attic writing as ΕΟΣ. which was semi-modernized as εἵως when the reformed orthography came into use. Adaptation of the current pronunciation to metrical use, Schwyzer's tentative explanation (*loc. cit.*), can hardly account for the rendering of a trochee as εω. Chantraine, for his part, ascribes the false diphthong to the 'analogy of ἕως', which has no diphthong. ῥεῖα presents a similar problem.[9] We must assume Aeolic ϝρᾶα (or ϝρᾶ), Ionic ῥῆα. ῥέα, which occurs nine times with synizesis, is suspect and presumably conceals the Aeolic form ϝρᾶ.

The problem of distraction or diectasis (e.g. ὁράᾳς, ὁρόωντες) continues to divide scholars. Such forms are peculiar to Homer, and Chantraine[10] is among those who would deny them any real existence. He leans towards Wackernagel's[11] explanation that the open forms (ὁράεις, ὁράοντες) were originally present and that when the contraction became habitual in the spoken language, metre was restored by a disyllabic rendering in recitation. Schwyzer[12] favours Kretschmer's[13] theory that the contracted vowel in current pronunciation had a double accent. Hermann[14] has argued in favour of the assimilation theory, according to which the Homeric forms present an intermediate stage between the open and the contracted forms. However, an example like ἕης for ἧς (Π 208) on the analogy of δο(ῦ) suggests that diectasis had become for later rhapsodists an artificial and arbitrary procedure.

When such errors of the tradition have been removed and the original text reconstituted the language still presents a strange appearance. The dialect is basically Ionic (ᾱ is in general replaced by η), yet unmistakably Aeolic features[15] are present (e.g. πίσυρες, πέλομαι, ἄμμε, ὔμμε, datives in -εσσι, perfect participles like κεκλήγοντες, etc., often disguised as -ῶτες, infinitives in -μεναι and -μεν, patronymic adjectives like Τελαμώνιος, third person plurals of the type ἤγερθεν for Ionic ἠγέρθησαν, and the athematic conjugation of contracted verbs such as φορήμεναι, κε for ἄν, etc.).

Some scholars would deny that forms such as ἱκέταο, λαόν, πολέμοιο are necessarily to be assigned to Aeolic. The Ionic of the Homeric poems, it has been argued, goes back to an earlier date than our earliest inscriptions,[16] so that -οιο may be the *Ionic* ancestor of later -οο, -ου, while -ᾱο may be ascribed to an Ionic earlier than the change of ᾱ to η and the quantitative metathesis. Monro even questioned whether -εσσι was a mark of Aeolic, pointing out that such datives occur in certain West Greek dialects, so that it may have been a general tendency which cannot be excluded from Ionic. There is, however, general agreement that such forms in West Greek are merely outcrops revealing the Achaean substratum in the Doric dialects of that region. After all possible concessions have been made to the archaists there remains a stubborn core of forms which must be classified as specifically Aeolic innovations: among these are the datives in -εσσι and the athematic forms of contracted verbs (φορήμεναι, etc.).

The Attic features present in our texts have been examined by

Wackernagel.[17] They are few and unimportant and it is clear that 'the Homeric epics were finished when they came to Athens and that only few and slight alterations and additions were made in Athens'.[18]

Various hypotheses have been put forward to account for the dialect-mixture in the epic language. Wholly untenable is the suggestion that a mixed dialect of this kind represents the spoken language of any historical Greek community.[19] It is true that the Ionians occupied certain originally Aeolic towns such as Smyrna and that the dialect-inscriptions of Chios show an admixture of Lesbian features (such as πρήξοισι for πρήξουσι). But no historical parallel has been produced for the type of mixture presented by the Homeric poems. It is difficult to believe that any spoken language possessed (to give only a few examples) at one and the same time three different genitive singulars for a single noun-type as -οιο, -οο, -ου, or that a personal pronoun could be optionally ὔμμε or ὐμέας or ὐμᾶς, or that it could use ἐλελίχθησαν in one sentence and ἐλέλιχθεν in the next. Dialect mixture can be observed even in a single word: στήθεσσιν has an Aeolic inflection but an Ionian ν-ephelkustikon. Further, if, as Nilsson points out,[20] Wilamowitz's theory were correct, 'it would be astonishing that Aeolisms appearing on Chios were absent from Homeric speech'.

August Fick and F. Bechtel, despite stubborn persistence, failed to convince scholars that the poems were originally composed in Aeolic and subsequently translated into Ionic forms, the Aeolic forms being left standing only if they were not metrically equivalent to the corresponding Ionic forms. The facts remained even more stubborn: in Z 106 we find ἐλελίχθησαν but ἐλέλιχθεν three lines later. Bechtel continued his endeavours to diagnose early and late sections on linguistic grounds but finally admitted that Ionic traces are evident even in the earliest parts of the *Iliad*.[21] The inescapable conclusion is that dialect mixture is a characteristic of the language in which the Homeric poems were actually composed. As P. Giles[22] pointed out, Homer comes at the end of an epoch not at the beginning, although 'many changes in his work were no doubt brought about by inaccurate recitation and by adaptation to Ionic and Athenian audiences'.

The thesis that the epic language is artificial received powerful support from the researches of Witte[23] and Meister.[24] Witte classified the archaic (Aeolic) phenomena according to their prosodic shape and place in the verse. Thus -αο and -αων occur predominantly at the end of the verse. The great majority of -οιο genitives occur before the feminine caesura or in the fifth and sixth feet. Patronymic adjectives precede the bucolic diaeresis or the end of the verse. Similar facts are adduced for poetical coinages: thus προσώπατα and προσώπασι occur before the bucolic diaeresis. Metrical convenience again governs the alternation of active and middle in εἰσορόωντι, εἰσοράασθαι; ἰκάνομαι; διώκετο, etc. The formulaic nature of Homeric diction (see section iii) reveals itself in numerous ways. We can observe a distinct tendency to make the different case-forms of a noun prosodically equivalent: 'Ἀντιφάταο, 'Ἀντιφατῆα; Αἰθιόπεσσι, Αἰθιοπῆας; εὐρέα πόντον, εὐρέϊ πόντῳ. Moreover 'formulae which had become fixed in certain places of the verse never move from this position'. For instance, the uncontracted forms ἔπλεε, ἦτεε occur before the bucolic diaeresis, and πάϊς is found forty-four times in the same position. Witte's conclusion from his researches is summed up in the paradoxical statement that 'the language of the Homeric poems is a creation of the epic verse'.

Meister, too, emphasized the importance of the metre: the analogical genitive πατέρος, for instance, occurs exclusively in the fourth and fifth feet, whereas there is no such restriction on πατρός. The same is true of the accusative εὐρέα (πόντον).

The inconsistent treatment of digamma [25] (against over 3000 places where the influence of this sound is metrically apparent, there are over 600 instances where it is neglected) is merely one more aspect of the artificiality of the epic language. Whether these divergent forms are chronologically or dialectically different elements, the explanation lies in a long bardic tradition. In the earlier period of verse-making digamma was pronounced in the spoken language and formulae were coined in which it played its part as a full consonant. In the course of time the sound was dropped in spoken Ionic, and, while the traditional formulae continued to make their influence felt, new verses were made in which digamma was neglected. As Chantraine [26] has written, 'tout se passe comme si les derniers aèdes avaient disposé d'un double jeu de formes, les unes plus archaïques, les autres plus récentes'.

While we may thus distinguish earlier and later linguistic forms, and most scholars would agree with Witte that 'centuries of poetic practice were required before the language of the Greek epic assumed the form which it presents to us', and indeed that an unbroken tradition of formulaic diction reaches back into the Mycenaean age,[27] philologists have not been able to present an acceptable chronological analysis of the poems based on linguistic criteria. As we have seen, Bechtel himself, one of the most stubborn defenders of Fick's hypothesis, was forced to admit Ionic influence even in the earliest strata of the *Iliad*. Indeed, it can be said that philologists in general have shared in the revolution which the 'Homeric question' has undergone since the turn of the century. The most recent authoritative survey[27a] of the linguistic aspect of the problem, in a paragraph headed 'Parties "récentes" et parties "anciennes" ', after some hesitant suggestions ('sans doute n'est il pas interdit de penser . . .') about late linguistic forms as symptoms of late composition, concludes with a reference to J. A. Scott's third chapter, in which the unitarian reaction reached its most hybristic intensity. Mazon, too, begins his own analysis with a virtual denial of the relevance of the linguistic evidence. The present writer was inclined to regard the different linguistic ingredients as so many colours on the palette of the artist; the history of pigments, it might be argued, has little relevance for a critic concerned with the design and composition of a picture.

It is, of course, possible that the oldest preserved Homeric verse was not composed until all the processes of linguistic development sketched above had ceased, and the interpretation of the linguistic evidence just adumbrated might command credence if the Homeric style and language were uniform. Witte,[28] however, was of the opinion that linguistic innovations provide a sure criterion for the separation of earlier and later strata. Bolling,[29] too, in his review of Meister's book, numbers himself among those 'who have hoped that the study of the Homeric language would contribute decisively to the solution of the Homeric question', and he gave as an illustration the distribution of the κ-forms of the aorist such as θήκατο, ἔδωκεν so frequently attested in the *Odyssey* and the later strata of the *Iliad*. G. P. Shipp[30] has made a systematic study of the distribution in the *Iliad* of forms classified as late in Chantraine's Grammar. He finds them predominantly in similes, digressions and 'comments'. His conclusion is: 'The similes of the *Iliad* are characterized by linguistic lateness. Late forms occur much more frequently than in narrative and archaisms are hardly found. More than half the similes of any length include late forms and no significant difference is observable between the similes of different parts of the poem.' On other evidence for the date of the similes see section i, n. 14. Shipp's evidence might perhaps be explained away as one more instance of ancient sensitivity to differences of genre. A more modern linguistic tone might be regarded as appropriate in similes drawn from contemporary life. This is, however, an unsatisfactory hypothesis, for it would be difficult to understand why a poet of such refined linguistic technique should give, for instance, the visit of the old women to the temple of Athena (Z 264ff) a linguistic 'new look', or that he should make the aged Nestor not merely garrulous but also neological. (Shipp has confirmed earlier impressions that the Nestorian passages contain many late forms.)

This last point leads on to another notable recent philological contribution. Professor M. Leumann[31] has attacked the problem of stratification from a different angle. The formulaic technique[32] often preserved words and phrases which no longer formed part of the spoken language. Hence they were liable to be misunderstood. A crass example from Alexandrian poetry is the pseudo-Theocritus' στήτα (*Syr.* 14) 'woman', which is due to a misinterpretation of διαστήτην ἐρίσαντε in A 6. Since no poet would so misinterpret his own work, such misunderstandings, if established, would appear to be incontrovertible evidence of stratification. Thus the negative compound adjective ἀταλάφρων is applied appropriately to Astyanax in Z 400 in the meaning 'timid', 'not steadfast' (cf. ταλάφρων N 300). This word was later interpreted as 'thinking like a child' and an adjective ἀταλός 'tender' was extracted (Y 222, λ 39). Now in the 'Shield' episode youths and maidens are dancing (ποσὶ σκαίροντες) and they are described as ἀταλὰ φρονέοντες (Σ 567). From this dancing context the adjective apparently came to mean 'skittish' and was applied to πῶλοι (so Y 222). Finally we find the word again in a dance context in the verse written on the Dipylon jug (IG 1. 492 a): *hος νυν ὀρχἐστōν παντōν ἀταλōτατα παιзει*. Here the meaning is apparently 'skilfully, gracefully', but the verse is evidently based on models of which Σ 567 is representative. Thus we have a long chain of re-interpretations starting from the transparent ἀ-ταλάφρων of Z 400 and ending in the verse on the Dipylon jug, which is dated to the eighth century B.C. (!) Again, in Π 471 παρήορος is used in its technical sense 'trace-horse'; in H 156 (a Nestorian passage) the phrase is misunderstood and the noun misinterpreted as an adjective meaning 'sprawling'. A similar misunderstanding of a technical word may occur in E 586, where κύμβαχος is used adjectivally of a man who falls on to his head in the deep sand, whereas in O 536 this word is a noun apparently denoting some part of the helmet. It remains to add that the hero in the passage where the word is apparently misunderstood is Antilochus, the son of Nestor.

Since the work of Shipp and Leumann has yet to be digested by the unitarians, the present report may conclude with a series of questions. If the similes are uniformly marked by linguistic lateness, on what hypothesis can we avoid the conclusion that the poet of the similes is late? If a series of misunderstandings terminates in the eighth century B.C., what lapse of time must we allow between the first and last stages, bearing in mind that the nature of the bardic tradition, with the rigorous apprenticeship necessary to acquire so elaborate a technique, would tend to favour conservatism rather than innovation? Finally, if two independent lines of research provide evidence that the Nestorian passages are late, may we not ask 'cui bono'? Is the answer 'Pisistratus', who claimed descent from the Neleids of Pylos?

v. Homer and the Archaeologists

BY DOROTHEA GRAY

In 1883 Arthur Evans met Schliemann and 'laughed a little at the odd little man with his preoccupation with Homer'.[1] Between 1870 and 1888 Schliemann discovered Troy, Mycenae, Orchomenus, and Tiryns, but was prevented from digging at Cnossus by the exorbitant demands of the landowners.[2] Wolfgang Reichel in *Homerische Waffen* (Wien, Hölder, 1894, 2nd ed. 1901) worked out in detail the application of the new finds to Homeric warfare, and his conclusions were largely adopted by Walter Leaf in his second edition of the *Iliad* (London, Macmillan, 1901-02). There was as yet no conception that about a thousand years separated the burials in the Shaft Graves at Mycenae on which Schliemann chiefly relied and the Peisistratean recension in which Leaf believed. Evans reported the astonishing success of his first year at Cnossus in *ABSA* 6 (1899-1900), and in 1905 was able to suggest the divisions and subdivisions of the Minoan civilization of Crete on which the chronology of the prehistoric Aegean has since been based.[3] Although great additions have been made to our knowledge since then, the Mycenaean Agamemnon had been discovered in the nineteenth century; one may say that the last half-century has rediscovered the Hellenic Homer.

It is not surprising that the first result of the discoveries was to set the Homeric poems back into the Bronze Age, with the elimination of any obstinate passages as interpolations. Schliemann, guided by Homer and Pausanias, went to look for the Homeric world where they said it should be, and found it. Later excavations have found remains of the same date on Greek sites which do not play a large part in that world, and overseas in countries which lay completely outside it, but it is still true that the main centres were those which are most important in legend, and that the chief of them were completely unimportant later. At first the only rival was Classical Greece, and the intervening stages —Submycenaean, Protogeometric, and Geometric—which differ far less both from the Homeric and from the Mycenaean world, even when they were recognized, were so obscure and unimpressive that their importance was slow to be realized. It is still much easier to suggest general accounts of the Late Bronze Age than of the Early Iron Age,[4] and unless some archaeologist is exceptionally lucky, the latter period is likely to remain relatively unrecorded; if a people did not build durable houses or bury their dead in well-stocked tombs, the spade cannot uncover colourful details about their life. There is in fact no history of this period, only a series of chronological problems, but there is a considerable body of evidence for their warfare and burial customs and their gradual renewal of contact with the east, and some for their interrelations as shown by their pottery, and for their temples, houses, settlements, and use of metals. This is collected and discussed in detail, along with the Mycenaean material, by Miss H. L. Lorimer in *Homer and the Monuments* (London, Macmillan, 1950), a book which not only gathers together practically all the previously scattered evidence for the material background of the poems, but has the great merit of giving equal weight to both periods and of distinguishing clearly between evidence and conclusions. It contains little about religion, but this aspect has been fully treated by M. P. Nilsson,[5] who interprets the thought behind the art with admirable caution; an account of Christianity based solely on medieval paintings would be singularly misleading, but even if we allow for such distortion, the art of the Bronze Age suggests primitive and superstitious beliefs from which the Homeric poems are free. Finally, the period ends with a discovery which may well prove to be the beginning of a new era in Homeric studies, the deciphering of the Mycenaean script.[6]

From the mass of material, it is only possible to note briefly a few of the main results directly relevant to Homer. On the Greek mainland important Mycenaean remains have been found in six main areas: — Mycenae itself, the earliest and most important, with a network of roads, forts, and settlements radiating out over the Argolid and into Corinthia and the Eurotas valley; the S.W. Peloponnese, with its centre in Messenian Pylos; Attica, where the wealth and strength of the Mycenaean settlement has come as a surprise; Boeotia, probably divided between Orchomenus and Thebes, though excavation in the latter is hampered by modern buildings; S.E. Thessaly, where Mycenaean influence spread out rather thinly from the country round Iolcus; and the West, especially Cephallenia and Aetolia, with modest remains from Ithaca.[7] It is true that the fertile plains are likely to be inhabited in any period, but the legendary importance of Mycenae, Tiryns, Pylos and Iolcus is inexplicable unless there was a tenacious memory of their historical greatness. After the fall of Mycenae there are few traces of civilized life in the Peloponnese or Boeotia, but the peripheral regions, Ithaca, Thessaly, and especially Attica, pass by a process of continuous development into the period marked by Protogeometric pottery. In the following, Geometric, period, Corinth, Argos, and Sparta become important, and Thessaly seems to fall behind; Ithaca has its period of greatest importance and is in touch with East Greece; there is little archaeological evidence for the prominence of Euboea, which is proved for the eighth century at least by its colonizing activities.[8] There were therefore places where the past could have been remembered continuously, and some of them had connections with the settlements in Asia Minor. Actual evidence of interest in the past is not found until the end of the eighth century, when offerings were made in Mycenaean tombs, and hero cults of Menelaus began at Sparta and of Agamemnon at Mycenae.⁹ At about the same time legendary scenes appear in art. Geometric vases have only centauromachies, double figures variously explained as Molione or as artistic space-filling, and sea and land battles which can as well be contemporary as mythical. A votive shield from Tiryns showing the death of an Amazon may belong to c. 700 B.C. A Protocorinthian vase with the death of Achilles is probably earlier than 680 B.C., and three Attic mythical scenes slightly later (Orestes and Aegisthus (?), killing of Nessus, and Achilles (?) and Cheiron). From the middle of the century come two representations of the blinding of the Cyclops, one certainly Argive, and from the third quarter an East Greek plate, with names, showing Hector and Menelaus fighting over the body of Euphorbus (P 70f). It cannot be proved that the artists were inspired by heroic poetry, still less by our *Iliad* and *Odyssey*; but a fragmentary Ithacan vase which 'cannot be much, if at all, later than 700 B.C.' is inscribed with a line of verse, probably a hexameter.[10]

Outside Greece, the Mycenaeans, succeeding to the position of the Minoan Cretans, spread over the Mediterranean, with settlements in Cyprus and Rhodes, in Syria, and in Asia Minor at least at Miletus and Colophon, and with trade and, possibly, settlements in Sicily and Macedonia.[11] Here there is disagreement with tradition; although Agamemnon is lord of many islands and all Argos, few islands take part in the war, Cyprus is outside the Achean sphere, the wanderings of Odysseus are natural if he is regarded as a pioneer in country recently opened up, but hardly if it was thought to have been long familiar to his contemporaries, and the Greeks would not have failed to claim that they were returning to their ancestral homes if they had known that Mycenaeans had ever possessed cities in Asia Minor. It is perhaps significant that the mainland traditions should have been the most persistent. Excavations at Smyrna have shown that the settlement goes well back into the tenth century[12] and suggested that the traditional date for the κτίσις 'Ιωνίας was not far wrong. The Protogeometric pottery there has strong affinities with Attica, and it seems that the settlers took most of their stories with them also and did not pick up local memories of wars in the Troad. It appears more and more that the Mycenaeans were members of an intercommunicating world of great powers, and especially were known to the Hittites as Ahhiava and to the Egyptians first as friendly traders and later as invading A-qi-wa-sa.[13] They shared their world's fate; the Dorian invasion[14] (which becomes more enigmatic as the gap between the destruction of Mycenae and the rise of the Dorian centres widens, and the innovations, which the newcomers were thought to have brought, are found to appear first in the areas into which they did not penetrate) takes its place in a general catastrophe which affected Egypt and Western Asia. In Homer there is a notable absence of great powers. While this makes dating more difficult, the fact itself agrees better with the isolation of Greece in the Early Iron Age, when the settlements in Asia Minor were cut off from the civilized kingdoms of the east by wild hillmen. Oriental influences began again in the second half of the eighth century, but at first they came indirectly, either through a Greek settlement on the Orontes at Al Mina, probably Posideium of Hdt. III. 91, or through Cyprus and the Phoenicians.[15] There are two exceptions. The *Odyssey* at least knows of Egyptian Thebes as a city from which friendly visitors could bring back rich presents, a situation which, however remembered, was in fact possible only before the early fourteenth century; it also knows of the river Aegyptus in a country which old men thought so remote that even a bird could not return from it in a year and young men visited in small flotillas prepared for trade or piracy, ideas which do not seem inconsistent with each other or with the absence of Greek pottery in Egypt before the foundation of Naucratis at the end of the seventh century.[16] More significant is the curious accuracy of the *Iliad* in its description of the city of Troy.[17] The settlers may have known the Troad, though the Homeric account of it actually presents difficulties, and have seen the ruined walls of Troy; but the account of the city goes far beyond this and differs from all we know of Early Iron Age architecture and town-planning. It seems to combine the power and wealth of Troy VI, destroyed by an earthquake c. 1300 B.C., with the fate of its poorer successor Troy VIIA, destroyed by an enemy c. 1200 B.C.

Certain objects and practices can be dated—not indeed without dissent but with some measure of agreement (page references to Lorimer, *op. cit.*):

(a) *Earlier than any possible date for the Trojan War*: A few epithets and incidents which suit only the body-shield (p. 133f, 181f).

HOMER

Silver-studded swords (p. 274f). Vessels like the cup of Nestor (p. 328f). ζῶμα in ξ 482 (p. 376).

(b) *Mycenaean generally*: Great wealth in precious metals. The technique of metal inlay.[18] Bronze weapons and tools. The single thrusting spear (p. 256f). The boar's tusk helmet (p. 212f). Helmets with φάλοι as well as λόφος, on the generally accepted interpretation of φάλος as *horn* (p. 227f, 239f). Probably the Cypriote corslet of Agamemnon and the corslet implied by χαλκοχίτωνες (p. 197f). The epithets for ships, though there is nothing in the narrative to distinguish them from ships on Geometric vases.[19] The plan of the house, but not its decoration (p. 406f).[20]

(b-c) *Mycenaean or Geometric*: The parry shield with single handgrip and telamon (p. 146f). The use of composite and self bows (p. 276f). The use of chariots in war (p. 307f). The χίτων as the dress of men in peace (p. 358f).

(c) *Geometric*: Cremation, either without indestructable goods of value or with weapons only (p. 103f). Pairs of throwing spears in fighting (p. 257f). Bronze θώρηκες and helmets, proved for the end of the Geometric period and invariable immediately after (p. 244f).[21] Leather shields with bronze face and no blazon, apparently characteristic only of the pre-hoplite type (p. 169). Iron axes, knives, and an arrow-head, and knowledge of iron-working shown in simile and metaphor (p. 111f). The assumption that precious objects are heirlooms or brought from abroad, usually by Phoenicians.[22] Wheeled tripods (p. 73). Temples of a simple type, not incorporated in a house (p. 433f). Women's dress (p. 377f). Illiteracy (p. 122f); the Mycenaeans were fully literate, but Homer either did not know writing or knew it as a new invention inappropriate to heroes.

(d) *Post-Geometric*: The lamp of Athena (p. 509f). The brooch of Odysseus (p. 511f). The procession to offer a robe to a seated statue of Athena (p. 442f). Any references to the hoplite equipment and tactics which revolutionized Greek warfare about 700 B.C. — perhaps B 543-4 and N 339-44, the gorgoneion on the shield of Agamemnon (p. 190f), and a few passages where the introduction of a bronze θώρηξ destroys the sense (p. 205f).

It is clear that Mycenaean and Geometric references cannot be used to break the poems up by scissors and paste methods; they are interwoven throughout. The Mycenaean elements chiefly occur as essential elements in the story or in formulaic passages or phrases, rarely in short descriptive passages, the geometric more frequently in the way that the poets tell the story or in similes. Though some things in the *Odyssey* are as old as anything in the *Iliad*, and some things in the *Iliad* as young as anything in the *Odyssey*, the Mycenaean content of the *Odyssey* is much smaller. So far as archaeology is concerned, this could be caused by difference of subject or of author or of date. In both poems the post-geometric element is small, and since our knowledge of geometric Greece, and still more of geometric Ionia, is defective, even the things listed are doubtful. The type of Odysseus' brooch (but not its design) is fairly securely dated in the seventh century, but a new and interesting form of brooch was likely to find its way into the poems where a striking token was needed for identification. The couplet describing the Gorgoneion seems to be an alternative devised to please a generation used to blazons. The *presentation of the robe* and the *moving of the arms* cannot be dated as post-geometric with certainty on archaeological grounds; the argument rests rather on their uneasy adjustment to their contexts and the accumulation of unusual features. Nothing which can be shown to be post-geometric is organically incorporated in the poems. Some post-Mycenaean elements obviously continued into the seventh century and later (e.g. the use of iron), but it is noticeable that the undoubtedly geometric custom of using two spears with a parry-shield slung on a telamon is not misunderstood as it is on seventh-century 'archaising' vases.[23] It seems established that the epic tradition admitted innovations freely until some date not far removed from 700 B.C. and then ceased to do so; opinions differ as to whether this could have happened if the poems were transmitted orally down to the middle of the sixth century.

Almost all the scholars mentioned in §§i–iii above took account of the archaeological evidence available when they wrote and thought that it supported, or at least could be reconciled with, their divergent theories. There are questions which archaeology cannot pretend to answer. The mass of evidence from Egypt to Scythia and from the Atlantic to the Euphrates with a range of dates over a millennium, and the disagreement of archaeologists on its interpretation, make it easy to concentrate on one group of facts or on one interpretation to the exclusion of others. The paucity of evidence from all countries from the decline of Mycenae until the late eighth century, and from some countries, notably the west coast of Asia Minor, in all periods, casts just suspicion on the *argumentum ex silentio*, and this suspicion is easily transferred to periods in which a solid body of positive evidence gives the negative argument real significance. For the Mycenaean period this has been increased by the discovery of isolated exceptions to some accepted generalizations, until some critics come perilously near to arguing that an object must have existed *because* it has not been found. By using these arguments, and by assigning all that is common to the Late Bronze and Early Iron Age to one of them, it is possible to reduce the contribution to the poems made by the other. But neither period can be eliminated, and such a combination of features of widely different date can be explained only by a tradition of oral poetry lasting for centuries and ceasing to develop at about the time when inscriptions in the Phoenician alphabet first appear. By establishing this, archaeology has largely contributed to the measure of agreement which has been reached.

I–III

[1] Jebb's book includes a useful sketch of the history of the Homeric question down to his time. For the period 1887–1923 there is a full critical bibliography in G. Finsler's *Homer*, third edition, Leipzig, Teubner, 1924. The developments of the next ten years are described by Nilsson in *Homer and Mycenae*, and by Delatte and Severyns in *L'Ant. class.* 2 (1933) 379ff; while A. Lesky's *Die Homerforschung in der Gegenwart* (Vienna, Sexl, 1952) gives an invaluable survey of recent work.

[2] By 1865 Mark Pattison could write 'We may safely say that no scholar will again find himself able to embrace the unitarian hypothesis' (*Essays*, 1.382). But in England, at least, a good many men of classical education continued, like Gladstone and Matthew Arnold, to cherish unitarian views.

[3] *Homer and the Epic* (1893); *Homer and his Age* (1906); *The World of Homer* (1910). Lang wrote with wit and elegance; but his interpretation of the culture described by Homer as belonging to a single 'age of transition' can no longer be sustained.

[4] *Die Bedeutung der Wiederholungen für die homerische Frage* (1890); *Die Bedeutung der Widersprüche für die homerische Frage* (1894); *Die Ilias als Dichtung* (1910); *Die Odyssee als Dichtung* (1914).

[5] Something not unlike the 'lay-theory' has recently been put forward by G. Jachmann ('Homerische Einzellieder', in the Festschrift for J. Kroll, *Symbola Colonien-sia*, Köln, 1949), for whom the *Iliad* is a 'Corpus' or 'conglutination' without any real architecture; but such views are nowadays exceptional. On the genesis of the *Kalevala* see Comparetti's edition, and his *Traditional Poetry of the Finns* (Eng. trans., London 1898).

[6] *Homer: an Introduction*, 104. Cf. Murray, *C.R.* 36 (1922) 75: 'we all believe in the unity of Homer: it is only when we try to explain what that unity is and how it has come about, that the Homeric Question begins'.

[7] *Introduction à l'Iliade*, par Paul Mazon avec la collaboration de Pierre Chantraine, Paul Collart et René Langumier (Paris, 'Les Belles Lettres', 1942); Theiler in *Festschrift Tièche* (Bern, Lang, 1947); P. Von der Mühll, *Kritisches Hypomnema zur Ilias* (Basel, Reinhardt, 1952).

[8] But it remains possible that the name belongs to some much earlier poet, to whom all the best epics were indiscriminately ascribed in Callinus' day (and down to the

fifth century). E. Bickel, in a book modestly entitled *Homer: die Lösung der homerischen Frage* (Bonn, Scheur, 1949), supposes Homer to be the man who invented the hexameter c. 1000 B.C. On the whole question of the name see Wilamowitz, *Die Ilias und Homer*, chap. 18, and E. Schwartz, 'Der Name Homeros', *Hermes* 1940.

[9] For the evidence see now Von der Mühll, op. cit., 369ff.

[10] Erich Bethe, *Homer: Dichtung und Saga*, vol. 1 (Leipzig, Teubner, 1914).

[11] *Praefatio ad Iliadem* xxviii.

[12] On the lateness of the Doloneia the observations of P. Chantraine (*Mélanges Desrousseaux*, 1937, 59ff), H. Heusinger (*Stilistische Untersuchungen zur Dolonie*, diss. Leipzig, 1939), and F. Klingner (*Hermes* 1940) appear decisive against Shewan's defence (*The Lay of Dolon*, London, Macmillan, 1911).

[13] Wilamowitz, *Die Ilias und Homer*, chap. 2. Schadewaldt's elaborate defence of Book VIII (*Iliasstudien*, Abh. Sachs. Akad. 1938, chap. 4) has not convinced the present writer that Wilamowitz was wrong.

[14] That the similes are the work of Ionian, not 'Achaean', poets was proved by Arthur Platt in an article in the *Journal of Philology*, 24 (1896) 28ff, which is still worth consulting. See also below, §iv.

[15] Sir Arthur Evans thought that the roots not only of Greek mythology but of the Greek epic went back to Mycenaean times (*J.H.S.* 32, 1912, 277ff). This speculation, which has been revived by Severyns (*Homère* II), will gain greatly in probability if it is finally established that the language of the Mycenaeans was Greek.

[16] For a criticism of the 'faded gods' hypothesis see Farnell, *Greek Hero Cults and Ideas of Immortality* (Oxford, Clarendon Press, 1921), chap. xi. Among Homeric figures Helen seems to be the only really convincing instance. The fantastic speculations of Charles Autran (*Homère et les origines sacerdotales de l'épopée grecque*, 3 vols., Paris, Denoel, 1938-44) have done nothing to enhance the probability of this type of view. The present writer can only regret its reappearance in a book whose first chapter makes an original and important contribution to the understanding of Homeric religion, Fernand Robert's *Homère* (Paris, Presses Universitaires de France, 1950).

[17] I quote the characteristically incisive judgement of Wilamowitz: 'any one who in regard to language or religion or manners throws *Iliad* and *Odyssey* into one pot can no longer claim to be seriously considered' (*Die Heimkehr des Odysseus*, 171).

[18] E. Bethe, *op. cit.* n10, vol. II (1922); E. Schwartz, *Die Odyssee* (München, Hueber, 1924); V. Bérard, *Introduction à l'Odyssée* (3 vols., Paris, 'Les Belles Lettres', 1924-25); P. Von der Mühll, art. 'Odyssee' in *R.E.* (1939); F. Focke, *Die Odyssee* (Stuttgart, Kohlhammer, 1943); R. Merkelbach, *Untersuchungen zur Odyssee* (München, Beck, 1951).

[19] On folklore in the *Odyssey* see also L. Radermacher, *Sitzb. Wien* 178 (1915) 1, and K. Reinhardt, 'Die Abenteuer der Odyssee', in his book *Von Werken und Formen* (Godesberg, Kupper, 1948). Rhys Carpenter's attractive book, *Folktale, Fiction and Saga in the Homeric Epics* (Berkeley, Univ. of California Press, 1946), contains some valuable chapters, but suffers from an excessive preoccupation with bears.

[20] On the date of Book XXIV, or rather of XXIII.297 to the end, the English reader may consult Allen's *Homer: the Origins and the Transmission*, 218ff, and Mackail's essay in *Greek Poetry and Life, Essays presented to Gilbert Murray*, 1ff (1936). As the latter points out, the 'Second Nekyia' is strikingly different in style from the rest; and there is something to be said for Schwartz's view that it was taken over by the Continuator from an older source.

[21] Consultation of a spirit seems to have been an element in the original folktale of the Wanderer's Return; but the abrupt changes in style, treatment, and scenery make it difficult to regard the present Nekyia as an imaginative unity.

[22] Von der Mühll has tried in the interest of simplicity to dispense with this assumption; but it may be doubted whether his analysis does full justice to the complexity of the evidence.

[23] See K. Meuli's brilliant essay, *Odyssee und Argonautika* (diss. Basel, 1921).

[24] Cf. Woodhouse, chaps. 8-16 (mainly from Wilamowitz).

[25] That the 'Telemachy' must have been composed as an expansion of the *Odyssey*, not as an independent poem, was already seen by Niese in 1882; but the authority of Kirchhoff and Wilamowitz has led analysts generally to accept the other view.

[26] See Schwartz, *op. cit.* (n18), 22ff.

[27] Cf. Leaf's judgement: 'the *Odyssey*, whatever the original materials on which it was based, is in its present form at least a poem due to a single poet', whereas 'the *Iliad* is a growth from a single poem'.

[28] Some of the reasons for attributing the present form of the *Odyssey* to the seventh century are stated by Carpenter, *op. cit.* (n19), chap. 5.

[29] See the introduction to Allen's *Homer: the Origins and the Transmission*.

[30] The classical statement of this point of view is the Abbé Bremond's *La poésie pure* (1925); but it was already widely held in France and England some years earlier.

[31] Engelbert Drerup, *Das Homerproblem in der Gegenwart* (Würzburg, Becker, 1921). He had already published in 1913 *Das fünfte Buch der Ilias, Grundlagen einer homerischen Poetik*.

[32] J. T. Sheppard (Sir John Sheppard), *The Pattern of the Iliad* (London, Methuen, 1922). Other unitarian writers with a mainly aesthetic approach are S. E. Bassett (*The Poetry of Homer*, Berkeley, Univ. of California Press, 1938) and E. T. Owen (*The Story of the Iliad*, New York, O.U.P., 1947) both of whom have made good observations on Homeric technique.

[33] The oversight has been convincingly explained by A. B. Lord, *T.A.P.A.* 69 (1938) 445, as due to the influence of a conventional motif – the aged father mourning his warrior son. Pylaemenes continues to be the favourite Aunt Sally of unitarians: both Bowra (*Tradition and Design* 97ff, *Heroic Poetry* 300f) and Fernand Robert (*Homère* 287) make great play with him, while passing in silence over more serious structural discrepancies.

[34] Readers should also be warned that, whether from an imperfect knowledge of German or from the carelessness engendered by apostolic fervour, Scott (*op. cit.* 76) actually attributed to Wilamowitz the view which the latter set out to refute, that the *Iliad* is 'a miserable piece of patchwork' (*Die Ilias und Homer* 322). The libel is unfortunately repeated in Bowra's *Tradition and Design*, p. 9.

[35] Examples are the dropping in the *Odyssey* of old cult-epithets whose meaning had long been forgotten, and of obsolete forms like the pronoun τύνη; and the outcropping of significantly new words like θεουδής, 'godfearing'. There is still need for a systematic and disinterested study of variations in vocabulary, grammar, and metre throughout the two poems, a study for which the new *Lexicon to Homer, Hesiod and the Older Epic*, now in preparation at Hamburg, ought to provide a secure foundation. Meanwhile, Leumann's exploration of semantic shifts within the poems (see below, §iv) points to conclusions which support the analysts.

[36] Sir Philip Macdonell, *C.R.* 55 (1941) 16. Hyperhistoricism of another sort pervades the singular book of Emile Mireaux, *Les poèmes homériques et l'histoire grecque* (2 vols., Paris, Michel, 1948-49). While tracing back the Trojan Cycle not to the Trojan War but to 'collective rites', he holds that both poems 'have well-defined political aims' in relation to the commercial ambitions of rival Greek states in the eighth and seventh centuries.

[37] Drerup, *Homerproblem* 273ff; Carpenter, *op. cit.* (n19), chap. 3. Among analysts, Bethe was equally sceptical; but the theory of displacement ('Sagenverschiebung') by which he accounted for the origin of the Trojan Cycle was severely (and justly) criticised by Drerup.

[38] W. Schadewaldt, *Von Homers Welt und Werk*, second (enlarged) edition, Stuttgart, Koehler, 1952, 177; H. T. Wade-Gery, *The Poet of the Iliad*, 7. Wade-Gery suggests that the invention is datable *a parte ante*, Homer's Hector being named after an historical Hector who once ruled in Chios (he thinks c. 800 B.C.). But the reverse relationship, assumed by Wilamowitz and Schadewaldt, seems at least equally probable; and if Ventris proves to be right in deciphering the name Hector on a Mycenaean tablet, the foundation of the argument will vanish.

[39] Nilsson, *op. cit.*, 33.

[40] Against the view of Leaf and Jacoby (*Sitzb. Berl.* 1933, 682ff) that the Catalogue is a late interpolation, V. Burr (NEωN KATAΛOΓOΣ, *Klio* Beiheft 39, 1944) thinks that Homer composed the Catalogue himself on the basis of a Mycenaean document; but it seems much likelier that it was transmitted in the tradition of heroic poetry (and subjected to some working over). See Bowra, *Tradition and Design* 70ff, and Wade-Gery, *op. cit.*, Appendix A.

[41] H. L. Lorimer, *Homer and the Monuments* 480. Both Miss Lorimer and Von der

Mühll (*op. cit.* n7, 159f) think that the Embassy was composed by Homer as an afterthought and was worked into the *Iliad* by the later and inferior poet who concocted Book VIII. This curious theory seems to rest on little more than the assumption that whatever is best in the *Iliad* must be 'Homer's'. But if Athens could within half a century give birth to three poets of genius, may not Ionia have produced more than one?

[42] 'Tradition und Geist im homerischen Epos', *Studium Generale* 4 (1951) 334ff.

[43] There are still last ditches occupied by Old Believers. The latest editor of the *Odyssey* (2 vols., London, Macmillan, 1947-48), W. B. Stanford, rejects virtually nothing, not even the Continuation (which Homer may have composed when he was 'aging or tired').

[44] See n19. It is hoped that Reinhardt will publish a book on Homer in English.

[45] J. T. Kakridis, *Homeric Researches* (Lund, Gleerup, 1949; written in English). The author's further speculations about the influence of the Meleager-poem on the *Iliad* may be thought less convincing.

[46] H. Pestalozzi, *Die Achilleis als Quelle der Ilias* (Zürich, Rentsch, 1945); E. Howald, *Der Dichter der Ilias* (*ibid.*, 1946); W. Schadewaldt, 'Einblick in die Erfindung der Ilias', *op. cit.* (n38), 155ff.

[47] One may fairly contrast the effective use of an *Aethiopis*-motif at *Iliad* XXII.208ff with the clumsy adaptation at VIII.80ff. On the possibility of reciprocal borrowing see Murray, *Rise of the Greek Epic*, 177ff, and §iii below.

[48] F. M. Combellack, *A.J.P.*, 71 (1950), 340. Milman Parry had uttered a similar warning, *Harvard Studies*, 1930, 75.

[49] A recent example is the suggestion that Penelope behaves so oddly in *Odyssey* XIX because she has correctly divined the stranger's identity, although by a 'subtle artistry' on the poet's part her discovery is never mentioned (P. W. Harsh, *A.J.P.*, 71, 1950, 1ff).

[50] For a criticism of the 'Fernverbindungen', of which Schadewaldt in particular has made a great deal, see Jachmann, *op. cit.* (n5).

[51] Parry acknowledged his debt to various predecessors, notably H. Düntzer in regard to the formulaic style and M. Murko in the comparative study of oral epic. Cf. also §iv below, on the work of Witte and Meister.

[52] Other important articles by Parry will be found in *T.A.P.A.*, 59 (1928), 233ff, and 64 (1933), 30ff.

[53] E.g. Richard Harder could say in 1942 that 'no one any longer doubts that Homer could write, and wrote his poetry down' (*Das Neue Bild der Antike*, ed. Berve, p. 102).

[54] See Nilsson's summary of Parry's work, *Homer and Mycenae*, 179ff, and his inferences regarding the development of Greek epic poetry, *ibid.*, 205ff; also Hermann Fränkel's inferences, *Dichtung und Philosophie des frühen Griechentums* (New York, A.P.A., 1951), 7ff.

[55] Bowra, *Heroic Poetry*, 241.

[56] Wade-Gery, *The Poet of the Iliad*, 39f.

[57] Parry, *Harvard Studies*, 1930, 137ff. On the unmetrical use of formulae see his *Les formules et la métrique d'Homère* (Paris, 'Les Belles Lettres', 1928); on their inappropriate use, *L'épithète trad.*, 146-81.

[58] This was noticed by Cauer, *Grundfragen der Homerkritik* (third ed., 2 vols., Leipzig, Hirzel, 1921-23), 451. Striking Odyssean examples are 1.29 ἀμύμονος Αἰγίσθοιο; 1.70 ἀντίθεον Πολύφημον; 14.18 ἀντίθεοι μνηστῆρες; 14.22 etc. συβώτης, ὄρχαμος ἀνδρῶν; and the misuse of Iliadic formulae at 14.419, 22.296, 308, and elsewhere (see Monro's edition of *Odyssey* XIII-XXIV, p. 328ff).

[59] H. Apoll., 172. Cf. Homer's Demodocus.

[60] Bethe, *Buch und Bild im Altertum* (Leipzig, Harrassowitz, 1945) 16, 110. Cf. Birt, *Antike Buchwesen*, 277, and Collart in Mazon's *Introduction à l'Iliade*, 7of.

[61] Carpenter, *op. cit.* (n19), 14. Cf. early Scandinavian poetry, which 'must have lived orally in Iceland for many generations before it was written down', although the runic script was available (G. Turville-Petre, *Origins of Icelandic Literature*, O.U.P., 1953, 7, 74).

[62] Cauer, *op. cit.* (n58), I.5: J. Wackernagel, *Sprachliche Untersuchungen zu Homer* (see below, §iv).

[63] Most of the ancient evidence is collected in Allen's *Origins and Transmission*, 226ff. That until then the poems were orally transmitted is specifically stated by Josephus, *c. Apion.* 1. 2. 12 (omitted by Allen).
[64] Lehrs, *Rh. Mus.* 17 (1862); Wilamowitz, *Hom. Untersuchungen* 235ff; Allen, *op. cit.* 239ff.
[65] See especially R. Merkelbach, *Rh. Mus.*, 1952, 23ff; also G. Thomson, *The Prehistoric Aegean* (London, Lawrence and Wishart, 1949) 568ff, and Carpenter, *loc. cit.*
[66] We hear of Greek rhapsodes doing this, schol. Pindar, *Nem.* 2.1. For expansion and compression in modern oral recitation cf. Chadwick and Chadwick, *Growth of Literature* II, 146, 250, and Fränkel, *op. cit.* (n54), 27.
[67] For the rapid growth of variants cf. e.g. Chadwick and Chadwick, *op. cit.*, II, 413ff; for examples of their conflation, *ibid.*, III, 163-70.
[68] As the Germans express it, 'Schichtenanalyse' will have to give way to 'Elementenanalyse'. The older analysts were misled by the analogy of excavation, in which it is often possible to expose untouched layers of earlier material. In a traditional oral poem we can never hope to find untouched layers.

IV

[1] P. Chantraine, *Grammaire homérique*, i. Phonétique et morphologie, 1942. ii. Syntaxe, 1953, Paris (Klincksieck). For word-formation we have an exhaustive survey in E. Risch, *Wortbildung der homerischen Sprache*. Berlin, 1937. Etymologies of a number of obscure Homeric words were contributed by F. Bechtel, *Lexilogus zu Homer*, Halle, 1914.
[2] D. B. Monro, *A Grammar of the Homeric Dialect*, 2nd edn., Oxford, 1891.
[3] J. van Leeuwen, *Enchiridium dictionis epicae*, Leyden, 1894.
[4] Useful surveys of linguistic work on Homer are given by P. Cauer, *Grundfragen der Homerkritik*, c. vi, 3rd edn., Leipzig, 1921; M. P. Nilsson, *Homer and Mycenae*, c. iv, London, 1933; P. Chantraine in P. Mazon, *Introduction à l'Iliade*, c. iv, Paris, 1942; A. Meillet in *Aperçu d'une histoire de la langue grecque*, 3rd edn., Paris, 1930.
[4a] *Rev. Et. Gr.*, 31, 1918, p. 277ff.
[5] M. Leumann, *Homerische Wörter*, Basel, 1950, p. 36ff.
[6] E. Schwyzer, *Griechische Grammatik*, I, München, 1939, p. 102f.
[7] *Loc. cit.*
[8] *Introduction*, p. 90.
[9] *Op. cit.*, p. 18.
[10] *Introduction*, p. 90f; *Grammaire*, I, p. 75ff.
[11] *Bezzenberger's Beiträge* 4, 1880, 25ff, and *Sprachliche Untersuchungen zu Homer*, p. 66ff.
[12] *Gr. Gram.* I, p. 104.
[13] A. Gercke and E. Norden, *Einleitung in die Altertumswissenschaft* I, 6 *Sprache*, 3rd edn., Leipzig, 1923, p. 93.
[14] E. Hermann, *Z.f. vergl. Sprachforsch.* 46, 1914, p. 241ff.
[15] Listed in Schwyzer, *Gr. Gram.*, p. 106ff.
[16] E. Meyer, *Forschungen zur alten Geschichte* I, 1892, p. 132. More recently upheld by G. H. Mahlow, *Neue Wege durch die griechische Sprache und Dichtung*, Berlin, 1926, p. 260ff.
[17] J. Wackernagel, *Sprachliche Untersuchungen zu Homer*, Göttingen, 1916.
[18] M. Nilsson, *op. cit.*, p. 162.
[19] U. v. Wilamowitz, *Sb. Berlin. Akad. Wiss.*, 1906, p. 61f., 'Ueber die ionisehe Wanderung'; T. W. Allen, 'Homer sang the language he spoke' (see section ii, p. 11).
[20] *Op. cit.*, p. 168.
[21] F. Bechtel, *Die Vocalcontraktion bei Homer*, Halle, 1908, in which the author repented of his earlier construction of a primitive Aeolic Iliad (in E. Robert, *Studien zur Ilias*, Berlin, 1901.)
[22] 'Was Homer a Chian?', *Cambridge Philol. Soc. Proceed.*, 1915, p. 7ff.
[23] Witte summed up his researches in Pauly-Wissowa *RE* VIII, 2213ff.
[24] K. Meister, *Homerische Kunstsprache*, Leipzig, 1921.
[25] See P. Chantraine, *Grammaire* I, p. 116ff.
[26] *Introduction*, p. 104.

HOMER

[27] It is too early yet to evaluate the Mycenaean inscriptions as presented in the decipherment of M. Ventris and J. Chadwick, *JHS* 73, 1953, p. 84ff. It is, however, noteworthy that the case endings -οιο, -δε and -φι are represented. If these should prove features of a primitive Arcado-Cyprian, it would reinforce the arguments based on the presence of Arcado-Cyprian words in Homeric vocabulary (see C. M. Bowra 'Homeric Words in Arcadian Inscriptions' *CQ* 20, 1926, p. 168ff, and Nilsson's discussion, *op. cit.*, p. 175f: 'there are words in the Homeric poems which go back to the Mycenaean Age'.

[27a] P. Chantraine, *Introduction*.

[28] *Loc. cit.*

[29] *Class. Phil.*, 1923, p. 266ff.

[30] G. P. Shipp, *Studies in the Language of Homer*, Cambridge, 1953.

[31] M. Leumann, *Homerische Wörter*, Basel, 1950.

[32] On Milman Parry's work see section iii.

V

[1] Joan Evans, *Time and Chance*, London, Longmans, Green, 1943, p. 263.

[2] C. Schuchhardt, *Schliemann's Excavations*, Tr. E. Sellers, London, Macmillan, 1891.

[3] Periods are distinguished by their characteristic pottery:

LATE HELLADIC or MYCENAEAN, c. 1600-1100 B.C. Contemporary with LATE Minoan in Crete and roughly dated by contacts with Egypt. See R. W. Hutchinson, '*Minoan Chronology reviewed*', *Antiquity* 28 (1954) p. 155f.

SUBMYCENAEAN. Transition from Bronze to Iron Age. Relative and absolute dates are very uncertain and vary from area to area. A. Furumark, *Mycenaean Pottery: Analysis and Classification* and *Chronology*, Stockholm, 1941; '*The Mycenaean III C pottery and its relations to Cypriote fabrics*', *Opuscula Archaeologica* 3 (1944), p. 194f.

PROTOGEOMETRIC, ?c. 1025-875 B.C. V. Desborough, *Protogeometric Pottery*, Oxford, Clarendon Press, 1952.

GEOMETRIC, to c. 700 B.C. P. Kahane, '*Die Entwicklungsphasen der attisch-geometrischen Keramik*', *AJA* 44 (1940), p. 464f. F. Matz, *Geschichte der griechischen Kunst* I, Frankfurt am Main, Klostermann, 1949.

PROTOCORINTHIAN, PROTOATTIC and PROTOARGIVE, seventh century. K. F. Johansen, *Les Vases sicyoniens*, Paris, Champion, 1923. H. Payne, *Necrocorinthia*, Oxford, Clarendon Press, 1931. J. M. Cook, '*Protoattic pottery*', *ABSA* 35 (1934-35), p. 165f.

[4] Arthur Evans, *The Palace of Minos* 1-5, London, Macmillan, 1921-36, is a classic for the whole Minoan-Mycenaean world. Summaries by G. Karo, '*Mykenische Kultur*', in *P-W Suppl.* 6 (1935), p. 583f, and Matz, *Die Ägäis*, in *Handbuch der Archäologie* 2.i. (1950), p. 179f. C. W. Blegen, '*Pre-classical Greece – a survey*', *ABSA* 46 (1951), p. 16f. J. L. Myres, *Who were the Greeks?*, University of California Press, 1930, and M. P. Nilsson, *Homer and Mycenae*, London, Methuen, 1933 (a useful short introduction) cover the whole period. For short accounts of the Early Iron Age, W. Kraiker and K. Kübler, *Kerameikos* I, Berlin, de Gruyter, 1939, p. 165f, and Desborough, *op. cit.*, p. 296f. For illustrations, H. Bossert, *The Art of Ancient Crete*, London, Zwemmer, 1937. F. Winter, *Kunstgeschichte in Bilder*, I. iii-iv, Neue Bearbeitung, Leipzig, Kröner, N. D. The chronology of the Late Geometric period depends on the validity of Thucydides' dates for the western colonies; see T. J. Dunbabin, *The Western Greeks*, Oxford, Clarendon Press, 1948, Appendix I.

[5] *The Minoan-Mycenaean Religion and its Survival in Greek Religion*, Lund, Gleerup, 1927, 2nd ed. (with much new material) 1950.

[6] See above §iv, n27.

[7] Karo, *op. cit.*, gives a convenient list of sites. The chief additions are: A. J. B. Wace, *Mycenae*, Princeton University Press, 1949 and '*Mycenae 1939-52*', *ABSA* 48 (1953) p. 3f; important finds by I. Papademetriou, including a new Grave Circle, *ILN*, 1952, vol. 221, p. 505-7, 1954, vol. 224, p. 259, 323-5, 363-5. Blegen, *Prosymna*, Cambridge, The University Press, 1937. O. Frodin and A. W. Persson, *Aeine*, Stockholm, 1938. Person, *New Tombs at Dendra near Midea*, Lund, Gleerup, 1942. S. S. Weinberg, '*Investigations at Corinth*', *Hesperia* 18 (1949), p. 156f. N. Valmin, *The Swedish Messenia Expedition*, Lund, Gleerup, 1938. Blegen, '*The Palace of Nestor*', *AJA* 57 (1953), p. 59f and '*Excavations at Pylos 1953*', *AJA* 58 (1954) p. 27f. I. T. Hill, *The Ancient City of Athens*, London,

HOMER

Methuen, 1953. F. H. Stubbings, *'Mycenaean pottery from Attica'*, *ABSA* 42 (1947), p. 1f. The most convenient account of Thebes is by F. Schober in *P-W* 5a, (1934), p. 1423f. On the Thisbe treasure, see Nilsson, *Minoan-Mycenaean Religion*[2], p. 40f. *'Excavations in Ithaca'*, *ABSA* 33, 35, 39, 40 (Summary), 44 (1932-49).

[8] Dunbabin, *'The early history of Corinth'*, *JHS* 68 (1948), p. 59f, but cf. *Hesperia* 18 (1949) p. 156f. R. M. Dawkins, *Artemis Orthia, JHS Suppl. Papers* 5, 1929, but cf. notes on chronology by E. A. Lane in *ABSA* 34 (1933-34), p. 99f. and S. Benton in *JHS* 70 (1950), p. 17f. C. Waldstein, *The Argive Heraeum*, Boston, Houghton Mifflin, 1902. For Ithaca, S. Benton, *'Further excavations at Aetos'*, *ABSA* 48 (1953) p. 255f, with previous references. J. Boardman, *'Pottery from Eretria'*, *ABSA* 47 (1952), p. 1f.

[9] Blegen, *'Post-Mycenaean objects in Mycenaean tombs'*, *AE* 1937, p. 377f. J. M. Cook, *'The cult of Agamemnon at Mycenae'*, Ἑταιρεία Μακεδονικῶν Σπουδῶν 9 (1953), p. 112f. Sanctuaries were likely to preserve memories, and there were Mycenaeans at Delphi and Delos, though not at Olympia or (as far as we know) Dodona. See especially H. Gallet and J. Treheux, *'Dépôt égéen et géometrique de l'Artemision à Délos'*, *BCH* 71-2 (1947-48), p. 148f.

[10] J. M. Cook, *'Early mythological representations in Greek art'*, *ABSA* 35 (1934-35), p. 206f. The authenticity of the shipwreck scene in R. Hampe, *Die Gleichnisse Homers und der Bildkunst seiner Zeit*, Tübingen, Neimeyer, 1952, Pl. 7-11, is unfortunately doubtful. The vases, etc., mentioned are shown in *ABSA* 35 (1934-35) Pl. 52, 42 (1947) Pl. 18a and p. 93, fig. 7, 43 (1948), p. 80-2 and Pl. 34, *CVA* Berlin i Pl. 5 and 18-21, *JHS* 73 (1953), p. 116, fig. 5, E. Pfuhl, *Malerei und Zeichnung der Griechen*, München, Bruckmann, 1923, 3 no. 65 and 117.

[11] Stubbings, *Mycenaean Pottery from the Levant*, Cambridge, The University Press, 1951; the literature is voluminous. For Crete, see J. D. S. Pendlebury, *The Archaeology of Crete*, London, Methuen, 1939, and P. Demargne, *La Crète dédalique*, Paris, de Boccard, 1947; apart from the legend of Minos, its chief *direct* importance for Homer is as a possible transmitter of traditions. Dunbabin, *'Minos and Daidalos in Sicily'*, *PBSR* 16 (1948), p. 1f. *FA* 7 (1954) nos. 737, 1945, and 2015. W. A. Heurtley, *Prehistoric Macedonia*, Cambridge, The University Press, 1939.

[12] *JHS* 72 (1952), p. 104. *ILN* 1953, vol. 222, p. 328-9.

[13] C. F. A. Schaeffer, *Stratigraphie comparée et chronologie de l'Asie occidentale*, London, Cumberlege, 1948, gives a survey of excavations which brings out their interconnection; for discussion of the conclusions see review-articles by G. Hanfmann, *AJA* 55 (1951), p. 355f, and 56 (1952), p. 27f, and Leonard Woolley, *Gnomon* 24 (1952), p. 57f. See also O. Gurney. *The Hittites*, Pelican Books, 1952, p. 46f, H. J. Kantor, *The Aegean and the Orient in the 2nd Millennium BC.*, *Arch. Inst. of America, Monograph* I, 1947, and G. A. Wainwright, *'Asiatic Keftiu'*, *AJA* 56 (1952), p. 196f.

[14] J. F. Daniel, O. Broneer and H. T. Wade-Gery, *'The Dorian Invasion'*, *AJA* 52 (1948), p. 107f.

[15] Sidney Smith, *'Al Mina'*, *The Antiquaries Journal*, 22 (1942) p. 87f. Woolley, *A Forgotten Kingdom*, Pelican Books, 1953. R. M. Cook, *'Ionia and Greece 800-600 B.C.'* *JHS* 66 (1946), p. 67f.

[16] R. M. Cook, *'Amasis and the Greeks in Egypt'*, *JHS* 57 (1937), p. 227f.

[17] W. Dörpfeld, *Troja und Ilion*, Athens, Beck and Barth, 1902. Blegen, *'New evidence for dating the settlements at Troy'*, *ABSA* 37 (1936-37), p. 8f. J. L. Caskey, *'Notes on Trojan chronology'*, *AJA* 52 (1948), p. 119f. Homer's Troy is also identified with Troy VI (Schaeffer) or removed from Hissarlik altogether (Ch. Vellay); the fourth volume of the report of the American excavations (Blegen and others, *Troy* 1-3, Princeton University Press, 1950-53), may settle the question.

[18] See especially Schaeffer, *Enkomi-Alasia* I, Paris, Klincksieck, 1952, p. 379f.

[19] G. S. Kirk, *'Ships on Geometric vases'*, *ABSA* 44 (1949), p. 93f.

[20] Wace, *'Notes on the Homeric House'*, *JHS* 71 (1951), p. 203f.

[21] A bronze helmet and θώρηξ have now been found at Argos in a Geometric burial of the late eighth century, *BCH* 78 (1954), p. 178 and fig. 38-39. For LMI bronze helmets, see M. S. F. Hood, *'Late Minoan warrior-graves'*, *ABSA* 47 (1952), p. 255f. If the Homeric bronze helmet is Mycenaean, it will, on present evidence, belong to group a.

[22] The Mycenaeans were a creative people. See Payne, *Perachora*, Oxford, Clarendon Press, 1940, p. 32f for the increase in imports after the middle of the eighth century.

[23] Lorimer, *'The hoplite phalanx'*, *ABSA* 42 (1947), p. 76f.

APPENDIX TO CHAPTER I
Sections i-iii

DURING the past fourteen years (1953-66) Homeric scholars have been active everywhere, and in the English-speaking world quite exceptionally so.[1] To name only substantial works dealing in English with central problems, we have had in rapid succession D. L. Page, *The Homeric Odyssey* (OUP, 1955); M. I. Finley, *The World of Odysseus* (first English edition, Chatto & Windus, 1956; also in Penguin Books); C. H. Whitman, *Homer and the Heroic Tradition* (Harv. Univ. Press, 1958); T. B. L. Webster, *From Mycenae to Homer* (Methuen, 1958); D. L. Page, *History and the Homeric Iliad* (Sather Classical Lectures, vol. 31, Univ. of California Press, 1959); A. B. Lord, *The Singer of Tales* (Harv. Univ. Press, 1960); *A Companion to Homer*, ed. A. J. B. Wace and F. H. Stubbings (Macmillan, 1962); G. S. Kirk, *The Songs of Homer* (CUP, 1962);[2] *The Language and Background of Homer*, ed. G. S. Kirk (Heffer, 1964); and J. A. Notopoulos, 'Studies in Early Greek Oral Poetry', (HSCPh 68, 1964, 1-77).

About the contentions of individual authors some brief indications are given below, but a word must first be said about the two collective works. The long-awaited *Companion*, planned by the late A. J. B. Wace before the last war, deals with almost every aspect of Homeric scholarship (except that, oddly enough, one misses any account of the world in which Homer himself is thought to have lived). All the sixteen contributors are specialists of high standing, and many of their contributions will be read with profit not only by sixth-formers and undergraduates (for whom the book was originally designed) but also by mature scholars. Intending users should, however, be warned that not all the articles are up to date (some were drafted in the nineteen-thirties), and in particular that the views expressed on literary questions reflect almost everywhere a pre-war 'unitarian orthodoxy' rather than the wider spectrum of current critical opinion: the arguments of 'unorthodox' scholars like Page, Finley and Kirk[3] are in general not answered but ignored. The serious student will do well to supplement the *Companion* by consulting the thirteen essays by eleven writers, originally published between 1947 and 1961, which are

APPENDIX 39

now assembled in *The Language and Background of Homer*. This is a less ambitiously comprehensive collection, but it provides a valuable introduction to several current controversies and, unlike the *Companion*, often gives the reader the wholesome opportunity of deciding for himself between conflicting views.

On what lines has the discussion developed since 1952? Only a few salient points can be noted here.

i. Although the unitarian approach is still on the whole the predominant one, nevertheless, as Lesky has noted, 'in late years Homeric analysis has vigorously claimed attention in almost all the old forms.'[4] Many weapons from the armoury of nineteenth-century analysts, rusty from long disuse, have been given a new cutting edge by D. L. Page.[5] From the Continent we have had B. Marzullo's radical book, *Il Problema Omerico*, and two uncompromising essays by Theiler;[6] more surprisingly, Schadewaldt, whose *Iliasstudien* has long been the bible of unitarians, has found to the chagrin of the faithful that he cannot explain the *Odyssey* without postulating two distinct Odyssey-poets.[7] The earlier of these he would identify with Homer, the author of the *Iliad*. But the opinion that the two poems have a separate authorship has been reinforced by the arguments of Heubeck and Page and seems to be gaining ground, at least on this side of the Atlantic.[8]

ii. Meanwhile, unitarian 'neoanalysis' (the exploration of 'Homer's sources') has been carried to its logical limit by W. Kullmann;[9] attempting systematically to distinguish traditional from invented material in the *Iliad*, he reaches the startling conclusion that virtually the whole of the so-called Trojan Cycle — *Cypria, Aethiopis, Iliou Persis* — existed as a pre-Homeric 'Grossepos' from which Homer borrowed extensively, and that in consequence the *Iliad* cannot have been composed before, at earliest, the latter part of the seventh century. In the same general category, though its methods are very different, may be placed Gabriel Germain's speculative but fascinating attempt to determine the ultimate sources of the various Odyssean folktales, for many of which he finds prototypes in the myths and rituals of Egypt and the Middle East.[10]

iii. While the old battles have thus continued, especially on the Continent, without much regard for Milman Parry's discoveries,[11] discussion in the English-speaking world has (as predicted) been focussed increasingly on the new questions which these discoveries raise, and in particular on the crucial transition from oral poetry to written text. Can we picture that transition without destroying the cherished belief that we possess to-day Homer's exact words? The comfortable assumption that Homer was an oral poet who had somehow learned to write has been firmly dismissed by the best contemporary experts on oral poetry, A. B. Lord and J. A. Notopoulos:[12] 'a poet is literary or oral, not both', the two techniques being mutually exclusive. But Lord's own notion that Homer must have dictated his poems to a conveniently literate collaborator is hardly more convincing.[13] Less conservative scholars like Page, Sealey and Kirk have accepted with or without qualms the likelihood that the poems passed through a longish period of oral transmission before being written down.[14] On the related problem of the 'Peisistratean recension' discussion also continues: the case against it has been most fully restated by Davison, the case in its favour (with certain modifications) by Sealey.[15] There is a gap in our knowledge here which can scarcely be filled save by more or less arbitrary guesswork.

iv. If Parry's discovery has influenced the recent course of Homeric debate, so also has Ventris's,[16] though perhaps with less reason. One may ask why the picture of Bronze Age civilization which scholars have tried to reconstruct from the accidentally preserved records of Mycenaean book-keepers should be expected to throw any light on the picture of that age drawn by Ionian poets four or five centuries later. Nevertheless, the search for links between the two has been actively pursued, especially by Webster, by several of the contributors to the *Companion*, and with different methods and somewhat greater caution by Page in *History and the Homeric Iliad*. The chief dissentient voice is that of M. I. Finley, who holds that 'the Homeric world was altogether post-Mycenaean, and the so-called reminiscences and survivals are rare, isolated and garbled'.[17] Without going so far as this, one may view with reserve much that has been written in recent years about 'Mycenaean epic' and similar subjects.[18] On Mycenaean and Dark Age elements in Homer, as on a good many other problems, the most sober and balanced judgement seems to the present writer to be Kirk's.[19] See further below, appendix to section v.

A few of the more important books and articles on specific topics remain to be listed.

APPENDIX

(a) Homeric religion: H. Schrade, *Götter und Menschen Homers* (Stuttgart, Kohlhammer, 1952); P. Chantraine, 'Le Divin et les dieux chez Homère', *Entretiens Hardt* I (1954) 47-94; A. Lesky, 'Göttliche und menschliche Motivation im homerischen Epos', SHA Phil.-hist.Kl. 1961, 4-52; B. C. Dietrich, *Death, Fate and the Gods, the development of a religious idea in Greek popular belief and in Homer* (Athlone Press, 1965); useful summary and bibliography by W. K. C. Guthrie in *CAH* 2nd ed., II, chap. xl (1961).

(b) Moral ideas: A. W. H. Adkins, *Merit and Responsibility, a study in Greek values* (OUP, 1960), chaps. 1-5.

(c) Ancient interpretations: F. Buffière, *Les Mythes d'Homère et la pensée grecque* (Paris, Les Belles Lettres, 1956).

(d) Scholia and transmission: H. Erbse, *Beiträge zur Überlieferung der Iliasscholien* (München, Beck, 1960); M. Van der Valk, *Researches on the Text and Scholia of the Iliad, Part I* (Leiden, Brill, 1963).

Finally, attention should have been drawn earlier to Richmond Lattimore's brilliant translation of the *Iliad* (Univ. of Chicago Press, 1951), which is still not so well known in this country as it deserves to be; the work of a scholar who is also a poet, it has been rightly described as 'a more or less standard version for our half-century'.[20] Nor can any survey leave unmentioned the mammoth *Lexikon des frühgriechischen Epos*,[21] which has taken ten years to reach the word ἄν in its fourth instalment. In its completed form the Homeric scholars of the twenty-first century will find it an invaluable aid; meanwhile we must make do with Ebeling (Teubner, 1885, reprinted Hildesheim, Olms, 1963) and the concordances of Prendergast and Dunbar (revised editions by B. Marzullo, Darmstadt, Wissenschaftliche Buchgesellschaft, 1962).

---

[1] See full critical bibliographies by A. Lesky in *Anzeiger f. d. Altertumswissenschaft*, 1953-65, covering current work, and by H. J. Mette in *Lustrum*, 1956 with addenda in subsequent issues, covering the years 1930-62. Much bibliographical information will also be found in the admirable chapter on Homer in Lesky's *History of Greek Literature* (Eng. trans., Methuen, 1966).

[2] Available also in a shortened version for the general reader under the title *Homer and the Epic* (CUP, 1965).

[3] Two important papers by Kirk appeared in 1960: 'Homer and Modern Oral Poetry' (CQ, N.S. 10) and 'Objective Dating Criteria in Homer' (MH 17), both now reprinted in *The Language and Background of Homer*.

[4] *History of Greek Literature*, 36.

[5] *The Homeric Odyssey, passim; History and the Homeric Iliad*, appendix on 'Multiple authorship in the *Iliad*'. Cf. also Kirk, *Songs of Homer*, chaps. 10 and 11.

[6] *Il Problema Omerico*, Florence, La Nuova Italia, 1952; W. Theiler, 'Noch Einmal die Dichter der *Ilias*' (*Festschrift Kapp*, München, 1954) and '*Ilias* und *Odyssee* in der Verflechtung ihres Entstehens' (MH 19, 1962).

[7] W. Schadewaldt, 'Der Prolog der *Odyssee*' (HSCPh 63, 1958, 15-32) and other studies preliminary to an expected book on the *Odyssey*.

[8] A. Heubeck, *Der Odyssee-Dichter und die Ilias* (Erlangen, Palm und Enke, 1954), stresses especially the wide difference between the religious worlds of the two poems, while Page, *The Homeric Odyssey* 149-59, emphasizes the difference of vocabulary and formulaic usage. Their separatist conclusions are shared by Finley, Kirk, Theiler, Stella (see n. 10 below), Burkert (RhM 103, 1960, 131) and others. But Page's extreme view that 'the *Odyssey* shows no awareness of the existence of the *Iliad*' is justly criticized by Webster, *From Mycenae to Homer*, 276 ff.

[9] W. Kullmann, *Die Quellen der Ilias* (*Troisches Sagenkreis*), Hermes Einzelschrift 14, 1960. Cf. the criticisms of Page, CR, N.S. 11 (1961) 205-9, and of U. Hölscher, *Gnomon*, 38 (1966) 113-27.

[10] G. Germain, *Genèse de l'Odyssée: le fantastique et le sacré* (Presses Universitaires de France, 1954). Other speculations on the relationship of oriental to early Greek poetry will be found in Luigea Stella, *Il Poema di Ulysse* (Florence, La Nuova Italia, 1955), with bibliography, and Webster, *op. cit.*, chap. 3.

[11] It is understandable that some respected veteran scholars like W. Theiler and the late Karl Reinhardt (*Die Ilias und ihr Dichter*, Göttingen, Vandenhoeck und Ruprecht, 1961) have felt unable to adjust their ideas to the new perspective; but one must regret, with Lesky, that younger men should apparently follow them in this.

[12] Lord, *The Singer of Tales*, 129; Notopoulos, HSCPh 68 (1964) 14 f.

[13] Lord, 'Homer's Originality: Oral Dictated Texts' (TAPA 84, 1953, repr. in *Language and Background* 68-78); cf. *Companion*, chap. 5. Lord's idea has been accepted by Sterling Dow (CW 49, 1956) and others, but the present writer is tempted to agree with Page (*Antiquity* 36, 1962, 308 ff.) that the picture of Homer dictating, like a modern Jugoslav bard to a 'Collector', 'will one day take its place among the curiosities of Homeric scholarship'.

[14] Page, *The Homeric Odyssey*, 138-45; R. Sealey, 'From Phemios to Ion', REG 70 (1957) 312-55; Kirk, 'Homer and Modern Oral Poetry' (n. 3 above), and *Songs of Homer*, chap. 4. Kirk has tried to minimize the resulting likelihood of post-Homeric changes in the text, but his arguments on this point have been challenged by Notopoulos, *op. cit.*, 14 and 68, and by Adam Parry, 'Have we Homer's *Iliad?*' (YCS 20, 1966).

[15] J. A. Davison, 'Peisistratus and Homer', TAPA 86 (1955) 1-21; R. Sealey, *op. cit.*, 342-51.

[16] The validity of Ventris and Chadwick's decipherment of Linear B is still denied by A. J. Beattie (*Companion*, 324) and one or two other scholars, but is accepted by the vast majority (including other contributors to the *Companion*).

[17] M. I. Finley, 'Homer and Mycenae: Property and Tenure', *Historia* 6, 1957, 159 (repr. in *Language and Background* 217).

[18] Cf. Sterling Dow's long and careful review of Webster's book, AJP 81 (1960) 422-34. Whitman's belief (shared to some extent by Webster) that '(prehistoric) Athens, and not Ionia, was the cradle of the Greek epic' (*Homer and the Heroic Tradition*, 58) seems to have even slighter evidential foundation.

[19] Kirk, 'Objective Dating Criteria' (n. 3 above) and *Songs of Homer*, chaps. 5-7. A comparable middle course is taken by Lesky, *History of Greek Literature*, 53-8.

[20] Kirk, *Language and Background*, xvi. Lattimore has in preparation a companion version of the *Odyssey*.

[21] Göttingen, Vandenhoeck und Ruprecht, 1953-. Now edited by Gerda Knebel.

Section iv

L. R. Palmer has contributed a general survey[1] of the language of Homer and P. Chantraine has added an appendix on *Les éléments dialectaux de la langue épique* (1957) to his *Grammaire homérique*.

APPENDIX 43

The general assessment of the epic language remains unchanged. Kirk[2] sums up a general consensus when he writes: '... the Iliad and the Odyssey are the culmination of a continuous tradition of oral poetry and ... their linguistic components are of diverse origin both in locality and date?' The question of the Aeolicisms has occasioned further discussion in the light of the evidence provided by the Linear B tablets.

C. J. Ruijgh[3] has taken up the old thesis of Meillet that the epic tradition started in the Mycenaean Peloponnese, where dialects ancestral to the Arcadian and Cyprian of classical times were spoken. Ruijgh's attempt to demonstrate the presence of such 'Achaean' elements has been carefully examined by E. Risch.[4] He concludes (rightly in my view) that no forms have been established which are specifically 'Achaean'. K. Strunk[5] has gone still further and maintains that the 'so-called Aeolicisms' in Homer are to be regarded as Mycenaean elements. Risch,[6] again, points out that such innovations as the datives in -εσσι, the perfect participles in -ων, -οντος and the change of $q^w e$ to *pe* are certainly post-Mycenaean and specifically, Aeolic. This is also the view of Chantraine and Palmer: there remains a stubborn core of forms which find their parallel only in the Aeolic dialects of historical times, and these forms are in some cases demonstrably post-Mycenaean. Palmer also takes the view that the new Mycenaean evidence entails little modification of previous hypotheses relating to the genesis of the epic dialect.[7]

V. Georgiev,[8] on the other hand, has argued that Mycenaean is a mixed dialect and that this is reflected in the dialect mixture of the Homeric poems. This is much like the thesis of Wilamowitz, who sought to account for the phenomenon by pointing to the dialect mixture presented by the inscriptions of Chios and Smyrna. It is to be rejected for similar reasons. The mixture is not the same in Homer as in the Linear B tablets.

J. Chadwick[9] seeks to pin down Mycenaean elements of vocabulary. His essay has been severely criticized by G. P. Shipp.[10] The difficulty is to establish when a word passed out of common use. Thus φάσγανον is certainly to be connected with the *pa-ka-na* of the Knossos Sword Tablets. The word was obsolete in post-Homeric times. But does such obsolescence justify the inference 'it is probably safe to assume that it was already obsolete at the time it was incorporated into the Homeric poems''? What we know is that the word was in ordinary use when Knossos was destroyed. We do not know when it ceased to be a part of everyday vocabulary. We do not know when it was incorporated in the Homeric poems.

The interrelations of the Greek dialects have historical implications which have their bearing on Homeric problems. The new Porzig-Risch thesis has found much favour. This seeks to impugn the long current idea that Arcado-Cypriot and Aeolic have so much in common that they are to be regarded as two branches, south and north, of a common 'Old Achaean dialect' group. Instead West Greek and Aeolic are combined and regarded as descendants of a one-time North Mycenaean, while Arcado-Cypriot and Attic-Ionic go back to South Mycenaean. Chadwick[11] has given currency to this new thesis and Risch's article has been reprinted in a collection edited by Kirk,[12] who refers to it as an 'already classic statement'. There has in fact been strong criticism of the new view by a number of scholars. At the first Mycenaean colloquium E. Benveniste[13] remarked that the hypothesis forces us to assume a period of intense development for the proto-Ionic of the Dark Age before the Ionian migration, whereas it implies for Arcado-Cypriot, which remained faithful to the postulated South Mycenaean, an even longer period of stagnation. Further difficulties have been discussed by Palmer[14] and others.[15] The fact is that the Linear B tablets already present developments which are incompatible with Attic-Ionic and indicate that the dialects of the Peloponnese were distinct from those of Attica in the Bronze Age. Thus the distinctively Arcado-Cypriot syntactic innovation of constructing 'from' propositions with the dative case is exemplified in the Linear B tablets. Again words like *to-pe-za* = τόρπεζα show that the sonant liquid $\underset{\circ}{r}$ had changed as early as the thirteenth century B.C. along a line which cannot lead to the Attic-Ionic τράπεζα. The divergence may be presented thus:

or   ra

To save the new linguistic hypothesis its proponents have recourse to a new *historical* hypothesis. In the Dark Age, before the migrations to Asia Minor, both the North Mycenaeans and the South Mycenaeans of Attica came under the influence of the

APPENDIX 45

'Dorians', who spoke West Greek. It was from them that the Ionians of Attica learned to say, for instance, εὔχεται, instead of the South Mycenaean εὔχετοι and τράπεζα instead of τόρπεζα. This historical hypothesis has a curious implication: the Dorians strongly influenced the Athenians who in the tradition repulsed them, whereas they failed to have this effect on the Arcadians whom they completely surrounded. The point is of importance not only to Homeric scholars but also to historians. They will be aware that an historical thesis devised to patch up the shortcomings of a linguistic hypothesis cannot be taken as 'supported by the linguistic evidence'.[16]

Kirk has emphasized the difficulty of establishing absolute dates for many of the 'late' features alleged by philologists. He examines[17] Shipp's thesis and finds that the facts relating to the concentration of such late linguistic elements in the similes are 'irrefutable'. The conclusion must surely be that the similes are an accretion which developed later in the tradition than the narrative parts. But the similes are one of the most characteristic features of the 'Homeric' poems. They may be regarded as an essential part of the culmination of a continuous tradition and ascribed to the 'great master(s).' I do not think, as Kirk apparently does, that by 'late' Shipp meant 'post-Homeric'. On the contrary, I think that he would agree with Kirk (as I should) that these advanced linguistic elements 'are simply "late" in relation to the whole history of the oral tradition, near the end of which came the great monumental poems'.

---

[1] In *A Companion to Homer*, ed. A. J. B. Wace and F. H. Stubbings, London 1962, pp. 75-178.
[2] G. S. Kirk, *The Songs of Homer*. Cambridge, 1962, p. 192.
[3] *L'élément achéen dans la langue épique*. Assen: Van Gorcum, 1957.
[4] *Gnomon* 30 (1958), 90-4.
[5] *Die sogenannten Äolismen der homerischen Sprache*. Diss. Köln, 1957.
[6] loc. cit.
[7] op. cit.
[8] 'Das Problem der homerischen Sprache im Licht der kreto-mykenischen Texte' in *Minoica und Homer*, ed. V. Georgiev und J. Irmscher, Berlin, 1961, pp. 10-19.
[9] 'Mycenaean Elements in the Homeric Dialect' in *Minoica*. Festschrift zum 80. Geburtstag von J. Sundwall, Berlin, 1958, pp. 116-23.
[10] *Essays in Mycenaean and Homeric Greek*. Melbourne, 1961.

[11] 'The Greek dialects and Greek prehistory', *Greece and Rome* N.S. 3, 1956, 38-50. Also *The Prehistory of the Greek Language* in *Cambridge Ancient History*, rev. ed., vol. 2, ch. 39, fasc. 15.
[12] *Language and Background of Homer*, Cambridge, 1964.
[13] *Études mycéniennes*, ed. M. Lejeune, Paris, 1956, p. 263: 'N'est-il pas plus plausible qu'à l'époque de nos tablettes, l'ionien (qui n'y est pas représenté) était déja plus ou moins largement différencié?'
[14] op. cit., pp. 86-94, and *The Interpretation of Mycenaean Greek Texts*, pp. 60-4:, to the references given ibid, p. 65, add R. Coleman, 'The Dialect Geography of Ancient Greece', *Transactions of the Philological Society*, 1963, 58-126.
[15] A. Tovar, 'On the Position of the Linear B Dialect', *Mycenaean Studies*, ed. E. L. Bennett, Madison, 1964, pp. 141-6.
[16] Cf. Coleman, op. cit., p. 105: '... it is unlikely that any period of contact between West Greek and Ionic speakers would have been sufficiently prolonged to bring about the kind of infiltration that Risch envisaged.'
[17] op. cit., pp. 201 ff.

Section v

New finds have modified the classification on pp. 28-9. Bronze body-armour is now established as Mycenaean; examples are few, but the range is wide; late fifteenth to early fourteenth century, helmet and ideograms of helmet and corslet from Knossos, heavy plate corslet, greaves and cheek-pieces from Argolis; late thirteenth to twelfth century, greaves from Achaea and Cyprus, ideograms from Messenian Pylos, helmets from Cyprus; Submycenaean, helmet from Argolis.[1] A very few cremations occur in predominantly inhumation cemeteries, mostly twelfth-century and in an area reaching from East Attica to the Cyclades.[2] A free-standing temple, containing about twenty approximately life-size statues, was founded on Keos by Minoan settlers in the Middle Bronze Age and remodelled in L.H. III.[3] A seventh-century aryballos, on which a hero in hoplite armour carries two spears, has strengthened the probability that hoplite fighting came in by stages and overlapped with the use of throwing spears.[4] New evidence has come from the impressive palace excavated at Messenian Pylos, Homeric in plan but not in decoration,[5] and from the intensive study of the Linear B tablets.[6] The view that the poems are almost wholly Mycenaean[7] gains some support from the new discoveries, though corslets and greaves seldom appear where they would be expected in actual Homeric fighting, and cremations and temples are abnormal in the Bronze Age. A fifteenth-century Minoan seal recently found on Naxos shows a warrior pouring libation at an altar beside which grows a graceful little palm tree;[8] it is a perfect illustration

APPENDIX

of *Odyssey* 6, 162f. but it does not prove the great antiquity of the simile. The opposite view[9] is taking a new form, accepting a Mycenaean tradition but claiming that it was grossly distorted, not by later practices, but by the imagination of poets and painters; so the hourglass shield was copied from the Mycenaean 8-shield seen on heirlooms or chance finds, Homeric chariot tactics were an attempt, in a society without war chariots, to make sense of Mycenaean chariot charges, and funerals on vases and in Homer reflected what were believed to be the customs of the Heroic Age. Sophisticated antiquarianism is hardly credible so early, and though misunderstanding is probable, nothing could be easier than a chariot charge. The accuracy of the literary and representational evidence has been further challenged by a full comparison of them with surviving weapons and armour,[10] raising an interesting question about the methods of poets and painters. Apparently the bronze-headed, ashen, single spear of Achilles was traditional; Homer keeps it, but makes Achilles throw it. If legend said that a hero killed two enemies with two spears, it is hard to see what a painter could do except give the hero a second spear, whether or not it was compatible with the rest of his armour. Both seem to draw on the present as far as the story allows, and sometimes further, and we are therefore justified in asking in what period any feature was 'contemporary'. But the criticism is salutary, and calls for a reappraisal of the validity of archaeological evidence in Homeric studies.

Numerous histories of the Bronze Age have been published.[11] New evidence is provided by the final account of the American excavations at Troy,[12] by widespread field work and excavation on Mycenaean sites,[13] and by work on the Linear B and other Bronze Age archives, which put some flesh on the bare bones of archaeology,[14] but they also draw largely on the literary tradition. The reconstructions differ widely, mainly because of the difficulty of determining the relative order of events within the thirteenth century. Troy to the Greeks was just 'Troy', not Settlements VI and VIIa-b, as London was 'London' before and after the Great Fire. If it was destroyed early in the century, its fall could be a unique triumph of Greek power, but if it fell about 1200 B.C., it becomes an incident in a destruction which embraced also Hittites, Egyptians and Greeks. The former is more Homeric, but the *Chanson de Roland* shows that an incident can be remembered as a triumph. The post-Mycenaean period is less well represented,[15] and the greatest need is probably for an impartial assessment of the fragmentary evidence for the history of the Geometric and Early Archaic periods. In studying the history of any period, it is safer to separate the literary and archaeological evidence. We have two short, independent accounts of the crucial transitional period,[16] using external and traditional evidence, and the differences are striking; on the one hand, a drift of nomadic herdsmen, aimlessly seeking new pastures over a long period, on the other, organized armies whose generals discuss the best route to cut off the enemy and meet to divide up the conquered territory.

There is additional evidence for an interest in legends in the eighth and seventh centuries: from Late Geometric graves on Ischia, a second 'Shipwreck' vase which removes the doubts expressed (p. 37, n. 10) about the Attic example and seems to repeat the theme of the 'sole survivor', and an inscription which refers to the Cup of Nestor as well known, and from Athens a Geometric scene very like later versions of the death of Astyanax; from the seventh century, from Eleusis a third 'Blinding of Polyphemus' and from Mykonos a lively picture of the Trojan Horse.[17]

---

[1] A. Snodgrass, *Early Greek Armour and Weapons*, Edinburgh U.P., 1964, pp. 3-4, 71-3. Ideograms, *B.I.C.S.* 6 (1959), pp. 47ff.
[2] V. R. d'A. Desborough, *The Last Mycenaeans and their Successors*, Oxford U.P., 1964, p. 71.
[3] J. L. Caskey, 'Excavations in Keos, 1964-1965', *Hesperia* 35 (1966), pp. 367ff.
[4] Snodgrass, *op. cit.*, p. 138 and Pl. 15. The evidence of the Chigi vase (Pl. 36) is ambiguous, since the front ranks have two spears of equal length, the other ranks one spear, and the soldiers still arming one long thrusting, and one short throwing spear.
[5] C. W. Blegen and M. Rawson, *The Place of Nestor at Pylos in Western Messenia*, vol. I, Princeton U.P., 1966 (not yet available), cf. my 'Houses in the Odyssey', CQ N.S. 5 (1955), pp. 1ff.
[6] M. Ventris and J. Chadwick, *Documents in Mycenaean Greek*, Cambridge U.P., 1956.
[7] In A. J. B. Wace and F. H. Stubbings, *A Companion to Homer*, Macmillan, 1962, post-Mycenaean evidence is virtually ignored. See my review in *Phoenix* 17 (1963), pp. 293ff.
[8] BCH 84 (1960), p. 810, fig. 2.
[9] M. I. Finley, *The World of Odysseus*, Chatto & Windus, 1956; G. S. Kirk, *The Homeric Poems as History*, *CAH*² fasc. 22. But see J. K. Anderson, 'Homeric, British and Cyrenaic chariots', AJA 69 (1965), pp. 349ff.
[10] Snodgrass, *op. cit.*
[11] Denys Page, *History and the Homeric Iliad*, University of California, 1959; T. B. L. Webster, *From Mycenae to Homer*, Methuen, 2nd ed., 1964; V. R. d'A. Desborough, *op. cit.*, n. 2; E. Vermeule, *Greece in the Bronze Age*, Chicago U.P., 1964; Lord William Taylour, *The Mycenaeans*, Thames & Hudson, 1964; F. H. Stubbings, *C.A.H.*² fasc. 18, 26, 39; G. E. Mylonas, *Mycenae and the Mycenaean Age*, Princeton U.P., 1966, cf. O. Broneer, 'The Cyclopean wall on the Isthmus of Corinth and its bearing on Late Bronze Age chronology', *Hesperia* 35 (1966), pp. 346ff.

[12] C. W. Blegen, *Troy IV*, Princeton U.P., 1958: *Troy*, *CAH*[2] fasc. 1: *Troy and the Trojans*, Thames & Hudson, 1963; M. I. Finley and others, 'The Trojan War', *J.H.S.* 84 (1962) pp. 1ff.; C. Nylander, 'The Fall of Troy', *Antiquity* 37 (1963), pp. 1ff; G. E. Mylonas, 'Priam's Troy and the date of its fall', *Hesperia* 33 (1964), pp. 352ff.
[13] R. Hope-Simpson, *A Gazetteer and Atlas of Mycenaean Sites*, BICS Suppl. 16, 1965.
[14] Cautious assessment by Page, *op. cit.*, n. 11.
[15] C. G. Starr, *The Origins of Greek Civilization*, Cape, 1962 (to 650 B.C.); A. R. Burn, *The Lyric Age of Greece*, Arnold, 1960.
[16] V. R. d'A. Desborough and N. G. L. Hammond, *The end of Mycenaean Civilization and the Dark Age*, *C.A.H*[2]. fasc. 13.
[17] (Ischia) Sir John Myres, *Homer and his Critics*, Routledge, 1958, Pl. 8; (Athens) E. T. H. Brann, *Antike Kunst*, 1959, pp. 35ff; (Eleusis) *A.J.A.* 59 (1955), Pl. 67 fig. (Mykonos) 3; BCH 86 (1962), Pl. 29.

CHAPTER II

EARLY GREEK LYRIC POETRY §

BY JOHN G. GRIFFITH

OF the great Greek lyric poets only Pindar survives in an independent manuscript tradition, so that until recently we relied largely on quotation and allusion in extant authors for our knowledge of this literature. It so happens that the first two papyrus discoveries in this field, which gave us portions of Alcman's Partheneion and of nineteen odes of Bacchylides, are still the most substantial, but these occurred before 1900 and fall outside the scope of this review, although recent work done on them will be mentioned in its place.[1] However since the first excavations in 1897, the papyri from Oxyrhynchus, supplemented by similar documents in Berlin,[2] Italy,[3] Strassburg, and elsewhere, have restored to us much of outstanding interest, including considerable passages from Pindar's Paeans, numerous though often disjointed fragments of Sappho and Alcaeus, some 160 lines of Corinna, of which about one-third is tolerably readable, a puzzling poem of Ibycus and, if they may be reckoned for this purpose as lyricists, a little of Archilochus and Tyrtaeus. Yet nothing new is attributed to Stesichorus and, surprisingly, very little to Simonides,[4] while Anacreon claims only one doubtful fragment, although
* more of the early Ionian poets is awaited from the next volume (XXII) of the Oxyrhynchus series.

In relation to the sustained efforts directed to these remains by many of the leading Hellenists of this century,[5] the substantive gains to our knowledge may seem disappointingly small, and serious perplexities await solution. We are still uncertain of the
* precise connotation of some fundamental terms; we cannot be sure of the originator[6] of the triadic structure of strophe, antistrophe, and epode; the music remains a mystery.[7] The dates of Alcman and Archilochus rest on doubtful evidence, while the personality of the significant Stesichorus is as misty as ever. Even with fresh evidence, the nature of Pindar's tactlessness to the Aeginetans which complicates the study of Nemean VII is still obscure, although that poem may now be read in the light of the offending

§ The marginal asterisks draw attention to supplementary notes to th˙ pp. 83–7 below.

passage of the sixth Paean. Overshadowing all questions of interpretation, technical problems of supplementing gaps in the papyri persist and demand as much insight as patience; all too often one can at best hope for no more than, in Gildersleeve's phrase, 'restoration to the semi-consciousness of square brackets'.[8] This is particularly true of the Oxyrhynchus rolls which were in many cases torn vertically in antiquity. This is why we have so many middles or ends of lines and so few complete ones.

Nevertheless there have been notable advances. Some of the fresh material is poetry of the highest order, while the finding of an Olympic victor-list[9] has fixed the date of the Ninth Olympian and also confirmed the computation of Pythiads for Pindaric chronology from 582, not 586 B.C. In consequence, the early dating of the Pythian odes must be abandoned; this error distorts the historical perspective in some editions still widely used, such as Gildersleeve's. The linguistic and metrical practices of the two Lesbian poets have been systematically examined and an 'abnormal' body of Sappho's poetry isolated.[10] How this phenomenon is to be understood is still not fully agreed, while Lobel's absolute exclusion of synonyms from Lesbian poetic vocabulary may have to be reconsidered in the light of new evidence.[11]

Space and difficulties of publication have necessitated the use in this account of a bare construe in place of continuous quotation in the original Greek, but substantive divergencies are indicated where possible. As foreign publications are not always readily available, in the notes to this chapter page references to C. M. Bowra's *Greek Lyric Poetry* (Clar. Press, 1936)[12] have been given for extracts (other than those from Pindar, Bacchylides and Archilochus) known at that date, or when applicable, to the same scholar's shorter treatment in J. U. Powell and E. A. Barber, *New Chapters in Greek Literature* (third series), pp. 1-67 (Clar. Press, 1933).[13] For Sappho and Alcaeus Lobel's distinctive numeration is cited first, with that of Diehl (designated by his initial) following.[14] For Pindar the references are to Bowra's text (Clar. Press, 1935; revised 1946), for Bacchylides to Snell's Teubner text of 1949. The remaining poets are cited from E. Diehl, *Anthologia Lyrica Graeca* (Leipzig, Teubner, 1925).[15] This account has not been further lengthened by references to such cardinal works as Wilamowitz, *Textgeschichte der griechischen Lyriker* (Berlin-Göttingen, 1900) or his *Sappho und Simonides* (Berlin, 1913). The doctrine contained therein has in essentials been assimilated into the main stream of criticism, and this single acknowledgment must suffice.

ALCMAN

* Both date and birthplace of Alcman are debated. Ancient authorities put his *floruit* in the 27th, 30th or 42nd Olympiad. Rohde long ago acutely observed that both the first two could be equated, on different ancient chronologies, with the seventh year of the reign of Ardys of Lydia: that is, if Gyges was killed in 652 B.C., 646 B.C. Thus Alcman would be a mid-seventh century figure. Discussion of his origin is vitiated for lack of evidence; if he had some Lydian connection, as a nebulous tradition suggests, he certainly lived and wrote in Laconia, in a language 'basically and preponderantly Laconian vernacular', with some epic contamination, so far as the fragments, with the possible exception of the interesting fr. 58, warrant inference.[16]

His Partheneion, discovered in 1855, has attracted to itself a large literature. A good conspectus of the issues and the present state of the various controversies is in D. L. Page, *Alcman, the Partheneion* (Cambridge, 1951); this gives a careful text that will be the basis of future research, with full exegetical information and a detailed discussion of the dialect. Where, however, so much divergence of opinion exists on problems of interpretation, it is well to read this book in the light of a review such as that of J. A. Davison.[19] It is generally agreed that the metrical unit is a 14-line stanza, and Page rightly questions the suggested triadic pattern of 2 strophes of 4 lines followed by a 6-line epode within it. The local mythology in the fragmentary beginning is well handled by Page (pp. 26-44), with its allusions to the sons of Hippocoon, to Aisa and Poros, to the daughter of Porcus (perhaps identified with Nereus) and the rest; Alcman may have rendered these old stories from a Laconian viewpoint, glorifying the local heroes where opportunity offered.

The interpretative quicksands of the latter part from line 36 to the end can be charted; scholars will continue to negotiate them by different routes as best they can. At least the attempt to distribute the lines between speakers can be given up, if only because the suggestions to hand yield such discrepant results,[17] quite apart from the lack of textual evidence. Also the principal problems may be met without recourse to so elaborate a *tour de force* of exegesis as Bowra's.[18] Page's main contentions are: (i) the choir is not split into hemichors, (ii) Hagesichora, Agido, and the eight girls named in lines 70-2 make up the 'decad' of 99, (iii) Agido is 'second in command' to Hagesichora, (iv) Aotis in 87 is the moon, perhaps to be identified with Ortheia, (v) in 61 the right reading is ὀρθρίαι φᾶρος ('the plough to the goddess of the morning twilight', although ὄρθριαι as nom. fem. plural is just conceivable), (vi) the Peleiades have nothing to do with the Pleiads, but are a rival Choir. If, however, objections such as Davison's,[19] based on doubts about the metaphorical use of μάχονται in 63, are sustained, then the Peleiades may not be a rival Choir after all, and we should be back where we started. But the case for one is strong on other counts and holds the field at present.

The urgency of the interpretative problems all too easily obscures the beauty of the poem, with its fresh imagery, verbal music (what girls ever had names that came lighter on the tongue than Vianthemis and her companions?) and homely, yet lively phrase. It is our only considerable literary witness to that interlude of brilliant civilization in seventh-century Spartan history that contrasts so strongly with the discipline and austerity of other days.

SAPPHO[20]

Her first book is now known from *POxy.* 1231 (fr. 56) to have consisted of 1320 lines or 330 Sapphic stanzas. Its opening poem 'Immortal Aphrodite of the rainbow throne ...' was familiar from Dionysius of Halicarnassus' quotation;[21] equally famous is the original of Catullus' 51st poem ('Ille mi par esse deo videtur ...'), the Greek of which is so well criticized by 'Longinus' in the tenth chapter of his essay *On the Sublime.* The occasion of this latter poem has been investigated, and it is generally agreed to have been a wedding feast at which Sappho was present because she has trained the choir which sings the hymeneals; though consistent with this conclusion, the linguistic analysis of Wilamowitz and Snell should not be pressed. Antiquity recognized the psychological interest of the piece; in this regard the comparison with two passages in Archilochus is suggestive. He uses Homeric idiom to describe the physical effects of his state of emotional tension, swooning and a mist over the eyes suggesting death; Sappho too is 'but little short of dying', but dispenses with epic phrasing to say so.[22]

From papyrus finds, and so less completely preserved but of

notable charm, is the propempticon to her brother, perhaps the Charaxus whose relations with the Egyptian courtesan Doricha-Rhodopis are mentioned by Herodotus (2. 135). Of transcendant loveliness, in spite of lacunae, is the poem to Anactoria which concludes with this miraculous stanza:

τᾶ]ς κε βολλοίμαν ἔρατόν τε βᾶμα
κἀμάρυχμα λάμπρον ἴδην προσώπω
ἢ τὰ Λύδων ἄρματα κἀν ὄπλοισι
πεσδο]μάχεντας.

I had liefer see her lovesome step and the bright radiance of her countenance than the chariots of the Lydians and infantrymen in armour doing battle.

This poem shows marked ring-form, that stylistic feature of archaic Greek poetry whereby the end of a poem (or a clearly marked-off section) verbally echoes the beginning. We find this elsewhere in Sappho; there is a particularly clear example in the last book of the *Iliad*.[23]

Our earliest witness to any part of her text is the ostracon of the second or early first century B.C., brilliantly deciphered by Medea Norsa,[24] which enables us to emend and combine two known fragments into what must have been, when complete, one of the most exquisite pieces of paradise-poetry in any literature. Discrepancies between the citations and the ostracon-text make restoration particularly hazardous in details, but a fair idea may be gained from D. L. Page's presentation in *Greek Literary Papyri* (Loeb) vol. I, pp. 376-8:

> '*Descending from Heaven* (?) ... *Come hither, I pray,* ye Cretans, to the holy temple, *where* is a lovely grove of
> 3 apple-trees and altars therein fragrant with frankincense. In it cool water babbles *quietly* (μαλίαν, see Hesych., *s.v.*) through the boughs and the whole place is overshadowed
> 6 with roses. About the shrine is the drowsy quiet of quivering leaves. In it a meadow that pastures horses (ἱππόβοτος) blooms with *oak* (? laurel) blossom, and dill-plants breathe
> 9 a honied scent. Come, Cypris, taking garlands do thou deign to grant me nectar as thou pourest it gracefully in chalices of gold, all mixed for the festival.

3–6 ('In it ... leaves') = Inc. Lib. 6: 5 D: *GLP.*, p. 203
9–11 ('Come ... festival') = α.6 App.: 6 D: *GLP.*, p. 200

If the reference to Cretans at the start were certain, the temple-grove might be that of Aphrodite Antheia, whose cult is known at Cnossus, and Sappho may have drawn her inspiration from a visit on her journey either to or from her exile in Sicily. Whatever the setting, the poem has features, as A. Turyn has well shown, common in later paradise-poetry. Pindar's dirge (fr. 114) gives a very similar picture with its lines:

> ... In meadows red with roses is the fringe of their city, overshadowed with frankincense and heavy with golden fruits.

It recalls too Vergil's description (A. 6. 637f) of the *amoena virecta* of Elysium. Indeed his *per campum pascuntur equi* and Pindar's phrase later in the same fragment 'some take their pleasure in horses' virtually guarantee the reading ἱππόβοτος in Sappho. Another eschatological passage is [Plato] Axiochus 371 c-d, especially its hierophantic 'meadows in the spring time clad in flowers of every hue', and later 'pure streams'. In this literature 'cool water' is symbolic of spiritual recreation (*refrigerium*). There is nothing impossible in Sappho having had a close link with this current of mystical ideas loosely called 'Orphic-Pythagorean'. The burden of her address to a rich lady of no literary taste[25]

> In death shalt thou lie, and there will be no remembrance of thee at any time, nor yearning for thee hereafter. Thou hast no share in the roses from Pieria...

is consistent with such a creed, whereby *pii vates* were placed in Elysium (Verg. A. 6. 662) but those *qui divitiis soli incubuere repertis* were excluded (*ibid.*, 610). However this may be, Sappho is praying for Aphrodite's inspiration and imagining a theophany against a paradise setting whose features later became conventional in this kind of writing. Noble as much later poetry in this vein is, it never surpassed the almost unearthly effect of these few lines of Sappho.[26]

Her second book was written, as Hephaestion tells us, entirely in the metre known to the ancients as '14-syllable Sapphic pentameter', a clumsy label which obscures its possible kinship to the glyconic, of which it may be ultimately an 'expanded' form. Its last poem, the ending of which is preserved in two papyri[27], was a narrative one on the wedding of Hector and Andromache, and written not in stanzas but line by line. It raises acute critical

problems, and not only because it shows the metrical and flexional 'abnormalities' that Sappho eschewed elsewhere,[28] except apparently in her other 'dactylic' work. On the strength of these and more particularly of an alleged but textually doubtful reminiscence of a phrase (κατ' αὔτμενα, if the reading is sound) in another fragment[29] as well as the undoubted trisyllabic neuter plural form πορφύρα (in Attic πορφυρᾶ) instead of the Lesbian πορφύρια, Lobel contended that this was by an Attic imitator, who had assimilated something of the spirit of the Lesbian poetic tradition, but not the mechanics of its versification. Before so detailed an attack judgment must be suspended, yet the case for its authenticity is not lost; it is good writing, and the author had a nice eye for detail. Furthermore it is explicitly attributed to Sappho by the two papyri and by Athenaeus (11.460d) who quotes line 10 of the fragment. The abnormalities may be licences (some, though not all, consistent with epic diction) which she may have allowed in an essentially narrative piece, though avoiding them elsewhere. This
* view does not lack supporters,[30] and one hopes that it is right.

Two poems of great loveliness are added to her fifth book. One[31] whose first surviving line is: 'Honestly I want to die' gives a haunting idea of the tenderness and depth of her affections; the other[32] includes a reference to her pupil-friend Atthis and speaking of a departed girl contains the memorable phrase:

νῦν δὲ Λύδαισιν ἐμπρέπεται γυναίκεσσιν, ὥς ποτ' ἀελίω δύντος ἀ
βροδοδάκτυλος σελάννα . . .

Now she shines out among the Lydian women as does the rosy-fingered moon when the sun is set . . .

This book was thought to consist of 3-line stanzas,[33] but this last piece resists such division and this whole 30-syllable phrase must form the metrical unit.[34] The glyconic seems to have been the highest common factor of the contents of this book, which will thus have been a series of variations upon this verse with additions and expansions to it.[35]

Other fragments might be mentioned, but the appeal of such poetry survives even divorce from context and the unsatisfactory and provisional nature of much of the restoration. Yet the perfection that comes from such unaffected simplicity and overwhelming felicity of phrase still dazzles the reader. Sappho's

Fig. 1 (a)
Birth of Athena

Fig. 1 (b)
Athena presenting Herakles to Zeus

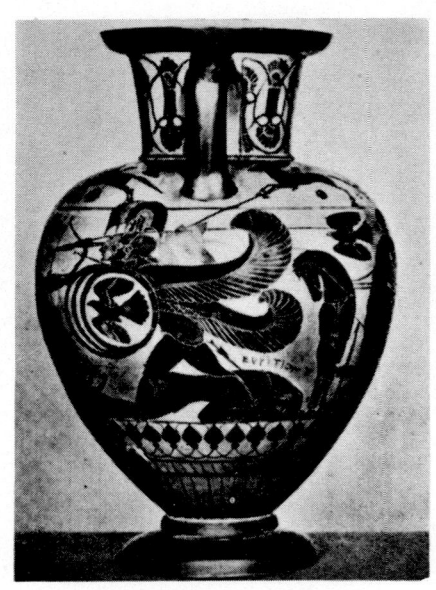

Fig. 2
Winged Geryon

Fig. 3
Herakles and the Chariot of the Sun

Plate II]

Fig. 4
Herakles in the Cup of the Sun

Fig. 5
Anacreon and Revellers

[Plate III

Fig. 6
Self-devotion of Croesus

Plate IV]

achievement is perhaps the more remarkable when account is taken of the strictness of her 'normal' versification. Besides the prosodiacal features characteristic of her 'normal' poems already referred to (p. 44 and cf. note 28), we find that she avoids hiatus, and that while the first two syllables of her glyconics are indifferently short or long, the last is not *anceps* but always long; also she does not use paragogic *nu* to 'make position'. Thus the task of her future editors, if their restorations are to satisfy these and other provisions, becomes more exacting.[36]

ALCAEUS[20]

Our impression of Alcaeus has been substantially corrected by new discovery. Allusions and the few significant fragments preserved in ancient authors had suggested a convivial, light-weight character: thus H. Weir Smyth[37] could write in 1900 'All Alcaeus' poetry is virtually sympotic'. Some of the additions certainly emphasize this side of the man, as the poem to Melanippus whom Herodotus (5.95) mentions in connection with Alcaeus' 'discretion' in the fighting against the Athenians at Sigeum: 'Drink and get tipsy, Melanippus, along with me...' This proceeds to enlarge on the theme *post mortem nulla voluptas* by the mythological example of Sisyphus. A sterner outlook is apparent in the political poems; here he comes out as an outspoken defender of the landowning *ancien régime*,[38] and is heartily against the mercantile tyrants of the day, Myrsilus and Pittacus. These both figure in a vigorous denunciation which runs: 'Let him, made kinsman by marriage to the children of Atreus, devour the city...' — a phrase which stigmatizes Pittacus' marriage above his station. In another poem he is accused of hypocrisy in that he had promoted legislation to discourage drinking, though of very questionable sobriety himself.[39]

Alcaeus, if born c. 620 B.C., was a boy when the civil upheavals in Lesbos began. In 612 his brothers helped to overthrow Melanchrus, but the successor, Myrsilus, had the best of a subsequent phase of the struggle, so that Alcaeus, now a combatant, and his friends had to retire for a time to Pyrrha,[40] some distance from the capital. At what point in these confused events the fighting against the Athenians at Sigeum occurred cannot be fixed, but from Alcaeus' Pyrrha-period may date the two latest published and longest consecutive fragments of his that we have. In the first of these in Alcaic stanzas, he calls upon three gods to deliver him and his associates from their troubles and for vengeance on the turncoat Pittacus, who has gone back on his solemn word.⁴¹

> ... *Where by a hill* seen from afar the Lesbians established this great precinct in common. In it they set altars of the Blessed Immortals and invoked Zeus of Suppliants and thee, glorious goddess Aeolian, thou that art the source from which all spring, and as the third they named Cemelius (= bountiful?) this Dionysus that feeds on raw flesh. Come ye, having a kindly heart hearken to our prayer and deliver us from these toils and sore exile. But let a Fury pursue yon son of Hyrrhas — a Fury sent by those of us when once, making sacrifices *of lambs*⁴² we foreswore *betraying* any of our comrades in any wise, but that we would either die and rest clad in earth at the hands of men who then *were uppermost* or when we had slain these same, thereafter deliver the folk from their troubles. This the Paunch bethought him as not to his liking, and with no qualms he tramples on the covenants and seeks to devour this city ... in no lawful wise. ... '

The name Myrsilus can be read in the fragmentary stanza that follows. The trinity Hera-Zeus-Dionysus (Thyone) may be the same as that in Sappho α.6 (28 D), but the title of Dionysus here (be it Cemelius or, against the papyrus-accentuation, Decemelius) is unexplained, if indeed it is a title at all. The general purport is however straightforward enough: it is a mordant but not unmanly hymn of hate — nascent hate perhaps, in so far as Pittacus' treachery is mentioned as if it were surprising news. The abusive epithet 'Physcon' was vouched for in Alcaeus by Diogenes Laertius (1.81), and we now have it in its context.

Perhaps from the same period is the singular poem surviving in column ii of the same papyrus. The poet has taken refuge at the extremity of the island near a precinct where competitions of female beauty are held; here he leads a yokel's life, missing the bustle of politics. Metre⁴³ suggests that the lines preceding this extract and mentioning a 'royal wall' (Hera's, according to the scholiast) came from another poem; we cannot be sure therefore of the localization of our piece, but it may have been the same. It runs:

Luckless I live, having a yokel's portion, while I crave to hear the assembly being announced, Agesilaidas, and the council. As for what my father and grandfather possessed and *grew old with*[44] among citizens that do each other despite — from this have I been evicted, in exile at the world's end. Like Onomacles in solitude did I inhabit a *hill*, I a *werewolf shunning* the war. For it is not *proper*[45] (οὐκ ἄ(ρ)με{ι}νον) to pick a quarrel with *stronger* men ... to the precinct of the Blessed Gods ... setting foot on the black earth, I, comforting myself in these gatherings do dwell, keeping my feet out of harm's way, in a place where the Lesbian lasses that compete in comeliness go with their trailing cloaks, and around murmurs the divine voice of women — the sound of their holy cry of joy at this season of the year.

This poem ended at the next stanza, as a *coronis* shows. The allusion to the werewolf is obscure and the adjoining words ill preserved. Lobel cites Hesychius' entry under *Pylaiides* ('women competing in beauty and winning') for the last lines; the precinct may thus have been near Mt. Pylaion, but unfortunately ancient descriptions do not fix the spot. The unexpected reference to this side of Lesbian feminine life brings the militant Alcaeus nearer to the world of Sappho; it is of course only coincidence that the epic reminiscence ἄχω θεσπεσία (line 27) recurs in her 'abnormal' poem[46] but the occurrence of στάσιν in the sense of 'quarrel' (line 19) is remarkable (see note 11). The metre too is interesting: two expanded glyconics of the form commonly called 'lesser Asclepiads', a glyconic lengthened by a syllable ('Hipponacteum') and an expanded 'glyconoid' element make up the stanza.[47]

The scholiast on a Berlin papyrus[40] speaks of a 'first exile' to Pyrrha, as a result of a plot against Myrsilus. This implies a second absence, so that Alcaeus seems to have returned to Mitylene, probably on the death of Myrsilus, over which he exults. The rise of Pittacus, who eventually became 'aesymnetes' in 590-580 B.C., would have been distasteful to Alcaeus; perhaps the voyage to Egypt mentioned by Strabo (1.37) may be an allusion to this second exile. Certainly his brother Antimenidas entered Babylonian service; if the tantalizing reference to Ascalon and Babylon on a papyrus scrap concerns him, he may have served in the Palestinian campaign of 597-6 B.C. against King Jehoiachim, or possibly in the later one of 586 B.C. We know nothing about Alcaeus' activities in his second exile, unless inferences may be drawn from this sinister allusion to Lydian gold:

> Father Zeus, the Lydians, distressed[48] at our misfortunes, gave us two thousand staters, in the hope that we could enter the sacred citadel, though in no wise had we as yet received any kindness from them or even knew them at all. Yet he, like a cunning fox, was hoping to hide, by putting forth easy speeches.

Whatever the upshot of this, he was recalled and generously forgiven by Pittacus; this act alone, apart from other accounts of the man, leaves us in no doubt that our poet's picture of him is grossly prejudiced. What Alcaeus did after his return is unknown, as is the date of his death.[49]

The comparison of the state to a ship at sea, familiar in other literature, seems to have been a favourite with Alcaeus. The lines referred in antiquity to the fight against Myrsilus develop a nautical allegory:

> I am puzzled by the rising[10] of the winds; one wave rolls from this side and another from that, while we drift in between in our black ship, sorely buffeted by a great storm. The bilge is up to the masthead, and the whole sail is already transparent and there are great rents in it.

This poem may have ended with nothing more stirring than a summons to his friend Bucchis to come and get drunk with him, though the connection of the fragments is not proved[50]. Another poem of the same period describes an emergency at sea, but this leads up to a rousing exhortation:

> Let us patch up the bulwarks as fast as may be and run for a safe haven. Let no weak fear overcome any one of us, for great is the task that lies plain before us. Remember our former disgrace; now let a man be proven and let us not shame by our cowardice our gallant parents that lie beneath the sod.

We can now emend and add with certainty to Alcaeus' works the scolion in the same vein preserved in a garbled form by Athenaeus (15.695a). This snatch is now shown by *POxy.* 2298 to have been from a longer poem; as Alcaeus wrote it, it may have run somewhat as follows:

> ... it is not right that squalls prevail (?). Nay, one must *rightly* forecast the sailing, whether a man has the power and skill of hand, since whenever he is at sea, he needs must abide the conditions ... *nor* is there any device ... *you must go* as the wind takes *you*.

For Alcaeus this was far from a conventional literary formula; it reads like a vivid presentation of his own experience.[51]

Two of his non-political pieces call for notice. One compares the errant Helen with the virtuous Thetis and draws the obvious moral: Thetis' son was 'noblest of the demigods', while Trojans and their city were ruined because of Helen. In a 'cletic' hymn to the Dioscuri summoning them from the 'Isle of Pelops' to the aid of storm-tossed sailors there is a description of the electrical phenomenon known to Mediterranean seafarers as 'St. Elmo's fire'. Whether this is earlier than the account of it in the 33rd Homeric hymn can not be settled, as this may also date from c. 600 B.C.[52]

Alcaeus' metric differs from Sappho's. It has been thought that he conceived his poems in 4-line units;[53] certainly the last line of his Sapphic stanza does not in the extant instances coalesce with the third, as hers not infrequently did. His vocabulary admits by-forms such as γαῖα, δῶμα, τέος, πύκινος as well as γᾶ, δόμος, σός, πύκνος to which Sappho limited herself. These and other divagations from her stricter norm are mostly explicable in terms of Homeric influence; they may also be due in part to the more mundane nature of much of his subject-matter and his robust and at times colloquial way of expressing it.

STESICHORUS[54]

So far no papyri supplement the 26 meagre fragments and the other allusions upon which our scanty knowledge of this great figure rests. To some extent, however, recent study of late seventh- and early sixth-century vase-painting compensates. The traditional date for him is thus incidentally corroborated: Suidas gives his birth in Olympiad 37 (632-29 B.C.) and his death in the 56th (556-53 B.C.), and it is precisely at this period and just after that myth-treatment in painting bears on what we know of these lost

lyric narrative poems. Certainly poet and painter may often be drawing independently on common saga-material, but in some cases the poet's influence is apparent. A striking instance is the Phrynos painter's cup (see fig. 1(a)): one panel shows the birth of Athena from the head of Zeus with the goddess already fully armed, a detail known from the scholiast on Apollonius Rhodius
* (4.1310) to be Stesichorean. Hephaestus too is represented, having done duty as *accoucheur*, and this one suspects may be an idea of the poet. The other side of the cup (fig. 1(b)) has Herakles, not as previously depicted armed with bow only, but complete with club and lion-skin; this we know originated with Stesichorus. Two (perhaps three) Stesichorean motifs on the same vase point strongly to conscious borrowing by the painter.⁵⁵

Features of his *Geryoneis* which can be illustrated from vases are the winged form of a three-bodied Geryon, appearing on two Chalcidean amphorae painted before 550 B.C. (see fig. 2), the episode of Herakles stopping the Sun or perhaps threatening it with his arrows (see fig. 3), and of his sitting in the Cup of the Sun (see fig. 4). Even if some vase-paintings are subsequent to the poet's lifetime, they testify to the persistence of his inventions. Almost all the known poems can be thus illustrated from vases or sculpture; extant artefacts apart, Pausanias' accounts of the Chest of Cypselus and the Amyclae Throne show that each of those monuments had four themes known to have been handled by Stesichorus, a proportion high enough to suggest direct influence.⁵⁶

A strong case can be made out for Stesichorus' having had close connections with Sparta and its politics. It explains the novel
* version he offered of the Helen-myth, with its surprising Palinode and imaginative variant whereby a Phantom Helen went to Troy in place of the real one. Features of his *Oresteia* that chime in with sixth-century Spartan politics included the localization of the death of Agamemnon in Lacedaemon, not in Mycenae; in other ways too he had considerable influence on the post-Homeric
* handling of the Orestes myth which is reflected in Attic tragedy.⁵⁷

To so inventive a genius one would readily ascribe the origin of triadic structure (see note 6), and with Alcman's claim disallowed (p. 40 above), this may be provisionally accepted. The long dactylic rhythms of the extant fragments have a sweep and dignity of their own, though one suspects that they would pall in continuous recitation. For an impression of what a complete lyric narrative of his may have been like, we still can do no better than think of the Argonaut story in lines 70-253 of Pindar's Fourth Pythian, its length doubled or trebled,[58] and some of its characteristically Pindaric features subtracted.[59]

IBYCUS

Ibycus, some thirty years junior to Stesichorus, inherited something of the Western Greek choral tradition, but is alone among the lyricists in that his reputation is somewhat diminished by new discovery. Quotations had shown his fondness for a romantic handling of his subject-matter, with his Achilles marrying Medea in Elysium, or Menelaus refraining from killing Helen because of her beauty. The love-symbolism of the quince-tree that underlies the longer of his two best-known fragments is consistent with this tendency, as is the elaborate comparison of Love to a hunting-net and the simile of the old racehorse that makes up the other. These two miniature masterpieces of limpid phrase have no peer outside Sappho. Elsewhere dactylic measures might recall the sterner Stesichorus, but his language, with its somewhat luscious compound adjectives, imparts a sensuous though not unattractive languor to the result, as is well shown in this picture of bird life, which makes one think of Aristophanes:

> On its topmost leaves there sit parti-hued ducks and shags of quivering neck that feed unseen in the dark and halcyons with their long wings.[60]

The new encomium to Polycrates is fairly certainly his, or if not by him, then by a close imitator. Language and content exclude Stesichorus, metre and style Anacreon, the only other likely author of a work on a person of that name. The manner is artificial and the total effect to us uninteresting, though perhaps the latest writer on it, D. L. Page, is over-severe on the defects of what never probably set out to be more than a slight piece of court-poetry. Of the forty-eight concluding lines we possess in a fairly continuous state, the bulk is an elaborate example of *praeteritio* — 'I will not praise the Greeks, or Paris, or Cassandra . . .' A tiresome break in the papyrus obscures the *dénouement*, but a reference to a 'son of Hyllis' (hardly the comely Nireus with an alternative genealogy, but an unknown beauty from the lost epic cycle) and to Troilus leads up to a climax of naive compliment: 'You too,

Polycrates, will have unfading glory, as far as lies with my song and my own glory.' Samian history,[61] in so far as we know it, suggests that this man is the son of the better known tyrant of this name; Himerius, the well-read sophist of the fourth century A. D., associates him with Anacreon at Rhodes, where he seems to have been a kind of viceroy to his father. We might wish that Ibycus had not written in such a vein, yet it is in an encomium that Pindar gives us his only extant confession of personal passion (fr. 108) and it seems that Ibycus preceded him in this *genre*.[62]

The dialect, once thought to be the mixed vernacular of Rhegium, is in fact a literary one with its variation in treatment of digamma, of 'weak position' and the like. These and other anomalies, together with features such as occasional Aeolisms, show this to be an early stage in the evolution of conventional choric idiom, with only as yet a veneer of Dorian on the epic foundation. The triadic structure exhibits 4-line strophes (strictly speaking, two metrical phrases, as synaphaea shows) and a 5-line epode. Dactyls predominate, though trochaic elements in the clausulae impart an Aeolic effect; thus the fourth line of the epode reads like a catalectic form of the metre used in Sappho β.2 (see p. 43 above).[63]

ANACREON

In view of the expectation of new additions to Ionic poetry in the next volume (XXII) of the Oxyrhynchus series, brief mention of Anacreon must suffice, as the current estimate of him may well need correction. The only papyrus fragment[64] so far associated with him is too doubtful in its attribution for useful discussion at present. A good account of his life and times is given by Bowra (in *GLP*, ch. VII), which takes cognizance of all relevant material, but is unsuitable for compression here. Anacreon's witty but mannerist style, with its many adjectives, proverbial turns of phrase and verbal conceits, such as the pun on the name Cleobulus, explains the fascination he had for later Greek poetasters who wrote the spurious but in places not unpleasing 'Anacreontea'. The tradition that he came in the course of his wandering life to Athens finds some confirmation in the Atticisms which occur in some of his poems, and he may well have had considerable influence upon Aeschylus, in whose lyrics he is said to have taken pleasure. At all events the characteristic and infectious Ionic metre which he used,[65] whether in its normal (⏑ ⏑ − − ⏑ ⏑ − ⏓) or 'anaclastic' form (⏑ ⏑ − ⏑ − ⏑ − ⏓), appealed to Aeschylus, who uses it in all his surviving tragedies except the *Eumenides*, often with, to our ears, telling effect. Anacreon has also a fortuitous interest for us in that his portrait (or at the least a near-contemporary representation) occurs on three Attic red-figure vases (see fig. 5), while a poem of the younger Critias and two epigrams show him remembered by later ages in the same convivial light.[66]

CORINNA[67]

To the scanty remains of Corinna a papyrus from Eschmunen adds 22 fairly legible lines out of 63 from a poem on the musical contest of Helicon and Cithaeron and 40 out of 142 from another on the daughters of Asopus. Yet it is an open question whether the authoress was an older contemporary of Pindar or lived in the Hellenistic age. She was not included in the Alexandrian Canon of Nine Lyricists, although a persistent but flimsy tradition associates her with Pindar; her lines rebuking Myrtis for vying with him do not, however, prove the early date. Critical analysis of the external evidence shows that no extant author of the second century B.C. or earlier was familiar with her works, although she was studied by grammarians of the first century B.C.

The internal evidence is also ambiguous. The 'reformed' Boeotian spelling of the fourth century has given the text a disconcerting appearance, with spellings such as κρατούνι (5.55 D) or ἐλέοθη (5.60: 8.2 D), and so forth. Relying on the evidence of Boeotian epigraphy, Page takes the -οι spelling of datives singular of o-stems in the papyrus to be significant for dating the document to 225-175 B.C. Initial digamma seems never neglected, but this feature is found in the inscriptions regularly down to c. 200 B.C., and does not prove an early date. On the other hand, her restriction of the 'short' form of the dative plural of 1st and 2nd declension to line-ends, and then only in immediate juxtaposition to a 'long' form in grammatical agreement, recalls the practice of Anacreon. Alien to her vernacular are her cavalier treatment of the augment, both temporal and syllabic, and her free use of paragogic *nu*, as well as her practice in regard to short vowels in 'weak position' and some points of pronominal usage.

From these and other details[68] it can be said that her dialect is notable in being a 'literary dialect in a vernacular dress'. This fact, taken with her absence from the Canon and the apparent date of the papyrus-text, warrants two alternative assumptions concerning her date: either she was a Hellenistic figure, or her work was indeed archaic but went out of circulation to be re-discovered about 200 B.C., when scholars transliterated it into the Boeotian spelling of the time. No consideration has so far been adduced to eliminate either hypothesis, and there the matter must be left.

Stylistically, her simple metrical systems,[69] the narrowly provincial interest of her subject-matter and unexciting yet clear form of expression might suggest folk-poetry. The unsporting way in which Helicon accepts his defeat may raise a smile, though the prophet Acraephen's forecast of the matrimonial experiences in store for Asopus' daughters has only antiquarian interest. In any event these fragments do not justify speculation on the nature of the lost prototypes of Greek epic, though if the date of their composition could be settled they would be of considerable value to the historian of Greek literature.

PINDAR[70]

* Successive editions have improved the text of the Epinicians and led to a sounder assessment of the manuscripts while three papyri (which include *P Oxy.* 1614 and 2092) throw a fitful light on the transmission of some passages in the Olympians. A saner approach to metrical questions, with emphasis on 'metrical context,' has replaced the arid discussions and extravagancies of J. H. H. Schmidt and his school in the last century. Archaeology has not perhaps cast as much light on Pindaric problems as might have been expected, though study of the re-carved inscription on the base of the Charioteer at Delphi bears upon the diplomatic activity of Theron and Hieron, Pindar's patrons, and Polyzelus, in the years 478-6 B.C.[71]

Since Wilamowitz's great work *Pindaros* (Berlin, 1922), perhaps the most arresting essay in interpretation is that of G. Norwood (*Pindar*, Berkeley, California, 1945). His detection of a hidden symbolism in most of the odes has a Verrallian ingenuity, though it is doubtful how far appreciation of, for example, Olympian VI is advanced by the concept of the Two Anchors alleged to be running through it, or of Pythian VIII by that of the Captive Bird. More arguable perhaps is the case for his fanciful 'rebus' on the initial letter of Theron's name and the Wheel of Fortune by which he interprets Olympian II. Yet however one views these imaginative flights, his account of Pythian XI in terms of the Bee-symbol offers a clue to that otherwise bizarre and obscure poem which had previously quite defied interpretation.[72] Perhaps the ancients were after all more sensitive to such associative conceits than we might think. For all its obvious dangers of subjectivity, Norwood's approach is an improvement on earlier ventures on these lines, such as the 'catchword theory' of Metzger, and cannot be set aside out of hand.

Pindar's style and methods of composition have been examined by various scholars, including W. Schadewaldt, L. Illig, and others; ring-form has been recognized more clearly and the lyricists' technique of telling a story by a series of pictures (often in a kind of reversed event-sequence) better appreciated.[73]

New papyrus material includes portions of Paeans (frs. 35-47: add perhaps 343), Dithyrambs (frs. 60-2), Partheneia (frs. 83-4) and possibly a hypocheme (fr. 124-5). Since Snell's brilliant junction of fr. 43 and fr. 46 and his proof that fr. 47 is rightly classed as a paean,[74] we have remains of 11 such pieces (not 12), excluding fr. 343. Three are for Theban occasions: I, ending with a prayer to Apollo to ensure good order, VII (very fragmentary) and IX, already known in part from quotation. This last was prompted by the eclipse of April 30th, 463 B.C.; hence the gloomy forebodings of catastrophe, whether political ('baleful *stasis*') or natural ('blight of crops' or even a deluge). In the new portion, Pindar, inspired by the nearness of the Ismenion, prays to Apollo, who begat the prophet Teneros upon the nymph Melia in this place. The prayer's wording is lost, for the papyrus ends with Pindar having, in his manner, swerved off into by-ways of Theban mythology. Enough however survives to give substance to Wilamowitz's view (*Pindaros*, p. 396) that this paean was written to avert political dangers of the day, particularly those which in 463 the new Periclean democracy might be thought to represent to Pindar's city and his own values.

Paean II (fr. 36) for the Abderites also mirrors events of the time. Since its foundation in 546 B.C. this colony had had hard struggles with its Thracian neighbours (here in line 39 loosely called 'Paeonian'). A novel genealogy for the eponymous hero

Abderus is followed by a striking reference to Athens and the Persian Wars:

> Fledgling among cities am I, yet nathless I have seen my mother's mother smitten with the fire of war.

Moralizing allusions to internal dissensions lead on to a reference to the critical battle the colonists fought before Mt. Melamphyllon, with a relevant *vaticinium ex eventu* by Hecate. A warm mention of Delphi, motivated, one suspects, by Delphi's consistent encouragement of Greek colonial ventures, follows; finally, giving ring-form to the whole, a prayer to Abderus to nerve the army in a final campaign. In Pyth. I, 61f Pindar had shown his power of transmuting constitutional matters into high poetry; here he does the same with recent history which, with local lore and a minimum of mythology, provides the inspiration. Critics have perhaps overstressed the poem's formal imperfections,[75] but its interest and some memorable lines deepen our knowledge of its author.

Paean IV (fr. 38) for the Ceans is certainly the poem promised in Isthmian I, 6f, but the date remains controversial. The Ceans would surely not have employed Pindar before Simonides' departure to Sicily in 476 B.C., perhaps not before his death nine years later; greater precision seems unattainable. The islanders' affection for their home is the theme of the paean; a phrase near the opening 'No horseman I, and in tending oxen not so very skilled' recalls Odysseus' praise of his native Ithaca (Od. 13. 242f). This affection is illustrated by a variant of the Melampus-story and at greater length by the resolute refusal of their king Euxantius to leave Ceos and rule in Crete. The excuse he gives is seismophobia, for Zeus and Poseidon had once wrecked his island, but his language is more convincing than his reason:

> In face of this am I to venture for wealth, and quite thrusting aside the ordinance of the Blessed Ones possess a great inheritance elsewhere? Set far from thee, heart of mine, the cypress-land and the pastures round Mount Ida.

The forceful yet measured phrasing gives a lively, plastic picture of the independent island-king; for equally effective characterization in lyric one would have to go to the interchange between Jason and Pelias in the Fourth Pythian.[76]

Another poem impinging on an extant ode is Paean VI (fr. 40). Pindar comes to Delphi for the Theoxenia to help his clansmen as 'spokesman', for he has heard that there are no men dancing at Castalia (line 8). An 'aition' on the origin of the Theoxenia follows, a famine (65) having been once averted by Delphian piety. Later in the poem Pindar, as we know from the scholiast on Nemean VII, fell foul of the Aeginetans for his way of referring to the Aeacid hero Neoptolemus. The papyrus gives the offending passage, and though the reading is doubtful at the crucial point, the possibilities are limited; nevertheless the precise nature of the tactlessness is not clear. Pindar mentions Neoptolemus' hubristic conduct at the fall of Troy when he leapt upon the aged Priam and killed him at an altar (lines 114-15). Thus he was not to return home or attain old age himself, but while he was wrangling with temple-servants περὶ τιμᾶν Apollo slew him in his own sanctuary at the earth's broad navel. Much turns on the adjective that went with τιμᾶν in line 118, whose first letter is illegible. No help comes from Nemean 7.42, where Pindar apologetically modifies this to 'a battle over meats', and makes a Delphian the slayer, not the god. The story was traditional, as Pindar insists; grieved as the Delphians were, Neoptolemus 'paid his debt to destiny' (Nem. 7.44). Thus neither the adjective μ]υριᾶν of the scholia-text (Drachmann, III p. 129) nor the emendation[77] κ]υριᾶν in line 118 carry any obvious point; μοιριᾶν is a shoddy conjecture made to the scholia-quotation before discovery of the papyrus (elsewhere Pindar uses, μοιρίδιος), while Πυθιᾶν, though going back to Zenodotus, does not fit the letter traces on the papyrus. It may be that the Aeginetans fastened upon some ambiguity in the language; whatever it was, Pindar took it seriously and in Nem. 7. 75-6 is ready to admit his fault: 'if, overwrought, I cried out too far in any wise, no unregenerate I in retracting'. Yet some of his characteristic intransigeance returns at the end (102-3): 'never will my heart admit that it mangled Neoptolemus with unseemly words'.

There the puzzle remains;[78] it is something of a relief to turn to the splendid eulogy of Aegina with which the Paean's last triad begins:

Island of high renown, thou art set as a queen in the Dorian sea, bright star of Zeus, the god the Greeks adore. Therefore we will not lay thee to sleep with no supper of hymns of praise, but receiving the surge of my songs thou shalt declare, whence thou didst get thy destiny of primacy at sea and of goodness that does right by strangers.

Irrelevant this may seem[79] in the light of our partial knowledge, but such eloquent wording has the true Pindaric throb, and its palpable warmth makes the Aeginetans appear either churlish or else hypersensitive in their unfriendly reception of the poem as a whole.

Of Paeans III (fr. 37), X (45) and V (39), only the last needs notice. Its 13 pleasant lines which survive show a simple non-triadic scheme; it has a reference to Euboea and was probably sung by a choir from that island at Delos.

As a result of Snell's[73] researches, Paeans VIII (fr. 43) and XI (fr. 46) must now be taken together. It is clear that in the opening lines preceding fr. 46 there were descriptions of the first and second temples at Delphi. Pausanias (10.5, 9f) gives the story; the first temple was of laurel, the second, made of bees' wax and bees' wings, was sent to the Hyperboreans, which explains the reference at the start of fr. 46. The story of the third temple of bronze (fr. 46. 6f) follows, with its architectural decoration of six singing Sirens of gold above the cornice; it was destroyed by an earthquake. Pindar naturally associated its building with Hephaestus: Pausanias in a later age was more sceptical. In the gap between the end of fr. 46 and the opening of 43 came the mention of the fourth temple and its architects Agamedes and Trophonius and the story of their father Erginus, king of Orchomenus, which underlies the scholiast of fr. 82 of the papyrus (col. I). The hitherto unexplained transition from this to the prophecy of Cassandra about the fall of Troy which forms fr. 43 is now to be read against the Delphic background that has been established for it. One imaginative variant from the familiar story appears: Cassandra makes Hecuba's dream-progeny not a firebrand, but a 'fire-bearing Fury with a hundred hands' (fr. 43, lines 11-12).

Snell has also shown[74] that fr. 47 is a Pindar Paean. It speaks of Naxian sheep being sacrificed to the Graces at Delos, and refers to Zeus' guarding of the place at the time of the birth of Apollo and Artemis. The language here rises more closely to the sustained 'strong' style of the Epinicians than anything so far observed in the Paeans:

By the bluff of Cynthus, where they say that Zeus of the dark cloud and white-flashing thunder sat and from above its peaks kept watch the while, when Coeus' kindly-hearted daughter was delivered of her sweet birth-pangs.

Only one (fr. 61) of the three new dithyrambic pieces (frs. 60-2) is noticed here. Its metre is regular dactylo-epitrite, so that Horace's 'numeris fertur lege solutis' argues defective knowledge, although it might apply better to the *vers libre* (ἀπολελυμένα) of later dithyramb. Horace's other feature, 'nova verba', is reflected in the astonishing σχοινοτένεια (known from quotation previously), but the piece's novelty lies in subject-matter rather than vocabulary. Puzzling as the 'song stretched like a rope' and the 'counterfeit ring of the letter San' are, the sequel is even more odd: the new gates (of song) open, Dionysiac instruments clang and torches blaze, whereupon Ares, Artemis (who has yoked lions for the occasion), and Athena delight Dionysus by engaging in Bacchic revelry. Such intrusion into the serenity of Olympus is a flight of imagination only conceivable in Pindar. Hence he passes, as the Muses' chosen 'herald of poetic words' (18-19), to tell of the Theban antecedents of Dionysus, with, presumably, an account of his birth, a usual theme of dithyramb. Almost every line deserves comment; in particular the use of Bacchic apparatus by gods in another's service is unparalleled in Greek, though Vedic literature (so Farnell) may show something similar. The association of the 'stately' Magna Mater with these rites reflects the fusion of the two strands of worship; the translation of the scene from earth to Olympus makes the Maenads for the nonce into Naiads (line 9). Stylistically, the concept of the 'countless snakes in Athena's aegis giving voice' (14-15) might in other hands have come perilously near the grotesque. Grammarians may note two cases of *schema Pindaricum* (concord of plural noun and singular verb) within a few lines (6-7, κατάρχει ... ῥόμβοι: 10, μανίαι τ'ἀλαλαί τ'ὀρίνεται). Both instances were obscured in the manuscripts of Strabo and Plutarch which quote the words; rare as this construction is in the epinicians it recurs twice in another dithyramb (fr. 63. 19, ἀχεῖ: 20, οἰχνεῖ).[80]

To us, for whom the Dionysiac cult suggests the ionic rhythms of Euripides' *Bacchae*, the contrast of that lovely but sensuous verse with Pindar's dignified Dorian cadences is almost uncanny; on every count this is a singular addition to our knowledge of Pindar.

Only the second of frs. 83 and 84 is certainly a Partheneion. The other, from its use of the verb in the first person singular with a masculine participle (φιλέων δ'ἄν εὐχοίμαν, 6), resembles rather an encomium or the like,[81] and may have been placed among the Partheneia only because it mentioned Aeoladas, who recurs in fr. 84. Classification of Pindar's poems in antiquity does not seem to have been strict, or the Eleventh Nemean, an encomium on a prytanis of Tenedos, would never have appeared, as it does, among the epinicia. Fr. 83 has some not untypical lines, with reflections on envy that goes with goodness and on human mortality.

In the other fragment Pagondas son of Aeoladas may have been the Theban general at Delium in 424 B.C. (Thuc. 4. 91); if so it is a work of Pindar's old age. The ritual, the escorting of a κωπώ (something like a maypole) to the temple of Apollo Ismenius by a troop of maidens accompanied by a boy whose parents are both alive and by an elderly man to carry the κωπώ, underlies the piece. It has some charm, and on the whole bears out the ancient judgment of Dionysius of Halicarnassus that the 'archaic "austere" harmony' elsewhere characteristic of Pindar was absent from the Partheneia. Yet there is something of his hard and allusive style in the invocation of the Sirens and the stilling of the winds in the first extant epode and second strophe (lines 9-15), though the text is doubtful. Pindar's praise of the family does not gloss over a certain unpopularity, perhaps political, though its members' integrity made all well in the end (lines 47-8). To most this is a blameless piece, not lacking in interest, but below the higher levels of Pindaric inspiration.[82]

Fragment 125 (cf. *NCGL III*, p. 51) is unplaced; it may possibly be from a hyporcheme. It has a graceful reference to the Locrian musical mode, on hearing which Pindar feels himself provoked to sing 'like a dolphin, whom the lovely music of flutes stirs in the waveless main'.

BACCHYLIDES

Bacchylides has been happy in his resurgence. Kenyon's *editio princeps* paved the way for Jebb's full-scale work (Cambridge, 1905), which is still the standard commentary. Recent trends are well reflected in B. Snell's revised Teubner text of 1943 (issued in 1949), with its informative introduction and full *apparatus criticus*, which is often exegetically helpful (e.g. on 3.48: 5.9: 5.142 and elsewhere). Bacchylides' literary qualities and shortcomings are now well known; though nothing offends, and granting that his descriptive passages such as that of the ghosts beside Cocytus (5. 64f) or Theseus' leap into the sea at Minos' behest (17. 75f) remain in the memory, he frankly is interesting rather than inspiring. Ancient critical opinion implied just so much, if 'Longinus' *de Sublim.* 33 is representative.

Particular interest attaches to his version in Ode 3 on the Death of Croesus, based probably on the Delian legend or the king's self-devotion; this, as Frazer showed, is one more in keeping with Oriental religious beliefs than the Delphic version in Herodotus, in which Cyrus consigns Croesus to the pyre. It is strange to find events of 546 B.C. turned into legend as soon as 468 B.C., and the comparison with the Myson painter's vase of c. 500 B.C. (see fig. 6) is interesting. One notes that here, as elsewhere, Bacchylides follows the painters rather than sets the example; in other ways too his originality is not above question, as we see from the unconcealed borrowing at the end of this ode (85f) from the exordium of Pindar's First Olympian, and of II 93, both poems written eight years before. However, ancient literary ethics were not as strict as our own.[83]

Apart from improvement in details of the papyrus text, the only noteworthy addition is the opening of an encomium (fr. 20B, Snell[2]) to Alexander son of Amyntas, who employed Pindar on occasion (see fr. 106). The papyrus adds six lines to the ten preserved in Athenaeus, and the four dactylo-epitrite quatrains make up the start of an elegant poem which again savours of Pindar (fr. 109).

ARCHILOCHUS

Though not included in the ancient canon of the Nine Lyricists, Archilochus is too important a figure to be passed over here. The material known before 1905 is reflected in Hauvette's monograph *Archiloque* (Paris, 1905). The remarkable Strassburg fragment, in which the poet wishes a perfidious friend shipwrecked on the Thracian coast, was sometimes attributed to Hipponax, whose manner it also suits. We now find that its phrase 'trampled his oaths underfoot' (line 13) is echoed in the new Alcaeus piece treated on p. 46 above, and as Alcaeus may have borrowed motifs from Archilochus elsewhere (e.g. the 'rhipsaspid' poet), we can be confident of the authorship of this 'curse-propempticon'.

It is entirely consistent with the outlook of the Archilochus who wrote (fr. 66 D)

> I know how to requite with fearful misfortune one that uses me despitefully.

It might be hoped that the inscription of one Demeas at Paros which gives an account of some events in Archilochus' life with quotations from him would help in solving some of the problems that arise in connection with the poet. The episodes are, however, trivial where they can be deciphered with certainty; a balanced account of their substance will be found in *NCGL III*, pp. 60-2. More adventurous reconstructions of the stone's text, such as that of J. M. Edmonds in *Elegy and Iambus* II, pp. 162f (Loeb), should be treated with caution. Archilochus' date turns on his mention of an eclipse (fr. 74 D). A. A. Blakeway argued for the earlier eclipse of 711 B.C., and sought to relate the historical allusions of the fragments to this time: the case for the later one of 648 B.C. is cogently put by F. Jacoby, and this date certainly seems to square better with the general course of Greek literary history.[84]

TYRTAEUS

Tyrtaeus' rugged elegiacs have exercised critics; Verrall,[85] arguing perversely from the wording of Lycurgus *Leocr.* 106, went so far as to contend that the extant pieces were a fourth-century forgery, referring to the third Messenian war. It may well be that the surviving Tyrtaean corpus contains accretions, but the latest addition to it (fr. 1 D³) is certainly early. These remarkable lines from a Berlin papyrus are treated in *NCGL III* (pp. 62-4); they include a mention of Messenians and a simile from chariot-racing (introduced at Olympia in 680 B.C.); they also give the names of the three Dorian tribes, Hylleis, Pamphyloi and Dumanes, thus carrying that distinctive feature of state-organization back to seventh-century Sparta. Independent enquiry[86] suggests that this may be a wide-spread Indo-European pattern, although confined in Greece to the Dorian elements. The poem shows the Dorian form ἀλοιησε-ῦ[μεν (line 55 D³) and the short scansion of the first declension accusative plural χαίτας (line 14 D³). Surprisingly it refers to a method of fighting with 'fenced shields', a tactic only mentioned incidentally in Homer, but pointless here unless familiar in

Tyrtaeus' day. It reads as much an exhortation to good order as a martial piece, but the first person plural (in lines 54f (D³): 'we will obey our leaders') identifies Tyrtaeus with his soldiery and bears on the question of his generalship.

For the remaining poems, as for those of the early elegists in general, current opinion is most conveniently reflected in C. M. Bowra's *Early Greek Elegy* (Oxford, 1936); W. Jaeger *Paideia* vol. I, ch. v and vიii (Eng. Trans. by G. Highet, Blackwell, Oxford, 1939, pp. 82f: 134f) should also be consulted, especially for his treatment of *arete* in Tyrtaeus.

METRE

This subject, as contentious as it is cardinal to any study of Early Greek Lyric, cannot be discussed in the space available here. A select list of works whose approach and doctrine commend themselves is given below, with no pretensions to completeness:

W. R. Hardie, *Res Metrica* (Oxford, 1920), especially pp. 118f.

P. Maas, *Griechische Metrik* (in Gercke-Norden, *Einleitung in die Altertumswissenschaft*, I. 7: Teubner 1929 (enlarged edn.)), and his *Die neuen Responsionsfreiheiten bei Bakchylides und Pindar* (Berlin, Weidmann; I, 1914: II, 1921).

cf. Snell, *Bacchylides*², Introd. pp. 18*-33*, for Maas' views: see now his *Pindarus*, pp. 305-21.

C. M. Bowra, *Greek Lyric Poetry* (Oxford, 1936), Appendix IV, pp. 453f.

J. A. Davison, 'Double Scansion in Early Greek Lyric' in C.Q. 28 (1934), pp. 183f for a rather different view and a good tabulation of Aeolic metres known at that time.

A. M. Dale, *Lyric Metres of Greek Drama* (Cambridge, 1938), especially chs. vიii-xii; cf. her articles 'The Metrical Units of Greek Lyric Verse' in C.Q. 44 (1950), pp. 138f: *ibid.*, 45 (1951), pp. 20f: 119f.

G. Thomson, *Greek Lyric Verse* (Cambridge, 1929), developing the views of W. Headlam in J.H.S. 22 (1902), pp. 209-27.

CONCLUDING REMARKS

The literary and historical interest of the new discoveries may obscure the importance of the study of Early Greek Lyric for the development of Greek thought. Homer, whatever his date, is in no sense a personality to us. There are, of course, flashes of autobiography in Hesiod, but Archilochus' intimate likes and dislikes shine out from his few surviving lines with a clarity inconceivable in an earlier tradition. The poet's own judgments count and serve as basis for argument: so Sappho can write:

> Some say a troop of horsemen or of infantry, others a fleet of ships is the fairest thing on earth ... but I say it is whatsoever one loves. (α.5: see p. 42 above and note 23.)

Myth and maxim are applied too to set the transient moments of personal experience against a more permanent or universal background. It has been well pointed out that archaic poets, especially in relating emotional experiences of their own, preface them with the word or idea 'again', and it is not fanciful to see in this the germ of a pattern-seeking reasoning verging on induction: 'know what ebb-and-flow (ῥυσμός) governs mankind', as Archilochus had said. Homeric man 'knew many things' without appearing to apprehend the connections between them; Solon and the lyricists first coin words of the form βαθύφρων, βαθύμητις, expressive of knowledge of a different order. Other concepts too are maturing: Achilles had complained that his commander had *dishonoured* him, stressing the respect due to his class; Archilochus says that a man has *wronged* him, showing by the one word quite a new concept of society. The notion of individual moral responsibility finds its first statement in Simonides' scolion to Scopas embedded in Plato's *Protagoras* (339a-347a). Much more could be said, but the significant originality of these poets is now becoming clear as it hardly was fifty years ago. We not only owe to them the first experiments in the metres and forms that later were to grow into Attic Tragedy, but have in them the earliest witnesses to the new direction Greek thought was taking.[87]

References to editions and matters of detail have been consolidated into notes at paragraph-ends where this has been possible without ambiguity.
[1] The Timotheus papyrus falls outside the purview of this account; it is conveniently treated by C. J. Ellingham in 'New Chapters in Greek Literature' (first series) pp. 59-65.
[2] Published in *Berliner Klassikertexte*, Heft V. 2 (=*BKT*), edited by W. Schubart and U. von Wilamowitz-Möllendorff (Berlin, 1907).
[3] In *Pubblicazioni della Società Italiana per la ricerca dei papiri greci e latini in Egitto*. Note especially Nos. 147 (vol. II) and 1300 (vol. XIII, fasc. 1).
[4] Unless the fragment 13.b D² is by him. See also D. L. Page, *Greek Literary Papyri* (Loeb) vol. 1, pp. 384-7: J. A. Davison in C.R. 48 (1934), p. 205f: B. Snell, *Bacchylides*²

EARLY GREEK LYRIC POETRY

fr. 60. For scraps from Simonides' epinicians on Runners, see Snell, Hermes, *Einzelschriften*, Heft 5 (1937), pp. 98-101.

[5] Particular mention must be made of B. P. Grenfell and A. S. Hunt, who together skilfully edited the first sixteen volumes of the Oxyrhynchus series (1898-1924), and of E. Lobel, who has done much for the later volumes and especially for Sappho and Alcaeus. In Germany W. Schubart, E. Diehl, R. Pfeiffer and B. Snell may be singled out; in Italy G. Vitelli and Medea Norsa. Others not themselves specialists in this field have often contributed valuable suggestions.

[6] The first certain instance is Ibycus fr. 3 D (see p. 52 above and note 63). It is not now thought to be present in germ in Alcman's Partheneion (see p. 40 above), and may be Stesichorus' invention. Yet the ascription of it to him might be due to a misunderstanding of the proverbial τρία Στησιχόρου, if this really referred to the three extant lines that are quoted as his celebrated Palinode (fr. 11 D: see note 59), as Crusius argued long ago. See B. L. Gildersleeve in A. J. Phil. 10 (1889), p. 382.

[7] The music published in 1650 by Athanasius Kircher and alleged to be that of Pindar, Pythian I is a forgery; see J. F. Mountford in C.R. 49 (1935), pp. 62-3, or more fully, P. Maas in Hermes 70 (1935), pp. 101-2.

[8] The conventions used in editing papyri are set out in *POxy*. vol. VI, p. xiii (repeated, vol. XXI, p. xiii). The most important are:
[ ] letters lost from the papyrus or no longer legible
⟨ ⟩ letters omitted in error by the scribe
{ } letters wrongly inserted by the scribe.
In the translations given here, words which render textually doubtful portions of the original are italicized.

[9] *POxy*. 222 (commentary in vol. II, p. 92).

[10] E. Lobel Σαπφοῦς Μέλη (=Σμ) (Oxford, 1925), pp. xxvf: see also his 'Αλκαίου Μέλη (=Αμ) (Oxford, 1927), pp. xf.

[11] Thus he argued ('Αμ p. xxxiii n) that τῶν ἀνέμων (?τὰν ἀνέμω) στάσιν in fr. 87 (30 D¹ = 46.a D²) must mean the 'quarter' in which the wind sits, not the quarrel of the winds, because the vernacular for the latter is λύα, not στάσις. This reasoning is no longer valid, now that στάσις occurs in the sense of 'quarrel' in *POxy*. 2165 fr. ii, line 19 (see p. 47 above). In fact B. Lavagnini in *Aglaia* (Paravia, Turin, 1937), p. 156 citing Polyb. I. 48, 2 suggested that the phrase ἀνέμων στάσις is a nautical term, perhaps the 'rising' of the winds.

[12] Referred to as *GLP*. This remains the most comprehensive treatment, though not including Corinna, Bacchylides or Pindar. Useful reviews are those of J. M. Edmonds in C.R. 50 (1936), pp. 169-70 and E. Kalinka in Berl. Phil. Woch. 1936, 1361-4. Also D. M. Robinson in C. Phil. 33 (1938), pp. 210f (mostly on very minor points, but some valuable art-references).

My debt to this book and to the essay cited in the following note will be obvious, and I gladly acknowledge it here.

[13] Referred to as *NCGL III*.

[14] The numeration of the 1936 (vol. I) and 1942 (vol. II) revisions of E. Diehl's *Anthologia Lyrica Graeca* (Leipzig, Teubner, 1925) shows only occasional changes. Where a difference has to be indicated, the latter is given as D¹, and the former as D². The third edition by R. Beutler has so far only covered the elegists and iambic poets (D³).

[15] The Loeb edition ('Lyra Graeca', 3 vols., 1921-27: vol. I reprinted 1928) by J. M. Edmonds offers too subjective a text of papyrus fragments to justify citation; it is useful for its full collection of *testimonia* and for a good essay on general topics of Greek lyric in vol. III, pp. 583-679.

Alcman

[16] Rohde's chronological reconciliation in Rh. Mus. 33 (1878), pp. 199f (cf. D. L. Page, *Alcman, The Partheneion*, p. 164 n1): Lydian connection, Page, *ibid.*, p. 167 (Appendix II): dialect, *ibid.*, p. 153: epic colour (e.g. ἵππον παγὸν ἀεθλοφόρον καναχάποδα) *ibid.*, p. 157f: fr. 58, *ibid.*, p. 159-62.

[17] E.g. those of J. T. Sheppard, in *Essays and Studies presented to William Ridgeway* (Cambridge, 1913), pp. 124f: J. B. Bury, C. A. H. 4, p. 501: Bowra, *GLP*, pp. 38-9.

[18] In *GLP*, pp. 41-58. He divides the choir of ten into two hemichors, identifying Alcman's choir with the Leucippides who are singing at a joint festival of Helen and Dionysus in competition with a rival choir of Peleiades. He accepts the reading ὀρθρίαι in line 61, but leaves the meaning of φᾶρος open.
[19] In C.R. 67 (1953), pp. 16f. On surviving evidence he is right to deny this metaphorical use of μάχεσθαι, νίκη, and cognate words. Yet the ceremonial background of the piece may have made all clear and justified what to us seems an extension of usage; ἀμύναι in 65 seems in particular to call for some such explanation.

Sappho

[20] Lobel's new edition of Sappho and Alcaeus is reported to be in an advanced state of preparation, and it is thus likely that the sections on these poets which follow here will have been outdated by the time they appear in print.
[21] α.1 App.: 1 D: *GLP*, pp. 190f: see now *POxy*. 2288. For a good analysis of the religious content of the poem, see A. Cameron in Harvard Theological Review 33 (1940), pp. 1-17. His conclusions differ from Bowra's; he discounts a 'deep emotional urgency', emphasizing conventional, sacral, and magical features of language and form.
[22] α.2 App.: 2 D: *GLP*, pp. 213f. Wilamowitz in *Sappho und Simonides*, pp. 58f: Snell in Hermes 66 (1931), pp. 71f.: Archilochus fragments, 104 D and 112 D. The comparison with Archilochus is well worked out by Bowra *GLP*, pp. 218f: see also B. Snell, *Entdeckung des Geistes* (Claasen und Goverts, Hamburg, 1948), p. 67 or in the English translation by T. G. Rosenmeyer (Blackwell, Oxford, 1953), p. 53.
[23] Propempticon, α.3: 25 D: *GLP*, pp. 229f: *NCGL III*, p. 6. Charaxus is named as her eldest brother by the anonymous biographer in *POxy*. 1800, who gives the other two as Larichus (cf. Athen. 10. 425 a) and Eriguius. This also states that her daughter was Cleis, called after Sappho's mother. Anactoria-poem, α.5: 27 D: *GLP*, pp. 204f: cf. *NCGL III*, p. 7. Ring-form: πεσδο]μάχεντας echoes the opening ο]ἰ μὲν ἱππήων στρότον, οἱ δὲ πέσδων . . . thus refuting T. L. Agar's reconstruction of a sixth stanza (C.R. 28 (1914), p. 190), which is based on flimsy evidence at best. Other instances in Sappho are: (i) α.1 App.: 1 D (line 25) ἔλθε μοι καὶ νῦν echoing ἀλλὰ τυίδ' ἔλθ' (line 5) (ii) α.2 App.: 2 D φαίνομαι (line 16) echoing opening word. See further L. Illig in work referred to in note 73 (esp. pp. 48f, 56f). Iliad example: 24. 601-19, where the Niobe digression is 'sealed off' by repetition of the idea of 'taking food' (δόρπου, 601: σίτου 613, 619) cf. ὄλοντο (603) and ὄλεσσαν (609).
[24] First published by her in *Annali della Regia Scuola Normale Superiore di Pisa*, II. 6 (1937), pp. 8-15. Republished in *PSI* XIII (1) No. 1300 with a good facsimile. See also R. Pfeiffer in Philol. 92 (1937), pp. 117f: W. Schubart in Hermes 73 (1938), pp. 297-303: other references in D. L. Page, *Greek Literary Papyri* vol. 1, pp. 376-8. The text translated here is based on Norsa's latest one, but there is serious dislocation at the opening. Did Sappho write δαφνίνοισ' in the third stanza, as Vergil's *odoratum lauri nemus* (A. 6.658) might perhaps suggest? (πρινινοισ' Norsa: ἠρινοισ' edd.).
[25] γ.3 App.: 58 D: *GLP*, p. 231. The epigram of Poseidippus quoted by Athenaeus (13. 596c) concerning Doricha and Sappho also has this idea of immortality conferred by song and may be indirectly inspired by her.
[26] Aphrodite Antheia, see L. R. Farnell, *Cults of the Greek States* (Oxford, 1895-1909) II, p. 632: A. Turyn in Trans. Am. Phil. Ass. 73 (1942), pp. 308f: refrigerium, see A. Dieterich *Nekyia*² (Berlin, 1913), pp. 95f, and authorities adduced by Turyn, *loc. cit.*, p. 313 n16. Orphism: since I. Linforth's book *The Arts of Orpheus* (Berkeley, California, 1941) one must be careful not to apply the adjective 'Orphic' indiscriminately; it should be reserved for ideas expressly associated with his name. However, in order to provide a label for a well-marked stream of mainly eschatological thought, the term 'Orphic-Pythagorean' may perhaps be kept and no harm done.
[27] *POxy*. 1232 and 2076. The poem is β.2: 55 D: see *GLP*, p. 236f and *NCGL III*, p. 10.
[28] These are summarized by Lobel in 'Aμ pp. xif. Note especially: (1) prosodiac hiatus (συνέταιροῖ ἄγοισ') (ii) short scansion before mute and liquid (ὄχλος, ἐλίχματα χρ): see, however, α.5 line 19, quoted on p. 42 above, ὄπλοισι (iii) gen. sing. in -οιο (Περάμοιο) (iv) 'short' form of dat. pl. (θέοις, φίλοις) (v) thematic formation (ὀνκαλέοντες) (vi) unaugmented tenses (ὀνόρουσε, ἐλέλυσδον) (vii) forms such as παρθενίκαν, ἐνί, πτόλιν, ὄσσαι ἰέρας, unapocopated κατά. See further Lobel Σμ p. xxvi: cf. *GLP*, pp. 236-7: *NCGL III*, p. 12.

²⁹ ε.2 App.: 99. 2 D.
³⁰ See H. Fränkel, *Gött. Nachr.* 1924, p. 64; A. Körte, *Arch. Pap.* 7 (1924), p. 126 and 10 (1931), p. 46: G. Perotta, *Saffo e Pindaro* (Bari, Laterza, 1935): Snell, *Entdeckung des Geistes*, p. 78 (Eng. Trans. p. 62).
³¹ ε. 3: 96 D: *GLP*, p. 196f: *NCGL III*, p. 8.
³² ε. 5: 98 D: *GPL*, p. 209f: *NCGL III*, p. 7.
³³ So Bowra, *NCGL III*, p. 4.
³⁴ For a different approach, see A. M. Dale 'The Metrical Units of Greek Lyric Verse' in C.Q. 45 (1951), p. 128.
³⁵ On metrical grounds two fragments, one in Milan and the other in Copenhagen, may have come from this book; they are unfortunately too disjointed for profitable discussion at present. See A. Vogliano in Philol. 93 (1938-9), pp. 277 (Milan fragment): E. Diehl in Rh. Mus. 92 (1943), p. 2 (Copenhagen fragment): C. Gallavotti in Riv. Fil. 69 (1941), pp. 161 (the two texts from the same poem?)
³⁶ Hiatus in Sappho: Lobel Σμ p. lxvi. Unlike Alcaeus, she allows overrun of word between third and fourth line of her Sapphic stanza, and so elision, not hiatus, at the end of the third line. Between first and second and second and third lines in this system hiatus is only licit for her if the open final vowel is long. Her glyconics differ from Anacreon's in that, though his always end in a long syllable, he has a preference for two long initial syllables; see W. R. Hardie, *Res Metrica* (Oxford, 1920), p. 172. Paragogic *nu*: see Lobel, Σμ p. xxxvii; there seems to be one exception (δ.1, 17). Alcaeus' practice in this differed (Lobel, *ibid.*, p. lxx).

Alcaeus
³⁷ *Greek Melic Poets* (Macmillan, 1900), p. 213.
³⁸ Hence perhaps the point of his 'parable' of the 'geomoroi' gathering their grapes too early (F 6: 117 D: *GLP*, p. 182).
³⁹ Melanippus-poem, B 10: 73 D: *GLP*, p. 168: *NCGL III*, p. 17. Myrsilus and Pittacus, D 12: 43 D: *GLP*, p. 154: *NCGL III*, p. 15. Marriage above one's station was a favourite motif in Greek lyric: cf. Alcman *Parth.* 17; A. *Pr.* 890f. Sobriety-legislation D 14: 45 D: *GLP*, p. 157.
⁴⁰ The evidence for a 'first exile' is in the scholiast on E 3 (p. 33 top, Lobel): cf. 37 D and *GLP*, p. 149 n1. Myrsilus too had his setbacks, as the phrase Μυρσίλου κάθοδον in a commentary on Alcaeus implies (*POxy.* 2306, col. i, line 19).
⁴¹ *POxy.* 2165 fr. i. Recent literature on this poem includes: E. Diehl in Rh. Mus. 92 (1944), pp. 2, 9f; C. Gallavotti in Riv. Fil. 70 (1942), pp. 163f: J. Kamerbeek in Mnemos. 13 (3rd series, 1947), pp. 94f, 161f.
⁴² Some supplement such as ἀμ[νοις μή] seems desirable, to provide an object for τόμοντες (so Kamerbeek, *loc. cit.*, p. 106).
⁴³ If line 7 of col. ii corresponded to the third line of this system, it would be short by a syllable, and there seems no obvious ground for altering the text at that point.
⁴⁴ The restoration here is puzzling: κα[γγεγή]ρᾶσ' is prosodiacally eccentric, and no other verb suggests itself. It may be that the relative clause τὰ πάτηρ ... broke off in anacolouthon without a verb; in that case κά[ς τὸ γῆ]ρας might be written and conceivably the apodotic δ' which appears necessary in line 16 points to this.
⁴⁵ οὐκ ἄμεινον pap. K. Latte in Mus. Helv. 4 (1947), pp. 141f, doubted the hyperbaton of the negative here in early poetry; further, if one discounts ionics in this system (see note 47), then the substitution of ... – ⏑ – ⏑ – ⏑ – for ... – – ⏑ ⏑ – ⏑ – is unlikely and there is much to be said for the emendation mentioned in passing by Latte, οὐκ ἄρμενον. ἄρμενος occurs in a Theocritean imitation of an Aeolic poem (29. 9) and as a noun in Alc. fr. 146 (40 D). For ἄρμενος with Infinitive, cf. Hes. *Erga* 785-6.
⁴⁶ β.2, line 27 (Lobel p. 78): 55 b. 7 D.
⁴⁷ Lobel sees ionics *a maiore* in the fourth line; I doubt the likelihood of this group in so preponderantly glyconic a context. I owe the useful term 'glyconoid' to cover metrical elements of this general type to Professor H. J. Rose.
⁴⁸ So restore, in the light of *POxy.* 2166 (c), ... ἐπα[σχάλαντες.
⁴⁹ Death of Myrsilus, fr. 93: 39 D: *GLP*, p. 151. Antimenidas, fr. 112: 50 D: *GLP*, p. 160. Ascalon and Babylon, B 20. 10: 82 D: *GLP*, p. 155. Lydian gold, D. 11: 42 D: *GLP*, p. 158: *NCGL III*, p. 16. Pittacus' forgiveness, Diog. Laert. 1. 75.
⁵⁰ See Lobel on D 15 (p. 29, top).

51 Nautical allegory, fr. 87: 30 D¹ = 46 A D²: *GLP*, p. 149. Exhortation, A 6: 120 D: *GLP*, p. 150: *NCGL III*, p. 14. For an excellent treatment of a small body of drinking songs in vogue at Athens at the turn of the sixth and fifth centuries B.C., of which this last passage was one, see *GLP*, pp. 402-33.
52 Helen and Thetis, B 14: 74 D: *GLP*, p. 178; *NCGL III*, pp. 18-19. Dioscuri, B 5: 78 D: *GLP*, p. 176: *NCGL III*, pp. 19-20.
53 Lobel Σμ p. xvi.

Stesichorus
54 The best discussion of the fragments and biographical data is by J. Vuertheim (Leyden, 1919). The chapter on Stesichorus in *GLP* (pp. 77-140) is particularly good, and the reader is referred to it for discussion of the art-evidence and related topics. The Tabula Iliaca (see *GLP*, pp. 105f) is too uncertain a witness for inclusion in this account.
55 For a delightful description of the Phrynos cup see J. D. Beazley, *Attic Black Figure* (London, Humphrey Milford, 1928), quoted in *GLP*, p. 112. Armature of Heracles, cf. Megacleides *apud* Athen. 12. 512f.
56 Winged Geryon (fig. 2): A. Rumpf, *Chalkidische Vasen* (Berlin, 1927) Taf. vii. Herakles and the Sun's chariot (fig. 3): skyphos from Taranto (7029) by Theseus painter; discussed in C. H. E. Haspels *Attic b.f. Lekythoi* (Paris) 1936, pp. 120f, where a different interpretation of the 'arrows' (i.e. that these are goad and sceptre) is given (p. 122, n6). Heracles in the Sun's Cup (fig. 4): Beazley, *Attic Red-Figure Vase Painters* (Oxford 1942) (= *ARV*), p. 296. Chest of Cypselus, Paus. 5. 17, 9f: Amyclae Throne, Paus. 3. 18, 10f.
57 Spartan politics; *GLP*, pp. 124f: Palinode, fr. 11 D. For Stesichorus' influence on Pindar and Attic Tragedy see the excellent account in the Introduction to Jebb's edition of Sophocles' *Electra* (pp. xvf).
58 We can only surmise that Stesichorus' poems were lengthy from the fact that the Alexandrian critics divided his *Oresteia* into two books (*GLP*, p. 129).
59 If we could be sure that the three lines of the Palinode (fr. 11 D) οὐκ ἔστ᾽ ἔτυμος λόγος οὗτος... were not independent but referred back to something said earlier in the same piece, we should have an anticipation of the abrupt transition so characteristic of Pindar, e.g. Ol. 1. 52 (rejection of the Tantalus-story), Pyth. 10. 48, etc.

Ibycus
60 Love and quince-tree, fr. 6 D: *GLP*, pp. 272-3. Race-horse, fr. 7 D: *GLP*, p. 276. Bird-life, fr. 9 D: *GLP*, p. 279.
61 The entry in Suidas is confused; it is better to emend the nominative of the name Polycrates to the genitive (which rectifies all) than to reject this witness altogether with P. Maas (Berl. Phil. Woch. 1922, 578).
62 Polycrates' encomium, fr. 3 D: *GLP*, pp. 262ff: *NCGL III*, pp. 31ff. Latest treatment, D. L. Page in Aegyptus 31 (1951), pp. 158ff, especially p. 165.
63 Dialect, Page *loc. cit.*, pp. 162ff: Aeolisms include forms Μοῖσαι and πεδά (never a Rhegine form for μετά) and third plural present Indicative active termination in -οισι(ν). Dorian veneer: papyrus accentuation and Infinitive form ὑμνῆν may not count for much, but the word ἔλευσαν (from ἐλεύθειν = 'bring') is only paralleled in the Cretan laws of Gortyn. For observations on the metre of the poem see *NCGL III*, pp. 35-6: P. Maas *Griechische Metrik* (see p. 63 above) §70.

Anacreon
64 *POxy.* 221 col. vii: cf. *NCGL III*, p. 66.
65 The normal form first occurs in Alcaeus (A 10: 123 D) and is familiar from Hor. *Carm.* 3, 12. In Anacreon it is frequent in conjunction with the anaclastic variant (e.g. 44 D). For its use in Aeschylus, cf. *Supp.* 1018f: *Pers.* 65f, 647f: *Th.* 721f: *Pr.* 128f, 399f: *A.* 447f, 691f: *Ch.* 327f.
66 Cleobulus, fr. 2 D: *GLP*, p. 293. Atticisms, (ἀγαθά=good things: θωρήσσειν: ἡβᾶν, etc.) *GLP*, pp. 311f. Vase representations, see G. M. A. Richter *Attic Red-figure Vases* (Yale University Press, 1946), pp. 44, 58. These are:
(i) Cup by Oltus in British Museum (E 18): see Beazley, *ARV*, p. 40, No. 69 (illustrated as fig. 5).

EARLY GREEK LYRIC POETRY

(ii) Lecythus signed by the potter Gales in Syracuse (26967), Beazley, *ibid.*, p. 31, No. 2 (top).
(iii) Calyx-crater by Cleophrades I (private possession), Beazley, *ibid.*, p. 123, No. 29. Critias, fr. 8: cf. *GLP*, p. 307-8.

Corinna

[67] I am much obliged to Professor D. L. Page for kindly allowing me a sight of an advance proof of his study of Corinna before this appeared (supplement to J.H.S. 73.) The account given above accepts his conclusions. Of the previous literature mention may be made of:
editio princeps, Wilamowitz in *BKT* V. 2, pp. 19-55. A revised text by W. Crönert in Rh. Mus. 63 (1908), pp. 166f. See also P. Maas in Pauly-Wissowa-Kroll *Realencyclopädie* s.v. Korinna (XI. 1393-7): *NCGL III*, pp. 21-30. The late date was first put forward by Lobel in Hermes 65 (1930), pp. 356f: Bowra in C.R. 45 (1931) p. 4 took the other view.

From PSI 1174 (5b D) we learn that one of her poems was entitled, rather surprisingly, *Orestes*. As only 5 fragmentary lines survive, little can be made of it.

[68] A perplexing form χρουσοφαῖς (4. 20-1 D) and an alleged Aeolic crasis κἄσσονθη (5. 63 D) are too disputable to serve as basis for any inference.

[69] fr. 4 D is in stanza-form of 5 regular *ionic a minore* dimeters acatalectic with a longer form for clausula (◡◡ - - ◡◡ - ◡◡ - -): fr. 5 shows polyschematist choriambic dimeters (with glyconics substituted in places) and pherecratean clausula.

Pindar

[70] References are to C. M. Bowra's Oxford Text (1935, revised 1946).
[71] Texts since B. L. Gildersleeve (Olympians and Pythians; 1895, last revision 1907) are: O. Schroeder (Teubner, 1923): C. M. Bowra (see previous note): A. Turyn (New York, 1944, reprinted with fragments added, 1948, 1950). The whole printing of B. Snell's new Teubner text was destroyed in an air raid, but, happily, was re-issued in 1953.
Useful translations are: (prose) J. E. Sandys (Loeb, 1924): L. R. Farnell (Macmillan, 1932; 'rhythmical prose'): C. M. Bowra and H. T. Wade-Gery (Nonesuch Press, 1928; Pythians only; contains some helpful historical notes); (verse) C. J. Billson (Oxford, 1928-30): (French prose) A. Puech (Budé, 1922; revised edition 1949-52).
Since Schroeder's full-scale work of 1923 and his commentary on the Pythians of 1922, the only exegetical edition for notice here is that of L. R. Farnell (Macmillan, 3 vols., 1930-32). This lacks an apparatus criticus and is not always up to date on details, but is particularly good on religion and kindred topics.
The only lexicon to Pindar is by J. Rumpel (1893); obsolete but see Snell, pp. 340f. The standard edition of the scholia is by A. B. Drachmann (Teubner, 3 vols., 1903-27). The following emendations not generally absorbed into texts may be noticed here: Ol. 1. 113, ἀλλοί(οι)σι for (ἐν) ἄλλοισι A. von Blumenthal in Hermes 69 (1934), p. 458: Pyth. 5. 15-16, repunctuation of H. J. Rose in C.Q. 35 (1939), pp. 69-70 (confirmed surely by the similar pause and word-placing in 5. 98): Nem. 3. 14 εἴραν for the gloss ἀγοράν (A. W. Mair: but see P. Maas, *Responsionsfreiheiten* I, p. 25).
Metre. See works cited on p. 63 above, especially P. Maas, *Griechische Metrik*, and, for latitude allowed in strophic correspondence, his *Responsionsfreiheiten bei Pindar und Bacchylides* I and II.

[72] Norwood might with advantage have expanded his note 26 on p. 251 on the intransitive use of the verb ταρασσέμεν (Pyth. 11. 42). He rightly cites Pl. *Rep.* 564b, but does not point out that the verb is there so used of drones; was it perhaps a technical term of the ancient apiarist?

[73] W. Schadewaldt, *Aufbau des pindarischen Epinikions* (Halle, 1928): L. Illig, *Zur Form des pindarischen Epinikions* (Berlin 1932). Ring-form to 'seal off' digression: cf. Pyth. 6. 26-42 or the narrative section of Pyth. 4 (lines 70-253) and see note 23.

[74] See Hermes 73 (1938), p. 431 (for fr. 47), pp. 432f (for frs. 43 and 46). He noticed that the letters of fr. 16 of *POxy*. 1792 (whence fr. 47, Bowra) were identical with some 11 letters of lines 134 and 136 of Paean 6 (fr. 40, Bowra), thus identifying both author and poem-type. (Turyn's text presents Snell's conclusions.)

[75] As Farnell, *op. cit.*, vol. 1, pp. 300-1.

82 EARLY GREEK LYRIC POETRY

⁷⁶ C. Gaspar, *Chronologie Pindarique* (Brussels, 1900), pp. 150f put Isth. I in 458 B.C., but on political allusions that do not clinch the matter. A date some years after 480 suits. For a good account of Euxantius, see Jebb, *Bacchylides*, pp. 448f.

⁷⁷ Housman's conjecture, C.R. 22 (1908), p. 12.

⁷⁸ Norwood's elegantly presented analysis (*Pindar*, p. 84) assumes that the offending paean was composed for Delphian ears *ad maiorem Apollinis gloriam*; why then the eulogy on Aegina if no Aeginetan was meant to hear it?

⁷⁹ So much so, that Farnell (vol. I, p. 313) suggested that the paean as we have it is a re-written version, with the triad containing the eulogy on Aegina added as a sop to offended feelings there—indeed a desperate expedient.

⁸⁰ For a good appreciation of the religious content of this poem, see Farnell, vol. I, pp. 329f. *nova verba*: cf. in the dithyrambs εὐάμπυκες (fr. 60. 13; this word recurs in what has been thought to be a paean, fr. 343. 20) and ἀκναμπτεί fr. 62. 12. Older treatments of *schema Pindaricum*, e.g. Gildersleeve, *Pindar*, p. lxxxviii: Jebb on S. *Tr.* 520. It can no longer be maintained that 'in this construction the singular verb precedes the plural subject'.

⁸¹ So Farnell, vol. II, p. 426: Wilamowitz (*Pindaros*, p. 437) took the other view.

⁸² For ritual see Farnell, vol. I, p. 332 (more fully in his *Cults of the Greek States* IV, pp. 284-6). Note especially the passage of Proclus (*Chrestom.* apud Phot. *Bibl.* p. 321b, Bekker) quoted there and in *NCGL III*, p. 53 n1. 'Austere harmony', see Dion. Hal. *Dem.* 39. Family politics: see *NCGL III*, pp. 54-5 (Pagondas as a Theban patriot is anti-Athenian).

Bacchylides

⁸³ Frazer, *Golden Bough*, 'Adonis, Attis and Osiris', vol. I, pp. 174-6 (Macmillan, 1927). Myson amphora: see Beazley *ARV*, p. 171 No. 47 (i).

Archilochus

⁸⁴ Strassburg fragment: 79 D: text in *NCGL III*, p. 58. Demeas' inscription: I.G. XII, 5. 445. Another new fragment (80 D: *NCGL III*, p. 60) concerning one Ariphantus and a Hipponax (not the iambist) is too uncertain in its reference for discussion here. Blakeway, see *Greek Poetry and Life* (*Essays presented to Gilbert Murray*) (Clar. Press. 1936), pp. 34-55: Jacoby, in C.Q. 35 (1941), pp. 97-109.

Tyrtaeus

⁸⁵ See C.R. 10 (1896), pp. 269f, and R.W. Macan's reply (C.R. 11 (1897), pp. 10-12) with Verrall's rejoinder (*ibid.*, pp. 185f).

⁸⁶ So G. Dumézil, *Jupiter, Mars, Quirinus* (Paris, Gallimard, 1941), pp. 254f.

⁸⁷ Sappho α.5: 27 D (cf. p. 42 above). Idea of 'again', Alcman fr. 101 D: Anacr. frs. 5, 17, 26, 45, 79 D: Sappho α.1 App. (1 D) end. ῥυσμός, Archil. 67 D. Achilles in Il. 1. 356: contrast Archil. 79 D line 13. Scopas-poem, Simonides 4 D: *GLP*, pp. 341f. See, for a detailed working-out of the points in this concluding section, Snell, *Entdeckung des Geistes* chs. 3 and 9 (Eng. Tr. pp. 43-70 and 208f) with authorities cited in his notes (Eng. Tr. p. 313f).

APPENDIX TO CHAPTER II

As systematic re-writing of this chapter to take account of work published since 1954 is not practicable, references to some of the more significant and readily accessible contributions to the subject are given in the supplementary notes below.

p. 38, para. 1 (also pp. 52, 61 above). This volume yielded two reasonably well-preserved pieces of Anacreon (P.Oxy. 2321, 2322) and a fair quantity of Archilochus, including one lengthy but mutilated fragment of iambics (P.Oxy. 2310).

p. 38 para. 2. For an objective critique of the traditional terms for ancient lyric forms, see A. E. Harvey, CQ N.S. v (1955), pp. 157-75. His conclusions are largely negative; he rightly stresses the serious divergences between the terminology of Alexandrian and later scholars and the usages valid at the time of composition of the poems which concern us.

p. 39 (and n. 12, p. 65). The second edition of this valuable work (Oxford, 1961) takes account of new material up to 1960 and incorporates some changes in doctrine. The more important of these are noted in a judicious and appreciative review by G. W. Bond in CR N.S. xiii (1963) pp. 140-4.

p. 39 (8 lines from bottom: also n. 20, p. 66). Authoritative texts covering recent accessions are: E. Lobel and D. L. Page, *Poetarum Lesbiorum Fragmenta* (Oxford, 1955); and D. L. Page, *Poetae Melici Graeci* (Oxford, 1962; an interesting review of this by H. Lloyd-Jones in CR N.S. xiv (1964) pp. 16 f).

For obvious reasons it has not been possible to incorporate references to the numerations in these works in the body of this chapter.

Alcman

p. 40 (and n. 16, p. 65). M. L. West (CQ N.S. xv (1965) pp. 188-94, working from references to the Spartan kings in the Alcman-commentary in P.Oxy. 2390 fr. 2, develops a powerful argument that at least one of Alcman's poems was composed not earlier than 620 B.C. and might be as late as 570. Ethnographical and geographical allusions in the fragments are consistent with a date for Alcman's activity in the last decades of the seventh century, or even the early years of the sixth.

p. 41, para. 1 (end). For a fresh and illuminating re-appraisal of the major controversies of this poem, see M. L. West, *ibid.*, pp. 194-202. On specific points, he may well be right about Aenisimbrota (pp. 199 f) and the meaning of τείρει in line 77 (= 'torments', emotionally). There may be some reluctance to abandon φάρος, whether in the sense of 'plough' or 'robe' in favour of φᾶϝος, in spite of West's careful and persuasive arguments.

p. 41, para 2. Some continuous portions of another Partheneion are recoverable from P.Oxy. 2387, fr. 3 (= *PMG* 3, lines 61-85). This shows some marked similarities to the other piece; see further *GLP*², pp. 33 f.

pp. 41-9, *Sappho and Alcaeus*

See now D. L. Page, *Sappho and Alcaeus* (Oxford, 1955). This gives a full treatment of the 12 best-preserved poems of Sappho with background essays, and detailed discussion of the fragments of Alcaeus, grouped into political poems (pp. 149-243) and non-political poems (pp. 244 f). Reviews in CR N.S. vii (1957) pp. 19-23 (Davison) and JHS 77, part II (1957) pp. 320 f (Beattie). See, too, article by A. W. Gomme, *ibid.* p. 255 f.

p. 41 (12 lines from bottom). A papyrus scrap from an unidentified work (commentary or literary essay) quotes the ending of this poem (α′ 2 = 31 L.-P.) and settles the reading of line 16 which proves to be φα]ίνομ' ἔμ' αὔτ[α. See M. Manfredi in *Dai Papyri della Societa Italiana* (Florence 1965) pp. 16-17.

p. 44, para. 1. Snell's acute correction of the curious ἀθύρματα (= toys) in line 5 of this poem to ἀθρήματα (see Glotta 37 (1958) pp. 283-5) is based on Hesychius' statement that this latter word was current in Lesbian in the sense of ὀπτήρια (sc. δῶρα). There seems no ground for doubting this observation, which, if relevant to this poem, would tell in favour of authenticity.

p. 46. The mysterious title of Dionysus yields to the pleasing emendation τὸν Σεμελήϊον of A. J. Beattie (CR N.S. vi (1956) pp. 189 f.).

Stesichorus

p. 49. Something is now known of the manner in which Stesichorus treated a situation analogous to that of *Odyssey* xv,

APPENDIX 85

43-181 from fragments in P.Oxy. 2360 (= *PMG* 209) which seem to come from his *Nostoi* (*GLP*², pp. 77-9). A glimpse of his *Suotherai* (or is it from *Pelias' Funeral Games*? See H. Lloyd-Jones in CR N.S. viii (1958) p. 17) appears in P.Oxy. 2359 (= *PMG* 222), a list of participants in, presumably, the Calydonian boar-hunt.

p. 50 line 7. Add P.Oxy. 2260 (= *PMG* 233) col. ii, lines 19-23.

p. 50, para. 3 (and n. 59, p. 68). The anonymous commentator preserved fragmentarily in P.Oxy. 2506 (see *PMG* 192 and 193) speaks surprisingly of Stesichorus having written not one but two palinodes, citing one Chamaelion, a not disreputable authority. See the treatment by C. M. Bowra in CR N.S. xiii (1963) pp. 245-52, and further F. Sisti in *Studi Urbanati*, 1965 pp. 301 f. (I owe this reference to Miss N. V. Dunbar.) The relation between the two palinodes remains obscure in some material points.

p. 50 (and n. 57, p. 68). From the anonymous commentator in P.Oxy. (vol. xxix) 2506 fr. 26, col. ii (= *PMG* 217) lines 7-14, we now know that the recognition by means of the lock of hair in Aeschylus' *Choephoroe* derived from Stesichorus. This source also confirms as Stesichorean the motif of Apollo giving Orestes a bow, and quotes Eur. *Or.* 268-9 (cf. schol. on 268), and possibly the pretext of marriage to Achilles for Iphigeneia's journey to Aulis (cf. Eur. *I.T.* 24-5: *I.A.* 454-9; cf. Eur. *El.* 1020 f.).

Ibycus

p. 51 (3 lines from bottom). The mysterious 'son of Hyllis' has been identified by an ingenious piece of detective work on the part of J. P. Barron (Cl. Rev. N.S. xi (1961) pp. 15-7) who restores the missing 14 letters of line 40 as

Καὶ Ζεύξιππος ὄν] ἁ χρυσεόστροφος Ὕλλις ἐγήνατο.

This is based on a corrected reading of Pausanias II. 6, 7.

Anacreon

p. 52 (cf. p. 38, para 1, end). On P.Oxy. 2322 (= *PMG* 347), see *GLP*² p. 278 f. where the relations between Anacreon and a boy-friend (presumably Smerdies) over the matter of a hair-cut are dexterously explored. Another interesting addition, P.Oxy. 2321 (= *PMG* 346), is similarly treated, *ibid.*, p. 286 f.

For a sensitive discussion of some features of Anacreon's language, as εὐκτίτου (fr. 5 D = *PMG* 358, line 5) and νηλεῶς (fr. 88 D = *PMG* 417, line 2) see A. E. Harvey in CQ N.S. vii (1957) pp. 211 f. This is a valuable article, showing how conscious the lyric poets were of the associations of epic diction.

Corinna
p. 53. For a judicious summing-up of recent literature on the questions raised, see A. Lesky, *History of Greek Literature* (English translation, Methuen, 1966) pp. 178-80. (This work also has good remarks on recent criticism of the other lyric and elegiac poets).

Pindar
P.Oxy. vol. 26 (1961) was devoted to fragments of Pindar; these were mostly scraps, but interesting, particularly P.Oxy. 2450: for an indication of their content see review by E. G. Turner in CR N.S. 13 (1963) pp. 268-70.

There is now a full treatment of the literary and historical aspects of Pindar's poetry in C. M. Bowra, *Pindar* (Oxford, 1964). On the Pythian odes see R. W. B. Burton, *Pindar's Pythian Odes* (Oxford, 1962). Add too J. Irigoin, *Histoire du Texte de Pindare* (Paris 1952). On E. L. Bundy, *Studia Pindarica* (Berkeley, 1962) see the well-tempered comments of G. M. Kirkwood in Gnomon 35 (1963) pp. 130-2.

Archilochus
Archilochus' importance for the study of early Greek poetry has hardly been recognized as it should have been, possibly because his versatile talent resisted classification. There are now editions by M. Treu (Tusculum Ausgabe, Munich 1959) and in the Budé series by F. Lasserre and A. Bonnard (Paris 1958); the latter gives generous citations of *testimonia* and has a full, if imaginative, introduction. The tenth volume in the series of *Entretiens sur l'Antiquité classique* published by the Fondation Hardt (Vandoeuvres, Geneva, 1963) is particularly important; in this seven contributors examine the cardinal problems. See especially for the crucial question of Archilochus' relation to the Oral Tradition, D. L. Page, *ibid.*, ch. IV, pp. 117-63 and discussion, pp. 164 f. Page argues that the elegiac remains are

APPENDIX

(p. 144) 'composed almost wholly in the traditional language of oral epic' with no indication that the use of writing has affected the technique of composition, and that 'where dactylic and iambic metres are mixed, the traditional language predominates in both components'. In the iambics and trochaic tetrameters (p. 161) a new literary language can be seen in process of formation by 'adapting "traditional" phrases combined with components of premeditated word-selection. In brief, the non-dactylic compositions of Archilochus reveal the transition from oral to written verse'. K. J. Dover (ibid. ch. V, pp. 206 f.) has interesting observations on Archilochus' attitude to the poet's task, and examines how far he is to be understood as speaking *in propria persona*.

p. 61 (8 lines from bottom). For a penetrating discussion of this piece and a comparison with Horace's Tenth Epode, see E. Fraenkel, *Horace* (Oxford, 1957) pp. 28 f.

p. 64 (6 lines from end of last paragraph). A recent discussion of this poem will be found in A. W. H. Adkins, *Merit and Responsibility* (Oxford, 1960) pp. 165 f.; 196 f.; 355 f. (where earlier treatments are reviewed).

CHAPTER III

GREEK TRAGEDY

BY T. B. L. WEBSTER

It would be interesting to trace the influence of Greek tragedy in recent years, to discuss such plays as *Mourning becomes Electra*, *La Machine Infernale*, and *The Family Reunion*, and to compare modern translations such as those of Murray, Watling, and Lucas. Here I mention these things to recall the fact that Greek tragedy is still alive and to remember that Eirik Vandvik's translation of the *Antigone* into Ny-Norsk and Jean Anouilh's *Antigone* were both in their different ways documents of the Resistance.

My task, however, is to give some account of scholarship in the last fifty years, and it is made easier by the existence of full bibliographies in the relevant volumes of W. Schmid's *Geschichte der griechischen Literatur*[1] and since the war by the very intelligent discussions of A. Lesky in the *Anzeiger für die Altertumswissenschaft*.[2] I can therefore confine myself to important new discoveries and to works of scholarship which either mark ground firmly won or point the way to new developments. I shall say more about post-war work than pre-war work because I want to give some picture of what is happening now. I propose therefore first to consider very briefly texts and editions, then new discoveries, then production, dramatic technique and origins, metre and music, language and style, and finally some particular problems of interpretation, which have been dealt with in works about Greek tragedy in general as well as in works about Aeschylus, Sophocles, and Euripides.

1. TEXTS AND EDITIONS

I need say little about texts except to note that Oxford, Loeb and Budé texts of each of the three tragedians have appeared in this period, and a new Oxford text of Aeschylus is promised. Sophocles' fragments have been published and discussed by Jebb and Pearson;[3] for the other two tragedians we still have only Nauck[4] but it is good to know that a new text is promised; commentaries on the fragments of Aeschylus and Euripides are badly needed. Among other commentaries E. D. M. Fraenkel's

Agamemnon[5] must be mentioned first. This great work not only gives the views of a very sound scholar on a great but extremely difficult play, but also records very fully the views of his predecessors, so that the whole process of argument through the centuries can be observed. Such a labour is justified for a play so important and difficult as the *Agamemnon*, and the editor elucidates in passing a great many other problems of Greek literature. Attention may also be called to P. Groeneboom's[6] Dutch commentaries on Aeschylus,the revised edition[7] of the Schneidewin-Nauck Sophocles, the Oxford editions[8] of Euripides, and to some commentaries on individual plays, J. Vürtheim's *Supplices*,[9] J. T. Sheppard's *Oedipus Tyrannus*,[10] J. Duchemin's *Cyclops*,[11] U. von Wilamowitz-Moellendorff's *Ion*,[12] J. U. Powell's *Phoenissae*.[13] Great help to future editors has been given by the manuscript studies of A. Turyn,[14] R. Aubreton,[15] and J. A. Spranger,[16] who has published facsimiles of the Euripidean manuscripts L, M, and P.

2. NEW INFORMATION

New information is provided by the papyrologists and archaeologists; the former produce new texts and the latter new illustrations. D. L. Page[17] in his Loeb *Greek Literary Papyri* gave texts and translations of practically all papyri published up to the war and Sir Arthur Pickard-Cambridge[18] commented in some detail on the finds up to 1933. I have therefore to say briefly what we have gained, including papyri published during or since the war. Two late and melodramatic plays of Euripides, *Antiope* and *Hypsipyle*, survive in fragments long enough to permit a plausible reconstruction and give us further instances of plays of the same general type as the *Ion*. The main lines of the *Alexander*, the first play of the trilogy containing the *Palamedes* and *Trojan Women*, can be ascertained from an extremely tattered papyrus with the help of the quoted fragments and fragments of Ennius' adaptation. It was an exciting play in which Paris after being victorious at the games is recognized when he is on the point of being murdered by Hecuba and Deiphobus. Gilbert Murray[19] has shown how the whole trilogy fits together: in the first play the Trojans mistook the Curse-child Alexander for the child of blessing; the second gave the curse upon the Greeks, who prefer false wisdom to true and murdered the innocent Palamedes; both curses were fulfilled in the *Trojan Women*, which showed the vanity of all received values but beyond them the new value of playing one's part to the end of agony and splendour.

The discovery from an inscription that Sophocles wrote at least one connected trilogy, Telepheia, is surprising; parts of the *Assembly of Achaeans*, which must have belonged to it, have also been identified in papyri.[20] But the chief gain for Sophocles is the satyr-play *Ichneutae*, in which the satyrs search for Apollo's lost oxen, are terrified by the sound of Hermes' newly invented lyre, arouse his nurse Cyllene, and then suggest that Hermes is the thief. It is an enchanting light-hearted play written in a sort of parody of Sophocles' own style. Miss Jane Harrison[21] illuminatingly noted the parallel between the arousing of Cyllene and the many vases which show an earth-goddess awakened by dancing or hammering satyrs.

Aeschylean-satyr plays have also been discovered. The best preserved is the *Diktyulkoi*.[22] In the first fragment two characters are on the sea shore; one discovered the chest in the sea and asks for help. This evidently comes from the beginning of the play; the chest contains Danae and the infant Perseus. In the second long fragment (of which one line is numbered 800) Danae has some difficulty with Silenus, who wants to marry her because he has been accepted cheerfully by the infant Perseus, and the satyr chorus propose to celebrate the wedding; she was perhaps finally rescued and the satyrs rewarded for saving her from the sea. A fragment of chorus[23] celebrates the gift of fire by Prometheus and looks forward to dances of the nymphs in gratitude. It probably comes from the satyr play *Prometheus Pyrkaeus*, which was produced with the *Persae* in 472; another moment of the same play is represented on a vase of 420-10 B.C. in Oxford,[24] on which the satyrs light their torches from the fennel stalk held by Prometheus. Sir John Beazley suggests that the vase-painter was inspired by a later production of the play, which seems also to have been acted in Lucania in the middle of the fourth century. A similar explanation may account for a vase of about 430 B.C. in Vienna,[25] which shows Talthybius visiting Achilles while he mourns for Patroclus, the Nereids bringing Achilles his arms (neither theme is known to Homer), and Priam coming to fetch Hector's body, three pictures inspired by the *Myrmidons*, *Nereids*, and *Phrygians*, which have long been assumed to be the Aeschylean trilogy. The *Myrmidons* also appear in papyri: a new fragment[26] comes from the beginning —

someone comes out of Achilles' quarters and prays for a good day which will bring a reconciliation. A fragment[27] published before the war tells us that the Greeks threatened to stone Achilles if he would not fight. Then presumably came the mission and death of Patroclus, and the vase shows Talthybius, Agamemnon's herald, visiting Achilles during his mourning.

Another of the new fragments[28] has been attributed by Miss M. L. Cunningham to the *Egyptians*, and if this is right it shows that Pelasgus was killed in this play and mourned by a chorus of women, the sons of Aegyptus being presumably a secondary chorus. A startling discovery is a didascalic notice[29] stating that Aeschylus won a victory with X, X, *Danaides*, and *Amymone*, and Sophocles was second. It is difficult to avoid the conclusion that the missing names are *Hiketides*, *Aigyptioi*, and that therefore the *Supplices* was not produced before 466. To suppose that the *Supplices* belonged to another trilogy or to suggest that the editor of this text of Aeschylus quoted a later production instead of the original production (for which the formula would surely have been different) seem to me desperate remedies to save the faces of the many scholars who (like myself) have dated the *Supplices* early on stylistic grounds. If the new date is accepted, we have rather to ask within what limits and on what occasions stylistic dating, which we have to use to date our many undated documents, is valid. At least three questions have to be asked: first, have we got a series? Secondly, can a logical series be converted into a chronological series? Thirdly, can criteria which have proved valid in constructing one series be used to construct another? For Aeschylus it is doubtful whether we have a series at all — the dated plays are only spaced over fourteen years when he was between the ages of 53 and 67; we may regard *Persae* and *Septem* as middle-aged Aeschylus and the *Oresteia* as old Aeschylus, but it is perilous to date the *Supplices* and *Prometheus* by them. Secondly, where we have a series, as we have for Euripides,[30] if we place the undated plays in relation to the dated plays at the exact points which the frequency of certain characteristics indicates, we convert a logical series into a chronological series, or in other words we assume that Euripides created in an absolutely regular way, that each work marked a step forward, and that he was never influenced by special circumstances, never bored or off colour, never hurrying over one part to lavish special care on another. Even with ample material probably finer dating than early, middle and late should not be attempted. Thirdly, a comparison of metrical statistics for Sophocles[31] shows that criteria which are valid for dating Euripides have no chronological significance for Sophocles.

This last point is relevant also to the discussion of a fragment[32] of a tragedy on the Gyges story (known from the first book of Herodotus). Candaules' wife tells how she had seen Gyges in the royal bedchamber at night and has summoned him after she had sent the king about his morning business. This tragedy of palace intrigue was dated by E. Lobel and D. L. Page early in the fifth century and by K. Latte in the third. Both parties invoke the same metrical arguments. The phenomena occur in Ionian writers of the seventh to sixth century, in Ion of Chios in the fifth century, and in Hellenistic tragedy, but scarcely at all in the three great tragedians. We can safely say therefore that the play was not by Aeschylus, Sophocles, or Euripides; but otherwise we can only say that on these grounds it could be Ionian of any date or Hellenistic. We are therefore reduced to other arguments; the only tragedies on historical themes that we know in the early fifth century have what may be called Battle of Britain themes, but there is some evidence for historical drama in the Hellenistic age[33] when such themes as Themistocles, Marathon, and Amastris had only a romantic interest, and here the Gyges-play could belong. Marathon is the subject of the *Persians* illustrated on the well-known Apulian vase in Naples. C. Anti[34] has recently revived the old theory that it is a picture of Phrynichus' *Persians* (a doubtful title of a poet of whom we know extremely little[35]); he supposes that the Apulian painter copied an Athenian painting celebrating Phrynichus' victory some century and a half before. The vase shows no trace of the style or composition of the supposed original and the assumption that it was inspired by a contemporary tragedy of about 330 B.C. is much more likely.

Fourth-century vases tell us something about new tragedy and quite a lot about revivals of old tragedies in Athens and South Italy. Most of the material (including fifth-century illustrations) is interpreted and illustrated in L. Séchan's admirable study.[36] Some has been added since, and through the labours of Sir John Beazley and A. D. Trendall dating and attribution is more accurate than it was twenty-five years ago. Aeschylus is represented by several plays in the early fourth century, and *Danaides, Oresteia*,

Bassarae, and *Niobe* were still being revived in the later fourth century. For Sophocles there is little evidence. Euripides is represented by *Medea, Hippolytus, Stheneboea, Andromeda, Hecuba, Hypsipyle, Iphigenia in Tauris, Meleager, Oenomaus, Telephus*. Although the South Italian evidence is fuller, it seems to agree with the evidence of vases, inscriptions, and other sources for Attica, and we find as we should expect that it was the exciting plays which were revived.

Variation on Euripidean themes is a general description of fourth-century tragedy in so far as we can reconstruct it. Thus a papyrus fragment of a *Septem*[37] shows Eteocles and Polynices debating their claims before Iocasta but consciously avoiding direct coincidence with Euripides. An anapaestic lament[38] of Andromache is strongly reminiscent of the *Trojan Women* and seems to have been the original of Ennius' *Andromache Aichmalotis*; it is possible that this is Antiphon's *Andromache*, in which the heroine tried to save Astyanax by giving him to someone else to bring up like Polydorus in the *Hecuba*. Several fourth-century *Medeas* are known: one is attested by a papyrus[39] and ascribed to the fourth century because it has the note 'Song of the chorus' instead of a choral ode — the chorus sang an interlude. As there is something about 'hidden' persons or things this may be Carcinus' *Medea* in which Medea hid her children; Chairemon's *Achilles Thersitoctonus* as illustrated by an Apulian vase.[40] Another *Medea* is the subject of the well-known Apulian vase in Munich.[41] In this version one child is saved; the ghost of Medea's father surveys the scene in horror; and Oistros (madness) is shown in a snaky chariot. Again we see embroidery and variation of the Euripidean play. We may also be able to say something about Astydamas' *Hector* and *Antigone*. The certain fragment of his *Hector* shows Hector saying farewell to Andromache (modelled on the sixth book of the *Iliad*). In two unconnected papyri[42] Hector asks for his arms, and his fatal fight with Achilles is described. In three as yet unpublished Hibeh fragments (which I mention with the permission of Professor E. G. Turner) there is a reference to a prophecy by Helenus, a description of Thetis bringing Achilles' new armour, and someone is told not to fight if he is afraid. The Hibeh group and the other two all seem to be fourth century and fit together with the certain fragment to form a plausible whole. A curious version of the Antigone story is preserved on an Apulian vase and by Hyginus:[43] it is a continuation of the Euripidean version and cannot be later than 330 B.C.; the only other author whom we know to have written an *Antigone* is Astydamas. Haemon had concealed Antigone, and when the play opens, their son is old enough to come to Thebes for the games; Creon recognized him and presumably ordered the execution of Haemon; Heracles intervened. The play had an obvious affinity with Euripides' *Alexander*. Astydamas was conscious of himself as a great creative writer. After him the influence of Lycurgus and Aristotle probably exalted old tragedy at the expense of new tragedy. At any rate when we next find an inscriptional record[44] of the festival, about the middle of the third century, we find that three old tragedies and three old satyr plays were presented instead of a single old tragedy in each year from 341 to 339 B.C. This evidence weighs more heavily than the many names but scanty fragments of Hellenistic tragedians.

3. PRODUCTION

The advance in our knowledge of the production of Greek tragedy can be clearly seen by comparing the later editions of Haigh's *Attic Theatre* with Sir Arthur Pickard-Cambridge's *Theatre of Dionysus*[45] and *Athenian Dramatic Festivals*. Major works had appeared in the intervening period and the names of M. Bieber, H. Bulle, and A. Wilhelm must at least be mentioned, but full bibliographies are included in Pickard-Cambridge's books and it will be more useful to state briefly the knowledge gained for tragedy. Before the middle of the fifth century the Athenian theatre had a background set in projecting wings; late in the century Periclean rebuilding embodied neither stone *skene* nor high stage (a few steps are perfectly possible) though it included the *ekkyklema*. Some idea of the normal palace background can be gained from South Italian vases of the first half of the fourth century if we admit that, just as the South Italians borrowed plays from Athens, so their scenery was inspired by Athens.[46] These simple wooden sets differ greatly from the elaborate and solid structures pictured in the interesting and imaginative reconstructions in a recent work[47] by H. Bulle and H. Wirsing, but are more convincing if we remember that the time allowed between plays cannot have been much more than half an hour: in Euripides' trilogy of 431 B.C., Medea's palace in Corinth was succeeded by Philoctetes' cave in Lemnos, and that by Dictys' palace in Seriphus.

A recent article by H. Kenner[48] has suggested that the rocks which appear in vase painting of the second quarter of the fifth century are inspired by stage-practice: such rocks could easily be painted on light screens and would make a quick change of scene possible. The building of a permanent background in stone belongs to the period of Lycurgus, and later still, possibly in the second century B.C., the action was transferred to a high stage. The introduction of the high-soled *kothornos* was equally late, but the masks with a tower of hair above the forehead were probably introduced in the time of Lycurgus as part of his glorification of fifth-century tragedy. Earlier monuments show no exaggeration in the masks, and the clothes seem to have followed the fashion of the day, simple in the mid-fifth century and very elaborate in the late-fifth century. In the fourth century Attic and South Italian costume seem to run parallel. *Athenian Dramatic Festivals* also contains a wealth of information on the conduct of the festivals, the records, audience, actors and chorus, and ends with an extremely useful chapter on the Hellenistic theatrical guilds.

4. DRAMATIC TECHNIQUE

When the texts are used as evidence (and they are often our only evidence) for scenery, properties, costume, and action, we must always ask whether the poet is writing primarily for the audience in the theatre or primarily for the audience who will read and see with the mind's eye. Aristotle by implication took the latter view. The former view was stated in an extreme form by Tycho von Wilamowitz-Moellendorff:[49] 'for a dramatist who must have considered presentation on the stage as the only object of his plays, it is only natural that the dramatic effect of the single scene and of the single situation should be more important than the unity and coherence of the whole'. In applying this view to Sophocles, however, he is not concerned so much with scenery and the like but with the influence of the single scene on the composition and the character-drawing or rather the subordination of plot and character-drawing to the effect of the single scene. All later Sophoclean criticism has had to take this book into account, and its influence is particularly clear in a recent but much less extreme study by A. J. A. Waldock.[50] An essentially similar approach to Euripides has been taken by W. Zürcher.[51] Briefly, he concludes that the minor figures of Euripides are often coloured entirely by the situation in which they appear, and for the major figures 'Euripides reveals and describes causes and results, expressions and intensities of particular feelings and emotions, but not the secret structure of the soul from which they come nor its inner relations and coherence as a personality'. These particular feelings he sees as part of human nature in general, not of the character of the individual. Interpretation in terms of the effect of the single scene seems to me more justifiable for Euripides than for Sophocles, and the good points in these studies are the refusal to read more into a character than the words of the dramatist justify (we must not ask how many children Lady Macbeth had) and the recognition that what Medea or Antigone says is conditioned by the tragic style and the kind of scene in which they are at the moment appearing. (It should also be noted that the dominance of style over individuality made it easier for actors to interpolate lines and harder for us to recognize interpolations.)[52] But with all these reservations Medea and Antigone still appear to us as great individuals whose actions and words are consistent with their greatness.

This, however, is compatible with the use of set forms and stylized language and these must never be forgotten in interpreting character. The forms were partly necessary, partly attractive to the audience (sometimes because they were very old). They have been much studied and only a few works can be mentioned here. Of necessary forms I mention only a very careful study of the introduction, i.e. the prologue and parodos, by W. Nestle,[53] in which he discusses all surviving tragedies; he considers the various forms (prologue speech, prologue speech with dialogue, pure dialogue), the relation of exposition to characterization, the kind of characters used and the amount of information given, and then the various forms of the lyric part of the introduction — purely choral or lyric dialogue — and their relations to the iambic parts; finally he assesses the different methods of the three tragedians. W. Schadewaldt[54] developed F. Leo's earlier study of the monologue into a long examination of self-expression in drama, showing how in the *Supplices* of Aeschylus the self-revelations are always appeals to the gods, in Sophocles they are appeals to someone distant or dead or to nature, but Euripides revives the Homeric form of soliloquy in which a character addresses himself to express what is going on in his mind. More recently J. Duchemin[55] has classified scenes of persuasion and debates, and has shown that

GREEK TRAGEDY 97

Sophocles only uses such scenes where the situation demands them, whereas Euripides introduces them into every play as part of his stock-in-trade; she also discusses the cross-influence of the law courts and the sophists on both tragedy and comedy. W. Kranz[56] shortly before the war studied all the surviving choruses of tragedy and the changes in metrical form, style, and content from earliest Aeschylus to latest Euripides. The three main divisions — old song (i.e. Aeschylus), choruses of classical tragedy (Sophocles and Euripides before the *Trojan Women*), new song (Euripides' *Trojan Women* and later plays) — are undoubtedly valid and much is valuable in Kranz's commentary on elements of cult in tragic choruses and on the relation of choruses to dialogue.

5. ORIGINS

Few will accept in its literal form Kranz's statement that steadiness of development is a basic law of Hellenic art (and his own main divisions belie it) or his deduction therefrom of two stages in pre-Aeschylean tragedy, an earliest tragedy, in which two parts of the chorus answered each other, and Thespis' tragedy, in which an actor was substituted for one part of the chorus, so that the so-called epirrhematic parts of tragedy preserve the original form used by Thespis. He has no satisfactory explanation of the difference in dialect between the sung strophe or antistrophe and the spoken epirrhema; the sung part is largely Doricised because Attic tragedians write in the tradition of Dorian choral lyric but in the spoken part they merely borrow particular words from other dialects;[57] the epirrhematic parts are not therefore very old in tragedy. The epirrhematic parts of Aeschylean tragedy were also examined after Kranz by A. Peretti,[58] who came to the conclusion that they were extraneous elements which came into tragedy with laments and other ritual songs. He includes also an interesting study of the spoken part (*rhesis*) of archaic tragedy, in which he finds clear formal resemblances to epic and to Ionian elegy. The lyric epirrhematic form of lamentation is Phrynichus' contribution; Thespis had added the *rhesis* to the choruses which sang to the gods — the hymns of which survivals can be seen in Aeschylean *parodoi*. Peretti finds an ancestor for the laments and invocations of the dead in Ionian laments; E. Bickel,[52] however, traces these back to the 'sufferings of Adrastus', which the Sicyonians honoured with 'tragic choruses'. We cannot then say anything very precise about the origin of the epirrhematic parts of tragedy, but it is important to establish that prayers to the gods and laments were existing forms which the tragedians borrowed and which therefore retained the flavour of their context when performed in the orchestra. This point is very well brought out in a recent and charming book by E. T. Owen:[60] 'the audience not only heard and saw a choir singing its ritual songs, but heard and saw also the issue effected by that ritual'.

If we are modest in our requirements, we find a satisfactory prehistory of tragedy in Themistius and the Suidas notices of Thespis and Phrynichus, which fits on to the technical history of tragedy in the *Poetics* itself. We can also enrich our appreciation of tragedy by realizing the flavour of the ritual songs and the Homeric quality of the early speeches. These flavours are stronger in Aeschylus than later, and stronger in the *Antigone* than in the *Philoctetes*. Much of the detailed work which has established this position has appeared since the publication of A. W. Pickard-Cambridge's *Dithyramb, Tragedy, and Comedy*;[61] it shows that, although Sir William Ridgeway was probably not justified in arguing that tragedy originated in performances at the tombs of deceased heroes, hero-cults, as he saw, certainly provided an important element in Aeschylean tragedy, and like ritual hymns were probably still a living influence in the fifth century. Gilbert Murray's[62] theory gives an origin in quite a different sense: he finds the origin of tragedy in a vegetation ritual in which the Year-God grows, sins, dies, and is born again. It is quite irrelevant to point out, as Pickard-Cambridge did, that 'it is only possible to find the forms in the extant plays if their order — Agon, Pathos, Messenger, Anagnorisis, Threnos, Theophany — which we were asked to observe, can be changed to almost any extent, and the very broadest meaning given to the terms themselves'. It would scarcely be expected that expert composers would repeat the theme without variations. The essential is a sequence of prosperity, suffering, and some more or less realized hope of renewed prosperity, which is the nerve of all Greek tragedies (as also of much Dionysiac ritual and of the Eleusinian mysteries).

So stated, Gilbert Murray's theory gives a persistent formal cause rather than an origin. It would give an origin if we could point to a pre-Thespian chorus which sang such stories in honour of Dionysus. Pickard-Cambridge suggests that Thespis found such a chorus in his native Icaria (from which we have a very fine mask of Dionysus of Thespis' time).⁶³ M. P. Nilsson,⁶⁴ however, says that tragedy belongs to the cult of Dionysus Eleuthereus (which is undoubtedly true), and the cult was introduced into Athens by Peisistratus (Pickard-Cambridge finds no evidence for this date); the god was called Melanaegis, which implies that his ministers put on the skins of the sacrificial goats and hence sang a 'goatsong'. Both Nilsson and Pickard-Cambridge dismiss as theorising Aristotle's statement that tragedy originated from the leaders of the dithyramb and that it developed from 'satyric'. Since the publication of Pickard-Cambridge's book the archaeological evidence has become a great deal clearer owing to the work of Beazley, Payne and others, and various scholars⁶⁵ have used it to justify Aristotle. First, Aristotle's 'dithyramb' has nothing to do with Bacchylides or Pindar but possibly something to do with Archilochus, who knew how to lead a dithyramb when his wits were thunderstruck with wine; similarly his 'satyric' has nothing to do with the classical satyr play. The classical satyr play was introduced by Pratinas and his satyrs had horse-tails and horse-ears; chorus men of this type appear on Attic vases from the beginning of the fifth century, and on the well-known Pronomos vase of the very end of the century their shaggy loincloths suggest a 'goat' ancestry, as does also their equation with goats in satyr plays by all three tragedians. They are led by a hairy satyr called Silenus. It would seem that Pratinas for the first time produced Silenus and satyrs in a form in which they had long been known to artists, presumably from descriptions in poetry. In the first half of the sixth century and a little before we find in the art of Athens, Corinth, Sparta, and elsewhere, besides satyrs and silens, padded dancers who behave like satyrs, occasionally turn up in Dionysus stories, and once dance round a goat and a mixing bowl. They therefore are men dressed as satyrs and are admirably suited to be led in a dithyramb by a drunken Archilochus, to have been Arion's satyrs, and to have been the goat choruses which sang the sufferings of Adrastus at Sicyon. Aristotle may have been thinking of them when he described the origin of tragedy. They survived in some Greek cities to his own time; they also gave their costume to the actors of comedy. For tragedy Buschor has suggested that we may read their development from Attic black figure vases, on which they gradually become slimmer and less distorted; these humanized 'goat-singers' of 'sufferings' Thespis found and revolutionized by the addition of an actor, so that those moments of agonized decision could be represented which B. Snell regards as the essential meaning of 'drama'.[66]

6. METRE

We have so far discussed the poet as a dramatist; we must now consider him as poet, musician, and thinker. The metres of dialogue, choral lyric, and monody used by the tragedians are to some extent an isolable chapter in the whole history of Greek metric, since increasingly, as the fifth century progressed, drama gathered up all that it could use of the metrical invention of the past and of other forms of poetry and of the new music, and developed and modified them to its own uses. It was the last, brilliant flowering of Greek creative genius in this field. The work of three German scholars, Wilamowitz, Schroeder, and Maas, in the early years of this century, established the study of metric on a sound footing by discarding the inorganic division into 'feet' and starting from the colon, the whole metrical phrase (sometimes further analysable into recurring 'metra', sometimes not), by getting rid of the obsession with 'ictus' and 'arsis' and 'thesis', and by closely relating the study of metric to textual criticism. Wilamowitz's great though ill-organized *Griechische Verskunst*[67] is still of basic importance and contains many analyses of tragic odes. All the lyrics in the extant plays of Aeschylus, Sophocles, and Euripides were analysed by O. Schroeder in the little volumes of his *Cantica*;[68] their usefulness is slightly diminished by the omission of all antistrophes, and his curious play with number patterns can safely be ignored. P. Maas' *Griechische Metrik*[69] gives an indispensable summary in concentrated and lapidary form of the present state of our knowledge. The iambic trimeter of dialogue has to be studied by statistical analysis; unfortunately the fullest work on the subject, J. Descroix' *Le trimètre iambique*[70] does not always apply the best methods to answer the questions which need answering. Useful details on the trimeter, the trochaic tetrameter, and the anapaestic dimeter can be gathered from W. J. W. Koster's rather over-schematic *Traité de Métrique Grecque*.[71] The lyric is treated in A. M. Dale's *Lyric Metres of Greek Drama*,[72] which without attempting to be systematic or exhaustive gives an account of each class of metre in turn, with some notes on characteristic usage in each of the three tragedians. Miss Dale also discusses such information as there is about the performance of Greek lyric verse and is laudibly sceptical of attempts to reduce different metres to a common denominator or to see metre as directly reflecting the emotion of the words. All the works mentioned so far proceed on the necessary assumption that Greek metre can be studied (not too unsatisfactorily) in the spirit of a grammarian, divorced from musical or orchestic accompaniment. Attempts to apply what little we know of Greek music to the elucidation of metre have mostly led in the past to arbitrary and subjective treatment which can lead us nowhere, but mention should be made of a recent more reasonable and suggestive approach by T. Georgiades.[73]

7. VOCABULARY AND STYLE

When we turn to the words which the poet uses, we find many studies of style. G. Björck in his *Alpha impurum*[74] makes some suggestions as to the kind of classification needed in a study of poetic language. He suggests that it shares with colloquial speech the quality of being more emotional than normal prose. Poets often use variations of form which make no difference to the sense. The freedom of poetic intuition may make for a certain lack of precision in expression. Slight changes may be made in expression to avoid associations which the poet does not require. Poetic words may be avoided because they have lost their freshness. These are hints which it is to be hoped will be developed into a study of tragic language. F. R. Earp in his *Style of Aeschylus*[75] uses the very simple categories, compound words, rare and epic words, and metaphors. This sensitive appreciation of Aeschylus' style brings out very well the peculiarities of the language of the *Supplices* as the most mannered and strained play of Aeschylus, a quality which need not be explained as a sign of early date. W. B. Stanford in *Aeschylus in his Style*[76] has much about the sources of Aeschylus' words and a discussion of dominant images in the plays; he ends with a characterization of Aeschylus from his style. Dominant imagery or rather the recurrence of certain striking images through the *Oresteia* has been studied in two articles by R. P. Winnington-Ingram[77] and among other stylistic phenomena by O. Hiltenbrunner.[78] Aeschylus thinks in pictures and the pictures are startling, often frightening symbols of themes which run through his plays and trilogies. Sophocles' imagery is quieter; he works with similes rather than metaphor. In *The Imagery of Sophocles' Antigone* R. F. Goheen[79] traces six main kinds of imagery — military, maritime, animals and their control, money and merchandise, marriage — through the play and shows how they are related to each other and to the characters and at the same time give a kind of framework through which the dramatist intended his work to be seen. F. R. Earp[80] discusses the details of vocabulary and style in his *Style of Sophocles*, and arrives at a characterization of Sophocles' earlier and later style — this in the main agrees with the characterization of K. Reinhardt,[81] who well speaks of 'the sound and imagery of the knightly world' in connection with the *Ajax*; of the later style Earp says, after analysing *O.C.* 607-28: 'we seem to be Oedipus and to share his thoughts and feelings, and to be speaking quite naturally. When this happens, rhetoric or any kind of obvious ornament would merely be distracting and out of place. Shakespeare in his later style, though he is often not so simple as Sophocles, can sometimes do the same kind of thing'. J. C. F. Nuchelmans[82] has done a very clear and careful piece of work in classifying Sophocles' nouns and adjectives. A rather similar classification of the vocabulary of Euripidean lyrics by W. Breitenbach[83] is extended to cover metaphor, pleonasm, antithesis, etc., and ends with a rather depressing description of Euripidean style as 'a true reflection of a distracted, emotion-riddled time and personality'. In a recent dissertation B. Meissner[84] studies the psychological terminology used by Euripides and defines his relation both to the old view that psychic disturbances were due to divine or daemonic powers and to the new view that knowledge of what is right will lead to doing it. This is a valuable semantic study which writes one clear chapter in the history of psychological terminology.

8. GENERAL WORKS AND POLITICAL BACKGROUND

Finally I want to consider four more general problems of the poet's attitude to his audience; what were the things that he wanted to tell them when he spoke to them through his characters and chorus on a great festival occasion in memorable language reinforced by music and song. I need not attempt to cover the whole field because two excellent general guides have been issued during the period: M. Pohlenz' *Griechische Tragödie*[85] in 1930 and H. D. F. Kitto's *Greek Tragedy: a literary study*[86] in 1939. Both in their different ways view tragedies in relation to the time in which they were created, so that the plays of Sophocles are interwoven with the plays of Euripides, whereas the more recent and shorter *Greek Tragic Poets* of D. W. Lucas[87] gives separate chapters to Aeschylus, Sophocles, and Euripides. This method shows the individuality of the poets more clearly; the other method allows interesting conclusions as to particular forms which were favoured at a particular time and particular approaches to subject matter which were favoured at a particular time. In general Kitto and Pohlenz agree in finding that in early tragedy, Aeschylus and early Sophocles, interest centres on the action rather than the characters or, to put this another way, on the impact of the gods on the characters rather than the characters themselves. They would both also recognize a middle period in which the interest centres on great and complex personalities, Medea and Oedipus; but it is much more difficult to find a common term for later tragedy. Kitto notes the strange individuality of characters in late tragedy and (wrongly in my opinion) takes Herakles in the *Trachiniae* as an example. Pohlenz speaks of the 'inner profanation of tragedy', which is not as it seems at first sight, a judgment of value but a suggestion that tragedy has now become a purely human drama, free of its religious background.

To the religious background of the three poets I shall return shortly. I want first to pose a question to which very differing answers have been given: how far it is justifiable to interpret Greek tragedy politically? I am not thinking here of interpretation of Greek tragedy in terms of a modern political theory of history as is done most eloquently by G. Thomson in *Aeschylus and Athens*.[88] I am rather concerned with references to contemporary political events. The tragic poet is writing for a great public religious festival. He may therefore be expected to show some reaction to great public events, and, as he is not deluded by any belief in the desirability or possibility of representing historical characters accurately, he is likely to colour his characters from his contemporaries. On the other hand, he is not a comic poet; he does not put his contemporaries on the stage nor does he refer to every petty event of the preceding year. It is difficult to find any clear criterion. Thus I have no doubt that in the *Oresteia* Aeschylus gives the Areopagus a sanction as a murder court and nothing more, and blesses the recent alliance between Argos and Athens by making the scene of Agamemnon's murder Argos instead of Mycenae. Sophocles seems to me to have coloured both Creon in the *Antigone* and Oedipus in the *Tyrannus* with traits from Pericles (the relation between Sophocles and Pericles is very sympathetically handled in a new book by V. Ehrenberg).[89] Euripides must have had the aggressive policy, which had destroyed Melos and was planning the Sicilian expedition, in mind when he wrote his Trojan trilogy. In these cases a political reference is forced on our attention. I remain however entirely sceptical about many contemporary references which have been seen,[90] such as the identification of Polynices in the *Septem* with Themistocles; I cannot see the *Ajax* as a reflection in myth of the contest between Sophocles and Aeschylus in 468; I see no relation between the plague at Athens and Phaedra's sickness, and I dare not identify Rhesus with Sitalkes of Thrace. There are two separate points. First, we must not try to see political references where there may be none, or assume a similar technique for the tragic and comic poet. Secondly we cannot use political references for dating because they are seldom sufficiently clear. If the late date for the *Supplices* is accepted, the reference which has been seen to the mission of Aristagoras vanishes. It is possibly doubtful whether we need see a reference to the Sicilian expedition at the end of the Euripidean *Electra* if other considerations suggest an earlier date. For the *Rhesus* two arguments, political references to Thrace as noted and strictness of metre, have been adduced to show that it is an early work of Euripides. Thrace was interesting in the fourth century as well as the fifth, and the metrical argument is only valid if the play is by Euripides. On the other hand it must be admitted that J. Geffcken's[91] careful study does not prove a fourth-century date, although this still seems to me the most likely.

9. AESCHYLUS AND ZEUS

One major problem of Aeschylean interpretation has been continuously discussed and seems to be a stage nearer solution: how is the Zeus who tortures Prometheus to be reconciled with the just governor of the Universe, whom we apprehend in the Zeus hymn in the *Agamemnon*? W. Schmid[92] adopts the heroic solution of supposing that the *Prometheus Bound* is a play written by a sophist within ten years of Aeschylus' death. But in spite of the difficulties of vocabulary and lyric metre, which among others F. R. Earp and A. M. Dale have noted in the works discussed above, this seems impossible; 'the narrations and predictions of Prometheus', as G. Thomson says in *Aeschylus and Athens*, 'have been handled with such artistic mastery of the material as to concentrate at the end of the play our whole attention on the sequel', and in the same way the *Prometheus Unbound* is unthinkable without a preceding *Prometheus Bound*. We must start from the sequence of two plays as original works by Aeschylus. Much has been written on their date and the nature of the play preceding or succeeding them, but as far as I can see no firm ground has been reached. The question of Zeus has, however, been discussed in two recent books. For F. Solmsen in *Hesiod and Aeschylus*[93] 'the Zeus of the *Prometheus Bound* is not Aeschylus' Zeus at all but the Zeus whose manifestations he found recorded in the *Theogony*'. Hesiod's Zeus is, however, also the father of Justice and of the Graces besides being the conqueror of the Titans. Solmsen suggests that Aeschylus saw the change from one state of affairs to the other as a development in time, and that the emergence of Justice took place during the reign of Zeus, not at its beginning. Solmsen has supported with new arguments the view that reconciliation is due not only to a change in Prometheus (of which the fragments of the sequel provide evidence) but also to a development in the character of Zeus. This view is held also by Pohlenz, Thomson, and others. D. W. Lucas speaks of 'Zeus as developing from the raw tyrant indulging a despotic power to something like a constitutional ruler under the divine law of his own making'. Gilbert Murray in *Aeschylus* says that 'it is Zeus who repents more than Prometheus' and then asks 'what if there is something quite wrong in the present condemnation of Zeus as he now is?'; his plan may be inscrutable to mortal thought. This second idea seems to me much easier to accept than the development in the character of Zeus. K. Reinhardt in his recent fascinating book, *Aischylos als Regisseur und Theologe*,[94] has pushed this suggestion a stage further. He says that the peculiarity of the gods is not that they develop but that they show two faces. Zeus shows the cruel face in the first play which we have and the gracious face in the second play which we have lost. This conception is found at the end of the Zeus hymn of the *Agamemnon* in the difficult lines, which may be paraphrased: 'there is something which we may call the grace of the gods, although they govern with strength from their majestic thrones'. So the sixth-century statue of Apollo at Delos carried a bow in one hand and little statues of the Graces in the other.[95] The *Oresteia* provides several other points of contact with the *Prometheus* besides the Zeus hymn, notably the conflict between the young gods and the old gods in the *Eumenides* and the sudden reconciliation of the Furies, achieved by Athena's whispered word. Some such sudden change in Prometheus and some such revelation of the other face of Zeus (to which the chorus of freed Titans must have borne testimony) seems more probable than the development of the character of Zeus.

10. SOPHOCLES AND THE GODS

It is probable that more single studies of Sophocles have been published in the last fifty years than of either of the other two tragedians. Tycho von Wilamowitz's study, which has been mentioned above, was a violent reaction against the psychological interpretation of the preceding fifty years. His implication that Sophocles wrote primarily for the effect of the individual scene at a single performance provoked reactions in its turn in Germany, Holland, Italy, and England. More recently discussion has centred on Sophocles' view of the relation between gods and men. Thus W. Vollgraff[96] attacks the traditional position that Sophocles was a pious believer and says that he is an anthropocentric individualist, while his gods are the gods of mythology and play the part which we assign to 'circumstances'. C. H. Whitman[97] takes a rather similar line, when he finds four 'levels of moral activity among which the plot creates tragic tensions', first, the sheer immorality of the clearly bad characters, secondly the everyday, maxim-guided chorus and the neutral characters; the third level is the level of the hero himself, whose *arete* 'is human because it is moral but its existence creates a process of becoming divine'; the fourth level is the deity itself; because it is above morality as it is above humanity, the relationship between it and the hero is one of keen life-and-death conflict. Whitman is entirely right in emphasizing the greatness of Sophocles' heroes and interprets them admirably; he quotes with approval the excellent passages in K. Reinhardt's book in which that author stressed their isolation from their fellows. I am not clear, however, in what sense they become divine except in the obvious case of Oedipus in the *Oedipus*

Coloneus. Nor am I clear that all those from Aristotle onwards who have found *hamartia* an ingredient in tragic heroes in general and Oedipus in particular have been wrong. Sir Maurice Bowra's treatment of Oedipus in *Sophoclean Tragedy*[98] seems to me more satisfactory, when he says that if Aristotle meant in the case of Oedipus that the *hamartia* was something like a fault of character which leads a man to see things wrongly, he came very near the truth. Oedipus killed an old man and all his staff in anger; without a moment's consideration he suspected Creon and Teiresias; great and sympathetic he certainly is and his disaster is out of all proportion to his merits, but he is not flawless. This brings us to the question of the relation of gods to men. Whitman makes two points: the Olympians are conventional symbols of an a-moral Deity (or even in some passages of irrational evil), and the attribution of justice to the gods is a sign of bourgeois morality in the chorus. Both are contrary to what seem to me to be the starting points of Sophoclean interpretation, his own attested piety and the traditional function of the chorus as the poet's mouthpiece. It is extremely difficult to formulate the relation of gods to man in Sophocles and therefore to describe the poet's own outlook on life. Bowra says 'King Oedipus shows the humbling of a great and prosperous man by the gods ... the gods display their power because they will. But since they display it, man may draw a salutary lesson'. The last sentence is surely right; about the first I am less happy if it implies that the gods intend to humble Oedipus; I suggest that the gods only act when man has made it necessary for them to act. Other authors, particularly Reinhardt in the book which has been mentioned and E. Turolla,[99] have emphasized the contrast between the blindness of the characters and the knowledge of the gods, the weakness of the characters and the strength of the gods, the appearance with which the characters deal and the reality with which the gods deal, an approach which naturally leads to a discussion of the relation between Sophocles and Heraclitus;[100] but it is, I think, easy to overstress this contrast. Sophocles' interest lies in human suffering; the behaviour of the gods has to be accepted piously. From this standpoint J. C. Opstelten[101] asks whether Sophocles can be described as a pessimist, and examines all passages which speak of the suffering of the innocent or the insignificance of human existence, noting their context and their tone of grief, bitterness, or resignation. Sophocles, he decides, was aware of the fragility of man, and so far was a pessimist, but his work is a religious and aesthetic victory over this awareness.

11. THE BACCHAE

Euripides is far more difficult to bring under a common denominator than Sophocles, and widely differing interpretations of his attitude towards the gods are still published. Thus L. H. Greenwood in *Aspects of Euripidean Tragedy*[102] thinks that Euripides is telling his audience what, if the tradition were trustworthy, and if the gods were like that, might have happened or even must have happened; for him the gods are phantasy and not even symbols of reality. A. Rivier[103] in his charming and sympathetic *Essai sur le Tragique d'Euripide* writes: 'the gods are perhaps cruel, they are terrible to men; but see — they act, they exist, one must therefore fear them, worship them, and try to live without provoking their anger', and in another place 'Euripides does not attack the religion of the myths, he affirms it in its essence and even in its mystery'. Both writers appear to me to oversimplify the problem; quite apart from the various attitudes of characters towards the gods — the piety of unawakened Ion, the criticism, scepticism, and rationalism of others — the gods who appear on the stage differ from each other, as a superficial consideration of Artemis and Aphrodite in the *Hippolytus*, Dionysus in the *Bacchae*, Hermes in the *Ion*, Athena in the *Trojan Women* will show. Nevertheless on one Euripidean problem, the interpretation of the *Bacchae*, considerable agreement will be found between three recent books by G. M. A. Grube,[104] E. R. Dodds,[105] and R. P. Winnington-Ingram.[106] After the rationalist interpretations of G. Norwood and A. W. Verrall, which failed because they were far too ingenious for any audience to have understood, but which in this country and in the first decade of the century were as good a spur to Euripidean scholars as Tycho von Wilamowitz's book was to Sophoclean scholars in the twenties, Gilbert Murray showed the way in *Euripides and his Age*[107] with his clear appreciation of the double nature of Euripides' Dionysus and his recognition that there is here 'a rather different attitude towards the pieties of the common man'. Winnington-Ingram's book is a running commentary which shows great sensitiveness to the language of the play, to the intricate themes which are interwoven in its texture, and to the dramatic effect of each situation both for itself and in its relation to the play. His general thesis is that the play is not primarily concerned with an ecstatic cult in Macedonia or Athens, although recent religious phenomena in Athens may have given it a topical interest, but is relevant much more widely to all emotional phenomena. The suppression of emotion in Pentheus and the Theban Bacchanals and the exclusive cult of emotions among the Asiatic Bacchanals lead to much the same results, which may be either an ecstasy of peace or a fury of violence. The characters and the chorus claim to have wisdom in regard to Dionysus, but all their wisdoms are variations of misunderstanding. The whole play communicates the wisdom of Euripides, which is to understand the beauty and the horror which are interdependently called forth if individual or group submits to the untrammelled emotion symbolized by Dionysus. It was not irreligious to present such a play at the god's own festival because it gave the god a reality which the thinking Athenian could recognize.

12. CONCLUSION

Rereading this summary I am aware how much I have left out, and I have probably omitted even more than I am conscious of. In particular I have said little about the tragedians in relation to the art, thought, and life of their times, which are discussed in the relevant parts of many more general books,[108] and I have perforce said nothing of many fine essays on individual plays. The discussion goes on and will continue to go on as long as we ask new questions based on our own experience of art and life. The achievement of the last fifty years is considerable, and, without predicting the new questions which will need answering in the next fifty years, the obvious immediate need is to make the new information available. We need first of all commentaries on the fragments which would include the new texts. We need secondly commentaries on the extant plays which take into account our new knowledge of production, metre, style, dramatic technique, ritual elements, and character drawing; for some plays certainly the form of Winnington-Ingram's running commentary on the *Bacchae* would be ideal. We need also a new edition of Schroeder's *Cantica* and a new history of tragic language. We need to reach some kind of clarity as to how far psychological interpretation is permissible, and there is no reason why the answer should be the same for all the tragedians or the same for the major and minor characters of any one of them. Finally, we need to try to define how the tragic poet works, how far it is justifiable to see a steady development, and where special considerations may be responsible for special results. Through the plays we must try to see the poet moulding his story in terms of his vision of gods and men into forms largely traditional but partly revolutionary.

I am grateful to the editor of *Diogenes* for permission to quote from my article on 'Modern Scholarship on Greek Tragedy'.
[1] Vols. 1, 2 (Aeschylus and Sophocles); 3 (Euripides). Munich, Beck, 1934 and 1940.
[2] 1 (1948), 65f, 99f; 2 (1949), 1f, 34f, 68f; 3 (1950), 195f; 5 (1952), 131f.
[3] Cambridge, University Press, 1917.
[4] Second edition, Leipzig, Teubner, 1888 (anastatic reprint, 1926).
[5] Oxford, Clarendon Press, 1950.
[6] Groningen, Wolters, 1903-44.
[7] E. Bruhn and L. Radermacher, Berlin, Weidmann, 1907-14.
[8] M. Platnauer, *Iphigenia in Tauris*, 1938; D. L. Page, *Medea*, 1938; J. D. Denniston, *Electra*, 1939; A. S. Owen, *Ion*, 1939; E. R. Dodds, *Bacchae*, 1944; A. M. Dale, *Alcestis*, 1954. In preparation: W. S. Barrett, *Hippolytus*.
[9] Amsterdam, H. J. Paris, 1928.
[10] Cambridge, University Press, 1920.
[11] Paris, Champion, 1945.
[12] Berlin, Weidmann, 1926.
[13] London, Constable, 1911.
[14] *Manuscript Tradition of the Tragedies of Aeschylus*, New York, Polish Institute, 1943; 'Manuscripts of Sophocles', Traditio, 2 (1944), 1; 'Sophocles Recension of Manuel Moschopulos', TAPA, 80 (1949), 94.
[15] *Démétrius Triclinius et les recensions médiévales de Sophocle*, Paris, Belles Lettres, 1949.
[16] CQ 33 (1939), 98 and 184.
[17] London, Heinemann, 1942.
[18] *New Chapters in the History of Greek Literature*, Third Series, 68f, Oxford, Clarendon Press, 1933.
[19] *Greek Studies*, 127, Oxford, Clarendon Press, 1946. The *Alexander* has been further discussed by F. Scheidweiler, Philologus 97 (1948), 321.
[20] Page, nos. 3 and 21, with bibliography.
[21] *Essays presented to William Ridgeway*, 136ff, Cambridge, University Press, 1913. Cf. also E. Buschor, SBAW, 1937, 32. A recent excellent study of the play by E. Siegmann, Hamburg, Hansischer Gildenverlag, 1941.
[22] Page, no. 2 with *Oxyrhynchus Papyri*, XVIII, no. 2161, London, Egypt Exploration Society, 1942. Cf. also E. Siegmann, Philologus 97 (1948), 71f; R. Cantarella, *I nuovi frammenti Eschilei*, Naples, 1950, Libreria del stato.
[23] *Oxyrhynchus Papyri*, XX, no. 2245, Oxford, Clarendon Press, 1952.
[24] AJA, 43 (1939), 618f. The vase is no. 187 in F. Brommer, *Satyrspiele*, Berlin, de Gruyter, 1944 (on which see my review, JHS, 70 (1950), 85).
[25] H. Kenner, JŒAI, 33 (1941), 1; and *CVA* Vienna, i, pl. 24.
[26] *Ox. Pap.* XX, 2253, identified by Professor Paul Maas. Also *Ox. Pap.* XVIII, no. 2163.
[27] Page, no. 20; cf. W. Schadewaldt, Hermes 71 (1936), 25.
[28] *Ox. Pap.* XX, 2251; cf. M. L. Cunningham, Rh M. 96 (1953), 223.
[29] *Ox. Pap.* 2256, fr. 3.
[30] E.g. the metrical researches of Th. Zielinski, *Tragodumenon*, 133f, Krakau, Polish Academy, 1925.
[31] E.g. those given by H. Siess, WS 36 (1915), 244; 37 (1916), 5.

GREEK TRAGEDY

[32] E. Lobel, PBA, 35(1950), 1; D. L. Page, *A new chapter in the history of Greek Tragedy*, Cambridge, University Press, 1951; K. Latte, Eranos 48 (1950), 131; A. Lesky, Hermes 81 (1953), 1.
[33] For Diphilus' *Amastris* see my *Studies in later Greek Comedy*, 153, Manchester, University Press, 1953.
[34] Arch. Class. 4 (1952), 23. For older bibliography see L. Séchan, *Etudes sur la Tragédie grecque*, Paris, Champion, 1926.
[35] Cf. in recent years F. Marx, Rh M 77 (1928), 340f; F. Stoessl, MH 2 (1925), 148.
[36] See note 34.
[37] Page no. 33.
[38] Page no. 30.
[39] H. J. M. Milne, *Catalogue of Literary Papyri*, no. 77, London, British Museum, 1927.
[40] Séchan, *op. cit.*, 528, fig. 156; J. D. Beazley, AJA, 54 (1950), 322.
[41] Séchan, *op. cit.*, pl. viii; O. Regenbogen, Eranos 48 (1950), 33.
[42] Page no. 29.
[43] Séchan, *op. cit.*, 274.
[44] A. W. Pickard-Cambridge, *Athenian Dramatic Festivals*, 123f, Oxford, Clarendon Press, 1953.
[45] Oxford, Clarendon Press, 1946.
[46] Cf. my article CQ,42 (1948), 15f and Pickard-Cambridge's reply CQ 43, (1949), 57f.
[47] *Szenenbilder*, Berlin, Mann, 1950.
[48] JŒAI, 39 (1952), 46.
[49] *Philologische Untersuchungen* 22 (1917), 39. See the criticism in J. C. Kamerbeek, *Studiën over Sophocles*, Amsterdam, H. J. Paris, 1934.
[50] *Sophocles the Dramatist*, Cambridge, University Press, 1951.
[51] *Darstellung des Menschen in Drama des Euripides*, Basel, Rheinhardt, 1947.
[52] Cf. D. L. Page, *Actor Interpolations in Greek Tragedy*, Oxford, Clarendon Press, 1934.
[53] *Struktur des Eingangs in der attischen Tragödie*, Stuttgart, Kohlhammer, 1930.
[54] *Monolog und Selbstgespräch*, Berlin, Weidmann, 1926.
[55] *L'Agon dans la tragédie grecque*, Paris, Belles Lettres, 1945.
[56] *Stasimon*, Berlin, Weidmann, 1933.
[57] See now G. Björck, *Alpha impurum*, Uppsala, Almquist och Wiksell, 1950.
[58] *Epirrema e Tragedia*, Florence, Le Monnier, 1939.
[59] Rh M. 91 (1942), 123.
[60] *The Harmony of Aeschylus*, Toronto, Clarke-Irwin, 1952.
[61] Oxford, Clarendon Press, 1927.
[62] A recent statement is given in *Aeschylus*, Oxford, Clarendon Press, 1940, and JHS 71 (1951), 120. G. Thomson in *Aeschylus and Athens* (London, Lawrence and Wishart, 2nd ed., 1948) looks rather to initiation ceremonies for an origin of the same kind.
[63] Published by W. Wrede, MDAI (A) 53 (1928), 66.
[64] His position is summarized in *Geschichte der griechischen Religion*, I, 218, Munich, Beck, 1941.
[65] I have found the following particularly useful: F. Brommer, *Satyroi*, Würzburg, Triltsch, 1937; K. Ziegler, *RE*, vi, 1906, s.v. *Tragoidia*; A. Lesky, *Griechische Tragödie*, Leipzig, Kröner, 1938; E. Buschor, *Satyrtänze*, Munich, Beck, 1943.
[66] 'Aischylos und das Handeln in Drama', Philologus Supplt. XX, 1928.
[67] Berlin, Weidmann, 1921.
[68] Leipzig, Teubner, Aeschylus, 1916; Sophocles, 1923; Euripides, 1928.
[69] Leipzig, Teubner, 1929.
[70] Paris, Klincksieck, 1931.
[71] Leyden, Sijthoff, 1936 (2nd edition, 1954).
[72] Cambridge, University Press, 1948.
[73] *Griechische Rhythmus*, Hamburg, Marion von Schröder, 1949.
[74] See above n 57.
[75] Cambridge, University Press, 1948.
[76] Dublin, University Press, 1942 cf. also J. Dumortier, *Les images dans la poésie d'Eschyle*, Paris, Belles Lettres, 1935.
[77] CR, 47 (1933), 97; JHS, 68 (1948), 130. Cf. also the treatment of legal imagery in B. Daube, *Zu dem Rechtsproblem in Aischylos' Agamemnon*, Zürich, Niehans, 1938.

[78] *Wiederholungs- und Motivtechnik bei Aischylos*, Bern, Francke, 1950.
[79] Princeton, University Press, 1951.
[80] Cambridge, University Press, 1944.
[81] Frankfurt, Klostermann, 3rd edition, 1948.
[82] *Nomina des Sophokleischen Wortschatzes*, Utrecht, Beyers, 1949.
[83] *Untersuchungen zur Sprache der Euripideischen Lyrik*, Stuttgart, Kohlhammer, 1934.
[84] *Mythisches und Rationales in der Psychologie des Euripideischen Tragödie*, Göttingen, Philosophische Fakultät, 1951.
[85] Leipzig, Teubner, 1930.
[86] London, Methuen, 2nd edition, 1950.
[87] London, Cohen and West, 1950.
[88] Cf. above n62.
[89] *Pericles and Sophocles*, Oxford, Blackwell (1954).
[90] The following instances will be found in F. Stoessl AJPh. 73 (1952), 113; A. von Blumenthal, *Sophokles*, Stuttgart, Kohlhammer, 1936; E. Delebecque, *Euripide et la guerre du Péloponnèse*, Paris, Klincksieck, 1951; R. Sneller, *De Rheso Tragoedia*, Amsterdam, H. J. Paris, 1949.
[91] Hermes 71 (1936), 394.
[92] *Untersuchungen zum Gefesselten Prometheus*, Stuttgart, Kohlhammer, 1929; see also *Geschichte der Griechischen Literatur*, I, 3, 281.
[93] Ithaca, Cornell University Press, 1949. See the admirable review by R. P. Winnington-Ingram in *Gnomon* 23 (1951), 414. See also article by O. J. Todd in CQ 19 (1925), 61f.
[94] Bern, Francke, 1949.
[95] Cf. R. Pfeiffer, Journal of the Warburg and Courtauld Institute, 15 (1952), 20.
[96] In *De Antieke Tragedie*, Leiden, Batteljee en Terpstra, 1947.
[97] Sophocles, Cambridge (Mass.), Harvard University Press, 1951.
[98] Oxford, Clarendon Press, 1944.
[99] *Saggio sulla Poesia di Sofocle*, Bari, Laterza, 1934.
[100] E.g. J. C. Kamerbeek in *Studia Vollgraff*, Amsterdam, North Holland Publishing Coy., 1948; H. Diller, *Göttliches und Menschliches Wissen bei Sophokles*, Kiel, Lipsius und Tischer, 1950.
[101] *Sophocles and Greek Pessimism*, Amsterdam; North Holland Publishing Coy., 1952.
[102] Cambridge, University Press, 1953.
[103] Lausanne, Rouge, 1944.
[104] *Drama of Euripides*, London, Methuen, 1941.
[105] *Bacchae*, Oxford, Clarendon Press, 1944.
[106] *Euripides and Dionysus*, Cambridge, University Press, 1948.
[107] London, Williams and Norgate, 1913 (new edition Oxford, Clarendon Press, 1946).
[108] E.g. W. Nestle *Vom Mythos zum Logos*, Stuttgart, Kröner, 1942; W. Jaeger, *Paideia*, Oxford, Blackwell, 1946; B. Snell, *Discovery of the Mind*, Oxford, Blackwell, 1953; E. R. Dodds, *The Greeks and the Irrational*, Los Angeles, University of California Press, 1951; T. B. L. Webster, *Greek Art and Literature*, Oxford, Clarendon Press, 1939.

APPENDIX TO CHAPTER III

Tragische Dichtung der Hellenen, Göttingen, 1964, is the second edition of A. Lesky's very valuable handbook on Greek tragedy for advanced students and covers the whole range of authors and problems with great sureness of judgment and an admirable assessment of modern scholarship in all languages. The following highly selective notes are greatly indebted to this and to the same author's *Geschichte der griechischen Literatur* and *Griechische Tragödie* (both now available in English). They follow the same lines as the preceding chapter (pp. 71ff.). *The Complete Greek Tragedies*, edited by R. Lattimore, S. G. Bernardete, D. Grene for the University of Chicago Press, 1959, seems likely and deserves to become the standard translation in English-speaking countries. Nauck's *Tragicorum Graecorum Fragmenta*[2] has been reissued (Hildesheim, 1964) with a supplement by B. Snell containing new fragments of Euripides and adespota quoted by ancient authors (but excluding papyrus texts). J. Jackson's volume of conjectures on the three tragedians, *Marginalia Scaenica*, Oxford, 1955, has been much praised.

1. *Texts etc.*

Aeschylus Texts: Oxford Classical Text, Gilbert Murray, 1955 (the surviving plays and fragments of plays from the same trilogy). Loeb, H. R. W. Smyth, 2nd edition, 1957, with a most useful supplement containing the papyrus fragments by H. Lloyd-Jones. H. J. Mette, *Die Fragmente der Tragödien des Aischylos*, Berlin 1959, a new complete edition with very full quotation of the citations and all the papyrus fragments (some rash supplements and attributions), translation, commentary, and reconstruction are given in *Der Verlorene Aischylos*, Berlin 1963. Commentaries: H. J. Rose, *A commentary on the surviving plays of Aeschylus*, Amsterdam, 1957-58; H. D. Broadhead, *The Persae of Aeschylus*, Cambridge 1960 (a good text with beautifully arranged apparatus and a very full and satisfying commentary); D. Page and J. D. Denniston, *Aeschylus Agamemnon*, Oxford 1957 (a very useful size for students; often brilliantly right and sometimes perversely wrong; the down-writing of Aeschylus as an original thinker, pursued also by H. Lloyd-Jones, JHS 76 (1956) 55, seems to some excessive). Tradition and Conjectures: R. G. Dawe, *The Collation and Investigation of the Manuscripts of Aeschylus*, Cambridge, 1964 (emphasizes the impossibility of constructing a stemma and the frequent appearance of good readings in late manuscripts.) He has also made a useful collection of modern conjectures, *Repertory of Conjectures on Aeschylus*, Leiden, 1965.

Sophocles Texts: Budé, A. Dain-P. Mazon, 1955-60. Commentaries: J. C. Kamerbeek, *Ajax*, Leiden 1953; *Trachiniae*, Leiden 1959 (both without text but very full and detailed; conservative in the handling of text); W. B. Stanford, *Sophocles' Ajax*, London 1963 (very full of information about Sophoclean usage in general, and extremely useful). Tradition: on the independent value of A (denied by Turyn) see J. C. Kamerbeek, *Mn.*, 11, 1958, 25; P. E. Easterling, CQ, 10, 1960, 51.

Euripides Texts: Budé, *Orestes*, F. Chapouthier and L. Méridier, 1959; *Bacchae*, H. Grégoire and J. Meunier, 1961. Commentaries: E. R. Dodds, *Bacchae*, Oxford 1960 (second, revised edition); and W. S. Barrett, *Euripides Hippolytos*, Oxford 1964 (a new text with useful introduction on history of the text, very full commentary); A. M. Dale, *Helen*, Oxford (1967). Tradition: A. Turyn, *The Byzantine Manuscript Tradition of the Tragedies of Euripides*, Urbana 1957, gives a detailed account of the manuscripts and their relation to each other; his assertion however that for the alphabetic plays P is a *gemellus* of L has been challenged by G. Zuntz, *An Inquiry into the transmission of the plays of Euripides*, Cambridge, 1965, who shows that P copied L; Zuntz has a full and fascinating discussion of the early history of the text and republishes with detailed commentary a papyrus of part of the *Helen*, the claims of which he perhaps rates too highly.

2. *New information*

B. Snell, *Scenes from Greek Drama*, Berkeley 1964, 1, 139, in his Sather lectures discusses Aeschylus, *Myrmidons*, and convincingly reclaims the papyrus (doubted by Page and Lloyd-Jones) of which he gives a new text (cf. above p. 73, n. 27). E. Fraenkel (*Eranos* 52, 1954, 61) ascribes *P.Oxy.* 2256 fr. 9 to the *Aitnaiai*, and it has been further discussed by Ph. Kakridis in *Eranos* 60, 1962, 111. For Sophocles a new and very difficult fragment of

APPENDIX 115

the *Inachos* (*P.Oxy.* 2369) describing the transformation of Io into a cow has been discussed by R. Pfeiffer (SBA, 1958) in relation to the old fragments (Page, no. 6 etc.): a satyr play still seems the most likely solution. *P.Oxy.* 2453 gives new fragments of the *Polyidos or Manteis*. *P.Oxy.* 2452 has been claimed on linguistic grounds for the *Theseus* (which is weakly attested) but may rather belong to Euripides' *Theseus*, where the new lyric dialogue between Ariadne and Eriboia fits admirably into the book fragments. The papyrus fragments previously associated with the *Assembly of the Achaeans* (above p. 73 n. 20) are now proved to belong to Euripides, *Telephos*. Four vases of the middle decades of the fifth century show Andromeda in Eastern dress led in by negroes and tied to a post or two posts; the coincidence suggests that Sophocles' *Andromeda* had a binding scene like the *P.V.* (BICS, 12, 1965, 29); the attitude of Perseus on one vase is parodied on the Vlastos oinochoe (*J.H.S.*, 65, 1945, pl. 5).

For Euripides the gain is greater. H. Van Looy has published a complete bibliography of the fragments (*AC*, 32, 1963, 162) and has given a new text, commentary, and reconstruction of the two Alkmaion plays, the two Phrixos plays, and the two Melanippe plays (*Zes Verloren Tragedies van Euripides*, Brussels 1964. The text is in Flemish, but a long summary in French is added). Some light is thrown on the two Phrixos plays by *P.Oxy.* 2456, a collection of very fragmentary hypotheses. These fix fr. 821 as prologue of *Phrixos A* and fr. 819 as prologue of *Phrixos B*. Tzetzes' statement that the *A* and *B* should be switched could be understood, if he was using a set of hypotheses which numbered the plays *not* chronologically but by their sequence in the story; thus a papyrus published by M. Papathomopoulos (*Récherches de Papyrologie*, III, 37) gives the end of a hypothesis of the *Peliades* (coinciding with Hyginus, *Fab.* 24) followed by the hypothesis of the *Medea* labelled *Medeia B*. If this is correct, the earlier *Phrixos A* will have dealt with a later stage of the story, perhaps Phrixos in Kolchis, than the later *Phrixos B*. G. W. Bond has published an excellent edition of the *Hypsipyle* (Oxford, 1963). New placing of some of the fragments and the addition of further lines to the prologue from a papyrus in Hamburg have made the outlines and some of the flavour of this long, late play clearer than before. It is possible that it was produced with the *Antiope* and *Phoenissae* in 411 or 410 B.C. B. Snell (*Scenes from Greek Drama*,

70) has reconstructed the *Antiope*, commenting particularly on the debate between Amphion and Zethos.

Besides the hypotheses (and the *Theseus*), *P.Oxy.*, vol. XXVII, contains fragments of Euripides' *Kresphontes* (2458), *Kretes* (2461), *Oidipous* (2459), *Telephos* (2460). The two fragments of the *Kresphontes* give a part of the prologue in which the young Kresphontes has returned and inquires of the situation from a sympathizer, and part of a later scene in which (cf. Hyginus, *fab.* 137) the chorus lament his supposed death after his lying recital to Polyphontes. (The speakers in the prologue are marked A and Γ, presumably first and third actor). Fr. 2* of the *Kretes* papyrus may come from the *parodos*, to which fr. 4 certainly belongs. Fr. 1 is a description of the Minotaur in stichomyth, perhaps Minos answering the leader of the chorus, who have been summoned to investigate the portent (?). The book fragments, papyri, testimonia, and illustrations have been conveniently collected and discussed by R. Cantarella, *I Cretesi di Euripide*, Milan, 1964. The *Oidipous* fragment describes the sphinx and then quotes her riddle in hexameters: this may come from the prologue. The *Telephos* fragments, which place the Berlin fragments previously ascribed to Sophocles' *Assembly of Achaeans* and probably also the Rylands fragment in this play, have been used with the old fragments, the Latin fragments, and the evidence of Aristophanes in an admirable reconstruction by E. W. Handley and J. Rea, BICS, Suppl. 5, 1957.

B. Snell devotes the last two chapters of *Scenes from Attic Drama* to the reconstruction and evaluation of the strange satyr-play *Agen*, which was played before Alexander on the Hydaspes. The reconstruction is convincing, and the play is shown to have had considerable political importance. An interesting glimpse of later tragedy is afforded by a silver cup in the British Museum published by P. E. Corbett and D. E. Strong, *B.M.Q.*, 22, 1960, 68: Orestes, Pylades, and Iphigeneia, pursued by Thoas, are saved by Chryseis, who persuades her son, the younger Chryses, not to surrender them because Orestes is his half-brother. The play was clearly written as a sequel to Euripides' *Iphigeneia in Tauris* and was the original of Pacuvius' *Chryses*.

3. *Production*

M. Bieber's second edition of *The History of the Greek and Roman*

Theater (Princeton, 1961) has a large number of new illustrations and full bibliography and references to publications. My 'Monuments illustrating tragedy and satyr play', BICS, Supp. 14, 1962, lists, dates, places and tries to interpret vases, terracottas, and other monuments illustrating actors and masks; *Griechische Bühnenaltertümer*, Göttingen, 1964, gives a selection of the material and includes theatres and inscriptions relevant to performances. F. Brommer, *Satyrspiele*[2], 1959 is a useful collection of pictures of satyrs on vases, although he is too ready to see a satyr play reflected in all scenes with satyrs. P. Arnott, *Greek Scenic Conventions in the fifth century B.C.*, Oxford 1962, takes a sensible conservative line in supposing a minimum of scenic apparatus but makes some egregious mistakes. A. M. Dale emphasizes the availability and advantages of the *ekkyklema* in fifth century tragedy in WS 69, 1956, 96. N. Hourmouziades discusses Euripides' use of the theatre and its machinery in *Production and Imagination in Euripides*, Thessaloniki, 1965. G. M. Sifakis argues for the use of the high stage, even for revivals of classical tragedy, from the early Hellenistic period in BICS, 10, 1963, 31; his *Studies in the Hellenistic theatre*, London, Athlone Press, 1966, is an extremely useful discussion and assessment of Hellenistic dramatic inscriptions, particularly in Delos and Delphi.

4. *Dramatic technique*

R. Lattimore in two very sensitive and sympathetic books (*The poetry of Greek tragedy*, Baltimore, 1958; *Story patterns in Greek Tragedy*, London, 1964) discusses the appeal to the imagination, as distinct from the intellect and the emotions, in tragedies from all three authors and the logic imposed on the plot by the kind of story chosen. G. H. Gellie has defined very well what can sensibly be said about character in Greek tragedy in *AUMLA*, 20, 1963, 241. Madame J. de Romilly in *L'Évolution du Pathétique d'Eschyle à Euripide*, Paris 1961, shows three different attitudes to suffering, particularly in spectacular scenes: Aeschylus emphasizes the act and gives a divine explanation; in Sophocles the suffering has the value of an ordeal; in Euripides man is alone with his misery, which is therefore all the heavier. A. M. Dale in *Classical Drama and its influence*, London 1965, 17, discusses the spoken intervention of the chorus in the action of the drama and the varying degrees of awareness of its presence shown by the actors.

M. Imhof in MH, 13, 1956, 125 interprets the scenes in trochaic tetrameters from Aeschylus to Euripides and finds that the long and lively metre is peculiarly suited to the late plays of Euripides.  A. Spira (*Untersuchungen zum Deus ex Machina bei Sophokles und Euripides*, Kallmünz, Opf., 1960) finds the essential element in the *deus ex machina* an epiphany which acts on the characters with compulsion like the epiphanies of gods in epic; he works out interestingly Euripides' use of a counter intrigue to produce a situation for the god to solve; the appearance of the god restores a just order (this is perhaps an overstatement).

5. *Origins*

The second edition of A. W. Pickard-Cambridge, *Dithyramb, Tragedy and Comedy*, Oxford 1962, includes a full list of all the vases, etc., which may throw light on the origins of drama and illustrates the most important of them, including a fragment of a vase found in Miletos, which shows that the much discussed padded dancers were performing in Ionia soon after 700 B.C. H. Patzer's difficult book on *Die Anfänge der griechischen Tragödie*, Wiesbaden 1962, which reinterprets and over-emphasizes the part of Arion, rightly stresses the importance of mythical narrative in choral lyric as one of the elements in the origin of tragedy. G. F. Else, *Hermes* 85, 1957, 17, usefully recalls the influence on early tragedy of dramatic recitation of epic at the Panathenaea (he develops the theme further in *The Origin and Early Form of Tragedy*, Harvard, 1965.)

6. *Metre*

The valuable and critical surveys of work on Greek Metre by A. M. Dale, *Lustrum* 2, 1957, 6 and by R. P. Winninton-Ingram on Greek Music, *Lustrum* 3, 1958, 5, discuss where relevant work on the metre and music of tragedy. P. Maas' *Griechische Metrik* (cf. above p. 83) has been translated with a few supplements by the author and translator, by H. Lloyd-Jones as *Greek Metre*, Oxford 1962. B. Snell, *Griechische Metrik*³, Göttingen, 1962, has been translated and adapted by T. G. Rosenmeyer in *The Metres of Greek and Latin*, London, 1963. D. S. Raven, *Greek Metre*, London 1956, is an extremely useful introduction for students and analyses a number of tragic choruses. W. Kraus, *Strophengestaltung in der griechischen Tragödie, I. Aischylos und Sophokles*,

APPENDIX 119

Vienna 1958, has analysed the structure of stanzas and reduced them to a number of comparatively simple patterns; much of this is valid and the book contains good incidental observations. H. Pohlsander (*Lyric Metres of Sophocles*, Michigan 1963) analyses all the choruses of Sophocles and comments on the metrical interpretations which have been published. A second edition of A. M. Dale, *Lyric Metres of Greek Drama*, is forthcoming.

7. Language and style

Three books should be mentioned: H. Friis Johansen, *General Reflection in tragic Rhesis*, Copenhagen 1959; W. Jens, *Die Stichomythie der frühen griechischen Tragödie*, Munich, 1955; L. Bergson, *L'Épithète ornamentale*, Uppsala 1956.

8. General works

Besides the three works of A. Lesky mentioned in the introduction and the works of R. Lattimore and Madame de Romilly quoted under Dramatic Technique, it should be noted that the general books (see above p. 85-6) of D. W. Lucas and H. D. F. Kitto have both had a second edition (the former in 1959 and the latter in 1961). The latter has also discussed the 'total impact' of the *Oresteia, Philoctetes, Antigone, Ajax* and contrasted them with *Hamlet* in *Form and Meaning in Drama*, London, 1956. An interesting book by John Jones (*On Aristotle and Greek Tragedy*, London 1962) re-examines the three tragedians in the light of Aristotle's *Poetics* and in particular attacks the concept of the tragic hero: he discusses particularly the three plays on the Elektra, Orestes, Klytaimnestra theme, and his phrasing of the problems in legal terminology often throws new light.

9. Aeschylus

J. H. Finley Jr. (*Pindar and Aeschylus*, Harvard 1955) compares the two contemporary poets who both think in images and both believe in a moral government of the universe. Madame J. de Romilly includes very fine interpretation of Aeschylean imagery in her study of *La Crainte et l'angoisse dans le théâtre d'Eschyle*, Paris 1958. On the *Septem* important discussions of the speeches about the champions have been published by E. Fraenkel in SBA 1957, of the second stasimon by G. R. Manton, in BICS 8, 1961, 77, and of the conclusion by H. Lloyd-Jones in CQ

53, 1959, 80; that the conclusion is by Aeschylus remains nevertheless improbable, and the most likely assumption is that it was added for a revival before the end of the fifth century. H. Lloyd-Jones has discussed the implications of the late dating of the *Supplices* (cf. above p. 74) in AC 33, 1964, 356, and R. P. Winnington-Ingram has given a reconstruction of the trilogy in JHS 81, 1961, 141. John Herington has interestingly suggested that the three Prometheus plays introduced each a different element: Ocean in the *P.V.*, Earth in the *P.L.*, and Ouranos in the *Pyrphoros* (*Phoenix* 17, 1963, 180, 236). Aeschylus' relations with Themistocles are defined rather boldly by W. G. Forrest, CQ, 10, 1960, 235f., 239f.

10. *Sophocles*

H. Friis Johansen's full report in English on Sophoclean literature, 1939-59, in *Lustrum* 7, 1962, is an infinitely valuable criticism with great sureness of touch; quite apart from its assessment of secondary literature, conjectures and interpretations on individual lines are listed and discussed under each play. Large books on Sophocles continue to pour out: S. M. Adams, *Sophocles the Playwright*, Toronto 1957; B. M. W. Knox, *Oedipus at Thebes*, Yale, 1957; G. M. Kirkwood, *A Study of Sophoclean drama*, Cornell, 1957; and on a more modest scale, very well argued and admirably restrained, H. D. F. Kitto, *Sophocles: Dramatist and Philosopher*, Oxford 1958. B. M. W. Knox, *The Heroic Temper*, Berkeley 1964, is a good general account of the Sophoclean hero and his predicament but overstresses the influence of hero-cults and personal religion; he discusses the *Ajax* in HSCPh, 65, 1961, 1. R. P. Winnington-Ingram considers how far the archaic world-picture may be attributed to Sophocles, *Classical Drama and its Influence*, London 1965, 30. I. M. Linforth has continued his sympathetic interpretations of individual plays in *California Publications in Classical Philology*, 1954, 1, Ajax; 1956, 95, Philoctetes, the play and the man; 1961, 183, Antigone and Kreon; 1963, 89, Electra's day. G. H. Gellie in BICS 11, 1964, 1 discusses motivation in Sophocles with special reference to the *Antigone* and *O.T.*; he finds that the large events of the action condition the character drawing in the latter play and the part played by the gods in the former. H. Pohlsander's argument from lyric metre (AJP 84, 1963, 280) that the *Trachiniae* should be dated between *Antigone* and *O.T.* and nearer *O.T.* is solider than the form-analysis of E.-R. Schwinge, *Die Stellung der Trachinierinnen*, Göttingen, 1962, which places it before the *Antigone*.

11. *Euripides*

A new text and commentary of Satyros' life is given by G. Arrigheti in *Studi Classici e Orientale*, 13, 1964. The large book by R. Goossens, *Euripide et Athènes*, Brussels 1962, relates Euripides' life and works to contemporary Athenian history and has much good detail and intelligent suggestions: it is marred by finding allusions everywhere to political events. Against this tendency a firm stand had been taken by G. Zuntz in the *Political Plays of Euripides*, Manchester 1955, although even he insists that one unique political ambience fits the *Heraclidae* and another the *Supplices*, but the book has good, detailed interpretation of both plays, an admirable classification of ancient Arguments, and a most important demonstration that the *Electra* has no allusion to the Sicilian expedition and must therefore be given its proper metrical date well before 415 B.C. The sequence: revival of *Choephori* — parabasis of *Clouds* (second edition) — Euripides' *Electra* (before 415 B.C.) — Sophocles' *Electra* — Euripides' *Helen*, 412 B.C. — Euripides' *Orestes*, 408 B.C. should now be regarded as established. *Fondation Hardt: Entretiens VI*, Geneva 1960, contains pleasant essays in English by G. Zuntz on the *Helen* and by R. P. Winnington-Ingram on the *Hippolytus*; J. C. Kamerbeek tackles the contrast between myth and reality in Euripides; A. Rivier perhaps overstresses the 'demonic' element in early Euripidean women; H. Diller shows Euripides' increasing preoccupation with place and ordinary people as factors in his drama; A. Lesky has an excellent discussion of Euripidean psychology. H. Strohm, *Euripides*, Munich 1957, analyses structural elements such as Discussions, Altar-scenes, and Recognitions. The relation between the two Hippolytus plays and the relation of the *Medea* and the second *Hippolytus* to Socrates are mentioned by Rivier, Winnington-Ingram, Lesky in the *Entretiens Hardt* and fully discussed by W. S. Barrett in his edition of the *Hippolytus* and by B. Snell (*Scenes from Greek Drama*, 23-69). Barrett attractively interposes Sophocles' *Phaedra* between the two Euripidean plays but denies the use of Seneca for reconstructing the *First Hippolytus*. Snell uses

Seneca freely. Neither states how Seneca handles his sources in other plays. Barrett denies the ethical dialogue, which Snell sees between Euripides and Socrates: neither notes that it is just at this period that the comic poets spoke of Socrates as helping Euripides make his plays; they evidently saw that their two bugbears were tackling the same problems. E. Fraenkel in SBA 1963 argues for large-scale interpolation in the *Phoenissae*, excluding, in particular, all references to the burial of Polyneikes; but was it possible after Sophocles' *Antigone* to omit this? H. Strohm argued in RhMus 87, 1959, 257 that the *Rhesus* is post-Euripidean: the arguments from dramatic forms etc. are attractive rather than compelling. W. Ritchie has re-examined the whole question in *The Authenticity of the Rhesus of Euripides*, Cambridge 1964. This very careful and extremely honest book claims the *Rhesus* for Euripides in his earliest period, 455-440 B.C. Strohm is only the last of a whole string of scholars who have felt that the whole spirit of the play is incompatible with Euripides. Ritchie's studies of vocabulary certainly show that the author knew his Euripides well. The strong argument against authenticity is metrical: the technique of the iambic trimeters fits well with earliest Euripides, but the trochaic tetrameters would date it after 415 B.C., if it were by Euripides, and the anapaestic opening is only paralleled in the posthumous *Iphigeneia in Aulis:* such a mixture of what in Euripides are clear chronological stages is impossible for Euripides.

CHAPTER IV

GREEK COMEDY

BY K. J. DOVER

A. METHOD

(1) *The Twentieth Century*

PAPYRI and inscriptions pose new problems and spring many surprises, but they may also answer questions already asked. The physical unearthing of new material is not in all circumstances more exciting than that kind of discovery which is ultimately the product of reflection; and a spark is often kindled by the mere juxtaposition of facts long familiar in isolation. For these reasons I propose to discuss in this section, A, progress in interpretation which may have been stimulated by the discovery of new material but was not dependent on this material for its success. In B I shall describe the three principal categories of discovery, and in C I shall try to summarize the present state of what seem to me the five most significant problems with which we are confronted by the old and the new material in combination.

A scholar who tries to explain a difficult passage of a Greek text may be conceived as exploring a complex of concentric circles; the innermost circle encloses the immediate context of the passage, the outermost the whole of human experience. The right path to pursue is long and spiral; the average interpreter of Greek Comedy in the nineteenth century tended to follow a path that was short and straight. Atomizing his text, he considered each sentence in its relation to the lexical, grammatical, and metrical norms continuously extracted by learning and devotion from his vast inheritance.[1]

Twentieth-century work on Comedy shows two characteristics which stand in particular contrast to the purely linguistic approach. One is the development of what I would call 'generic studies', the extension to literary form of the methods of collection and classification previously applied to linguistic data; these methods have been particularly fruitful when applied to recurrent dramatic situations.[2] The second characteristic is the realization, as yet imperfect and erratic, of the full implications of the simple truism that Comedy is *drama*; these implications will be discussed in (2) below.

In contrasting one century with another one necessarily commits a double injustice: an injustice to the past, in that the most stimulating and fruitful of modern enquiries may turn out to be no more than the following up of hints long unheeded but plainly given by individual scholars a century ago; and an injustice to the present, in that anyone who still sees Comedy through the eyes of a Kock or a Blaydes may share the credit which rightly belongs to those who do not. Nevertheless, if the nineteenth-century scholars who were influential in their own day are viewed in contrast with the twentieth-century scholars who have been influential in ours, I believe that the distinction made above is valid.

If the historian of the future is ever asked whether there was any one man in this century whose influence on the study of Comedy was outstanding, he may well say: Wilamowitz. Superficially, this may seem a surprising choice, for the bulk of Wilamowitz's work on Comedy is not large, and there are others — Alfred Körte most obviously — who might reasonably claim prior mention.[3] But Wilamowitz was no waster of words, and methodologically he has had no equal; much of his work should be read not as a systematic exposition of data but as intellectual protreptic illuminated by provocative examples. He owed his understanding of Comedy to his sustained determination to take the Greeks as he found them and to his refusal to believe that metre and politics, palaeography and religion, cannot be studied by the same man at the same time.

(2) *Action and Language*[4]

Van Leeuwen was long perplexed by the dramaturgy of *Acharnians*, but in his edition of 1901 he solved the problem to his own satisfaction: *Dicaeopolidem . . . in ipsa urbe celebrare parva Liberalia, quorum tempus legitimum dudum praeteriit, fingentem se rure versari . . . Lamachum autem et Euripidem vicinos* (sic) *Dicaeopolidi fingendo comicus fines arti suae concessos non est egressus*. Now, van Leeuwen was an intelligent editor who had gone far to free himself from purely verbal preoccupations,[5] but he had not freed himself from the characteristic attitude of the nineteenth century towards dramaturgy: the acceptance of the 'three unities' as fundamental and the grudging admission of occasional departures from these unities by virtue of 'comic licence'. The fact is that in Old Comedy the moment and the episode were everything, and all consistency of place, time, character, personality, and logic could be sacrificed to them.[6] It might be said that Aristophanes made great demands on the imagination of his audience — provided we understand that the poet did not regard himself as asking for a concession and his audience was not conscious of granting one. This concentration on the comic moment is characteristic of several types of popular comedy in our own day. Perhaps the man who is brought up on Molière and Shaw, who listens in to *Studies in Interpretation* but never to *Take It From Here*, is not altogether to be trusted with Aristophanes.

The reader who makes a serious effort to put himself in the place of the ancient audience will find Aristophanic dramaturgy at once more acceptable. Progress in the archaeology of the Greek theatre[7] has facilitated this imaginative effort, but in interpreting a text it is also necessary that we should always see in the mind's eye the movements and gestures of the speakers and hear in the mind's ear the sound of their voices.[8] It is an encouraging sign that in the Teubner third edition of Menander the *actio* appears above the apparatus; but we are still unskilled in visualizing gesture. Editors of *Frogs* do not seem to remember that line 1434 ὁ μὲν σοφῶς γὰρ εἶπεν, ὁ δ'ἕτερος σαφῶς was spoken by a live man with mobile hands, so that data on μέν and δέ are of limited relevance.

In many nineteenth-century scholars the mind's ear was as undeveloped an organ as the mind's eye. In fr. 1 K of Antiphanes a speaker is declaiming in tragic style; someone else at last exclaims τί λέγεις; and he replies τραγῳδίαν περαίνω Σοφοκλέους. And here is Kock's comment: *non video cur non maluerit scribere* περαίνω Σοφοκλέους τραγῳδίαν, *versu haud paullo modulatiore*. With a sudden shock we realize that to Kock Greek was not a real noise that once issued from the mouths of real men, but a set of visual symbols to be manipulated by rules which were excellent up to a point but defective in so far as they were based on only a portion of the relevant facts. It is strange that when so much work has been devoted to the vocabulary of Greek Comedy so little thought has been given to its characteristic groupings of words and structure of phrase,[9] and for this deficiency our reluctance to speak the words of the text aloud is to blame.

Study of vocabulary has concentrated on the distribution of words; in Menander to establish his relation to the Koine[10] and in Aristophanes to uncover the different literary and cultural strata which make up his astonishing edifice of poetry. The substratum of Aristophanic language is presumably colloquial, though the boundaries of colloquial Greek are much harder to determine than those of colloquial Latin. It may often be identified by expressions which recur in the popular speech of Byzantium and modern Greece,[11] or by terminations of a type associated with colloquialism in Latin.[12] Overlying this substratum is the language of parody. Parody of serious poetry, especially of Tragedy, is comparatively easily detected and isolated,[13] but a more subtle parody, or a kind of allusion which shades into parody, is seldom completely absent from any passage of Aristophanes. In particular, many words and terminations[14] are associated with certain specialized vocabularies, e.g. with medicine or philosophy or formal rhetoric; it has been well remarked that the editor of Aristophanes needs inverted commas.[15]

The late nineteenth-century school which regarded linguistic abnormality as aesthetically objectionable or even morally depraved is not a good master in the study of Comic language. Just as in metre the divergence of Comic practice from Tragic has to be recognized,[16] and premature theorizing has merely hindered the essential task of discerning and describing metrical phenomena, so in language the student of Comedy must adopt a non-committal and positivistic approach. Even in the field of vocabulary the essential material has not yet been wholly reduced to a serviceable form. We have an Index to Aristophanes,[17] but — while it is ungracious to carp at a work which we use not only with gratitude but also with relief that we did not have to do the job ourselves — it is to be deplored that all such indices for the sake of a few hours' more work and a few shillings more in printing costs omit the plausible variants. No comprehensive index to the Comic fragments has been compiled since the mid-nineteenth century.[18] Furthermore, most of the existing studies of Comic vocabulary would be of shorter length but greater weight if their authors, before labelling a word 'colloquial', 'technical', 'poetic', etc., on the purely positive evidence had asked and answered the vital question: 'How else could the poet have said it?'

(3) Comedy and Society

Not all the humour of Comedy is verbal, and not all the verbal humour is readily appreciated without effort. The analysis of humour is never popular, thanks to the superstition that a joke explained is no joke. Fortunately useful classificatory work has been done on some obvious types of humour in Comedy,[19] but there is much in the Greek sense of humour and sense of fantasy which is elusive. The enjoyment of tremendous indecency in close conjunction with refined literary criticism no longer presents a serious problem, for the unparalleled restraint imposed on the written word by the convention of the nineteenth century has died the death of all excesses; contemplation of the cold and arrogant savageries which our own world perpetrates makes us turn with something like relief to Aristophanic lechery. For the understanding of those aspects of Comedy which are really alien to our own culture we cannot do better than look to the modern Greeks. Anyone who has seen dancing in a Greek village will not discount the final clause in *Wasps* 1524-1530 τὸ Φρυνίχειον ἐκλακτισάτω τις ὅπως ἰδόντες ἄνω σκέλος ὤζωσιν οἱ θεαταί. On a more sophisticated level, there is hardly an incident, hardly even a phrase, in Nikos Kazantsakis' novel *Zorba the Greek* which has not an alien ring to ears which know only English, but no one who has read Aristophanes will raise his eyebrows at a remark such as 'Many are the joys of this world — women, fruit, ideas', which the *New Yorker* picked out for sarcastic comment.

Though the attention paid to the audience's sense of humour has been scanty, much has been paid to its intellectual attainments, and it is commonly represented as sceptical in religion and intimately conversant with great poetry. The case for its scepticism rests primarily on its tolerance of the discomfiture of Poseidon in *Birds* and the discreditable antics of Dionysus in *Frogs*. Yet the conclusion that Athenian society in the late fifth century was in general sceptical of traditional religion[20] is not easily reconciled with the evidence from other sources, and rests on a failure of the imagination. To understand pre-Christian religious attitudes requires a great imaginative effort, and those who make it are commonly regarded as impostors by those who cannot. The intimate association of the gods with the fabric of ordinary Greek life is something which might be better understood by a Papuan than by a bishop, and perhaps best of all by the medieval Christian, whose humour was full of casual blasphemy[21] and prompt to interweave the comic and the tremendous.[22] The fact is that the Greek gods had human pleasures and understood laughter; at the right time and place they could take a joke.[23]

The case for the literary discrimination of the Athenian audience rests on the fondness of Comedy for literary topics[24] and above all for parody. But it has been remarked that criticism of poetry in Comedy tended to be criticism of the poet's person (real or conventionalized) rather than of his art;[25] and the humour of paratragedy lies not in the choice of the particular tragic passage but in the use of tragic language as such in a comic context. The audience could detect that tragedy was being parodied without identifying lines from *Telephus* or *Medea*, and the stance and voice of the actor would show them that it was there to be detected.[26] Even if they recognized the original and remembered its source, it may be that the majority of the allusions in Comedy are allusions to lines which the poet knew from experience were widely disseminated;[27] and to remember ἡ γλῶσσ' ὀμώμοχ' ἡ δὲ φρὴν ἀνώμοτος is not the same thing as forming a critical judgment on *Hippolytus*. Again, the poet may often have amused himself by recondite allusions which he did not expect his audience to appreciate;[28] experience of the modern 'little' revue suggests that the uninformed majority will readily join in the laughter of the few and feel more flattered than insulted by an appeal to their discrimination.

Attempts to use Comedy as evidence for Athenian society and economy are valuable and productive,[29] but the material needs very cautious handling. It is not only that the closest attention must be paid to the context, for that is a necessary principle of all interpretation. The sociologist using Comedy must deal with two special difficulties, the autonomous comic myth and the nature of comic statement. The fidelity of Comedy to ordinary life can be overrated; as well as the farmer of real life, there is the conventional farmer of Comedy, and the two may differ. Comic conventions tend to lag behind the times; in the comic papers of our own day sergeant-majors wear waxed moustaches, countrymen chew straws, and dons spend their whole adult life in serene senility. In comic statement there is no room for judicious accuracy; it must be forceful and slick and capture the audience's interest. Antiphanes (fr. 191 K) says that everyone was familiar with the stories of Tragedy, Aristotle (*Poet.*, 1451b) that few were.

Even making allowance (which way, incidentally?) for their difference in date, they cannot both be right, and no one who reads the Antiphanes fragment with attention can hesitate long on which to believe. Thus the sociologist who takes Comic convention and Comic statement at face value will go very wide of the mark; but he can make very good use of Comedy if he is prepared to ask what makes a joke a joke, and what presuppositions must be shared by author and public if Comedy is to be intelligible.[30]

Much of what has been said above applies also to the political historian's use of Comedy. The history of the discussion of such passages as *Knights* 173-4 ('Cast your right eye on Caria and your left on Carthage') or the embassies to and from Persia in *Ach.* 61-124[31] emphasizes the complexity of the issues involved and the difficulty of deciding between the claims of pure fantasy, faithful parody of actual events, and exploitation of ideas that were in the political air. The whole methodological problem was attacked in 1873 by Müller-Strübing's *Aristophanes und die historische Kritik* with a determination and acumen only slightly vitiated by an undertone of mad laughter and a number of unlikely solutions of particular difficulties; it is perhaps due for an equally thorough re-examination.

It is always hard to interpret a political allusion until one knows what axes the writer is grinding, and at first sight Old Comedy appears to have ground one large axe busily and continuously. Aristophanes is still popularly regarded as a conservative who used Comedy as a medium for glorifying the Athens of Aeschylus and attacking all that was new in politics, literature and philosophy. Now, no reasonable man will deny the presence of a serious element in Comedy, quite apart from the personal feud between Aristophanes and Cleon. The fact that the privilege of Comic ridicule was suspended by law from 440/39 to 437/6 shows that it was not always regarded as a light-hearted family game; nor can we read Aristophanes without becoming aware of passages which strike home in a way that fun does not. Such subjective feelings are a poor basis for argument, but they are facts and we must take cognizance of them.

The common view of Aristophanes as a preacher has to contend with the coincidence that to judge from the fragments the other poets of Old Comedy all belonged to the same crusted minority. Croiset[32] attempted to meet this difficulty by suggesting that

Comedy was traditionally the favoured art-form of the conservative, suspicious Attic farmers, and that its character and development were determined by the sympathies of this appreciative audience.

But the presentation of Aristophanes, to say nothing of other poets, as spokesman or instrument of a party or class is easier to sustain on a first reading than on a second. Any consistent picture of his views which can be constructed from snippets of chorus or dialogue, chosen without regard for speaker or context, can be confronted by different pictures constructed on the same principle. Aristophanes was a dramatist of genius; he had a keen eye for the absurdities inherent in all conflicts of temperaments and ideas, and he was concerned, *qua* dramatist, to exploit them.[33] Thus in *Clouds* his purpose was not to persuade his audience of the immorality of Socrates but to bring together Strepsiades, Pheidippides and Socrates, each in his own way an ass, and work out, with dramatist's logic, what happens.

Moreover, Comedy by its very nature makes certain demands on its practitioners. In Aristophanes, as in popular comedy of all ages, people are presented as they appear to the Common Man, who is tough but comfort-loving, shrewd but uneducated, caustic but unpolished, irreverent and intolerant of the unfamiliar. With the Common Man as foil, 'Euripides' and 'Socrates' are composite characters exhibiting the features popularly attributed to the intellectual, and their individuality is to some extent suppressed in order to secure their conformity to accepted comic types.[34]

It may also be true that the good comic writer is almost inevitably committed to rebellion — or reaction; it does not matter which we call it — against the established order and the fashions and movements of his day.[35] The same facet of his mind that makes him fertile in comic invention makes him sceptical and independent. Wit and cant do not live comfortably together, and for all its fierce virtues Athenian public life was not lacking in cant.

B. DISCOVERY

(1) *The Text of Aristophanes*

The pursuit of manuscripts in the libraries of Europe, or the reexamination of manuscripts last collated by Bekker or Dindorf, is no less an act of discovery than the extraction of a papyrus fragment from the sands of Eygpt, and I make no further apology for dealing at this point with the establishment of the text of Aristophanes.

Comparatively speaking, we are now well informed on the manuscripts of Aristophanes,[36] but little of the essential data was available before the end of the nineteenth century. Important collations were then made by von Velsen, Zacher and Zuretti, and later by White, Cary[37] and Coulon. The Oxford Text of Hall and Geldart[38] was defective even for its time; for the sake of brevity it suppressed much of value in the apparatus, though room was found for many mediocre conjectures. Coulon's Budé edition[39] is the first which gives an accurate and discriminating apparatus. Much remains to be done,[40] especially on what were in Byzantine eyes the major plays, *Plutus*, *Clouds*, and *Frogs*, and until it is done final judgment on the stemmata so far proposed[41] should be reserved. The upper reaches of the stemma are unlikely to be seriously refashioned, but for the lower reaches we have to take our editors' work on trust; it is a pity that Coulon did not publish a systematic *eliminatio*.

The contribution of the papyri has been interesting but not exciting.[42] A Berlin papyrus[43] gives us some help with the dialect of the Megarian in *Acharnians*, and warns us of the complexity of the tradition by agreeing in error with the Codex Ravennas at *Ach*. 791. It is satisfactory, but not surprising, that a papyrus of *Thesmophoriazusae*[44] refers to the old man in the play as κηδε, i.e. κηδεστὴς Εὐριπίδου, not as 'Mnesilochus',[45] and preserves a stage-direction ολολυ[at 277;[46] the same papyrus tantalizingly gives us only the first few letters of the difficult line 809, which van Leeuwen pusillanimously deleted.

The editor of Aristophanes can profit more than the editor of any other Greek author from the citations of the text in other authors, and from the scholia. Coulon's edition is the first which presents the material from these sources satisfactorily in the apparatus. The citations have now been catalogued,[47] and apart from the right readings which they sometimes afford they throw some light on the interrelation of the extant manuscripts; this is particularly true of the numerous citations from Aristophanes in Suidas.[48]

A definitive edition of the scholia is in preparation, the only complete edition to date being Dübner's of 1842, which is not adequate. The scholia on *Birds* have been edited separately by White.[49] Rutherford's *Scholia Aristophanica*[50] unfortunately comprised only the scholia of the Codex Ravennas. The Ravennas is a handsome and venerable manuscript, but its scholia are for the most part an abbreviated and garbled version of what appears in a fuller and more intelligible form in the Codex Venetus. To publish them by themselves, with only passing references to the Venetus, was absurd; and though the absurdity was quickly and decisively exposed,[51] it imposes on undergraduates to this day.

Before proper use can be made of scholia something must be known of their origin, and here the papyri have provided many helpful clues. The bare format of early dramatic texts brings home to us the magnitude of the ancient commentators' responsibilities; fragments of learned commentaries and of texts with a greater or smaller degree of marginal annotation reveal not only the nature of the commentaries themselves but also the possible relationships between separate commentary and marginal note. The outlines of the history of the ancient study of Aristophanes are now tolerably clear.[52] White believed that a late commentary on Aristophanes was transferred wholesale to the margins of an Aristophanes codex in the fourth or fifth century A.D., and that this codex was sole ancestor of the minuscule archetype of our extant manuscripts.[53] What we know of codices, Christian and secular, from the fourth to the ninth century A.D., does not support this hypothesis,[54] and the fact that the extant scholia on a given passage often repeat the same explanation several times, introducing each repetition by ἄλλως, suggests that the archetype in fact accumulated its scholia from the relatively sparser marginalia of not one but many earlier manuscripts.[55] Thus although the Aristophanes scholia are ultimately the product of the ancient study of Aristophanes, the genealogy of any given scholion may be very different from that of its immediate neighbour.

(2) *The Text of Menander*[56]

Until the end of the nineteenth century the Greek text of Menander was known only by the very numerous citations in later authors and anthologies; and these, being mainly gnomic in character, gave little idea of the sight and sound and movement of a Menandrean play. In 1897 a papyrus fragment containing eighty lines of *Georgus* was discovered; a few years earlier a parchment fragment at St. Petersburg had been identified as belonging to *Phasma*. A fragment of *Colax* was published in 1903 (a second was to come in 1914), and then in 1905 came the discovery of the mutilated Cairo codex, comprising very substantial parts of *Epitrepontes*, *Periciromene*, and *Samia*, with some smaller items, including the hypothesis and opening scene of *Heros*.

Of these plays *Epitrepontes* has attracted the most attention — for which its quality as well as its comparatively extensive preservation is responsible — and a summary of its history since 1905 may serve as a specimen of the work devoted in this century to the constitution of the text of Menander.[57]

The Cairo codex was originally made up of quaterniones, and each quaternio consisted of four sheets folded and placed one inside another to make sixteen pages. When the codex was found, the quaterniones had been separated from each other, and many lost; those that had not been lost were largely disrupted, and what remained was pieces of half-sheets. It was found that the best preserved half-sheets could be placed in an approximate order either by their physical configuration or on the grounds of their content. From this it emerged that within each quaternio the four sheets had originally been so placed that a side with vertical fibres uppermost alternated with a side with horizontal uppermost; thus when the quaternio was completely made up pages 1 and 16 would have had horizontal fibres, pages 2 and 15 vertical fibres, 3 and 14 vertical, 4 and 13 horizontal, 5 and 12 horizontal, and so on. This naturally reduced the number of alternative positions possible for the fragments which were not easy to place by content. Körte's second Teubner edition of 1912 was able to print ten of the original pages (i.e. the greater part of three folded sheets) in their correct order in the first half of the play, and four (i.e. one folded sheet) in the second; mutilated pieces of another four half-sheets were given an approximate location, and the position and extent of the completely missing portions were accurately estimated.

The Cairo half-sheet known as Z, which had been excluded from *Epitrepontes* by Körte and placed by others in the early part of the play, was then given its correct place by the observation that it bore the marginal number ς'. This was not a page-number, for the half-sheet of *Heros* bore the page-numbers κθ' and λ' while Z's number was on one side only. But considered as the first sheet of the sixth quaternio, or by its content — Pamphile is being urged by her father to divorce her husband — it fits well into the gap between Smicrines' realization of his son-in-law's bad behaviour and Habrotonon's recognition of Pamphile.

An Oxyrhynchus papyrus (*POxy*. 1236) published in 1914 gave us a mutilated portion of the text of *Epitrepontes* which overlaps the text of one of the best-preserved Cairo half-sheets and one of the minor Cairo fragments. This at once introduced order into a part of the play which in Körte's 1912 edition had been extremely uncertain.

The parchment fragment in Russia which contained a piece of *Phasma* exhibited also forty-odd lines of a play which van Leeuwen and Capps recognized as *Epitrepontes*. Körte in 1912 did not admit these lines, and those who referred them to *Epitrepontes* were not agreed on the position in the play which they should occupy. It is now accepted that they give us the end of the original first act and the beginning of the second, and thus precede the parts extant in the Cairo codex.

Mention must also be made of a papyrus first published by Weil in 1879 and for long attributed (as it was by its ancient copyist) to Euripides. It is not itself a fragment of a dramatic text, but a speech transcribed from a play; a daughter is addressing her father who has evidently urged her to divorce her husband. The ascription to Euripides was palpably wrong, and Prof. Robertson[58] suggested that the speech is not merely the work of Menander but is actually Pamphile's reply to her father in *Epitrepontes*. The argument is persuasive, and if two lines had been irrecoverably mutilated it might well have won general acceptance; those lines, however (19-20) ἀλλ' ἔστ' ἐμοὶ μὲν χρηστός, ἠπόρηκε δέ· σὺ δ' ἀνδρί μ', ὡς φῄς, ἐκδίδως νῦν πλουσίῳ are not quite the point which Pamphile would have made in her actual situation. Körte, while accepting Menander's authorship on linguistic grounds,[59] has excluded the speech from *Epitrepontes* in his third edition. Interest in the particular problem of whether we are concerned here with Pamphile's reply to Smicrines seems to have allayed the more general suspicion which should have been aroused by the fact that so long and serious a speech in a style so near Tragedy is without parallel in New Comedy.[60]

Apart from the plays already mentioned, fragments of *Citharista*,[61] *Coneiazomenae*,[62] *Perinthia*,[63] *Misumenus*,[64] and *Theophorumene*[65] have been identified by content on grounds of varying cogency; in the *Theophorumene* fragment the coarsely abusive ἱππόπορνε strikes a discordant note for Menander. The Cairo codex also gives us some sixty lines of a play not yet identified, and the so-called *Comoedia Florentina*,[66] stylistically the essence of Menander, does not very readily suggest any of the known titles.

(3) *Didascaliae and Similar Records*

Fragments of inscriptions which recorded victories at dramatic festivals or names of poets and actors were known well before the end of the last century, but it was not until 1906 that Wilhelm was able to determine the precise nature of the original inscriptions and assign the fragments their relative positions.[67] Wilhelm's conclusions have since been corrected or augmented in minor details,[68] and a few additional fragments have been recovered.[69] We are concerned with four types of document, three from Athens and one from Rome. The Athenian documents are:

(i) The so-called 'Fasti', in which were recorded the names of the victorious διδάσκαλος and χορηγός in Tragedy and Comedy at the Dionysia each year.[70]

(ii) The Didascaliae, which recorded under each archon-year all the plays performed at the festival concerned, in the order of the prizes obtained, together with the names of the poets and the protagonists.

(iii) The victor-lists; these included a list of all the Comic poets who had ever won the first prize at the Dionysia, arranged in order of first victories, and a similar list for the Lenaea. In both lists the total number of his victories at the festival concerned was entered against each poet's name.

The fragments from Rome appear to come from a document which listed all the Comic poets with the titles of their plays, each poet's plays being dated and arranged in order according to the prizes obtained.

The extant fragments of the Fasti give us the names and dates of seven victorious Comic διδάσκαλοι from Magnes in 473/2 to Alexis in 348/7; they also record the fact that an old play was revived in 340/39 and that this was the first occasion of such an occurrence. The Didascaliae give us no certain information on Comedy before 313/2; 289/8 is well preserved; after which, excepting a few undatable fragments, we pass to the early second century. Although in that century Comedy was presented at the Dionysia in only one year in three, and on each occasion an old play was revived, we can also see that five new plays were performed on each occasion; the record appears to have ended in the last quarter of the century. The victor-lists of Comic poets are well preserved for both Dionysia and Lenaea in the fifth century, and for the Lenaea in the fourth. Thanks to the literary evidence and the few but valuable pieces of the Fasti, some fixed points in the chronology of the victor-lists can be established, and it can be stated with certainty that Comic poets first competed for prizes at the Dionysia between 490 and 480 (probably 486) and at the Lenaea about 440. The problem of the two Apollodori is also settled by the occurrence of the name Apollodorus with a first Lenaean victory c. 320 and a first Dionysian victory at least forty years later.

The extant portions of the inscription from Rome provide valuable information on the chronology of the plays of Callias in the fifth century and Anaxandrides in the fourth, and somewhat scrappier information on Teleclides, Lysippus and Aristomenes.

C. HISTORY OF COMEDY

(1) *Genre and Individual*

The epigraphic records combined with the literary evidence have made it possible to construct an outline chronology of Greek Comedy,[71] and unless new material is discovered it is unlikely that any substantial additions will be made to what is now generally accepted. But to arrange titles in chronological order is not the same thing as interpreting the extant fragments and discovering what the plays themselves were about. Wherever we have a title and handful of fragments, in almost every case we have inherited from Meineke, Bergk, and Kock a more or less tentative and partial reconstruction of the play. These reconstructions are sometimes brilliant and persuasive, but it is to be regretted that many of them have now crystallized into dogma; unthinkingly we tend to accept even the numerical order of the fragments of a play in Kock as giving their original relative position. All the Comic fragments need now to be re-examined from top to bottom and the traditional reconstructions treated — for their own good — with the utmost scepticism. In particular, the manifold contextual possibilities of each fragment should be taken into account, and we should resist the temptation to draw too facile a conclusion, chronological or otherwise, from the allusion in a fragment to a known person or historical event.[72]

One of many reasons for undertaking such an examination is the desirability of knowing where to draw the boundaries between Aristophanes and Aristophanic Comedy and between Menander and Menandrean Comedy. Until recently the bulk of our evidence for New Comedy was the Roman adaptations, and although it was known who had written the originals of many of the adaptations, it was hard to draw essential distinctions between these original authors and impossible to avoid speaking of New Comedy in generic terms. It would be quite untrue to say that the papyri represented a merely quantitative accession of material.[73] They allow us at least to form a positive conception of Menander[74] independently of the Roman adaptations, and it is interesting that the best-preserved of the Cairo plays happens also to show us a character, Habrotonon in *Epitrepontes*, entirely remote from the 'stock-types' commonly regarded as characteristic of New Comedy.[75]

Nevertheless, to characterize Menander in contrast with the Romans is not equivalent to characterizing him in contrast with his contemporaries. The attribution of individual characteristics to Philemon, Diphilus, or Apollodorus of Carystus still rests primarily on interpretation of the Roman plays,[76] and sometimes requires an assumption of uniformity of structure and treatment within the work of a given author which may be a right assumption but cannot as yet be conclusively justified.[77] The papyri stimulated interest in the separation of Greek from Roman elements in the Roman plays, but this work has been most fruitful when its purpose has been to construct a positive picture of the Roman element;[78] attempts to give an equally positive picture of the Greek element[79] tend to be vitiated by an oppressively subjective assumption that the Greeks were dramaturgically impeccable.

The generic nature of the study of New Comedy is well shown by a simple pragmatic test: we now possess about thirty papyrus fragments, some of them of considerable extent, which can clearly be assigned to New Comedy, but we cannot assign them to particular authors. Moreover, in a genre which flourished for so long we cannot clearly distinguish even the main stages of development. For example, an anonymous prologue[80] shows us a light kind of literary criticism familiar in Roman prologues, but we do not know whether it belongs to the time of Menander or to a century and a half later. It would be pleasant to think that another prologue[81] which expounds the situation in lines beginning successively with α, β, γ, etc., belonged to a very late and degenerate stage of the genre, but the papyrus itself, written at the end of the third century B.C., imposes a terminus.

Turning now to Old Comedy, I suppose that if we had ever been able to choose what papyri should be discovered we might have recalled Horace's triad (*Sat.* 8. 4. 1) *Eupolis atque Cratinus Aristophanesque poetae*. Fortune has been kind; we now have a substantial fragment of Cratinus's *Pluti*,[82] half the hypothesis of his *Dionysalexander*,[83] several good portions of Eupolis's *Demi*,[84] and a fragment[85] which has been assigned solely on the strength of the words (ll. 5-6) καὶ φράζεθ' οἷα τἀνθάδ' ἔστ [⏑ – ⏑ –] Προσπαλτίοισιν to Eupolis's *Prospaltii*. In all significant respects this new material confirms the conclusion already drawn from the citations: that Old Comedy combined a relative uniformity of structure with great variety of theme.

The earlier plays of Aristophanes exhibit a strong community of structure which in one element, the parabasis, can be pursued into detail. Although no two plays present the same constituents in exactly the same order, it is possible to construct an ideal schema from which each play deviates in one respect or another;[86] the later plays deviate increasingly, and *Frogs*, *Ecclesiazusae*, and *Plutus* cannot be accommodated under the same schema without impairing its usefulness. Among the new fragments, Aristides' treatment of the Sycophant in *Demi* 61-100 not only recalls the episode *Ach.* 909-28 but by its apparent position in the development of the 'plot' conforms to the structure of *Ach.*, *Peace*, and *Birds*, in which the crisis of the action is followed by a series of episodes illustrating the state of affairs brought about by the crisis. The hypothesis of *Dionysalexander* tells us that in the parabasis the chorus addressed the audience περὶ τῶν ποιητῶν, which recalls *Knights*, *Clouds*, *Wasps*, and *Peace*. Only *Pluti* strikes an unfamiliar note by the chorus' address to the audience in the *parodos*. In general the shorter citations often permit us, by coincidence of metre, form, and subject, to assign them to one place rather than another in their original plays.[87]

GREEK COMEDY 139

In theme, however, the position is quite different. We know that mythological burlesque and political allegory, combined in *Dionysalexander*, were common in Old Comedy, but they are absent from the extant work of Aristophanes; the pre-Aristophanic 'Οδυσσῆς of Cratinus possessed some features which induced Hellenistic scholars to associate it with 'Middle Comedy',[88] and Aristophanes' late plays *Aeolosicon* and *Cocalus* appear to have resembled their contemporary *Plutus* no more closely than the plays of the Archidamian War.[89] In full recognition of this variety and inventiveness we should be at least as cautious of generalization about Old Comedy as about, let us say, Aeschylean Tragedy.

(2) *The Origins of Comedy*

If we possessed a dozen complete plays by different poets of Old Comedy from the period 460-430 B.C. it might be possible to discover by extrapolation how the genre began. As it is, we cannot extrapolate from Aristophanes. Although Comedy changed in his hands, the change was not necessarily in the same direction as the developments before his time; it is therefore unsafe to argue from his early plays that the sequence prologue-agon-parabasis was his inheritance from the early days of Comedy.[90] The chorus' address to the audience in the *parodos* of Cratinus' *Pluti* does not imply that the role of the chorus was larger before Aristophanes, but only that the relation between chorus and audience which exists in the Aristophanic parabasis may originally have existed in other parts of the play. The known variety of themes in Old Comedy also discourages extrapolation.

Mention should here be made of Cornford's argument[91] that Comedy originated as a ritual representing the triumph of the new year over the old and that sequences in this ritual were ultimately responsible for features inherited and preserved by Aristophanes. Cornford's book owed a great deal to the influence of Jane Harrison[92] and to the essentially wise realization of the late nineteenth century that anthropological evidence has a bearing on Greek studies. But the value of anthropology lies in its capacity to suggest possibilities, and Cornford's bland dishonesties and sheer unreasonableness in the use of evidence were not a very good advertisement for it. Throughout the book we are unhappily aware of the great gulf between him and Aristophanes;[93] if only he had sat down to write a comedy before writing about the Origin of Comedy! The starting point for the study of Comic origins is the fact that Aristophanic Comedy shows us a regular combination of extremely dissimilar elements, which entitles us to assume that the origin of the genre is complex. The search may be conducted separately through literary evidence and through iconography. Aristotle (*Poet*. 1449a) saw the origin of Comedy in οἱ ἐξάρχοντες τὰ φαλλικά, and says (1448a, cf. 1449b) that the Dorians claimed its invention, a claim partly supported by the early date of Epicharmus. Our evidence on the performances of ἰθύφαλλοι and φαλλοφόροι reveals no dramatic element, though there were φαλλοφόροι who 'made fun of the bystanders',[94] and this, combined with the association of Dionysus with phallic ritual,[95] may point at least to a possible origin of the parabasis. In the dramatic element in Comedy the two recurrent features which engage our attention are the agon, involving two actors or one actor and the chorus, and the episodes. The attempt to discover a specific origin for the agon[96] is probably mistaken, for contest is hard to separate from drama, and the Greek love of contest is manifest throughout their literature.[97] For the episodes it is natural to look to Epicharmus and the Dorians. Epicharmus,[98] whose fragments show no sign of literary immaturity or undeveloped technique,[99] wrote at least one piece which required three characters,[100] but there is no good evidence that he wrote also for a chorus.[101] He was the first man known in later times to have put comedies into written form, but it is doubtful whether he created the genre from nothing,[102] and the existence of rudimentary comic drama in Dorian communities is indicated by the evidence relating to Sparta[103] and Megara.[104]

So far, so good. The literary evidence points to a combination of an indigenous chorus (presumably called a κῶμος and associated with Dionysus, probably also associated with him as part of a phallic ritual) with an episodic drama introduced from the Dorian world. We should beware of extending this dependence on Dorian Comedy from form to matter. Indigenous fairy-tales certainly made their contribution, and comic narrative had an Ionian ancestry; the citations from Archilochus and the new papyri of Hipponax[105] reveal a colourful ferocity of language and a startling obscenity which are strongly reminiscent of Old Comedy.

GREEK COMEDY

The archaeological enquiry into Origins begins from the costumes of actors and chorus.[106] The extant plays, together with many titles of lost plays, imply that the chorus most frequently represented animals, women, foreigners, or abstractions. Choruses of men disguised as animals, dancing in unison to a flute-player, appear on Attic black-figure vases much earlier than Comedy as we know it;[107] the vases tell us nothing of the god or festival with whom such choruses were associated, and in particular there is no known point of contact between them and phallic ritual.

No representation of the comic actor exists which can be referred with certainty to the fifth century, but two red-figure vases of the very early fourth century[108] show that he wore (a) a grotesque mask, (b) tights, with a padded stomach and buttocks, (c) a large artificial phallus. The internal evidence of Aristophanes points also to the phallus as a common, if not universal, feature of the actor's costume.[109] These elements appear singly or in combination on Corinthian vases of the early sixth century. Most important are two figures which appear in a representation of the return of Hephaestus with Dionysus;[110] they have grotesque faces, with wild hair and beards, prodigious phalli, and short chitons which throw stomach and buttocks into prominence. In isolation this vase would justify the suggestion that the actor's costume in Old Comedy originated in the portrayal of a kind of satyr, but there is other evidence which complicates the issue. On another Corinthian vase[111] we find (a) a flute-player with a dancer who wears a mask and a short padded chiton, (b) two creatures called Εὔνους and Ὀφέλανδρος, naked and of normal shape except for Ophelandrus' unduly large phallus, carrying a wine-jar, (c) a naked figure called Ὀμρικός, with a very large phallus, (d) two naked men in the stocks, with a woman standing by, and a wine-store. The names point to Dionysiac demons,[112] and the natural interpretation of the vase is that it portrays a story about them. As often in vase-painting, the kind of association intended between demons and dancer is open to very different interpretations, but at the least we can say that masked padded dancers existed in sixth-century Corinth and were considered by a painter an appropriate subject for association with a story about Dionysiac demons, and at the most it can be argued that the scene on the vase portrays a comic performance[113] — which does not explain Comedy but only raises its date and associates it with

Corinth. Unmasked padded dancers, without the phallus, are common on Corinthian vases and appear on Attic vases, under Corinthian influence, in the mid-sixth century;[114] they are occasionally associated with Dionysus,[115] and once with a figure who wears the phallus as well as padding.[116] The discovery of early sixth-century comic masks at Sparta,[117] which accord well with the literary evidence for rudimentary drama there, has no archaeological point of contact with the Corinthian iconographic tradition.

The abundant evidence adduced in the last fifty years has not solved the problem but at least it has clarified the questions which need answering. It seems probable that the actor's costume was in origin a portrayal of a kind of satyr, and that this portrayal was practised in the Peloponnese in the sixth century; it seems certain that comic episodes, in which the actors used masks, were also practised then in the Peloponnese; but when and why were the two combined, so that a man dressed in imitation of a satyr when he was portraying the doings of beings other than satyrs? Secondly, when and why were characteristics of the animal-chorus and the φαλλοφόροι combined in one chorus — or has Aristotle's ἐξάρχοντες τὰ φαλλικά put us on a wrong scent?[118] Thirdly, when and why were the two elements, actors and chorus, each perhaps of a double origin, combined in the same performance?

(3) *The Structure of New Comedy*

The Cairo codex gives us fifty well-preserved lines of the prologue of *Periciromene*, spoken by the personified Agnoia. In this prologue the situation from which the plot develops is expounded in detail, and in ll. 7-8 we read: . . . τῆς παιδός, ἣν νῦν εἴδετε ὑμεῖς . . . In other words, a scene preceded the appearance of Agnoia. So in *Heros* the play opens with a scene between Getas and Daos; after fifty lines, the text is mutilated, but in the *dramatis personae* Ἥρως θεός is listed third, after Getas and Daos. Similarly, in the prologue of the '*Comoedia Florentina*' Tyche says (ll. 3-4) οὗ δ' εἰσελήλυθ' ὁ θεράπων ἐν γειτόνων ἀδελφὸς οἰκεῖ . . . It thus appears to have been Menander's practice to open the play with a dramatic scene and arouse the interest of the audience before entrusting the clarification of the situation to the speaker of the prologue.[119] Roman Comedy exhibits this feature only in *Cistellaria*, whose original, as we now know, was Menander's

GREEK COMEDY

Synaristosae.[120] The treatment of the prologue in the other poets of New Comedy is discernible only by inference from the Roman evidence.

In the St. Petersburg fragment of *Epitrepontes* (32-5) Simmias says to Chaerestratus: 'Let's go in here to see Charisius', and Chaerestratus replies 'Yes, let's go. There's a gang of young men coming this way, half-drunk, and I think it's not a good time to get in their way.' This is followed in the text by the word XOPOY; after which Onesimus enters and begins a monologue in which (apparently) no reference is made to the 'gang of young men half-drunk'. Similarly in *Periciromene* 71-6 (141-6 A) Daos calls out to the slaves indoors 'A whole lot of drunken young men are coming ... I must go and look for my master ...' and off he goes to find Moschion. Then comes XOPOY in the text, immediately followed by a well-preserved dialogue between Daos and Moschion in which nothing is said of drunken young men. At *Epitrepontes* 242 (201 AJ), *Samia* 270 (413 A), *Comoedia Florentina* 45, and in an anonymous fragment,[121] the entry XOPOY occurs without any reference in either the preceding or the following words to the presence or nature of the chorus; at *Heros* 54 (p. 300 A) and in a second anonymous fragment[122] the lines preceding and following XOPOY are unreadable; and at *Epitrepontes* 584 (764 A) the presence of XOPOY in the original is an inference from the spacing of the preserved right margin.

These facts appear to warrant three generalizations. First, that the chorus continued to be used in New Comedy, but as an entr'acte and not as a participant in the action; secondly, that at least in Menander it was represented as a κῶμος; and thirdly, that its presence and nature might be referred to on its first appearance but not on its subsequent appearances. The limited basis of these generalizations is obvious; their strength is the fact that the instances of XOPOY are preserved by the purest chance and not to illustrate a thesis. Körte tried to implicate the chorus more closely in the action[123] by suggesting that, for example, at *Periciromene* 76 (146 A) they were the friends of Polemon mentioned at 55-6. But the attempt to identify the composition of the possible choruses in Menander (especially *Epitrepontes*) and the Roman adaptations made it necessary to suppose that the same group of dancers appeared in different guises in the same play and that on occasions a group was present on the stage during part of the action, in readiness for an entr'acte, but not referred to in the dialogue.[124] Körte later retracted his argument.[125] None the less, it was pointed out[126] that a passage of Terence, *Heaut.* 170 sqq., suggests at least one occasion in Menander[127] in which the chorus was something more than a passing κῶμος. Chremes there says: 'I must go and remind Phanias to come and have dinner with me.' He goes off; the stage is empty; he returns, saying 'They tell me he's come to me already . . . Well, I'm keeping my guests waiting . . .' His departure from the stage is not dramatically necessary in Terence's play; in Menander's, it could have been the cue for the entry of his guests as a κῶμος and their performance of a song and dance, after which they would have entered his house.

When the presence of the chorus was recognized as a characteristic of New Comedy, the question of its relevance to the traditional five acts was naturally raised. The five-act division as we know it in Terence is very old,[128] and Donatus *Praef. Ad.* 1.4 *quinque actus . . . choris divisos a graecis poetis* suggests that if we had a play of Menander absolutely intact we should find XOPOY four times, dividing the play into five blocks of approximately equal dramatic weight. Roman Comedy for the most part, though not without some awkwardness at times, admits of this partition.[129] Of the originals, we can only say that it suits *Epitrepontes* very well and is reconcilable with what we know of the other plays. Considerations other than the extant texts certainly support it. Once the role of the chorus had become stereotyped, we should expect a large measure of agreement on the amount of work that could fairly be demanded of it. The 'laws' of Greek drama, such as the 'law' of three actors in Tragedy, had their origin not in legislation or in ritual but in economic fair play. What could be expected of the choregus and the State helped to determine what was expected of the poet.

(4) *Middle Comedy*

XOPOY is a phenomenon not confined to the new Menander. It has always been there in the text of the two latest extant plays of Aristophanes, *Ecclesiazusae* and *Plutus*; which shows that the virtual elimination of the chorus from the action in New Comedy was the end of a process begun in Aristophanes' own day. The intermediate process may be inferred from one fragment of Alexis and another which *may* be Alexis. In the former (fr. 107 K) we recognize the formula which we saw in Menander: 'I see a κῶμος approaching...'¹³⁰ The latter is a papyrus fragment¹³¹ attributed to Alexis on the admittedly slender grounds that it has (ll. 22-3) εὖ γε καὶ [παλ]αιστρικῶς and Phrynichus *Ecl.* 218 says παλαιστρικός· "Ἀλεξίν φασιν εἰρηκέναι, ὁ δὲ ἀρχαῖος παλαιστικὸν λέγει. It presents a scene in which a group of people is addressed as ἄνδρες (ll. 18, 26) and replies as ἡμεῖς οἱ παρόντες (l. 24); XOPOY occurs also in a mutilated context. It does not follow that the ἄνδρες, of whom all but one could be mute characters, were also the performers of the choral entr'acte (cf. the *advocati* of Plautus, *Poen.* 504-816), but the fragment constitutes *some* evidence that Alexis may represent the turning-point in the history of the comic chorus.

The attempt to trace through the fragments of the fourth-century comic poets the development of elements common to Old and New Comedy and the origins of elements characteristic of New Comedy constitutes the true study of Middle Comedy. As a positive category, 'Middle Comedy' is unsatisfactory¹³² — for us, though not for the ancients. It was ignored by Kock, who thought it a label devised by the Hadrianic age. In this he was historically wrong,¹³³ but methodologically justified. The poverty of our positive conception of Middle Comedy is well illustrated by the readiness with which an anonymous papyrus fragment is assigned to Old or New Comedy but not to Middle. Our knowledge of Middle Comedy rests on the citations, on a papyrus fragment,¹³⁴ and on the *Persa* of Plautus, the original of which should probably be dated earlier than Alexander — not because of its historical allusion, which is not as specific as it looks,¹³⁵ but on negative grounds, the difficulty of dividing it into five 'acts'¹³⁶ and the difference of its theme and treatment from what we regard as characteristic of New Comedy.

Hellenistic theory regarded as typical of Middle Comedy the absence of political criticism and the popularity of the mythological burlesque.¹³⁷ This generalization is acceptable provided that it is not interpreted too rigidly. Mythological burlesque was much older than the fourth century, and the Ὀδυσσῆς of Cratinus was described as 'Middle' just as Aristophanes' *Cocalus* looked forward to the plots of New Comedy. We should therefore think of Middle Comedy not as generating several wholly new types of plot but as establishing a preference for some old types of plot over others.

Extant titles suggest that plays no less political in theme than *Acharnians* and *Knights* continued to be written for the first two decades of the fourth century,[138] and the citations show many acrimonious political allusions down to the last quarter of the century.[139] That ancient theory concealed the gradualness of the decline in political content may be due to the rapid reduction of the role of the chorus and the consequent elimination of the type of parabasis in which the chorus, irrespective of the content of the rest of the play, spoke directly to the audience of matters of contemporary political interest.[140] The reason for the change suggested in antiquity, the temporary suppression of free speech in 404-3, is unacceptable.[141] We know there were political plays in the twenty years after 404; and if we did not know it, we should naturally have supposed that the democratic restoration of 403 brought with it a redoubled enthusiasm for outspoken criticism. If a political reason must be sought, it is legitimate to recall that the unique position of Pericles created an abnormal political situation in the quarter-century after his death. Men prominent in political life were ambitious to achieve a comparable προστασία. In such a society politics tend to be conceived in terms of personal prestige. The political orgasm of 404-3 made a break with the past and inaugurated a fresh tradition; the audience of *Plutus* did not think politically in the same terms as the audience of *Knights*.

Alternatively, the reason might be literary. Since the ageing but infinitely adaptable Aristophanes was in the vanguard of the change, it is worth entertaining the idea that he consciously envisaged a dissemination of Attic Comedy in the Greek-speaking world comparable to the dissemination of Tragedy; and if Comedy was to achieve this, it could do so only in a form such that a knowledge of Athenian political personalities was not necessary for its appreciation.

Turning from generalizations to details, the student is constantly struck by the essential continuity of Comedy. The *Miles Gloriosus* recalls Lamachus in *Acharnians*.[142] An incident in an anonymous fragment (conceivably Philemon),[143] where one speaker seems to be deliberately mystifying another by conveying information a syllable at a time, reminds us of the verbal game of the slaves in

Knights 21-6. In a fragment of Timocles[144] a ghastly pun compels one speaker to break the dramatic illusion and cry to the audience 'Stop, for heaven's sake! No whistling!' The two houses of *Ecclesiazusae* foreshadow the New Comedy stage, though the spirit of Old Comedy is lively enough to allow them to be a different pair in different parts of the play.[145] The essential continuity of the comic tradition in manner as well as substance strikes the ear at once if Eupolis fr. 159 K and Terence, *Eunuchus* 247 sqq. are read side by side;[146] in the one, a chorus of κόλακες describe their way of life, and in the other the parasite Gnatho describes his.

Let me pursue in greater detail one final example of comic continuity. At one end of the scale, the Aristophanic parabasis frequently tends away from specific personalities and towards generalized social and political criticism; at the other, the *sententiae* of New Comedy include reflections on contemporary morality. These two extremities are linked by an example from the latest stage of Old Comedy, Plato fr. 22 K, 'Our laws are like cobwebs . . .', and one from Middle Comedy, Xenarchus fr. 4 K, 'Our young men are intolerable! . . .'[147] To these we may now add the telling words from an anonymous fragment:[148] κἄπειτα τῆς ἐκκλησίας κατηγορεῖ ἕκαστος ἡμῶν, ἧς ἕκαστος αὐτὸς ἦν.

The apparent continuity of a literary tradition may, however, reflect only persistent elements in the society which provided the material for Old and New Comedy alike. In *Wasps* 1351-9 Philocleon says to the flute-player: 'Be nice to me, and one day I'll buy you as my concubine . . . I can't do it yet, because I've no property of my own . . . My son keeps an eye on me, and he's a hard, mean man . . . I'm the only father he's got!' We recognize here a comic reversal of a situation familiar in New Comedy: the dissolute son, the courtesan, the strict father. Yet I should be reluctant to infer that this situation was already familiar in Comedy by the time of *Wasps*.[149] The reference is rather to a situation which occurred in real life, or was commonly believed to occur; compare Thurber's drawing of a man saying to a girl in a crowded hotel lounge: 'You wait here, and I'll bring my etchings down.'

The change from Old to New Comedy was not in all respects leisurely and logical. The fourth century hastened the pace by two distinct innovations; one was the rapid rise of the hetaera as a comic character,[150] and the other was the revolutionary change in comic costume. Between Old Comedy and New the comic actor abandoned the short chiton and padding and phallus for ordinary dress.[151] The date and circumstances of the change are not known, but evidence has been adduced from the so-called Phlyakes vases from South Italy.[152]

Φλύακες were South Italian performers of burlesque.[153] As a literary form, these burlesques are associated particularly with the third-century writer Rhinthon; but the vases concerned are anything up to a century earlier. They show scenes of mythological burlesque or of everyday life; the male characters wear sometimes a short chiton, sometimes tights, nearly always a prodigious phallus. As the scenes are often being enacted on a low stage reached by steps, it seems likely that the grotesque features of the characters are meant to be masks, though they differ from real masks in wearing the expression appropriate to the moment. In one scene the three participants are uttering words which can be put together to make one and a half iambic trimeters.[154] A vase which stylistically is dated late in the series portrays an old man without the phallus.[155] If this single example were supported by others, so that it became possible to say for certain that the phallus disappeared from the phlyakes vases about such-and-such a date the argument for their connection with Middle Comedy would be immeasurably strengthened, and an approximate date could be given for the essential change in comic costume at Athens. As matters stand, the connection is doubtful. The stage portrayed on the vases is not the Attic theatrical stage, but similar to one which appears on an Attic vase portraying a non-dramatic solo dancer;[156] at the most, therefore, the phlyakes vases would show us the adaptation of Attic Comedy to a South Italian stage. But while it is often possible to describe a phlyakes-vase scene as representing a known Middle Comedy, it is never necessary; and when we recall Epicharmus in the early period and Rhinthon later, it is difficult to see in the phlyakes vases anything but a drama wholly Western Greek in inspiration.[157] So far as the physical appearance of the characters is concerned, iconographic burlesque independent of dramatic burlesque may have exercised some influence; the Kabeirion vases from Thebes prove that such an iconographic tradition existed in the fourth century.[158]

Pollux iv, 143-154, describing the masks of Comedy, presents us with a set of highly-developed conventions which may well go back to the late fourth-century practice at Athens. Representations of masks in the middle or early fourth century[159] are too few to enable us to trace the growth of the Pollucian conventions. A few experiments in designing comic masks will soon show that there are not an infinite number of distinguishable grotesqueries, and to point out the affinities of specimens from different places and dates is not necessarily to reveal a historical connection between them.[160]

(5) *Comedy and Tragedy*

The Tragic affinities of New Comedy were recognized in antiquity, and Satyrus' *Life of Euripides*[161] summarizes them thus: '... quarrels between husband and wife, father and son, servant and master, or situations involving sudden change of fortune, substitution of children, violation of girls, and recognition by rings and necklaces; for all this is really the mainstay of New Comedy, and it was Euripides who perfected it.' The taste of the fourth century, as is independently demonstrated by Aristotle's *Poetics*, differed from ours in admiring one element in Tragedy above others: the dramatic recognition. From Tragedy this theme passed into Comedy, with the difference that whereas in Tragedy the outcome of the plot was predetermined by myth and the poet's choice of means necessarily limited, in Comedy only the *kind* of outcome could be known and the changes which could be rung on the means were almost unlimited.[162]

It must not be supposed that at any particular moment in the fourth century the development of Comedy was interrupted by a swift and decisive turning away from the Comic tradition towards the Tragic. As already remarked, Aristophanes himself used a recognition-plot, and the characteristic plots of New Comedy emerged by a process of selection, not revolution, from the infinite variety of Old and Middle Comedy. Furthermore, many Tragic features in New Comedy which at first appear independent are probably to be interpreted as necessary consequences of the new type of plot. This is certainly true of the expository prologue, demanded by the complexity of the plot; the purely Comic element in the ancestry of the prologue is not important.[163] Again, a complex narrative plot cannot be reconciled with the discontinuities of time and place allowed by the inventive fantasy of Old Comedy. A character in New Comedy must be something more than a series of reactions to episodes designed to be enjoyed individually; it is therefore not surprising that Menander's technique of characterization reminds one of Euripides.[164]

Despite Philemon's remark (it comes from an anthology, and the original context is unknown)[165] Εὐριπίδης . . . ὃς μόνος δύναται λέγειν, New Comedy does not present any obvious linguistic or stylistic affinities with Euripidean Tragedy. The comic confections of the Aristophanic vocabulary have gone, and what remains is effortless and elegant, less colourful, but essentially colloquial; and verbal reminiscences of Euripides which have been detected in Menander are not impressive either in numbers or in fidelity.[166]

New Comedy is best regarded as the product of a long-standing convergence of Comedy and Tragedy. Just as we found it possible to trace the development of certain recurrent features throughout Old, Middle, and New Comedy, so it is possible to trace many of them beyond Old Comedy to Tragedy. For example, the severance of choral lyrics from the development of the action, which for us first appears in *Ecclesiazusae*, cannot be considered in isolation from the irrelevant ode in Eur. *Hel.* 1301-1368 and Aristotle's attribution to Agathon of the introduction of ἐμβόλιμα into Tragedy (*Poet.* 1456a).[167] This important structural development can be supported by a number of minor details. It is amusing (but perhaps no more) to recognize in Eur. *Phoen.* 196 what might be regarded as the Tragic prototype[168] of the formula 'Here comes a crowd — let's get out of the way.' The *narratio convivialis*, which may be discerned as the context of many citations from Comedy, has a splendid ancestor in *Wasps* 1299-1323, but in reading that passage of *Wasps* we are at once reminded of Eur. *Alc.* 747-772.[169] The same point is illustrated by consideration of the parallel development of the monologue[170] and the narrative speech[171] in Tragedy and Comedy.

Similarities of detail between Tragedy and Comedy should not be taken as necessarily implying a consistent one-way influence. They do, however, remind us that Tragic and Comic poets were familiar with each other's work and wrote for performance before the same audience in the same theatre. The demands made by this co-existence in identical theatrical conditions were the same demands, and often found the same solutions.

'The curse of specialization' is nowadays a *locus rhetoricus*, and

GREEK COMEDY

for that reason may before long command no more respect than *loci* of more impressive pedigree. It suffers from the disadvantage that whereas farmers really are happier than tyrants and a philosophical turn of mind really does confer more lasting pleasure than a discriminating palate, it is not altogether obvious that Classical studies will prosper if everyone renounces the standards which he knows to be attainable only by specialization. But if any lesson is to be drawn from this brief survey of Greek Comedy, we might do worse than to recollect the end of Plato's *Symposium*. Aristophanes may have agreed with Socrates' argument, in so far as it applied to poets, only for the sake of peace and quiet; but had the argument been applied to scholars, he might well have opened both eyes to agree τοῦ αὐτοῦ ἀνδρὸς εἶναι κωμῳδίαν καὶ τραγῳδίαν ἐπίστασθαι ἐξηγεῖσθαι.

In referring the reader to books and articles I have tried to preserve a balance between two different and often conflicting criteria: importance in the history of the study of Greek Comedy, and accessibility to the British reader in the nineteen-fifties. I have often omitted works which in their time represented significant progress in favour of accessible modern works which summarize the results of half a century's study.

In the citation of Comic fragments:
K refers to Kock's *Comicorum Atticorum Fragmenta*,
D „ to Demianczuk's *Supplementum Comicum*,
S „ to Schröder's *Novae Comoediae Fragmenta*,
P „ to Page's *Greek Literary Papyri*.

In addition to the abbreviations current in *L'Année Philologique* I have used the following special abbreviations:
DFA Sir Arthur Pickard-Cambridge, *The Dramatic Festivals of Athens*, Oxford, 1953.
DTC A. W. Pickard-Cambridge, *Dithyramb, Tragedy, and Comedy*, Oxford, 1927.
NCh M. Platnauer, *Comedy*, in *New Chapters in the History of Greek Literature, Third Series*, Oxford, 1933.
SLGC T. B. L. Webster, *Studies in Later Greek Comedy*, Manchester, 1953.
Wil., *Ar.* U. von Wilamowitz-Möllendorf, *Aristophanes Lysistrate*, Berlin, 1927.
Wil., *Men.* id., *Menander: Das Schiedsgericht*, Berlin, 1925.

[1] Cf. S. G. Owen's obituary of Blaydes in JAW 32 (1909), pp. 37-9.
[2] F. Leo, *Der Monolog im Drama*, AGG N.F. 10.5 (1908), especially pp. 113-19, on the investigation of poetic forms in general; W. Kock, *De Personarum Comicarum Introductione*, Breslau, 1914; K. Kunst, *Studien zur griechisch-römischen Komödie*, Wien-Leipzig, 1919; A. Perkmann, *Streitszenen in der griechisch-römischen Komödie*, WS 45 (1926-27), 46 (1927-28).
[3] We must also be aware of the presence of a ghost: Georg Kaibel, who died in 1901 in the prime of life. It is not easy to set a limit to the services which his prodigious scholarship would have rendered to the study of Greek Comedy had he been given another thirty years of life.
[4] No complete exegetical editions of Aristophanes have appeared since those of J. van Leeuwen (Leyden, 1893-1906) and B. B. Rogers (London, 1901-06). Rogers' scholarly equipment was defective, and though the force and ingenuity of his translation endeared him to the amateur he has not been taken seriously by the professional; but he sometimes hit the nail on the head (cf. Ed. Fraenkel, Eranos, 48 (1950), p. 84 n1, on *Birds* 267). Of the editions of separate plays the most significant are: W. J. M. Starkie's *Wasps, Acharnians*, and *Clouds* (London, 1897, 1909 and 1911 respectively),

R. A. Neil's *Knights* (Cambridge, 1901), Wil., *Ar.*, L. Radermacher's *Frogs* (SAWW 198.4 (1921)), and K. Holzinger's commentary on *Plutus* (SAWW 218.3 (1940)). Of contributions in periodicals: Wilamowitz, *Ueber die Wespen des Aristophanes*, SPAW 1911; V. Coulon's articles in REG 35 (1922) – 44 (1931); K. Holzinger, *Erklärungen umstrittener Stellungen des Aristophanes*, SAWW 208.5 (1928) and 215.1 (1933).

[5] Wil., *Ar.*, p. 7 is grossly unfair.
[6] F. Krause, *Quaestiones Aristophaneae Scaenicae*, Rostock, 1903; Wilamowitz, SPAW 1911, pp. 481-5, and Hermes 64 (1929), pp. 470-6; W. Kranz, Hermes 52 (1917), p. 585 n1; O. J. Todd, *Quomodo Aristophanes Rem Temporalem in Fabulis suis Tractaverit*, HSPh. 26 (1915).
[7] A. W. Pickard-Cambridge, *The Theatre of Dionysus at Athens*, Oxford, 1946.
[8] Wil., *Ar.*, pp. 7, 38-9, and Hermes 64 (1929), pp. 466-470.
[9] Wil., *Men.*, p. 156; W. Dittmar, *Sprachliche Untersuchungen zu Aristophanes und Menander*, Weida, 1933, is a step in the right direction.
[10] Chr. Bruhn, *Ueber den Wortschatz des Menanders*, Jena, 1910; D. B. Durham, *The Vocabulary of Menander*, Princeton, 1913.
[11] G. P. Anagnostopoulos, Γλωσσικὰ 'Ανάλεκτα I, 'Αθηνᾶ 36 (1924), esp. pp. 42-4.
[12] *Ibid.*, pp. 52-7.
[13] A. C. Schlesinger, *Indications of Parody in Aristophanes*, TAPhA 67 (1936) and AJPh 58 (1937).
[14] C. W. Peppler's articles in AJPh 28 (1907), 31 (1910), 37 (1916), 39 (1918), 42 (1921).
[15] J. D. Denniston, *Technical Terms in Aristophanes*, CQ 21 (1927).
[16] J. W. White, *The Verse of Greek Comedy*, London, 1912, gives valuable data on metres κατὰ στίχον, but his analysis of lyric metres is too theoretical; on problems of responsion, Wilamowitz, *Griechische Verskunst*, Berlin, 1921, pp. 470-486, and M. Platnauer, *Antistrophic Variations in Aristophanes*, in *Greek Poetry and Life*, Oxford, 1936, pp. 241-256.
[17] O. J. Todd, *Index Aristophaneus*, Cambridge (Mass.), 1932.
[18] Demianczuk's *Supplementum Comicum* and Jensen's and Körte's editions of Menander contain *indices verborum*. K. Klaus, *Die Adjektiva bei Menander*, Leipzig, 1936, is an excellent analysis of part of Menander's vocabulary.
[19] H. Steiger, *Die Groteske und die Burleske bei Aristophanes*, Phil. 89 (1934); H. W. Miller, *Comic Iteration in Aristophanes*, AJPh 66 (1945), cf. 65 (1944).
[20] G. Keller, *Die Komödien des Aristophanes und die athenische Volksreligion seiner Zeit*, Tübingen, 1931, esp. p. 16; M. P. Nilsson, *Greek Piety*, Oxford, 1948, p. 77.
[21] P. Lehmann, *Die Parodie im Mittelalter*, München, 1922, pp. 39-40, 55-6, 208.
[22] E.g. the persistent intrusion of comic elements in the Alsfeld Passion Play (ed. R. Froning, *Das Drama des Mittelalters* vols. 2-3, Stuttgart, n.d.: cf. P. Scherer, *Geschichte der deutschen Litteratur*, Berlin, 1883, pp. 247-8) or the comic treatment of Noah and his family in *The Chester Pageant of the Deluge* (ed. E. Rhys in *Everyman and Other Interludes*, London 1909); cf. G. Murray, *Aristophanes*, Oxford, 1933, p. 2.
[23] Wilamowitz, *Der Glaube der Hellenen*, Berlin, 1931, vol. 1, p. 43 and vol. 2, pp. 96-8; H. Kleinknecht, *Die Gebetsparodie in der Antike*, Stuttgart-Berlin, 1937, pp. 116-22.
[24] G. W. Baker, *De Comicis Graecis Litterarum Iudicibus*, HSPh. 15 (1904).
[25] A. E. Roggwiller, *Dichter und Dichtung in der attischen Komödie*, Zürich, 1926, pp. 18-28.
[26] A. Römer, *Ueber den litterarisch-ästhetischen Bildungsstand des attischen Theaterpublikums*, ABAW 22 (1905), esp. p. 68.
[27] *Ibid.*, pp. 76-8.
[28] Schlesinger, pp. 313-14; Roggwiller, p. 7.
[29] V. Ehrenberg, *The People of Aristophanes*, Oxford (ed. 1) 1943, (ed. 2) 1951.
[30] I have argued this at greater length in a review of Ehrenberg's book in *Cambridge Journal* 5 (1952).
[31] H. Weber, *Aristophanische Studien*, Leipzig, 1908, pp. 30-43; Ed. Meyer, *Geschichte des Altertums*, Stuttgart-Berlin, 1901, vol. 4, pp. 366-7; A. Ruppel, *Konzeption und Ausarbeitung der Aristophanischen Komödie*, Darmstadt, 1913, p. 6.
[32] M. Croiset, *Aristophane et les Partis à Athènes*, Paris, 1906 (English tr. by J. Loeb, London, 1909).
[33] A. W. Gomme, *Aristophanes and Politics*, CR 52 (1933).

GREEK COMEDY 153

[34] W. Süss, *De Personarum Antiquae Comoediae Atticae Usu atque Origine*, Bonn, 1905, pp. 10-22; A. Weiher, *Philosophen und Philosophenspott in der attischen Komödie*, München, 1913, p. 16.
[35] Cf. 'Beachcomber' and 'Timothy Shy'.
[36] Listed by J. W. White, *The Manuscripts of Aristophanes*, CPh 1 (1906).
[37] E. Cary, *The M nuscript Tradition of the Acharnians*, HSt 18 (1907); J. W. White and E. Cary, *Collations of the Manuscripts of Aristophanes' Aves*, HSt 29 (1918), and *Collations of the Manuscripts of Aristophanes' Vespae*, HSPh. 30 (1919); cf. O. Bachmann's preface (pp. vi-xxx) in K. Zacher's edition of *Peace*, Leipzig, 1909.
[38] F. W. Hall and W. M. Geldart, (ed.) *Aristophanis Comoediae*, Oxford (ed. 1), 1900, (ed. 2), 1906.
[39] V. Coulon, (ed.) *Aristophane*, Paris, 1923-30, five vols., with French translation by H. van Daele.
[40] See now D. Mervyn Jones, *The Manuscripts of Aristophanes' Knights* (I), CQ N.S. 2 (1952).
[41] Van Leeuwen, *Prolegomena in Aristophanem*, Leyden, 1908, pp. 270-9; Coulon, vol. 1, pp. xii-xviii; G. Pasquali, *Storia della Tradizione e Critica del Testo*, Firenze, 1952 (ed. 2), pp. 194-201; cf. Mervyn Jones, pp. 172 n1, 175-6.
[42] Pasquali, pp. 196-8, somewhat exaggerates their importance.
[43] *BKT* V 2 (1907), pp. 100-5.
[44] *PSI* 1194.
[45] Cf. van Leeuwen on the *dramatis personae* of *Thesmophoriazusae*.
[46] Cf. the Ravenna Scholiast: ὁλολύζουσι· τὸ ἱερὸν ὠθεῖται.
[47] W. Kraus, *Testimonia Aristophanea*, Wien. Akad. Denkschr. 70.2 (1931).
[48] Coulon, *Quaestiones Criticae in Aristophanis Fabulas*, Strasburg, 1907.
[49] *The Scholia on the Aves of Aristophanes*, Boston, 1914.
[50] Three vols., London, 1896.
[51] A. Römer, *Studien zu Aristophanes und den alten Erklärern Desselben*, Leipzig, 1902; note especially (p. 2) the amusing example *Wasps* 1326.
[52] Wilamowitz, *Einleitung in die griechische Tragödie* (= *Euripides Herakles*, vol. 1 chh. 1-4), Berlin, 1907, pp. 179-184; P. Boudreaux, *Le Texte d' Aristophane et ses Commentateurs*, Bibl. Ec. Fr. Ath. 114 (1919); J. Steinhausen, Κωμῳδούμενοι, Bonn, 1910; White, *Verse &c.*, pp. 384-421; A. Gudeman, *Scholien (Aristophanes)*, RE 2 II cols. 672-80. The mention in a recently published letter of the second century A.D. of 'books vi and vii of Hypsicrates' Κωμῳδούμενοι' is an interesting glimpse beyond the great ancient scholars whose names we already knew (*POxy.* 2192).
[53] *Scholia &c.*, pp. lxvii-lxxii.
[54] G. Zuntz, *Die Aristophanes-Scholien der Papyri*, Byzantion 13 (1938) and 14 (1939).
[55] Zuntz, pp. 601-4; cf. Boudreaux, pp. 171-88.
[56] The most recent critical text is A. Körte's third Teubner edition, 1938 (K³); C. Jensen's, Berlin, 1929 (J), is extremely useful and more easily obtainable in this country than Körte's. F. G. Allinson's Loeb edition (A), Cambridge (Mass.), 1921, is the only text really accessible in this country, but it is out of date in some important respects. K³ and J include only the plays known from papyrus and parchment fragments; the citations have now (1954) appeared in the Teubner series.
[57] Pp. 9-13 A; pp. ix-xi, xix-xxi J; pp. viii-x K³.
[58] D. S. Robertson, *An Unrecognized Fragment from Menander's Epitrepontes?*, CR 36 (1922); *NCh* p. 168; fr. 34 P; p. 132 J; p. 143 K³.
[59] *Euripides oder Menander?*, Hermes 61 (1926).
[60] Page *ad loc.*
[61] P. 370 A; p. 96 J; p. 104 K³.
[62] P. 398 A; p. 110 J; p. 120 K³.
[63] P. 420 A; p. 120 J; p. 130 K³.
[64] P. 408 A plus fr. 52 P; p. 112 J; p. 122 K³; *NCh*, p. 169; add now W. Schubart, BSAW 97.5 (1950), no. 22; *SLGC*, p. 184.
[65] P. 101 K³; fr. 55 P.
[66] *PSI* 126; p. 128 J; p. 138 K; fr. 54 P; Schubart, *loc. cit.*; E. Ulbricht, *Kritische und exegetische Studien zu Menander*, Leipzig, 1933, pp. 4-26.
[67] A. Wilhelm, *Urkunden dramatischer Aufführungen in Athen*, Sond. öst. arch. Inst. 6, (1906); reviews by E. Capps, AJPh 28 (1907), and Wilamowitz, GGA 1906.

68 A. Dittmer, *The Fragments of Athenian Comic Didascaliae* (sic) *Found in Rome*, Leyden, 1923; IG ii² (1931), 2318-2325; the material is now published and discussed in *DFA* pp. 103-26.
69 *Hesperia* 7 (1938), pp. 116-18, and 12 (1943), pp. 1-11.
70 The victorious tribes in the men's and boys' choruses were also recorded, and after c. 450 the victorious tragic protagonist; the Comic διδάσκαλος was normally, but not necessarily, the poet.
71 P. Geissler, *Chronologie der altattischen Komödie*, Berlin, 1925; H. Oellacher, *Zur Chronologie der altattischen Komödie*, WSt 38 (1916); Webster, *Chronological Notes on Middle Comedy*, CQ N.S. 2 (1952); R. J. T. Wagner, *Symbolarum ad Comicorum Graecorum Historiam Criticam Capita Quattuor*, Leipzig, 1905.
72 I have attempted a specimen re-examination in *Plato Comicus: Presbeis and Hellas*, CR 64 (1950).
73 The thorough characterization of New Comedy by Ph. -E. Legrand, *Daos*, Lyon-Paris, 1910, pp. 64-324, serves to show the relation between the highest common factor of the Roman plays and the highest common factor of Roman plays plus Greek.
74 A. W. Gomme, *Essays in Greek History and Literature*, Oxford, 1937, pp. 249-95; Webster, *Studies in Menander*, Manchester, 1950.
75 H. Hauschild, *Die Gestalt der Hetäre in der griechischen Komödie*, Leipzig, 1933, pp. 40-9 (cf. pp. 31-40 on Thais in *Eunuchus*).
76 *SLGC*, pp. 4, 125-83, 205-32.
77 P. W. Harsh, review of Webster's *Studies in Menander*, Gn 25 (1953).
78 Leo, *Plautinische Forschungen* (ed. 2), Berlin, 1912, ch. 3; Fraenkel, *Plautinisches im Plautus*, Berlin, 1922; cf. H. W. Prescott, *Criteria of Originality in Plautus*, TAPhA 63 (1932).
79 G. Jachmann, *Plautinisches und attisches*, Berlin, 1931, W. E. J. Kuiper, *Grieksche Origineelen en Latijnsche Navolgingen*, Amsterdam, 1936; cf. Gomme, 251 n2; G. E. Duckworth, *The Nature of Roman Comedy*, Princeton, 1952.
80 Adesp. fr. 14 D; fr. 7 S; fr. 60 P; *NCh*, p. 178.
81 Adesp., fr. 22. 2 D; p. 63 S; fr. 72 (2) P; *NCh*, pp. 172-3.
82 *PSI* 1212; fr. 38 P; W. Schmid, *Geschichte der griechischen Literatur* 1.4, München, 1946, pp. 81-2.
83 pp. 31-2 D; *NCh*, pp. 159-161; Schmid, pp. 86-8.
84 Eupolis frr. 7-12 D plus Adesp. fr. 40 D plus *POxy*. 1240; fr. 40 D P; *NCh*, pp. 161-3; Schmid, pp. 124-132.
85 *PSI* 1213; fr. 41 P; Schmid, pp. 114-15, speaks as if not only were the identification certain but the interpretation of the fragment simple and obvious — which is not the case.
86 Th. Zielinski, *Die Gliederung der altattischen Komödie*, Leipzig, 1885; P. Mazon, *Essai sur la composition des comédies d' Aristophane*, Paris, 1904; *DTC*, pp. 292-328.
87 M. Whittaker, *The Comic Fragments and their Relation to the Structure of Old Attic Comedy*, CQ 29 (1935).
88 Platonius, Περὶ Διαφορᾶς Κωμῳδιῶν 7; Schmid, p. 80.
89 Schmid, p. 221.
90 *DTC*, pp. 240-4, 292-311, argues by extrapolation.
91 F. M. Cornford, *The Origin of Attic Comedy*, London, 1914; cf. *DTC*, pp. 329-49.
92 Murray, *Francis Macdonald Cornford*, 1874-1943, Proc. Brit. Acad. 29, pp. 1-6.
93 e.g. pp. 17, 34, which are vital to his argument.
94 Semus of Delos *ap.* Athen. 622d; *DTC*, pp. 233-7.
95 Nilsson, *Geschichte der griechischen Religion*, I, München, 1941, pp. 557-61.
96 H. E. Sieckmann, *De Comoediae Atticae Primordiis*, Göttingen, 1906, referred it to Epicharmus.
97 Radermacher, *Frösche*, pp. 21-34; Wil., *Ar.*, p. 14.
98 For the text of Epicharmus see Kaibel, *Comicorum Graecorum Fragmenta*, 1.1, Berlin, 1899, and A. Olivieri, *Frammenti della Commedia Greca e del Mimo nella Sicilia e nella Magna Grecia*, 1, Napoli, n.d. (expansive where Kaibel is austere, but adds little of real importance); on the poet in general, Kaibel, *Epicharmos*, RE 6 coll. 34-41; *DTC*, pp. 353-415; E. Wüst, *Epicharmos und die alte attische Komödie*, RhM 93 (1950).
99 Kaibel, coll. 37-9.
100 Fr. 6 (Kai)=3 (Ol.); *DTC*, pp. 389-90.

101 *DTC*, pp. 405-6; Wüst, p. 342.
102 Kaibel, col. 39.
103 *DTC*, pp. 228-30.
104 *DTC*, pp. 274-84.
105 Archil. fr. 28, Hippon. fr. 14 A, 1-9; cf. Schmid, p. 70 nn 14, 16.
106 Körte, *Archäologische Studien zur alten Komödie*, JDAI (1893); A. Greifenhagen, *Eine attische schwarzfigurische Vasengattung und die Darstellung des Komos im VI Jahrhundert*, Königsberg, 1929; Humfry Payne, *Necrocorinthia*, Oxford, 1931, pp. 118-24; E. Buschor, *Satyrtänze und frühes Drama*, SBAW 1943.5.
107 J. Poppelreuter, *De Comoediae Atticae Primordiis*, Berlin, 1893; M. Bieber, *History of the Greek and Roman Theater*, Princeton, 1939, figs. 76, 77, 79; *DTC*, pp. 245-6, figs. 16-18. The vase which shows men riding on real dolphins and ostriches (Bieber, fig. 78) is of very doubtful relevance for drama; E. Bielefeld, *Ein Delphinreiter Chor*, AA 1946/47, answers the ill-conceived suggestions of F. Brommer, *Delphinreiter*, AA 1942.
108 Bieber, fig. 121; (*DTC*, fig 32 is expurgated) and S. P. Karouzou, AJA 50 (1946), pp. 132-8 and fig. 10.
109 *DFA*, p. 234, n2; more cautiously, *DTC*, p. 237, n1, Körte, pp. 65-9, Wüst, PhW 1942, col. 460. See now W. Beare, CQ N.S. 4 (1954), pp. 64 sqq.
110 Bieber, fig. 83; Payne, pp. 121-2 and fig. 44G; Buschor, pp. 20-1 and fig. 10; Greifenhagen, p. 60.
111 Körte, pp. 90-2; Bieber, fig. 85; *DTC*, pp. 273-4; Greifenhagen, pp. 57-9, 66, n128; Payne, p. 122.
112 Cf. Anecd. Bekk., i, p. 224, οἱ δὲ 'Ομβρικὸς ὑπὸ 'Αλικαρνάσσεων Βάκχος.
113 Payne seems to have thought this, *loc. cit.*
114 Greifenhagen, pp. 65-6; CVA Pays-Bas, Musée Scheurleer, 26, 4-5, shows some men dressed as women among padded dancers.
115 Payne, pp. 121-2.
116 Payne, pl. 34, no. 2.
117 *DTC*, pp. 254-6.
118 Nilsson, pl. 35, nos. 2-3, shows a red-figure vase on which there are two representations of the ritual phallus being drawn along on wheels by a crowd of men; in one scene, a giant silenus stands over the phallus, in the other a naked giant man with rounded stomach. H. Herter, *Vom Dionysischen Tanz zum komischen Spiel*, Iserlohn, 1947, p. 17, sees in this figure the link between phallic ritual and the dancers with padded stomachs.
119 Wil., *Men.*, pp. 142-9.
120 Fraenkel, *Das Original der Cistellaria des Plautus*, Phil 87 (1932).
121 Adesp. fr. 17 D; fr. 3.III S; fr. 66 (e) P.
122 Adesp. fr. 23 D; fr. 4 col. V S; cf. fr. 65 (*ad fin.*) P.
123 Körte, Χοροῦ, Hermes 39 (1904).
124 E. Bethe, *Der Chor bei Menander*, BSG 60 (1908).
125 *Komödie*, RE 11, col. 1268.
126 R. C. Flickinger, Χοροῦ in *Terence's Heauton*, CPh 7 (1912), p. 24; K. J. Maidment, *The Later Comic Chorus*, CQ 29 (1935), pp. 20-1.
127 Cf. the didascalia to *Heaut.: Graeca est Menandru*.
128 Legrand, pp. 464-7; Wil., *Men.*, pp. 120-1.
129 Legrand, pp. 467-90.
130 Leo, Χοροῦ, Hermes 39 (1904).
131 fr. 48 P; *NCh*, p. 166.
132 Leo, *Monolog*, pp. 38-46.
133 Körte, *Komödie*, coll. 1257-8.
134 n131 above, and fr. 47 P, probably from the Διὸς γοναί of Philiscus: memorable for the line ἔχρησε γὰρ Κρόνῳ ποθ' 'Απόλλων δραχμήν; *NCh*, pp. 164-6.
135 H. W. Prescott, *The Interpretation of Roman Comedy*, CPh 11 (1916), p. 135 n2; Fraenkel, *Plautinisches*, p. 89 n2; but cf. Maidment, p. 15 n8.
136 Wil., *Men.*, p. 121 n1.
137 Platonius 11.
138 *SLGC*, pp. 26-8.
139 *SLGC*, pp. 37-49.
140 Cf. Platonius 8.

[141] Platonius 4, but cf. Maidment, pp. 3-7.
[142] F. Wehrli, *Motivstudien zur griechischen Komödie*, Zürich-Leipzig, 1936, p. 101.
[143] Adesp. fr. 16 (h) D; fr. 2 (e) S; fr. 64 (4) P; *NCh*, p. 176.
[144] Timocles fr. 2 D; fr. 22 S; fr. 51 (b) P.
[145] Wil., *Ar.*, p. 206; Fraenkel, *Dramaturgical Problems in the Ecclesiazusae*, in *Greek Poetry and Life*, Oxford, 1936, pp. 257-76.
[146] Fraenkel, *De Media et Nova Comoedia Quaestiones Selectae*, Göttingen, 1912, p. 74.
[147] *Ibid.*, p. 88.
[148] Adesp. fr. 12b D; fr. 45 (a) P.
[149] This inference is drawn by Wehrli, p. 24.
[150] Hauschild (v. n75 above).
[151] *DFA*, pp. 234-5.
[152] Webster, *South Italian Vases and Attic Drama*, CQ 42 (1948).
[153] E. Wüst, Φλύακες, RE 20, coll. 292-306; L. Radermacher, *Zur Geschichte der griechischen Komödie*, SAWW 102.1 (1925).
[154] Bieber, fig. 381; Webster, p. 25.
[155] Bieber, fig. 394; Webster, p. 20; cf. also Bieber, figs. 357, 392, 402?
[156] JHS 65 (1945), pl. V; but I am not sure that *DFA*, p. 237, is right to associate this with dancers on tables (JHS 59 (1939), p. 25) or small table-like objects (*ibid.*, p. 10).
[157] Pickard-Cambridge, *South Italian Vases and Attic Drama*, CQ 43 (1949); *DFA*, pp. 236-8.
[158] Bieber, figs. 90-1.
[159] Bieber, figs. 122-35.
[160] Webster, *The Masks of Greek Comedy*, BRL 32.1 (1949), arguing from widely-distributed fourth-century terracotta statuettes, extends the Pollucian conventions as far as possible into Middle and Old Comedy.
[161] von Arnim, *Supplementum Euripideum*, Bonn, 1913, p. 5.
[162] Cf. Antiphanes fr. 191 K.
[163] Legrand, pp. 495-8, makes the most of it; cf. Aristophanes fr. 335 K (Schol. *Thesm.* 298), Philyllius fr. 8.
[164] Pasquali, *Menandro ed Euripide*, A & R 21 (1915), argues for a more direct derivation of characterization from Euripides.
[165] Philemon, fr. 3 D; fr. 23 S; fr. 50 (b) P.
[166] Collected by E. Sehrt, *De Menandro Euripidis Imitatore*, Giessen, 1912; but many of his examples are inappropriate or exaggerated; *Georgus* 79 sqq.~Eur. *Hipp.* 403-4 is not very happy, and Men. fr. 348 K is a paratragic commonplace (cf. Ar. frr. 1, 155 K).
[167] Flickinger, CPh 7 (1912), pp. 31-4.
[168] Körte, *Komödie*, col. 1268.
[169] Fraenkel, pp. 13-32.
[170] Leo, *op. cit.*, esp. p. 36.
[171] Fraenkel, pp. 6-12.

APPENDIX TO CHAPTER IV

THE study of Greek comedy during the last few years has been dominated by the discovery of more Menander. We now have *Dyskolos* virtually complete (first published as *Papyrus Bodmer IV* in 1958; edited as an Oxford Classical Text by Hugh Lloyd-Jones in 1960; edited with an extensive introduction and commentary by E. W. Handley [London, 1965]), substantial portions of *Sikyonios* (edited by R. Kassel in the 'Kleine Texte' series, 1965) and new fragments of *Misoumenos* (edited by E. G. Turner, BICS Suppl. XVII). *Dyskolos*, produced in 316 B.C., is not a great play, but as an item in the history of comedy it is full of interest, not only in its formal aspects (it is divided into five parts by four irruptions of a chorus [cf. p. 117], and its final scene is composed mainly in iambic tetrameters) but also in its characterization and in some of the sentiments and attitudes which it expresses.

New discoveries in the field of Old Comedy have been confined to the mediaeval manuscripts. A Paris manuscript (Suppl. gr. 463) has corrections and scholia which are in the hand of Demetrius Triclinius himself (W. J. W. Koster, *Autour d'un manuscrit d'Aristophane écrit par Démétrius Triclinius* [Groningen, 1957] — but the suggestion that the main text is also written by Triclinius has not been generally accepted). A hitherto unnoticed manuscript, Holkhamensis 88, proves to be a good copy of the Triclinian edition of eight plays of Aristophanes (N. G. Wilson, CQ N.S. xii [1962], 32ff.). The publication of the scholia on Aristophanes, under the general editorship of Koster, has so far given us only Johannes Tzetzes' scholia on *Plutus, Clouds, Frogs* and *Birds* (Groningen and Amsterdam, 1960-1964), but the preparatory work has brought to light from fourteenth century mss. undeniably ancient scholia which are missing or curtailed in the Ravennas and Venetus, and a coherent picture of Byzantine editions of Aristophanes is beginning to emerge (see the articles by Koster and Holwerda in *Mnemosyne* from 1952 onwards).

Frogs has been edited, with a commentary, by W. B. Stanford (London, ed. 2, 1963), and *Peace* by M. Platnauer (Oxford, 1964). The late J. M. Edmonds' edition of *The Fragments of Attic Comedy*, published in four volumes (Leiden, 1957-1961), is not at all what was wanted; it abounds in mistakes, confusions, superficial judgments and irresponsible emendations, and the editor's belief that he could read a marginal and interlinear paraphrase (vol. IIIB, Appendix) in the Cairo codex was a delusion.

The evidence for the origins of comedy is now presented in T. B. L. Webster's substantially revised edition (Oxford, 1962) of Pickard-Cambridge's *Dithyramb, Tragedy and Comedy*. Problems of production are discussed in Webster's *Greek Theatre Production* (London, 1956) and P. D. Arnott's *Greek Scenic Conventions in the Fifth Century B.C.* (Oxford, 1962). Webster's book contains a short list of works of art which, in one sense or another, 'illustrate' comedy, and he has published complete lists in BICS Suppl. IX and XI. A. M. Dale in JHS lxxvii (1957), 205ff., has argued that only one door into the σκηνή was available to Aristophanes, and that this holds good even for those scenes (notably in *Acharnians*, *Clouds* and *Ecclesiazusae*) where the words of the text imply more than one door; there are (in the present writer's opinion; cf. Proc. Camb. Phil. Soc. 1966, 2 ff.) weighty arguments against this hypothesis, but its opponents must admit that it has forced upon us a salutary reappraisal of Aristophanic theatrical production.

Among the numerous books written during the last ten years on various aspects of the art of Aristophanes three are noteworthy: C. F. Russo, *Aristofane autore di teatro* (Florence, 1962), which, although marred by errors of detail, investigates practical theatrical problems of the kind which editors of texts often ignore; H.-J. Newiger, *Metaphor und Allegorie* (Munich, 1957), which deals with types and degrees of personification in Aristophanes; and J. Taillardat, *Les Images d'Aristophane* (Paris, ed. 2, 1965), an exceedingly thorough account of Aristophanes' vocabulary, with many illuminating comments on individual passages.

CHAPTER V

THE GREEK PHILOSOPHERS

BY SIR DAVID ROSS

THE best general work covering the whole history of Greek philosophy is that of Zeller, which, begun far back in the nineteenth century, continued to come out in new editions in the twentieth. The first two volumes of a valuable new edition with Italian translation and notes by R. Mondolfo were published in 1932 and 1938. [To these, Mondolfo has since added Vol. I, Part 4, *I presocratici: Eraclito*. The following have also appeared: II, 6, *Aristotele e i Peripatetici più antichi* (Armando Plebe); III, 6, *La filosofia post-aristotelica: Giamblicho e la scuola di Atene* (Giuseppe Martano). The Roman numerals correspond to Zeller's volumes. It is understood that there will be eighteen parts in all.] Another general history, much less detailed and more popular in style but with real learning behind it, is that of T. Gomperz, which was translated into English and published in that form in 1901-12. Ueberweg-Praechter's *Grundriß der Geschichte der Philosophie* is particularly useful because of the bibliographies it contains.

Along with these works must be mentioned the articles on particular schools and on individual philosophers in Pauly-Wissowa's *Realencylopaedie*, which as regards the less known philosophers is often the most complete source of information at our command. The sketch of the history of Greek philosophy by L. Robin, *La Pensée Grecque*,[1] should also be mentioned, and with it three books dealing with particular questions, though not confined to particular schools or individuals — Edward Caird's *Evolution of Theology in the Greek Philosophers*,[2] J. I. Beare's *Greek Theories of Elementary Cognition from Alcmaeon to Aristotle*[3] and E. Kapp's *Greek Foundations of Traditional Logic*.[4]

When we are dealing with authors whose works exist only in fragments, the foundation of all research is a full and well-arranged collection of these fragments, and of the *testimonia* of other writers referring to them. For the Pre-Socratics this invaluable foundation was laid by Hermann Diels in his *Fragmente der Vorsokratiker*, which appeared first in 1903, and of which the latest (7th) edition including a very full index, was issued in 1954.⁵ In this country a brilliant account of the Pre-Socratics had been given by John Burnet in 1892, ed. 4, 1930 (repr. 1945) — a real tour-de-force for a man of twenty-eight; and his further thoughts were expressed in his *Greek Philosophy: Thales to Plato*.⁶ In both books he showed originality and vigour in his treatment of his subject. The emergence of philosophy from theology and mythology was treated with characteristic brilliance, and with less than his caution of later years, by F. M. Cornford in his *From Religion to Philosophy*;⁷ and the same side of the early philosophers, down to and including Anaxagoras, Diogenes of Apollonia, and the Sophists, has been discussed by Werner Jaeger in *The Theology of the Early Greek Philosophers*;⁸ he had already dealt, less methodically, with the early philosophers in his *Paideia*.⁹ Other works dealing with the Pre-Socratics are H. Cherniss, *Aristotle's Criticism of PreSocratic Philosophy*;¹⁰ A. Schmekel, *Die positive Philosophie in ihrer geschichtlichen Entwicklung*;¹¹ W. Kranz, *Vorsokratische Denker*¹² (a selection of fragments, with a German translation); F. M. Cornford, 'Was the Ionian Philosophy scientific?';¹³ O. Gigon, *Der Ursprung der griechischen Philosophie von Hesiod bis Parmenides*;¹⁴ W. H. S. Jones, *Philosophy and Medicine in Ancient Greece*;¹⁵ K. von Fritz, 'Νοῦς, Νοεῖν and their derivatives in PreSocratic Philosophy'.¹⁶

When we come to Socrates, we come to one of the questions that have most acutely divided the opinion of scholars in this century. Up to 1911 the generally accepted view was that Socrates had no constructive philosophy, that he was a moralist pure and simple, interested in combating the unsettling influence of the Sophists and in setting ideals of virtue before his fellow-citizens, and that it was partly as a tribute to his master in that respect, and partly because the conventions of the dialogue did not allow him to make himself a character in his dialogues, that Plato put the theory of Ideas in Socrates' mouth. In 1911 two books appeared in which this interpretation was challenged. Burnet in his edition of the *Phaedo*,¹⁷ and Taylor in his *Varia Socratica*,¹⁸ set themselves to proving that Socrates was the real author of the theory of Ideas, and that the early dialogues, down to and including the *Republic*, are strictly historical. This thesis Burnet maintained again in *Greek Philosophy: Thales to Plato*, and Taylor maintained in several later works. Taylor in his preface to

Varia Socratica expresses his thanks to Burnet, and I believe that he regarded Burnet as the originator of this view.

Much discussion has ranged round this thesis. It did not, I believe, meet with much favour on the Continent; Robin and Ritter, the leading Platonists in France and in Germany, did not accept it. In the Proceedings of the Sixth Congress of Philosophy in 1926, Robin, fresh from an intensive study of the *Phaedo*, joined three leading students of Plato in America in denouncing the theory; R. C. Lodge pointed out that Taylor had gone somewhat further than Burnet — as he certainly did later when he treated the *Timaeus* also as not expressing Plato's own views, but as an attempt at reconstructing the cosmology of Timaeus the Pythagorean. On the whole, the reaction of scholars has tended to be the same as that of these four; the position was accurately stated by Burnet's friend J. A. Smith when he wrote 'upon the whole it may be said that, while from some competent scholars the thesis has won enthusiastic adherence, it is by most regarded as paradoxical and respectfully rejected'.

The thesis was doomed to failure; its doom was sealed by Aristotle's words in the *Metaphysics*: 'Two things may be fairly ascribed to Socrates — inductive arguments and general definition, both of which are concerned with the starting-point of science; but Socrates did not make the universals or the definitions exist apart; his successors, however, gave them separate existence, and this was the kind of thing they called Ideas.' There was, apparently, a Burnet-Taylor theory in Aristotle's time, and he here sets himself deliberately and with full knowledge (for he was 'the mind' of the Platonic school) to point out in what respect those who held this view went too far, in ascribing the theory of Ideas to Socrates. There is, however, another remark by Aristotle that has to be borne in mind: τοῦτο δ' (the theory of Ideas) ἐκίνησε μὲν Σωκράτης διὰ τοὺς ὁρισμούς, 'Socrates stirred this matter up', or 'Socrates gave the impulse to this theory', 'by reason of his definitions'. That leaves room for much enquiry as to the precise nature and extent of the impulse that Socrates gave. The picture Aristotle thus presents, along with those presented by Plato, by Xenophon, who makes Socrates a rather commonplace moralist, and by Aristophanes, who makes him a figure of fun, form the quadrilateral within which the true Socrates is to be found. It was on the basis of Aristotle's judgments that I in editing thought for instance holds that none of the dialogues is earlier than the death of Socrates, while another takes the opposite view.

A minor controversy about Plato, confined to this country, arose in the twenties. It was concerned with the famous passage in the *Republic* about the Sun, the Idea of Good, the Line, and the Cave. It started with an article in *C.Q.* 5 (1911) 73-88 by J. L. Stocks (another scholar who died before his time) — an article in which he argued that, from the ratios mentioned by Plato as existing between parts of the Line, it follows that the two intermediate parts must be equal in length, and inferred that Plato did not mean the faculty for which the third part stands (διάνοια) to be any better than that for which the second part stands (πίστις). Stocks's article was followed by a series of articles by A. S. Ferguson,[30] and others joined in the fray. It cannot be said that any general agreement has been reached on the subjects raised in this discussion, but it would be agreed that the famous passage is very rich in content, and that the discussion has brought to light aspects of it which had been ignored before. Perhaps the most systematic attempts that have since been made to arrive at its meaning are those made by H. W. B. Joseph[31] by N. R. Murphy[32] and by me in *Plato's Theory of Ideas*.[33]

The general tendency in the study of Aristotle, until this century, has been to regard all his works, with the exception of the dialogues, as belonging to the latest period of his life, that of his headship of the Lyceum (335/4-322); and the dialogues, because of their great divergence from the doctrines expressed in the other works, had sometimes been regarded as not being by Aristotle at all. But in 1910, in a study which, appearing not as a book but as an article in the *Encyclopaedia Britannica*, and being the work of one who had a well-deserved reputation for eccentricity, attracted little attention from scholars, Thomas Case was able to show that there was evidence of change of view between one work of Aristotle and another. In particular, he showed that the analysis of the judgment in the *De Interpretatione* is more primitive than that in the *Prior Analytics*, and more akin to that of Plato in the *Sophistes*. He also showed that the ethical theory of the *Eudemian Ethics* is more Platonic than that of the *Nicomachean*. Thus he rescued two works, the *De Interpretatione* and the *Eudemian Ethics*, which had been believed or suspected to be spurious, and showed that they belonged to a comparatively early stage of Aristotle's the *Metaphysics*[19] and Professor Field in writing *Plato and his Contemporaries*[20] criticized the Burnet-Taylor theory; and Professor Field added to this a valuable analysis of the tradition handed down in the Academy, which confirms Aristotle's account.

On the minor Socratic schools there is not a great deal to report, and indeed the materials for new work are scarce. C. M. Gillespie wrote well on the Megarians.[21] On the Cynic school we have D. R. Dudley's *History of Cynicism*.[22] On Antisthenes, in particular, we have articles by G. Rodier, by Gillespie, and by K. von Fritz.[23] On Diogenes the Cynic we have F. Sayre's *Diogenes of Sinope*, and articles by von Fritz.[24] The Aristippus who founded the Cyrenaic school has now been distinguished from his grandfather who was a companion of Socrates, and on the grandson we have the work of G. B. L. Colosio, *Aristippo di Cirene*.[25] The edition of Aeschines Socraticus by H. Dittmar should also be mentioned.[26]

Burnet rendered a great service to the study of Plato by publishing a text[27] which was a great improvement on any earlier text, and which has not been superseded. He had also a scheme, which he partly carried out (but without publication), of constructing an Index Platonicus worthy of comparison with Bonitz's magnificent *Index Aristotelicus*; I understand that such a scheme is being undertaken in Germany.

The best (almost) complete text that has appeared since Burnet's — a text accompanied by introductions and translations — is the Budé text, of which perhaps the high-water marks are the *Phaedo*, the *Symposium*, and the *Phaedrus*, all by Robin.[28] The whole of Plato has also been done in the Loeb series (text and translation).

The order of writing of Plato's works is a real enigma to students of him. The only method of approaching the question that has yielded firm results is the stylometric method introduced by Lewis Campbell in his edition of the *Sophistes* and the *Politicus*.[29] This has been largely adopted by other students, and has led to almost complete agreement about the order of the later works. The order most generally accepted places the *Republic* about the middle of Plato's life as a writer, and supposes it to have been followed by the other works in this order: *Phaedrus, Parmenides, Theaetetus* (or *Theaetetus, Parmenides*), *Sophistes, Politicus, Timaeus, Philebus* (or *Philebus, Timaeus*), *Laws*. With regard to the works earlier than the *Republic* there is no approach to agreement; one school of thought, and formed a bridge between Plato and the later Aristotle.

In 1912 Werner Jaeger published his monograph on the *Metaphysics*,[34] in which he dissected that work with great skill, showing which parts belong to the main scheme and which do not, and which are early, which late. In 1923 he published his famous *Aristoteles: Grundlegung einer Geschichte seiner Entwicklung*,[35] in which (independently of Case's work, which he did not know) he reached results similar to Case's but covered much wider ground. He showed that in Aristotle's writing there is a general trend away from Plato's unworldiness to a growing interest in the phenomena of the world around us. He classified Aristotle's works under three periods — his life in the Platonic Academy (367-347) (aet. 17-37), his life in the Troad, in Lesbos, and in Macedonia (348/7-335/4), and his life in Athens as head of the Peripatetic school (335/4-322). To the first period he assigned the dialogues, except the *De Philosophia*, which he dated in the second period; and he showed how in these Aristotle set forth a distinctive view of life and of the world. To the second period he assigned the greater part of the *Metaphysics*, the *Eudemian Ethics*, the earliest parts of the *Politics*, the greater part of the *Physics*, and the *De Caelo* and the *De Generatione et Corruptione*. To the third period he assigned the remainder of the works, including those concerned with biology and with psychology, except the third book of the *De Anima*, which he dated earlier.

Thirteen years before Jaeger's book appeared, D'Arcy Thompson had in a prefatory note to his translation of the *Historia Animalium*[36] called attention to the frequent references in the work, and (though in a lesser degree) in the other biological works, to places in Lesbos, in Macedonia, and on the coast of Asia Minor, all the way from the Bosphorus to the Carian coast. This is just the region in which Aristotle spent the *Wanderjahre* mentioned above. Thompson drew the conclusion that Aristotle's 'work in natural history was antecedent to his strictly philosophical work'. This is probably too broad a statement; it is not likely that throughout this period Aristotle had given up the interest in philosophy already manifested in the dialogues. But at least it seems clear that the biological treatises, which, even without the psychological treatises, form about a quarter of the whole genuine Aristotelian *corpus*, were in the main written during the intermediate period and not, as Jaeger maintained, in the latest.

The next large attempt at a dating of Aristotle's works is that of F. Nuyens, in his *Ontwikkelingsmomenten in de Zielkunde van Aristoteles*[37] (later reissued under the title *L'Évolution de la Psychologie d'Aristote*).[38] While Nuyens's main subject is the development of Aristotle's psychology, he deals incidentally with the whole question of the chronology of Aristotle's works. He considers Thompson to have shown that the *Historia Animalium* dates from the middle period of Aristotle's writing, and he holds that the other biological works, though later than the *Historia* (the collection of facts on which they were based), still belong in the main to the same period. On this basis he considers the psychological writings — the *De Anima* and the *Parva Naturalia*. He finds that the last part of the *Parva Naturalia* belongs to the biological period, while the *De Sensu* and the *De Memoria*, and the three treatises on sleep and dreams, belong, like the *De Anima*, to the last period.

Nuyens has made a strong case for assigning the *De Iuventute* to the same period as the biological works; the points of contact, e.g. the treatment of the heart as the seat of all the activities of soul, are very striking. He seems to be less successful when he assigns the other treatises of the *Parva Naturalia* to the same period as the *De Anima*. These treatises clearly work on the basis of a two-substance theory of soul and body; the *De Anima*, on the other hand, or rather the central part of it, the second book, clearly proceeds on the basis of the soul's not being a distinct substance, but the 'first *entelecheia*' of the body, the characteristic or complex of characteristics which distinguishes a living body from one that is dead or has never lived. That is the conception which marks Aristotle's furthest movement away from the Platonic view of soul, and there is no trace of it in the *Parva Naturalia*.

One result seems to follow from the criticism of Nuyens, A. Mansion, and other scholars: that Jaeger was mistaken in supposing that most of Aristotle's work in philosophical theory was achieved during his middle period, and that the final period was almost entirely given up to the organization of scientific and historical research; a deep interest in philosophy, such as he undoubtedly had, is not so easily lost or suppressed as that. We should, I believe, think of his mind as being occupied during both the middle and the final period both with scientific and with philosphical studies. But much of Jaeger's brilliant reconstruction still holds good.

Let me finish with a few general observations. In the nineteenth century most of the solid work in the interpretation of Greek philosophy had been that of German scholars. Fine work had been done by Grote, Jowett, Bywater, Jackson, and others, but I can think of only one discovery of major importance that British scholarship had made — Campbell's discovery that the clue to the dating of Plato's later dialogues lay in minute observation of stylistic changes; this has led to a dating of the later dialogues which has in the main won general assent. In the present century British, French, and latterly American, Italian, Belgian, and Dutch scholarship has played a larger part than hitherto. German scholarship has fallen somewhat into the background, though German scholars domiciled in Great Britain or in the United States have continued the great German tradition, and classical scholarship in Germany itself will undoubtedly revive.

In Great Britain, and perhaps most of all in Oxford, the nature of the curriculum has tended to concentration on the great central figures, Socrates, Plato, and Aristotle. This has led to a great narrowing of my own knowledge, and I have thought it best in this sketch to concentrate mainly on these philosophers, and as regards the others simply to indicate where the best guides are to be found. We have had scholars who have worked in these other fields; Burnet and Cornford have worked on the Pre-Socratics, Bevan on the Stoics and the Sceptics, Dean Inge and Professor Dodds on the Neoplatonists; and it is likely that in the future British scholarship will turn in larger measure to these, for it, comparatively unworked fields.

A point which has occurred to me in writing this sketch is the fact that sometimes a question which seems at first sight very difficult has been solved by dwelling on one fact of primary importance. I have given one instance, the settling of the Burnet-Taylor controversy by attention to Aristotle's very plain statement (buttressed, of course, by other considerations that have led to the same conclusions). I will add two others. It was at one time very doubtful what it was that led to Aristotle's discovery of the syllogism. Maier thought he had found the answer, in deriving this from the Platonic method of division, but that answer was by no means convincing. Shorey discovered the true answer by noticing that Aristotle several times uses the word ἐπιφέρειν or the word συνεπιφέρειν to express the dragging in of one term by another, in other words to express the notion of implication, and that this is undoubtedly borrowed from Plato's usage of ἐπιφέρειν in the *Phaedo* to express the dragging in of one Idea by another. What Plato put forward as a metaphysical doctrine, Aristotle turns to a new account by making it the basis of his logical theory.

A third example comes to light in a still more puzzling context. Plato's theory of Idea-numbers remains a great problem, but we are certainly taken some way towards the solution of it by noting that the phrase 'the great and small' which Aristotle constantly uses in describing the theory is undoubtedly borrowed from the *Philebus*. That seems to me to show that Plato's doctrine took its origin not from the *Sophistes* as has sometimes been supposed, but from the account of the ἄπειρον in the *Philebus*. I do not, of course, suggest that there is always some one passage or phrase that will solve our problem, but I think it probable that there is often one, if we could only find it; and others may be able to think of other instances illustrative of the point.

[1] Paris, 1923, ed. 2 1948; Engl. tr. London, 1928.
[2] Glasgow, 1904.
[3] Oxford, 1906.
[4] New York, 1942.
[5] With W. Kranz, Berlin (Weidmann).
[6] London, 1914.
[7] London, 1912, repr. New York, 1957. [But see also the unfinished *Principium Sapientiae, a study of the origins of Greek philosophical thought*, ed. W. K. C. Guthrie, Cambridge U.P., 1952.]
[8] Oxford, 1947.
[9] Three volumes in Engl. tr., Oxford (Blackwell), 1939 and 1945; German ed., two vols., 1934 and 1947.
[10] Baltimore, 1935.
[11] Berlin, 1938.
[12] Berlin, 1939.
[13] JHS, 62 (1942).
[14] Basel, 1945.
[15] Baltimore, 1946.
[16] *C. Ph.*, 40 (1945) and 41 (1946).
[17] Oxford, 1911.
[18] Oxford, 1911.
[19] *Aristotle's Metaphysics*, text and commentary by Sir W. D. Ross, two vols., Oxford, 1924.
[20] London, 1930.
[21] AGPh, 24 (1911). [See also article *Megarikoi*, by Stenzel and Theiler, in Pauly-Wissowa, vol. 15 (1931), col. 217-220; and the recent writings on Stoic Logic which are mentioned on p. 178 below.]
[22] London, 1938.
[23] Année Philos. 1906 and 1911; *A.G. Ph.* 26 (1913) and 27 (1914); *Hermes* 62 (1927) and *Ph. M.* 84 (1935).
[24] Sayre, *Diogenes of Sinope*, Baltimore, 1938; von Fritz, *Philol.*, supplbd. 18 (1926) and *SIFC* 5 (1927).

[25] Turin, 1925. [See also Gabriele Giannantoni, *I Cirenaici*, Firenze, Pubbl. dell' Istituto di Filosofia dell'Univ. di Roma V.]
[26] [See also A. E. Taylor, *Philosophical Studies*, ch. 1 'Aeschines of Sphettus'.]
[27] Oxford, 1899-1901.
[28] Paris (Belles Lettres), 1926, 1929 and 1933.
[29] Oxford, 1867.
[30] *CQ* 15 (1921), 16 (1922), 28 (1936).
[31] *Knowledge and the Good in Plato's Republic*, Oxford (Classical and Philological Monographs), 1948.
[32] *The Interpretation of Plato's Republic*, Oxford, 1951.
[33] Oxford, 1951.
[34] *Entstehungsgeschichte d. Metaph. des Aristoteles*, Berlin, 1912.
[35] Berlin, 1923; Engl. tr. (Oxford), 1924, 2 ed. 1957.
[36] *Works of Arist.*, vol. 4, Oxford, 1910.
[37] Nijmegen-Utrecht, 1939.
[38] Louvain, The Hague and Paris, 1948.

APPENDIX TO CHAPTER V

BY DONALD J. ALLAN

Some verbal changes have been made in Sir David Ross's chapter, which are not noted; and some additions made which have been indicated by brackets. His bibliography of later Greek philosophy will still be found useful but is not here reproduced. In this appendix covering the period from 1954 to the middle of 1966 I aim rather at description of the movement of opinion, with some comment thereupon, than at a full record of detail.

Philosophy before Plato. In his learned and admirable review of research in pre-Socratic philosophy from 1953 to 1962 inclusive,[1] G. B. Kerferd singles out the following as the most important themes: (i) the authority of Aristotle and Theophrastus for the understanding of the pre-Socratics, (ii) the place to be assigned to the religious and mythical component in their thinking, (iii) the correct assessment of the rational element unquestionably present in the thought of individual pre-Socratics whatever its extent or limitations. How far back is the metaphysical as distinct from the physical mode of theorizing to be traced? To Parmenides, by general agreement, but perhaps even earlier? Were these thinkers scientists, and were they the first scientists? Did any of them seek to establish their doctrines by experiment, as distinct from mere observation, and if they did not, were there others in the sixth- or fifth-century Greek world who did so? Kerferd adds a further question, arising on a different level since it is not openly discussed by those concerned. Is it advisable for the historian of thought frankly to approach the study with philosophical interests of his own? If he does, there is a risk of distortion of fact and false evaluation, but if, remaining philosophically neutral, he records the achievements of these thinkers as cosmologists, it may be felt that something is missed. 'The only remedy is eternal vigilance and the determined use of the whole apparatus of scholarship applied to all the evidence before any interpretation is propounded—mere intuitive accounts can no longer be accepted as sufficient.'

I must send the reader to Kerferd for all detail of work devoted to pre-Socratic thought and the Sophists during the nine years covered by his review. Within the last years the second volume of Guthrie's history including the account of the Eleatics, Empedocles, Anaxagoras and the atomists has been published. Michael Stokes breaks new ground with a comparison between the cosmology of Hesiod and that of the three early Milesian thinkers.[2] Professor C. J. de Vogel, in a reconstruction of early Pythagoreanism,[3] makes use of evidence now often regarded as suspect, though it rests on the authority of historians of the fourth century B.C. There are some new publications on Parmenides.[4] After a burst of activity concerning Anaxagoras, several scholars have now taken part in a debate on the interpretation of the cosmic cycle in Empedocles's theory,[5] with reference especially to the genesis of plants and animals; and the first parts of an interesting work on this philospher by J. Bollack[6] have appeared. I return below to the point mentioned by Kerferd concerning Theophrastus as a historian of opinion.

Kerferd is able to mention numerous works written from 1953 onwards on the individual sophists. He holds that 'while there is a growing recognition of the philosophic importance of the major sophists, this has yet to be reflected in any large-scale treatment which will present the detailed evidence and not at the same time give a distorted or eccentric view of the movement as a whole.'[7]

Socrates. Sir David Ross is right in maintaining (p. 161 above) that the thesis of Burnet regarding the historical Socrates is now defunct. The common assumption is that Plato's Apology has only a remote relation to the actual speech of Socrates at the trial.[8]

Plato and the Academy. Anyone who has engaged as scholar or philosophical critic in Platonic study with some faint hope of making a contribution of his own knows that the first hindrance is the crippling weight of already existing literature. It is a convenient, but surely weak and unscientific, course to limit the range of one's vision to the work of admired teachers and compatriots. Those who are thus embarrassed can for the present follow behind two oecumenically minded guides: Professor Harold Cherniss in two successive volumes of *Lustrum*[9] has summarized with some critical comment the books and articles published between 1950 and 1957; Dr. E. M. Manasse has reviewed in separate articles[10] (i) the literature on Plato in the German language between, roughly, 1930 and 1962 and (ii) that

APPENDIX

during the same period in English. I presume that there is a third instalment in preparation. The author says he did not accept the language division without some hesitation. But his policy conforms to the facts and is realistic.

Is there any progress — is there a path through the maze? It is now just a century since Campbell in the Introduction to his edition of the Sophistes and Politicus adopted the method of fixing the order of composition of the dialogues by a statistical study of style and vocabulary. He and later practitioners of the method independently reached certain conclusions. The Phaedrus is not a work of Plato's youth. The Theaetetus and Parmenides were written after the Phaedo and Republic. Next, but probably after an interval, come the Sophistes and Politicus, in which Socrates has been superseded as the leading speaker. Finally, there is a group of writings, to which the Timaeus and Critias belong, wherein some features of style already visible in the Sophistes are accentuated. In one of these (Philebus) Socrates again conducts the discussion.

The problem since about 1900 has been how to give on this basis an account of Plato's development, especially in the theory of knowledge, which shall be plausible from both a biographical and a philosophical point of view. This is what in their day C. Ritter and Stenzel, Taylor and Cornford, Diès and Robin were seeking to do. Some spoke of a continuous golden thread, others found signs of a fresh start by the sexagenarian philosopher after a phase of ambitious construction. Some others believed in no real development at all. Some spurned, and some sympathetically accepted, the help of Aristotle.

A useful sample of more recent interpretation of Plato is provided by the collection of twenty articles published under the title *Studies in Plato's Metaphysics*.[11] (Most of these were previously published in journals, some in 1930-40, the majority since 1950.) Considering the collection as a whole, I do not think there has been a remarkable shift in the range of discussion. Even if one or two essayists are trying to shake the modern consensus of opinion about the sequence of the dialogues, the formulation of topics continues to have some reference to it. But the analysis of the meaning of words and structure of arguments is more searching, and in consequence the range of possible explanations is not quite the same today as it once was. I think it is also the case that passages of a logical nature in such a dialogue as the Sophistes have yielded up some of their meaning to modern philosophers worried by similar problems.

The Parmenides is a particularly hard nut to crack. G. Vlastos, in a paper reproduced in the volume mentioned, makes a determined assault on the problem whether the Third Man argument is a valid refutation of the separate Forms. He and others, by a precise presentation of this criticism, have made it clear what assumptions on the part of the maintainer of the Forms will make it valid. It could then in turn be asked whether Plato previous to writing the Parmenides usually made those assumptions; if so, whether he was aware that it was they which made him vulnerable to the objection; and if he did know this (perhaps, as a matter of fact, he was perplexed, and wrote the dialogue for precisely that reason), whether he nevertheless continued to make them (here the chronology of the dialogues comes in).

Various and opposite answers to these last questions are given by the contributors to the above-mentioned volume, and the disputes are not ended by the citation of particular passages, since each wants to read these in his own manner. A related discussion by no means terminated yet concerns the date of the Timaeus and its relation to other dialogues.[12]

Whether or not the separate Forms are still asserted in the Philebus, we see Plato at work there with a procedure apparently independent of them and of the horizontal division of the world which they bring with them: namely, the use of the principles limit, unlimited, and cause of mixture. With them also he operated in the lecture or lectures entitled 'On the Good', given either to selected followers or to all who cared to hear. The facts are obscure. While English-speaking scholars have remained rather sceptical about this unwritten Platonism, or at least, about the possibility of recovering it, H. J. Krämer in an important work[13] has endeavoured to show that Plato held an esoteric doctrine, which he deliberately reserved as a precious secret for the few; that this was by no means a late development, since it can be detected by reading between the lines of most of the dialogues; and that the title 'On the Good' is significant. The dualistic derivation from principles provided a basis for judgments of value. K. Gaiser assists Krämer by bringing together the evidence

APPENDIX

for the scientific activity of the Academy and showing its connection with the doctrine of principles,[14] and E. Berti (in a book, however, which will be more conveniently considered under another heading) stresses the importance of the same doctrine as a link between Plato and Aristotle. This recent research is in my opinion to be welcomed. It may be questioned whether what is novel in the conclusions is wholesome. But it is also fairly plain that it has not yet received the attention it deserves in the English-speaking world.

The writers just mentioned assume the genuineness of the VIIth Epistle. Thirty-five years ago this opinion had the weight of authority behind it and looked like an encouraging conquest of modern scholarship. About fifteen years ago an attentive observer could see fluctuations and a current beginning to move in the other direction; and now it is low tide again.[15] One must not despair. But it might be wise to look at the possibility that this and others among the Platonic letters are composite products. Agreement about their genuineness may be hard to secure because there is real force in the arguments used on both sides.

There have also appeared much-needed commentaries and other good expository work in abundance.[16]

Aristotle and Theophrastus. I begin with studies devoted to Aristotle's development, and take up the story where it was left by Sir D. Ross, pp. 163-5 above. Jaeger's presentation of Aristotle's earliest philosophy was coloured by his confident belief that in both the Eudemus and Protrepticus Aristotle subscribed to the doctrine of the separate Forms. He set apart, as a later dialogue, the de philosophia, in which these were certainly criticized. As he did not discuss in any detail the works de Ideis and de bono, he did not make clear where he thought they fitted into the series. Fifteen years ago it was still usual to regard this part of Jaeger's reconstruction as sound, whatever doubts might be felt about his resolution of the treatises into strata.

Our information about the de Ideis is, however, comparatively full. It was brought into the picture by some scholars in 1930-40; and recent inquirers have continued this work besides devoting attention to the de Bono. They have also — nearly all[17] assuming that the passages in Iamblichus's Protrepticus were rightly assigned by Bywater and Jaeger to Aristotle's work of that name — looked afresh at the passages noted as Platonic by Jaeger. As a result, it has become the fashion to say that Aristotle at no time subscribed to the belief in the Forms; and that the de Ideis is to be dated c. 355 B.C. and perhaps associated with the Platonic Parmenides itself as an expression of dissatisfaction with the two-world theory.

But now the roads divide. In his edition of fragments of the Protrepticus[18] as well as in previous writings, I. Düring finds already visible Aristotle's later philosophy of nature and his tenets about practical reason. According to him not only are the Forms absent, but several key conceptions of the mature Aristotle are present, and the work is no *Jugendschrift*. Others regard it as more significant that, Forms or no Forms, the language and style of thought in the Protrepticus (if indeed a single strain of music is heard there and it was not a dialogue) is highly Platonic. To identify Platonism with acceptance of the separate Forms is rather superficial. If so, Jaeger's characterization of the first phase is not so wide of the mark.

This is the outcome of an admirably planned and informative work by E. Berti on the philosophy of the younger Aristotle,[19] a book written with clarity and philosophical insight, which gives a fair and intelligent, and I think exhaustive, review of previous research. Berti rejects Jaeger's dating of the de philosophia, which he sees as closely related to Plato's Timaeus, agrees with the critics who hold that Aristotle never professed the separate Forms, and regards the Protrepticus as the work of an Aristotle now near to maturity. And yet — the general outcome is that he was a loyal member of the Academy whose entire literary output was, in one way or another, for a long time concerned with the public defence of its educational ideals. (He took the lead in controversy with the school of Isocrates). If he would have nothing to do with the transcendent Forms, he took over and built into his own physics the equally Platonic doctrine of principles. His early dialogues, so far as now accessible to us, and his master's late dialogues gain by being seen in close relation to one another.

But in this sphere of research, movement is rapid and, to take one instance, the last two years have seen three more notable studies concerned with de philosophia.[20]

I now proceed to note, with what may seem arbitrary selection, some work on the Aristotelian system. The Physics is a treatise which has not been studied with much enthusiasm or comprehension in the modern world. But Ross's commentary (1937)

APPENDIX

was valuable, and one may now record the appearance of two works of fine scholarship, in a sense complementary to one another. F. Solmsen[21] explains clearly in what way Aristotle and Plato diverge in the concepts they use for the interpretation of nature, commencing with an account of the revival of physical science after the blows it had received from Parmenides. W. Wieland,[22] concerned more with the relevance of Aristotle's argument to modern inquiry into the foundations of science, enlarges upon the undoubtedly true observation that what was superseded at the time of the Renaissance was his cosmology, rather than that sort of analysis which fills the treatise on Physics. Today, when there is doubt concerning the principles of physics and when linguistic philosophy flourishes, we can better understand what Aristotle endeavoured to do. He did not set about the construction of an all-inclusive system of nature, but tried to elicit by analysis what human beings from the first carry in their minds — the structure that is presupposed as they watch natural processes and represent their experience in words. Judging by Aristotle's actual procedure, he thought the explanatory 'principles' of physics were to be ascertained largely by scrutiny of the forms of speech. Wieland thus gives an exposition which has the effect of releasing physics from the chaperonage of metaphysics — making it *prior* to the latter, as the ancient title implies. This involves a break with tradition.

A judicious commentary accompanies the new German translation of the de anima by W. Theiler.[23] The thesis of Nuyens regarding the development of Aristotle's psychology, stated above by Ross (p. 165) and favourably viewed by him, has been independently criticized by I. T. Block and W. F. R. Hardie.[24] They hold that Aristotle might well have employed at one time, but for different purposes, a form-matter and a user-instrument description of the relation between soul and body, because these are not inconsistent with one another. I think that Theiler also would agree in this.

Nuyens's principles are, on the other hand, approved and applied by R. A. Gauthier and J. Y. Jolif in the Introduction to their commentary on the *Nicomachean Ethics*.[25] After describing Aristotle's evolution in what must now be classed as conservative terms, in the manner of Jaeger, they maintain that the treatise is not founded upon Aristotle's late psychology and theory of the intellect, but on the psychology of the time of transition. In the department of Aristotelian ethics, these years have been remarkably productive. Besides the fine commentary (with translation) just mentioned, F. Dirlmeier has translated with a first-rate commentary not only the Nicomachean version, but the *Magna Moralia* and *Eudemian Ethics*.[26] While he proceeds on the assumption of the genuineness of the *Magna Moralia*, apart from possible shaping by an editor, this is questioned by the present writer, and now in an interesting and thorough work by P. L. Donini.[27]

The Politics is the subject of a volume representing the *Entretiens* held at the Fondation Hardt in the summer of 1965.[28] A version of book III, with Introduction, by Richard Robinson, appears in a new series issued by Oxford University Press and designed for philosophical students.[29] Aristotle's work and influence in the field of history, biography and theory of historical writing are surveyed in a masterly manner by K. von Fritz.[30]

The Topics was the subject of a Symposium Aristotelicum held at Oxford in 1963, of which the proceedings will shortly be published. A previous symposium held at Louvain resulted in the volume *Aristote et les problèmes de méthode*.[31] J. L. Ackrill has translated, for the Oxford series mentioned just above, the Categories and de interpretatione.[32] In a work on Aristotle's theory of science, M. Mignucci[33] takes up the important question whether Aristotle's formal logic can be pronounced quite free from metaphysical assumptions.

The ever-fascinating subject of Aristotle's philosophy of action has attracted several writers.[34]

Bywater's text of the Poetics (1st ed. 1909, 2nd ed. 1911) has now been superseded in the series of Oxford texts.[35] The new editor, R. Kassel, makes use of the fourteenth-century Florence manuscript Riccardianus 46, known to, but neglected by, his predecessor. He also brings in the evidence of the thirteenth-century Greek-Latin version, the text of which has been edited from manuscripts subsequent to Bywater, who even denied its existence. The treatise is the subject of interesting books by G. F. Else and J. Jones.[36]

Jaeger's text of the Metaphysics appeared in 1957 in the series of Oxford texts.[37] While no doubt most aspects of Aristotle's 'first philosophy' have been discussed somewhere during these years, what is most to the front is the meaning and possible

APPENDIX

chronological development of his views concerning the province of the supreme philosophical study. The debate goes back to the Greek commentators. Some expositors leave Aristotle with both a general ontology and a theology, either of which he might term, on occasion, first philosophy. Others, relying on texts from book E ch. 2, and book K, leave him with the latter only. According to these, to study 'being *qua* being' is to study immaterial substance, because this is the ground of physical substance, which in turn is the ground of being in the other categories. I shall not try to summarize the discussion further, and will refer the reader to the work of the contestants themselves.[38]

Emerson Buchanan, in an interesting essay,[39] questions the effectiveness of the vocabulary used by English translators of the Metaphysics, which is of course in some cases inherited from Latin translators. He may well be right in this, but I do not think it affects what has just been described. P. Aubenque sees Aristotle in this department as a raiser of problems, who does not expect to achieve solutions.[40]

The Kuratorium of the Free University Berlin resolved in 1965 upon the establishment of an Aristoteles-Archiv in its *Seminar für klassische Philologie*; this is under the directorship of Professor Paul Moraux. The main field of research is the transmission of the Greek text of Aristotle. An index of manuscripts has already been compiled, a full collection of microfilms of those previous to A.D. 1600 is being formed, and the ultimate aim will be to publish a precise description of the preserved manuscripts.

Coming to Theophrastus, I take up first from p. 170 above the point that he has been regarded as an unreliable historian of ideas because his judgments and criticisms seem to echo those of Aristotle. Diels, besides showing that later summarizers of doctrine drew their material from the Φυσικῶν Δόξαι, held that what has come down to us as the de sensu is probably a section drawn intact from that work, and again that Simplicius, quoting Theophrastus through one or two intermediaries, reproduces him accurately. He held that the work rested on more specialized studies of individual philosophers, of which the titles are known to us. Finally, he represents Theophrastus as collecting and conforming to the judgments in his master's treatises.

These statements are, I think, now sometimes repeated, with unfortunate results, without reservations which Diels attached to them. Firstly the de sensu is more critical than the Φυσικῶν Δόξαι, as a whole, appears to have been. Secondly, it is going beyond the evidence to explain every concord of Aristotle and Theophrastus in an historical judgment by the subservience of the latter. The probability is that Aristotle saw and used his colleague's work, so far as it had been completed. Every passage must be examined with this possibility in mind.

The physical system of Theophrastus is the subject of a recent work by P. Steinmetz;[41] the same scholar has edited the Characters;[42] so, also, has R. G. Ussher.[43] Some researches of G. Senn,[44] on the order of composition of the botanical treatises, have been published posthumously.

Stoicism. The student of logic can now turn to Benson Mates, as well as to the Greek chapters in the history of logic by William and Martha Kneale,[45] for a sympathetic account of the Stoic system, which is now universally seen as a genuine advance beyond Aristotle. In a somewhat similar fashion, S. Sambursky, in a work on the physics of the Stoics,[46] points out that the modern interest in ancient atomism, which is easy enough to explain, has brought about some neglect of the rival system. His thesis is that, even though physics to the Stoics themselves was of less importance than logic, they developed an original and consistent system of physical concepts and applied it to the whole body of their teaching. In these we find anticipated basic ideas which have governed physical thought since the eighteenth century. They were the theorists of the continuum, and they viewed the continuum not so much spatially as dynamically. The main theory was erected by Zeno and Chrysippus, the most important later additions — that is, the concepts of pneuma and of 'sympathy' — were due to Poseidonius. Finally, G. Verbeke expounds Stoic opinion concerning progress in history.[47]

---

[1] 'Recent Work on PreSocratic Philosophy', *American Philosophical Quarterly*, vol. 2, no. 2, (1965), pp. 1-11.
[2] 'Hesiodic and Milesian Cosmogonies', *Phronesis*, vol. VII, no. 1 (1962), pp. 1-37 and vol. VIII, no. 1 (1963), pp. 1-34.
[3] *Pythagoras and Early Pythagoreanism* — an interpretation of ancient evidence, Assen (Van Gorcum), 1966.
[4] *Parmenides' Auffahrt zur Göttin des Rechts*, [Abh. Mainz Akad. d. Wiss., 1958], Wiesbaden, 1959, by K. Deichgräber. *Die Offenbarung des Parm. und die menschliche Welt*, Assen (Van Gorcum), 1964, by M. J. Mansfeld. Parmenides, a text with trans.,

commentary and critical essays, Princeton Univ. Press (1965), by Leonardo Tarán. *Der Logosbegriff bei Heraklit und Parmenides, Phronesis*, vol. XI (1966), pp. 81-98, by W. J. Verdenius.
[5] I refer only to the last, which is the article of F. Solmsen in *Phronesis*, vol. X (1965), pp. 109-148.
[6] *Empédocle*, vol. I, *Introd. à l'ancienne physique*, vol. II, *Les origines* — Texte, traduction, commentaire, by Jean Bollack, Paris (1965).
[7] There is now an English translation of M. Untersteiner's work on the Sophists (Oxford, 1954 (Blackwell)).
[8] Thomas Meyer, *Platons Apologie*, Stuttgart, 1962 (Tübinger Beiträge zur Altertumswiss. 42), shows that Plato in the Apology and elsewhere some rhetorical tropes which are found in the orators; by raising them to a higher level he makes them practically less effective. Gilbert Ryle in *Plato's Progress* (Cambridge U.P., 1966) wishes to connect the Apol. with an inferred prosecution, either of Plato himself, or of someone closely connected with him, on a charge of defamation; this was successful, and led to the cessation of Plato's instruction of young men in dialectic, and so of that kind of dialogue in which this had been reflected. Ryle explains passages in the Meno and Gorgias which seem loosely attached to the context as additions made to the written version of these works after such a prosecution. It would be dated *c.* 375-370, which means giving the Apol. a later date than scholars usually accept. On the Socratic problem in general, see review by O. Gigon of two works by V. de Magalhaes-Vilhéna, *Gnomon* 27 (1955) 259-66.
[9] *Lustrum*, vol. 4 (1959), and 5 (1960).
[10] *Philosophische Rundschau*, Tübingen, vol. V, Beiheft I and IX Beih. II, 1957 and 1961.
[11] *Studies in Plato's Metaphysics*, ed. by R. E. Allen, London (Routledge), 1965.
[12] See article on date of Timaeus by G. E. L. Owen and criticism thereof by H. Cherniss in the volume mentioned in last note. Owen from various indications judges that Tim. belongs philosophically, as it seems to do in its dramatic setting, to the Republic-Phaedo group. It is especially significant that one passage asserts the horizontal division between knowledge and opinion and their objects. Owen turns aside the evidence from vocabulary by giving preference to other tests still of a stylistic nature. It is, however, fair to urge (i) that perhaps this only shows that Plato did not formally abandon the Forms, and (ii) that to prise out Tim. from the later dialogues is to weaken the structure on which the critic is otherwise still standing. Should we not accept the sovereignty of stylometry unless we definitely want to return to the competitiveness of the state of nature? I express no personal opinion.
[13] *Aretê bei Platon und Aristoteles*, Abh. Heidelberg phil. hist. Kl., 1959. The criticism of Vlastos in *Gnomon* 35 (1963), 541-55 ought perhaps to be read in conjunction with K.'s *Retraktationen zum Problem des esoterischen Platon*, M.H. 21 (1964), 137-67. See now also K. von Fritz in *Phronesis*, vol. XI (1966), 117-53, who while defending the authenticity of the philosophical passage in *Ep.* VII, denies that it gives confirmation to the theory of a secret doctrine deliberately witheld from the outer world.
[14] *Platons ungeschriebene Lehre*, Stuttgart, 1963. By same author — *Die Elegie des Aristoteles an Eudemos, Mus. Helv.*, vol. 23 (1966), 84-106.
[15] G. Boas, *Philosophical Review*, LVII (1948), 439-57, claims to prove misunderstanding of the dialogues by the writer of *Ep.* VII. In Germany, its authenticity was questioned by G. Müller, *Archiv für Philosophie*, III (1949) 251ff. Gilbert Ryle, *op. cit.* (note 8 above) argues that the writer is unsuccessfully disguising the fact that Plato's invitation to Syracuse came from the elder Dionysius, not his son. He suggests that some of the Epistles were forged in the interest of Dion's followers.
[16] Text with commentary — *Gorgias*, E. R. Dodds, Oxford, 1959; *Meno*, R. S. Bluck, Cambridge U.P., 1961. Among other services these rectify a fault in Burnet's collation of F. *Parmenides*, R. S. Brumbaugh, *Plato on the One*, New Haven, Yale U.P., 1961 (new collation of manuscripts). *Epinomis*, E. des Places, Paris, 1956 (Collection Budé, Tome XII, 2me partie).

Exposition mainly concerned with one dialogue — *Plato's Cretan City*, Glenn R. Morrow, Princeton U.P., 1960; *Plato's Use of Fallacy*, Rosamund K. Sprague, London (Routledge), 1962; *Plato's Republic*, R. C. Cross and A. D. Woozley, London (Macmillan), 1964.

English translations — various. There is a revised ed. of Morrow's *Epistles*, Library of Liberal Arts, 1961.
Index: *Lexique de la langue philosophique et religieuse de Platon* (Tome XIV in Budé edition of Plato) by E. des Places, Paris, 1964. Not offered as a complete Lexicon which would supersede that of Ast. Of more general scope — *An Examination of Plato's Doctrines* (two vols.), I. M. Crombie, vol. I 1962, vol. II 1963, London (Routledge); *Plato's Later Epistemology*, W. G. Runciman, Cambridge, 1962.

[17] This is disputed by W. Gerson Rabinowitz, *Arist.'s Protrepticus and the sources of its reconstruction*, Berkeley, 1957 (Univ. Calif. Publ. in Classical Philology 16).

[18] *Arist.'s Protrepticus — an attempt at reconstruction* — Studia Graeca et Latina Gothoburgensia XII, 1957. References to the author's earlier writings will be found there. See also — J. D. Monan, *La connaissance morale dans la Protreptique d'Aristote*, Rev. Phil. de Louvain 58 (1960) 185-219; A. H. Chroust, *Arist. Protrepticus* — a reconstruction, Notre Dame, Indiana, 1964; the contributions of E. de Strycker and S. Mansion in *Aristotle and Plato in the mid-fourth century* (ed. Düring and Owen), Göteborg, 1960; and the critical notice of this by Ch. Lefèvre, *Du plàtonisme à l'aristotélisme*, Rev. Phil. de Louvain 59 (1961).

[19] *La filosofia del primo Aristotele*, Univ. di Padova, Pubbl. Fac. di Lettere e di Filosofia, vol. XXXVIII, 1962.

[20] M. Untersteiner, Arist. *Della filosofia*, Collect. Temi e Testi, 10, Roma, 1963; P. Moraux, article *Quinta Essentia*, Pauly-Wissowa, 47, Halbbd., (1963), col. 1171-1266; J. Pépin, *L'interprétation du de Philosophia d'Aristote*, REG LXXVII (1964), 445-88; W. Haase, *Ein vermeintliches Aristotelesfragment* in *Synusia* — Festgabe für W. Schadewaldt, ed. H. Flashar and K. Gaiser, Tübingen, 1965.

[21] *Arist.'s system of the physical world* — a comparison with his predecessors, Cornell Studies in Classical Philology XXXIII, 1960.

[22] *Die Aristotelische Physik*, Göttingen, 1962. Critical notice by E. Tugendhat in *Gnomon* 35 (1963), 543-55. In expansion of what is said in the text, I refer to my own review CR XVI (1966) 168-71. Wieland has a provocative section on teleology in Aristotle — for this see also Marjorie Grene, *Portrait of Aristotle*, London (Faber), 1963; D. M. Balme, *Arist.'s use of the teleological explanation*. Inaugural Lecture, Queen Mary College, Univ. of London, 1965; L. Bourgey, *Observation et expérience chez Aristote*, Paris, 1955; I note here also the appearance of the Oxford text of *de generatione animalium* ed. by H. J. Drossaart Lulofs, Oxford, 1965; of ed. 2 of the commentary of Verdenius and Waszink on *de gen. et corr.* (1966); and of editions of the *de Caelo* by P. Moraux (Collection Budé, 1965) and L. Elders *Aristotle's Cosmology*, Assen (Van Gorcum), 1966.

[23] *Aristoteles Werke in deutscher Übersetzung* herausgeg. Ernst Grumach, Berlin (Akademie-Verlag), Band 13, 1959.

[24] *The Order of Arist.'s psychological writings*, AJP 82 (1961), 50-77; 'Arist.'s Treatment of the Relation between the Soul and the Body', *Philosophical Quarterly*, vol. 14 (1964), pp. 53-72.

[25] *L'Éthique à Nicomaque*, three vols., Louvain 1958-9. Shorter work by R. A. Gauthier, *La Morale d'Aristote*, Paris, 1958.

[26] Same Collection as named in note 23 — Band 6, *Nikomachische Ethik* (1956), Band 8, *Magna Moralia* (1958), Band 7, *Eudemische Ethik* (1962).

[27] D. J. Allan in *Gnomon* 38 (1966) 138-49; P. L. Donini, *L'Etica dei Magna Moralia*, Torino, 1965.

[28] *Entretiens de la Fondation Hardt*, Genève-Vandœuvres, 1965.

[29] *Politics* books III and IV, trans. with Introd. and comments, Oxford (Clarendon Aristotle), 1962.

[30] *Arist.'s contribution to the practice and theory of historiography*, Univ. of California Publ. in Philosophy, vol. 28 (1958), pp. 113-38. Berkeley.

[31] Ed. by S. Mansion, Louvain, 1961 (Collection Aristote-traductions et études.)

[32] *Categories* and *de Interpretatione*, trans. with notes and glossary, Oxford (Clarendon Aristotle), 1963.

[33] M. Mignucci, *La teoria aristotelica della scienza*, Pubbl. della Fac. di. Magistero della Univ. di Padova: Firenze (Sansoni), 1965.

[34] E. M. Michaelakis, *Arist.'s Theory of Practical Principles*, Athens (Cleisiounis), 1961; P. Aubenque, *La prudence chez Aristote*, Paris, 1963; J. J. Walsh, *Arist.'s conception of*

APPENDIX

moral weakness, Paris (Presses Universitaires), 1963; Takatura Ando, *Arist.'s Theory of Practical Cognition*, ed. 1 1958, ed. 2 1965. The Hague (Nijhoff).

[35] *Aristotelis de arte poetica* recogn. R. Kassel, Oxford, 1965.

[36] *Aristotle's Poetics: the argument*, Cambridge (Harvard U.P.), G. F. Else (whose 'Survey of Work on Aristotle's Poetics,' 1940-1954' in CW 48 (1954-55), 73-82, may here be mentioned; *Aristotle and Greek Tragedy* by John Jones, London (Chatto and Windus) 1962. Here it is argued that commentators, ignoring Arist.'s positive statement that a tragedy is an imitation of an *action*, have read the tragic hero into the Poetics. They have then looked for him in the tragedies themselves, and have, of course, found him.

[37] *Aristotelis metaphysica* recogn. W. Jaeger, Oxford, 1957. Critical notice by R. Walzer, *Gnomon* 31 (1959), 586-92.

[38] Joseph Owens, The Doctrine of Being in the Aristotelian Metaphysics, ed. 1 1951, ed. 2 1963 with new Foreword: Toronto (Pontifical Institute of Medieval Studies) 1963; P. Merlan, *From Platonism to Neo-Platonism*, ed. 1 1953, ed. 2 1960, The Hague; A. Mansion, *L'objet de la science philosophique suprême d'après Arist. Métaph.* E 1, in Mélanges de Phil. Grecques offerts à Mgr. A. Diès, Paris (Vrin) 1956, also *Philosophie première* . . . *chez Arist.* in *Rev. phil. de Louvain* 56 (1958), 165-221; V. Décarie *L'objet de la métaphysique selon Aristote*, Montreal (Institut d'études médiévales) and Paris (Vrin), 1961.

[39] *Aristotle's Theory of Being*, Univ. of Mississippi Publications, 1962.

[40] *Le problème de l'être chez Aristote* — essai sur la problématique aristotélicienne. See J. Brunschwig, 'Dialectique et ontologie chez Aristote', *Rev. Philos. de la France et de l'étranger*, Paris, 1964.

[41] *Die Physik des Theophrastus von Eresos*, Bad Homburg, 1964.

[42] Theophr. Charaktere hrsg. und erklärt von P. Steinmetz, München (das Wort des Antike), 1960.

[43] Theophr. Characters, ed. R. G. Ussher, London (Macmillan), 1960.

[44] *Die Pflanzenkunde des Theophrastos von Eresos*, hrsg. von O. Gigon, Basel, 1956. I have not seen Theophrastus *On Stones*, Introd., text, trans. and comm. by E. R. Caley and J. F. C. Richards, Columbus (Ohio), 1956. Texts only are mentioned, as it is impossible to review here the extensive literature concerning Theophrastus during these years.

[45] B. Mates, *Stoic Logic*, Univ. of California Press, 1961; William and Martha Kneale, *The Development of Logic*, Oxford, 1962.

[46] *The Physics of the Stoics*, London (Routledge), 1959.

[47] *Les Stoïciens et le progrès de l'histoire*, Rev. Phil. de Louvain 62 (1964) 5-38.

Postscript. To the surveys of literature on Plato mentioned in notes 9 and 10 there should be added: *Vingt années d'études Platoniciennes*, by P-M. Schuhl, in *Études Platoniciennes* (Paris, 1960). This is a reprint of an address given in 1953. The range of this Appendix has been limited by a double ἀνάγκη, that of space, and that of the author's knowledge. It should no doubt have been rounded off by a survey of progress in the study of post-Aristotelian philosophy as a whole, and especially of neo-Platonism. Enquirers can, however, be directed to two volumes in the *Entretiens sur l'antiquité classique* published by the Fondation Hardt, Vandœuvres-Genève: Tome V (1960) *Les sources de Plotin*, and Tome XII (1966) *Porphyre*. The Cambridge History of Later Greek and Early Mediæval Philosophy edited by A. H. Armstrong made its appearance after the period covered by this Appendix.

CHAPTER VI

THE GREEK HISTORIANS[1]

BY G. T. GRIFFITH

FIFTY years ago the tranquil surface of classical studies in the field of the Greek historians was still dancing with the waves created by the re-discovery of the Aristotelian *Constitution of Athens*; and the ripples are still to be seen to this day. Every Greek scholar must reserve a corner of his heart for Egypt, and live always in the hope of a new papyrus. These fifty years have not produced in this field another *Constitution*, but they have not treated us badly. True, the papyrus 'finds' of Greek historical writings that are both new and exactly identifiable are comparatively few and small, though they include the Didymus commentary on Demosthenes with its wealth of reference to and citation from historians of the fourth and third centuries B.C., and they include interesting fragments of Hellanicus, Philistus, Ephorus, Theopompus, Sosylus and (?) Phlegon.[2] But the finds which must still be labelled *Adespota* are more impressive, headed as they are by *Hellenica Oxyrhynchia*, that considerable fragment of a very considerable historian, whether we choose to call him Theopompus or Ephorus or Cratippus or Daimachus of Plataea, or plain Mr. X. And smaller discoveries have added to knowledge, and whetted the appetite, in matters so diverse as tyranny at Sicyon, Polycrates of Samos, the history of Boeotia and of the fourth century B.C., the activities of Alexander the Great and of more than one of his successors or *Epigonoi*, the history of the Ptolemies, of the Second Punic War, and of a Roman expedition against Ethiopians. To the Oxyrhynchus historian we shall return. For information on the lesser discoveries the reader must be referred in the main to the special studies which they have inspired.[3]

One of the solemn thoughts suggested by these new fragments of knowledge as they appear is, how small a portion of the whole corpus of Greek historical writing has in fact survived. The assembly of the Greek historians is full of ghosts. These are the writers known to us only by the citations from their works, or references to them, which we find in the writings of authors who

THE GREEK HISTORIANS

do survive; the writers whose character must necessarily remain relatively indistinct and unsubstantial, and in some cases positively vague. Yet one of the first tasks of modern scholarship, in these fifty years as before it, has been to collect, analyse, assess, and use to the full every scrap of information available concerning this world of ghosts; not only from a natural desire to make their better acquaintance, but also because, though ghosts for us, they were alive for most of their Greek successors in the writing of history, and in fact provided their successors with much of their material. It is vital (to take an example) to know what Ptolemy was like as a historian, in order to arrive at a fair judgment of Arrian who used his book. One modern figure pervades this world and marshals (as it were) the spirits: Felix Jacoby, whose monumental *Fragmente der griechischen Historiker* comprises, in so far as the work of one man can, the sum of human knowledge in this field.[4]

Nowhere in the study of Greek historical writings is this consciousness of absent friends more strong than in its very beginnings. For of History, no less than of the Epic, it is true to say that we are presented with it in full flower, and are left to guess at its seed-time and the shoot and the bud. Of the historical element in the Epic itself this is not the place in which to speak. But the beginnings of Greek prose writing, had those early works come down to us, would certainly be beyond price. Herodotus and Thucydides, both in style and in outlook, are completely mature writers. Though it may be true that no genuine *historian*, who wrote before them, has perished, yet no one will doubt that the authors or transmitters of *stories* (*logoi*) in prose represented a formative period which was either very long or very intense (or even both), and of which only some of the later representatives, those who committed stories to writing, are known to us even by name. Originating in a desire to entertain, the spoken story, transmitted by word of mouth, must be nearly as old as speech itself. When the desire to instruct is added, the story becomes material to some one (or more) of a number of serious pursuits, among them history. The man who focuses his attention on particular topics, or particular places or periods of time, and writes down the stories that he has been able to collect about them, is not yet an anthropologist or a geographer or a historian, but he has taken the first steps, and has marked a path for those who follow. These early storytellers have been studied to good purpose by Aly and others, not only for their own sake but also for the relation in which they stand to the History of Herodotus;[5] for the fact that Herodotus never mentions earlier writers except occasionally to disparage them cannot be taken to mean that he made no use of them. On the contrary, it is hard to see from where much of the material of his earlier books can have been taken if not from them. Xanthus of Lydia and especially Hecataeus of Miletus suggest themselves as writers whom Herodotus is likely to have consulted;[6] and though his debt to Xanthus seems slighter than a remark of Ephorus would lead us to expect, that to Hecataeus is important. Although its extent has been the subject of controversy which began long before the present century, and in which the very genuineness of the Hecataeus fragments has been called in question, the issue will probably never again be in doubt.[7] Herodotus used the *Periegesis* of Hecataeus extensively, though by no means slavishly, as his occasional expressions of dissatisfaction sufficiently show. But to judge from the fragments that survive, Herodotus far surpassed Hecataeus and other predecessors, and also indeed his younger contemporary Hellanicus of Lesbos, in (among other things) the literary quality of his writings. It was his archaic simplicity of style that chiefly accounted perhaps for the eclipse of Hecataeus for many generations after Herodotus wrote. Hellanicus too, and for the same reason, though he lived long and wrote much, made comparatively little impression on his nearest posterity. The valuable work which has been done on him in the last fifty years underlines the previously existing picture of him as the last and most versatile of the writers of *Logoi*, his twenty-four known titles covering works purely mythological, works dealing with particular regions or peoples including the interesting *Atthis* which will be mentioned later, works mainly chronological, and one or more works (four titles are known) bearing on ethnology in general.[8] But nothing has arisen from the study of his surviving fragments, apart perhaps from the *Atthis*, to make us think that the customary line of demarcation should be rubbed out, the line that separates the last of the 'storytellers' from the first of the historians.

It is perhaps inevitable that a writer so attractive as Herodotus should have been from time to time a target for attack by later writers, from Plutarch onwards, who pursued narrower objectives than he, and perhaps pursued them with a more selfconscious (though not necessarily more real) seriousness of purpose. Such

THE GREEK HISTORIANS

attacks were not lacking among the studies of Herodotus that appeared in the late nineteenth century, some of which found grave fault with his credibility in general; a historian who failed to indicate his debts to earlier writers or to apply tests of veracity to the stories that he collected on his travels, who seemed to lack consistent criteria for judging evidence or determining causation, and who certainly lacked the practical experience of affairs so valuable to the describer of a great war.[9] These were the more important issues raised by his detractors. They did not, however, go unanswered even at that time. The sympathetic study of Macan reacted, perhaps even too far, against the fault-finding; and the comprehensive work of Hauvette not only passed a balanced judgment on these matters, but also served as a basis from which the work of the twentieth century has proceeded on various lines of enquiry.[10]

It has continued to seem (and it undoubtedly is) of first importance to establish so far as possible the how, the where, and the when of the History's composition; for only so is it possible to arrive at an understanding of the historian's development and achievement.[11] Even the modern aids to travel and research could not bring a work of this scope into the world quickly, and it is agreed that for Herodotus it must have been the labour of very many years. By the external evidence which comes from our knowledge, albeit scanty, of his life and travels, combined with the internal evidence of cross-references, occasional inconsistencies, and very occasional reference to contemporary events, the date of composition of particular sections has been hazarded and sometimes established. But how subjective even research of this kind can be is to be judged by the fact that the two views, that Books VII–IX were composed last, and that they were composed first, could be, and still are, maintained simultaneously.[12] Nor is it a merely academic problem. On the contrary, on the answer a man finds for this problem depends his view of the whole development of the world's first historian. Thus, if *we* could be transposed in time and place so as to find ourselves in Herodotus' shoes, with just the same evidence and resources, without doubt we should write Books VII–IX first (the evidence there being the easiest to collect and to check); and only gradually should we be driven back into the remoter and obscurer past, braving its greater dangers in the hope of learning and showing for certain how the great struggle with

Persia ever arose. But if in doing this we imagined ourselves to be imitating Herodotus we might be wrong, just as one of the acutest of the moderns was doubtless wrong when he wrote '... the Greek historian's method precludes him from choosing his subject. He cannot, like Gibbon, begin by wishing to write a great historical work, and go on to ask himself what he shall write about. The only thing he can write about is the events which have happened within living memory to people with whom he can have personal contact. Instead of the historian choosing the subject, the subject chooses the historian.'[13] This is probably wrong just *because* it is modern. And in the same way any reconstruction of Herodotus' composition which attributes to him a 'grand design' from the start or from near the start of his labours[14] seems less likely to be right than one which allows the History as we have it to have been not only composed but actually conceived piecemeal, whether as a series of originally unconnected *logoi* (Lydian, Egyptian, Assyrian, and so on),[15] or as an original *Persica* into which were interwoven contributory digressions great and small and upon which was eventually superimposed the crowning struggle of the Persian invasions of Greece.[16] Even the great are beginners once: and they may be expected to begin perhaps beyond, but not so very far beyond, where their predecessors and contemporaries leave off.

Whatever the final decision about the composition of the History as we now have it, it is certain that it contains much material which could well have been assembled by Hellanicus or an earlier writer of *logoi*, and which we now should describe as material for the geographer, the ethnographer, or the anthropologist.[17] It is the ultimate use made by Herodotus of this material, its blending into the great unity, as it appeared ultimately to him, of the story of Graeco-Persian relations, that distinguishes him from his predecessors and makes him a historian; because it pre-supposes in him a realization of the historical process. How good a historian he was remains to be determined, and this is perhaps the most important result of the work of the last fifty years; it has been, broadly speaking, a work of rehabilitation in the main successful.

The more important matters at issue here are, the methods used by Herodotus in collecting and treating his evidence, his performance *vis-à-vis* the problem of historical causation, and his performance as a literary artist. These questions have been in the forefront of all the general studies, and many of the particular studies, of modern years. His debt to earlier writers has been mentioned, but no one now will under-estimate the important part taken by his own travels, too, in the collection of his information. His reliability as an eye-witness has in general been established, even regarding some of those wonders of the Orient concerning which he was formerly most suspect.[18] On his ability to sift and interpret evidence which he got from foreigners by word of mouth, different views are still possible. No one will deny (to mention outstanding examples) that in his Egyptian stories he left us insufficient guidance for distinguishing myth from history even if he could so distinguish them himself; or that his picture of the army and fleet of Xerxes in 480 B.C. is false, even though the sources from which he drew it were sound; or that his account of the Ionians was distorted by the influence (presumably) of his Samian sources. But in his record of Greek affairs there is still no unanimity as to just how much to allow for its colouring by Athenian influence in general and by that of certain Athenian families in particular. His own twice-stated avowal of what he conceived to be his duty to the evidence remains a problem, and one not only of why he put many things in, but also of why he left some things out (as Myres has recently urged).[19] Finally, where rehabilitation has been least successful is on his work as a military historian; after all the interpretations and explanations of the moderns, the conclusion stands inescapable, that Herodotus left them too much which needed to be interpreted and explained.[20]

That Herodotus understood something of causation is apparent from the opening sentence of his History, and is to be expected of one who knew (who can doubt it?) of the works of the Ionian philosophers. But as between Fate, or Fortune, or the direct intervention of gods, or the power of Man to control his destiny by his own unaided efforts, it has always been, and it still is, hard to say just where he laid the ultimate or the chief responsibility.[21] Perhaps it is not unfair to conclude from the modern studies of these things that any interpretation which arrives at a perfectly coherent picture of the state of his mind is in danger of misleading us. It would indeed be extremely surprising if the first writer (so far as we know) who ever posed the question of causes to history *had* been able to supply a perfectly coherent answer; and just as we are not surprised when he occasionally explains some particular series of great events by trivial human causes, so it should not surprise us if we cannot reconstruct for him a secure philosophy of history in general.

The literary genius of Herodotus has never been in doubt. The uninterrupted flow of studies great and small embodying research into all aspects of his writing testifies to the fact that of all Greek writers he remains one of the most *read*.[22] His affinities with the Epic mode of exposition have been well brought out;[23] and it has been shown that there is reason to think that he was not untouched by the influences of the Tragic drama.[24] The speeches which he incorporated in his narrative have been the object of special study, though Rhetoric in the normal sense of the word as it is applied to Greek prose writers, passed him by — thank goodness:[25] though it seems almost certain that he must have heard speakers in the new style, he had the great good sense, for purposes of his own composition, to take no notice of them whatever. The highest tribute to his technical skill has been paid by so fine a judge as Denniston, and the standards applied by Denniston to his prose style can be applied just as fearlessly to his literary artistry in general.[26] He stands today as perhaps the most admired, as well as the most loved, of all Greek prose writers.

An age like this is not the age to neglect Thucydides; the twentieth century has studied him closely. And although for him, as for Herodotus, a problem of composition (and problems arising therefrom) has always been in the forefront, yet he has been well served too by the eminent scholars who have offered more comprehensive interpretations of him in recent years. Gomme and Finley, to name only two, have produced works of distinction; and Gomme's *Commentary*, when it is complete, will stand as a model of learning and sound judgment.[27]

The composition question itself, however, ever since Ullrich's work on the subject over 100 years ago,[28] has been one of controversy between those who have held that the History as we have it was composed at widely different times (the extremes being indicated by those passages in it which seem of necessity to have been written comparatively early in the Peloponnesian War, and certain other passages which must have been written late in the War and some of them after it was over), and those who have believed it to be mainly late work composed in the light of notes and researches made during two or three decades and of the ultimate result of the War itself.[29] The attraction of the first view, argued brilliantly by Schwartz and less successfully by Pohlenz and Schadewaldt, lies partly in the insight which it can be made to offer into a broadening and deepening of the historical consciousness of Thucydides as the long war proceeded.[30] The attraction of the second is in the coherence which it professes to find in the historical thought of the whole work, which could only spring, it is argued, from a mature experience of the problems, discernible equally in the first chapters of Book I and the last chapters of Book VIII and expressing itself regularly throughout in terms which often recall and occasionally even repeat one another.[31] After exhaustive examination and argument the 'unitarians' in recent years have appeared sometimes to be winning, for it may be said that one exponent or another of this view has explained all or nearly all the passages which had seemed on the face of it to be 'early'. But appearances may be deceptive. The 'second introduction' (Book V, 26.1) can be explained, but not perhaps explained away. And there still remain, to reinforce the ingenuity of Schwartz, the sober promptings of common sense. For the fact surely is that this History of Thucydides reads much more like a book written in thirty years than a book written in three. The passages most concerned in these arguments come, nearly all, in speeches or other pieces of analytical writing; and there are big tracts of narrative containing nothing whatever to suggest either a late or an early date of composition. Despite assertions to the contrary, a skilful writer can 'patch' almost anything — and often will, rather than write an entirely new version incorporating what he wants to add to an existing one. It would not be surprising if the view were yet to prevail of an early version, composed during and shortly after the first half of the War and containing perhaps comparatively few speeches or analytical passages, many of these latter being worked in to the existing fabric at a much later date when the plan for completing the whole work down to the end of the whole War had been put into operation, never (alas) to be completed.[32]

The debate on the composition has raised incidentally most of the major issues concerning Thucydides' historical method in general; his conception of the duties of a historian, his criteria of relevance, of accuracy (this including his new chronological method), of causation, the part assigned by him to the speeches and to the analytical passages which suggest the motives behind the actions and the generalizations which govern the particulars, and especially the factors which ultimately inspired and shaped this study in war, politics, and imperialism.[33] Particularly fruitful have been those studies which have aimed at penetrating to the influences in contemporary life and thought which help to explain his personality and genius. Natural science (and especially perhaps the science of medicine) has been rightly stressed as a discipline underlying not only some mannerisms of thought but also the great stride forward which Thucydides made in the examination and testing of evidence 'in order to know something exact'.[34] The attempt to suggest that he (perhaps unconsciously) thought of and presented the story of imperial Athens in terms of the Tragic drama was entertaining, but it has not carried conviction.[35] But the influences of the contemporary sophistic movement with its pretensions to providing the means for directing human activities by the application of certain rules of probability or expediency or human nature, on both his thought and his literary style, have been established beyond dispute.[36]

Where one writer is so pre-eminent as a source for our knowledge of a period as is Thucydides, all work done on that period must necessarily be in some sense a commentary on him. Especially is this so of the epigraphical discoveries of recent years, containing as they do many important additions to our knowledge of the affairs especially of the Athenian empire, and of Athenian finance. That Thucydides made some use of official records is plain from the treaty texts which he incorporates, and from his dating of events anterior to the outbreak of the War, where he seems to depend on a list of archons preserved at Athens, and to have knowledge of similar records preserved elsewhere. That he made little use of the records of decrees of the Athenian assembly regulating the affairs of the empire of Athens in the period of its growth and expansion is not surprising, because his account of that period is deliberately brief and summary. But it *is* surprising that he fails to use such sources fully for the years of the War itself, and most of all in the sphere of finance, the importance of which he himself stresses at the outset, and thereafter unaccountably neglects. That great publication of recent years, *The Athenian Tribute Lists*, crowns for the time being the achievements of modern archaeology and epigraphy in this field, and provides the basis for a thorough revaluation in the near future of many related problems, in many of which Thucydides will be concerned, whether for what he wrote or for what he failed to write.[37]

The text, the language, and the style of Thucydides have continued to be a fruitful field for classical scholarship in the fifty years now under review.[38] The papyri, though they attest the fact that he was still read and used in Egypt in the Hellenistic and Roman period, contribute comparatively little of value to modern textual criticism, though the Oxyrhynchus Commentary is of no little interest.[39] Speaking generally, the best modern studies of his literary style have been those which have been also studies of the subject-matter in the wider connections already indicated, for of no writer is it more patently true to say that the style is the man. For the speeches this is self-evident. But it is not less true for the narrative also (τὰ ἔργα τῶν πραχθέντων), always bearing in mind the aim expressed by the writer himself, of recording them with the greatest possible exactitude. It has always been recognized that the high lights in this narrative of events can claim a place among the really great performances of historical writing. But the skill with which he narrates the ordinary and the unexciting, this too is a significant and on the whole a neglected aspect of him as an artist.

Nothing has occurred in the past fifty years to challenge the view that Greek historiography reached its peak with Herodotus and Thucydides, who though they may appear superficially to be opposites are in reality complementary in their contributions to the ideal figure of the historian that that age was capable of producing.[40] In antiquity the conception of history as the exposition of the knowable facts arrived at by methodical judgments on evidence collected by methodical research never did come into existence. Research, in this sense, into the past never was practised; perhaps the researches of Thucydides into the contemporary came near to achieving the methodical. It is possible to argue, though, that Herodotus was the *purer* (incomplete) historian of the two, because he appears to tell the story purely for the story's sake. If it were true, as has been alleged, that Thucydides' *real* interest in life was to illustrate by his story the prevalence of certain laws of human nature in the sphere of politics, and this perhaps with a view to instructing posterity as to their behaviour (I, 22.4); if his speeches (for example) were not the very thing, or even the sort of thing, that the speaker really said but rather the sort of thing that in the writer's own view best illustrated the 'law' that at this point he wanted to illustrate, then one must surely agree with Collingwood that his work represents a retrogression, and that Herodotus as a pure historian had no successor.[41] Thucydides himself tells us what he *meant* to do (1. 22.1-3). But did he achieve it? Did he even try to achieve it? In this matter of the speeches many have thought he did not. In the matter of Cleon, or even in a wider field, some have thought that he failed to be objective.[42] The answer lies for each of us in the text of Thucydides himself, enlightened often and occasionally darkened by the counsel of the moderns upon it.

The publication in 1907 of the celebrated fragment from the writer who must still be called the Oxyrhynchus historian has promoted one of the most entertaining controversies of the literary history of antiquity, and one which suggests some chastening reflections. This excerpt of some 600 lines from a book which from internal evidence must have been written before 346 and most probably before 356 B.C., and which was evidently a conscious continuation of the History of Thucydides undertaken on a scale larger than that of the *Hellenica* of Xenophon, this surely could not present an insoluble problem of identification.[43] It should be added that three shorter fragments of the same work (amounting to some ninety lines in all) published in 1949 do not assist towards the solution, though they give some useful confirmation on other points.[44] Xenophon apart, the known continuators of Thucydides are only two, Theopompus (in his *Hellenica*) and Cratippus; and the third prominent early contender in this battle of authorship was Ephorus.[45] The strength of the claim of Cratippus lay partly in the fact that so little is known of his life and especially of his work that refutation by a comparison of this *Hellenica* with identified specimens of his writing was impossible. Its weakness was that not everybody believed (or believes) that he was really, as he appears to be, a younger contemporary of Thucydides; the view has been strongly argued that he was a fairly late Hellenistic writer posing as one whose *floruit* was 400 B.C. or a few years later.

THE GREEK HISTORIANS 193

This view, even with the powerful support of Schwartz and Jacoby, is not shared by the present writer, who feels obliged to count Cratippus still as a *possible* author of the new *Hellenica*.[46] The case with Theopompus and Ephorus is very different. Theopompus did write a *Hellenica* continuing Thucydides; but the briefest comparison of the received fragments of his writings with the Oxyrhynchus work makes it abundantly clear that he did not write *this Hellenica*. This prose of Oxyrhynchus is plain, unrhetorical (almost entirely), and on the whole dull; as different from all that we know of Theopompus, whether by experience or by repute, as chalk from cheese. The conclusion is inevitable that it was mainly the authority of Eduard Meyer (and in the early days of the controversy of Wilamowitz too) that led Theopompus to be taken seriously in this matter.[47] His claim nowadays has lapsed.[48] With Ephorus the difficulties are different in character, though not in magnitude.[49] The prose of Oxyrhynchus could be, on a superficial examination at least, the prose of Ephorus, though a closer study has revealed differences which are striking without being perhaps absolutely conclusive.[50] But how can the arrangement of Ephorus in his Greek History, treated 'by subjects' within a broad chronological framework, be reconciled with the arrangement seen in the Oxyrhynchus writer, where the most significant feature of the whole work as we have it is the strict adherence to the Thucydidean scheme of narrative by 'summers and winters', a scheme rejected (we are told) by historians after Thucydides in general?[51] And how could the writing of this description of events in 396-5 B.C. be done by Ephorus before 356 (or even before 346 B.C.), dates which disagree with everything else we know about the progress of his work? Moreover a new Ephorus papyrus[52] showing remarkable *verbal* agreement with Diodorus (who used Ephorus here as a source) has revealed the weakness of the arguments from the *factual* agreements of *Hellenica Oxyrhynchia* with Diodorus (using Ephorus here too as a source); the two kinds of agreement are quite different. In short, despite so great an authority as that of Schwartz, the claim of Ephorus may be said to have lapsed also.[53]

The view that the author was Androtion need not detain us, though it, too, had distinguished sponsors.[54] But the remaining candidate who cannot be eliminated is Daimachus of Plataea, who was suggested, and is still supported, by Jacoby.[55] The title

M

or subject of the history of Daimachus is not known, but we are reliably informed that Ephorus used it (and indeed used it unscrupulously), and one of the attractions of Daimachus for this purpose is the presence, by a wonderful stroke of luck, in the surviving fragments of *Hellenica Oxyrhynchia* of that invaluable summary of the institutions of the Boeotian League. Who but a Boeotian would have turned aside to tell us this? Decidedly, Daimachus must be a possibility.

Nevertheless the writer must remain, for the present, 'the Oxyrhynchus historian'. But what sort of historian? A more than respectable one, it would appear. In style, dull but unobjectionable; in chronological exactness superior to Xenophon and, of course, to Ephorus whose method no doubt helps to account for the chronological vagaries of Diodorus; superior to Xenophon also in width of interest and depth of insight into politics, and even in grasp of the essentials of a military and naval situation in war, though perhaps his inferior (of this we cannot be certain) in accuracy of detail in his description of the operations of Agesilaus in Asia. If such a historian as this is in fact one who is not even known to us by name, this is a sobering thought; indeed the thing seems improbable, despite the reasoning of Bloch.[56] But the importance of *Hellenica Oxyrhynchia* in these years since its rediscovery goes beyond this question of authorship, and beyond the new information it has yielded; it lies most of all in the stimulus it has given to the study of the fourth-century historians in general, and to the lessons which it has taught us here.[57] It has taught us to know (among other things) our own limitations.

That other great gift of the papyri, *Athenaion Politeia*, has continued to inspire fruitful studies even after the intense activity of its first twenty years subsided. Here the question of authorship may be considered of secondary importance, since it has never been in doubt that this is the work which antiquity itself recognized as Aristotle's *Constitution*. What has been called more and more in question, by further detailed inquiry into the sources which it used for Athenian history before the fourth century, is the reliance to be placed on the work by us. Especially misleading had been an original assumption which passed unquestioned for many years, that it derived information ultimately from an ancient priestly chronicle (of *Exegetae*) comparable to those at Rome and summarised by an entirely unknown writer about the year 380.[58]

Variant accounts by fourth-century writers of (e.g.) Solon's constitutional enactments make extremely questionable the existence for them of any writings based on sixth-century records, or of the early laws themselves if they had become obsolete in the meantime.[59] It seems more probable that this *Constitution*, in its historical account of the Athenian development, depended entirely on the published work of earlier writers, and that its value for us therefore depends partly on the quality of these literary sources and partly on the quality of the criticism to which they were subjected by the author. The sources themselves were coloured by the political differences that manifested themselves violently in Athens in the last twenty years of the fifth century and were never completely extinguished thereafter, with the result that Athenian interpretations of even the remote past bear signs of political bias varying from the oligarchic (exemplified by the Draconian Constitution which survives in *Ath. Pol.* 4) to the radical democratic which was perhaps responsible for the picture of Solon as father of the democracy.[60] It is the unskilful blending of these discrepant traditions in the historical part of this *Constitution* that has prompted the view that this is but mediocre history, and even the extreme view (which however has much to commend it) that Aristotle himself can have had nothing to do with its composition;[61] for why should a first-rate philosophical mind become suddenly third-rate when it devoted itself to history? The second part of the *Constitution*, however, concerned with the contemporary working of the democracy at Athens and hence derived from sources of information exactly known and verifiable, belongs to a different order altogether, and perhaps deserves even more attention than it has received hitherto.[62]

Undoubtedly the most important historiographical result of the appearance of *Ath. Pol.* was the stimulus which it provided to the study of its own sources above-mentioned, which prove to be certain of the writers of Athenian history (*Atthides*) of the generation immediately before Aristotle's own.[63] The prototype of these writers was Hellanicus, whose comparatively brief 'Attic history', despite the slighting reference to it by Thucydides, no doubt was valuable in its collection and crystallization of much oral tradition that might otherwise have faded or perished. The line of his successors did not commence till some fifty years after his own publication (a fact perhaps to be explained by the appearance within one generation of the considerable mass of historical writing on the early history of Athens by Herodotus and Thucydides besides that of Hellanicus himself, which collectively may have been felt for the time being to be authoritative); but thereafter it continued unbroken during nearly a century. Not the least of the services of Jacoby has been his learned and skilful handling of these writers, showing the common characteristics of subject, method and treatment, without submerging in these common factors the essential characteristics of the individuals, who differed sometimes widely from each other (as might be expected) in temper and in their particular fields of interest, and above all in their viewpoint on the politics of the present, which seems invariably to have been reflected in their interpretation of the politics of the past.[63a] What seems established beyond question is that they are to be regarded not as mere antiquarians but as real historians in this restricted sphere of their choosing. Inevitably this local history of Attica has become better known to us than that of any other region of the Greek world, but as a product of Greek local patriotism the *genre* was widespread, with exponents of particular distinction (for example) among the Sicilian Greeks.[64] Presumably the great collection of *Constitutions* promoted by Aristotle must have been based at least in part on the 'local' literature of this kind. In Athens itself a logical development in the direction of genuine documentary research resulted from the establishment of the Peripatetic school, with its encyclopaedic tendency producing in this field the περὶ νόμων of Theophrastus and the περὶ τῆς 'Αθήνησι νομοθεσίας of Demetrius, works the survival of which would have been invaluable to us, and especially perhaps for their treatment of the earliest laws of Athens concerning which error was (and is) so easy. Craterus in his collection of Athenian ψηφίσματα was on safer ground.[65]

Although the age of Herodotus and Thucydides, naturally, was responsible for second-rate writers too, among whom the names of Stesimbrotus, Ion, Ctesias, and the Old Oligarch will come readily to mind,[66] nevertheless the pre-eminence of the fifth century in historiography as in many other matters, has not been undermined by work done in the last fifty years on historians of the fourth century. The Sophists had done their work, and the school of Isocrates was to continue it. But Xenophon himself, who ought to be our best friend, proves to be, too often, a broken reed. This is no new discovery indeed (Grote was fully alive to his shortcomings); but besides the study of Xenophon's historical writings themselves, the study of other sources for the first forty years of the fourth century has done something to bring home what an opportunity it was that Xenophon missed. The author of *Hellenica Oxyrhynchia* in two pages of a modern text gives us more unequivocal information about the institutions of Boeotia at that time than Xenophon ever gives in his *Hellenica* about those of Sparta, Athens, or any other Greek state; to say nothing of the new light that was thrown on Agesilaus' war in Asia when this historical fragment was discovered. The decree of Aristoteles forms the basis for our study of the Second Athenian Confederacy, the creation of which (like the founding of Megalopolis) Xenophon did not think fit even to mention. And scholars of previous generations are easily forgiven for a failure to find in the *Hellenica* the evidence for the existence in the first half of the century of a new concept in the international relations of Greek cities, the concept usually referred to now (as it was then by certain other contemporary writers) in the words *Koine Eirene*. The realization that this phrase, in the mouth of the orator Andocides or from the pen of historians used as sources by Diodorus Siculus in his surviving history, was not just vaguely descriptive but was the correct term for a peace embodying principles of what came to be known in the twentieth century as collective security — this has been a really notable advance of the last twenty-five years or so.[67] Few more telling reminders could be found of the truth that the history of every age worth writing about needs to be written by historians of each generation in turn; it needed scholars used to the ideas and the practice of a League of Nations to penetrate to the truth (and perhaps even beyond the truth) about *Koine Eirene*, its failures and its shams as well as the genuine ideas behind it, where their predecessors, with the exception of Adolf Wilhelm, had considered it little.

Here Xenophon availed nothing; and his reputation as a historian cannot be said to have recovered from the criticisms of the nineteenth century. Nevertheless both as a writer of charm and versatility and as a mirror of his times he has retained, as a glance through the bibliographies will show, a considerable attraction for scholars,[68] who moreover have not been deterred by the problems of dating the composition of his major works and indeed, in the case of the *Hellenica*, of dating the different sections of which that work has been alleged to be made up.[69] Although some of these questions probably still do not admit of a definitive answer, the labour expended on them has been by no means wasted, because of the light which has been shed from time to time on important aspects of Xenophon's writing, whether linguistic or stylistic, aspects which concern the relation of one work to another, or which concern the political viewpoint and the thought of the man himself.[70] It is perhaps significant that two most recent studies stress the importance of Thucydidean influence on Xenophon in his historical aim in the *Hellenica*, and constitute a reaction from the earlier view that, in this as in other of his more important books, the aim was at least in part propagandist. To aim, however, is not to hit the mark; and even if it be conceded that he saw and approved the better it is hard to avoid the conclusion that he often followed the worse. The truth perhaps is that Xenophon's best qualities were not those of the pure historian so much as of the storyteller, and that incomparably his best work was the *Anabasis*, regarded not as a history of a campaign (though it has been well appreciated as such by a practical soldier)[71] but as a story of adventure written by one who with this theme before him really knew how to write.[72]

The Hellenistic writers of history, with the one great exception of Polybius, are known to us only by fragments of their writings, or when it can be perceived that their writings have been followed closely by a later writer whose work has come down. The great collection of Jacoby has been of the utmost service in making these fragments themselves easily accessible and indicating in the commentary something of the state of modern knowledge and opinion on the innumerable individuals concerned.[73] Perhaps one of its greatest merits is that it does treat them all as individuals, and not as so many examples of so many types. When it is a question of trying to apprehend a multitude of shadowy forms, the instinct to classify and to label is irresistible, and indeed really necessary. The classification of these historians by the subject-matter of their histories or by the titles is a simple and salutary *aide-memoire*. More insidious is the fashion of labelling a writer as pragmatic, or Peripatetic, or Isocratean, or Asianic in style, as a means of summing up what we have been able to find out about the way in which he thought or wrote. For the fact is that we know *for certain* and in detail comparatively little about the writings of even such famous exponents as Timaeus or Phylarchus or Posidonius. If even half of a book of Timaeus himself were to be discovered, it might well be that our idea of him (to which the adverse comments of Polybius cannot fail to contribute) would need to be radically changed, just as our idea of Sosylus (whom Polybius also disparaged) was changed by the discovery of one small fragment from his 4th book.[74]

Generalization, then, about these Hellenistic historians as individuals is dangerous. Granted that there is reason to believe that the sensational tends to predominate in one writer, the ethical in another, or in a third mere rhetoric, it would no doubt be a mistake to think of these swiftly-taken likenesses as genuine portraits. And the more sober and sensible characters among them are in some ways inevitably the most obscure. The figures of (say) Diyllus the Athenian or even Hieronymus of Cardia remain still indistinct, even though the periods of which they wrote have been greatly clarified by the modern historians of the late fourth century, using primarily the last surviving books of Diodorus Siculus, which were based on the accounts of those lost writers.[75] In one particular corner of Hellenistic historiography it has been possible to go farther, because there by the accident of survival *several* late writers are preserved, providing a wider basis for comparison and evaluation of their Hellenistic sources; and although this corner is concerned with only a short period of history, it is an important period, and moreover the light that can be thrown upon its historians is more than ordinarily instructive.

Nowhere is the great spread of Hellenistic historiography better exemplified than in the historians of Alexander.[76] His own thought for the record is shown by the Journal (Ephemerides) for the keeping of which Eumenes of Cardia was responsible,[77] and by the presence in the camp and at court of the historians Callisthenes of Olynthus and Anaximenes of Lampsacus. Then there were the men of action or affairs, also present, who turned historian later in life: Nearchus, Onesicritus, Aristobulus, Ptolemy, Chares of Mytilene, to name no more. These men who were (to a greater or less degree) eyewitnesses represent the fountain head whence flowed and spread the history of Alexander, through (among others) Clitarchus of Alexandria, through Diodorus

Siculus and Plutarch, through the Romans Pompeius Trogus (*via* Justin's abstract) and Curtius Rufus, and above all through Arrian of Nicomedia writing in the second century A.D., down to the modern historian. These fifty years have seen much progress in the sifting and evaluation of the sources of our sources, which are (mainly) the surviving works of Arrian, Diodorus and Plutarch. Especially the claim of Arrian has been vindicated, that he went to the purest source of which he knew, the history of Ptolemy, which (we see) he supplemented from time to time by that of Aristobulus;[78] and that he departed from these sober and knowledgeable writers only in instances which he clearly indicates: here is an 'official' tradition, based partly (in the case of Ptolemy) on access to the Journal, favourably disposed of course to Alexander, but reasonably objective and above all aloof from controversy, rhetoric, and nonsense.[79] Callisthenes on the contrary provoked controversy in his life (and his death) on the spot, which moreover influenced the Peripatetic school of philosophy to view Alexander as a tyrant and a bad example, a view which survives here and there in Diodorus and Plutarch (and more in Curtius Rufus).[80]

Of the other writers who had accompanied Alexander there is no individual who has been detected as having influenced his successors profoundly. But the sensationalism and irresponsibility which seem to have characterized the book of Onesicritus, making of it a historical novel rather than a history,[81] may be taken as symptoms prevalent among writers, contemporary and later, who aimed above all at getting the greatest possible amount of excitement out of events and places and peoples themselves intrinsically exciting. The 'paradoxology', as Aeschines called it, of Alexander's lifetime went even farther than the orator himself (with his eyes primarily on Greece) thought to press it: indeed it ended up, as is well known, in a work of almost pure fiction, the Alexander Romance.[82] But the romantic element as an ingredient of what may be called popular *history* has been traced most clearly in the (lost) work of Clitarchus, that most discussed of figures among the Alexander-historians.[83] From being regarded as an eyewitness and the principal source used by Diodorus in his 17th Book he has been degraded by Tarn to a writer of the second generation (writing not before 280) and one whom Diodorus used merely as a secondary source from time to time.[84] Though this drastic treatment may not commend itself to everyone, there seems no doubt that his importance for the tradition had been inflated beyond anything that can be justified either by what we are told about him from antiquity or by the actual citations that have come down. He owed his survival (for he was read) perhaps to his instinct for the popular taste in the manner as well as in the matter of his writing.

The greatest gain from this reconsideration of Clitarchus was the reconsideration of Diodorus which Tarn also undertook, arriving at conclusions attractive in themselves and particularly weighty because they correspond with conclusions of others who have worked independently on other parts of Diodorus' History (see below). His Book XVII (according to this view) is not a simple transcription or abbreviation of (mainly) Clitarchus, but 'rather a complex structure' deriving from two main sources used consecutively, but also from a number of less important sources, of which Clitarchus is the chief, used from time to time. The novelties of Tarn's view, apart from the relegation of Clitarchus himself, are the advancement of what he calls the 'Mercenaries' Source', a Greek writer who used mainly information from the Persian side up to the death of Darius, to the position of first principal source, and the substitution of Aristobulus for Clitarchus as the succeeding principal source thereafter.[85] For Plutarch's *Life* the position is less satisfactory. Its sources, too, present a complex problem, and one which may be insoluble; at all events it seems unlikely that it has been solved completely as yet.[86]

For the period after Alexander's death and the early third century B.C. the loss of Hieronymus of Cardia is one comparable with that of Ptolemy's history of Alexander, though it is partially redeemed by a vicarious survival in the preserved books XVIII-XX of Diodorus.[75] But the sole survivor of the Hellenistic historians, Polybius, has naturally received the attention that sole survivors deserve; attention which has done nothing to shake the established belief in his own stout qualities to which his preservation must be partly due.[87] Among writers who, most of them, thought too much in rhetorical or ethical or dramatic terms and too little as historians, Polybius stands out from his environment as one who not only understood most of the things which a historian should do but also was able to avoid the most serious obstacles to their accomplishment: by some happy freak of personality (in that age) he had been able to realize that a man who writes like an ass is unlikely to think like a man of sense. The study of his literary style has suggested that though he was by no means indifferent to stylistic considerations he was content that the style should be the servant (the very humble servant, as it turned out) of the historical material and not its master.[88]

A man of action and of affairs, intent on writing history for the practical instruction of men like himself, impatient of his predecessors who had sometimes described things which they did not fully understand and had taken insufficient trouble to learn about, this was the man who by the accident of his exile and his intimacy with leading Romans became in a position to find out and understand everything, or nearly everything, about this people which now held the future of the civilized world in its immature hands. How well did he succeed? This is the ultimate question to which all the important Polybian studies have led up. His grasp of the Mediterranean world as now (in effect) a political entity in a sense more definite than the vaguer unity of the *Oikoumene* already suggested by Alexander's conquests; his evident intention of writing history impartially, successful in the main in the Roman sections and failing only occasionally when he wrote of Greek affairs;[89] his skilful use of earlier writers, and of some documentary evidence, for the period before his own lifetime, and of oral evidence and that of his own experience for the contemporary history — these are things which were known fifty years ago, and have not been assailed. In this last connection the importance of Laelius has been stressed as a source of information:[90] and the Polybian dating of the first Roman Treaty with Carthage, though it has been attacked, has not been conclusively overthrown.[91] A recent study has nicely appreciated his understanding of the principles of historical causation, where his strength lies in his division of interest between the historical weight (so to speak) of great men and that of institutions, in the allowance which he gives to other lesser factors also, and in his agnostic allocation of what are sometimes called to-day 'the imponderables' to Tyche and to no other.[92] His understanding of military matters and the accuracy of his descriptions has continued to stand the test of time, despite the long controversy over the Alpine passes and a few problems of local topography which he has left us.[93] Indeed an important claim has been staked, though not as yet established, for him as 'the creator of the geography of the West'.[94] All these and other

THE GREEK HISTORIANS

questions may be expected to be summarized and enriched by the forthcoming Commentary of Walbank.

On the composition of his History controversy has continued, and probably will continue. Despite the plainness of his original intention to record the years 220-168, and the presence in the earlier books of certain passages which evidently were written before the events of 146, no certain chronological scheme indicating stages of composition can be put forward, beyond suggesting a probability that the first fifteen books were completed before 146.[95] Various theories have been advanced postulating a revision, or even revisions, of an original draft, performed later in life and after the forty-book scheme carrying the work down to 146 had been undertaken;[96] but the evidence for a revision of the earlier books in reality amounts to little.[97] Even the much-debated 6th Book where Roman institutions are described from two points of view which have appeared contradictory has recently been re-interpreted in a way which calls these apparent contradictions in question.[98]

Whatever may be conjectured of the lost works of Ptolemy I or Hieronymus of Cardia, Posidonius, or even Strabo, there can be little doubt that Polybius was the most important of all the Hellenistic historians. His work became authoritative in a way which recalls the authority of Thucydides for the history of his age, and in particular its authority for Livy is a matter of urgency for the student of Roman historiography.[99] The one thing which no interpretation yet (not even Glover's) has been able to supply for Polybius is one single spark of genius.[100] With all his virtues, worthy, diligent, shrewd and comprehending as he was, he has remained *par excellence* the scholar's historian, because he lacked the skill or the touch to set the mind alight in the common reader.

If Polybius was, in the sense suggested above, the Thucydides of the Hellenistic age, Plutarch, the other great figure among Greek historical writers that remains to be discussed, resembles Herodotus at least in the wealth of his collection of material, so widely spread in time and place; a Herodotus whose travels (for our purpose) were performed in a world of books.[101] He was a repository of information not only from Hellenistic sources but from the great classical writers too, and also (though less copiously) from the Romans. It has long been recognized that Plutarch was not a systematic or scientific collector of facts, still less a scientific interpreter or critic; research and criticism in the modern sense are far removed from his method. Nor was the convention of ancient biography so closely allied as that of the modern to the writing of genuine history,[102] to which indeed he specifically disclaimed any pretension (*Alex.* 1). Nevertheless to exclude him on this account from a discussion of the Greek historians would be pedantic, partly because his *Lives* are more valuable to us than all the works of Greek historians that are lost and even than some that survive, and partly because the very considerable volume of work on them in the last fifty years (for he remains, as he has always been, a popular writer) itself repays attention.[103]

The conventional view that Plutarch turned to historical studies in his old age and wrote most if not all of his *Lives* in a period of about ten years in the principate of Trajan is probably incapable of proof; it may be true, but the evidence for it is extremely slight.[103] More important, to us, is to know *how* he wrote them. He gives the impression of being a very well-read, if not a positively learned man. A pronounced tendency of modern research, however, has been to discount the appearance of a multiplicity of past writers whose names are mentioned in the *Lives*, and to advance the view that Plutarch's method in writing them was the simpler one of following mainly one writer (perhaps even the writer of an earlier biography) for the narrative parts of any particular *Life*, and thereafter to enrich this skeleton with anecdote particularly illustrative of character, this material also derived perhaps from collections already in existence;[104] anyone who wrote as much in his life as Plutarch (we know) did, cannot also have found time to read as much as he would seem to have done on his own showing.[105] This method of approach has two weaknesses. In the individual *Lives* it is seldom possible to name convincingly the one source used by Plutarch for his 'skeleton'. And secondly it implies in him a lack of ingenuousness concerning his sources which seems totally at variance with the impression of his character conveyed by all his many writings in general. Here if anywhere, one would say, goes an honest man. It is to be hoped that over this tendency of the past generation a reaction on the lines suggested by Gomme in his brief but acute study will prevail.[106] In the meantime valuable work has been done on individual *Lives*, on the 'comparisons' between pairs of *Lives*, and also on textual problems.[107]

Finally it remains to consider the late writers of Universal

THE GREEK HISTORIANS

Histories and the like, of whom Diodorus Siculus is the most important survivor.[108] Nobody, one supposes, ever loved Diodorus for himself alone; but the fact remains that there are quite long periods of Greek History where we should be very badly off without him. It has long been recognized that his value depends entirely on the value of the sources that he happens to be using at any particular moment, for he himself has nothing of criticism, of judgment, or even of style that adds in any way to our comprehension of the events he describes. Even with good sources he was liable to error and to muddle, especially in matters of chronology (a difficult problem for him admittedly); and he did not always choose the best sources.[109] Thus in the books where he owes much to Ephorus and nothing directly to Thucydides, there has appeared no cause to revise the received opinion that Diodorus contributes remarkably little to our knowledge of the period recorded by Thucydides himself.[110] For the succeeding century, where he had more works available on which to draw, the position is somewhat different. Besides the new view (already mentioned) of Tarn about his Book XVII, valuable studies by (among others) Accame and Hammond have suggested that the problem of his sources is in reality a little more complex than Schwartz had proposed.[111] And that the same may be true of his Books XVIII-XX, long recognized as owing most to the highly-esteemed Hieronymus of Cardia supplemented by Diyllus, is made possible by the controversy as to the origin of the ὑπομνήματα of Alexander cited at 8.4, if, as seems the more probable, the document he referred to here was spurious.[112] The surviving fragments of his lost later books do not suffice to contribute to this source question more than the obvious, namely that he used such well-known and authoritative histories as those of Polybius and Posidonius. One may suspect, however, that future work on the surviving books may yet establish the opinion that Diodorus was perhaps a more conscientious, though not a more able writer than had been generally supposed.

One further valuable service of Diodorus needs to be mentioned: his preservation, in the notices which he regularly gives of Roman and Italian events, of the earliest Roman tradition that was committed to writing, that of the first group of annalists, who wrote in Greek.[113] The Greek interest in the early history or legends of Rome goes back as far as (among prose-writers) Hellanicus, but naturally it is among those who specialized in Western history that it most appeared. Antiochus of Syracuse, writing about 420, found occasion to mention the Romans, and Timaeus is known to have devoted much space to them. The Pyrrhic and Punic Wars had given opportunities for the writing of their contemporary history by Greeks, whose work was used by Plutarch (Hieronymus in *Pyrrhus*) and by Polybius.[114] Posidonius had continued the story where Polybius left off. But a bolder design still was attempted by Dionysius of Halicarnassus, the celebrated literary critic and man of letters, when he settled in Rome in 30 B.C. and prepared to write a Greek history of the Romans from their origins down to the beginning of the First Punic War. By this time to search for the real truth about early Rome in the writings of the Roman annalists was like looking for a needle in a haystack, and moreover Dionysius' knowledge of Latin and his literary associations in Rome led him to go for his material not only or primarily to the best annalists (the earliest, the Greek-writers) but to the most recent, who were also the most copious and the most misleading. Although opinions have varied as to which individuals he drew from most, there is no cause to revise radically the verdict given by Schwartz more than fifty years ago.[115] Gifted though Dionysius was with literary skill and with some judgment, his book is of far more value as an involuntary contribution to literary history, illustrating the growth of a legend, than for the true story of early Rome.[116] Interesting verbal correspondences between the text of Dionysius and citations from the Roman History of Juba the learned king of Numidia are more likely to have arisen from the use of a common source than from the use of the one by the other.[117]

The problem of the Roman sources was never absent for the later Greek writers also who essayed histories of Rome; and the results are the more serious because the Greeks themselves never thoroughly realized the existence of the problem at all. It is for this reason that the Histories of Appian and of Dio Cassius are of such variable value in their different parts. Appian in particular was a historian no better than Diodorus, though possessed of a somewhat livelier approach. Writing when he did (second century A.D.) of the Republican wars he easily fell into errors which it would have required a good critical historian to avoid, besides others which seem due to negligence; and always he was

THE GREEK HISTORIANS 207

at the mercy of his sources, whichever he might chance to choose. Nevertheless the work done on him in the last fifty years, though it has not equalled in volume that on Diodorus, has shown some tendency towards a comparable result, in that, while Appian's reputation may not have been increased by it, it has been somewhat changed.[118] It had been assumed that he wrote his accounts of the different wars by transcribing or abridging one appropriate source;[119] and frequent examples of correspondence with Plutarch seemed best explained by the view that the two writers were following here the same source. But the difficulty of agreeing, in the case especially of the *Civil War*, what Appian's main source really was, gave rise to many expressions of views; and it was long before the most probable view was put forward, that in reality he commonly used more sources than the one. The detection, in his account of the Gracchi, of material deriving originally from a source contemporary with those events and of peculiar value, a due emphasis on differences as well as correspondences between Appian and Plutarch, and finally, in his account of Caesar's life and the events that followed his death, the indications of three separate points of view, suggesting three different sources — all these factors, added to an occasional unwillingness to decide (as it seems) between discrepant versions at his disposal, would appear to point to a method of composition not of the very simplest.[120]

A more considerable historian, however, was Dio Cassius both in the grand scale of his Roman history from origins to his own day and in the equipment which he brought to its execution.[121] True, he was incapable of scientific criticism, in the modern sense, of the Republican annalistic tradition;[122] and his Republican history (to judge by the surviving books) was a somewhat lifeless composition as of one describing an age with which he had little in common. But with the Principate his firmer touch is exemplified by the increasing scale till finally he is writing what is in effect contemporary history to which authority is lent by his own experience. Detailed work on his chronology for the Imperial period reinforces the general impression that he aimed at an accurate and systematic reconstruction with results in the main reliable.[123] Less satisfactory is the impression derived from modern studies which have sought to throw light on the reliability of Dio's interpretation of events, especially in the early Principate. It has long been generally accepted that Dio wrote as one who took the Principate for

208   THE GREEK HISTORIANS

granted after two centuries of its existence, and that this led him sometimes into misunderstanding of the evolutionary character of the Principate in its early stages. As an extreme example may be taken the celebrated speech which he attributes to Maecenas in Book LII, a speech so far removed from the realities of the year 29 B.C. that it has been taken to be appropriate propaganda for the realities of the reign of Severus Alexander when Dio wrote it, and even to look forward to later developments of the third century.[124] Though this view in its extremest form may have gone too far, there still remains no doubt that failures of interpretation due to this cause constitute the most serious defect in Dio's valuable History.[125] More surprising, in a writer of his station and experience in life, is a charge that he reveals ignorance of an important point of Roman law, an ignorance suggesting that in this instance he followed his sources with too little circumspection; but the charge seems to be well founded.[126]

Nevertheless Dio provides, together with Arrian whose work on Alexander has been mentioned already, a worthy conclusion to the line of the classical Greek historians. Herodian remains something of a mystery, though sometimes a useful one.[127] Dexippus would have been more useful still had he survived. But the two great pillars of ancient historiography in decline stand as a somewhat striking memorial of what could still be done at this late date by two men of an intellectual discipline which made them aware of truth as an abstract quality that could be aimed at; men moreover whose powers of judgment in big affairs had been well exercised in the course of distinguished careers in Roman public life. Arrian's choice of Ptolemy as his principal source for Alexander, and his genuine attempt to understand an age so remote in time and in character from his own, will stand comparison with the performance of any other writer of antiquity faced with similar problems. It must be concluded that the loss of his works of contemporary history is to be regarded as serious.[128]

So the story ends, for the time being. It will continue, for there is no sign of any loss of interest in the Greek historical writers; but the probability is that it will continue on unspectacular and evolutionary lines. Short of the discovery of some more *Constitutions* of Aristotle or his school or of (say) a book or two of Theopompus, it is hard to see that any sudden or drastic reorientation should take place. Texts will be studied — and if the labours of textual scholarship have received insufficient attention in this chapter, exigencies of space besides error of judgment must be pleaded by the writer. Sources will be probed, and in this direction, well-trodden though it is, there is still room here and there for views that are both new and true. Especially, it is hoped, the minds and the natures of these writers of another world will be approached and understood. *Tout comprendre c'est tout pardonner.* In the writings of the Greek historians, let us face it, there is much to pardon, for Thucydides and Herodotus were never reborn in their spiritual descendants; but even so the rewards of understanding are great.

---

[1] Space does not permit the mention in text or notes of the many modern writers who in general or particular works on ancient history have illuminated incidentally the interpretation of Greek historians whom they have used as their sources. References are confined, generally speaking, to works, or sections of works, specifically directed to the study of the historians themselves.

I am much indebted to Dr. A. H. McDonald for allowing me to see his chapter on 'The Roman Historians' at an early stage; and to the Editor for his vigilance and learning, which have supplied me with several titles that I had missed.

[2] Details of publication in R.A. Pack, *The Greek and Latin literary texts from Greco-Roman Egypt*, Ann Arbor (Michigan U.P. 1952): see especially nos. 241 (Didymus), 258 (Ephorus), 334 (Hellanicus), 1056 (Philistus), 1061 (Phlegon), 1162 (Sosylus), 1700 (tyranny at Sicyon and Athens), 1702 (Polycrates), 1703 (Boeotia), 1704 (Sicyon), 1711-12 (*Hellenica Oxyrhynchia*), 1713 (a fourth-century history), 1714 (*Anonymi Philippica*), 1716-19 (Alexander), 1721 (letter to a king of Macedonia), 1724 (Third Syrian War), 1725 (Siege of Rhodes), 1728 (Ptolemaic history), 1729 (Second Punic War), 1731 (Rome and Ethiopia).

See also in general J. U. Powell and E. A. Barber (edd.), *New Chapters in Greek Literature*, Oxford (Clarendon) 1921, 122ff (E. M. Walker), 142ff (J. U. Powell); *op. id.* (Second Series), 1929, 65ff (E. M. Walker), 76ff (G. C. Richards); F. Bilabel, *Historici: Die kleineren Historikerfragmente auf Papyrus* (Kleine Texte, 149), Bonn, 1922.

[3] For the Lindian Temple-Chronicle, discovered in 1904, see n64.

[4] F. Jacoby, *Die Fragmente der griechischen Historiker*, (FGrH) I, Berlin 1923 (Weidmann); II. A and C, 1926: II. B and D, 1929-30; III. A, B, C, Leiden 1940-50 (Brill).

A useful catalogue of sources has been compiled by A. Calderini, *Le fonti per la storia antica greca e romana*, I, 1947, Milan.

[5] E. Bux, RE s.v. *Logographen* (1) 13, 1021ff (1927).

W. Aly, *Volksmärchen, Sage und Novelle bei Herodot und seine Zeitgenossen*, Göttingen, 1921; *id., Formprobleme der frühen griechischen Prosa*, Ph Suppl. 21, 3, 1929; F. Jacoby, 'Über die Entwicklung der griechischen Historiographie', Kl 9 (1909), 8off; *id.,* 'Griechische Geschichtsschreibung', *Die Antike*, II (1926), 1ff; E. Howald, 'Ionische Geschichtsschreibung', H 58 (1923), 113ff; W. Schmid, *Geschichte der griechischen Literatur*, I, 21, 683ff (1929), (Müllers Handbuch). L. Pearson, *The Early Ionian Historians*, Oxford, 1939 (Clarendon).

On Pherecydes, U. von Wilamowitz-Möllendorff, SPAW 1926, 125ff; A. Momigliano, 'Per l'età di Ferecide Ateniese', RFC 10 (1932), 346ff; R. Laqueur, RE 19 s.v. Pherekydes (3), 1991ff (1938); F. Jacoby, 'The first Athenian Prose Writer', Mn (1947), 13ff.

[6] For Xanthus, Pearson *op. cit.,* 109ff (Bibliography 137f); P. Södel, *De fabellis ad Croesum pertinentibus*, Diss. Göttingen 1911; L. Alexander, *The Kings of Lydia*, Diss. Princeton, 1913.

[7] Fragments, F. Jacoby FGrH I, no. 1, 1ff; 317ff (Commentary); *id.,* RE 7 2667-750 (1912); L. Pearson, *op. cit.,* 25ff (Bibliography 106ff); J. V. Prasek, 'Hekataios als Herodots Quelle zur Geschichte Vorderasiens', Kl 4 (1904), 193ff; J. Wells, 'The

genuineness of the Γῆς Περίοδος of Hecataeus', JHS 29 (1909), 41ff; M. O. B. Caspari, 'On the Γῆς Περίοδος of Hecataeus', JHS 30 (1910), 236ff; C. Sourdille, *La durée et l'étendue du voyage d'Hérodote en Égypte*, Paris, 1910; B. Schulze, *De Hecataei Milesii fragmentis quae ad Italiam meridionalem spectant*, Diss. Leipzig, 1912; F. Windberg, *De Herodoti Scythiae et Libyae descriptione*, Diss. Göttingen, 1913; A. W. Gomme, 'The Legend of Cadmus and the λογογράφοι', JHS 33 (1913), 53ff, 223ff; J. Grosstephan, *Beiträge zur Periegese des Hekataios*, Diss. Strassburg, 1915; V. Ehrenberg, 'Zu Herodot', Kl 16 (1920), 318ff; W. Aly, 'Die Entdeckung des Westens', H. 62 (1927), 299ff, 485ff; A. Momigliano, 'Il Razionalismo di Ecateo di Mileto', A and R 12 (1931), 133ff; G. de Sanctis, 'Intorno al Razionalismo di Ecateo', RFC, N.S. 11 (1933), 1ff; W. A. Heidel, 'Hecataeus and the Egyptian priests in Herodotus, Book II', Mem. Amer. Acad. of Arts and Sciences, 18. 2. (1935), 53ff; D. W. Prakken, 'Herodotus and the Spartan King Lists', TAPhA 71, (1940), 460ff.

[8] Fragments, F. Jacoby FGrH I, no. 4, 104ff; 430ff (Commentary). In general *id.*, RE 8. 104ff (1912); L. Pearson, *op. cit.*, 152ff (Bibliography, 233ff); Jacoby, *Atthis*, Oxford (Clarendon) 1949, especially 79ff.
Cf. also C. F. Lehmann-Haupt, 'Chronologisches zur griechischen Quellenkunde; I. Hellanikos, Herodotos, Thukydides', Kl 6 (1906), 127ff; F. Rühl, 'Die Zeitansätze für Hellanikos', RhM 61 (1906), 473ff; W. Aly, 'Barbarika nomima', Ph 85 (1929), 42ff.

For the new *Atlantis* fragment, A. S. Hunt, *P. Oxyrh.* 8. 1084 (1910) = FGrH, F. 19b.; A. von Blumental, *Hellanicea: de Atlantide*, Diss. Halle, 1913. Pearson (*op. cit.*, 177ff) is sceptical about the attribution.

[9] E.g. A. H. Sayce, *Herodotus* I-III, London, 1883 (Macmillan); *id.*, *The Egypt of the Hebrews and Herodotus*, London (Rivington) (1895).

[10] R. W. Macan, *The History of Herodotus*, IV, V, VI, London (Macmillan) 1895; VII, VIII, IX, London (Macmillan) 1908; A. Hauvette, *Hérodote historien des guerres médiques*, Paris, 1894; W. W. How and J. Wells, *A Historical Commentary on Herodotus* (2 vols.) Oxford (Clarendon), 1912, 2nd ed. (1928).

[11] Among early studies, see especially A. Kirchoff, *Über die Entstehungszeit des herodotischen Geschichtswerkes* (2nd ed.), Berlin, 1878; A. Bauer, *Die Entstehung des herodotischen Geschichtswerkes*, Berlin, 1878.

[12] By (e.g.) Macan, *op. cit.*, and F. Jacoby, RE Suppl. 2 s.v. Herodotos (2) 205ff (1913) respectively.

[13] R. G. Collingwood, *The Idea of History*, Oxford (Clarendon), 1946, 26-7.

[14] M. Pohlenz, *Herodot, der erste Geschichtsschreiber des Abendlandes*, Berlin, 1937.

[15] Jacoby, *op. cit.,*. 281ff, 330ff.

[16] G. de Sanctis, 'La composizione della storia di Erodoto', RFC 54 (1926), 289ff; F. Focke, *Herodot als Historiker*, Stuttgart, 1927; cf. also T. Braun, *Das Geschichtswerk des Herodot*, Leipzig, 1927. J. E. Powell, *The History of Herodotus*, Cambridge (University Press), 1939.

[17] J. L. Myres, *Herodotus: Father of History*, Oxford, (Clarendon) 1953, especially chap. 3; Jacoby, *loc. cit.*; 343ff, 398f, 467ff; J. O. Thomson, *A History of Ancient Geography*, Cambridge (University Press), 1948, chap. 2; K. Trüdinger, *Studien zur Geschichte der griechisch-römischen Ethnographie*, Basel, 1918, 14ff.

[18] For a summary, Myres, *op. cit.*, 25, 31. Of the works mentioned below, not all are favourable to Herodotus on particular points at issue.

On Babylonia, H. C. Tolman, 'A historical note on Hdt. 1. 106', TAPhA 31 (1900), XVIIff; *id.*, 'The Temple of Ζεὺς Βῆλος (Hdt. 1. 181)', *ibid.*, 32 (1901), XCVIff; J. Oppert, 'L'étendue de Babylon', CRAI 1903, 611ff; C. F. Lehmann-Haupt, 'Zu Herodot 1. 183', Kl 7 (1907), 447ff; F. Delitzsch, 'Zu Herodots babylonischen Nachrichten', *Festschrift E. Sachau* (ed. G. Weil), Berlin, 1915, 87ff; R. Koldeweg, 'Das Stadtbild von Babylon nach den bisherigen Ausgrabungen', JDAI 1918, 73ff; J. Weissbach, s.v. *Kyros* (6) RE Suppl. Bd. 4, 1129ff (1924); E. Unger, 'Herodotos und der alte Orient', *F & F* 3 (1927), 258ff; O. E. Ravn, *Herodotus' description of Babylon*, Copenhagen, 1942.

On Scythia, J. N. Svoronos, 'Explication des trésors de la tombe royale de Solokha', *Journ. Intern.* 17 (1915), 3ff; M. Rostovtzeff, *Iranians and Greeks in South Russia*, Oxford, 1922; K. Meuli, 'Scythica', H 70 (1935), 121ff; A. Baschmakoff, 'Étude paléoethnologique sur le peuple iranien des Scythes d'Hérodote, dits Scolotes', BAGB 51 (1936),

3ff; P. E. Legrand, 'Hérodote historien de la guerre Scythique', REA 42 (1940) (*Mélanges G. Radet*), 219ff; J. Coman, 'Quelques traits indo-européens des Scythes selon Hérodote', REI 3 (1943), 95ff. On Egypt, C. Sourdille, *Hérodote et la réligion de l'Egypte*, Paris, 1909; J. Vogt, *Herodot in Aegypten*, Stuttgart, 1929; W. Spiegelberg, *Die Glaubwürdigkeit von Herodots Beschreibung von Aegypten*, Berlin, 1921 (2nd ed. 1926: English Translation by A. M. Blackman, *The Credibility*, etc., Oxford, 1927, Blackwell); G. Bérard, 'Remarques sur une erreur historique d'Hérodote', REG 50 (1937), 289ff; R. M. Cook, 'Amasis and the Greeks in Egypt' *JHS* 57 (1937), 229ff; W. G. Waddell, *Herodotus, Book 2*, London, 1939 (Dent); H. de Meulenaere, *Herodotos en Egypte*, Diss. Louvain, 1946; C. Roebuck, 'The organization of Naucratis', CPh 46 (1951), 212ff; J. L. Myres, *op. cit.*, 152ff. F. W. von Bissing, 'Naucratis', BSAA 39 1951, 33ff; G. A. Wainwright, 'Herodotus II 28 on the sources of the Nile', *JHS* 73 (1953), 104ff.

[19] *Op. cit.*, chap. 4. On Hdts' use of sources and historical method in general, cf. W. Schmid, *op. cit.*, I, 2. 628ff (1934); Jacoby, *op. cit.*, 410ff; cf. also C. F. Lehmann-Haupt, 'Chronologisches zur griechischen Quellenkunde II', Kl 7 (1907), 61ff and 299ff; E. Howald, *art. cit.*, H 58 (1923), 113ff; J. Wells, *Studies in Herodotus*, Oxford, 1923 (Blackwell); *id.*, 'Herodotus and Athens', CPh 23 (1928), 317ff; F. Focke, *Herodotus als Historiker*, Stuttgart, 1927; K. M. T. Chrimes, 'Herodotus and the reconstruction of history', JHS 50 (1930), 89ff; G. de Sanctis, 'Aristagora di Mileto', RFC 9 (1931), 48ff; P. E. Legrand, 'De la "malignité" d'Hérodote', *Mélanges Glotz*, II, 535ff; O. Regenbogen, 'Herodotus in seinem Werke', *Die Antike* 6 (1930), 202ff; H. Kleinknecht, 'Herodot und Athen', H 75 (1940), 241ff; G. Nenci, 'Le fonti di Erodoto sull' insurrezione ionica', RAL 5 (1950), 106ff; H. Volkmann, 'Die Inschriften im Geschichtswerk des Herodot', in *Convivium* (Festschrift K. Ziegler), Stuttgart, 1954 (Drachenmüller), 41ff.

[20] See especially G. B. Grundy, *The Great Persian War*, London, 1901 (Murray); A. Boucher, 'La bataille de Platées d'après Hérodote, RA 2 (1915), 257ff; C. F. Lehmann-Haupt, 'Herodots Arbeitsweise und die Schlacht bei Marathon', Kl 18 (1918), 65ff, 303ff; J. Kromayer (and others), *Antike Schlachtfelder*, 4, Berlin, 1924; 5, 229ff (1931); J. A. R. Munro, *Cambridge Ancient History*, 4, 229ff, Cambridge, 1926; Sir F. Maurice, 'The size of the army of Xerxes', JHS 50 (1930), 210ff; *id., ibid.*, 52 (1932), 13ff; F. Miltner, 'Der taktische Aufbau der Schlacht bei Salamis', JŒAI 26 (1930), 115ff; G. Sotiriadis, 'The campaign of Marathon according to a recent critic', PAA 17 (1933), 377ff; H. Grégoire, 'La légende de Salamis, ou comment les philologues écrivent l'histoire', LEC 21 (1935), 519ff; W. Marg, 'Herodot über die Folge von Salamis', H 81 (1953), 196ff.

[21] W. Nestle, *Herodots Verhältnis zur Philosophie und Sophistik*, Progr. Schönthal 1908; I. M. Linforth, 'Herodotus' avowal of silence in his account of Egypt', Univ. of California Stud. in Class. Philol., 7 (1924), 269ff; C. Sourdille, 'Sur une nouvelle explication de la discrétion d'Hérodote', REG 38 (1925), 289ff; K. A. Pagel, *Die Bedeutung des aitiologischen Momentes für Herodots Geschichtsschreibung*, Diss. Berlin, 1927; O. Regenbogen, *op. cit.*; H. Bischoff, *Die Warner bei Herodot*, Diss. Marburg, 1932; F. Hellmann, *Der Kroisos 'Logos'*, Berlin, 1934; H. Panitz, *Mythos und Orakel bei Herodotos*, Greifswald, 1934; K. Wüst, *Politisches Denken bei Herodotos*, Diss. Munich, 1935; G. de Sanctis, 'Il logos di Creso', RFC 64 (1936), 1ff; K. von Fritz, 'Herodotus and the growth of Greek historiography', TAPhA 67 (1937), 315ff; R. Lattimore, 'The wise adviser in Herodotus', CPh 34 (1939), 24ff; *ibid.*, 357ff; L. Pearson, 'Credulity and scepticism in Herodotus', TAPhA (1941), 335ff; G. C. J. Daniels, *Religues-historische Studie over Herodotus*, Antwerp, 1946.

[22] Editions: H. Kallenberg, I, 1894, II, 1899, *id.*,[2] 1924-33 Leipzig (Teubner); C. Hude (2 vols.), Oxford, 1908; *id.*,[2] Oxford, 1926; Edition with Commentary: B. A. van Groningen, I-V, 1946-52, Leiden (Brill).

Text with Translation: A. D. Godley, I-IV London (Heinemann-Loeb Library), 1921-24; P. E. Legrand, I-VIII, Paris (Budé), 1932-48.

Translations: A. J. Evans, *The Penguin Herodotus*, New York (Penguin), 1941; J. E. Powell, *Herodotus* (2 vols.), Oxford (Clarendon), 1948; (French) H. Berguin, *L'enquête d'Hérodote d'Halicarnasse* (2 vols.) Paris (Garnier), 1932.

Text and language: A. Calderini, 'Tentativi di ricerche linguistiche in Erodoto', RIL (1908), 737ff; W. Aly, 'Ein Beitrag zur Textgeschichte Herodots', RhM 64 (1909), 591ff; H. Richards, 'Notes on Herodotus', CR 19 (1905), 290ff, 340ff; *ibid.*, 27 (1913),

157f; F. Hartmann, 'Über die Grundlagen zur Beurteilung von Herodots Dialekt', VDPh (1929), 113f; *id.*, ZVS 60 (1932), 89ff; Z. Trenker, 'La λέξις εἰρομένη d'Hérodote' [in Polish], *Charisteria G. Pazychocki*, Warsaw, 1934; L. Weber, 'Curae Herodoteae ad L. Vallam pertinentes', RFC 13 (1935), 356ff; *id., ibid.*, 15 (1937), 377ff; *id.*, 'Lectiones Herodoteae', PhW 57 (1937), 219ff; 58 (1938), 495ff; E. Arend, *Verbalabstrakte bei Herodot und ihre Vorgeschichte*, Diss. Berlin, 1936; J. E. Powell, 'Studies on the Greek reflexive: Herodotus', CQ 27 (1933), 208ff; *id.*, 'Emending Herodotus', PhW 57 (1937), 1199ff; *id.*, *A lexicon to Herodotus*, Cambridge (University Press), 1938; *id.*, 'Notes on Herodotus III', CQ 32 (1938), 211ff; P. E. Legrand, 'Herodotea', REA 40 (1938), 225ff; *id.*, *Herodotus* (transl.), Critical Appendix, II, 687ff; A. Colonna, 'Tradizione manoscritta e critica congetturale in Erodoto', Athenaeum, 7 (1940), 11ff; A. H. R. E. Paap, *De Herodoti reliquiis in papyris et membranis Aegyptiis servatis*, Leyden (Brill), 1948; M. Untersteiner, *La lingua di Erodoto*, Bari (Adriatica), 1949.

[23] Jacoby, *op. cit.*, 378ff, 486ff.

[24] J. L. Myres, 'Herodotus the Tragedian', *Mackay Miscellany*, Liverpool, 1914, 88ff; H. Fohl, *Tragische Kunst bei Herodotus*, Rostock, 1932.

[25] W. Nestle, *op. cit.*; A. Deffner, *Die Rede bei Herodot und ihre Weiterbildung bei Thukydides*, Munich, 1933; E. Schulz, *Die Reden in Herodot*, Greifswald, 1933; L. Solmsen, 'Speeches in Herodotus' account of the Ionian Revolt, AJPh 64 (1943), 194ff; *id.*, 'Speeches in Herodotus' account of the battle of Plataea, CPh 39 (1944), 241ff.

[26] J. D. Denniston, *Greek Prose Style*, Oxford (Clarendon), 1952, 5ff. In general (besides works already cited), A. Hausrath, 'Die ionische Novellistik', NJW 33 (1914), 441ff; W. Pohlmann, *De arte qua fabulae Herodoteae narratae sunt*, Diss. Göttingen, 1912; E. Weber, 'Herodotos als Dichter', NJW 21 (1908), 669ff; J. A. K. Thomson, *The art of the Logos*, London, 1935 (Allen and Unwin).

[27] A. W. Gomme, *A Historical Commentary on Thucydides*, I, Oxford (Clarendon), 1945; J. H. Finley, Jr., *Thucydides*, Cambridge, Mass. (Harvard), 1942. Cf. also (general works), F. M. Cornford, *Thucydides Mythistoricus*, London (Arnold), 1907; G. B. Grundy, *Thucydides and the History of his Age*, London (Murray), 1911, 2nd ed., 2 vols., Oxford (Blackwell), 1948; Ed. Meyer, *Thukydides und die Entstehung der wissenschaftlichen Geschichtsschreibung*, Vienna, 1913; W. M. Lamb, *Clio Enthroned*, Cambridge (University Press), 1914; A. Thibaudet, *La campagne avec Thucydide*, Paris, 1922; F. Taeger, *Thukydides*, Stuttgart, 1925; G. F. Abbott, *Thucydides, A Study in historical reality*, London (Routledge) 1925; E. Täubler, *Die Archaeologie des Thukydides*, Leipzig (Teubner), 1927; B. W. Henderson, *The Great War between Athens and Sparta*, London (Macmillan), 1927; C. N. Cochrane, *Thucydides and the Science of History*, Oxford (Clarendon), 1929; W. Kolbe, *Thukydides im Lichte der Urkunden*, Stuttgart, 1930; H. Berve, *Thukydides*, Frankfurt-am-Main, 1938; W. Jaeger, *Paideia*, I, 479ff. Berlin-Leipzig (de Gruyter) 1934 (transl. G. Highet, Oxford (Blackwell), 1939); J. de Romilly, *Thucydide et l'impérialisme athénien*, Paris (Belles Lettres), 1947; W. Schmid (Schmid-Stählin), *op. cit.*, I, 5, Munich (Biederstein), 1948, 1-223.

[28] F. W. Ullrich, *Beiträge zur Erklärung des Thukydides*, Progr. Hamburg, 1846.

[29] Summarized and discussed by J. H. Finley, Jr., 'The Unity of Thucydides' History', *Athenian Studies presented to W. S. Ferguson* (HSPh, Suppl. vol. 1), 255ff. Among earlier studies, see especially U. von Wilamowitz-Möllendorff, 'Thucydides VIII', H 43 (1908), 576ff; *id.*, 'Der Waffenstillstand von 423 v. Chr.', SPAW 1915, 607ff; *id.*, 'Das Bündnis zwischen Sparta und Athen', *ibid.*, 1919, 934ff; F. Jacoby, 'Thucydides und die Vorgeschichte des Peloponnesischen Krieges', NGG, 1929, 1ff.

[30] E. Schwartz, *Das Geschichtswerk des Thukydides*, Bonn, 1919 (2nd ed. 1929); M. Pohlenz, 'Thukydidesstudien', NGG, 1919, 96ff; 1920, 56ff; W. Schadewaldt, *Die Geschichtsschreibung des Thukydides*, Berlin, 1929; N. G. L. Hammond, 'The composition of Thucydides' History', CQ 34 (1940), 146ff; *id.*, 'The arrangement of thought in the Proem and in other parts of Thucydides I', *ibid.*, 2 (1952), 127ff.

[31] A. Grossinsky, *Das Programm des Thukydides (Neue Deutsche Forschungen*, Abt. Klass. Phil.), Berlin, 1936; H. Patzer, *Das Problem der Geschichtsschreibung des Thukydides und die thukydideische Frage (N.D.F. Abt.Kl.Ph.)*, Berlin, 1937; F. Bizer, *Untersuchungen zur Archäologie des Thukydides*, Diss. Tübingen, 1937; J. H. Finley, Jr., *Ferguson Studies*, *loc. cit.*

[32] Cf. also, on composition, G. B. Grundy, *op. cit.*, I², 387-534; A. von Domaszewski, 'Eine Urkunde bei Thukydides', SHAW, ph.-hist. Kl. 11 (1920), 5; M. Pieper, 'Thuky-

didesforschung in den letzten Jahren', *Sokrates*, 29 (1924), 104ff; E. Täubler, *Die Archäologie des Thukydides*, Stuttgart, 1927; K. Ziegler, 'Der Ursprung der Exkurse in Thukydides', RhM 78 (1929), 58ff; W. K. Prentice, 'How Thucydides wrote his history', CPh 25 (1930), 117ff; A. Momigliano, 'La composizione della storia di Tucidide', MAT 68 (1930), 1ff; G. de Sanctis, 'Postille Tucididee', RAL 6 serie, 6, (1930) 299ff; R. Zahn, *Die erste Periklesrede*, Diss. Kiel, 1934; A. Rehm, 'Über die sizilischen Bücher des Thukydides', Ph 43 (1934), 133ff; H. Münch, *Studien zu den Exkursen des Thukydides*, Heidelberg, 1935; H. G. Strebel, *Die Wertung und Wirkung des thukydideischen Geschichtswerkes in der griechisch-römischen Welt*, Diss., Munich, 1935; R. Laqueur, 'Forschungen zu Thukydides', RhM 86 (1937), 316ff; H. Bogner, *Thukydides und das Wesen der altgriechischen Geschichtsschreibung*, Hamburg, 1937; O. Luschnat, *Die Feldherrnreden im Geschichtswerk des Thukydides*, Leipzig, 1942.

[33] See also the works cited at note 27 above.

Add: E. Ciaceri, 'Intorno alla obbiettivita storica nei discorsi Tucididei', RFC 38 (1916), 67ff; A. B. West, 'Thucydidean chronology anterior to the Peloponnesian War', CPh 20 (1925), 216ff; F. Jacoby, *op. cit.* n 29; O. Danninger, 'Über das εἰκός in den Reden bei Thukydides', WS 71 (1931), 12ff; G. Méautis, 'Le dialogue des Athéniens et des Méliens', REG 48 (1935), 250ff; G. F. Bender, *Der Begriff des Staatsmannes bei Thukydides*, Diss. Würzburg, 1938; V. Bartoletti, 'Il dialogo degli Ateniesi e dei Melii nella Storia di Tucidide', RFC 17 (1939), 301ff; G. Deininger, *Der Melier-Dialog*, Diss. Erlangen, 1939; S. Mazzarino, 'Tucidide e Filisto sulla prima spedizione ateniese in Sicilia', BSC 4 (1939), 5ff; S. B. Smith, 'The economic motive in Thucydides', HSPh 51 (1940), 267ff; L. Pearson, 'Thucydides as reporter and critic', TAPhA 78 (1947), 37ff; F. M. Wassermann, 'The Melian dialogue', TAPhA 78 (1947), 18ff; E. Bayer, 'Thukydides und Perikles'. WJA 3 (1948), 1ff; H. Ll. Hudson-Williams, 'Conventional forms of debate and the Melian dialogue', AJPh 71 (1950), 156ff. H. D. Westlake, 'Thucydides and the Athenian disaster in Egypt', CPh 45 (1950), 209ff; V. Ehrenberg, 'Thucydides on Athenian colonization', CPh 47 (1952), 143ff; P. A. Brunt, 'Thucydides and Alcibiades', REG 65 (1952), 77ff; M. Treu, 'Athen und Karthago und die thukydideische Darstellung', *Historia* 3 (1954), 58ff.

[34] Especially C. N. Cochrane, *op. cit.* On the Plague, see especially W. Ebstein, *Die Pest des Thukydides*, Stuttgart, 1899; J. Ehlert, *De verborum copia Thucydidis*, Diss. Berlin, 1910; B. von Hagen, 'Die sogennante Pest des Thukydides', Gymnasium 49 (1938), 120ff; J. F. D. Shrewsbury, Bull. Hist. Med. 24 (1950), 1ff; D. L. Page, 'Thucydides' description of the Great Plague at Athens', CQ 3 (1953), 1ff.

[35] F. M. Cornford, *op. cit.*

[36] W. Nestle, 'Thukydides und die Sophistik', NJW 25 (1914), 649ff; W. R. M. Lamb, *op. cit.*; J. H. Finley, Jr., 'Euripides and Thucydides', HSPh 49 (1938), 23-68; *id.*, 'The Origins of Thucydides' Style', *ibid.*, 50 (1939), 35-84.

[37] On official records, A. Kirchoff, *Thukydides und sein Urkundenmaterial*, Berlin, 1885; Schwartz, *op. cit.*, 11ff (*et passim*). For the modern discoveries and their interpretation, see especially W. Kolbe, *op. cit. supra*; H. Nesselhauf, *Untersuchungen zur Geschichte der delisch-attischen Symmachie* (Kl Beiheft 30, Leipzig, 1933); L. Highby, *The Erythrae Decree* (Kl Beiheft 36, Leipzig, 1936); W. Kolbe, 'Thukydides und die Urkunde, *IG* 1² 63', SPAW, 1937, 172ff; B. D. Meritt, H. T. Wade-Gery, and M. F. McGregor, *The Athenian Tribute Lists*, I, Cambridge, Mass. (Harvard U.P.), 1939; II, Princeton, 1949; III, 1950; IV (containing full bibliography) 1953.

For the list of archons, B. D. Meritt, *Hesperia* 81 (1939), 59ff; T. J. Cadoux, 'The Athenian archons from Kreon to Hypsichides', JHS 68 (1948), 70ff; F. Jacoby, *Atthis*, 169ff, 345ff. For other such lists elsewhere, Jacoby, *ibid.*, 176ff, 352ff.

[38] Editions: H. Stuart-Jones (2 vols.) Oxford (Clarendon), 1900-01; J. Classen–J. Steup, 5th edition, 1914-22; H. Stuart-Jones, J. E. Powell, *ibid.*, 1942; C. Hude (2 vols.), Leipzig (Teubner), 1913-25; *ed. minor*, 1930-36; *Scholia*, 1927. Text with Translation: C. F. Smith (4 vols.), London (Heinemann-Loeb Library), 1919-23; J. de Romilly, vol. 1 Paris (Belles Lettres - Budé), 1953.

Translations: A. S. Way, *Speeches in Thucydides and funeral orations*, London (Macmillan), 1934; J. Voilquin–J. Capelle (2 vols.), Paris, 1936 [French]; H. Weinstock (2 vols.), Stuttgart, 1938 [German]; R. W. Livingstone, *The History of the Peloponnesian War*, Oxford (Clarendon), 1943;

On the text, etc., I. C. Vollgraf, 'Thucydidea', Mn 33 (1905), 57ff, 421ff; (1906)

411ff; (1908), 187ff; N. Festa, 'Sulla pubblicazione della storia di Tucidide', RLC 21 (1918), 3ff; R. J. Bonner, 'The book divisions of Thucydides', CPh 15 (1920), 73ff; J. Weidgen, 'Zum Thukydidestext', RhM 76 (1927), 180ff, 307ff, 347ff; *ibid.*, 77 (1928), 384ff; A. Dain, 'Liste des manuscrits de Thucydide', REG 46 (1933), 20ff; V. Bartoletti, *Per la storia del testo di Tucidide*, Florence, 1937; J. E. Powell, 'The archetype of Thucydides', CQ 32 (1938) 75ff; *id.* 'The Cretan manuscripts of Thucydides', *ibid.*, 103ff; B. Hemmerdinger, 'La division en livres de l'œuvre de Thucydide', REG 58 (1948), 104ff; D. M. Lewis, *Towards a Historian's Text of Thucydides*, Diss. Princeton, 1952; K. J. Dover, 'The Palatine Manuscript of Thucydides', CQ 4 (1954), 53ff.

On language and style, of the general works cited earlier, see especially Lamb, *op. cit.*, Finley, *op. cit.* Add: W. Lüdke, *Untersuchungen zum Satzbau des Thukydides*, Diss. Kiel, 1930; J. E. Powell, 'Studies on the Greek reflexive: Thucydides', CQ 28 (1934), 159ff; W. Woessner, *Die synonymische Unterscheidung bei Thukydides und den Politischen Rednern der Griechen*, Würzburg, 1937; J. Ros, *Die METABOAH (Variatio) als Stilprinzip des Thukydides*, Paderborn, 1938; M. den Hont, 'Studies in early Greek letter-writing', Mn 45, 2 (1949), 19ff.

[39] E. Voltz, *Die Thukydidespapyri*, Diss. Strassburg, 1911; F. Fischer, *Thucydidis reliquiae in papyris et membranis Aegyptiacis servatae*, Diss. Leipzig, 1913; C. Hude, 'Les papyrus et le texte de Thucydide', SBA Copenhagen 6 (1925), 579ff; J. E. Powell, 'The Papyri and the text of Thucydides', *Actes du V congrès international de papyrologie*, Brussels, 1938, 344ff; R. A. Pack, *op. cit.*, 55-6 (Nos. 1176-1205). The Oxyrhynchus Commentary on Thuc. II, 1-45 (*P.Oxy.* 6, 853) = Pack No. 1205; cf. H. Bloch, in *Ferguson Studies*, 314f.

[40] U. von Wilamowitz-Möllendorff, *Greek Historical Writing*, Oxford (Clarendon), 1908; R. W. Macan, CAH 5, chap. 14, Cambridge (University Press), 1927; F. Rosanelli, 'Le relazioni fra Erodoto e Tucidide', A & R 11 (1930), 115ff, 151ff. Cf. in general, J. B. Bury, *The Ancient Greek Historians* (Macmillan), 1909, 36-149. A. W. Gomme, *The Greek Attitude to Poetry and History* (Sather Classical Lectures), Berkeley and Los Angeles (Univ. of California), 73ff.

[41] R. G. Collingwood, *op. cit.*, 28-31.

[42] E.g. R. W. Macan, *op. cit.*, *ibid.*; A. H. M. Jones, 'The Athenian democracy and its critics', *CHJ* 20 (1953), 1ff; G. E. M. de Ste. Croix, 'The Character of the Athenian Empire', *Historia* 3 (1954), 1ff, especially 31ff.

[43] Editions: B. P. Grenfell and A. S. Hunt, *P.Oxy.* 5, 842; *id.*, *Hellenica Oxyrhynchia*, Oxford (Clarendon), 1909; F. Jacoby, FGrH 2A, no. 66, 17-35; 2C, 6ff; E. Kalinka, *Hellenica Oxyrhynchia*, Leipzig (Teubner), 1927; M. Gigante, *Le Elleniche di Ossirinco*, Rome (Gismondi), 1949. V. Bartoletti, I understand, has a new edition in preparation. Cf. especially the admirable paper of H. Bloch, 'Studies in historical literature of the fourth century B.C.', *Ferguson Studies*, 303-41, with good bibliography of works published 1926-40: for earlier bibliography, Kalinka, *op. cit.*

[44] *PSI* 13, 1304; A. Calderini, *Aegyptus*, 28 (1948), 222-3; *id.*, CE 48 (1949), 348-50; F. Jacoby–P. Maas, 'The authorship of the *Hellenica* of Oxyrhynchus', CQ 44 (1950), 1ff; M. Gigante, 'I frammenti delle Elleniche di Ossirinco', *Maia* 2, 1949, 208ff; V. Bartoletti, 'Nuovi frammenti dello Storico di Ossirinco', *RSI* 61 (1949), 236ff; S. Accame, 'Trasibulo e i nuovi frammenti delle Elleniche di Ossirinco', *RFIC* 28 (1950), 30-49; A. Fuks, 'Note on the Nova Hellenicorum Oxyrhynchiorum Fragmenta', CQ NS 1, 1951, 155.

[45] For the attributions of authorship summarized, see Bloch *loc. cit.*, 306f.

[46] E. Schwartz, 'Die Zeit des Ephoros', H 44 (1909), 481ff (and especially 496ff); F. Jacoby, FGrH II, c, p. 64; *id.*, CQ *loc. cit. supra* (n44). In favour of Cratippus (among many others) W. A. Goligher, 'The new Greek historical fragment attributed to Theopompus or Cratippus', *EHR* 23 (1908), 277ff; A. von Mess, 'Die Hellenika von Oxyrhynchos', RhM 63 (1908), 370ff; L. Pareti, 'Cratippo e le Elleniche di Oxyrhynchos', SIFC 19 (1912), 398ff; K. J. Beloch, *Griechische Geschichte* I, 1², 28; III, 1², 44ff, 62ff; J. H. Lipsius, *Der Historiker von Oxyrhynchos*, BSAW 67 (1915), 45ff; E. Kalinka, *op. cit.*, 1912. See also A. W. Gomme, 'Who was "Kratippos"?', CQ NS 4 (1954), 53ff.

[47] Especially, E. Meyer, *Theopomps Hellenika*, Halle, 1909. On the stylistic considerations, see Grenfell and Hunt (*ed. princeps*); G. de Sanctis, 'L'Attide di Androzione e

THE GREEK HISTORIANS

un papiro di Oxyrhynchos', Atti r. accad. Torino, 43 (1908), 209ff; A. Franz, *Ein Historikerfragment aus Oxyrhynchos*, Progr. Prague, 1910; G. Bauer, 'De sermone Hellenicorum Oxyrhyncho repertorum', *Diss. philol. Vindobonenses*, XI, 1913.

[48] The arguments against it are best perhaps stated by F. Jacoby, 'Der Verfasser der Hellenika von Oxyrhynchos', NGG, 1924, 13ff. Surprising is the adherence to it thereafter of R. Laqueur, RE 2 Reihe, 5, s.v. Theopompos (9), 2193ff (1934).

[49] In favour of Ephorus as author: E. M. Walker, *The Hellenica Oxyrhynchia*, Oxford (Clarendon); *id.*, in *New Chapters* 1 (1921), 124ff; E. Cavaignac, 'Sur l'attribution des fragments etc.' *REA* I (1927), 176-81; *id.*, 'Réflexions sur Ephore', *Mélanges Gustave Glotz* I, 149ff, Paris, 1932. B. P. Grenfell in Grenfell and Hunt, *P.Oxy.* 13 (1919), 112f; Ed. Schwartz, 'Geschichtsschreibung und Geschichte bei den Hellenen', *Die Antike* 4 (1928), 22; J. G. Winter, *Life and Letters in the Papyri*, 1933, 240ff.

Against: (especially) G. L. Barber, *The historian Ephorus*, Cambridge (University Press), 1935; P. Treves, Athenaeum (review of Barber), 15, (1937), 126ff; S. Accame, 'Le fonti di Diodoro per la guerra Deceleica', *RAL Ser.* 6, 14 (1938), 347ff.

[50] A. Franz, *op. cit.*, at n47; G. Bauer, *op. cit., ibid.*, especially 27ff.

[51] Dion. Hal. Περὶ Θουκυδίδου, 9.830. 18 U.-R. The importance of this observation has been discussed by most of the best studies on *Hell. Oxy.*; for résumé, see Bloch, *op. cit.*, 308ff.

[52] *P.Oxy.* 13, 1610 (= Jacoby FGrH 2A, 96-7, F 191); G. L. Barber, *op. cit.*, 53ff; M. Gigante, *Frammenti sulla Pentacontaëtia*, Naples, 1948.

[53] Still in one of his latest publications, 'Die messenische Geschichte bei Pausanias', Ph 92 (1937), 21, n3.

[54] G. de Sanctis, *loc. cit.*, *supra* (at n47); *id.*, 'Nuovi studi sulle "Elleniche" di Ossirinco', *ibid.*, 66 (1931), 157-94; A. Momigliano, 'Androzione e le "Elleniche" di Ossirinco', *ibid.*, 29-49. The refutation of this attribution is summarized by Bloch, *op. cit.*, 328ff.

[55] F. Jacoby, 'Der Verfasser der Hellenika von Oxyrhynchos', NGG, 1924, 13ff; *id.*, FGrH 2A, 17-35; C 6-20; *id.*, CQ 44 (1950), 1ff.

[56] *Op. cit.*, 334ff. Among early studies on the question of authorship, several declined to name an author. Among more recent ones (since 1920) only Wilamowitz maintained this view, in *Reden und Vorträge* II[4], 224. W. Otto, who had maintained it in 1922 (HZ 125, 483), in 1926 declared himself in favour of Daimachus (Busolt–Swoboda, *Griechische Staatskunde* II, 1577, note on p. 81, n2).

[57] For Theopompus, in addition to works already cited, see especially R. Laqueur RE 2 Reihe, 5, s.v. Theopompos (9), 2176ff (1934); A. Momigliano, 'La storia di Eforo e le Elleniche di Teopompo', RFC (1935), 180ff.

[58] U. von Wilamowitz-Möllendorff, *Aristoteles und Athen* I (1893), 260ff; cf. O. Seeck, 'Quellenstudien zu der Aristotelischen Verfassungsgeschichte Athens', Kl 4 (1904), 292ff; A. von Mess, 'Aristoteles 'Αθηναίων Πολιτεία und die politische Schriftstellerei Athens', RhM 66 (1911), 356ff.

For criticism of the view of Wilamowitz and of works written more or less under its influence, see especially F. Jacoby, *Atthis: the local chronicles of Ancient Athens*, Oxford (Clarendon), 1949, chap. 1. For other views on *exegetae*, especially R. Laqueur *RE* 13, s.v. *Lokalchronik*, 1083ff (1927); K. von Fritz, 'Atthidographers and Exegetae', TAPhA 71 (1940), 91ff. J. H. Oliver, *The Athenian expounders of the sacred and ancestral law*, Baltimore, Johns Hopkins Univ. Press, 1950, especially chaps. 2-4. The controversy still continues.

[59] C. Hignett, *A History of the Athenian Constitution to the end of the fifth century B.C.*, Oxford (Clarendon), 1952; J. H. Oliver, 'Greek Inscriptions', *Hesperia* 4 (1935), 5ff. In general, the studies of U. Kahrstedt on the Athenian Constitution, *Studien zum öffentlichen Recht Athens* I, 1934; II. 1936, Stuttgart-Berlin; *id.*, 'Untersuchungen zu athenischen Behörden I', Kl 30 (1937), 10ff; II, *ibid.*, 31 (1938), 1ff; III, *ibid.*, 32 (1939), 148ff; IV, *ibid.*, 33 (1940), 1ff; H. T. Wade-Gery, 'Studies in the structure of Attic society', CQ 27 (1933), 17ff; A. Ledl, *Studien zur älteren athenischen Verfassungsgeschichte*, Heidelberg, 1914.

[60] P. Cloché, 'Remarques sur la prétendue "Constitution de Dracon"', REA 42 (1940), 64ff; (Mélanges G. Radet); F. E. Adcock, 'The source of the Solonian chapters of the *Athenaion Politeia*', Kl 12 (1912), 1ff; Ch. Rogge, 'Zur Interpretation der Gedichte Solons und der Πολιτεία 'Αθηναίων des Aristoteles', PhW 1924, 794ff.

And below, n63a.
⁶¹ E.g. (most recently) Hignett, *loc. cit.*.
⁶² Especially, H. Hommel, *Heliaia* (Ph Suppl. Bd. 19. 2), Leipzig, 1927. The most important editions, translations and commentaries are: J. E. Sandys, 2nd ed.; a revised text with an introduction, critical and explanatory notes, etc., London, 1912; F. Blass–T. Thalheim (Teubner), Leipzig, 1914; F. G. Kenyon (Oxford), 1920; G. Mathieu–B. Haussoulier (Text and French translation), Paris, 1922 (Budé); Blass–Thalheim–H. Opperman (Teubner), Leipzig, 1928; H. Rackham (Loeb, Text and Translation), London (Heinemann), 1935; K. von Fritz–E. Kapp (Translation, with Introduction and Commentary), New York 1950.
See further, G. Mathieu, *Aristote, Constitution d'Athènes* (Essai sur la méthode suivi par Aristote dans la discussion des Textes), Paris, 1935; E. Drerup, 'Ist die *Athenaion politeia* des Aristoteles vollendet?', Mn, 1941, 1ff.
Studies of particular passages and questions are too numerous to mention; especially on the revolution of 411 B.C.
⁶³ In addition to the works cited at n58 above, see E. Schwartz, RE II, 2 (1896), 2180-3; P. Foucart, *Étude sur Didymos*, Paris, 1907; G. de Sanctis, *Atthis*, Padua, 1912; Christ–Schmid, *Gesch. d. griech. Lit.*⁶ II, 1. 1920, 109ff; M. Lenchantin, 'Nuovi frammenti di Filocoro,' RFC 10 (1932), 41ff; R. Laqueur, RE 19.2 (1938), 2434-42; L. Pearson, *The Local Historians of Attica*, Philadelphia, 1942. H. Bloch, *loc. cit., supra*, esp. 341ff.
For collected fragments, Jacoby FGrH, 3B, Nos. 323a (Hellanicus), 328 (Philochorus), 41ff.

⁶³ᵃ Jacoby, *Atthis*, esp. 71ff, 290ff, where earlier views are discussed.
⁶⁴ Jacoby, FGrH, 3B, 540ff; Christ–Schmid, 2. 1. 225ff (1920). For the Lindian Temple-Chronicle of the Rhodian Timachidas, see C. Blinkenberg, *La chronique du temple Lindien*, Copenhagen, 1912 (and *Kleine Texte*, no. 131, Bonn, 1915); *id.*, Lindos II, Copenhagen, 1941, 149ff.
Cf. also G. S. Richards in J. U. Powell–E. A. Barber (edd.), *New Chapters* (second series, 1929), 76ff.
⁶⁵ Jacoby, *ibid.*, no. 228; Bloch, *op. cit.*, 355ff.
⁶⁶ On the Old Oligarch, especially G. Hofmann, *Beiträge zur Kritik und Erklärung der pseudo-xenophontischen* Ἀθηναίων Πολιτεία, Progr. Munich, 1907; L. Siegel, 'Zur pseudoxenophontischen Ἀθηναίων Πολιτεία', WS 32 (1911), 914ff; E. Kalinka, *Die pseudoxenophontische* Ἀθηναίων Πολιτεία, Leipzig, 1913; E. Bruhn, 'Die oligarchische Denkschrift über die Verfassung Athens als Schullekture', Neue Jahrb. 24 (1921), 17ff; G. Stail, *Über die pseudoxenophontische* Ἀθηναίων Πολιτεία, Diss. Würzburg, Paderborn, 1921; M. Kupferschmid, *Zur Erklärung der pseudoxenophontischen* Ἀθηναίων Πολιτεία, Diss. Hamburg, 1932; K. Münscher, 'Kritischer Nachlass zur pseudo-xenophontischen Ἀθηναίων Πολιτεία', RhM 81 (1932), 209ff; H. Instinsky, *Die Abfassungszeit der Schrift vom Staate der Athener*, Freiburg, 1933; K. I. Gelzer, *Die Schrift vom Staate der Athener*, H. Einzelschr: 3, 1937; E. Rupprecht, *Die Schrift vom Staate der Athener*, Kl Beiheft 44, 1939; A. Meder, *Der Athenische Demos zur Zeit des peloponnesischen Krieges im Lichte zeitgenössischer Quellen*, Diss. Munich, 1939; M. Volkening, *Das Bild des attischen Staates in der pseudoxenophontischen Schrift vom Staate der Athener*, Diss. Munster, 1940; A. W. Gomme, 'The Old Oligarch', HSPh (*Ferguson Studies*) 1940, 211ff; H. Frisch, *The Constitution of the Athenians*, Copenhagen, 1942; E. Hohl, 'Zeit und Zweck der pseudoxenophontischen Ἀθηναίων Πολιτεία', CPh 45 (1950), 26ff.
⁶⁷ The more important works are: F. Taeger, *Der Friede von 362/1*, Stuttgart, 1931; G. de Sanctis, 'La pace del 362/1', RFC 12 (1934), 145ff; A. Momigliano, 'La κοινὴ εἰρήνη dal 386 al 338', RFC 12 (1934), 485ff; *id.*, 'Della storia publicistica sulla κοινὴ εἰρήνη nel IV secolo', ASNP Ser. 2, 5 (1936), 97ff; F. Hampl, *Die griechischen Staatsverträge des 4 Jahrhunderts v. Chr.*, Leipzig, 1938; W. Nestle, *Der Friedensgedanke in der antiken Welt* (Ph Suppl. Bd. 31. i); 1938; V. Martin, 'Le traitement de l'histoire diplomatique dans la tradition littéraire du IVème siècle', MH 1 (1944), 13ff, 34ff; S. Accame, *La Lega Ateniense nel IV secolo a.C.*, Rome, 1941; *id.*, *Richerche intorno alla guerra Corinzia*, Turin, 1951; M. Sordi, 'La pace di Atene del 371/0 a.c.', RFC 29 (1951).
⁶⁸ Bibliography, E. Richter, JAW 142 (1909), 341ff; 178 (1919), 1ff; J. Mesk, *ibid.*, 203 (1925), 1ff; 230 (1931), 1ff; 251 (1936), 1ff; J. Penndorf, 268 (1940), 1ff; and (for some of the later work) J. Luccioni, *Les idées politiques et sociales de Xénophon*, Paris, 1947.

THE GREEK HISTORIANS 217

Editions, Translations, etc.: Teubner: W. Gemoll, *Expeditio Cyri*, 1909; C. Hude, *Expeditio Cyri, ed. maior*, 1931; *ed. minor*, 1936; *id., Historia Graeca, ed. maior*, 1930; *ed. minor*, 1938. J. Thalheim, *Scripta minora* (2 vols.), 1910-12. Oxford: E. C. Marchant, I, *Historia Graeca*, 1900; III, *Expeditio Cyri*, 1904; V, *Opuscula*, 1908; Budé: P. Masqueray, *Anabase*, Paris, 1930; J. Hatzfeld, *Helléniques*, Paris, 1936-39; P. Chantraine, *Économique*, Paris, 1949; Loeb Library; C. L. Brownson, *Hellenica* and *Anabasis*, 1918-22; E. C. Marchant, *Scripta Minora*, 1925 London (Heinemann); J. Luccioni, *Hiéron*, Paris, 1948 (ed. with introduction, translation and commentary); F. Ollier, Xénophon: *La République des Lacédémoniens*, Lyon-Paris, 1934; J. H. Thiel, Ξενοφῶντος Πόροι (ed. with commentary), Diss. Amsterdam, 1922; W. H. D. Rouse, *The March up-Country* (transl.), London (Nelson), 1947; R. Warner, *Persian Expedition* (Penguin Books, 1949). Cf. also A. W. Persson, 'Zur Textgeschichte Xenophons', Acta Univ. Lund., 1914; H. Richards, *Notes on Xenophon and others*, London (Grant Richards), 1907; G. Pierleoni, *Xenophontis respublica Lacedaemoniorum*, Berlin, 1905.

[69] T. Marschall, *Untersuchungen zur Chronologie der Werke Xenophons*, Diss. Munich, 1928; M. Pohlenz in Gerke-Norden, *Einleitung* I (1927), 103ff. On *Anabasis*, A. Körte, 'Die Tendenz von Xenophons Anabasis', NJW 25 (1922), 1, 15ff; A. Kappelmacher, 'Zur Abfassungszeit von Xenophons Anabasis', AAWW ph.-hist. Kl 60 (1923), 15ff.; J. Mesk, 'Die Tendenz der xenophontischen Anabase', WS 43 (1922-23), 212ff; A. Gwynn, 'Xenophon and Sophaenetus', CQ 23 (1929), 39ff; E. Delebecque, 'Xénophon, Athènes et Lacédémone', REG 69 (1946), 71ff.

On *Hellenica*, B. Niese, 'Chronologische und historische Beiträge zur griechischen Geschichte der Jahre 370-64', H 39 (1904), 83ff; L. Lohse, *Quaestiones chronicae ad Xenophontis Hellenica pertinentes*, Diss. Leipzig, 1905; R. Müller, *Quaestionum Xenophontearum capita duo*, Diss. Halle, 1907; A. Banderet, *Untersuchungen zu Xenophons Hellenika*, Diss. Berlin, 1919; A. Rapaport, 'Xenophontea', Eos, 27 (1924), 19ff; K. Vorrenhagen, *De Orationibus quae sunt in Xenophontis Hellenika*, Diss. Münster, 1926; J. Hatzfeld, 'Notes sur la composition des Helléniques', RPh 57 (1930), 113ff, 209ff; G. de Sanctis, 'La genesi delle Elleniche di Senofonte', ASNP Ser. 2, 1 (1932), 15ff; G. Colin, *Xénophon historien d'après le II livre des Helléniques*, Paris, 1933; M. MacLaren, Jr., 'On the composition of Xenophon's *Hellenica*', AJPh 55 (1934), 121ff; M. Sordi, 'I Caratteri dell'Opera storiografica di Senofonte nelle Elleniche', Athenaeum N.S. 28 (1950), 1ff; 29 (1951), 273ff.

[70] See, in addition to works cited at nn67 and 69, L. Gautier, *La langue de Xénophon*, Geneva, 1911; E. Scharr, *Xenophons Staats-und Gesellschaftsideal und seine Zeit*, Halle, 1919; A. Kappelmacher, 'Xenophon und Isokrates', WS 43 (1922-23), 212ff; G. Colin, 'Sur la véracité de Xénophon dans les Helléniques', CRAI, 1931, 343ff; A. Momigliano, 'L'egemonia tebana in Senofonte e in Eforo', *Atene & Roma*, 37 (1935), 101ff; W. Nestle, 'Xenophon und die Sophistik', Ph 94 (1940), 31ff; A. Delatte, 'La formation humaniste selon Xénophon', BAB 35 (1949), 505ff; H. R. Breitenbach, *Historiographische Anschauungsformen Xenophons*, Diss. Basel, 1950.

[71] M. Sordi, *op. cit.*, *supra* (n69); H. R. Breitenbach, *op. cit.*, *supra* (n70).

[72] G. Cousin, *Kyros le Jeune en Asie Mineure*, Paris-Nancy, 1905; A. Boucher, *L'anabase de Xénophon, avec un commentaire historique et militaire*, Paris, 1913; T. R. Glover, *From Pericles to Philip*, especially 106ff, London (Dent), 1917.

Among other works of interest not yet cited are: T. Thalheim, 'Zu Xenophons kleineren Schriften', H 43 (1908), 427ff; W. Schwahn, 'Die xenophontischen Πόροι und die althenische Industrie im vierten Jahrhundert', RhM 80 (1931), 253ff; A. Wilhelm, 'Untersuchungen zu Xenophons Πόροι', WS 52 (1934), 18ff; A. Momigliano, 'Per l'unita logica della Λακεδαιμονίων πολιτεία di Senofonte', RFC, 14, 1936, 170ff; K. M. T. Chrimes, *The* Respublica Lacedaemoniorum *ascribed to Xenophon*, Manchester (University Press), 1948; K. Münscher, *Xenophon in der griechisch-römischen Literatur*, Philologus Suppl. Bd. 13 (1920).

[73] F. Jacoby, FGrH., especially 2A Nos. 73 (Diyllus), 76 (Duris), 81 (Phylarchus), 84 (Neanthes), 86 (Agatharchides), 87 (Poseidonius), 88 (Timagenes), 90 (Nicolaus), 91 (Strabo); *ibid.*, 3A No. 566 (Timaeus).

[74] In general, P. Scheller, *De hellenistica historiae conscribendae arte*, Diss. Leipzig, 1911; R. Schubert, *Die Quellen der Geschichte der Diadochenzeit*, Leipzig, 1914; A. von Mess, 'Die Anfänge der Biographie und der psychologischen Geschichtsschreibung in der griechischen Literatur', RhM 70 (1915), 317ff; 71 (1916), 79ff; Christ-Schmid, *Gesch. der*

*griech. Lit.*⁶ 2. 1. 204ff (1920); and the forthcoming study of certain Hellenistic historians by T. S. Brown.

Cf. also G. Misch, *Geschichte der Autobiographie* I, 120ff, Teubner, Leipzig and Berlin, 1907; R. Reitzenstein, *Hellenistische Wundererzählungen*, Leipzig, 1906. There is an English translation of Misch's book by E. W. Dickes: *A History of Autobiography in Antiquity*, 2 vols., London (Routledge and Kegan Paul), 1950.

⁷⁵ For Diyllus, especially A. Rohde, *De Diyllo Atheniensi Diodori auctore*, Diss. Leipzig, 1909; W. Schwahn, 'Diyllos', Ph 86 (1931), 145ff; A. Momigliano, 'Due problemi storiografici', RIL 65 (1932), 573ff; and n112, *infra*.

For Hieronymus, F. Jacoby, RE 8.2 s.v. Hieronymos (10), 1540ff. (1913); R. Schubert, *op. cit.*, *supra* (n74); C. Bottin, 'Les sources de Diodore de Sicile pour l'histoire de Pyrrhus, des successeurs d'Alexandre le Grand et d'Agathocle', RBPh 7 (1928), 1307ff; P. Treves, 'Ieronimo di Cardia e la politica di Demetrio Poliorcete', RFC (1932), 194ff; T. S. Brown, 'Hieronymus of Cardia', AHR 52 (1946-47), 684ff. For the Heidelberg epitome, see G. Bauer, *Die Heidelberger Epitome*, Leipzig, 1914; F. Jacoby, FGrH 2B, 835ff; 2D, 548ff (no. 155).

⁷⁶ 'Fragments' in Jacoby FGrH, IIB, Nos. 117-53; D. 403ff; cf. especially W. W. Tarn, *Alexander II: Sources and Studies*, Cambridge (University Press), 1948; C. A. Robinson, Jr., *The History of Alexander the Great*, I, Brown University Press, 1953.

⁷⁷ Jacoby, FGrH, *ibid.*, no. 117; J. Kaerst, 'Ptolemaios und die Ephemeriden Alexanders des Grossen', Ph 56 (1897), 334ff; *id.*, RE 5. 2. s.v. *Ephemerides*, 2749ff (1905); C. F. Lehmann-Haupt, 'Zu den Ephemeriden Alexanders des Grossen, H 36 (1901), 319ff; C. Wachsmuth, 'Alexanders Epheremiden und Ptolemaios', RhM 56 (1901), 220ff; C. A. Robinson, Jr., *The Ephemerides of Alexander's expedition*, Providence, 1932.

⁷⁸ See (in addition to relevant works cited n77), E. Schwartz, RE 2. 1 s.v. *Aristoboulos* (14), 911ff (1895); Ed. Meyer, 'Arrians Geschichte Alexanders des Grossen', H 33 (1898), 648ff; F. Reuss, 'Arrian und Appian', RhM 54 (1899), 446ff; H. Endres, *Die offiziellen Grundlagen der Alexanderüberlieferung und das Werk des Ptolemäus*, Würzburg, 1913; F. Wenger, *Die Alexandergeschichte des Aristobul von Kassandreia*, Würzburg, 1914; H. Strassburger, *Ptolemaios und Alexander*, Leipzig, 1934; E. Kornemann, *Die Alexandergeschichte des Königs Ptolemaios I von Aegypten*, Leipzig and Berlin, 1935; P. Treves, 'L'œuvre historique du roi Ptolemée', REA 39 (1937), 267ff.

⁷⁹ Jacoby, RE 11 s.v. Kallisthenes (2) part 1, 1674ff (1919); *id.*, FGrH, no. 124; P. Cossen, 'Das angebliche Werk des Olynthiers Kallisthenes über Alexander', Ph 74 (1917), 1ff; C. A. Robinson, Jr., 'The seer Aristander', AJPh 50 (1929), 195ff; J. A. O. Larsen, 'Alexander at the Oracle of Ammon', CPh 27 (1932), 70ff, 274ff; P. Jouguet, 'Alexandre à l'oasis d'Ammon et le témoignage de Callisthène', BIE 26 (1943-44), 91ff; Tarn, *loc. cit.*, *supra*, 350ff; T. S. Brown, 'Callisthenes and Alexander', AJPh 77 (1949), 225ff.

⁸⁰ E. Schwartz, RE 4. 2 s.v. Curtius (31), 1871ff (1901); A. Ruegg, *Beiträge zur Erforschung der Quellenverhältnisse in der Alexandergeschichte des Curtius*, Basel, 1906; G. Radet, 'La valeur historique de Quint Curce', CRAI 1924, 356ff; Tarn, *loc. cit.*, *supra*, 116ff.

On 'hostile' tradition, W. Hoffmann, *Das literarische Porträt Alexanders des Grossen im griechischen und römischen Altertum*, Leipzig, 1907; L. Eiche, *Veterum philosophorum qualia fuerint de Alexandro Magno judicia*, Rostock, 1909; F. Weber, *Alexander der Grosse im Urteil der Griechen und Römer*, Leipzig, 1909; J. Stroux, 'Die stoische Beurteilung Alexanders des Grossen', Ph 88 (1933), 222ff; M. H. Fisch, 'Alexander and the Stoics', AJPh 58 (1937), 59ff.

⁸¹ T. S. Brown, *Onesicritus*, Berkeley (California, U.P.), 1949; cf. G. Radet, 'Notes sur l'histoire d'Alexandre', REA 27 (1925), 11ff, 81ff, 183ff; A. Körte, 'Anaximenes von Lampsakos als Alexanderhistoriker', RhM 61 (1906), 476ff; F. Pfister, 'Das Nachleben der Überlieferung von Alexander und den Brahmanen', H 76 (1941), 143ff. (And see on Clitarchus, n83.)

⁸² W. Kroll, RE 11 s.v. Kallisthenes (2) part 2, 1707ff (1919); *id.*, *Historia Alexandri Magni (Pseudo-Callisthenes)*, I, Berlin, 1926. A. Ausfeld, *Der griechische Alexanderroman*, Leipzig, 1907; E. Mederer, *Die Alexanderlegenden* (Würzburger Studien, No. 8), Stuttgart, 1936; B. Axelson, *Zum Alexanderroman des Julius Valerius*, Lund, 1936; A. Kurfess, 'Zu Pseudo-Callisthenes', PhW 59 (1939), 287ff, 942f.

[83] F. Reuss, 'Aristobul und Kleitarch', RhM 57 (1902), 581ff; id., 'Hellenistische Beiträge: Kleitarchos', RhM 63 (1908), 58ff; P. Schnabel, *Berossos und Kleitarchos*, Leipzig, 1912; Jacoby, RE 11 s.v. *Kleitarchos* (1922). Cf. also C. A. Robinson, Jr., *The Historian Chares*, New York, 1928.

[84] Tarn, *loc. cit.*, *supra*, especially, 1-55.

[85] *ibid.*, 63ff. See in general E. Schwartz, RE 5. 1. s.v. Diodoros (38). 663ff (1903); and many of the works cited above; also T. S. Brown, 'Clitarchus', AJPh 71 (1950), 134ff.

[86] Especially, J. E. Powell, 'The sources of Plutarch's *Alexander*', JHS 50 (1939), 229ff; Tarn, *loc. cit.*, 296ff.

[87] Bibliography in E. Mioni, *Polibio*, Padua (Cedam), 1949. General works: O. Cuntz, *Polybius und sein Werk*, Leipzig, 1902; C. Wunderer, *Die psychologischen Anschauungen des Historikers Polybios*, Erlangen, 1905; id., *Polybios, Leben und Weltanschauung aus dem 2. vorchristlichen Jahrhundert*, (Das Erbe der Alten) Leipzig, 1927; E. Schwartz, *Charakterköpfe aus der Antike*, 78ff, Leipzig, 1910 (= *id.*, ed. J. Stroux, Leipzig, 1943, 73ff); R. Laqueur, *Polybius*, Leipzig, 1913; B. Stumpo, 'Il pensiero di Polibio', Athenaeum, 9 (1921), 273ff; *ibid.*, 10 (1922), 153ff; G. de Sanctis, *Storia dei Romani*, III, 1, 200ff, Turin, 1917; T. R. Glover, CAH 8, 1ff; Cambridge (University Press) 1930; E. Sihler, 'Polybius of Megalopolis', AJPh 48 (1927), 38ff; W. Siegfried, *Studien zur geschichtlichen Anschauung des Polybios*, Leipzig, 1928; E. Ibendorff, *Untersuchungen zur darstellerischen Persönlichkeit des Polybios*, Rostock, 1930; K. Lorenz, *Untersuchungen zum Geschichtswerk des Polybios*, Stuttgart, 1931; K. Glaser, *Polybios als politischer Denker*, Vienna, 1940.

[88] On style in general, Mioni, *op. cit.*, 131ff. Cf. (in addition to works cited above), C. Wunderer, *Polybianische Forschungen. Beiträge zur Sprach- und Kulturgeschichte*, 1, 1898; 2, 1901; 3, 1909, Leipzig; Th. Büttner-Wobst, 'Der Hiatus nach dem Artikel bei Polybios', Ph 16 (1903), 541ff; H. F. Allen, *The infinitive in Polybius*, Chicago, 1907; K. Reik, *Der Optativ bei Polybios und Philo*, Diss. Leipzig, 1907; R. Limberger, *Die Nominalbildung bei Polybios*, Stuttgart, 1923; K. Lorenz, *Studien zu den Proömien der Bücher I und III des Polybios*, Diss. Halle, 1931; A. Feldmann, *Zum Aufbau der Geschichtserzählung bei Polybios*, Berne, 1929.

[89] Cf. especially de Sanctis, *op. cit.*, *supra* (n87); Mioni, *op. cit.*, especially chaps. 6 and 7; H. Ullrich, *Die Reden bei Polybios*, Zittau, 1905; *id.*, *De Polybii fontibus Rhodiis*, Leipzig, 1908; K. J. Beloch, 'Polybius' Quellen im dritten Buche', H 50 (1915), 357ff; Ed. Meyer, 'Zur Geschichte des Zweiten Punischen Krieges', SPAW 1915, 935ff; (1916), 1068ff; U. Kahrstedt, 'Zwei Urkunden aus Polybios', NGG 1923, 93ff; E. Bikermann, 'Notes sur Polybe', REG 50 (1937), 217ff; F. W. Walbank, Φίλιππος Τραγῳδούμενος, JHS 58 (1938), 55ff; *id.*, *Philip V of Macedon*, Cambridge (University Press), 1940, 278ff, and *passim*; F. W. Wood, 'The Tradition of Flaminius' selfish ambition in Polybius and later historians', TAPhA 70 (1939), 93ff; A. Aymard, 'Le fragment de Polybe "sur les traîtres",' REA 42 (1940), 9ff; I. V. A. Fine, 'The Background of the Social War of 220-17 B.C.', AJPh 61 (1940), 129ff; W. Hofmann, 'Ein Papyrusfund zum Frieden von 203', H 76 (1941), 270ff (discussing P. Rylands, 3, 491); M. Feyel, *Polybe et l'histoire de Béotie au III siècle a.C.*, Paris, 1942; J. P. V. D. Balsdon, 'Some questions about historical writing in the second century B.C.', CQ 3 (1953), 158ff.

[90] E. Meyer, *op. cit.*, *supra* (n89); R. Laqueur, 'Scipio Africanus und die Eroberung von Neukarthago', H 56 (1921), esp. 207ff. On documentary evidence, see also A. Schulten, 'De ratione quae intercedit inter Polybium et tabulas publicas', *Diss. philol. Halenses* 19 (1910), 167ff.

On Fabius Pictor, C. Sisto, 'Influenza di Fabio Pittore sull'opera di Polibio', A & R 33 (1931), 176ff.

[91] Especially, de Sanctis, *Storia* II, 252; L. Wickert, 'Zu den Karthagerverträgen', Kl 31 (1938), 349; R. L. Beaumont, 'The date of the first treaty between Rome and Carthage', JRS 29 (1939), 74ff.

[92] Mioni, especially chap. 6 and 8; cf. also W. Warde-Fowler, 'Polybius' conception of Tyche', CR 17 (1903), 445ff; P. Shorey, 'Tyche in Polybius' CPh 16 (1921), 280ff; E. Täubler, *Tyche*, Leipzig, 1926, 75ff; J. Laureys, *De Tyche en Polybius*, Diss. Louvain, 1943.

[93] See, besides discussions in general histories, G. Grasso, 'Il Λίβυρνον ὄρος polibiano ... etc.', RFC 30 (1902), 438ff; S. Wilkinson, 'Note on Polybius 3. 47-50 and

Livy 21, 31-32', CR 28 (1914), 123ff; W. Sontheimer, 'Der Feldzug Hannibals in Oberitalien bei Livius und Polybius', Kl 27 (1934), 84ff.
[94] Mioni, *op. cit.*, 127; cf. R. Thouvenot, 'Défense de Polybe', Hespéris 35 (1948), 79ff; J. O. Thomson, *op. cit.*, 183ff, 209ff.
[95] So already K. J. Neumann, 'Polybiana', 31 (1896), 519ff. See in general K. Swoboda, 'Die Abfassungszeit des Geschichtswerks des Polybios', Ph 72 (1913), 462ff; R. Laqueur, *op. cit.*, *supra* (n87); *id.*, 'Scipio Africanus und die Eroberung von Neukarthago', 56 (1921), 131ff; *id.*, 'Die Flucht des Demetrios aus Rom', 65 (1930), 129ff; M. Holleaux, 'Polybe et le tremblement de terre de Rhodes', REG 36 (1923), 480ff; E. Cavaignac, 'Sur l'économie de l'histoire de Polybe d'après Tite Live', RPh 50 (1926), 103ff; E. Hohl, 'Zu Polybios XXXI, 12' H 66 (1931), 91ff; F. W. Walbank, 'Polybius, Philinus and the first Punic War', CQ 39 (1945), 1ff; E. Mioni, *op. cit.*, chap. 3; P. Pédech, 'Sur les sources de Polybe: Polybe et Philinos', REA 54 (1952), 246ff; A. Klotz, 'Studien zu Polybios', H 80 (1952), 325ff.
[96] The most extreme views were those of Lacqueur, *opp. citt.*, *supra*: *contra* (*e.g.*), Holleaux, Hohl, Walbank, Mioni.
[97] The arguments are well resumed by Mioni, *loc. cit.*
[98] K. Glaser, *op. cit.*, 16ff; Mioni, *op. cit.*, chap. 4: see in general P. Zillig, *Die Theorie von der gemischten Verfassung*, Diss. Würzburg, 1915, 53ff; E. Ciaceri, 'Il trattato di Cicerone *De Republica* e le teorie di Polibio sulla costituzione romana', RAL 27 (1918), 237ff, 266ff, 303ff; F. Taeger, *Untersuchungen über das Weiterwirken des VI Buches des Polybius in der griechisch-römischen Literatur*, Diss. Tübingen, 1921; E. Kornemann, *op. cit.*, *supra* (n92); H. Staeglich, *Darstellung der Staatstheorie des Polybius und des M.T. Cicero*, Diss. Leipzig, 1933; L. Zancan, 'Dottrina delle costituzioni e decadenza politica in Polibio', RIL 69 (1936), 499ff; F. W. Walbank, 'Polybius and the Roman Constitution', CQ 37 (1943), 73ff; W. Theiler, 'Schichten im 6 Buch des Polybios', H 81 (1953), 296ff. Cf. also G. C. Richards, 'Polybius, the Greek admirer of Rome', CJ 40 (1944-45), 274ff.
[99] See Mioni, *op. cit.*, 161f (bibliography, IX — *Polibio e Tito Livio*).
[100] T. R. Glover, *loc. cit.*, *supra* (n87). For text and language, Mioni, 162ff (bibliography xii and xiii).
[101] In general, R. Hirzel, *Plutarch* (Das Erbe der Alten, 4), Leipzig, 1912; J. J. Hartmann, *De Plutarcho scriptore et philosopho*, Leiden, 1916; Christ–Schmid, *Geschichte der griechischen Literatur*[6], II, 1, 485-534, Munich, 1920; O. Göldi, *Plutarchs sprachliche Interessen*, Zurich, 1922; E. R. Dodds, 'The portrait of a Greek gentleman', *Greece and Rome* 2 (1933), 97ff; I. N. Barbu, *Les procédés de la peinture des caractères et la vérité historique dans les biographies de Plutarque*, Paris, 1934; H. C. Girard, *Essai sur la composition des Vies de Plutarque*, Thèse Paris, 1945; H. Schläpfer, *Plutarch und die klassichen Dichter*, Zurich, 1950; K. Ziegler, *Plutarchos von Chaironeia*, Stuttgart 1949; = RE21, s.v. Plutarchos (2), 636ff, and especially 895ff (1951).
[102] F. Leo, *Die griechisch-römische Biographie*, Leipzig, 1901; A. von Mess, *loc. cit.*, *supra* (n74).
[103] Christ–Schmid[6], II, 1, 519f; cf. also F. Focke, *Quaestiones Plutarcheae*, Diss. Münster, 1911, 50ff; C. Stolz, *Zur relativen Chronologie der Parallelbiographien Plutarchs*, Diss. Lund, 1929.
[104] For writers named by Plutarch, Christ–Schmid[6], *ibid.*, 522f.
[105] W. Graf Uxkull-Gyllenband, *Plutarch und die griechische Biographie*, Stuttgart, 1927; A. Weizsäcker, *Untersuchungen über Plutarchs biographische Technik*, Berlin, 1931.
[106] A. W. Gomme, *A Historical Commentary on Thucydides*, I, 54-84; cf. G. H. Stevenson, 'Ancient historians and their Sources', JPh (1920) 204ff; Gomme rightly stresses, too, that different *Lives* called for different methods of composition.
[107] On the text, especially K. Ziegler, *Die Überlieferungsgeschichte der verglichenen Lebensbeschreibungen Plutarchs*, Leipzig, 1907; *id.*, 'Plutarchstudien', i-xxi, RhM 63 (1908), 68 (1913), 76 (1927), 81 (1932), 82 (1933), 83 (1934), 85 (1935), 87 (1938): A. J. Kronenberg, 'Ad Plutarchi *Vitas*', Mn 55 (1927), 66ff; Ser. 3, 1 (1934), 161ff; 65 (1937), 303ff; C. Lindskog–K. Ziegler (ed.) *Plutarch: Vitae parallelae*, 4 vols., Leipzig (Teubner), 1914-39; English translation by A. Stewart-G. Long, 4 vols., London (Macmillan), 1906; B. Perrin (Loeb), 11 vols., London and Cambridge (Mass.) (Heinemann, Harvard U.P.), 1914-26; A. H. Clough, *Plutarch's Lives. The Translation called Dryden's*. Corrected and revised by AHC (5 vols.) Oxford (Clarendon), 1902.

Editions, commentaries and translations of individual *Lives* are too numerous to mention here.
Among particular studies (especially on sources) may be mentioned: W. Soltau, *Die Quellen Plutarchs in der Biographie des Valerius Poplicola*, Progr. Zabern 1905; J. J. Hartinan, 'De Plutarchi studiis Latinis', Mn 34 (1906), 307ff; L. Peper, *De Plutarchi Epaminonda*, Diss. Jena, 1912; F. E. Adcock, *art. cit.*, Kl 12 (1912), 1ff; *id.*, 'The source of Plutarch *Solon*', xx–xxiv, CR 28 (1914), 38ff; W. Uxkull-Gyllenband, *Die Quellen in Plutarchs Kimon*, Diss. Heidelberg, 1923; E. Bux, 'Zwei sozialistische Novellen bei Plutarchus', Kl 19, 1925, 413ff; R. Zimmermann, 'Die Quellen Plutarchs in der Biographie des Marcellus', RhM 79 (1930), 56ff; A. Klotz, 'Die Quellen der plutarchischen Lebensbeschreibung des Marcellus', RhM 83 (1934), 289ff; *id.*, 'Die Quellen Plutarchs in der Lebensbeschreibung des T. Quinctius Flamininus', *ibid.*, 84 (1935), 46ff; *id.*, 'Über die Quellen... etc. Q Fabius Maximus', *ibid.*, 125ff; *id.*, 'De Plutarchi vitae Caesarianae fontibus', Mn Ser. 3, 6 (1938), 313ff; *id.*, 'Zu den Quellen, etc. ... Camillus', RhM 90 (1941), 282ff; F. R. B. Godolphin, 'The source of Plutarch's thesis in the *Lives* of Galba and Otho', AJPh 56 (1935), 324ff; H. D. Westlake, 'The sources of Plutarch's Timoleon', CQ 32 (1938), 65ff; *id.*, 'The sources etc. ... Pelopidas', *ibid.*, 33 (1939), 11ff; J. E. Powell, 'The sources of Plutarch's Alexander', JHS 59 (1939), 229ff; R. E. Smith, 'Plutarch's biographical sources in the Roman Lives', CQ 34 (1940), 1ff; *id.*, 'The Cato Censorius of Plutarch', *ibid.*, 105ff; *id.*, 'The sources of Plutarch's Life of Titus Flamininus', *ibid.*, 38 (1944), 88ff; P. v.d. Mühll, 'Antiker Historismus in Plutarchs Biographie des Solon', Kl 35 (1942), 89ff; F. Robert, 'La réhabilitation de Phocion et la méthode historique du Plutarch', CRAI 1945, 526ff; G. Delvaux, 'Les sources de Plutarque dans les Vies parallèles des Romains', Diss. Brussels, 1946; R. Flacelière, 'Sur quelques passages des Vies de Plutarque, I Thésée-Romulus', REG 61 (1948), 67ff; 'II Lycurgue-Numa', *ibid.*, 391ff; P. de Lacy, 'Biography and Tragedy in Plutarch', AJPh 73 (1952), 159ff.
On συγκρίσεις, K. Prieth, *Einige Bemerkungen zu den parallelen Biographien Plutarchs, mit besonderer Berücksichtigung der* συγκρίσεις; Progr. Wels 1908; F. Leo, *op. cit.*, 149ff; R. Hirzel, *op. cit.*, 71ff; M. A. Stiefenhofer, *Die Echtheitsfrage der biographischen Synkriseis des Plutarch*, Diss. Giessen, 1915.

[108] On Posidonius, see Jacoby, FGrH 2A, No. 87, 222ff; *ibid.*, 2C, 154ff; G. D. Ohling, *Quaestiones Poseidonianae ex Strabone collectae*, Diss. Göttingen, 1907; H. Binder, *Dio Chrysostomos und Posidonios*, Diss. Tübingen, 1907; E. Norden, *Die germanische Urgeschichte in Tacitus Germania*, Berlin, 1920 (2nd ed., 1921); K. Reinhardt, *Poseidonios*, Munich, 1921; A. Mühl, *Poseidonios und der plutarchische Marcellus: Untersuchung zur Geschichtsschreibung des Poseidonios von Apameia*, Berlin, 1925; J. Morr, *Die Quellen von Strabons drittem Buch*, Ph Suppl. 18.3 (1926); R. Munz, *Poseidonios und Strabon, I Voruntersuchungen*, Göttingen, 1929; G. Pasquali, 'Cesare, Platone e Posidonio', SFC 8 (1931), 297ff; G. Stümpel, *Name und Nationalität der Germanen, Eine neue Untersuchung zu Posidonios, Cäsar und Tacitus*, Kl Beiheft 25, Leipzig, 1932; M. Truscelli, 'I Κελτικά di Posidonio e loro influssi sulla posteriore etnografia', RAL 11 (1935), 609ff; A. Vogliano-L. Salvestroni, 'Sulle orme di Posidonio', La Parola di Passato 2 (1947), 90ff; K. Reinhardt, RE 22.i. s.v. Poseidonios (3), 558ff, and especially 630ff, 822ff (1953).
On Nicolaus of Damascus, Jacoby, FGrH 2A, No. 90, 324ff; *ibid.*, 2C, 229ff; P. Jacob, *De Nicolai Damasceni sermone et arte historica*, Diss. Göttingen, 1911; R. Laqueur RE 17 s.v. Nikolaos (20), 362ff (1937).

[109] Edition: F. Vogel and C. T. Fischer, Teubner 5 vols. (1887-1906).
A. B. Drachmann, *Diodorus: Römische Annalen bis 302 a.Chr. samt dem Ineditum Vaticanum*, Bonn, 1912. English translation (Loeb) C. H. Oldfather, R. M. Geer, C. L. Sherman 1-5, 9, London (Heinemann), 1933-48.
On text and language: H. Kallenberg, *Textkritik und Sprachgebrauch Diodors*, Berlin, 1901; R. Kapff, *Der Gebrauch des Optativus bei Diodorus Siculus*, Diss. Tübingen, 1903; H. Kallenberg, 'Textkritisches zu Diodor', RhM 63 (1908), 260ff; R. Laqueur, 'Untersuchungen zur Textgeschichte des Diodor', NGG 1906, 313ff; E. L. Green, 'Der Optativ bei Diodor', TAPhA 34 (1903), 40ff; S. Peppink, 'De Diodori codice antiquissimo', RFC 12 (1934), 156ff.
Some general studies: E. Schwartz, RE 5. i. s.v. Diodoros (38), 663ff (1903); A. von Mess, 'Untersuchungen über die Arbeitsweise Diodors', RhM 60 (1905), 244ff; R. Laqueur, 'Zur griechischen Sagenchronographie', H 42 (1907), 513ff; M. Kunz, *Zur*

Beurteilung der Prooemien in Diodors historischer Bibliothek, Zürich, 1935; B. Farrington, *Diodorus Siculus universal historian*, Swansea (University of Wales), 1937; E. Troilo, 'Considerazioni su Diodoro Siculo e la sua Storia universale', AIV (1940-41), 17ff; G. Vlastos, 'On the pre-history in Diodorus', AJPh 67 (1946), 51ff.

[110] A. Scherr, *Diodors XI. Buch, Compositions- und Quellenstudien*, Bottrop, 1933; W. Kolbe, 'Diodors Wert für die Geschichte der Pentekontaetie', H 72 (1937), 241ff.

[111] N. G. L. Hammond, 'Diodorus' narrative of the Sacred War and the chronological problems of 357-352 B.C.', JHS 57 (1937), 44ff; *id.*, 'The Sources of Diodorus Siculus XVI', I, CQ 31 (1937), 79ff; II, *ibid.*, 32 (1938), 137ff; S. Accame, 'Le fonte di Diodoro per la guerra Decelaica', RAL, S. 6, 14 (1938), 347ff. Cf. also K. Uhlemann, *Untersuchungen über die Quellen der Geschichte Philipps von Makedonien . . . im 16. Buch Diodors*, Diss. Strassburg, 1914; E. Cavaignac, 'Réflexions sur Éphore', *Mélanges G. Glotz*, Paris, 1932, I, 143ff; A. Momigliano, 'Le fonti della storia greca e macedone nel libro XVI di Diodoro', RIL 65 (1935), 523ff; L. Robert, 'Diodore XIV 84.3 — Études d'épigraphie grecque', RPh 60 (1934), 43ff; D. E. W. Wormell, 'The literary tradition concerning Hermias of Atarneus', YClS 5 (1935), 57ff; P. Treves, 'Per la critica et l'analisi del libro XVI di Diodoro', ASNP, Ser. 2, 6 (1937), 255ff; M. Tonev, 'Die Chronologie des dritten heiligen Krieges und die Jahreseinteilung im XVI Buch Diodors', *Stud. hist.-phil. Serdicensia* I, 165ff (Sofia), 1938.

[112] H. Endres, 'Krateros, Perdikkas, und die letzten Pläne Alexanders. Eine Studie zu Diodor XVIII, 4. 1-6'. RhM 72 (1918), 437ff; W. W. Tarn, 'Alexander's ὑπομνήματα and the "World-kingdom",' JHS 41 (1921), 1ff; *id.*, 'Alexander's Plans', JHS 59 (1939), 124ff; *id.*, *Alexander the Great, II Sources and Studies*, 378ff; U. Wilcken, 'Die letzten Pläne Alexanders des Grossen', SPAW 24 (1937), 192ff.

For Diodorus as a source for Alexander in general see p. 169 *supra*.

For Books xviii-xx, G. Mehret, *De Duride Samio et Hieronymo Cardiano Diodori Siculi auctoribus eorumque arte et ratione*, Diss. Leipzig, 1921: C. Bottin, 'Les sources de Diodore de Sicile', RBPh 7 (1928), 1307ff; W. Schwahn, 'Diyllos', Ph 86 (1931), 145ff; A. Momigliano, 'Due problemi storiografici', RIL 65 (1932), 569ff; A. Wilhelm, 'Diodoros XIX, 45', RhM 84 (1935), 250ff; T. S. Brown, 'Hieronymus of Cardia', AHR 52 (1946-47), 684ff.

[113] On the Roman sections: G. Sigwart, 'Römische Fasten und Annalen', Kl 6 (1906), 269ff, 341ff; P. Varese, 'La fonte annalistica di Diodoro per l'età della prima guerra punica', SSAC (1910), 219ff; R. Laqueur, 'Diodors Bericht über die Schlacht an der Allia', PhW 41 (1921), 861ff; A. Rosenberg, *Einleitung und Quellenkunde zur römischen Geschichte*, Berlin, 1921, 118ff; A. Klotz, 'Diodors römische Annalen', RhM 86 (1937), 206ff; *id.*, *Livius und seine Vorgänger, III*, Leipzig, 1941; F. Altheim, 'Diodors römische Annalen', RhM 93 (1950), 267ff.

[114] In general, on the third century, M. Holleaux, *Rome, la Grèce, et les monarchies hellénistiques* Paris, 1927, chap. 1-2.

[115] Edition: C. Jacoby, IV, 1905; *Suppl.* (*Indices*) 1925, Leipzig (Teubner).

Translation: E. Cary, *Dionysius of Halicarnassus, The Roman Antiquities* (Loeb), 1-7, London (Heinemann) and Cambridge (Harvard U.P.) 1937-50.

Cf. also A. G. Roos, 'De fragmentis nonnullis Antiquitatum Romanorum libris postremis', Mn (1910), 281ff; S. Peppink, 'De duobus Dionysii Antiquitatum codicibus Vaticanis', RFC 13 (1935), 226ff; S.Ek, *Herodotismen in der Archäologie des Dionys von Halikarnass*, Lund, 1942; B. L. Ullman, 'Dionysius on Saturnian verse', CPh 39 (1944), 47ff; H. J. Rose, 'Unmetrical "Triumph-songs" ', *ibid.*, 258; S.Ek, 'Eine Stiltendenz in der römischen Archäologie des Dionysios von Halikarnass', Eranos, 7 (1945), 198ff (Mélanges Löfstedt).

[116] E. Schwartz, RE 5. 1. s.v. Dionysios (113), 934ff (1903); F. Halbfass, *Theorie und Praxis in der Geschichtsschreibung von Dionysio von Halikarnassos*, Diss. Münster, 1910; E. Skard, 'Epigraphische Formeln bei Dionys von Halikarnass', *Symbolae Osloenses* 11 (1932), 55ff; E. Gaida, *Die Schlachtschilderungen in den Antiquitates Romanae des Dionys von Halikarnass*, Breslau, 1934; A. Klotz, 'Zu den Quellen der Archaiologia des Dionysios von Halikarnassos', RhM 87 (1938), 32ff; *id.*, *Livius und seine Vorgänger, III*, Leipzig, 1941.

[117] F. Jacoby, RE 9. 2. s.v. Iuba (2), 2384ff, and especially 2393ff (1916).

[118] See, first, E. Schwartz, RE 2.1. s.v. Appianus (2) 216ff (1895).

[119] E. Kornemann, *Die neue Liviusepitome*, Kl Beiheft 2, Leipzig, 1904 [on P. Oxyrh.

THE GREEK HISTORIANS 223

4. 668]; F. Münzer, 'Anmerkungen zur neuen Liviusepitome', Kl 5 (1905) 137ff; A. Schulten, *Numantia* III (Exkurs I: *Die Quellen von Appians Iberica*, 1-43) Munich, 1927; E. Meyer, *Caesars Monarchie und die Prinzipät des Pompeius*, Stuttgart, 1918, 603ff; L. Piotrowicz, *Plutarque et Appien. Recherches sur les Sources de l'histoire romaine à l'époque des révolutions*, Posen, 1921 [In Polish]; E. Kornemann 'Die unmittelbare Vorlage von Appians Emphylia', Kl 17 (1921), 33ff.

[120] Especially, I. N. Barbu, *Les sources et l'originalité d'Appien dans le deuxième livre des Guerres Civiles*, Paris, 1934. Cf. also W. Ensslin, 'Appian und die Liviustradition zum ersten Bürgerkrieg', Kl 21 (1925), 415ff; J. H. Thiel, 'Deux notes sur l'histoire des Gracques' (à propos d'Appien Guerres Civiles, 1. 12. 47-54) Mn (1933-34) 61ff; A. Klotz, *Appians Darstellung des zweiten punischen Krieges*, Paderborn, 1936; R. M. Geer, 'Plutarch and Appian on Tiberius Gracchus', Class. and Med. Studies in honour of E. K. Rand, New York, 1937, 117ff; I. Calabi, 'I commentarii di Silla come fonte historia', MAL 8 Ser. 3 (1950), 245ff.

Edition: P. Viereck, *Historia romana*, vol. II (ed. alt. correctior), Leipzig (Teubner), 1905. Text with English Translation: H. White, *Appian's Roman History* (4 vols.), London (Heinemann-Loeb), 1912.

[121] Editions: U. P. Boissevain, vol. 3, 1901; 4 (H. Smilda-Index), 1926; 5 (W. Nawijn-Index graecitatis), 1931; J. Melber, vol. 3, Leipzig (Teubner), 1928. Translation: E. Cary, *Dio's Roman History* (9 vols.), London (Heinemann-Loeb), 1914-26.

Cf. also H. von Herwerden, 'Spicilegium Dionis', RhM 64 (1909), 161ff; J. B. Ullrich, *Über die Latinismen des Dio Cassius*, Progr. Nuremberg, 1912; A. G. Roos, 'Über einige Fragmente des Cassios Dio', Kl 16 (1916), 75ff; H. I. Botshuyver, *Der Optativgebrauch bei Cassius Dio*, Diss. Amsterdam, 1923.

[122] E. Schwartz, RE 3 s.v. Cassius 40 (1899), 1684ff; Ed. Meyer, *Caesars Monarchie*, 605f; A. Klotz, 'Uber die Stellung des Cassius Dio unter den Quellen zur Geschichte des zweiten punischen Krieges', RhM 85 (1936), 68ff.

[123] W. F. Snijder, 'On chronology in the imperial books of Dio's Roman history', Kl 33 (1940), 39ff.

Cf. also for D's methods of composition and performance: D. R. Stuart, 'The attitude of Dio Cassius toward epigraphic sources' UMS, (1904), 101ff; J. C. P. Smits, *Die Vita Commodi und Cassius Dio*, Leiden, 1914; G. Vrind, *De Cassii Dionis vocabulis quae ad ius publicum pertinent*, Diss. Amsterdam, 1923; id., 'De Cassii Dionis historiis', Mn 54 (1926), 321ff; M. Hammond, 'The significance of the speech of Maecenas in Dio Cassius Book LII', TAPhA 63 (1932), 88ff (cf. P. Meyer, *De Maecenatis oratione a Dione ficta*, Diss. Berlin, 1891); H. A. Andersen, *Cassius Dio und die Begründung des Principats*, Berlin, 1938; D. M. Pippidi, 'Dion Cassius et la religion des empéreurs', Rev. hist. du Sud-Est européen 19 (1942), 407ff; A. Freixas, 'La divinación imperial en Dion Cassio', AILC 2 (1940-44), 15ff (Buenos Aires); H. Hagendahl, 'The mutiny of Vesonto', C & M 6 (1944), 1-40; K. Heinz, *Das Bild Kaiser Neros bei Seneca, Tacitus und Cassius Dio*, Diss. Berne, 1948.

[124] Especially, M. Hammond, *loc. cit., supra* (n123).

[125] H. A. Andersen, *op. cit., supra* (n123); cf. E. Cornelius, 'Zum politischen Testament des Augustus', PhW 59 (1939), 735.

[126] P. S. Rogers, 'Ignorance of the law in Tacitus and Dio. Two instances from the history of Tiberius', TAPhA 64 (1933), 18ff.

[127] Edition (Teubner): K. Stavenhagen, *Ab excessu divi Marci libri octo*, Leipzig, 1922. Cf. also E. Baaz, *De Herodiani fontibus et auctoritate*, Diss. Berlin, 1909; J. C. P. Smits, *De Geschiedschrijier Herodian en zijn Bronnen*, Leiden, 1913; H. Schultz, RE s.v. Herodianus (3), 954ff (1913); A. G. Roos, 'Herodian's method of composition', JRS 5 (1915), 191ff; E. Hohl, 'Die Ermordung des Commodus. Ein Beitrag zur Beurteilung Herodians', PhW 52 (1932), 1135ff; id., 'Die "gotische Abkunft" des Kaisers Maximinus Thrax', Kl 34 (1941), 92ff; G. M. Bersanetti, 'Sulla guerra fra Septimio Severo e Pescennio Nigro in Erodiano', RFC 16 (1938), 357ff.

[128] K. Hartmann, 'Über das Verhältnis des Cassius Dio zur Parthergeschichte des Flavius Arrianus', Mn (1946), 73ff.

Editions: A. G. Roos, 1 *Anabasis*; 2 *Scripta minora et Fragmenta*, Leipzig (Teubner), 1907-28.

THE GREEK HISTORIANS

Text with English translation: E. I. Robson, *Anabasis and India I*, 1929; 2, 1933, London (Heinemann-Loeb). Cf. also (in addition to works cited above, nn77-8) F. Bersanetti, *L'Anabasi di Arriana. Studio critico-filologico*, Turin, 1904; C. Patsch, 'Arrians *Periplus Ponti Euxini*', Kl 4 (1904), 68ff; A. G. Roos, *Prolegomena ad Arrians Anabaseos et Indicae editionem criticam edendam*, Groningen 1904; *id.*, *Studia Arrianea*, Leipzig, 1912; *id.*, 'Ad U.P. Boissevain septuagenarium epistula de Arriani Periplo Ponti Euxini', Mn (1926), 101ff; *id.*, 'De Arriani Indicae dialecto Ionica', *ibid.*, 55 (1927), 23ff; J. Meunier, 'Les sources de la monographie d'Arrien sur l'Inde', MB 19 (1922), 5ff; V. Chapot, 'Arrien et le Périple du Pont-Euxin', REG 34 (1921), 129ff; C. Fries, 'Zu Arrians Anabasis Alexandri', PhW 58 (1938), 590f; G. Radet, 'Notes sur l'histoire d'Alexandre IX', REA 43 (1941), 33ff; A. Stein, 'On Alexander's route into Gedrosia', GJ 102 (1943), 193ff; J. Dziech, 'De Graecis Brahmanum aestimatoribus', Eos 44, 1 (1950), 5ff.

K. Latte, 'Ein neues Arrianfragment', NGG ph.-hist. Kl 1950, 3, shows good cause for believing that PSI 12.2, No. 1284 (ed. V. Bartoletti) is a fragment of Arrian's τὰ μετ' Ἀλέξανδρον, and not of Hieronymus.

APPENDIX TO CHAPTER VI

Since 1954 work on all the main Greek historians, including some of the non-survivors, has given good results. Important books on the foundations of Sicilian history and chronology by R. van Compernolle; on Thucydides by A. W. Gomme, J. de Romilly, F. E. Adcock and E. Delebecque; on Xenophon by Delebecque; on Aristotle's *Athenaion Politeia* by J. Day and M. Chambers, and on his *Politics* by R. Weil; on Timaeus by Truesdell S. Brown; on Polybius by F. W. Walbank and P. Pédech; on Phylarchus by T. W. Africa; on Posidonius by M. Laffranque; on the lost histories of Alexander by L. Pearson; on the Roman chronology of Diodorus Siculus by G. Perl; on the Siceliot historians by G. de Sanctis; on Plutarch's historical methods by M. A. Levi and P. A. Stadter; on Appian by E. Gabba; on Dio Cassius by F. Millar; on the technique of Herodotus, Thucydides, Xenophon and Arrian by H. Montgomery—the list speaks for itself: and it is a 'short list' at that.[1] The spoken word of some distinguished historians of antiquity who met in 1956 under the auspices of Fondation Hardt adds its significant testimony.[2]

Meanwhile the articles have appeared in profusion. For the central figures of this chapter, Herodotus and Thucydides, I am absolved from evaluation in detail by the admirable surveys which have appeared in these years in *Classical Weekly*, from the pens of F. M. Wassermann, P. M. MacKendrick and M. Chambers.[3] For Herodotus, the trend continues to be favourable, with a few exceptions, to his reputation both as an historian and as an artist. Thucydides, having almost the least in common of all Greek writers with the common man, remains partly for that reason impenetrable; or at least not entirely penetrable. To understand what he meant to say is one thing. It is another thing to know whether he was too much the aristocrat himself, too much the highbrow, too much the exile really to understand the (mostly) much more ordinary people that he wrote about. Unfair to Cleon? Yes clearly, on one plane; but on another plane, was it really *possible* to be unfair to Cleon? Dilemmas such as this continue to haunt the modern interpreter. Encouraging is the persistence (revival, even?) in some form of a view that Thucydides wrote what he did at 1.22.1 (on his method of writing the speeches) to enlighten his readers and not to bamboozle them. This seems such plain good sense that it must always have stood a fair chance of being the truth, even if not the kind of truth that is sure to prevail.

The 'Themistocles Decree' from Troezen has aroused great interest; and the questioning by H. B. Mattingly of the chronological framework for the development of the Athenian empire constructed by the editors of the *Athenian Tribute Lists* has led to a stimulating exchange of views, which may lead to some interesting reappraisals. Both these topics, however, fall outside the scope of this Appendix. The sector in which, as it seems to me, a radical reappraisal has taken place since 1954 is that of the Alexander historians, where the view of Alexander himself is affected greatly by a revaluation of what may be called the non-official strands in the tradition, and by a more sceptical attitude to the official tradition preserved especially by Arrian. Articles by E. Badian and others have changed the picture substantially; the *Heldenleben* has come to verge on Elizabethan tragedy, and this may indeed be of the truth. What is certain is that those contemporaries of Alexander who knew the whole truth cannot be trusted entirely to have told it in what they wrote, and not always for the same reasons. The war must go on (and I am sure it will).

A select bibliography follows for the years since 1954 (I have included in it a few titles of 1954 itself or earlier which were not available to me when I wrote the original chapter). All books and articles on Greek history, other than the purely popular or derivative, are concerned with the Greek historians, and the task of selecting titles for this list is invidious. My aim has been to try to choose those works which I knew of, whatever their titles, which had a bearing on the historians themselves both direct and considerable. For example, a group of articles on the popularity (or unpopularity) of the Athenian empire are included here (for their bearing on Thucydides), whereas a series of articles by G. L. Cawkwell which contribute notably to fourth-century interpretations are not. In making these decisions I am bound to have made some mistakes, for which I apologize in anticipation.

APPENDIX

On early historians:
R. van Compernolle, *op. cit. infra*, n. 1.
G. Nenci, *Hecataei Milesii Fragmenta*, Florence, 1954; *id.*, 'Una riposta delfica alla metodologia ecataica (Pindaro, *Olimpica* I, 28-36)', CS 3 (1964), 269ff. P. Tozzi, 'Ecateo di Mileto in Eustazio', *Athenaeum* 39 (1961), 26ff: *id.*, 'Studi su Ecateo di Mileto', I, *ibid.*, 41 (1963), 39ff; II, *ibid.*, 318ff; III, *ibid.*, 42 (1964), 101ff; IV, *ibid.*, 44 (1966), 41ff.
H. Diller, 'Zwei Erzählungen der Lyder Xanthos', *Navicula Chiloniensis* (Festschr. Jacoby), Leiden, 1956, 66ff; H. H. Scullard, 'Two Halicarnassians and a Lydian', *Ancient Society and Institutions. Studies presented to V. Ehrenberg*, Oxford (Blackwell), 1966, 225ff; F. P. Rizzo, 'Racconto della spedizione ateniese a Corcira in Ellanico e Tucidide', RFC 94 (1966), 273ff; A. Momigliano, 'Ellanica e gli storici d. guerra d. Peloponneso', *Athenaeum* 44 (1966), 134ff.
F. Jacoby, *FGrH* III C 2, Leiden, 1958, includes Xanthus (no. 765).

On Herodotus:
General—T. S. Brown, 'H. and his profession', AHR 59 (1953-54), 829ff; A. W. Gomme, *The Greek attitude to Poetry and History*, Berkeley, 1954, 73ff; K. Latte, 'Die Anfänge der griechischen Geschichtsschreibung'; *Entretiens Hardt*, 4 (1965), 3ff; A. Lesky, *Geschichte der griechischen Literatur*, Berne, 1958, 286ff; A. Momigliano, 'The place of H. in the history of historiography', *History* 43 (1958), 1ff; J. Wikarjak, *L'histoire générale d'H.'*, Posen, 1961; A. de Sélincourt, *The world of H.*, London and Boston, 1962; A. R. Burn, *Persia and the Greeks*, London and New York, 1962; C. Hignett, *Xerxes' invasion of Greece*, Oxford, 1963.
Editions, Language, etc.—P. E. Legrand, *Hérodote* IX, Paris, 1954; *id.*, X (Index analytique), Paris, 1964; A. Thumb, A. Scherer, *Handbuch der griechischen Dialekte*, Ed. 2, Heidelberg, 1959, 194ff; H. B. Rosén, *Eine Laut- und Formenlehre der herodoteischen Sprachform*, Heidelberg, 1962.
Composition, methods, causation, etc.—H. Volkmann, 'Die Inschriften im Geschichtswerk des H', *Convivium* (Festgabe Ziegler), Stuttgart, 1954, 41ff; R. Lattimore, 'The composition of the history of H.', CP 53 (1958), 9ff; H. Erbse, 'Tradition und Form im Werke H.s', *Gymn.* 68 (1961), 239ff; H. Immerwahr, 'Historical action in H.', TAPA 85 (1954), 16ff; *id.*, 'The Samian stories of H.', CJ 52 (1957), 312ff; *id.*, 'Aspects of historical causation in H.',

TAPA 87 (1956), 241ff; *id.*, 'Ergon: History as a monument in H. and Thucydides', AJP 81 (1960), 261ff; R. Crahay, *La littérature oraculaire chez H.*, Paris, 1956; G. Nenci, *Introduzione alle guerre persiane e altri saggi di storia antica*, Pisa, 1958; A. E. Wardman, 'H. on the causes of the Greco-Persian wars', AJP 82 (1961), 133ff; H. T. Wallinga, 'The structure of H. 2. 99-142', *Mn* N.S. 12 (1959), 204ff. H. Homeyer, 'Zu den Anfänge der griechischen Biographie', *Eranos* 60 (1962), 132ff; M. Miller, 'The Herodotean Croesus', *Klio* 41 (1963), 58ff; F. J. Groten, 'H.'s use of variant versions', *Phoenix* 17 (1963), 79ff; H. Fahr, *Kambyses, Ein Beitrag zur Herodotinterpretation*, Diss. Hamburg, 1959; H. Barth, *Methodologische und historiographische Probleme der Geschichtsschreibung des H.*, Diss. Halle, 1963; P. T. Brannan, 'H. and history. The constitutional debate preceding Darius' accession', *Traditio* 19 (1963), 427ff; K. H. Waters, 'The purpose of dramatisation in H.', *Historia* 15 (1966), 157ff.

Herodotus and Athens—G. Vlastos, 'Isonomia', AJP 74 (1953), 337ff; H. Strasburger, 'H. und das perikleische Athen', *Historia* 4 (1955), 1ff; A. E. Wardman, 'Tactics and the tradition of the Persian Wars', *Historia* 8 (1959), 49ff; H. Erbse, 'Anmerkungen zu H.', *Glotta* 39 (1960-61), 215ff.

Herodotus and Foreign Peoples—E. Leudekkers, 'H. und Aegypten', ZDMG 29 (1954), 330ff; O. Seel 'Herakliden und Mermnaden', *Nav. Chil.* (Jacoby Festschrift), Leiden, 1956, 37 ff.; H. Diesner, 'Scythische Religion und Geschichte bei H.', RhM 104 (1961), 202ff; D. Herminghausen, *H.'s Angabe über Aethiopien*, Diss. Hamburg, 1963; H. Klienknecht, 'H. u. d. maked. Urgeschichte *Hermes* 94 (1966), 134ff.

Religion and ethos—W. Pötscher, 'Götter und Gottheit bei H.', WS 71 (1958), 5ff; A. Dihle, 'Aus H.s Gedankenwelt', *Gymn.* 69 (1962), 22ff; *id.*, 'H. und die Sophistik', *Philologus* 106 (1962), 207ff; L. Hüber, *Religiöse und politische Beweggründe des Handels in der Geschichtsschreibung des H.*, Diss. Tübingen, 1963.

Chronology and Topography—N. G. L. Hammond, 'Studies in Greek chronology of the Sixth and Fifth Centuries B.C.', *Historia* 4 (1955), 370ff; *id.*, H. Strasburger, 'H.s Zeitrechnung', *Historia* 5 (1965), 129ff; F. Mitchel, 'H.'s use of Genealogical Chronology', *Phoenix* 10 (1956), 48ff; H. U. Instinsky, 'H. und der erste Zug des Mardonius gegen Griechenland', *Hermes* 84 (1956), 477ff; W. K. Pritchett, 'New light on Platea', AJA 61 (1957), 9ff; *id.*, 'New

light on Thermopylae', *ibid.*, 62 (1958), 203ff; *id.*, 'Xerxes' route over Mount Olympus', *ibid.*, 65 (1961), 369ff; *id.*, *Marathon*, U. Cal. Publ. Cl. Arch. 4. 2, Berkeley, 1960; H. Kaletsch, 'Zur lydischer Chronologie', *Historia* 7 (1958), 1ff; M. Miller, 'The earlier Persian dates in H.', *Klio* 37 (1959), 29ff.
Reliability—A. Blamire, 'H. and Histiaeus', CQ, N.S. 9 (1959), 142ff; F. Haible, *H. und die Wahrheit. Untersuchungen zur Wahrheitsbegriff, Kritik und Argumentation bei H.*, Diss. Tübingen, 1963; G. Gottlieb, *Das Verhältnis der ausserherodoteischen Ueberlieferung zu Herodot*, Diss. Bonn, 1963; M. White, 'The duration of the Samian Tyranny', JHS 74 (1954), 36ff, cf. T. J. Cadoux, *ibid.*, 76 (1956), 105f; J. P. Barron, 'The sixth-century tyranny at Samos', CQ, N.S. 14 (1964), 210ff; T. S. Brown, 'H. speculates about Egypt', AJP 86 (1965), 60ff.

On Thucydides:
General—J. de Romilly, A. W. Gomme, F. E. Adcock, *op. cit. infra*, n. 1; A. W. Gomme, *The Greek Attitude to Poetry and History*, Berkeley, 1954, 116ff; *id.*, *More Essays in Greek History and Literature* Oxford (Blackwell), 1962, 112ff; H. Strasburger, 'Die Entdeckung der politischen Geschichte durch T.', *Saeculum* 5 (1954), 395ff; W. Eberhardt, 'Die Geschichtsdeutung des T.', *Gymn.* 61 (1954), 306ff; F. M. Wassermann, 'Die Warnung des T.', *Neues Abendland* 10 (1955), 267ff; R. Syme, 'Thucydides', PBA 48 (1963), 39ff.
Text, etc.—O. Luschnat, *Thucydides* I (Bks. 1 and 2), Leipzig (Teubner), 1954; L. Bodin, J. de Romilly, *Thucydide* VI and VII, Paris, 1955 (Budé); J. de Romilly, *Thucydide* II Paris, 1962 (Budé); B. D. Meritt, 'Indirect tradition in T.', *Hesperia* 23 (1954), 185ff; B. D. Hemmerdinger, *Essai sur l'histoire du Text de T.*, Paris, 1955; A. Kleinlogel, *Geschichte des Thukydidestextes im Mittelalter*, Berlin, 1965.
Language, Style, etc.—P. Moreaux, 'T. et la rhétorique. Étude sur le structure des deux discours III. 37-48', LEC 22 (1954), 3ff; C. Meister, *Die Gnomik im Geschichtswerk des T.*, Diss. Basel, 1955; J. T. Kakridis, *Der Thukydideische Epitaphios. Ein stilistischer Kommentar*, Munich, 1961; J. E. Ziolkowski, *T. and the tradition of funeral speeches at Athens*, Diss. N. Carolina, Chapel Hill, 1963.
Aims—J. de Romilly, 'Utilité de l'histoire selon T.' *Entretiens Hardt* 4 (1956), Geneva, 1958, 41ff; F. Egermann, 'Zum historiographischen Ziel des T.', *Historia* 10 (1961), 435ff.

Accuracy—R. Sealey, 'The great earthquake in Lacedaemon', *Historia* 6 (1957), 368ff; cf. N. G. L. Hammond, *ibid.*, 8 (1959), 490; D. W. Reece, 'The date of the fall of Ithome', JHS 82 (1962), 111ff; S. Dow, 'T. and the number of Acharnian *Hoplitai*', TAPA 92 (1961), 66ff; W. E. Thompson, 'Three thousand Acharnian Hoplites', *Historia* 13 (1964), 300ff; A. R. Burn, *ibid.*, 14 (1965), 376; W. K. Pritchett and B. L. van der Waerden, 'Thucydidean time-reckoning and Euctemon's Seasonal Calendar', BCH 85 (1961), 17ff; B. D. Meritt, 'The seasons in T.', *Historia*, 11 (1962), 436ff. W. K. Pritchett, 'T. v. 20', *Historia* 13 (1964), 21ff; *id.*, 'The Thucydidean summer of 411 B.C.', CPh 60 (1965), 259ff.

Finance—H. T. Wade-Gery and B. D. Meritt, 'Athenian resources in 449 and 431 B.C.', *Hesperia* 26 (1957), 163ff; R. Sealey, 'P. Strassburg 84 Verso', *Hermes* 86 (1958), 440ff; M. Chambers, 'Four hundred and sixty talents', CP 53 (1958), 26ff; M. F. McGregor, 'T. and A. W. Gomme', *Phoenix* 13 (1959), 58ff.

Scientific method (and Medicine)—K. von Fritz, 'Der gemeinsame Ursprung der Geschichtsschreibung und der exakten Wissenschaften bei den Griechen', *Philosophia Naturalis* 2 (1952), 200ff; K. Weidauer, *T. und die hippokratischen Schriften*, Heidelberg, 1954; C. Lichtenthaeler, *Thucydide et Hippocrate*, Geneva, 1965; W. P. MacArthur, 'The Athenian plagues. A medical note', CQ, N.S. 4 (1954), 171ff; cf. D. L. Page, *ibid.*, 174; F. W. Mitchel, 'The Athenian plague. New evidence inviting medical comment', GRBS 5 (1964), 101ff.

Causation—G. M. Kirkwood, 'T.'s words for Cause', AJP 73 (1952), 37ff; L. Pearson, 'Prophasis and Aitia', TAPA 83 (1952), 205ff; R. Sealey, 'T., Herodotus, and the causes of the War', CQ, N.S. 7 (1957), 1ff; A. Andrewes, 'T. on the causes of the War', *ibid.*, 9 (1959) 223ff.

Aspects of composition—P. K. Walker, 'The purpose and method of the Pentekontaetia in T. Book I', CQ, N.S. 7 (1957), 27ff; R. Katicic, 'Die Ringkomposition im ersten Buche des thukydideischen Geschichtswerkes', WS 70 (1957), 179ff; (cf. *id.* 'Die Ringkomposition in der vorklassischen attischen Prosa', Ž Ant. 10 (1960), 41ff;) H. Erbse, 'Zur Geschichtsbetrachtung des T.', A & A 10 (1961), 19ff; H. D. Westlake, 'T. II. 65. 11', CQ, N.S. 8 (1958), 102ff; H. Strasburger, 'T. und die politische Selbstdarstellung der Athener', *Hermes* 86 (1958), 17ff; K. Rohrer,

APPENDIX

'Ueber die Authentizität der Reden bei T.', WS 72 (1959), 36ff; A. Andrewes, 'The Melian Dialogue and Pericles' last speech', PCPS 186 (1960), 1ff; *id.*, 'The Mytilene Debate', *Phoenix* 16 (1962), 63ff; *id.*, 'T. and the Persians', *Historia* 10 (1961), 1ff; G. T. Griffith, 'Some habits of T. when introducing persons', PCPS 187 (1961), 21ff; F. Sieveking, 'Die Funktion geographischer Mitteilungen im Geschichtswerk des T.', *Klio* 42 (1964), 73ff.

Politics and Speeches—H. Erbse, 'Ueber eine Eigenheit thukydideischer Geschichtsbetrachtung', RhM 96 (1953), 38ff; F. M. Wassermann, 'T. and the disintegration of the Polis', TAPA 85 (1954), 46ff; *id.*, 'Post-Periclean Democracy in Action:... (Thuc. 37–48', *ibid.* 87 (1956), 27ff; *id.*, 'The voice of Sparta in T.', CJ 59 (1964), 289ff; H. Herter, 'Pylos und Melos', RhM 97 (1954), 316ff; H. D. Westlake, 'T. and the Pentecontaetia', CQ, N.S. 5 (1955), 53ff; R. Reimer-Klaas, *Macht und Recht bei T.*, Diss. Tübingen, 1962; F. Kiechle, 'Ursprung und Wirkung der machtpolitischen Theorien im Geschichtswerk des T.', *Gymn.* 70 (1963), 289ff; B. X. de Wet, 'Periclean imperial policy and the Mytilenean debate', A Class 6 (1963), 106ff.

The Athenian empire—M. Treu, 'Athen und Melos und der Melierdialog des T.', *Historia* 2 (1953/4), 253ff; *id., ibid.*, 3 (1954/5), 58ff; W. Eberhardt, 'Der Melierdialog und die Inschriften,... ', *ibid.*, 8 (1959), 284ff; G. E. M. de Ste Croix, 'The character of the Athenian empire', *ibid.*, 3 (1954), 1ff; D. W. Bradeen, 'The popularity of the Athenian empire', *ibid.*, 9. (1960), 257ff; H. W. Pleket, 'Thasos and the popularity of the Athenian empire', *ibid.*, 12 (1963), 70ff; T. J. Quinn, 'T. and the unpopularity of the Athenian empire', *ibid.*, 13 (1964), 257ff; J. de Romilly, 'T. and the cities of the Athenian empire', *Univ. of London Inst. of Class. Stud. Bull.*, 13 (1966), 1ff; R. Sealey, 'The origin of the Delian League', *Ancient Society and Institutions. Studies V. Ehrenberg*, Oxford (Blackwell), 233ff; N. G. L. Hammond, 'The origins and the nature of the Athenian Alliance of 478 B.C.', JHS 87 (1967), forthcoming.

Athenian leaders, etc.—A. W. Gomme, 'Thucydides and Kleon. The second battle of Amphipolis', Ἑλληνικά, 1954: now in Gomme, *More Essays in Greek history and literature*, Oxford (Blackwell), 1962, 112ff; A. G. Woodhead, 'T.s portrait of Cleon', Mn 4 ser. 13 (1960), 289ff; H. D. Westlake, 'Hermocrates the Syracusan', BRL 41 (1958), 239ff; *id.*, 'Athenian aims in Sicily',

Historia 9 (1960), 385ff; *id.*, 'T. and the fall of Amphipolis', *Hermes* 90 (1962), 276ff; J. de Romilly, 'L'optimisme de T. et le jugement de l'historien sur Périclès (T. 2. 65)', REG 78 (1965), 557ff; H. Vretska, 'Perikles und die Herrschaft der Würdigsten—T. II. 37. 1', RhM 109 (1966), 108ff.

H. D. Meyer, 'Vorgeschichte und Begründung des delisch-attischen Seebundes', *Historia* 12 (1963), 405ff; analyses the evidence of Herodotus and of T. on this topic. M. L. Paladini, 'Considerazioni sulle fonte della storia di Cleone', *Historia* 7 (1958), 48ff, shows that later historians preserve no tradition alternative to that of Thucydides.

Fourth-century historians, excluding Atthis *and* Alexander:
Hellenica Oxyrhynchia—V. Bartoletti, *Hellenica Oxyrhynchia*, Leipzig, 1959 (Teubner); *id.*, 'In margine agli *H.O.*', A & R, N.S. 10 (1965), 161ff; I. A. F. Bruce, *An historical commentary on the H.O.*' Cambridge, 1967 (forthcoming); *id.*, 'The political terminology of the O. historian', *Emerita* 30 (1962), 63ff; *id.*, 'Chios and P.Sl 1304', *Phoenix* 18 (1964), 272ff; T. R. C. Weaver, '*H.O.* and some related problems', AUMLA 7 (1957), 20ff; S. Perlman, 'The causes and the outbreak of the Corinthian War', CQ, N.S. 14 (1964), 64ff.

Xenophon (and 'Old Oligarch')—E. Delebecque, *op. cit. infra*, n. 1; W. Klug, 'Zwei Reden des X. (*Anabasis* III. 1. 15-25 und III. 2. 8-32)', Festschr. Regenbogen, Heidelberg, 1956, 117ff; D. Lotze, 'Die chronologischen Interpolationen in X.'s *Hellenika*', *Philologus* 106 (1962). 1ff; R. D. Barnett, 'X. and the wall of Media', JHS 83 (1963), 1ff; O. Lendle, 'Der Bericht X.s über die Schlacht von Kunaxa', *Gymnasium* 73 (1966), 429ff; F. Stark, *Alexander's Path*, London, 1958, 203ff; J. K. Anderson, 'Xenophon, Respublica Lacedaemoniorum 1. 11. 10', CPh 59 (1964), 175ff; H. D. Westlake, 'Individuals in X., *Hellenica*', BRL 49 (1966), 246ff. F. Schroemer, *Der Bericht des Sophainetos über den Zug der Zehntausend,* Diss. Munich, 1954.

M. Gigante, *La costituzione degli Ateniesi. Studi sullo pseudo-Senofonte*, Naples, 1953; H. Haffter, 'Die Komposition der pseudo-xenophontischen Schrift vom Staat der Athener', *Navic. Chil.* (Festschr. Jacoby), Leiden, 1956, 79ff; J. de Romilly, 'Le pseudo-X. et Thucydide, étude sur quelques divergences de vues', RPh 36 (1962), 225ff.

APPENDIX

Ephorus—K. B. J. Herbert, *Ephorus in Plutarch's Lives*, Diss. Harvard, 1954; résumé HSPh 63 (1958), 510ff; W. R. Connor, *Studies in Ephorus and other sources for the causes of the Peloponnesian War*, Diss. Princeton, 1961; R. Drews, 'Ephorus and history written κατὰ γένος', AJPh 84 (1963), 244ff.

Theopompus—A. E. Raubitschek, 'Theopompus on Thucydides the son of Melesias', *Phoenix* 14 (1960), 81ff. (And see under 'Scylax', below.)

Philistus—R. Lauritano, 'Ricerche su Filisto', *Kokalos* 3 (1957), 98ff; G. de Sanctis, *op. cit. infra*, n. 1.

'Scylax'—A. Peretti, 'Eforo e Pseudo-Scilace', SCO 10 (1961), 5ff; *id.*, 'Teopompo e Pseudo-Scilace', *ibid.*, 12 (1963), 16ff.

Ctesias—J. M. Bigwood, *Ctesias of Cnidus*, Diss. Harvard, résumé HSPh 70 (1965), 263ff.

On Atthis *and* Aristotle, Athenaion Politeia:

Atthis *tradition*—F. Heidbuechel, *Die Chronologie der Peisistratiden in der Atthis*, Diss. Cologne, 1955; A. E. Raubitschek, 'Theophrastus on ostracism', C & M 19 (1958) 78ff; H. Bloch, 'F. Jacoby, FGr H. 3 B' [review], *Gnomon* 31 (1959), 487ff; K. J. Dover, 'Androtion on ostracism', CR 13 (1963), 256ff; A. J. Podlecki, 'The political significance of the Athenian "Tyrannicide" cult', *Historia* 15 (1966), 129ff.

Ath. Pol.; *general*—*Edition*—C. A. Viano, *Politica e Constituzione di Atene*, Turin, 1955. K. von Fritz, 'Die Bedeutung des Aristoteles für die Geschichtsschreibung', *Entretiens Hardt*, 4 (1956), 85ff; R. Weil, *op. cit. infra*, n. 1; *id.*, 'Philosophie et histoire: la vision de l'histoire chez A.', *Entretiens Hardt*, 11 (1964), 159ff; J. J. Keaney, *The structure, dating and publication of Aristotle's AP.*, Diss. Harvard, résumé HSPh 65 (1961), 362ff; *id.*, 'The structure of Aristotle's AP', HSPh 66 (1963), 115ff; M. Chambers, 'A.'s forms of democracy', TAPA, 92 (1961), 20ff; J. Day, 'Accidents in A., *Ath. Pol.* 26. 1', *ibid.*, 52ff; J. Day and M. Chambers, *op. cit. infra*, n. 1.

Ath. Pol.; *particular*—A. L. Boegehold, 'A.'s *Ath. Pol.* 65, 2. The official token', *Hesperia*, 29 (1960), 393ff; K. Kraft, 'Zur Uebersetzung und Interpretation von A. *Ath. Pol.* Kap. 10', JNG 10 (1959-60), 21ff; G. V. Sumner, 'Notes on chronological problems in the Aristotelian A.P.', CQ, N.S. 11 (1961), 31ff, 129; R. Seager, 'Herodotus and A.P. on the date of Cleisthenes' reforms,' AJPh 84

(1963), 287ff; F. P. Rizzo, 'La costituzione di Draconte . . .',
Mem. di Ist. Lomb. Acc., Cl. di lettre etc., 27, 4 (1963), 271ff;
E. Ruschenbusch, 'Ephialtes', *Historia* 15 (1966), 369ff.

The Alexander historians:
  General—C. A. Robinson, *The history of Alexander the Great*, I,
1953, II, 1963, Providence; L. Pearson, *op. cit. infra*, n. 1; J. E.
Atkinson, 'Primary sources and the Alexanderreich', A Class 6
(1963), 125ff; F. Pfister, 'A. der Große, Die Geschichte seines
Ruhms im Lichte seiner Beinamen', *Historia* 13 (1964), 37ff;
P. Treves, *Il mito di A. e la Roma d'Augusto*, Milan, 1953; E. Badian,
'A. the Great and the Unity of Mankind', *Historia* 7 (1958),
425ff; *id.*, 'The death of Parmenion', *TAPA* 91 (1960), 324ff;
id., 'Harpalus', *JHS* 81 (1961), 16ff.
  Ephemerides, etc.—L. Pearson, 'The Diary and Letters of Alexander', *Historia* 3 (1955), 429ff; F. Pfister, 'Das Alexander-Archiv
und die hellenistisch-römische Wissenschaft', *ibid.*, 10 (1961),
30ff; A. E. Samuel, 'Alexander's "Royal Journals"' *ibid.*, 14
(1965), 1ff.
  Ptolemy/Arrian—J. R. Hamilton, 'The cavalry battle at the
Hydaspes', *JHS* 76 (1956), 26ff; W. B. Kaiser, *Der Brief A's des
Großen an Dareios nach der Schlacht bei Issos*, Diss. Mainz, 1957;
C. Gorteman, 'βασιλεὺς φιλαλήθης', *CE* 33 (1958), 256ff;
A. B. Breebart, *Enige historiografische aspecten van Arrianus' Anabasis
Alexandri* (with résumé in English), Diss. Leiden, 1960; C. B.
Welles, 'The reliability of Ptolemy', Festschr. A. Rostagni,
Turin, 1963, 101ff.
  A. Gitti, 'L'unitarietà della tradizione su Alessandro Magno
nella ricerca moderna', *Athenaeum* 34 (1956), 39ff; P. A. Brunt,
'Persian accounts of Alexander's campaigns', *CQ*, N.S. 12
(1962), 141ff.
  Clitarchus/Diodorus—J. R. Hamilton, 'Clitarchus and Aristobulus', *Historia* 10 (1961), 448ff; E. Badian, 'The date of Clitarchus',
PACA 8 (1965), 5ff; R. Wolf, *Die Soldatenerzählungen des Kleitarch bei
Q. Curtius Rufus*, Diss. Vienna, 1964; M. J. Fontana, 'Il problema
delle fonte per il XVII libro di Diodoro Siculo', *Kokalos* 1
(1955), 155ff; *id.*, 'Sulla cronologia del XVII libro di D.', *ibid.*,
2. (1956), 37ff; C. B. Welles, *Diodorus*, 8 (Bks. 16. 66-17), London
and Cambridge, U.S.A., 1963 (Loeb), Introduction.

'*Peripatetic*' *tradition?*—A. I. Wardman, 'Plutarch and A', CQ, N.S. 5 (1955), 96ff; E. Mensching, 'Peripatetiker über A'., *Historia* 12, (1963) 274ff.

Metz epitome—P. H. Thomas, *Incerti auctoris epitoma rerum gestarum Alexandri Magni* etc., Leipzig, 1960 (Teubner); L. Ruggieri, 'L'Epitoma . . . , etc. A proposito della recente edizione di P. H. Thomas', *Athenaeum* 39 (1961), 285ff.

Hellenistic historians:
General—F. W. Walbank, 'Tragic history. A reconsideration', BICS 2 (1955), 4ff; *id.*, 'History and Tragedy', *Historia* 9 (1960), 216ff. N. Zegers, *Wesen und Ursprung der Tragischen Geschichtsschreibung*, Diss. Cologne, 1959; C. O. Brink, 'Tragic history and Aristotle's school', PCPS, N.S. 6, 1960, 14ff.

Duris—M. J. Fontana (see under 'Alexander historians': Diodorus); L. Ferrero, 'Tra poetica e istorica. Duride di Samo', Miscell. Rostagni, Turin, 1963, 68ff; E. Manni (see under *Timaeus*, below).

Messenia—L. Pearson, 'The pseudo-history of Messenia and its authors', *Historia*, 11 (1962), 397ff.

Timaeus—T. S. Brown, *op. cit. infra*, n. 1.; A. Momigliano, 'Atene nel III secolo A.C. e la scoperta di Roma nella Storie di T. di Tauromenio', RSI 71 (1959), 529ff; E. Manni, 'T. e Duride e la storia di Agatocle', *Kokalos* 6 (1960), 167ff; A. Alföldi, 'T.s Bericht über die Anfänge der Geldprägung in Rom', MDAI(R) 68 (1961), 64ff.

Phylarchus—J. Kroymann, 'Phylarchos', RE Suppl. 8 (1956), 471ff; E. Gabba, 'Studi su Filarco. Le biografie plutarchee di Agide e di Cleomene', *Athenaeum* 35 (1957), 3ff, 193ff; T. W. Africa, *op. cit. infra*, n. 1.

Polybius:
Edition, etc.—P. Pédech, *Polybe, Histoires, Livre XII*, Paris, 1961 (Budé); A. Aymard, 'Un fragment de Polybe mal classé (XVIII 40. 1-4)', *Pallas* 4 (1956), 3ff; J. M. Moore, *The Manuscript Tradition of P.*, Cambridge, (1965).

General—F. W. Walbank, *op. cit. infra*, n. 1; P. Pédech, *op. cit., ibid.*, M. Geltzer, *Ueber die Arbeitsweise des P.* SHAW 1956, 3, Heidelberg, 1956; I. Devroye and L. Kemp, *Over de historische methode von Polybios*, Brussels, 1956 (résumé in French); H. H. Schmitt,

Hellenen, Römer und Barbaren. Eine Studie zu P., Wiss. Beil. z. Jahresber. 1957-58 des Hum. Gymn., Aschaffenburg; A. Mauersberger, 'Der historische Aspekt des P.,' *Altertum* 10 (1964), 75ff.

Criticism of historians—R. Koerner, *P. als Kritiker früheren Historiker*, Diss. Jena, 1957 (résumé Wiss Zschr. Univ. Jena 6, 1956-57, 547f); F. W. Walbank, 'Polemic in P.' JRS 52 (1962), 1ff; M. A. Levi, 'La critica di P. a Timaeo', Miscell. Rostagni, Turin, 1963, 195ff; B. Shimron, 'P. and the reforms of Cleomenes III', *Historia* 13 (1964), 147ff.

Political views—K. von Fritz, *The theory of the mixed constitution in antiquity*, New York, 1954; A. T. Cole, *The political theory of P. and its sources*, Diss. Harvard, résumé in HSPh 65 (1961), 356ff; K.-W. Welwei, 'Demokratie und Masse bei P.', *Historia* 15 (1966), 282ff.

Polybius on Rome—C. O. Brink and F. W. Walbank, 'The construction of the Sixth Book of P.', CQ, N.S. 4 (1954), 97ff; F. W. Walbank, 'P. and Rome's eastern policy', JRS 53 (1963), 1ff; *id.*, 'P. and the Roman State', GRBS 5 (1964), 239ff; A. T. Cole, 'The sources and composition of P. VI', *Historia* 13 (1964), 440ff.

Polybius on the Seleucids—P. Pédech, 'Deux campagnes d'Antiochus III chez P.', REA 60 (1958), 67ff; H. H. Schmitt, 'P. und seine Quellen', *Untersuchungen zur Geschichte Antiochos des Großen und seiner Zeit, Historia* Einzelschr. 6, Wiesbaden, 1964, 175ff; T. S. Brown, 'P.s account of Antiochus III', *Phoenix* 18 (1964), 124ff.

Miscellaneous—A. Reveri, 'Tyche in P.', *Convivium* 24 (1956), 275ff; P. Pédech, 'La géographie de P. Structure et contenu du livre XXXIV des *Histoires*', LEC 24 (1956), 3ff; *id.*, 'Notes sur la biographie de P.', *ibid.*, 29 (1961), 145ff; H. Erbse, 'Polybios—Interpretationen', *Philologus* 101 (1957), 269ff.

Posidonius:

M. Laffranque, *op. cit. infra*, n. 1; *id.*, 'P. d'Apamée et les mines d'Ibérie', *Pallas* 5 (1957), 17ff; *id.*, 'P., Eudoxe de Cyzique et la circumnavigation de l'Afrique', R. Philos 153 (1963), 199ff; F. Altheim, 'P. und Sallust', *Studi Francisci*, Milan, 1956, 101ff; G. Pfliegersdorfer, *Studien zu P.*, SAWW 232, 5, Vienna, 1959; J. J. Tierney, 'The Celtic ethnography of P.', *Proc. Royal Irish Acad.* 60, C, 5 (1960), 189ff; A. D. Nock, 'Posidonius', JRS 49 (1959), 4ff; J. Heurgon, 'P. et les Étrusques', *Hommages à A.*

Grenier, Brussels, 1962, 799ff; A. Dihle, 'Der fruchtbare Osten', RhM 105 (1962), 97ff; *id.*, 'Zur hellenistischen Ethnographie', *Entretiens Hardt* 8 (1962), 205ff; H. Strasburger, 'P. on problems of the Roman Empire', JRS 55 (1965), 40ff.

Manetho:
W. Helck, *Untersuchungen zu Manetho in den ägyptischen Königslisten*, Berlin, 1956.

Dionysius of Halicarnassus:
E. Gabba, 'Studi su D. da Alicarnasso. I. La costituzione di Romolo', *Athenaeum* 38 (1960), 175ff; II. 'Il regno di Servio Tullio', *ibid.*, 39 (1961) 98ff; III. 'La proposta di legge agraria di Spurio Cassio', *ibid.*, 42 (1964), 29ff; H. Hill, 'D. of H. and the origins of Rome', JRS 51 (1961), 88ff.

Diodorus Siculus (see also, for Book 17, under *Alexander Historians*, above):
Loeb Classical Library—Vols. 4 and 6 (C. H. Oldfather), 8 (C. B. Welles), 10 (R. M. Geer), 11 (F. R. Walton), London and Cambridge, U.S.A., 1954-63. G. Perl, *op. cit. infra*, n. 1; J. Palm, *Ueber Sprache und Stil des D. von Sizilien*, Lund, 1955; F. R. Walton, 'Notes on D.', AJPh 76 (1956), 274ff, 408ff; R. Lauritano, 'Sileno in D.?', *Kokalos* 2 (1956), 206ff; E. Manni, 'Da Ippi a D.', *ibid.*, 3 (1957), 136ff; M. Sordi, 'La terza guerra sacra', RFC 36 (1958), 134ff; *id.*, 'La cronologia delle vittorie persiane e la caduta di Ermia di Atarneo, in D. S.', *Kokalos* 5 (1959), 107ff; R. Laqueur, 'Diodorea', *Hermes* 86 (1958), 257ff; W. Spoerri, *Späthellenistische Bericht über Welt, Kultur und Götter. Untersuchungen zu D. von S.*, Basle, 1959; A. E. Astin, 'D. and the date of the embassy to the East of Scipio Aemilianus', CPh 54 (1959), 221ff; C. Dolce, 'D. e la storia di Agatocle', Kokalos 6 (1960), 124ff; M. Pavan, 'La teorisi storica di D. S.', RAL 16 (1961), 19ff, 117ff; L. C. Smith, 'The chronology of Books XVIII-XX of D. S.', AJPh 82 (1961), 283ff; R. Drews, 'D. and his sources', *ibid.*, 83 (1962), 383ff; *id.*, *op. cit.*, under *Ephorus*, above; T. T. B. Ryder, 'Spartan relations with Persia after the King's Peace', CQ, N.S. 13 (1963), 105ff; R. K. Sinclair, 'D. S. and the writing of history', PACA 6 (1963), 36ff; *id.*, 'D. S. and Fighting in Relays', CQ N.S. 16 (1966), 249ff.

Josephus:
L. Feldman, *Scholarship on Philo and Josephus (1932-1962)*, New York, 1963.

Plutarch:
K. Ziegler, *Vitae parallelae* I1, I2, II1, Leipzig, 1957-64 (Teubner); E. Flacelière, E. Chambry, H. Juneaux, *Vies* I and II, Paris, 1957 and 1961 (Budé); Flacelière, Chambry, *Vies* III, 1964 (Budé); H. Erbse, 'Textkritische Beiträge zu den Biographien P.s', RhM 100 (1957), 271ff.
General—A. Dihle, *Studien zur griechischen Biographie*, Göttingen, 1956; C. Theander, 'Zur Zeitfolge der Biographien P.s', *Eranos* 56 (1958), 12ff; P. A. Stadter, *Plutarch's historical methods. An analysis of the* Mulierum Virtutes, Cambridge, U.S.A., 1965.
Sources—T. Tzannetatos, 'Ὁ Θουκυδίδης ὡς πηγὴ παρὰ τῷ Π. βιογραφοῦντι', EEAth 8 (1957/8) 429; *id.*, 'Ὁ Θουκυδίδης παρὰ τῷ Πλουτάρχῳ φιλοσοφοῦντι', *Athena* 72 (1958), 204ff; F. Frost, 'Some documents in P.'s *Lives*', C & M 22 (1961), 182ff; J. R. Hamilton, 'The letters in P.'s *Alexander*', PACA 4 (1961), 9ff; H. Homeyer, 'Beobachtungen zu den hellenistischen Quellen der Plutarch-Viten', *Klio* 41 (1963), 145ff; E. Gabba, *op. cit.*, under '*Phylarchus*'; K. B. J. Herbert, *op. cit.*, under '*Ephorus*'.
Aspects of P.'s methods—Mr. L. Paladini, 'Influenza della tradizione dei Sette Savi sulla *Vita di Solone* di P.', REG 69 (1956), 377ff; M. Muehl, 'Solon gegen Peisistratos. Ein Beitrag zur peripatetischen Geschichtsschreibung', RhM 99 (1956), 315ff; R. J. Shoeck, 'More, P., and King Agis. Spartan history and the meaning of Utopia', PhQ 35 (1956), 366ff; K. Berger, *Characterbilden bei Tacitus und P.*, Diss. Cologne, 1962.
Individuals—E. Meinhardt, *Perikles bei P.*, Diss. Frankfurt a.M., 1957; H. Martin, 'The character of P.'s Themistocles', TAPA 92 (1961), 326ff; L. Gil, 'La semblanza de Nicias en P.', E Clás 6 (1962), 404ff; E. Gabba, *op. cit.* under *Hellenistic historians: Phylarchus*.
P. on Rome—E. Valgiglio, *P., Vita dei Gracchi*, Rome, 1957; K. B. J. Herbert, 'The identity of P.'s lost *Scipio*', AJPh 78 (1957), 83ff; R. Flacelière, 'Rome et ses empéreurs vus par P.', AC 32 (1963), 28ff; D. A. Russell, 'P.'s Life of Coriolanus', JRS 53 (1963), 21ff.
Synkrisis—S. Constanza, 'La synkrisis nello schema biografico di Plutarco', *Messana* 4 (1955), 127ff; H. Erbse, 'Die Bedeutung

der Synkrisis in den Parallelbiographien P.'s', *Hermes* 84 (1956), 398ff.

Date of composition—C. P. Jones, 'Towards a chronology of P.'s works', JRS 56 (1966), 61ff., and especially 66ff.

Appian:
H. White, *Roman history* IV, London and Cambridge, U.S.A., 1955 (Loeb); E. Gabba, *Bellorum civilium liber primus*, Florence, 1958; P. Viereck, A. G. Roos, E. Gabba, *Historia Romana*, I, Leipzig, 1962 (Teubner).
P. Meloni, *Il valore storico e le fonti del libro Macedonico di A.* AFLC 22, Rome, 1955; E. Gabba, 'Note appianee', *Athenaeum* 33 (1955), 218ff; *id.*, *op. cit. infra*, n. 1; *id.*, 'Sul libro siriaco di A.', RAL 12 (1957), 339ff; *id.*, 'Storici greci dell' impero romano da Augusto ai Severi', RSI 71 (1959), 361ff; T. J. Luce, 'A.'s magisterial terminology', CPh 56 (1961), 21ff; *id.*, 'A.'s Egyptian History', *ibid.*, 59 (1964), 259ff; G. Wirth, *op. cit.* under '*Arrian*'; I. Hahn, 'A. et le cercle de Sénèque', A Ant Hung 12 (1964), 169ff.

Arrian (see also under '*Alexander historians*'):
G. Marenghi, 'Sulle fonti del *Periplo* di A.', SIFC 29 (1957), 217ff; *id.*, 'Caratteri e intenti del *Periplo* di A.', *Athenaeum* 35 (1957), 177ff; G. Wirth, 'Anmerkungen zur Arrianbiographie. Appian-Arrian-Lukian', *Historia* 13, 1964, 209ff.

Dio Cassius:
C. Questa, 'Tecnica biografica e tecnica annalistica nei libre LXII-LXIII di C. D.', Stud Urb 31 (1957), 37ff; J. Guey, 'À propos de la fondation de Lyon. D. C. et le s.c. d'avril 43 av. J. C.', BSAF 1959, 128ff; F. Millar, 'Some speeches in C. D.', MH 18 (1961), 11ff; *id.*, *op. cit. infra*, n. 1; G. B. Townsend, 'Traces in D. C. of Cluvius, Aufidius and Pliny', *Hermes* 89 (1961), 227ff; *id.*, 'Some rhetorical battle-pictures in D.', *ibid.*, 92 (1964), 467ff; J. Bleicken, 'Der politische Standpunkt D.s gegenüber der Monarchie', *ibid.*, 90 (1962), 444ff; J. Morris, 'Senate and emperor', *Studies G. Thomson*, Prague, 1963, 144ff.

Polyaenus:
O. Seel, 'Trogus, Caesar und Livius bei Polyaenus', RhM 103 (1960), 230ff.

Herodian:
F. Cassola, 'Sulla vita e sulla personalità dello storico Erodiano', NRS 41 (1957), 213ff; E. Hohl, *Kaiser Commodus und H.*, SDAW 1954, 1, Berlin; *id.*, *Kaiser Pertinax und die Thronbesteigung seines Nachfolgers im Licht der Herodiankritik*, *ibid.*, 1956, 2, Berlin; F. J. Stein, *Dexippus et Herodianus . . . quatenus Thucydidem secuti sint*, Diss. Bonn, 1957.

Aspects of historiography:
E. Wolf, *Griechisches Rechtsdenken* III. 2. *Die Umformung des Rechtsgedankens durch Historik und Rhetorik*, Frankfurt, 1956; R. C. Dentan (ed.), *The idea of history in the ancient Near East*, New Haven, 1955; P. Munz, 'History and myth', Philos Q 6 (1956), 1ff; A. E. Wardman, 'Myth in Greek historiography', *Historia* 9 (1960), 403ff; J. G. A. Pocock, 'The origins of study of the past', CSSH 4 (1961-62), 209ff; A. Momigliano, 'Storiografia su tradizione scritta e . . . sur trad. orale', AAT 96 (1961-62), 186ff; F. Chatelet, *La Naissance de l'histoire*, Paris, 1962; M. I. Finley, *The Greek Historians*, London, 1959, 1ff.

T. S. Brown, 'The Greek sense of time in history, as suggested by their accounts of Egypt', *Historia* 11 (1962), 257ff; E. J. Bickerman, *La cronologia nel mondo antico*, Florence, 1963.

G. Avenarius, *Lukian's Schrift zur Geschichtsschreibung*, Diss. Meisenheim, 1956; H. Strasburger, 'Komik und Satire in der griechischen Geschichtsschreibung', *Festg. P. Kirn*, Berlin, 1963; 13ff; A. Momigliano, 'Some observations on causes of war in ancient historiography', *Acta Congr. Madvigiana*, I, 199ff.

A. Dihle, *Studien zur griechischen Biographie*, Göttingen, 1956.

F. Jacoby, *Abhandlungen zur griechischen Geschichtsschreibung* (ed. H. Bloch), Leiden, 1956, is a selection of Jacoby's articles and essays. *Id.*, *Griechische Historiker*, Stuttgart, 1956, is a selection of his major RE articles.

---

[1] R. van Compernolle, *Étude de chronologie et d'historiographie Siceliotes*, Brussels, 1960; J. de Romilly, *Historie et raison chez Thucydide*, Paris, 1957; A. W. Gomme, *Historical Commentary on Thucydides*, II and III, Oxford, 1956; F. E. Adcock, *Thucydides and his history*, Cambridge, 1963; E. Delebecque, *Thucydide et Alcibiade*, Aix-en-Provence, 1965; *id.*, *Essai sur la vie de Xénophon*, Paris, 1957; J. Day and M. Chambers, *Aristotle's history of Athenian democracy*, Berkeley, 1962; R. Weil, *Aristote et l'histoire. Essai sur la Politique*, Paris, 1960; T. S. Brown, *Timaeus of Tauromenium*, Berkeley, 1958. K. von Fritz, *The theory of the Mixed Constitution in antiquity. A critical Analysis of Polybius' political ideas*,

New York, 1954; F. W. Walbank, *A Historical Commentary on Polybius*, I, Cambridge, 1957; P. Pédech, *La méthode historique de Polybe*, Paris, 1964; T. W. Africa, *Phylarchus and the Spartan revolution*, Berkeley, 1961; M. Laffranque, *Posidonios d'Apamée*, Paris, 1965; L. Pearson, *The lost histories of Alexander the Great*, New York, 1960; G. Perl, *Kritische Untersuchungen zu Diodors römischer Jahrzählung*, Berlin, 1957; G. de Sanctis, *Ricerche sulla storiografia siceliota*, Palermo, 1958; M. A. Levi, *Plutarco e il V secolo*, Milan, 1955; P. A. Stadter, *Plutarch's historical methods. An analysis of the Mulierum Virtutes*, Cambridge, U.S.A., 1965; E. Gabba, *Appiano e la storia delle guerre civile*, Florence, 1956; F. Millar, *A study of Cassius Dio*, Oxford, 1964. H. Montgomery, *Gedanke und Tat: zur Erzählungstechnik bei Herodot, Thukydides, Xenophon und Arrian*, Lund, 1965.

[2] *Histoire et historiens dans l'antiquité*: Entretiens sur l'antiquité classique, IV, Fondation Hardt, Geneva, 1956.

[3] F. M. Wassermann, 'Thucydidean scholarship, 1942-1956', CW 50 (1966-57), 65ff, 89ff; P. MacKendrick, 'Herodotus 1954-1963', *ibid.*, 56 (1963), 269ff; M. Chambers, 'Studies on Thucydides 1957-1962', *ibid.*, 57 (1963), 6ff. W. Drause, 'Herodot, Forschungsberichte', *Anz. Alt.* 14 (1961), 25ff, covers the years 1934 to about 1960.

CHAPTER VII

GREEK ORATORS AND RHETORIC

BY H. Ll. HUDSON-WILLIAMS

I. THE ATTIC ORATORS

(a) *General*

DURING the second half of the nineteenth century considerable progress was made in improving the texts and elucidating the subject-matter of the Attic Orators. In England Jebb[1] revived a waning interest in the subject by his elegant survey of the Orators before Demosthenes. These two volumes, although of greater interest to the general reader than to the specialist, have been of permanent value. More specialized work was done in Germany by Blass. Most research on this subject since the turn of the century is indebted to his painstaking accuracy and almost unbelievable industry. His critical editions in the Teubner series (for which he edited all the Orators except Lysias and Isaeus) still provide the majority of our standard texts or have formed the basis of those which superseded them. The four volumes of his great work, *Die Attische Beredsamkeit*,[2] make arid reading, but they show uncompromising thoroughness and sound judgment. They still provide the only comprehensive work on Attic Oratory, and no attempt has been made during the present century to replace them.

Studies on this massive scale have been rare in the twentieth century. Wyse's edition of Isaeus[3] is a notable exception. Distinguished work of a less ambitious kind has, however, not been lacking. Papyrological discoveries[4] during this century and the last provided material for evaluating manuscripts and improving texts, and their importance is reflected in modern editions. A new school of Italian scholars has done useful work, mainly in commenting on the subject-matter of the speeches. Excellent articles on the Orators have appeared in *Pauly-Wissowa*. Bibliographical surveys in *Bursians Jahresbericht* and Marouzeau's *L'Année Philologique*, etc., have considerably lightened the work of scholars. Commentaries on the legal speeches have benefited from the progress made in the study of Attic law, particularly by the great work of Lipsius[5] on this subject.

A short survey of Attic Oratory and its development was provided by Dobson,[6] but there have been few books of a general nature on individual orators other than Demosthenes. A significant contribution of the age has been the publication of editions in the Loeb and the Budé series which are designed to assist the general reader rather than to provide definitive texts. The Loeb Classical Library now includes all the Attic Orators; the quality of these editions varies considerably, but they have made the Orators more easily accessible to the English-speaking public. Most of the Orators have also been edited in the Budé series; these editions are more ambitious and are indispensable to the scholar as well as to the general reader; some of the translations in this series are easily the best that have yet appeared in any language.

(b) Individual Orators
Antiphon

An interesting and important addition to the works of Antiphon was provided by the discovery in Egypt of a papyrus fragment of his last speech, delivered in his own defence. This was first edited in 1907 by Nicole.[7] His attempts to restore the mutilated text were bold and have since been improved upon. This fragment was included in Thalheim's revision of Blass's Teubner text, which was published in 1914. There has been much discussion as to the authenticity of the *Tetralogies*. Probably most scholars now believe that these speeches are genuine, but the controversy still continues.[8] The difficulty of comparing purely literary speeches with genuine ones inevitably makes an argument, which is largely concerned with stylistic points, inconclusive. Two books deserve mention in a review of work done on Antiphon, although they cover a wider field. Solmsen,[9] in investigating the origins of Attic legal oratory, discussed and analysed the subject-matter and composition of Antiphon's speeches. Aly,[10] in examining the various forms of early Greek prose, devoted a considerable part of his work to the speeches of Antiphon, including recently discovered fragments. He was particularly concerned with establishing the identity of the orator and sophist of this name. Few would now agree with his conclusion, but he probably provided the best case that has been made in support of this thesis. A recent article by Dover[11] has helped to determine the date, or at least the order, of certain speeches.

Andocides

Fuhr has systematically revised and enlarged Blass's edition,[12] adding a number of conjectures of his own and of others. The dearth of commentaries on the subject-matter of the speeches made Dalmeyda's Budé edition[13] particularly welcome. His text may not satisfy the exacting needs of a specialist as he took drastic measures to emend difficult passages, but the needs of the general reader are well provided for and there is much to interest the scholar. There has been some discussion as to the authenticity of the speech *Against Alcibiades*. It is generally agreed to be spurious, but opinions as to its date and authorship have varied. Some, like Dalmeyda, have believed it to be a student's exercise of the early fourth century, others have assigned it to the Hellenistic period.

Lysias

At the beginning of the century Thalheim[14] produced an edition which superseded Scheibe's and supplied an urgent need by taking full advantage of work done on Lysias during the second half of the nineteenth century. Since then Hude[15] has published his excellent Oxford text based on an independent study of the manuscripts. These are now the two standard texts of Lysias. There has been a good Budé edition by Gernet and Bizos;[16] the second volume has useful notes on the content and setting of the fragments which papyrological discoveries have made available; these fragments have added substantially to our knowledge of Lysias' lost speeches. During the past twenty-five years several editions of individual speeches have appeared in Italy. In Germany Müller[17] has made an exhaustive enquiry into the date and purpose of the obviously spurious Eighth Speech. The authenticity of the *Epitaphius*, a more difficult problem, was investigated by Walz;[18] he argued that the speech was genuine by pointing out various Lysianic characteristics and ascribing divergencies from Lysias' forensic style to the epideictic nature of the work. A question of more general interest was discussed by Ferckel[19] who tried to discover whether Lysias abused his position as a guest of Athens. In this book Lysias appears in a distinctly less attractive light than in his own writing.

Isocrates

The discovery of papyrus fragments, particularly of the *Peace*, has provided new material for assessing the relative merits of the manuscripts, but little work of primary importance has been done on the text. Blass's revision of Benseler's work (1878-79) is still the standard edition. The first volume of an elaborate edition by Drerup[20] was published in 1906. This contained an exceptionally full discussion of the manuscripts and much relevant information from ancient and modern sources on individual speeches. Scholars have questioned the soundness of Drerup's judgment on many points in this volume, but its wealth of detail makes it an important work and it is to be regretted that it was not continued. Since 1928 three volumes of the Budé edition[21] have been published; brief introductions, which reflect the findings of modern scholarship and the good sense of the editors, correct many misapprehensions; the translation is certainly the most accurate that has yet appeared of the speeches concerned.

Annotated editions include Forster's *Cyprian Orations*,[22] Laistner's *Peace* and *Philip*[23] (the first English commentary on these speeches), and Treves' *Panegyricus*[24] and *Philip*.[25] These were intended mainly for use in schools, but the editions of Treves deserve the attention of more advanced scholars. An edition of the *Trapeziticus* by Bongenaar[26] contained a copious and detailed commentary dealing chiefly with the legal aspects of the case.

Wyse in the introduction to his edition of Isaeus, like many other scholars, lamented the lack of a good index to Isocrates. The publication of Preuss's *Index*[27] in 1904, probably the most satisfactory index to any of the Orators, was an event of importance. Preuss did not merely give references (as he had done in indexing Demosthenes), but also classified the references according to grammatical usage. It is unfortunate that this valuable volume is now almost impossible to obtain.

There have been numerous doctoral dissertations and articles in journals on such subjects as Isocrates' debt to the early Sophists, his relations with Plato, Alcidamas, and Aristotle, and the authenticity of the *Letters* and of the τέχνη ascribed to him. Most scholars now reject the fragments of the τέχνη as spurious, but accept all, or nearly all, the *Letters* as genuine. Wilcox[28] has dealt in some detail with the mutual recriminations between Isocrates and contemporary rhetoricians. Hudson-Williams[29] has discussed his method of literary composition and pointed out evidence in his works which shows that they were intended for a listening as well as a reading public. Wersdörfer[30] has studied the meaning of semi-technical terms used by Isocrates; his analysis is chiefly useful because it shows that these words have a different meaning in different contexts and that certain passages have been misunderstood by editors who did not realize this. A somewhat ingenuous work by Gisela Schmitz-Kahlmann[31] considered Isocrates' use of past history to support his arguments. Isocrates' influence on Cicero, Dionysius, and Aristides was discussed in a book by Hubbell;[32] he was mainly concerned with Isocrates' views on the scope and purpose of oratory and did not deal with his influence on the style of later writers.

Modern scholars tend to be out of sympathy with Isocrates and his ideals; he is often dismissed as a second-rate thinker remarkable only for the virtuosity of his style. He has, however, not been without his admirers. Mathieu[33] wrote a sympathetic, but well-reasoned, account of his political views and their historical background; Burk,[34] a pupil of Drerup, defended Isocrates' teaching with unbounded enthusiasm, contending that he was the father of humanistic education; Jaeger[35] in *Paideia* portrayed him as a great educationalist and political thinker.

Isaeus

Two important editions of Isaeus appeared in the opening years of the century. Thalheim's Teubner text,[36] although ostensibly based on Scheibe's edition, was largely an independent work. It was soon followed by Wyse's edition.[3] This was planned on a vast scale with all the apparatus of modern scholarship. In this work a meticulously prepared text, rather less conservative than that of Thalheim, is accompanied by a detailed discussion of the manuscripts. The bulk of the book is taken up by an exhaustive commentary on the subject-matter of the speeches with a mass of illustrative material. One of Wyse's main objects was to prove that modern writers on Greek law had attached undue importance to statements in the speeches, forgetting that the purpose of legal oratory was to persuade, not to tell the truth. It is surprising that in such an elaborate edition Wyse did not, like Thalheim, include the fragments of lost speeches; he did, however, make full use of them in compiling his commentary. Wyse's edition is obviously one of the major works of classical scholarship in the twentieth century. It replaced Schömann's famous commentary which had appeared over seventy years earlier; it is itself unlikely to be superseded for a long time.

Other work on Isaeus has inevitably been on a lesser scale. The Greek scholar P. S. Photiades devoted many years to a study of the speeches and published various notes in Greek periodicals; he would probably have achieved considerably more had not much of his unpublished material been lost in the destruction of Smyrna in 1922. An index to the speeches by W. A. Goligher and W. S. Maguiness appeared in issues of *Hermathena* between 1938 and 1949. This was badly needed as Isaeus, alone of the Orators, had not been indexed. It is to be hoped that it will be published again in a more convenient form. Isaeus can only have a limited appeal, but during the century translations have appeared in English, French, German, and Italian. There is still room for a general book assessing his place in Greek Oratory, an aspect neglected by Wyse.

Lycurgus

Since Blass published his Teubner edition in 1899 the most important work on Lycurgus has been Durrbach's Budé edition[37] with its excellent introductory matter and carefully prepared text. Durrbach's study of Lycurgus' life, still a standard work, appeared as far back as 1889; his edition was published posthumously in 1932. Broadly speaking his collation of the two chief manuscripts merely confirmed the accuracy of Blass's work, but in one important respect his text was superior. Blass wrongly credited Lycurgus with a scrupulous regard for euphony and emended the text accordingly, particularly by the systematic elimination of hiatus. It is generally agreed that Durrbach was right in restoring the manuscript readings in many places.

There has been no attempt to rival the scholarly detail of Rehdantz's work on the speech *Against Leocrates*, but two less ambitious commentaries deserve mention. Petrie[38] produced the first edition in England since the eighteenth century, with useful notes on the text, language, and subject-matter. Treves' edition,[39] although erratic on linguistic points, has excellent notes on the subject-matter.

Aeschines

Comparatively little work has been done on Aeschines. A second edition of Blass's Teubner text appeared in 1908. Heyse[40] has investigated the textual tradition, having studied in particular the text of the speech *Against Timarchus*. The importance of his work on the manuscripts was acknowledged by the editors of the two Budé volumes,[41] but they questioned his system of classification, basing their objections mainly on papyrological evidence. The Budé edition included the spurious *Letters* which had previously been edited by Drerup in 1904. The need of an English translation was met by Adams' Loeb edition.[42]

Hyperides

It is little more than a hundred years ago that the speeches of Hyperides began to emerge from the sands of Egypt. By 1892 six speeches had been recovered, in whole or part. These were edited by Blass in his Teubner text of 1894. Material of such exceptional interest has naturally attracted the attention of scholars in the twentieth century and much work of distinction and importance has been done. In 1906 Kenyon, who had already played a prominent part in restoring the text, brought out his Oxford edition[43] of the six speeches, based on a new collation of the papyri. In 1917 Jensen, having studied the papyri afresh with great care and thoroughness, produced what was in effect an entirely new Teubner edition.[44] For specialists this must be considered the authoritative text and, unless new papyri are discovered, will presumably continue to be so for some time.

Two works on the language of Hyperides, by Gromska[45] and Pohle,[46] appeared within a short space of one another, in 1927 and 1928. Both were scholarly studies and were of particular interest and importance because Hyperides reflects, more conspicuously than other writers of his time, the intermediate stages of the process by which Attic was absorbed into a new common language.

During the past twenty-five years Colin has played an outstanding part in the work done on Hyperides. In 1934 he produced a most interesting book[47] in which he tried to reconstruct from the fragmentary papyri the argument of the speech which Hyperides delivered against Demosthenes in connection with the Harpalus scandal. In 1938 he published a long and detailed article[48] on the *Epitaphius* and considered its relation to other extant speeches of this genre. Valuable work on the *Epitaphius* has also been done by Hess.[49] His scholarly attempt to establish the text and elucidate the subject-matter was published in the same year as Colin's article. Colin's Budé edition[50] of the six speeches, the result of many years' work on Hyperides, appeared in 1946; the introductions which discuss the matter of the speeches and their historical setting are particularly valuable. De Falco[51] provided a full commentary on the speeches *For Euxenippus* and *Against Athenogenes*.

Hyperides is one of the outstanding literary finds of modern times and it can fairly be claimed that during the past fifty years scholars have made good use of the material bequeathed to them.

Demosthenes

It is generally agreed that Blass's Teubner text (1888-92) has serious shortcomings, in particular because it reflects a misplaced confidence that Demosthenes consistently followed certain principles of prose-rhythm. This and other reasons made the gradual appearance of the Oxford text[52] particularly welcome. The first two volumes were edited by Butcher, the last two by Rennie. A more ambitious edition,[53] in the Teubner series, was started by Fuhr in 1914 and continued by Sykutris in 1937. These two volumes, all that have appeared, contain the first twenty-six speeches. Although much valuable work has been done a complete definitive text of Demosthenes is still lacking.

There have been several new annotated editions of individual speeches. Among the more important are Goodwin's editions of the speeches *On the Crown*[54] and *Against Midias*;[55] these, although published early in the century, are still indispensable for their commentary on the subject-matter. More recently Treves' edition of the speech *On the Crown*,[56] although weak on linguistic points, has provided excellent discussions of the political, legal, and historical aspects. Schwahn's study of the speech *Against Aphobus*,[57] in which he tried to solve difficulties and discrepancies by employing methods of modern accounting, was notable not so much for the validity of its conclusions as for the novelty of its approach.

An article by Treves[58] in 1936 discussed works of doubtful authenticity. Treves, differing from the conclusions of Sykutris in an earlier article, rejected the *Epitaphius* as spurious. In 1938 the difficult question of the composition and authorship of the *Fourth*

Philippic and its relation to the speech *On the Chersonese* were considered by Adams[59] in an important article. An interesting point was treated by Dorjahn.[60] He tried to show from extant speeches that Demosthenes could, and to some extent did, speak without previous preparation. Admiration for Demosthenes' mastery of style has been quickened by a recent book of Gilberte Ronnet,[61] although her attempts to relate the development of his style to that of his character, based on a statistical analysis of his political speeches, are somewhat forced and unconvincing.

The large number of more general books on Demosthenes shows the extent to which he, alone of the Orators, has captured popular imagination. Many writers have been impressed by the parallels between the age of Demosthenes and the twentieth century, so much so that some books have been little more than a camouflage for political propaganda. In 1914 the relevance of Demosthenes in modern times was stressed by Pickard-Cambridge,[62] an enthusiastic admirer of his subject, in a popular, but scholarly, work. Elsewhere Demosthenes has appeared in a much less favourable light. Drerup in *Aus einer alten Advokatenrepublik*,[63] published in 1916, pictured him as an unscrupulous lawyer-politician. He continued his onslaught in *Demosthenes im Urteile des Altertums*,[64] in which he claimed that our estimate of Demosthenes should be based on the evidence of his contemporaries, which is almost entirely unfavourable to him, rather than on Plutarch and later sources, for whom Demosthenes had become a romantic legend. Drerup's polemics were much criticized at the time, not least by German scholars, but, if allowance is made for bias and prejudice, there is much of lasting value in these two books. At the other extreme was Clemenceau's fiery panegyric[65] published in 1924. In more recent books the spirit of extremism and propaganda seems to have waned. Treves[66] gave a clear-cut picture of Demosthenes and some of his contemporaries marked by sober sense and sound judgment. A more detailed work by Cloché[67] examined Demosthenes' career and achievements, defending his honesty while admitting his faults, and clarified several controversial problems. An important book by Jaeger[68] traced the origin and development of Demosthenes' political views. One should also mention two excellent little handbooks on Demosthenes, intended for the general reader, by Adams[69] and Mathieu.[70]

Dinarchus

Dinarchus was edited by Blass and indexed by Forman in the latter part of the last century. Little interest has been shown in him since then, but those who wish to study the incipient decline of Attic Oratory now have an easily accessible text and translation in a recently published Loeb volume.[71]

Demades

In 1932 De Falco[72] edited the fragments attributed to Demades and the *testimonia*. Shortly afterwards Treves[73] studied the fragments and tried to reconstruct something of his personality and political career. Demades is included in the same Loeb volume (*Minor Attic Orators* ii) as Dinarchus.

2. RHETORIC

(a) General

Any bibliographical survey under the heading 'rhetoric' must inevitably be arbitrary in its selection and incomplete in its treatment. For this term, when applied to Greek literature, is almost unlimited in its connotation, being inseparably connected with various other subjects, such as educational theory, literary criticism, and style. If one considers work done during the century on the more technical side of rhetoric the first feeling must be one of regret that two important gaps have not been filled. In the first place there is still no satisfactory book on Greek rhetoric and its historical development. The second edition of Volkmann's book[74] is still the standard work on the subject, but it is unsatisfactory, not merely because it is out of date, but because it is incomplete and makes little attempt to trace the historical development of rhetoric. The sections on epideictic writing, for instance, give no account of the early history of this genre and neglect important evidence in pre-Aristotelian writers. It is to be hoped that the new 'Müller Handbuch' on rhetoric, which has been in preparation for many years, will soon be published. The first historical survey which gave a clear idea of the successive stages in the development of Greek rhetoric was Kroll's learned and brilliant article in *Pauly-Wissowa*, first published as a separate article in 1937,[75] but this was necessarily only a summary. The second major gap is a lexicon of Greek rhetorical terms; recourse must still be had to Ernesti's work which was published in the eighteenth century. This deficiency has been alleviated by the excellent glossaries in Rhys Roberts' editions of Dionysius, Demetrius, and 'Longinus' and the indices to Teubner editions of Greek rhetoricians.

In other respects there has been plenty of important work on rhetorical subjects. Norden's magnificent survey[76] of the development of artistic prose came just before the beginning of the century. It is unlikely to be superseded for a long time, but a scholar who revised it in the light of modern scholarship and enlarged the rather scanty early chapters would perform a more than welcome service. Atkins' *Literary Criticism in Antiquity*,[77] published in 1934 and recently reprinted, has been a useful aid to the study of rhetoric, although not primarily intended for the specialist. An admirable little handbook by Rhys Roberts on *Greek Rhetoric and Literary Criticism*[78] makes one regret that this eminent scholar did not write a more detailed book on the subject. An important achievement of the century has been the publication of several volumes in a new Teubner corpus of *Rhetores Graeci* which, as far as it goes, shows an immeasurable advance on the series edited by Walz. The Paderborn *Rhetorische Studien* under the general editorship of Drerup has provided a useful series of monographs on miscellaneous subjects connected with ancient rhetoric; Krumbacher,[79] to mention one example of this series, gave an interesting summary of methods of voice-training employed by ancient rhetoricians.

(*b*) *Pre-Aristotelian Rhetoric*

The Sicilian origins of rhetoric were studied in great detail by Kowalski,[80] but it must be admitted that the gain was unsubstantial. Corax and Tisias remain little more than names. The subject was more realistically treated in a short article by Hinks.[81] The growth at Athens of the seed imported from Sicily has been more effectively studied. An admirable book by Navarre[82] published at the beginning of the century described the development of rhetoric at Athens and attempted to reconstruct a τέχνη which reflected fourth-century rhetorical teaching before Aristotle formulated a scientific system. The more detailed aspects of this development have provided scholars with abundant material for research. Their work has been made easier by the publication of volumes which collected together in a convenient form much of the ancient evidence. Diels' great work, *Die Fragmente der Vorsokratiker*, of which there have been six editions during the course of the century, includes many relevant texts, particularly those of the early Sophists; the full *testimonia*, and the index of significant words in the third volume have made it invaluable to the student of rhetoric as well as of philosophy. To some extent this was supplemented by Untersteiner's collection of texts relating to the Sophists.[83] Recently Radermacher[84] has edited fragments and excerpts illustrating early rhetorical theory. Many of these, having no philosophical import, were not included in Diels' collection. Anyone who has worked on early Greek rhetoric must be conscious of the time saved by having this material assembled together in a convenient form. The volumes which have appeared in the last twenty-five years of Schmid and Stählin, *Geschichte der Griechischen Literatur*,[85] have provided a useful *subsidium* for the student of fifth-century rhetoric, particularly because of the numerous references to rhetorical terms and forms. If, to take an example at random, one wants to find examples of paradoxical encomia in Euripides, one can do so by consulting the index to the third volume.

Attempts have been made to trace the early development of the three forms of oratory distinguished by Aristotle, a subject neglected by nineteenth-century scholars. Solmsen[9] enquired into the origins and growth of legal oratory, basing his study mainly on the evidence in Antiphon's speeches. It has been commonly supposed that early rhetoricians taught only legal oratory, but Wilcox[86] drew attention to innumerable examples which show that Gorgias and others prepared their pupils for the ecclesia as well as the law-courts. Hudson-Williams[87] discussed the largely extempore nature of political speeches in the fifth and early fourth centuries B.C. and its influence on the manner in which Thucydides and Isocrates composed their purely literary speeches. No satisfactory account has been given of the origins and early development of epideictic speeches. Burgess's *Epideictic Literature*[88] well described the later development of the various branches of epideictic prose, but made little attempt to trace the early history of the elements out of which this genre was formed.

The importance of the early Sophists for the study of rhetoric was recognized by the younger Gomperz in his book *Sophistik und Rhetorik*;[89] scholars have found some of his theories untenable, but this detailed treatment of a neglected subject was a contribution of some importance. Süss's book *Ethos*[90] discussed a miscellaneous assortment of subjects connected with pre-Aristotelian rhetoric, including a number of controversial questions; his treatment was discursive and disorderly and many of the solutions which he offered were highly improbable, but the book cannot be altogether disregarded. Many problems connected with this period are concerned with the relations between Isocrates, Alcidamas, and Plato, and in particular with various difficulties raised by the *Phaedrus*. Every aspect of these problems has been discussed at length by modern scholars without, it must be admitted, very tangible results. Two works on the *Phaedrus* deserve mention because they clarify the issues involved, if they do not give the final solutions. Robin's lengthy introduction to his Budé edition[91] of this dialogue includes a good review of its rhetorical implications. The introduction and commentary which accompany Hackforth's translation,[92] although primarily concerned with the philosophical aspects of the dialogue, treat the rhetorical side realistically. However, a new edition of the *Phaedrus* with a full commentary from the rhetorical angle is badly needed.

The stylistic contribution of the early rhetoricians, which was somewhat cursorily treated by Norden in *Die Antike Kunstprosa*, has since been studied in some detail. At the beginning of the century Drerup[93] discussed the subject at length with reference to Thrasymachus and his school, Gorgias, Antiphon, and Theodorus of Byzantium. Two commentaries on Gorgias' writings may be mentioned: Immisch[94] produced a small, but useful, edition of the *Helen*; recently Vollgraf[95] devoted a whole book to a commentary on the short fragment, some twenty lines, of the *Epitaphius*. Aly[10] has studied the various forms of early rhetorical prose. Lamb's *Clio Enthroned*,[96] although ostensibly concerned with Thucydides' style, has a much wider interest; in an elegant survey which conceals much learning Lamb described the impact of rhetoric on fifth-century prose in its successive stages. In the first chapter of his book on *Greek Prose Style* Denniston[97] provided what is probably the best short analysis in any language of the elements which influenced fifth-century prose. Reference should also be made to two long and very interesting articles by Finley[98] on 'Euripides and Thucydides' and 'The origins of Thucydides' style'. Whether one agrees or not with the general conclusions of these two articles

GREEK ORATORS AND RHETORIC

about the character of Thucydides' speeches and their historical accuracy, their detailed examination of the elements which influenced Thucydides' style has made a valuable contribution to the study of early rhetoric. An important point stressed by Finley and other modern scholars is that traces of the so-called 'rhetorical influences' are to be found in Athenian literature before Gorgias' visit to Athens in 427, and must not necessarily be ascribed to the importation of Sicilian rhetoric to Athens.

The study of pre-Aristotelian rhetoric has an interest and importance which go far beyond the narrow limits of the subject itself. In the fifth and early fourth centuries the art of persuasion was a living force and the fascination it exercised is reflected in the literature of the period. A knowledge of rhetorical conventions and rhetorical usage is essential for the interpretation of passages in Thucydides, Isocrates, Plato, and many of their contemporaries. Nineteenth-century scholars tended to neglect this early period of rhetoric and concentrated on Aristotle and later theorists. Recently pre-Aristotelian rhetoric has received more attention, but the work done is widely dispersed in periodicals and dissertations. A book is badly needed which will make the results of such work in this field more accessible.

(c) Aristotle and Later Theory

Römer's Teubner edition which was published towards the end of the last century is still the most detailed and authoritative critical work on Aristotle's *Rhetoric*. There has been no detailed commentary since that of Cope and Sandys in 1877, but a great deal has been done, largely in the form of annotated translations, to make this difficult and obscure work more intelligible. A translation made by Jebb in the last century was published for the first time in 1909 under the editorship of Sandys who added numerous notes.[99] Progress made towards a better understanding of the *Rhetoric* was reflected in Rhys Roberts' translation,[100] with footnotes, which was published in 1924. It is generally agreed that this was a significant improvement on all earlier renderings and is still probably the best. Since then the *Rhetoric* has been edited in the Loeb series by Freese[101] and bks. i and ii in the Budé series by Dufour.[102] There has also appeared a free translation with a running commentary by Lane Cooper,[103] designed to help those who know little or nothing about the subject.

The so-called *Rhetorica ad Alexandrum*, at one time attributed to Aristotle, is generally agreed to be the work of Anaximenes. A papyrus fragment found in Egypt and published by Grenfell and Hunt in 1906 has supplemented the manuscript evidence and helped to confirm the fourth-century origin of this work. Forster[100] provided an excellent English translation together with some valuable textual notes. It has been edited by Rackham[104] in the Loeb series with a fuller apparatus than is generally found in Loeb volumes. Rackham, more reluctant than most modern scholars to ascribe the work to Anaximenes, would not commit himself to a positive opinion about its authorship. The sources from which this handbook was drawn and other questions connected with the rhetorical works of Anaximenes were discussed by Wendland[105] in a book published in 1905.

Important work has been done on Aristotle's conception of rhetorical style and its development by his peripatetic successors. An article by Hendrickson[106] in 1904, which studied and analysed the stylistic principles of Aristotle and Theophrastus, helped to clarify a neglected and obscure subject and stimulated other scholars to enlarge on his work. In 1910 Mayer[107] edited the scanty fragments of Theophrastus' work *On Style* and tried to reconstruct the original from them. An edition of these fragments was badly needed, but Mayer's attempted reconstruction was found to be unsound. A much more important book by Stroux[108] appeared two years later. Ostensibly concerned with Theophrastus' stylistic theory, it had a far wider significance as it did much to explain the development of rhetoric generally from Aristotle to Roman times. Stroux was the first to give a convincing and coherent account of the way in which Aristotelian theory was adapted and systematized by Aristotle's successors. More recently the Aristotelian influence on later stylistic theory has been profitably discussed by Barwick[109] and Solmsen.[110] An excellent summary of its historical development is to be found in Kroll's *Pauly-Wissowa* article.

Particularly fruitful has been the interest shown by scholars in Dionysius, Demetrius, and 'Longinus'. Usener and Radermacher[111] performed an invaluable service by editing Dionysius' essays on rhetoric and literary criticism in the Teubner series and taking account of work done on the text since Reiske's edition in the eighteenth century. The first volume of this edition appeared in 1899, the second in 1904, and the work was concluded in 1929 by the publication of a supplementary fascicule containing a preface and indices. The subject-matter and background of these essays were discussed in a learned work by Egger[112] which was published in 1902. Rhys Roberts supplied exceptionally full and scholarly editions of the letters to Ammaeus and Pompeius,[113] and of the essay *On Literary Composition*.[114] These editions included an excellent translation, a discussion of the manuscripts, a commentary on the subject-matter, abundant references to modern works, and useful glossaries of technical terms. More recently Bonner[115] has examined Dionysius' critical methods in individual essays and tried to trace an improvement and development in his technique. The date and order of composition of the various essays are, however, still uncertain. A book on the subject by Pavano[116] appeared in 1942, but it cannot be said to have solved this much discussed problem. There is still need of a complete English translation of these essays; they might well be included in the Loeb series.

The fragments of Dionysius' contemporary Caecilius of Calacte were edited by Ofenloch[117] in 1907. His edition included nearly everything which had ever been ascribed to Caecilius and little attempt was made to distinguish the probably authentic from the almost certainly spurious, but it was, nevertheless, a useful contribution to the study of later rhetoric.

At the beginning of the century two editions of Demetrius' essay *On Style* appeared almost simultaneously, those of Radermacher[118] and Rhys Roberts.[119] Although radically at variance on many points, both made an important contribution to the elucidation of the text and subject-matter. Both texts were based on a new and independent study of the Paris manuscript. Unlike Radermacher, whose edition was essentially designed for specialists, Roberts aimed at interesting a wider public and included in his commentary several illustrations from modern writers. In 1927 he produced another edition of Demetrius' essay in the Loeb series in which he revised his earlier text and translation and supplemented the bibliography. Several articles on Demetrius have been written by Orth who in 1923 supplied the first German translation[120] of this essay.

The twentieth century has seen a marked revival of interest in 'Longinus'. New editions of the essay *On the Sublime* have appeared in many languages and discussion as to the name and date of the author has been frequent in periodicals. This interest was stimulated in England by the publication in 1899 of Rhys Roberts' edition,[121] the first English edition for over sixty years. Vahlen[122] in 1905 and again in 1910 produced new editions of his revision of Jahn's text which were remarkable for their meticulous accuracy and sound judgment. Prickard's Oxford text,[123] much praised by reviewers, was published in 1906 and his translation in the same year. New editions have since been published in England, France, Germany, Italy, Holland, and Greece; there have also been several new translations. The many attempts to find the author of this essay are chiefly notable for the diversity of their conclusions; the only point on which there seems to be agreement is that the author was not Cassius Longinus. The danger of trying to derive this essay from definite sources was shown by Mutschmann[124] in a book published in 1913; in particular he pointed out that the supposed influence of Caecilius on 'Longinus' was based on very slender evidence. The least important part of this book was Mutschmann's attempt to ascribe the essay to a pupil of Theodorus of Gadara.

It is impossible to do justice in this chapter to the 'Second Sophistic' period. Most of its literature might come under the headings 'rhetoric' or 'oratory', and a review of scholarship covering such a wide field would be disproportionately long. It must be enough to consider briefly the work done on the more technical side of rhetoric. The results of this work are to a great extent to be found in a number of volumes which have appeared in the new Teubner corpus of *Rhetores Graeci*. Schmid[125] edited the two rhetorical treatises attributed to Aelius Aristides. Like other editors in this series he provided an invaluable index of rhetorical terms. His text and critical notes completely superseded the work of his predecessors. As regards the authorship he concluded that the two works were by different persons and that neither was written by Aristides. Even more important was the work done by Rabe on Hermogenes, his successors, and his ancient commentators. In 1913, after publishing several papers on Hermogenes during the early years of the century, Rabe produced an edition of his works in the Teubner series.[126] Since then he has edited in the same series the *Progymnasmata* of Aphthonius,[127] the *Commentary on Aphthonius* by Bishop Johannes of Sardis,[128] and a collection of introductions to various rhetorical works.[129] In this narrow field, much of it a dreary waste of repetitious pedantry, Rabe produced order out of chaos. Probably no man has contributed so much to the study of this later period of rhetoric. His editions are models of painstaking care and unrelenting thoroughness. Other volumes which have appeared in the new Teubner corpus are Felton's edition of the *Progymnasmata* of Nicolaus[130] and Camphausen's edition of Romanus' work Περὶ τοῦ ἀνειμένου.[131] In 1939 an anonymous commentary on two works of Hermogenes, Περὶ στάσεων and Περὶ εὑρέσεως, was edited for the first time by Kowalski.[132]

---

[1] R. C. Jebb, *The Attic Orators from Antiphon to Isaeus*², London, Macmillan, 1893.
[2] F. Blass, *Die Attische Beredsamkeit*², Leipzig, Teubner, 1887-98.
[3] W. Wyse, *The Speeches of Isaeus*, Cambridge, The University Press, 1904.
[4] For a discussion of the more important papyrological discoveries see *New Chapters in Greek Literature* I, edited by J. U. Powell and E. A. Barber, Chapter VII, Oxford, The Clarendon Press, 1921 and F. G. Kenyon 'Greek Papyri and their contribution to Classical Literature' and B. P. Grenfell, 'The value of papyri for the textual criticism of extant Greek authors', JHS 39 (1919).
[5] J. H. Lipsius, *Das attische Recht und Rechtsverfahren*, Leipzig, Reisland, 1905-15.
[6] J. F. Dobson, *The Greek Orators*, London, Methuen, 1919.
[7] J. Nicole, *L'Apologie d'Antiphon*, Geneva and Bâle, Georg, 1907.
[8] For two recent articles expressing contrary views see P. von der Mühll, 'Zur Unechtheit der antiphontischen Tetralogien', MH 5 (1948) and G. Zuntz, 'Once again the Antiphontean Tetralogies', MH 6 (1949).
[9] F. Solmsen, *Antiphonstudien. Untersuchungen zur Entstehung der attischen Gerichtsrede*, Berlin, Weidmann, 1931.
[10] W. Aly, 'Formprobleme der frühen griechischen Prosa', Ph Suppl. Bd. 21, Heft 3 (1929).
[11] K. J. Dover, 'The chronology of Antiphon's speeches', CQ 44 (1950).
[12] F. Blass and C. Fuhr, *Andocidis Orationes*, Leipzig, Teubner, 1913.
[13] G. Dalmeyda, *Andocide: Discours*, Paris, 'Les Belles Lettres', 1930.
[14] T. Thalheim, *Lysiae Orationes*, Leipzig, Teubner, 1901.
[15] K. Hude, *Lysiae Orationes*, Oxford, The Clarendon Press, 1912.
[16] L. Gernet and M. Bizos, *Lysias: Discours*, Paris, 'Les Belles Lettres', 1924-26.
[17] P. A. Müller, *Oratio Quae inter Lysiacas Fertur Octava*, Monasterii Westfalorum, 1926.
[18] J. Walz, 'Der lysianische Epitaphios', Ph Suppl. Bd. 29, Heft 4 (1936).
[19] F. Ferckel, *Lysias und Athen*, Würzburg, Triltsch, 1937.
[20] E. Drerup, *Isocratis Opera Omnia* I, Leipzig, Weicher, 1906.
[21] G. Mathieu and E. Brémond, *Isocrate: Discours* I-III, Paris, 'Les Belles Lettres', 1928-42.
[22] E. S. Forster, *Isocrates: Cyprian Orations*, Oxford, The Clarendon Press, 1912.
[23] M. L. W. Laistner, *Isocrates: De Pace and Philippus*, New York, Longmans, Green, and Co., 1927.
[24] P. Treves, *Isocrate: Il Panegirico*, Turin, Paravia, 1932.
[25] P. Treves, *Isocrate: A Filippo*, Milan, Signorelli, 1933.
[26] J. C. A. M. Bongenaar, *Isocrates' Trapeziticus*, Utrecht, Dekker en van de Vegt, 1933.
[27] S. Preuss, *Index Isocrateus*, Leipzig, Teubner, 1904.
[28] S. Wilcox, 'Criticisms of Isocrates and his φιλοσοφία', TAPhA 74 (1943) and 'Isocrates' fellow-rhetoricians', AJPh 66 (1945).

[29] H. Ll. Hudson-Williams, 'Thucydides, Isocrates, and the rhetorical method of composition', CQ 42 (1948) and 'Isocrates and recitations', CQ 43 (1949).
[30] H. Wersdörfer, *Die φιλοσοφία des Isokrates im Spiegel ihrer Terminologie*, Leipzig, Harrassowitz, 1940.
[31] G. Schmitz-Kahlmann, 'Das Beispiel der Geschichte im politischen Denken des Isokrates', Ph Suppl. Bd. 31, Heft 4 (1939).
[32] H. M. Hubbell, *The Influence of Isocrates on Cicero, Dionysius, and Aristides*, New Haven, Yale University Press, 1913.
[33] G. Mathieu, *Les Idées Politiques d'Isocrate*, Paris, 'Les Belles Lettres', 1925.
[34] A. Burk, *Die Pädagogik des Isokrates*, Würzburg, 1923.
[35] W. Jaeger, *Paideia* III, Oxford, Blackwell, 1945.
[36] T. Thalheim, *Isaei Orationes*, Leipzig, Teubner, 1903. This was reviewed in great detail by Wyse in CR 18 (1904).
[37] F. Durrbach, *Lycurgue: Contre Léocrate, Fragments*, Paris, 'Les Belles Lettres', 1932.
[38] A. Petrie, *Lycurgus: The Speech Against Leocrates*, Cambridge, The University Press, 1922.
[39] P. Treves, *Licurgo: L'Orazione contro Leocrate*, Milan, Signorelli, 1934.
[40] M. Heyse, *Die Handschriftliche Überlieferung der Reden des Aeschines*, Ohlau, 1912.
[41] V. Martin and G. de Budé, *Eschine: Discours*, Paris, 'Les Belles Lettres', 1927-28.
[42] C. D. Adams, *The Speeches of Aeschines*, London, Heinemann, 1919.
[43] F. G. Kenyon, *Hyperidis Orationes et Fragmenta*, Oxford, The Clarendon Press, 1906.
[44] C. Jensen, *Hyperidis Orationes*, Leipzig, Teubner, 1917.
[45] D. Gromska, *De Sermone Hyperidis, Studia Leopolitana* III, 1927.
[46] U. Pohle, *Die Sprache des Redners Hypereides in ihren Beziehungen zur Koine*, Leipzig, Harrassowitz, 1928.
[47] G. Colin, *Le Discours d'Hypéride contre Démosthène sur l'Argent d'Harpale*, Paris, 'Les Belles Lettres', 1934.
[48] G. Colin, 'L'oraison funèbre d'Hypéride; ses rapports avec les autres oraisons funèbres athéniennes', REG 51 (1938).
[49] H. Hess, *Textkritische und erklärende Beiträge zum Epitaphios des Hypereides*, Leipzig, Harrassowitz, 1938.
[50] G. Colin, *Hypéride: Discours*, Paris, 'Les Belles Lettres', 1946.
[51] V. de Falco, *Iperide: Le Orazioni in difesa di Eussenippo e contro Atenogene*, Naples, Libreria Scientifica, 1947.
[52] S. H. Butcher and W. Rennie, *Demosthenis Orationes*, Oxford, The Clarendon Press, 1903-31.
[53] C. Fuhr and J. Sykutris, *Demosthenis Orationes* I-II, 1, Leipzig, Teubner, 1914-37.
[54] W. W. Goodwin, *Demosthenes: On the Crown*, Cambridge, The University Press, 1901.
[55] W. W. Goodwin, *Demosthenes: Against Midias*, Cambridge, The University Press, 1906.
[56] P. Treves, *Demostene: L'Orazione per la Corona*, Milan, Signorelli, 1933.
[57] W. Schwahn, *Demosthenes: Gegen Aphobos*, Leipzig, Teubner, 1929.
[58] P. Treves, 'Apocrifi Demostenici', Ath 14 (1936).
[59] C. D. Adams, 'Speeches VIII and X of the Demosthenic Corpus', CPh 33 (1938).
[60] A. P. Dorjahn, 'On Demosthenes' ability to speak extemporaneously', TAPhA 78 (1947). Dorjahn continued the theme in TAPhA 81 (1950) and 83 (1952).
[61] G. Ronnet, *Étude sur le Style de Démosthène dans les Discours Politiques*, Paris, de Boccard, 1951.
[62] A. W. Pickard-Cambridge, *Demosthenes and the Last Days of Greek Freedom*, London, Putnam, 1914.
[63] E. Drerup, *Aus einer alten Advokatenrepublik*, Paderborn, Schöningh, 1916.
[64] Würzburg, Becker, 1923.
[65] G. Clemenceau, *Démosthène*, Paris, Plon, 1924.
[66] P. Treves, *Demostene e la Libertà Greca*, Bari, Laterza, 1933.
[67] P. Cloché, *Démosthène et la Fin de la Démocratie Athénienne*, Paris, Payot, 1937.
[68] W. Jaeger, *Demosthenes: The Origin and Growth of his Policy*, Cambridge, The University Press, 1938.
[69] C. D. Adams, *Demosthenes and his Influence*, London, Harrap, 1927.

GREEK ORATORS AND RHETORIC

[70] G. Mathieu, *Démosthène: L'Homme et L'Œuvre*, Paris, Boivin, 1948.
[71] J. O. Burtt, *Minor Attic Orators* II, London, Heinemann, 1954.
[72] V. de Falco, *Demade Oratore: Testimonianze e Frammenti*, Pavia, 1932.
[73] P. Treves, 'Demade', Ath 11 (1933).
[74] R. Volkmann, *Die Rhetorik der Griechen und Römer*[2], Leipzig, Teubner, 1885. The so-called third edition (in the Müller Handbuch series) was merely a summary of the earlier edition.
[75] W. Kroll, *Rhetorik*, Stuttgart, Metzler, 1937.
[76] E. Norden, *Die Antike Kunstprosa*, Leipzig, Teubner, 1898.
[77] J. W. H. Atkins, *Literary Criticism in Antiquity*, Cambridge, The University Press, 1934. Reissued by Methuen, London, 1952.
[78] W. Rhys Roberts, *Greek Rhetoric and Literary Criticism*, New York, Longmans, Green, and Co., 1928.
[79] A. Krumbacher, *Die Stimmbildung der Redner im Altertum*, Paderborn, Schöningh, 1921.
[80] G. Kowalski, *De Arte Rhetorica* I, Lwow, Gubrynowicz, 1937.
[81] D. A. G. Hinks, 'Tisias and Corax and the invention of rhetoric', CQ 34 (1940).
[82] O. Navarre, *Essai sur la Rhétorique Grecque avant Aristote*, Paris, Hachette, 1900.
[83] M. Untersteiner, *I Sophisti, Testimonianze e Frammenti* I-II, Florence, 'La Nuova Italia', 1949.
[84] L. Radermacher, *Artium Scriptores*, SAWW 227, 3, Vienna, Rohrer, 1951.
[85] W. Schmid and O. Stählin, *Geschichte der Griechischen Literatur* I, i-v, Munich, Beck, 1929-48.
[86] S. Wilcox, 'The scope of early rhetorical instruction', HSPh 53 (1942).
[87] H. Ll. Hudson-Williams, 'Political speeches in Athens', CQ New Series 1 (1951).
[88] T. C. Burgess, *Epideictic Literature*, Chicago, The University of Chicago Press, 1902.
[89] H. Gomperz, *Sophistik und Rhetorik*, Leipzig, Teubner, 1912.
[90] W. Süss, *Ethos*, Leipzig, Teubner, 1910.
[91] L. Robin, *Platon: Phèdre*, Paris, 'Les Belles Lettres', 1929.
[92] R. Hackforth, *Plato's Phaedrus*, Cambridge, The University Press, 1952.
[93] E. Drerup, 'Die Anfänge der rhetorischen Kunstprosa', JKPh 27 (1902).
[94] O. Immisch, *Gorgiae Helena*, Berlin and Leipzig, De Gruyter, 1927.
[95] W. Vollgraff, *L'Oraison Funèbre de Gorgias*, Leiden, Brill, 1952.
[96] W. R. M. Lamb, *Clio Enthroned*, Cambridge, The University Press, 1914.
[97] J. D. Denniston, *Greek Prose Style*, Oxford, The Clarendon Press, 1952.
[98] J. H. Finley, HSPh 49 (1938) and 50 (1939).
[99] R. C. Jebb and J. E. Sandys, *The Rhetoric of Aristotle*, Cambridge, The University Press, 1909.
[100] *The Works of Aristotle Translated into English* XI, Oxford, The Clarendon Press, 1924.
[101] J. H. Freese, *Aristotle: The Art of Rhetoric*, London, Heinemann, 1926.
[102] M. Dufour, *Aristote, Rhétorique* I-II, Paris, 'Les Belles Lettres', 1932-38.
[103] L. Cooper, *The Rhetoric of Aristotle*, New York, Appleton, 1931.
[104] H. Rackham, *Rhetorica ad Alexandrum* (together with W. S. Hett, *Aristotle, Problems* II), London, Heinemann, 1937.
[105] P. Wendland, *Anaximenes von Lampsakos*, Berlin, Weidmann, 1905.
[106] G. L. Hendrickson, 'The peripatetic mean of style and the three stylistic characters', AJPh 25 (1904).
[107] A. Mayer, *Theophrasti περὶ λέξεως Libri Fragmenta*, Leipzig, Teubner, 1910.
[108] J. Stroux, *De Theophrasti Virtutibus Dicendi*, Leipzig, Teubner, 1912.
[109] K. Barwick, 'Die Gliederung der rhetorischen τέχνη und die horazische Epistula ad Pisones', H 57 (1922).
[110] F. Solmsen, 'The Aristotelian tradition in ancient rhetoric', AJPh 62 (1941).
[111] H. Usener and L. Radermacher, *Dionysii Halicarnasei Opuscula*, Leipzig, Teubner, 1899-1929.
[112] M. Egger, *Denys d'Halicarnasse*, Paris, Picard, 1902.
[113] W. Rhys Roberts, *Dionysius of Halicarnassus: The Three Literary Letters*, Cambridge, The University Press, 1901.
[114] W. Rhys Roberts, *Dionysius of Halicarnassus: On Literary Composition*, London, Macmillan, 1910.

[115] S. F. Bonner, *The Literary Treatises of Dionysius of Halicarnassus*, Cambridge, The University Press, 1939.
[116] G. Pavano, *Sulla Cronologia degli Scritti Retorici di Dionisio d'Alicarnasso*, Palermo, 1942.
[117] E. Ofenloch, *Caecilii Calactini Fragmenta*, Leipzig, Teubner, 1907.
[118] L. Radermacher, *Demetrii Phalerei Qui Dicitur de Elocutione Libellus*, Leipzig, Teubner, 1901.
[119] W. Rhys Roberts, *Demetrius: On Style*, Cambridge, The University Press, 1902.
[120] E. Orth, *Demetrios: Vom Stil. Deutsche Übersetzung*, Saarbrücken, 1923.
[121] W. Rhys Roberts, *Longinus: On the Sublime*, Cambridge, The University Press, 1899.
[122] O. Jahn and J. Vahlen, Διονυσίου ἢ Λογγίνου περὶ ὕψους, *De Sublimitate Libellus*, Leipzig, Teubner, 1905 and 1910.
[123] A. O. Prickard, *Libellus de Sublimitate Dionysio Longino Fere Adscriptus*, Oxford, The Clarendon Press, 1906.
[124] H. Mutschmann, *Tendenz, Aufbau, und Quellen der Schrift vom Erhabenen*, Berlin, Weidmann, 1913.
[125] W. Schmid, *Rhetores Graeci V. Aristidis Qui Feruntur Libri Rhetorici II*, Leipzig, Teubner, 1926.
[126] H. Rabe, *Rhetores Graeci VI. Hermogenis Opera*, Leipzig, Teubner, 1913.
[127] H. Rabe, *Rhetores Graeci X. Aphthonii Progymnasmata*, Leipzig, Teubner, 1926.
[128] H. Rabe, *Rhetores Graeci XV. Joannis Sardiani Commentarius in Aphthonii Progymnasmata*, Leipzig, Teubner, 1928.
[129] H. Rabe, *Rhetores Graeci XIV. Prolegomenon Sylloge*, Leipzig, Teubner, 1931.
[130] J. Felton, *Rhetores Graeci XI. Nicolai Progymnasmata*, Leipzig, Teubner, 1913.
[131] W. Camphausen, *Rhetores Graeci XIII. Romanus Sophista*: Περὶ τοῦ ἀνειμένου, Leipzig, Teubner, 1922.
[132] G. Kowalski, *Commentarius Codicis Vaticani Gr. 107 in Hermogenis* Περὶ στάσεων *et* περὶ εὑρέσεως *opera*, Lwow, 1939.

APPENDIX TO CHAPTER VII

The Orators

CONTROVERSY whether there were one or two Antiphons continues.[1] D. M. Macdowell[2] has attempted to reconcile the well-known discrepancy between Athenian homicide law and homicide law as it appears in the *Tetralogies*. More scholarly work on Andocides has appeared during the last few years than during the entire first half of the century. This is mainly to be found in U. Albini's editions of the *De Reditu* and *De Pace*,[3] and D. M. Macdowell's edition of the *De Mysteriis*.[4] Albini's work concentrates on the stylistic and lexical aspects; Macdowell's edition is particularly valuable for its full discussion of the historical, religious, and legal background to the case.

Characteristic of the recent Italian and Spanish interest in the Orators is a complete critical edition of Lysias by U. Albini together with a translation,[5] and the first volume of a similar work by M. F. Galiano.[6] Lesser publications include two articles by J. J. Bateman,[7] on Lysias' attitude to the law and on the form in which he framed his arguments, and an interesting study of Lysias' character-drawing by S. Usher[8] who points out that in many speeches there is no attempt at individual characterization.

Opinions on Isocrates vary as widely as ever. In E. Mikkola's account of his views[9] he appears as an original thinker who only wrote when he had something important to say. At the other extreme is G. A. Kennedy's disparaging estimate ('He was tiresome, long-winded, and above all superficial').[10] From the historical and political viewpoint M. A. Levi and P. Cloché[11] have drawn somewhat idealized portraits of him, the latter showing considerably more reason and moderation. D. L. Clark[12] stresses the importance of his educational influence on later antiquity. Among the more important works on Isocrates is E. Buchner's commentary on the *Panegyricus*,[13] in which he makes original and interesting discoveries about the structure of the speech as well as discussing its historical background. In 1962 the final volume of the excellent Budé edition of Isocrates was published.

U. Schindel in an interesting study of Demosthenes' *Nachleben*[14] shows the remarkable attraction Demosthenes had for 18th-century scholars. He has fallen in popularity today in comparison with the other great prose-writers, and there has been comparatively little work of importance done on him recently. His attitude to panhellenism is discussed in a book by J. Luccioni.[15] Shorter studies cover the following subjects: the accuracy of Dionysius' dates for some of Demosthenes' Speeches,[16] his use of the dependent infinitive as a stylistic device,[17] the facts about the case against Midias,[18] arguments for dating the 4th *Philippic* earlier than the *De Chersoneso*,[19] the development of his technique of argument.[20] Some Belgian scholars have tried to use psychological criteria in analysing the structure of his speeches and those of other orators.[21]

In general while there have been no spectacular new views or discoveries on the Attic Orators, some impressive work has been done, particularly in the form of critical editions and commentaries.

Rhetoric

G. A. Kennedy's excellent book[10] on the general development of Greek oratory and rhetoric has met a real need. There is still room for a more detailed work on this subject. It has a wide appeal judging by the large number of recent publications on various aspects of ancient rhetoric, both technical and general.[22] Some scholars stress its relevance to modern literary criticism. With this apparently in mind H. Lausberg[23] has attempted the ambitious, but impossible, task of compiling a comprehensive *ars rhetorica* for students of modern literature based on Greek and Latin sources.

V. Buchheit's detailed study[24] of the theory and development of epideictic oratory is welcome, although many of the controversial problems it raises remain unsolved. Two recent editions of Aristotle's *Rhetoric* should be mentioned, namely Sir David Ross's Oxford text[25] and A. Tover's Spanish edition with an extensive commentary.[26]

The most significant work on the post-Aristotelian period deals with style and literary criticism rather than rhetoric in the narrower sense. G. M. A. Grube, who in his more detailed publications has done much to advance the study of this subject, has provided a good general survey of the ancient literary critics.[27] Two books on Demetrius, *On Style* introduce new ideas, namely Grube's translation with its long and detailed introduction,[28] and a volume of miscellaneous studies by D. M. Schenkeveld.[29] There has been a renewal of controversy about the date of this work.[30] Important and original work continues to be done on 'Longinus'; particular mention should be made of D. A. Russell's text and full-scale commentary.[31] Lesser publications include W. Bühler's penetrating study of certain chapters,[32] H. D. Blume's interesting and original attempt to analyse the style,[33] and two articles by G. J. De Vries[34] on points of text and elucidation. Speculation about the author of this essay continues.[35]

In connection with the technicalities of the later Greek rhetoricians D. Mattes's work on Hermagoras[36] is of primary importance and supersedes much previous work on him. Reference should also be made to R. Nadeau's investigations into the *stasis* theory[37] and D. Hagedorn's study of the *ideai* of Hermogenes.[38]

---

[1] See E. R. Dodds, CR 4 (1954), 94-95; J. S. Morrison, PCPhS 7 (1961), 49-58; S. Luria, Eos 53 (1963), 63-67.
[2] *Athenian Homicide Law in the Age of the Orators*, Manchester, the University Press, 1963.
[3] *De Reditu*, Florence, Le Monnier, 1961; *De Pace*, Florence, Le Monnier, 1964.
[4] Oxford, Clarendon Press, 1962.
[5] Florence, Sansoni, 1955.
[6] Barcelona, Ediciones Alma Mater, 1953.
[7] TAPhA 89 (1958), 276-85 and Phoenix 16 (1962), 157-77.
[8] Eranos 63 (1965), 99-119.
[9] *Isokrates, seine Anschauungen im Lichte seiner Schriften*, Helsinki, 1954.
[10] *The Art of Persuasion in Greece*, Princeton University Press (London, Routledge and Kegan Paul), 1963.
[11] M. A. Levi, *Isocrate: Saggio Critico*, Milan, Istituto Editoriale Cisalpino, 1959 and P. Cloché, *Isocrate et son Temps*, Paris, 'Les Belles Lettres', 1963. For historical and political aspects see also S. Perlmann, 'Isocrates' Philippus. A reinterpretation', Historia 6 (1957), 306-17, and K. Bringmann, *Studien zu den politischen Ideen des Isokrates*, Göttingen, Vandenhoeck and Ruprecht, 1965.
[12] *Rhetoric in Greco-Roman Education*, New York, Columbia University Press, 1957.
[13] *Der Panegyrikos des Isokrates* (Historia Einzelschriften 2), Wiesbaden, Steiner, 1958.
[14] *Demosthenes im 18. Jahrhundert* (Zetemata 31), Munich, Beck, 1963.
[15] *Démosthène et la Panhellénisme*, Paris, Presses Universitaires, 1961.
[16] R. Sealey, REG 68 (1955), 77-120.
[17] B. Gaya Nuño, *Sobre un giro de la lengua de Demóstenes*, Madrid, 1959
[18] H. Erbse, H 84 (1956), 135-51.
[19] S. G. Daitz, CPh 52 (1957), 145-62.
[20] L. Pearson, Phoenix 18 (1964), 95-108.
[21] Particularly M. Delaunois in *Le plan rhétorique dans l'éloquence grecque d'Homère à Démosthène*, Brussels, Palais des Academies, 1959.

[22] For details of publications up to 1963 see two useful surveys by C. S. Rayment in CW 52 (1958-59), 75-91 and 57 (1963-64), 241-51.
[23] *Handbuch der literarischen Rhetorik*, Munich, Hueber, 1960.
[24] *Untersuchungen zur Theorie des Genos Epideiktikon von Gorgias bis Aristoteles*, Munich Hueber, 1960.
[25] Oxford, Clarendon Press, 1959.
[26] Madrid, Instituto de Estudios Políticos, 1953.
[27] *The Greek and Roman Critics*, London, Methuen, 1965.
[28] *A Greek Critic: Demetrius On Style*, Toronto, the University Press, 1961.
[29] *Studies in Demetrius On Style*, Amsterdam, Hakkert, 1964.
[30] See G. P. Goold, 'A Greek professorial circle in Rome', TAPhA 92 (1961); 168-92. J. M. Rist, 'Demetrius the stylist and Artemon the compiler', Phoenix 18 (1964), 2-8; G. M. A. Grube, 'The date of Demetrius On Style', Phoenix 18 (1964), 294-302; also Schenkeveld *op. cit.*
[31] *'Longinus', On the Sublime*, Oxford, Clarendon Press, 1964.
[32] *Beiträge zur Erklärung der Schrift vom Erhabenen*, Göttingen, Vandenhoeck and Ruprecht, 1964.
[33] *Untersuchungen zu Sprache und Stil der Schrift* περὶ ὕψους, Göttingen, 1963.
[34] Mnemosyne 12 (1959), 54-72 and 18 (1965), 225-68.
[35] See M. J. Boyd, 'Longinus, the philological discourses and the essay on the Sublime', C.Q. 7 (1957), 39-46 and G. M. A. Grube, 'Theodorus of Gadara', AJPh 80 (1959), 337-65.
[36] His long and detailed article 'Hermagoras von Temnos 1904-1955', Lustrum 3 (1958), 58-214, is far more than a bibliographical commentary. This was followed by his edition of the fragments (Leipzig, Teubner, 1962).
[37] See particularly 'Classical systems of *stases* in Greek: Hermagoras to Hermogenes', GR and BS 2 (1959), 51-71.
[38] *Zur Ideenlehre des Hermogenes*, Göttingen, Vandenhoeck and Ruprecht, 1964.

CHAPTER VIII

HELLENISTIC POETRY

BY E. A. BARBER

MUCH progress has been made during the last half-century in the study of Hellenistic, or, as it used to be called, Alexandrian Poetry. The change in nomenclature is itself significant. Earlier scholars used the term Alexandrian, because most of the poets from this age whose works survived in any considerable amount through the Roman and Byzantine periods were known to have resided for a longer or shorter time at Alexandria and to have been connected with the Ptolemaic Court there and with the Library and Museum which the dynasty established in the city. However more than a century ago J. G. Droysen used the word *Hellenismus* to denote the period extending from Alexander the Great down to Augustus, and since his time the term Hellenistic has been generally employed by historians to describe the age in question. Its transference to the literature and in particular to the poetry of the period is more recent. In fact the Italian scholar Cessi[1] seems to have been the first to use it in the title of a study of these poets. He was followed by Wilamowitz (1924) and Körte (1925), but both Rostagni[2] (1916) and Legrand (1924) retained the description Alexandrian. On the whole the change seems justified. It is not of great importance that some of the well-known poets, for example Aratus, Euphorion, Nicander, appear not to have visited the Egyptian capital, since their work undoubtedly conforms to 'Alexandrian' standards, but much contemporary epic poetry, now lost, seems not to have accepted those standards, and further the papyri have proved the existence during these centuries of a more popular type of verse, either moralizing or intended to distract and amuse the crowd.

The debt which the student of Hellenistic Poetry owes to the papyri-discoveries of the last half-century of course goes far beyond the differentiation just mentioned. Thanks to them we now know much more about the political, social, and economic background of this literature than we did previously. Secondly great additions have been made from the same source to the poetical texts themselves. Their number and importance can be best appreciated by perusing the invaluable registers of Oldfather[3] (1923) and Pack[4] (1952). Among Hellenistic poets of the first rank the chief beneficiaries from this largesse have been Herodas, Callimachus, and Theocritus. More will be said later about Herodas, who was known by a few fragments only till in 1891 Kenyon published the *editio princeps* of his *Mimiambi*. Of Callimachus the manuscript tradition has preserved for us the six *Hymns*, some sixty epigrams, and a large number of fragments from lost poems. This was the situation when in 1870-73 Schneider[5] produced his edition of the poems and fragments, which with all its faults marked a notable advance in Callimachean scholarship. The first addition to the contents of Schneider's two volumes came not from papyri, but from a wooden tablet containing substantial remains of the *Hecale*, which were published by Gomperz[6] in 1893. In 1904 Nicole edited from a papyrus fragments of an elegiac poem, which he claimed to be the *Aetia* of Callimachus, but which Pfeiffer[7] has since identified with the Funeral Elegy on his wife Arete composed by a much later Hellenistic poet, Parthenius. The same year saw the publication of a few lines from an Oxyrhynchus papyrus, which we now know to come from Callimachus' *Iambi*. These small and misleading beginnings were the prelude to much greater things. In 1910 Grenfell and Hunt gave to the world the famous papyrus[8] which contains a large amount of the *Aetia* and of the *Iambi*. Since that date down to 1952 comparatively few years have not witnessed the publication of new fragments of Callimachus. Though far too many problems both of text and of interpretation remain unsolved, we now possess substantial portions of the poet's *Aetia*, *Iambi*, *Lyrica*, *Lock of Berenice*, and other occasional elegies such as the *Victory of Sosibius*. We have also further additions to the *Hecale*. Besides restoring to us so much of Callimachus' poetry the papyri have also preserved ancient scholia on it and considerable fragments of a particularly valuable work, the self-entitled *Diegeseis*[9] (*Expositions*), covering *Aetia*, Books III (end) and IV, the *Lock*, *Iambi*, *Lyrica*, *Hecale*, and *Hymns* I and II. This last document not only quotes the first line of each *Aetion*, etc., but also summarizes the content, thus enabling us to get a much clearer picture of each work as a whole and of the order of the parts. For example we now see that in the *Aetia* there was no such orderly sequence of topics as was once imagined. Instead Callimachus passed from one *Aetion* to another with little or no attempt at connection, though no doubt on occasion two or even more similar stories might follow each other. In the *Iambi*, as Dawson[10] and others have shown, there is proof of more deliberation and artistic purpose in the grouping of the poems within the 'book', but the criterion is the metre rather than the matter, which is typically miscellaneous. Besides all this fresh material the papyri also supply fragments of all the *Hymns* except *Hymn* V, and Pfeiffer believes that it is merely an accident that this is still unrepresented. A good many minor and some major and rather startling changes have had to be made in the manuscript text of the *Hymns* in the light of this new testimony. Another surprise due to the papyri is the revelation that Catullus' version of the *Lock* was far from being a literal and complete translation of the Greek.[11] To pass to Theocritus, it was already known from the list given by Suidas and from a few fragments that the manuscripts did not contain all the works attributed to him in antiquity. Further, some of the manuscripts themselves state that Id. XXIV is incomplete, and now a papyrus from Antinoe establishes that some thirty lines followed line 140. The remains are fragmentary, but it is clear that the poem ended with a succinct account of Heracles' Labours, his apotheosis and marriage to Hebe, as foretold by Teiresias in lines 79ff. What is more, the last two lines contained an invocation of Heracles and an appeal to the god to ensure that the poet, like himself, might prove victorious over his adversaries. Thus Id. XXIV was a Hymn, like Id. XXII, however much it approximates to an *epyllion*, the modern term for a short epic narrative. A still more surprising addition from the same papyrus is a fourth lyric poem in Aeolic to follow Id. XXX. The remains are even sparser than for Id. XXIV, but there can be little doubt that the content was similar to that of the two preceding παιδικά, Id. XXIX and Id. XXX. It is possible that the papyrus once contained other lost poems of Theocritus, for example the *Berenice*, but there can be no certainty since it arranges the poems *more suo* like the other papyri. Of the nine Theocritean papyri four are of real importance. Like those of Callimachus' *Hymns* they contain many new readings, a goodly number of which are preferable to those of the manuscript tradition.

The other leading Hellenistic poets have been much less well served by the papyri. About a dozen of these have added to our knowledge of the text of the *Argonautica* of Apollonius Rhodius,[12] but we have nothing new from his lost works; six containing parts of Aratus' *Phaenomena* have come to light, but again there is nothing from his lost poems, which were apparently more numerous than those of Apollonius. Very little from Lycophron's *Alexandra* or from the *Theriaca* and *Alexipharmaca* of Nicander has been discovered, but a commentary[13] on lines 377-95 of the *Theriaca* contains learned citations from other poets and shows how closely even so repellent a work as this was studied by posterity.

If we turn to less well-preserved writers and to the epigrammatists, we find, and the fact should be noted, that there is nothing new from the first generation of Hellenistic poets, Philitas, Hermesianax, Phanocles, Alexander Aetolus, Simias, and Asclepiades. There are minor additions[14] to the epigrams of Leonidas of Tarentum and Antipater of Sidon and more important ones[15] to those of Posidippus of Pella, including poems on the Pharos at Alexandria and the temple of Arsinoe-Aphrodite-Zephyritis. The same papyrus which contains old and new epigrams of Leonidas and Antipater also includes two by an unknown poet, Amyntas. It belongs to the first century A.D. and clearly formed part of an anthology in which epigrams varying the same theme were grouped together, a principle that differs from that observed by Meleager in arranging his *Garland*. Two new and interesting epigrams[16] are contained in a papyrus which its editors styled *Un Livre d'Écolier*. The first describes in highly technical language the restoration of a fountain, adorned with sculptures of a Ptolemy and an Arsinoe; the second apparently commemorates the dedication, mentioned by Aelian, of a temple to Homer by Ptolemy IV Philopator. Two more,[17] one in elegiacs and the other in iambics, are epitaphs for a courageous hound belonging to Zenon, agent of the celebrated Apollonius, the Ptolemaic minister of finance. It is enlightening to see the new bureaucracy appearing as patrons of verse. Another supporter of the Ptolemaic régime has emerged from the twilight as a result of papyri-discoveries. This is Philicus of Corcyra, a member of the Tragic Pleiad and priest of Dionysus at Alexandria. We knew already that Philicus had composed a *Hymn to Demeter* in a rare metre, choriambic hexameters, and our authority, Hephaestion, quotes the first two lines of it. In 1927 Medea Norsa published some fifteen lines from a Hymn to Demeter in this very metre. There can hardly be any doubt that they come from Philicus' poem.[18] The Hymn was no more intended to accompany cult than was *Hymn* VI of Callimachus. Like the latter, it was, as Page says, 'an exercise in poetry — especially in metre — intended for a learned audience', in fact the γραμματικοί whom Philicus addresses in the opening lines preserved by Hephaestion. By an odd coincidence a different papyrus has yielded a sepulchral epigram[19] on Philicus, written apparently by a contemporary, i.e. about the middle of the third century. Yet another Hymn to Demeter[20] was published by C. H. Roberts in 1934. This is in the metre of Horace, *Odes* I, 7 and 28 and *Epodes* 12 (dactylic hexameter and tetrameter) and so far remains the only example of its use in Greek. Echoes of Callimachus are evident and since the papyrus was written in the third century B.C. are worthy of note.

The additions made by the papyri to our knowledge of minor Hellenistic epic are disappointing. We have nothing new of Rhianus, which is a pity. Three new fragments[21] of Euphorion are no compensation. Of the two first one describes Heracles bringing Cerberus from Hades, the other contains a list of imprecations and apparently formed part of the poem entitled 'Curses or the Goblet-thief'. The third,[22] which comes from a different source, is considerably longer but hardly more attractive. When intact the roll to which it belongs seems to have contained several poems of Euphorion arranged in alphabetical order according to the title of each. In what remains we have the conclusion of the *Thrax* and the beginning of the *Hippomedon Maior*. The former deals with two stories of unhappy love, both of which are summarized by Parthenius,[23] whose titles cite Euphorion as having treated them in the *Thrax*. The second story ends with an appeal for the restoration of Peace and Justice in the style of Hesiod and some rather heavy moralizing on the latter's formidable strength.[24] From anonymous authors we have some eighteen lines of a poem[25] where the speaker talks like the Hecale of Callimachus, about forty-seven of a bucolic poem[26] which has resemblances to the sixth Eclogue of Virgil, and some twenty-two of a poem[27] dealing with Egyptian botany. We have also scraps of short narrative poems dealing with Diomede and perhaps Actaeon and Telephus.[28]

At this point something must be said about the additions to our knowledge of two writers who because of their date are not generally classed among the Hellenistic poets, but who were much discussed by the literary critics of that age. The first is Antimachus[29] of Colophon, born about 444 B.C. A papyrus from Hermupolis contains fragments of an erudite commentary on his *Artemis* (end) and *Thebais* (beginning) with seventeen *lemmata* from Antimachus' text. These confirm the opinion derived from the earlier fragments that several characteristics of the learned Hellenistic Poetry, e.g. the 'interpretation' of Homer, the contamination of different myths, and the obscure vocabulary, were already to be found in Antimachus, despite Callimachus' disparagement of him. Erinna, the poetess of Telos, who probably lived at the end of the fourth century B.C., is a writer very unlike Antimachus. Her masterpiece was a hexameter poem in three hundred lines, entitled the *Distaff*, in which she lamented the death soon after marriage of her friend Baucis and recalled the childhood which they had spent together. Though later poets were loud in their praise of the *Distaff*, the surviving quotations from it are very few. Now a papyrus[30] has given us the remains of over fifty lines and though many of them are sadly incomplete skilful restoration and interpretation have succeeded in presenting a clear enough picture of at least this section of the poem and so making a welcome addition to the more intimate poetry of the fourth to third century B.C.

Mention has been made earlier of the two types of verse which existed in the Hellenistic age alongside the 'cyclic' poetry of the traditionalists and the new style championed by Callimachus, namely a popular moralizing verse and another type equally popular but eschewing any moral purpose. We knew little of either type till the papyri enlightened us, and it is only now that we realize the significance of the scanty information that we did possess. What has come to light of the verse intended to amuse or thrill a popular audience is naturally anonymous, but among the moralists two writers have become prominent, Cercidas[31] of Megalopolis and Phoenix of Colophon. Literary sources had preserved only nine short fragments of the former's verse. Now the survival in an Oxyrhynchus papyrus of substantial remains from his *Meliambi*, that is poems lyrical in form, but satiric in content, has thrown a flood of light on his personality and qualities as a poet. We knew already that he had played a leading part in the troubled political life of the Peloponnese during the third century. The new fragments show that though a member of the governing and property-owning class he voiced in his poetry the grievances of the poor and took his Cynic creed seriously. His style too is largely Cynic and recalls that of the prose *Diatribe*, supposed to be an invention of the wandering philosopher, Bion the Borysthenite; but Cercidas borrowed some elements, e.g. new and lengthy compounds, from other sources. A. D. Knox[32] argued that Cercidas was the editor of an anthology of moralizing verse preserved in several papyri, and perhaps the author of some of the pieces written in the choliambic or scazon metre. This metre seems to be the only one employed by Phoenix,[33] a poet known to us previously from one reference in Pausanias and five quotations in Athenaeus. Two of the latter (a moralizing commentary on the well-known epitaph of Ninus, and the *Chough-Beggars*) run to more than twenty lines each and give a more favourable idea of Phoenix's powers than is provided by the new *Iambus* of twenty-two lines, an attack on wealth. Phoenix is thought to be a little prior in date to Callimachus and since there is some coincidence in themes between the two, though their development of them is different, the latter's *Iambi* may owe something to those of Phoenix. The other additions to the moralizing verse of the period are inconsiderable. There are more Γνῶμαι (*Prudential Maxims*) of that shadowy figure, Chares,[34] and fragments of Pseud-Epicharmea,[35] moral rules which it was the custom since the end of the fifth century B.C. to father on Epicharmus. It is disappointing that nothing new has turned up from the verse of the professional philosophers, Crates, Cleanthes, and Timon of Phlius, each in his own way a personality of whom we should like to know more. Equally we have nothing fresh of Sotades, a more ambiguous character.

Passing to the verse which was devoid of any moral purpose we find that the new discoveries, though for the most part fragmentary and late, are fairly numerous, and that by the light of them and the previous evidence we now get a much better idea of what was composed in this vein. It is difficult for obvious reasons to classify these productions, but perhaps we may start from the distinction which the ancients themselves made between the spoken and sung Mime. Examples of the former are a Mime[36] with the same sordid subject as the fifth Mime of Herodas and a Farce[37] which seems to parody the *Iphigeneia in Tauris* of Euripides, both preserved in an Oxyrhynchus papyrus. Most of the Farce is written in prose though it breaks into a medley of verse towards the end; the Mime is all in prose except for the last line. Mimody, as the sung Mime was called, is better represented in the papyri. Aristoxenus[38] tells us that Mimody was divided into two types, Hilarody and Magody, the former being a burlesque of Tragedy and the latter of Comedy. We might then class the Oxyrhynchus Farce as a specimen of Hilarody except for the preponderance of prose in it. But Tragedy and Comedy were not the only ancestors of Mimody. The papyri have revealed several compositions whose affinities are rather with lyric poetry. The most famous is that known as the *Alexandrian Erotic Fragment* or *Fragmentum Grenfellianum*,[39] an emotional appeal, largely in dochmiacs, by a deserted *hetaira* to be readmitted to her lover's house. The general resemblance to Id. II of Theocritus is clear, but it is uncertain whether the *Fragment* imitates Theocritus or whether both writers are inspired by a popular type. Another find coming within the sphere of Mimody consists of eight lines[40] inscribed on a temple door (of all places!) between Gaza and Jerusalem. The contents confirm the statement of Athenaeus[41] that Phoenicia was full of the so-called Locrian Songs, which are, he tells us, songs with adultery for their theme. Other scraps of popular lyric have turned up in various quarters. The most attractive pieces are two sailors' songs,[42] a boy's lament[43] for his lost cock, and the drinking-song[44] in 'tapering' hexameters which merits the attention that has been bestowed upon it.

The stimulus given to the study of Hellenistic Poetry by the discovery of all this new material has naturally been very great. During the nineteenth century scholars, especially in Germany, had been active in producing better texts of the Alexandrian poets. Ahrens's edition (1855-59) of the *Bucolici* reduced the chaos of the manuscripts to order and improved the dialect. Schneider's edition of Callimachus has been mentioned already. That of Apollonius' *Argonautica* by Merkel (1854) has still to be replaced. In 1856 Schneider published Nicander with the Scholia, while in 1881 Scheer edited Lycophron and in 1908 completed his task by publishing the Scholia on that author. Maass performed a similar service for Aratus (Text 1893, Scholia 1898). Nor were the *poetae minores* neglected. Meineke's pioneer work (*Analecta*

Alexandrina, 1843) on Euphorion, Rhianus, Alexander Aetolus, and Parthenius still has value and so has Hiller's *Eratosthenis carminum reliquiae* (1872). Timon of Phlius was edited by Wachsmuth (1885) and by Diels (1901); Leonidas of Tarentum by Geffcken (1896). Stadtmüller's edition (1894-99-1906) of the *Palatine Anthology* was unfortunately cut short by his death and has never been completed, so that we depend on the editions of Dübner-Cougny (1864-72-90), Paton (Loeb, 1916-18), and Waltz (Budé, 1928-44), the last of which at present covers Books I-VIII only. While the Germans were thus laying the critical foundations for further study, the French had been concerned rather with the literary history of the time or the characteristics of individual authors, witness the elegantly written book of Couat, *La Poésie Alexandrine* (1882) and Ph. E. Legrand's *Étude sur Théocrite* (1898). The Germans had not been idle in this department either. Rohde's great work[45] on the Greek Novel, which first appeared in 1876, threw a new light on certain aspects of Alexandrian Poetry, as did the *Epigram und Skolion* of R. Reitzenstein, published in 1893. Finally 1891-92 saw the publication of Susemihl's indispensable work of reference, *Geschichte der griechischen Litteratur in der Alexandrinerzeit*. It must be admitted that nothing comparable to such works was being produced in this country during the same period. In fact only one name need be mentioned. J. P. Mahaffy was certainly a great man, but as a scholar he spread himself too widely to be a master of any one subject. Nevertheless his books on post-classical Hellenism, especially *Greek Life and Thought from the Age of Alexander to the Roman Conquest* (Ed. 1, 1887, Ed. 2, 1896), were the first introduction of many English students to the Hellenistic age and its literature.

This growing interest in post-classical Greek poetry was quickened by the re-discovery of Herodas in 1891. Here, it seemed, was something quite different from the conventional idea of Alexandrian Poetry. This 'Realist of the Aegean', to borrow the description given him by Sharpley,[46] exhibited qualities very unlike those of Callimachus or Apollonius or even Theocritus. No doubt the art, not to say artificiality, of Herodas was for a long time seriously under-estimated, but the important point is that scholars were compelled to re-consider their opinion of the literary world to which he belonged. Further, the editing of his text and of all the other discoveries that followed made new and exacting demands on classical students, especially in view of the fact that in the early stages of papyrology the mechanical aids which are now employed were not yet available. However scholarship rose to the opportunity and it is no disparagement of the work done in other countries, particularly Germany and Italy, to say that the acquisition by this country of the finds from Oxyrhynchus and the inspired labours of Kenyon, Grenfell, Hunt, Milne, and Lobel, to mention only the protagonists, have made the British contribution pre-eminent. Not only were the new texts successfully deciphered, but in order to restore, explain, and illustrate them it was necessary to scrutinize afresh all the relevant evidence on the subject that had come down from antiquity in other texts, scholia, and citations of every sort. Naturally this could not be done in a day, and, where, as in the case of Callimachus, the new material came to light piece-meal, it was difficult to form a clear idea of the whole. At last, however, we seem to have reached a state of comparative stability and the time for definitive editions has obviously arrived.

For two poets, Theocritus and Callimachus, such editions are already available. In his day Wilamowitz rendered valuable service to Theocritus and the other *Bucolici* by his text,[47] which first appeared in 1905, and also by his important book[48] (1906) on the text's history. Wendel not long afterwards both edited the scholia[49] and elucidated their origin and transmission.[50] Edmonds' *The Greek Bucolic Poets* appeared in the Loeb Classical Library in 1912, and in 1919 Cholmeley re-edited his *Theocritus*, which had first been published in 1901. This was soon followed by the *Bucoliques Grecs* (Budé, 1925-27) of Legrand, the chief value of which lay in the fuller *apparatus criticus* and the separate introductions. But the most important additions from the papyri were yet to come, and it was not till after the Second World War that an up-to-date text was produced by Gallavotti,[51] who not only included the new material from the papyri, but also vastly improved the *apparatus criticus* after a far more thorough examination of the manuscripts than any of his predecessors had attempted. Gallavotti's edition appeared in 1946, but was apparently not available to Latte,[52] who in 1948 produced a school-text of Theocritus only. Gow on the other hand, who in 1950, after a gestation of sixteen years and a series of valuable articles which goes much further back, gave to the public the edition[53] of Theocritus for which it had been impatiently waiting, made full and fruitful use of Gallavotti's labours. A second edition of his book was called for in 1952 and in the same year Gow edited a text of all the *Bucolici* for the Clarendon Press. Other scholars may not always agree with Gow's choice of readings, but the masterly introduction and the commentary which very rarely overlooks a difficulty and brings a wealth of new information to explain and illustrate the text are not likely to be superseded in this generation or the next.

Callimachus, as we have seen, was treated more scurvily by the accidents of time than Theocritus, and the problem confronting his editors has always been different. After Schneider the most distinguished of them was again Wilamowitz, whose text[54] long held the field. Meanwhile the Loeb edition of A. W. Mair (1921) and the Budé edition of Cahen (Ed. 1, 1922; Ed. 2, 1940) helped by including some of the new material. But the scholar destined to produce the definitive edition was revealed in 1921 when Pfeiffer published *Callimachi Fragmenta Nuper Reperta* (Ed. maior, 1923), which was followed up by his valuable *Kallimachosstudien* (1922). His task was a long and arduous one, constantly interrupted by the discovery of new material; but in 1949 Pfeiffer was able to bring out vol. I containing the Fragments and in 1953 vol. II containing the Hymns, with their scholia, the Epigrams, and impressive Prolegomena and Addenda.[55] For the purposes of the second volume besides incorporating the papyrus material he re-examined the whole of the manuscript tradition, in which undertaking he was greatly helped by the earlier labours of Smiley.[56] There is this difference between Pfeiffer's two volumes that, whereas the understanding of the Fragments is assisted by explanatory notes, the Hymns and Epigrams are edited without such aid to the reader. An up-to-date commentary on the Hymns therefore remains a *desideratum*, since that of Cahen[57] was not altogether satisfactory even when it appeared. The same thing may be said about the Epigrams, despite the work of Veniero and Hauvette.[58] Not even a Pfeiffer could be expected to supply an answer to all the problems of reading and interpretation raised by the poems of Callimachus as they have reached us, but he has solved very many of them and for the rest he has enormously facilitated the task of future scholars who venture on the fascinating game of bringing back Callimachus from the shades.

Apollonius Rhodius still awaits an editor of this calibre, but it is understood that he will not have to wait long. The editions[59] of R. C. Seaton are now out of date. That of Mooney[60] (1912) is still useful and so is Gillies' edition[61] (1928) of Book III only, but much work[62] on various aspects of the *Argonautica* has been published during the last forty years, and the future editor will have the advantage of being able to use Wendel's exemplary edition[63] (1935) of the Scholia. Aratus was edited by G. R. Mair[64] in 1921, but otherwise has not attracted much attention. Lycophron was edited by A. W. Mair in the same volume of the Loeb Library and by Mooney,[65] also in 1921. Nicander had long been shunned by most students and in consequence the edition[66] of Gow and Scholfield, while modestly claiming to provide no more than first aid, is extremely welcome. Editions of Herodas since the discovery of the *Mimiambi* have been very numerous. Half a dozen or more followed the *editio princeps* in quick succession. That of Nairn[67] (1904) held the field in this country until in 1922 Headlam and Knox brought out their lavish edition,[68] to which the illustrative material collected in the notes gives a permanent value. Seven years later Knox included Herodas in the volume of the Loeb Library containing the Choliambic Poets. Meanwhile in 1926 Herzog,[69] an expert on the antiquities of Cos, had re-edited one of Crusius' many editions. Less has been heard of Herodas since 1930, but two Italian editions have appeared recently.[70] Cercidas and Phoenix were re-published by Knox in the Loeb volume mentioned above and also found a place in the *Collectanea Alexandrina* of J. U. Powell and the *Anthologia Lyrica* of E. Diehl, as did most of the minor Alexandrians. Separate dissertations on some of the latter have also appeared from time to time, for example on Philitas by A. Nowacki (1927) and G. Kuchenmüller (1928), on Simias by H. Fränkel (1915), on Asclepiades by O. Kauer (1935). Representative Hellenistic epigrams are included in the selections of Mackail[71] (Ed. 3, 1911), Geffcken[72] (1916) and Gabathuler[73] (1937), but the edition of all the Epigrammatists of this age, which Powell had planned as a continuation of his *Collectanea*, still awaits some enterprising scholar. Meanwhile Oehler[74] has edited the epigrams of Meleager's *Garland* with a German verse-translation (1920). Three renderings into English verse, namely of Leonidas by E. Bevan, of Callimachus' *Epigrams* by G. M. Young, and of Asclepiades by W. and M. Wallace, which appeared in 1931, 1934, and 1941

HELLENISTIC POETRY 279

respectively, also include the Greek text. Finally the fragments of Parthenius' verse together with his collection in prose of 'Unhappy Love-stories' were edited by S. Gaselee in a volume of the Loeb Library (1916).

Such in brief being the additions to Hellenistic poetical texts and the output of editions and commentaries in the last sixty years it remains to be considered what the literary historians have done to bring their criticism up to date. An account of the new finds and their significance is given in the three volumes of *New Chapters in the History of Greek Literature*.[75] A supplementary chapter by Cahen, added to J. Loeb's English translation (1931) of Couat's *La Poésie Alexandrine*, follows the latter book chapter by chapter, recording and commenting on the fresh material as it was known some twenty years ago. Earlier the present writer had stressed the existence in Hellenistic times of verse other than that known as Alexandrian in an essay[76] on Alexandrian Literature and had contributed a longer account of that literature to vol. VII of the *Cambridge Ancient History*. The papyri-discoveries, so far as then available, were naturally brought into the picture in the more important works of Christ and Schmid, Legrand, Wilamowitz, Körte, and Trypanis. The sixth edition (1920) by W. Schmid of W. von Christ's *Geschichte der griechischen Literatur*, vol. II, 1, is still indispensable, though so much new material has come to light since it was published. The small book by Legrand[77] (1924) is truly an *aureus libellus* and remains the best introduction to Alexandrian Poetry. The literary histories from the pens of Wilamowitz and Körte are on a larger scale. The former's work in two volumes, published in 1924 and entitled *Hellenistische Dichtung in der Zeit des Kallimachos*, reveals the master's hand on every page and contains countless fresh suggestions and novel illustrations, but can be properly appreciated only by readers already well-acquainted with this poetry and its problems. Körte's book, *Hellenistische Dichtung*, published in 1925 (English translation by J. Hammer and M. Hadas, 1929), gives a readable account of Hellenistic Poetry, including Menander and the New Comedy, marked by independence of judgment and enlivened by numerous examples in translation. That of Trypanis[78] (1943) has the advantage of being later in date than those just mentioned and is thus able to make use of the material published up to the beginning of the Second World War, but has unfortunately remained incomplete. The one volume which has appeared deals admirably with the general character of the age and its poetry, Elegy before Callimachus, Callimachus himself, and the Epigram. In *A History of Later Greek Literature* (1932), F. A. Wright gives a lively account of Hellenistic Poetry, but does not go very deep. H. J. Rose devotes Chapter X of his work, *A Handbook of Greek Literature* (1934), to the same topic and has interesting things to say. Detailed studies of individual poets have not been lacking, the most notable being that of Callimachus by Cahen[79] (1929) and of Theocritus by Bignone[80] (1934). The latter scholar had previously published a volume[81] on the Greek Epigram, which has the merit of including examples from the collections of epigrams, gathered *ex lapidibus*, made by Kaibel (1878) and Hoffmann (1893). It is impossible to list here all the work that has been done in recent years on particular features of Hellenistic Poetry, for example its vocabulary, use of mythology, interest in geography and 'origins', etc., but a word must be said about the study of the metrical refinements introduced by these poets. The foundations of this were well and truly laid by P. Maas in his contribution to vol. I of Gercke-Norden's *Einleitung in die Altertumswissenschaft* (Ed. 3, 1927), and important work on these lines has been published by, among others, H. Fränkel[82] and Wifstrand.[83]

This is not the place to register the results of recent research about the influence of Hellenistic Poetry on Roman, but two books which are primarily concerned with Latin literature may nevertheless be mentioned. The first is the collection of essays by W. Kroll, *Studien zum Verständnis der römischen Literatur* (1924), which contains much of value about the poetic theory and practice of the Hellenistic writers. *Lucilius und Kallimachos* (1949) by Puelma Piwonka traverses some of the same ground, but the comparison between the two poets is far-fetched. The second of the two books mentioned above is that of A. A. Day, *The Origins of Latin Love-Elegy* (1938), which includes the fullest and most sensible discussion of the much debated question whether the 'subjective' elegy of the Romans had its counterpart and model among the Alexandrians. Nothing has been discovered since 1938 to shake the conviction of those who maintain that it did not, but the story (from the *Aetia*) of the love of Phrygius and Pieria, as re-constructed by Pfeiffer,[84] has introduced us to another heroine of

Callimachus' narrative elegy, who is considerably more attractive than the colourless Cydippe.

A third work which bridges the gap between Hellenistic and Roman Poetry is *The Epyllion from Theocritus to Ovid* (1931), by M. M. Crump. This shows a better knowledge of Latin than of Alexandrian literature. The authoress nowhere indicates that the use of the word ἐπύλλιον to mean 'short poem' is only once (Athen. 2, 65A) found in any ancient writer, cf. Heumann, *De Epyllio Alexandrino*, p. 7; its employment to mean a short poem written in hexameter verse is wholly modern, but has been generally adopted for its convenience. This does not imply that the Alexandrians invented a definite genus of short narrative poetry which they insisted should conform to certain rigid rules of composition. In such matters each poet enjoyed complete liberty of action.

To sum up the present position, there is pretty general agreement about the ideals and methods of the Hellenistic poets who can be called Alexandrians. No one would deny that Alexandrianism was characterized by an avoidance of big themes and long books, that is lengthy, *continuous* poems, and a preference for what is small and fine; or that it was directed to a limited public of appreciative connoisseurs and not to the *profanum vulgus*; or that Callimachus was the protagonist in the new movement and that he left his contemporaries and posterity in no doubt about what he was striving for. There is more dispute about the extent and success of the revolution. Ziegler[85] argued that even in the third century the prevailing taste was for long epics and supported his argument by citing the mythological epics with traditional themes, the encomia of tribes and cities, and the few panegyrics of reigning monarchs, mention of which has come down in ancient authorities or is recorded by inscriptions. Unfortunately these are all lost except for a few odd lines, and Ziegler's attempt to re-construct their content and style by comparison with the *Annales* of Ennius, the Pergamene sculptures, Hellenistic historiography with its predilection for the dramatic, and the poetry of Nonnus and his school, is ingenious, but quite unconvincing. On the other hand it has long been admitted that the Golden Age of Alexandrian Poetry was short-lived, lasting from about 290 to 240 B.C. After the latter date there are a few *epigoni* such as Euphorion, Eratosthenes, Rhianus (if he belongs here), Moschus, Bion, and the epigrammatists, but during the second century Alexandrianism, as indeed poetry generally, seems to have been at a discount, and it was not till Parthenius brought the gospel to Rome in the age of Sulla that the ideals of Callimachus again became influential. There are no Ptolemaic papyri of Callimachus, Theocritus, Apollonius Rhodius, or Aratus.[86] That even in Callimachus' lifetime the opposition was not confined to the 'rebel' Apollonius was suggested by the ancient evidence and is now confirmed by the *Invective* (Pfeiffer, Fr. 1) directed against his critics, whom he terms *Telchines*, that is Malicious Demons. The Florence Scholia on the passage name some of the critics. Unfortunately the text is imperfect, but among other persons unknown to us, it seems to include Asclepiades of Samos and certainly mentions a Posidippus, who may be the epigrammatist, since both he[87] and Asclepiades[88] praise the *Lyde* of Antimachus, which Callimachus[89] criticized severely. The last name on the list is that of Praxiphanes, the Peripatetic philosopher from Mytilene, and it is thus established that the work of Callimachus with the title Πρὸς Πραξιφάνην was a controversial tract directed against the Peripatetic, who professed literary criticism as well as philosophy.[90] But it is impossible with our present evidence to re-construct the famous quarrel between Callimachus and Apollonius. Certainly Apollonius is convicted of plagiarizing[91] from the Argonaut episode in the *Aetia*, as well as from the *Hecale*, and this fact coupled with personal friction due to Callimachus' position at the Library being subordinate to that of Apollonius, who was apparently Chief Librarian,[92] goes a long way to explain the trouble.

Another matter in which modern students of Hellenistic Poetry are more cautious than their predecessors is chronology. The dates of certain historical events, for example the death of Queen Arsinoe, are now known from papyri and inscriptions, and can be used to give a *terminus ante* and *post quem*, but such external testimony is still very sparse and the internal evidence is interpreted differently by different critics. Thus Gow believes that in Id. XIII and Id. XXII Theocritus is improving on earlier versions by Apollonius in the *Argonautica* of the Hylas and Amycus stories, while Pfeiffer[93] more plausibly maintains that Theocritus' treatment of the episodes is prior to that of Apollonius. The truth is that despite all the new discoveries and indeed because of them we realize better today the limits of our knowledge. We have been bitten so often that we are shy of definite assertions and final judgments. It is not a very exciting attitude, but it is probably a wise one.

Nevertheless much has been accomplished. It is nearly fifty years since the present writer as a young undergraduate made his first acquaintance with the Alexandrian Poets. In those far-off days the aids available to the student for the understanding of what was still regarded as a remote and rather unattractive subject were immeasurably less than they are today. An attempt has been made above to outline the varied activity of so many scholars which has brought about this happy result. But like most other things literary appreciation is subject to fashion and it may be that concern with Hellenistic Poetry has temporarily reached a zenith. It is undeniable that most of the Alexandrians consciously resorted to an ivory tower[94] and this reaction to world-shaking events cannot expect to escape criticism. Yet it is to be hoped that the good work will be carried on and that there will never be wanting a succession of persons eager and able to extend our knowledge and appreciation of what was written by the scholar-poets of Alexandria.

[1] C. Cessi, *La poesia ellenistica*, 1912.
[2] A. Rostagni, *Poeti alessandrini*.
[3] C. H. Oldfather, *The Greek Literary Texts from Greco-Roman Egypt*. University of Wisconsin Studies in the Social Sciences and History, No. 9, 1923.
[4] R. A. Pack, *The Greek and Latin Literary Texts from Greco-Roman Egypt*. University of Michigan General Library Publications, No. 8, 1952.
[5] O. Schneider, *Callimachea*, 2 vols.
[6] Th. Gomperz, *Aus der Hekale des Kallimachos*.
[7] CQ 37 (1943), pp. 23-32.
[8] P. Oxy., 1011.
[9] Ed. 1, M. Norsa and G. Vitelli, Διηγήσεις di Poemi di Callimaco, 1934; Ed. 2, A. Vogliano in *Papiri della R. Università di Milano*, pp. 66 sqq., 1937.
[10] C. M. Dawson, *The Iambi of Callimachus*. Yale Classical Studies, vol. XI (1950), pp. 1-168. A full and valuable edition, but vol. I of Pfeiffer's *Callimachus* was not available to the author.
[11] See R. Pfeiffer, *Callimachus*, vol. I, Fr. 110 and vol. II, Addenda to Fr. 110; E. A. Barber in *Greek Poetry and Life*, pp. 343-63, 1936.
[12] See H. Fränkel, AJPh (1950), pp. 113-33.
[13] P. Oxy., 2221.
[14] No. 107 in D. L. Page, *Greek Literary Papyri*, vol. I, Loeb Classical Library, 1942. Henceforward cited as Page.
[15] Page, 104.
[16] Page, 105.
[17] Page, 109.
[18] Page, 90. See K. Latte, Mus. Helvet. 11 (1954), pp. 1-19.
[19] Page, 106.
[20] Page, 91.
[21] Page, 121.

[22] See A. Barigazzi, Aegyptus 27 (1947), 1-2, pp. 53-107; Athenaeum 26 (1946), 1-2, pp. 34-64.
[23] xiii and xxvi.
[24] For the latest fragments of Euphorion see P. Oxy., 2219 and 2220.
[25] Page, 122.
[26] Page, 123.
[27] Page, 124.
[28] Pp. 71-8 in J. U. Powell, *Collectanea Alexandrina* (1925). Henceforward cited as Powell, CA.
[29] B. Wyss, *Antimachi Colophonii Reliquiae*, 1936.
[30] Page, 120; E. Diehl, *Anthologia Lyrica Graeca*, ed. 2, i.4, pp. 207-11; C. M. Bowra, *Problems in Greek Poetry* (1953), pp. 151-68.
[31] A. D. Knox, *Herodes, Cercidas, and the Greek Choliambic Poets*. Loeb Classical Library. 1929; Powell, CA, pp. 201-19; J. U. Powell and E. A. Barber, *New Chapters in the History of Greek Literature*, i, pp. 1-12. Henceforward cited as New Chapters.
[32] *The First Greek Anthologist*, 1923.
[33] A. D. Knox, *Herodes, Cercidas etc.*; Powell, CA, pp. 231-6; New Chapters, i, pp. 12-16; G. A. Gerhard, *Phoinix von Kolophon*, 1909.
[34] Powell, CA, pp. 223-7; New Chapters, i, p. 18.
[35] Page, 102; Powell, CA, pp. 18-21; New Chapters, i, pp. 18-21.
[36] Page, 77; New Chapters, i, 122-3.
[37] Page, 76; Powell, CA, p. 181 (end only); New Chapters, i, p. 121.
[38] *Ap.* Athen., 621C.
[39] Powell, CA, pp. 177-80; New Chapters, i, pp. 54-5.
[40] Powell, CA, p. 184; New Chapters, i, p. 55.
[41] 679B.
[42] Page, 97, 98; Powell, CA, pp. 195-6; New Chapters, i, pp. 58-9.
[43] Page, 75: Powell, CA, pp. 182-4; New Chapters, i, p. 56.
[44] Page, 125; T. F. Higham in *Greek Poetry and Life*, pp. 299-324, 1936.
[45] E. Rohde, *Der griechische Roman und seine Vorlaüfer*. Ed. 3, 1914.
[46] H. Sharpley, *A Realist of the Aegean; being a verse-translation of the Mimes of Herodas*, 1906.
[47] Oxford Classical Texts. Ed. 2, 1910.
[48] *Die Textgeschichte der griechischen Bukoliker*, 1906.
[49] C. Wendel, *Scholia in Theocritum Vetera*, 1914.
[50] *Überlieferung und Entstehung der Theokrit-Scholien*, 1920.
[51] C. Gallavotti, *Theocritus Quique Feruntur Bucolici Graeci*, Rome, 1946.
[52] K. Latte, *Theocriti Carmina*, Iserlohn, 1948.
[53] A. S. F. Gow, *Theocritus*. Vol. I, Introduction, Text and Translation; vol. II, Commentary, Cambridge, 1950.
[54] *Callimachi Hymni et Epigrammata*, Berlin, Ed. 4, 1925.
[55] R. Pfeiffer, *Callimachus*, Clarendon Press, 1949-53.
[56] M. T. Smiley, 'The Manuscripts of Callimachus' Hymns', CQ 14 (1920), pp. 1-15, 105-22; 15 (1921), pp. 57-74, 113-25.
[57] E. Cahen, *Les Hymnes de Callimaque*, 1930.
[58] A. Veniero, *I poeti de l'Antologia Palatina secolo III a.c.*, vol. I, part 1, 1905; A. Hauvette, REG 20 (1907), pp. 295-357.
[59] Oxford Classical Texts, 1900; Loeb Classical Library, 1912.
[60] G. W. Mooney, *The Argonautica of Apollonius Rhodius*, Longmans, 1912.
[61] M. M. Gillies, *The Argonautica of Apollonius Rhodius, Book III*, C.U.P., 1928.
[62] E.g. by A. Platt, JPh 33 (1917), pp. 1-53; 34 (1918), pp. 129-41; 35 (1919), pp. 72-85; H. Fränkel, Gött. Nachr. (1929), pp. 164-94; D. A. van Krevelen, Eranos 47 (1949), pp. 138-47 and SIFC 25 (1951), pp. 95-103.
[63] C. Wendel, *Scholia in Apollonium Rhodium Vetera*.
[64] A. W. Mair, *Callimachus and Lycophron*; G. R. Mair, *Aratus*.
[65] G. W. Mooney, *The Alexandra of Lycophron*.
[66] A. S. F. Gow and A. F. Scholfield, *Nicander*. See also Gow, CQ, N.S., vol. I (1951), pp. 95-118.
[67] J. A. Nairn, *The Mimes of Herodas*.
[68] W. Headlam and A. D. Knox, *Herodas*.

69 R. Herzog, *Die Mimiamben des Herodas*.
70 Q.Cataudella, *Eroda, I Mimiambi*, 1948: G. Puccioni, *Herodae Mimiambi*, 1950.
71 J. W. Mackail, *Select Epigrams from the Greek Anthology*, Longmans, 1890.
72 J. Geffcken, *Griechische Epigramme*.
73 M. Gabathuler, *Hellenistische Epigramme auf Dichter*.
74 A. Oehler, *Der Kranz des Meleagros*.
75 Series i, 1921; ii, 1929; iii, 1933. Clarendon Press.
76 *The Hellenistic Age*, pp. 31-78. Cambridge. Ed. 2, 1925.
77 Ph. E. Legrand, *La Poésie Alexandrine*.
78 K. A. Τρυπάνης. Ἡ ᾿Αλεξανδρινὴ Ποίηση, Τόμος Α'.
79 E. Cahen, *Callimaque et son Œuvre poétique*.
80 E. Bignone, *Teocrito*.
81 E. Bignone, *L'Epigramma Greco*.
82 H. Fränkel, Gött. Nachr. (1926), pp. 197-229.
83 A. Wifstrand, *Von Kallimachos zu Nonnos*, 1933.
84 Frr. 80-3, and vol. II, Addenda to Fr. 80 and Fr. 82.
85 K. Ziegler, *Das Hellenistische Epos*, 1934.
86 See C. H. Roberts, Museum Helveticum 10 (1953), 3-4, p. 269. The whole article (pp. 264-79), entitled 'Literature and Society in the Papyri', is most informing, especially as regards the difference in the Ptolemaic period between the literary taste of Alexandria and that of provincial Egypt.
87 AP xii, 168.
88 AP ix, 63.
89 Fr., 398.
90 See K. O. Brink, CQ 40 (1946), 1-2, pp. 11-26.
91 Pfeiffer, *Callimachus*, vol. II, pp. xli-ii.
92 P. Oxy., 1241.
93 *Callimachus*, vol. II, pp. xlii-iii.
94 See Roberts, *op. cit.*, p. 271.

NOTE: For further information about Hellenistic Poetry the reader may consult the articles in *The Oxford Classical Dictionary* (1949) on the various poets and the relevant subjects, e.g. Alexandrian Poetry, Epyllion, Greek Pastoral Poetry, etc.

APPENDIX TO CHAPTER VIII

BY G. GIANGRANDE

BARBER's chapter on Hellenistic poetry is such a well-balanced *mise au point*, and the assessment it provides still so valid, that I felt unable to modify it in order to bring it up to date: I judged that this purpose could be best served by adding an Appendix. It will be obvious to the reader that I have written it having especially in mind prospective classics research students — a species now rapidly multiplying, to my intense pleasure, in British universities: I hope they will find it useful not only as an indication of what has been done so far, but also of what needs doing. To this aim I have, besides including the new material published after Barber's survey, also selected as best I could and indicated certain older items which still constitute the fundamental tools for future research.

Texts, Commentaries, Stylistic Studies

The long awaited edition of Apollonius' Argonautica by H. Fränkel appeared in 1961 (OCT; revised reprint 1964). This work (on which cf. H. Erbse, *Gnom.* 1963, p. 18 ff., and G. Giangrande, CR 1963, p. 153ff.) has established the mss. tradition on a much more detailed basis than was the case before (52 mss. and several papyrus fragments have been scrutinized), abounds in original contributions offered by the editor, Keydell, Lloyd-Jones and P. Maas, and represents an immeasurable improvement upon Seaton's. Fränkel has solved as many textual problems as he has unmasked obscurities: the elucidation of these latter will be the exciting task of future research. The editor could hardly be accused of conservativism in his approach to the *Überlieferungsgeschichte* (his main conclusions are expounded in *Einleitung zur krit. Ausgabe der Argonautika des Apollonios*, Abh. Akad. Wiss. Gött., Phil.-hist. Kl., Dritte Folge, 55, 1964), and his emphasis on the ancient stage of the transmission being one of fluidity (in the Pasqualian sense) has given rise to many problems, chiefly in relation to the misplacement or otherwise of lines and the question of the two ancient editions. Future researchers will find ample ground for investigation in this field (cf. especially Erbse, Rh Mus 1963, p. 229ff).

Two useful commented editions of the third book of the Argonautica have been added to Gillies' (Ardizzoni, Bari 1958, and Vian, Paris 1961): both these editions are centred on the poet's diction, a field which in many respects still holds out a promise of abundant harvest (Boesch, *De Apoll. Rhod. elocutione*, Diss. Berlin 1908 is excellent, but not sufficiently detailed and in any case outdated; the best monograph is now G. Marxer, *Die Sprache des Apollonios Rhodios in ihren Beziehungen zu Homer*, Diss. Zürich 1935, but there remain very considerable problems, cf. Erbse, *Hermes* 1953, p. 163 ff. and van der Valk, *Researches on the Text and Scholia of the Iliad*, Part i, Leiden 1963, p. 258ff).

The Anthology has been published by Beckby in the *Tusculum* series (München, Heimeran, 1957-58; revised edition now in progress) with a critical apparatus made especially valuable by the account it gives of the important and hitherto hardly accessible *Marc.* 481; this edition contains a valuable Introduction to the genre *Epigram* and an extremely useful *Namen- und Sachverzeichnis* for which every researcher will be thankful. The Hellenistic epigrams of the Anthology have been published, in a critical text and with an ample commentary, by Gow and Page (Cambridge, 1965). This work, undoubtedly one of the major achievements of British scholarship in this century (cf. G. Giangrande, CR 1967, p. 17f.) offers a commentary, dealing both with diction and *Realien*, on almost 5,000 lines of Hellenistic poetry which had remained so far, apart from certain exceptions, devoid of any adequate illustration. The task of future researchers will be to enlarge the analysis offered by the two editors, probing deeper into the various epigrammatists by means of single monographs such as Seelbach's commented edition of Mnasalcas and Theodoridas (*Klass.-Philol.-Studien* 28, Wiesbaden 1964). This type of probing at the deepest possible level, concentrating on a limited area, is particularly suited to the proper focusing of Hellenistic poetry, which was *Buchpoesie*: it will be no doubt the canonic method of research in the foreseeable future; outstanding examples of the fruits borne by this procedure are Bühler's commentary on Moschus' Europa (*Hermes Einzelschriften* 13, Wiesbaden 1960), and Lloyd-Jones' commentary on the *Seal of Posidippus* (JHS 1963, p. 75ff.).

Aratus' *Phaenomena* have been edited, with a critical text and a commentary, by Martin (Florence 1956); the editor's text is not startlingly different from Maas', but the *Überlieferungsgeschichte* has now been more amply clarified (Martin's results are expounded in his *Histoire du texte des Phénomènes d'Aratos*, Paris 1956). What remains to be done now is a good monograph on the language of Aratus, considered both in itself and its relationship to the other Hellenistic poets (Loebe, *De elocutione Arati Solensis*, Diss. Halle 1864 will be the necessary starting point, outdated and incomplete as it is).

Lycophron's *Alexandra* has now appeared in a critical edition by Mascialino (Leipzig, Teubner, 1964): the editor is more conservative than Scheer, and gives a fuller account of the mss. tradition in his apparatus. An analysis of Lycophron's vocabulary and syntax in its relation to the other Hellenistic poets is still lacking: J. Konze (*De Lycophron. dictionis proprietate in universum ratione simul habita Homeri et tragicorum*, Diss. Münster 1870) and G. Walter (*De Lycophrone Homeri imitatore*, Diss. Basel 1903) have already provided good points de repère.

Callimachus' Hymns and his diction in general are still waiting to be investigated: a team of researchers under G. Giangrande is preparing a commentary on the Hymns and an analysis of the poet's syntax (on the model of Linsenbarth, *De Apoll. Rhod. casuum syntaxi comparato usu homerico*, Diss. Leipzig 1887 and Wåhlin, *De usu modorum apud Apoll. Rhod.*, Diss. Lund 1891). Another study urgently needed is a survey of Callimachus' vocabulary in general (Bredau, *De Callimacho verborum inventore*, Diss. Breslau 1892 is outdated, not least in view of papyrus discoveries): much material has been usefully collected by Lapp, *De Callimachi tropis et figuris*, Diss. Bonn 1965. On the specific question of Callimachus' attitude to Homer the best essay still remains Herter's *Kallimachos und Homer*, Bonn 1929: its methodological approach could fruitfully be extended to Apollonius. Good material has been collected by H. Kranz, *Kallimachos und die Sprache Homers: eine Untersuchung der Hymnen auf Apollon und auf Delos*, Diss. Wien 1939. Callimachus' sense of humour and irony have been studied by K. J. McKay (*The Poet at Play*, Leiden 1962, and *Erysichthon, a Callimachean Comedy*, Leiden 1962).

Nicander's style, so far neglected perhaps because of the unprepossessingness of the subjects treated by the poet, has now been analysed by H. Schneider (*Vergleichende Untersuchungen zur sprachlichen Struktur der beiden erhaltenen Lehrgedichte des Nikander*, Klassisch-philol. Studien 24, Wiesbaden 1962): this work shows the very interesting ways in which a didactic poet like Nicander sought to enliven his diction, and one is left wondering whether an investigation along the same lines of Aratus's poem would bear fruit.

Theocritus is still waiting for a comprehensive essay showing *in concreto* the poet's uncommon ability in the manipulation of his dialect mixture according to the requirements of theme, context and characters: on this feature, well known in its general outlines (cf. V. Pisani, *St. della lingua greca*, in *Encicl. classica* ii, v. 1, Torino 1960, p. 115 ff.) there is ample room for detailed analysis, as is shown by C. Gallavotti, *Lingua, tecnica e poesia negli Idilli di Teocrito*, Rome 1952.

Aristotle's *Poetics* has now appeared in a critical edition by Kassel (OCT, 1965); the editor is on the whole conservative; his apparatus is particularly important in view of the account taken of the *Riccardianus* 46 and the Arabic versions (these latter underrated by Rostagni, as a reaction to Gudeman's excesses). The rivalry between the branch of mss. tradition represented by the *Riccardianus* and the other branch is a challenging subject for textual studies. Else's Commentary on the Poetics (*Aristotle Poetics: the Argument*, Cambridge, Mass. 1957) is not only a useful critical survey of results arrived at and theories propounded by previous scholars, but also contains many new ideas, not seldom heretic but always stimulating: future research will greatly benefit from this work.

Literary History

The question of the rivalry between Callimachus and Apollonius has now been reassessed by Eichgrün (*Kallimachos und Apollonios Rhodios*, Diss. Berlin 1961). This work will now be the convenient starting point for any future research on this problem, which is admittedly very elusive owing to the obliqueness of the asides and allusions which Hellenistic poets employed as ammunition for their literary battles. Eichgrün provides a sensible survey of the material, including of course the papyrus evidence, and, whilst his work leaves many points unsolved, many others are convincingly dealt with. What in particular is needed now is a detailed and comprehensive analysis of the Apollonian and Callimachean passages in which there is coincidence, with a view to clarifying any 'versteckte Kritik' (Knaack); it will be necessary to draw Theocritus into the picture, as is evident especially from Köhnken, *Apollonios Rhodios und Theokrit (Hypomnemata,* 12, Göttingen 1965) whose detailed analysis of the Theiodamas episode is very instructive in this respect, and also from G. Schlatter, *Theokrit und Kallimachos,* Diss. Zürich 1941 (interesting material).

The well proven introductory monograph by Körte has now been published in a much revised second edition by Händel (*Hellenistische Dichtung,* Stuttgart 1960): the portions relating to the major poets (Apollonius, Callimachus and Theocritus) are those more drastically revised and brought up to date; the choice of bibliography is excellent. For the special angle of the relationship between poetry and visual arts (a relationship especially relevant to Hellenistic taste, cf. G. Huber, *Lebensbeschreibung und Kleinmalerei im hellenistischen Epos,* Diss. Basel 1926) the best monograph is now Webster, *Hellenistic Poetry and Art,* London 1964, which contains, alongside a full treatment of its main subject, numerous enlightening insights into purely literary problems.

Apollonius Rhodius has been the subject of extensive investigation relating to his narratory technique: Carspecken has given a good analysis of the 'romantic' approach by Apollonius to the traditions of epic narratory technique as established by Homer (*Apollonius Rhodius and the Homeric Epic, Yale Class. Stud.,* 1952, 33 ff.), whilst such features as motivation and utilization of mythological material in the economy of the poem have been treated by Händel (*Beobachtungen zur epischen Technik des Apollonios, Zetemata* 7, München 1954); H. Faerber had already studied the Apollonian similes (*Zur dichterischen Kunst in Apollonios Rhodios' Argonautika: die Gleichnisse,* Diss. Berlin 1932), and now Drögenmüller has filled a lacuna by studying the technique of similes in Hellenistic epic poetry (*Die Gleichnisse im hellenistischen Epos,* Diss. Hamburg 1956); an investigation of Theocritus' similes, which are perhaps the most complex, would probably yield good fruit.

On the subject of the influence of Hellenistic poetry on the Romans mention must be made of Wimmel, *Kallimachos in Rom* (*Hermes Einzelschriften* 16, Wiesbaden 1960: dealing with the apologetic themes), M. Hügi, *Vergils Aeneis und die hellenistische Dichtung* (Diss. Bern 1952; analyses Vergil's allusions to Apollonius, perhaps with a tendency by the author to overstate his case), B. Otis, *Virgil, a Study in Civilized Poetry* (Oxford 1963: good insights into the poet's mind), and the second volume of the *Entretiens Hardt* (Geneva 1953).

Hellenistic poetry, with its gusto for subtle irony, recondite or overt allusion, subtle evocativeness, *kleinmalerisch* formal polish, appeals to us moderns (cf. Rostagni, *Poeti Aless.*, Torino 1963, p. 33 ff.) just as strongly as Homer's statuesqueness and the tragedians' *gravitas* appealed to Victorian taste: there is no doubt that the 'zenith' now reached by Hellenistic studies, to use Barber's word, will last. I can think of no better way to conclude this short survey than to refer the reader to Pfeiffer's illuminating article '*The Future of Studies in the Field of Hellenistic Poetry*', JHS 1955, p. 69 ff. = *Ausgew. Schriften*, München 1960, p. 148 ff.

CHAPTER IX

ROMAN DRAMA

BY W. A. LAIDLAW

One may readily infer the lively interest which the learned world has taken in Roman drama during the last half-century from the vast output in Europe and America of books and articles concerning all its aspects. Within the confines of this chapter it is possible only to indicate the various trends of research and 'climates of opinion', to mention the most significant books and articles, and to refer to the bibliographies where the multifarious material may be traced.

Inevitably the most labour has been expended on those authors the text of whose dramas has wholly or in great part survived, that is, on Plautus, Terence, and Seneca. Inevitably too the greater activity has been displayed in the field of the earlier dramatists, on aesthetic and philological grounds, though the comparative lack of interest in Seneca's tragedies has been made good in more recent years.

Roman drama is read, in the last analysis, to be enjoyed — as some American and British scholars have recently emphasized. But there are many possible lines of approach, especially to the earlier drama. The scholars of the last half-century have been active in these fields:

(a) Collation of MSS. and production of sounder reference works and texts; better commentaries and translations; surveys of general character.
(b) Examination of problems relative to stage presentation.
(c) Analysis of the structure of plays and of dramatic technique; the relation of Plautus and Terence to their New Comedy sources and other possible sources; criteria of originality, and the relative merits of Plautus and Terence.
(d) Chronology, its problems and results.
(e) Investigation of metre and prosody, the relation of ictus and accent.
(f) Investigation of language, grammar, and style.
(g) Historical and sociological data of comedy.

(h) The decline of early tragedy, the problems of Senecan tragedy.
These are the main lines of investigation. It is not implied that they are all mutually exclusive, much less that all problems have been solved. The relation of Roman comedies to their 'models' is still, in the absence of any complete piece of New Comedy, a thorny question. Not less ardently disputed has been the relation of the Latin accent (itself imperfectly known) to the ictus of dramatic verse. And in the field of tragedy the authorship of the *Octavia* has been keenly debated. The inevitable specialisation in many particulars, pursued by scholars in many countries, has tended to make works of a general and more comprehensive character necessary.' In the summary which follows an effort is made to survey the fields of inquiry already listed (a) to (h).

(a) Since 1900, the year of Lindsay's large edition of the *Captivi*, there has been much activity in the editing and re-editing of Roman drama. Ritschl's epoch-making Plautus has been partly re-issued in a second or a third edition in the Teubner series (Loewe-Goetz-Schoell, 1902-22). Lindsay's Plautus (O.C.T., 1903) was re-issued in a new edition seven years later. In the comprehensive classical series of texts and translations, Paul Nixon was responsible for Plautus in the Loeb Classical Library (1916-38)[1] and A. Ernout for Plautus in the 'Collection Budé' (1932-40); both works are valuable alike for the humanist and the scholar. Modern editions of separate plays of Plautus are too numerous to mention in this survey,[2] apart from those, which, conceived on a grander scale, are more notable landmarks in the field of scholarship. Of the latter we note W. M. Lindsay, *The Captivi of Plautus* (London, Methuen, 1900), to which is prefixed an important introduction; Fr. Marx, *Plautus Rudens, Text u. Commentar* (Leipzig, Hirzel, 1928); and, of the less popular comedies, P. J. Enk, *Plauti Mercator cum Prolegomenis, Notis Criticis, Commentario Exegetico* (Leiden, Sijthoff, 1932, two vols.): G. E. Duckworth, *T. Macci Plauti Epidicus*, edited with critical apparatus and commentary (Princeton, Prin. Univ. Pr., 1940), which contains a valuable bibliography, pp. 429-53; and, lastly Professor Enk's two-volume edition of the *Truculentus* (Leiden, Sijthoff, 1953). Of the most popular plays of Plautus there have been many editions.[3]

The Oxford text of Terence edited by R. Y. Tyrrell (1902) was superseded by that of R. Kauer and W. M. Lindsay (1926). Text and commentary have appeared twice: S. G. Ashmore, *The Comedies of Terence* (2nd edition, O.U.P. — New York, 1910) and the edition of G. Coppola (Torino, Chiantore, 1927). J. Sargeaunt was the translator of the Loeb Terence (1912). A valuable introduction, with bibliographical notes, is prefixed to the Budé Terence of J. Marouzeau (1942-49). There have been editions and re-editions of the separate plays of Terence, the most recent being that of the *Andria* by A. Thierfelder (Heidelberg, Kerle, 1951).[4]

Provision has been made for the Latin-less reader. Apart from the translations provided in the Loeb and Budé series, there have been published in England, U.S.A. and elsewhere translations of Plautus and Terence in prose and verse. Groups of Plautine comedies were done into English by Sir R. Allison (London, Humphreys, 1914) and by F. A. Wright and H. L. Rogers (London, Routledge, 1925); a complete German prose translation was done by L. Gurlitt (Berlin, Propyläen Verlag, 1922, 4 vols.). Prose translations of Terence were done by F. Perry (O.U.P., 1929), and E. Chambry (Paris, Garnier, 1932), and a verse translation by W. Ritchie (London, Bell, 1927). A translation in prose and verse, R. W. Hyde and E. C. West, *The Menaechmi of Plautus* (Harvard U.P., 1930) has been highly praised 'because of its colloquial nature and also because it presents in verse the more lyrical portions of the original'.[5] This translation is incorporated in a remarkable recent publication, G. E. Duckworth, *The Complete Roman Drama* (New York, Random House, 1942, 2 vols.). The scope of this work is given as 'a variety of prose and verse translations by various hands with notes and glossary'. It is to be classed therefore among the books of more general appeal to which reference is made elsewhere in this review.

The fragments of early Roman tragic poets, last edited by O. Ribbeck in 1897-8, are now re-edited by A. Klotz (1953). A new edition and translation is found in E. H. Warmington, *Remains of Old Latin* (Loeb edit., vols. 1 and 2, 1935-36). The dramatic fragments of Ennius are available in J. Vahlen, *Ennianae Poesis Reliquiae* (Leipzig, Teubner, 3rd edition, 1928). The fragments of Pacuvius are separately treated in C. Faggiano, *Pacuvius, Ricostruzione dei drammi e traduzzione dei frammenti* (Galatina: Marra e Lanzi, 1930).

Three of the tragedies of Seneca (*Hercules Furens, Troades, Medea*) were edited together by H. M. Kingery (New York, Macmillan, 1908). Complete text and translation by F. J. Miller appeared in the Loeb Classical Library in 1917. In the Teubner series the tragedies were re-edited by R. Peiper and G. Richter in 1921. And in the same decade were published the editions of H. Moricca (Torino, Paravia; 2nd ed., 1947) and L. Herrmann (Paris, Budé, 1924-26). There have been several editions of the supposedly Senecan *Octavia*, besides that of L. Herrmann, *Octavie, tragédie prétexte*. (Paris, Les Belles Lettres, 1924.)

So much for the actual editions of Roman drama in this century. Much preparatory investigation has been carried out on the MSS. themselves and many important works published concerning text-tradition, notably that of Plautus, Terence, and Seneca. Lindsay broke ground with his *Palatine Text of Plautus* (Cl. Pr., 1896), which was followed by his *Codex Turnebi of Plautus* (Cl. Pr., 1898), and his *Ancient Editions of Plautus* (Oxford, Parker, 1904), in which the relations of the famous Ambrosian palimpsest (*A*) and the 'Palatine family' were examined. The MS. tradition of Plautus had already been surveyed in the introduction to his edition of the *Captivi* (1900). Recent summaries are found in Pauly-Wissowa-Kroll, RE 14 (1928) col. 118-124, and in the introduction to Ernout's Budé edition of Plautus (I, xxiv-xxxiv). And for bibliography see P. J. Enk, *Handboek der Latijnse Letterkunde*, II, i, 113-17.

The effect of *retractatio*, i.e. reworking of the text in the revival period, was examined in C. C. Coulter's *Retractatio in the Ambrosian and Palatine Recensions of Plautus* (Bryn Mawr, Pen., 1911). The bearing of *retractatio* on Plautine criticism is immediate.[6] Miss Coulter examined five plays of Plautus (*Persa, Poenulus, Pseudolus, Stichus, Trinummus*) and she appeared to prove that the activity of the *retractator* affected the Ambrosian recension, a conclusion disturbing to those who hoped to find in *A* the *verba ipsissima* of the dramatist.

Even greater activity has been displayed on the text-tradition of Terence. It might be said to originate from the labours of K. Dziatzko and Fr. Leo in the latter part of the last century, and to begin with articles of R. Kauer, 'Zu Terenz', Wiener St. XX (1898), 252-76, XXII (1900), 56-114. Soon the American scholars Weston and Watson and the German O. Engelhardt published work on the illustrated Terence manuscripts. Over twenty years later came the important work of L. W. Jones and C. R. Morey.[7]

In the discussion of the chief families of MSS. and recensions of the text the pre-eminence of the famous codex Bembinus (*A*) has not remained unchallenged. Here are noted only the most important contributions to the discussion: R. H. Webb, 'An attempt to restore the Archetype of Terence MSS.' (HSCP, XXII (1912), 55-110; L. Jachmann, *Die Geschichte des Terenztextes in Altertum* (Basel, Reinhardt, 1924), J. D. Craig, *Jovialis and the Calliopian text of Terence* (Oxford, Blackwell, 1927): L. W. Jones, 'Ancient Texts of Terence' (ClPh, 25 (1930), 318-27). At the outset of the last article it was remarked: 'There is hardly an important Latin author whose text is in worse condition today than that of Terence. His very popularity has worked against him; in the Middle Ages manuscripts of his plays were multiplied in such quantity and in such manner as to obscure completely their origin and relationships.' The writer goes on to praise the editors of the Oxford text for advances in textual knowledge, but declares that the Oxford text leaves much to be desired. (*Ibid.*, p. 318.) Jones opposed the view of Craig that the codex Bembinus was the text held in honour in the fourth century A.D. and that it was necessarily a superior text. In 1934 an important examination of the relevant scholia was published: J. F. Mountford, *The Scholia Bembina* (Liv. U.P.). Next the problem of interpolation was faced in P. Fehl, *Die interpolierte Recension des Terenztextes* (Berlin, Junker, 1938). A notice of new unexamined MSS. appeared in an article by J. Andrieu, 'Nouveaux manuscrits de Térence' (REL 18 (1940), 546). A valuable survey of the whole textual field is given by Marouzeau in his introduction to the Budé Terence (I, 68-95); and see also Herescu, *op. cit.*, 25-8.

The needs of the research scholar have been furthered by the compilation of indices verborum. Plautine scholars are grateful for G. Lodge's *Lexicon Plautinum* (Leipzig, Teubner, 1901-33). The smaller companion volume for Terence is Jenkins, *Index verborum Terenti* (Chapel Hill, Univ. of North Carol. Pr., 1932). The corresponding publication for Seneca's dramas is W. Oldfather, A. S. Pease, H. V. Canter, *Index verborum quae in Senecae fabulis necnon in Octavia praetexta reperiuntur* (Univ. of Illin. Stud., 1918).

The survey of Roman drama in the last half-century has been

so widespread and so detailed, and has revealed so many problems, that need has arisen for monographs of a comprehensive character or else devoted to some wider aspect of the field. There are the comprehensive articles of Pauly–Wissowa–Kroll, RE, and the critical surveys contained in Bursian's Jahresbericht;[8] but these are the quarry of the specialist. A valuable, clear account of Roman comedy was given in G. Michaut: *Histoire de la Comédie Romaine: sur les tréteaux latins* (Paris, Fontemoing, 1912); but indeed an English reviewer (CR (1913), p.172) sadly noted, 'in all the dictionary of Roman drama there is hardly a term that can be exactly and satisfactorily defined'!

The present intention is to refer to some other publications, which, while wholly scholarly, have an appeal beyond the professional scholar. These are mainly in English and French; their content is factual or critical or both; they supplement the accounts available in histories of Latin literature and allow scope for a fuller, perhaps idiosyncratic, appreciation. They began to be published after the First World War. One of the first to appear was G. Michaut: *Histoire de la poésie latine: Plaute* (Paris, Fontemoing, 1920, 2 vols.). A little later came P. Lejay: *Plaute* (Paris, Boivin, 1925), an excellent book. Just before this had been published G. Norwood: *The Art of Terence* (London, Blackwell, 1923), a very lively, but — for most readers — biased assessment by one to whom Plautus was grossly inferior as an artist to Terence.[9] The same prejudice informs his *Plautus and Terence* (London, Harrap, 1932), which Professor Beare has summed up as 'readable and independent, if somewhat extreme', Professor Duckworth as 'both inadequate and misleading, especially in its treatment of Plautus'. Lovers of Plautus do not like to be told that he wrote plays like a blacksmith mending a watch.

Before the end of the last war there appeared in the United States two books intended to provide the general reader with a survey, in translation, of Roman drama, firstly G. E. Duckworth: *The Complete Roman Drama* (New York, Random House, 1942, 2 vols.)[10] and, secondly, P. W. Harsh: *A Handbook of Classical Drama* (Stanford, Cal., Stan. Univ. Pr., 1944), in which are included full analyses of the comedies of Plautus and Terence.

Two more recent books have surveyed the field of Roman drama from different angles, and are in some measure complementary — W. Beare: *The Roman Stage. A Short History of Latin*

Drama in the time of the Republic (London, Methuen, 1950) and G. F. Duckworth: *The Nature of Roman Comedy. A Study in Popular Entertainment* (Princeton, Prin. Univ. Pr., 1952). The method of Professor Beare may perhaps be called objective; in his preface he says, after a reference to E. Fraenkel's *Plautinisches im Plautus*, 'I found, however, in the course of time that my interest lay not so much in the relation of the Latin plays to their Greek originals, or in those linguistic, metrical and textual studies associated with the names of W. M. Lindsay and E. A. Sonnenschein, as in the light thrown by the plays on the theatre for which they were intended. It seemed to me that nearly all modern discussions of Latin drama rested on certain assumptions, conscious or unconscious, which might seem reasonable in themselves but were incapable of proof and sooner or later led to serious difficulty. Ever since the Renaissance the scholars of Western Europe, even while basing their standards on the supposed practice of the Greeks and Romans, have in fact allowed contemporary habits of thought to colour their conception of classical antiquity.' His book covers comedy (*palliata, togata*, and mime) and tragedy throughout the Republic, examines the actual conditions of the Roman theatre and the modes of presentation of plays, and considers the problems for modern scholarship arising therefrom; and the value of the book is enhanced by its apt illustrations. No recent book covers the field of Roman Republican drama so succinctly; and for good measure it supplies an epilogue on drama under the Empire.

Professor Duckworth's book was written about the same time. The emphasis on popular entertainment in both these books is significant of a swing from the philological approach to Roman comedy which marked the work of Ritschl, Lindsay, and other scholars overlapping the twentieth century. Duckworth's book is primarily a study of the plays of Plautus and Terence, the difference of whose techniques is considered at great length, but it is not intended for the specialist — 'it is directed primarily to those who are interested in classical literature in a more general way, and to all readers of ancient and modern comedy' (*ibid.*, Pref.). It is abreast of modern scholarship, is very well documented, has a good index and the best bibliography of Plautus and Terence available in one volume. Prior to these was published an Italian survey of Roman comedy: F. Arnaldi: *Da Plauto a Terenzio* (Napoli, Loffredo, 1946-47), 2 vols.[11]

ROMAN DRAMA

No critical consideration of Plautus and Terence ever loses sight of Greek New Comedy. The best one-volume survey is that of P. E. Legrand's *Daos. Tableau de la comédie grecque pendant la période dite nouvelle* (Lyon, Rey, 1910), translated by J. Loeb as *The New Greek Comedy* (London, Heinemann; N.Y., Putnam, 1917), though it is fair to add that Tenney Frank charges the author with the 'mistake of treating the Greek and Roman New Comedy as a single phenomenon' (*Roman Life and Literature*, p. 73). There is a rewarding chapter on Menander in A. W. Gomme: *Essays in Greek History and Literature* (Oxford, Blackwell, 1937), in which, as in *Daos*, there are frequent references to Plautus and to Terence.

The output of books and articles on Roman comedy has vastly exceeded that on tragedy, nor is there the same demand for books of general character on Roman tragedy. If one considers the cultural development of Western Europe this is not astonishing. F. Leo broke fresh ground with his *De tragoedia Romana* (Göttingen, Dieterich, 1910). Roman tragedy for the modern world shrinks to the Senecan drama, and of this the only comprehensive survey in English is C. W. Mendell's *Our Seneca* (New Haven, Yale Univ. Pr., 1941). There have been, of course, a large number of specialized studies of Senecan drama, which will be noticed, in part, in the sequel. Nor is the interest of our Elizabethan forefathers in Senecan tragedy forgotten.

Finally, among works of a general character regarding theatrical productions must be mentioned C. Saunders: *Costume in Roman Comedy* (New York, Columb. Univ. Pr., 1909),[12] J. T. Allen, *Stage Antiquities of the Greeks and Romans and their influence* (Berk., Cal., Longmans, Green, 1927), and the standard illustrated work on the theatre, M. Bieber, *Die Denkmäler zum Theaterwesen im Altertum* (Berlin-Leipzig, de Gruyter, 1920), subsequently translated as *The History of the Greek and Roman Theater* (Princeton, Prin. Univ. Pr., 1939).

(*b*) Much has been written about the actual staging of Roman plays. Old problems, such as those of the wing-entrances and of the wearing of masks, have been re-examined.

At the outset be it remarked that the conditions and problems of presentation are admirably reviewed by Beare (*op. cit.*, chs. XIX-XXVI, and App.) and by Duckworth (*op. cit.*, ch. IV, 'Presentation and Staging', ch. V 'Stage Conventions and Techniques'). There is a wealth of information in Miss Bieber's book already mentioned; and J. T. Allen's little book, also cited, is not less useful from having a comparative slant.

But to return: one of the earliest contributions to the subject of staging was F. Bauer: *Quaestiones scenicae Plautinae* (Strasbourg, Hertzer, 1902). Then in 1909 came Miss Saunders' book on costume of Roman comedy. Costume should, or might, include masks; and to refer to masks is to stir up a veritable hornet's nest of controversy. In her article 'The Introduction of Masks on the Roman Stage', AJPh, 32 (1911), 58-73, Miss Saunders remarked: 'If ancient testimony concerning the introduction of masks on the Roman stage were as consistent as it is abundant one of the troublesome problems in the history of the Roman theatre would never have arisen' (*ibid.*, p. 88). The evidence being confusing, one might ask, what might one have expected? It might have been expected that the Romans, in imitation of the Greeks, would have taken over the convention of wearing masks — the advantages, and the disadvantages, of which are summed up by Michaut, *Histoire de la Comédie romaine*, 419ff. Perhaps the most obvious advantage of masks was that their use would facilitate the combining of roles, if players were hard to come by, as they might have been when comedies were staged a few times only during the year.[13]

But even C. M. Kurrelmeyer, who emphasizes the smallness of the troupe in her book, *The Economy of Actors in Plautus* (Graz, Deutsche Vereins-Druckerei, 1932), rejects the use of masks in Plautus' day. The traditional view is that masks were not worn on the Roman stage until after the death of Terence; but the view is rejected by Beare[14] and others, who range themselves in support of Festus. Duckworth (*op. cit.*, 94) concludes that 'the evidence for the late introduction of masks in Roman comedy is weak. Latin grammarians, perhaps eager to point out as many differences between Greek and Roman usage as possible, developed conflicting theories as to who made the innovation. The problem may never be solved, but the probabilities favour their use from the earliest period of Roman drama. Such a view explains the passage in Festus, accounts for the presence of the word *persona* in Plautus and Terence and best accords with the history and nature of Roman comedy.' He regards as plausible the theory of a small troupe, and takes Miss Kurrelmeyer to task for her patronage of mute substitutes; but he warns us that the attempts of scholars to assign the parts in a given play seldom agree (*op. cit.*, 97).

The conventions of the actual staging of a Roman comedy have been the object of much investigation. For example, with regard to the coming and going of actors (who, by convention, returned, if at all, by the same way as they quitted the stage), internal evidence reveals how many doors are required in addition to side-entrances (*parodoi*). 'In comedy the normal setting requires two doors, but a few plays need three and a few only one. No comedy requires more than three doors' (Beare). And the three doors were a fixed convention of the back scene (Beare, *op. cit.*, App. G). The old theory that actors knocked before coming out of a stage 'house' was rejected years ago,[15] but it has been left for Professor Beare to demolish the view that house doors opened outwards on to the stage (*ibid.*). A general investigation of stage movements in Roman comedy is contained in Professor Mary Johnston's *Exits and Entrances in Roman Comedy* (New York, W. F. Humphrey Press, 1933), and it reaches the conclusion 'that on the stage of the Roman theatre the side-entrance to the right of the spectators was used for entrances and exits of characters from and to the city and the forum, and that the side-entrance to the left of the spectators was used for entrances and exits of characters moving from and to the port and foreign parts, and, probably, from and to the country as well' (p. 151). This conclusion involves, as Beare notes, a discrepancy between Greek and Roman usage as far as the harbour was concerned. In her discussion too she says, 'An alley or passage (*angiportum*) was supposed to lead back from the street between two houses' (*ibid.*, 15). But Beare rejects this oft-repeated view, declaring that *angiportus* (*angiportum*) is a street, not a *cul-de-sac*, invisible and necessary.[16] The problem of the *angiportus* and its congeners is discussed elsewhere.[17]

If the *angiportus* is not then a lane between houses, it cannot have provided a retreat for that eavesdropping of which Terence availed himself more than Plautus.[18] Equally unreliable seems now the conclusion that there were no seats for the spectators in Plautus' time, in spite of some ancient evidence and Ritschl's conclusion.[19]

(*c*) The mention of eavesdropping brings up, in a humble way, the whole question of dramatic technique in comedy, a big subject, of which only the salient features can be noticed here.

Discussion ranges over the nature and the devices of exposition, the use of link- and other kinds of monologue, the functional purpose of certain roles, and so forth.

A fairly recent American book, D. E. Fields, *The Technique of Exposition in Roman Comedy* (Chicago, Univ. Library, 1938), is concerned with pre-suppositions of the plot, not with development of action within the play. Concerning that development, some critics have emphasized the artificiality of our Act and Scene divisions, with the corollary of uninterrupted action, as does C. C. Conrad, *The Technique of Continuous Action in Roman Comedy* (Menasha, Banta Publ. Co., 1915). It is not to be supposed that the stage was never empty, and indeed there is the clear evidence of *Bacch.* 107 and *Pseud.* 573, the latter passage providing evidence of some kind of musical interlude; but in the opinion of Conrad such interludes or other pauses, when the action is intermitted, are not evidence of act-division; comedy was written for continuous action. This is feasible, at any rate, if the number of actors was unlimited (cf. Schanz and Hosius, I, 146), but if roles had to be doubled it might well be necessary for the dramatist to devise bridging scenes. This was thought to be the purpose of some inorganic scenes introducing a slave-boy ruminating, a kind of monologue.[20] Continuity of action and continuity of time should not, of course, be equated. J. N. Hough, in an article, 'The Continuity of Time in Plautus' (ClPh 31 (1936), 244-52), complains that the voluminous literature on the subject has rarely preserved a careful distinction between the two. To return to monologue: the purpose of monologue in comedy is at least three-fold — 'to retain the speaker for the coming scene, to provide opportunity for eavesdropping, to fill intervals of time' (J. N. Hough). Another American critic, H. W. Prescott, has devoted three articles[21] to the study of both link-monologues and exit-monologues; the latter he finds about as numerous as link-monologues, the total being about one hundred; entrance-monologues are nearly three times as numerous. Clearly it is link- and exit-monologues which have more to do with continuity of action. Prescott wrote: 'The external form of a Roman comedy is misrepresented in all modern editions of Plautus and Terence except in Leo's edition of Plautus. Modern texts mislead the reader into thinking that a Roman comedy is divided into acts and scenes like a modern comedy. On the contrary, with some exceptions, the action is continuous, devoid of curtain falls or regularly recurring pauses of any length: and of scene divisions the spectator in the time of Plautus and Terence probably had little or no consciousness.' (ClPh, 34 (1939), 3). And again: 'The metrical form of the exit monologue is remarkably uniform and corresponds in this respect to the link monologue . . . It serves as one of many devices to prevent a vacant stage and a substantial pause by filling an interval of time which might have been achieved by act division' (*ibid.*, 36 (1942), 20).

Horace laid down the precept that a play must have five acts; but, as Beare says, 'the most careful researches of modern scholars have been unable to discover clear evidence of five-act division in any Greek play which has reached us complete, or in the plays of Plautus or Terence' (*op. cit.*, 188). And this negative conclusion was admitted in R. T. Weissinger's *A Study of Act Divisions in Classical Drama* (Iowa St. in ClPh, No. 9, Scottdale, 1940), a work which Beare praises for forcing attention again to fundamental conditions and conventions.

Turning to the minor characters, in another article (ClPh, 15 (1920), 265-81) Prescott discussed the inorganic roles in Roman comedy: 'They assist in the exposition of situation, in the quick reversal of action, and in the solution of complications. They provide entertainment, especially in the case of buffoon roles, such as parasites, cooks, and *pueri delicati*. They fill intervals of time . . . Seldom do they serve exclusively any one of these various purposes' (*ibid.*, 280). The complement to this article is O. L. Wilner's 'The Characteristic Treatment of Inorganic Roles in Roman Comedy' (ClPh, 25 (1930), 56-71). Prescott has also examined the silent roles in comedy (ClPh, 31 (1936), 97-119). G. E. Duckworth has investigated the unnamed characters in the plays of Plautus (ClPh, 23 (1938), 267-82), and found them to total some forty persons.

These articles are general in scope; and there are studies dealing with characterization as a whole.[22] Also, there have been many studies of individual comedy types: the running slave,[23] the *leno*,[24] the parasite,[25] and a recent appraisement of these types in the economic setting of Rich Man *versus* Poor Man.[26]

The Roman comic dramatists had such stock types and others with which to deal; but the fact that the *œuvre* of Terence is so different from that of Plautus gives rise by implication to the problem of the originality of Roman comedy.

First, as to the difference of technique of the two comedians: while it is admitted that the prologues of Terence are genuine and a vehicle for self-justification against detractors rather than for plot-exposition, the authenticity and scope of the extant prologues of Plautus has been matter of controversy since the discussion of them by Leo in his *Plautinische Forschungen*[2], 188-247.[27] Apart from the prologue, informatory or otherwise, the dramatist must give his audience enough foreknowledge to be at least as well informed as the characters, but not so well-informed as to miss the pleasures of surprise. How the dramatist dealt with the problem — presuppositions of the plot — is the theme of many studies, for example the work of D. E. Fields already cited and of P. W. Harsh, *Studies in Dramatic 'Preparation'* (Diss., Univ. of Chicago, 1935).[28] It is clear that the more an audience knows in advance the less tension and surprise and the more comic irony are in store. The traditional view that Plautus by his technique gave away tension and surprise, Terence the possibility of comic irony, has been shown from analysis to be untenable, or to need considerable modification. Nor indeed is it likely that the method of Plautus should continue throughout his long career unaltered; prologues may be missing from some plays because he preferred to eliminate them in the interest of dramatic surprise. In general, more careful attention has been paid to the dramatic structure of his plays.[29]

It has been argued that Caecilius was a transitional figure between Plautus and Terence, that he was responsible for the Terentian rejection of the expository prologue and the development of the elements of suspense and surprise — and Norwood was of opinion that Menander himself was working towards this goal (*Greek Comedy*, 353f). But the hypothesis regarding Caecilius has been controverted by several.[30] It might be that Terence was too faithful to Plautus' more subtle methods![31]

Tenney Frank, writing on 'Terence's Contribution to Plot-Construction' (AJPh, 49 (1928), 308-22), expressed himself cautiously when he said that Terence 'despite his fondness for the Greek originals and his outspoken claim of fidelity to them, seems consciously to have striven for a suspended dénouement. He does not entirely suppress dramatic irony, but he reduces its scope, he eliminates the expository prologue completely, he is chary about giving information to the spectator, preferring to keep him under tension for a part if not for the whole of the play.' Terence has been regarded as a painstaking translator,[32] but Norwood, Frank himself, Beare, and other writers have invoked Terence's dramatic technique as proof of his originality.[33]

With regard to plot-construction there remains the much-discussed problem of *contaminatio*, to which Terence's own statements give rise. There is agreement neither about the connotation of the term nor the method of construction it implies.[34] If Terence did indeed follow precedent in botching one play from more than one model, then it might be well to sift the plays of Plautus in search of *contaminatio*. And this has been fervently done, perhaps incautiously, if, as Beare thinks, Terence was not telling the truth. Such critical analysis has been the concern in the main of German scholars. F. Leo in his chapter on Plautus' sources (*PF*, III, 'Plautus und seine Originale') investigated *Miles Gloriosus* and *Poenulus*, the chief quarries for such investigation. Ed. Fraenkel (*op. cit.*, IX 'Contaminierte Stücke') adds *Stichus* and *Casina*. Jachmann devotes a chapter of his book *Plautinisches und Attisches* to an analysis of *contaminatio* and discusses the *Rudens, Casina, Aulularia, Miles Gloriosus, Poenulus, Epidicus* and *Trinummus*. He points out that the *Miles* is the best play for his purpose, as indeed other studies indicate.[35] But G. E. Duckworth in his article 'The Structure of the *Miles Gloriosus*' (ClPh, 30 (1935)) registers a stern protest.[36] Indeed, few Plautine plays have escaped the charge of *contaminatio*.[37] But the pendulum is swinging in another direction. Professor Beare has in various writings[38] produced a novel theory regarding Terence which bears on Plautus by implication. He takes the extreme position that Terence did not practise *contaminatio* in the sense of interweaving plots; he merely adapted borrowed scenes. To interweave plots would involve the Latin dramatist in 'original work of a complicated character', whereas to the upholders of the practice he is incapable of such work. The American critic, H. W. Prescott, in an article, 'Criteria of Originality in Plautus' (TAPhA, 63 (1932), 103-25) tilts at Ed. Fraenkel for providing himself a relatively insecure basis for determining what is *Plautinisches*. Duckworth, after citing the basic weaknesses of those who see *contaminatio* everywhere in Plautus (*Nature of Roman Comedy*, 206f), says that 'many of the conclusions of Leo, Fraenkel, Jachmann, and others have been discredited; the pendulum has swung in the opposite direction but, like most healthy reactions, it has perhaps gone too far. Most scholars today would hesitate to deny contamination to Plautus as completely as Beare does'.

The urge to find *contaminatio* in Roman comedy is in fact one revelation of a widely-held judgment, especially among German critics, that all the weaknesses — repetitions, inconsistencies and so forth — are due to the Roman imitator. And the unverifiable hypothesis of Greek perfection is weaker still if the very nature and origins of New Comedy have been misapprehended. So Tenney Frank is highly critical of Jachmann's work: 'most of it seems to me misspent labour based upon unreasonable premises: the assumption that the originals were perfect, that all flaws are attributable to the incapacity of Plautus, and that these plays should be judged by criteria applicable to work meant for literary publication' (AJPh, 53 (1932), 81). H. W. Prescott wrote a series of articles aimed against misapprehensions regarding Hellenistic and Roman comedy.[39] And T. Frank tilted against Leo's doctrine that New Comedy merely borrowed its devices of prologue, fate, recognition and the rest from tragedy. 'Prescott's incisive criticism', he wrote, 'of that view must stand, with its insistence that we take Sicilian antecedents, Aristophanes, and environment into account' (AJPh, 49 (1928), 315). And a passage of Prescott has the honour of being cited by both Duckworth and Enk: 'Scholars are prone to ascribe to Hellenistic comedy a relatively faultless form and structure. Then analysing Roman comedies these same scholars when they find in the Latin plays various structural weaknesses are quick to stamp such defects as the botchwork of the Roman adapters. In view of our ignorance of the antecedents of Hellenistic comedy, and considering the scanty remains of the Greek type, this procedure is reckless.' (ClPh, 18 (1923), 23.)

Finally, another debatable point in the technique of comedy: the origin of the double-plot. Plautus brought on often a pair of characters (like Rosencrantz and Guildenstern), but seems to have little aptitude for a double plot, though the *Bacchides* and the *Poenulus* provide some evidence. Terence in his later plays reveals the technique perfected; Norwood (*Plautus and Terence*, 147) went so far as to attribute to him its introduction; but the fact that the *Bacchides* has a Menandrian original is ominous. Norwood wrote, indeed, not about double-plot but 'duality method', which he regarded as central, 'the focus of the Terentian art and the Terentian spirit' (*ibid.*). Whichever term be used, it seems safe to believe that Terence was not its inventor.

(*d*) No doubt our appreciation of Plautus would be enhanced if we knew the order in which the plays were written. The problem of Plautine chronology has been examined intermittently for the last half-century. It was originally considered in Ritschl's *Parerga* in 1845. A dissertation, V. Puttner, *Zur Chronologie d. plautinischen Komödien* (XXXV Prog. Ried, 1905-06), contains the bibliographical material to date.[40] The discussion was resumed some twenty years later, and has been maintained in general or in particular since, the chief and recent landmark being the work of C. H. Buck, *A Chronology of the Plays of Plautus* (Baltimore (Diss.), 1940). The other scholars who have contributed most to the discussion are Sedgwick, Hough, and Enk. It might seem probable that observations of contemporary allusions in the plays would be most fruitful; this historical method has been the basis of the work of Enk and Hough, but, as Duckworth has observed, it can produce very divergent results; *Menaechmi*, *Rudens* and *Amphitruo* have been considered, from allusions noted, either early (Enk) or late plays (Buck).

Other criteria have been used. In 1925 Sedgwick suggested a tentative chronology based on the relative frequency of lyrics, the number of the *cantica* increasing, it seemed, as the dramatist attained more independence of style.[41] In publishing a revised chronology[42] in 1949 he wrote: 'I think we have now reached a stage in which we can point to definite results, and a chronology which can claim to be in the main established with only a small margin of error.' Sedgwick found himself in general agreement with the American scholar Hough, who, while unwilling to put forward specific dates, has argued for three periods of production, early, middle, and late. Hough used a variety of criteria; he maintained that later work is characterized by a subtler use of Greek words, a more skilful use of intrigue and decreasing amount of explanation, a more skilful employment of link-monologues, an increase in vulgar humour and Roman allusions. If Hough is right, Plautus in his maturer work showed greater independence and greater skill. This seems a reasonable conclusion.[43] Controversy has admittedly been acute regarding the date of the *Casina* and its revival performance, with special regard to the meaning of *novi nummi*.[44] Beare defends the priority of the *Mer-*

cator,[45] and the author of a recent thesis returns to the investigation of the first years in which the comedies were staged.[46]

The chronology of Terence's six plays has not been so much debated in the last half-century. But problems of chronology arising from his own prologues, and ancient comment upon them, were considered again by the American scholar R. C. Flickinger, and by N. Terzaghi, who went so far as to argue that Terence wrote other comedies which have not survived. Other departures from the traditional chronology were advocated by other Italian critics, whose views did not commend themselves to their fellow-countryman, Arnaldi.[47]

(e) The problems of metre and prosody which emerge in the field of Roman comedy are both thorny and fascinating. The biggest problems are those raised by the so-called law of *Breves Breviantes* (or *Iambenkürzung*) and the relation of verse-ictus with the accent of ordinary speech. Only a summary account is possible here of the great output of learned comment in this field, a field the more rewarding, of course, if we can catch the very intonations of contemporary Roman speech. Before the turn of the century, the work of Klotz, *Grundzüge altrömischer Metrik* (Leipzig, Teubner, 1890), loomed large. But its deficiencies were noted in the trenchant preface of W. M. Lindsay's *Early Latin Verse* (Oxford, Clar. Press, 1922), an indispensable work even for those who criticize it adversely, and containing an important (if select) bibliography. The second edition of Leo's *Plautinische Forschungen* (1912) had much comment on metre and prosody, especially hiatus and synaloephe, but in his review of the book Sonnenschein complained (CR 27 (1913), 237), 'we are left without any clear conception of Leo's view as to the fundamental question of Old Latin prosody — the doctrine of "iambic shortening" as it is generally called in German, or "breves breviantes" as it is called in France.' (It was Havet who coined the term.) Lindsay once wrote: 'the law of Breves Breviantes is an imposing (and repellent) name for the characteristic slurred pronunciation of everyday life at Rome' (AJPh 42 (1921), 336). But again Sonnenschein complained in his review of *Early Latin Verse* that Lindsay nowhere formulated a doctrine of 'Breves Breviantes', and that if Plautine verse is quantitative and not accentual (as Lindsay admitted) then the theory of B.B. 'falls to the ground *as an explanation of the structure of old Latin verse*'.[48]

It is partly the old problem of Roman utterance wedded to Greek prosody, of everyday speech and metrical forms. Is B.B. in fact a phonetic or a metrical law? G. Jachmann made out (*Studia Prosodiaca*, Habilitations-schrift, Marburg, 1912)[49] that B.B. (Iambenkürzung) was avoided in crucial places in the verse (e.g. near the end of the line); but his theories were later rejected by O. Skutsch in his *Prosodische und metrische Gesetze der Iambenkürzung* (Göttingen, Vanderhoek and Ruprecht., 1934); the quantitative nature of Plautine verse is not impaired by B.B. And when B.B. is discussed reference must be made to an article by Sonnenschein, 'The law of *breves breviantes* in the light of Phonetics' (ClPh, VI (1911), 1-11), to a modified doctrine of B.B. of A. Brenot, *Les Mots et Groupes iambiques réduits dans le Théâtre latin* (Paris, Champion, 1923), and to F. Vollmer, *Über die sog. Iambenkürzung bei den skenischen Dichtern der Römer* (S. Ber. bayr. Akad. Philos., 1924, 4 Abh.).

In 1919 appeared a significant article by E. Sturtevant, 'The coincidence of Accent and Ictus in Plautus and Terence' (ClPhil, 14 (1919), 234-44); references were given for the relevant material of discussion since 1870.[50] A summary of the problem of metrical ictus (with references to date) was contained in J. F. Mountford's article 'Some neglected evidence bearing on the *ictus metricus* in Latin verse' (TAPhA 56 (1925), 150-61). The problems of the relation of ictus and accent were faced in two elaborate works, E. Fraenkel's *Iktus und Akzent in lateinischen Sprechvers* (Berlin, Weidmann, 1928) and H. Drexler's *Plautinische Akzentstudien* (Breslau, Marcus, 1932-33), 3 vols.; both important, if extreme.[51] Fraenkel accepts the coincidence in dialogue of verse ictus and the accent of colloquial speech, with the implication for at least one reviewer that 'Plautus and Terence were not quantitative poets at all' (Radford). Drexler retreats from Fraenkel's position to a compromise, itself rigid, of a stressed group-accent reflected in the poet's verse ictus. In either work a highly ingenious effort is made to escape the objectionable clash of ictus and accent in the verse of comedy; but the ingenuity has provoked much adverse comment.[52] Still, it must be admitted that the substitute theories of some who reject the work of Fraenkel and Drexler — e.g. R. Kauer, 'Iktus und Akzent im lat. Sprechvers', WS 47 (1929), 68-78, E. Vandvik, *Rhythmus und Metrum: Akzent und Iktus* (Symbol. Osl., fasc. suppl. VIII, Oslo, 1937, 237ff) have not been well received.

If there were no stress ictus in dialogue verse, the problem of clash might prove to have been misconceived, as K. M. Abbott points out in his 'Ictus, Accent and Statistics in Latin Dramatic Verse' (TAPhA 75 (1944), 127-40).[53] This article and much of the relevant literature concerning the supposed clash of accent and ictus is noted in the Introduction to P. W. Harsh: *Iambic Words and Regard for Accent in Plautus* (Standford, Cal. U.P., 1949).[54]

An interesting theory in support of diaeresis after certain feet in dialogue verse — sometimes called *loci Jacobsohniani* — was propounded by H. Jacobsohn in his *Quaestiones Plautinae metricae et grammaticae* (Göttingen, 1904). But there is insufficient evidence to show that it is valid for Plautus or for Terence.[55]

Finally may be mentioned some works of general character in this field: G. Ramain, 'Métrique Plautinienne', Rev. de Phil., 29 (1905), 205-26, W. A. Laidlaw, *The Prosody of Terence* (London, St. Andrews Univ. Publ., 40, 1938), L. Nougaret, 'Le métrique de Plaute et de Térence', *Mémorial des Études Latines offert à J. Marouzeau* (Paris, Les Belles Lettres, 1942), 123-48, and W. B. Sedgwick, 'The Origin and Development of Roman Comic Metres', C & M, 10 (1949), 171-81.[56]

After the long verse of comedy, the *cantica*. If, as the epitaph records, his *numeri innumeri* bewailed the death of Plautus, it is not surprising that his *cantica* which reveal them should have attracted much attention, both for themselves and for their possible origin.[57] In a sense the problem of the source of the Plautine *cantica* is an aspect of the main problem of criticism of Roman comedy — the degree of its dependence on, or independence of, Greek models. It is on the other hand a peculiarly Plautine problem in so far as his great rival Terence wrote comedies almost devoid of *cantica*. And, supposing their origin known, we have still to ask how they were performed on the stage. The strange tale of the assistant musician (Livy, VII, 2.10) was tacitly accepted by Lindsay (*E.L.V.*, 263n) and by W. B. Sedgwick (CR 39 (1925), 55-8), but W. Beare has protested (CR 54 (1940), 70-2) that distinction of actor and singer would render some scenes unstageable; and the same conclusion is reached by Duckworth (*Nature of Roman Comedy*, 364).

The discussion of *cantica* in comedy begins with Ritschl (Rh.Mus., 1871, 599-637) and F. Leo (*Die plautinischen* Cantica *und die hellenistische Lyrik* (Berlin, Weidmann, 1897). To Leo, wrote

Lindsay (*E.L.V.*, 261), we all owe a truer appreciation of Plautine *cantica*. It was in 1896 that Grenfell published his Hellenistic song in dochmiacs (*An Alexandrian Erotic Fragment*) and this clearly influenced Leo towards the view that Plautus found his models in contemporary music-hall songs of Southern Italy,[58] traceable to the lyrics of Euripides' plays. But clearly Euripides might have similarly influenced many of the New Comedy dramas not extant, which Plautus is known to have copied, as was objected by H. H. Law in her *Studies in the Songs of Plautine Comedy* (Diss., Univ. of Chicago, 1922). E. Fraenkel rejected Leo's view; his own thesis is briefly that Plautus had in fact his material in the dialogue of the Greek original, but converted dialogue into song. Why? He, like Ennius, was inheriting a principle of older Roman dramatists introduced perhaps by a tragedian (*P. im P.*, 321-73). The discussion was continued by O. Immisch, whose theory attempted to combine the views of Leo and Fraenkel.[59] And in his articles in Philologus H. Roppenecker discussed the adaptation by Plautus of the metre to sense and feeling.[60] Duckworth has complained that Fraenkel's theory seems unsatisfactory: 'There are no lyrical meters in the few fragments extant of pre-Plautine comedy, and even if Naevius or Livius Andronicus did make the innovation, Fraenkel's solution merely pushes the problem back to the very beginnings of formal Roman drama. Why was the dialogue verse of Greek comedy changed to song? Why did the Roman spectators prefer song and dance to straight dialogue?' (*Nature of Roman Comedy*, 378). But he admits the tendency of subsequent views towards pre-literary forms; Lejay, for example, found the source of the Plautine *canticum* in dramatic *satura* of which Plautus developed the musical element (*Plaute*, 1925, 28ff). Marx found in the Plautine song and dance an inheritance from Etruria (*Plaut. Akz.*, II, 363ff). Others have suggested the fusion of more than one source: e.g. native *satura* and Hellenistic song.

The note of uncertainty is sounded still. Sedgwick pointed out (CR, 39 (1925), 58n) that the considerable fragments of Roman tragedy extant have not the polymetrical character which the theory of Fraenkel might lead us to expect. T. Frank later observed: 'The student of Naevius' tragic fragments will be inclined to believe with Fraenkel (*P. im P.*, 344) that the *canticum* was invented by one of the predecessors of Plautus. His criticism of Leo is valid, but the problem does not yet seem to me to be solved. There is still the possibility that Naevius may have seen musical comedies in Sicily, during his campaigns there' (AJPh, 49 (1928), 316n). Beare, concluding his chapter on 'Music and Metre', declares, 'The much debated question as to the origin of the *cantica* would seem to be largely unreal. Whatever metrical hints the Latin dramatists gathered from external sources, their use of the metres is characteristically Roman. Professor Fraenkel has rightly exorcised the phantom of "Hellenistic opera" conjured up by the imagination of Leo and Wilamowitz (*P. im P.*, 333). Unfortunately he himself clings to the view that Plautine comedy is distinguished from its Greek originals by its 'interchange of spoken and sung scenes' (*op. cit.*, 323).[61] And if the chronology of the plays is sound enough to prove that the earliest plays had the fewest *cantica*, the latest ones the most, then the deliberate choice of the dramatist enters into the matter at least as much as tradition.

Another problem still affects the *cantica*. A propos of responsion and symmetry Lindsay remarked (*E.L.V.*, 315), 'The time is not ripe for an analysis of all the Plautine *cantica*.' F. Marx, in his edition of *Rudens* (254ff), considered the possibility that Plautus may have had models of polymetrical *cantica* in New Comedy. Fr. Crusius in his work *Die Responsionen in den Plautinischen* Cantica (Phil. Suppl. xxi. 1, 1929)[62] essayed to demonstrate the strophic structure of *cantica*, not perhaps without damage to text and structure. Writing at the same time (Philol. 84, 1929) H. Roppenecker urged caution: 'Es fehlt also noch die abschliessende Erkenntniss des formalen Aufbaus der Lieder.' But it is now generally admitted that at least some responsion in the *cantica* is certain.

(*f*) It is convenient to take as the source, or beginning, of the half-century's investigation into the language, grammar, and style of comedy F. Leo's *Analecta Plautina: De figuris sermonis* (Göttingen, Dieterich, 1896, 1898, 1906, 3 parts). Then Lindsay's book *The Syntax of Plautus* (Oxford, Parker, 1907; Repr. N.Y., Stochert, 1936) not only broke fresh ground but provided a synthesis of some earlier work.[63] This was followed by C. E. Bennett, *Syntax of Early Latin* (Boston, Allyn, 1910-14, 2 vols.) and by J. T. Allardyce, *Syntax of Terence* (London, St. Andrews Univ. Pub., 27, 1929). Articles of a general character were, E. Löfstedt, 'Plautinischer Sprachbrauch und Verwandtes', Glotta, 3 (1912), 171-91; F. Echstein, 'Syntaktische Beiträge zu Plautus', Philol.

NS31 (1921), 142-73; 'Neue Untersuchungen zu Plautus und Terenz', *ibid.*, 34 (1925), 410-36; J. Marouzeau, 'Plaute et la première crise du latin', REL, 1926, 99ff. A work hovering between grammar and style is H. Haffter, *Untersuchungen zur altlateinischen Dichtersprache* (Berlin, Weidmann, 1934). Other studies are concerned with the diminutives of Plautus,[64] with word-play,[65] with proper names,[66] with pleonasm,[67] and even the erotic vocabulary and humour of Plautus.[68] There are many other articles dealing with details grammatical or stylistic of comedy, for which cf. J. P. Enk, *op. cit.*, II, 2, 294-308 and the larger bibliographical works.

The use of parody is a recognized weapon in the armoury of the writer of comedy. Parody is a feature of the style of Plautus — not Terence. There is parody of tragedy in general — τραγική λέξις — or of particular passages of individual poets. It is the frivolous Roman reaction to Greek mythology; a fair example is the jesting on the Tale of Troy from the lips of Chrysalus in the *Bacchides*. The subject of parody is discussed by Leo, Fraenkel, Sedgwick, and Thierfelder.[69] Leo observed that Plautus in his use of parody allows us to recognize that the continuity between Old and New Comedy is unbroken (*op. cit.*, 138); Plautus is adapting from New Comedy, but there are echoes from the Old Comedy which he cannot have known. Often, of course, parody may exist in Plautus undetected by his modern reader. T. Frank thought he found in act V of *Mercator* a parody of Pacuvius' *Teucer* (CQ 21 (1927), 88). The contemporary popularity of tragedy makes it likelier that Comedy should parody it.[70] Parody is a form of the comic in expression. The humour of Plautus and Terence, their exploitation of the comic in its varying aspects, are discussed in every appreciation of Roman comedy. Perhaps there is not much new to be said, nor is it possible here to refer to the many scattered observations on this subject. There are articles on the comic in Plautus,[71] it has been claimed that Plautus makes more and better jokes in his later plays,[72] and there is another consideration of the *vis comica* of Terence.[73]

(g) Though the comedies are read primarily as works of dramatic art they are also read with an eye to discovering information regarding ancient life. Evidence has been derived concerning the operation of law, partly Greek law of the original, partly Roman law of the adapted comedy.[74] The situation in the *Trinummus*, the legal authority of Megaronides in the absence of his friend abroad, provided matter for investigation.[75] Investigation has sometimes been concentrated on one author, on one play, or on some aspect of law; for example, the law of sale or of inheritance, or the legal incapacity of actors.[76] It is clear that in the adaptation of a Greek model cases might arise where Greek law was unintelligible to a Roman audience, or else dramatically unsuitable. 'Plautus as well as Terence', says M. Radin, 'accepts Greek legal situations only where they are dramatically indifferent. In other cases, their law must be assumed to be Roman law, since when it is Greek law, it is rendered intelligible by some form of explanation.'[77]

Apart from law, information of diverse kinds has been gathered from Roman comedy. Useful collections have been made by C. Knapp of references to painting, plays, players, and playwrights.[78] Knapp assembled too the evidence gleaned from Plautus and Terence about travel.[79] Another collection bears on allusions to literary topics, often for the sake of parody, appearing in Roman comedy; a number in Plautus have a bearing on Latin literature.[80] The American scholar, J. N. Hough, considered the use of Greek words occurring in Plautus, and by analysing the scenes in which they occur, suggested a means of assessing the development of the dramatist's art. Later he noted the usage of Terence.[81]

The scrutiny of law in Roman comedy noted above is part of the wider examination of life as it was lived in the time of Plautus and Terence, of which the comedies themselves provide some evidence. This was the theme of a dissertation of G. W. Leffingwell, *Social and Private Life at Rome in the time of Plautus and Terence* (Columbia Univ. Stud., N.Y., Longman, 1918). A more limited theme is pursued in D. R. Lee, *Childlife, adolescence, and marriage in Greek New Comedy and in the comedies of Plautus* (Diss., Madison, Wisconsin, 1919). The most recent and the most arresting survey of social life depicted in the comedies is that contained in the work of the American writer, P. L. Dunkin, *Post-Aristophanic Comedy* (Urbana, Univ. of Ill. Press, 1946). Here the assessment is related almost entirely to economic determination, and Plautus is the author's hero because he is the Poor Man's champion. It is not new to say that Terence followed in the wake of Menander, but it is perhaps startling to condemn the whole *ethos* of Terence as the Rich Man's friend. 'Plautus ridiculed the Rich Man of his original in cruel caricatures; Terence exalted the Rich Man with many a flattering touch. Plautus' hero is an ingeniously scheming Poor Man who must so behave in order to keep alive at all; Terence's villain is a stupid scheming Poor Man who is wicked through mere malice. Plautus found only a morbid resignation in the philosophy of his original, and so he passed it over or ridiculed it; Terence found that philosophy congenial, and he saturated his plays with it. Plautus created an art for money's sake; Terence created an art for art's sake' (p. 138).[82]

Dunkin by a very different route (for he is not concerned with aesthetic values) reaches the same goal of an unabashed partisanship which is reached by Norwood in his *Plautus and Terence*.

But the stage not only supplies some contemporary evidence of social conditions; it may reveal a state of lively tension between itself and the body politic. In an article, 'The theatre as a factor in Roman politics under the Republic' (TAPhA 38 (1907), 49ff) Abbott pointed out that in Cicero's time lines from tragedy and comedy were cited (with Gallic relish, no doubt) as applicable to contemporary politics. The possibility of stage censorship, at which Plautus hints in *M.G.* 211f, is re-examined by T. Frank, who, writing on 'Naevius and Free Speech' (AJPh 48 (1947), 105-10), suggested that the imprisonment of Naevius was due to a merely temporary censorship, the outcome of war strain. But the view has since been propounded that censorship was the rule, not the exception, in the last two centuries of the Republic.[83]

(*h*) The somewhat contemptuous attitude to Roman tragedy which prevailed in the nineteenth century has been traced to the influence of Nisard, who declared that in his opinion and that of all critics there was, accurately speaking, no Roman tragedy. His successors in France denigrated the tragedies of Seneca, and pointed out that Roman tragedy reached its peak in the Republic with Accius and at once declined. Why? In a re-examination of the problem ('The Decline of Roman Tragedy', CJ 12 (1916-17), 176-87), T. Frank rejected the solutions that tragedy was too exotic a form, or that the audience had become debauched by the arena-shows, or that there was a scarcity of genius. 'The real reason seems to be that the Roman dramatists had exhausted their material, that is, the material suitable in their day for their purposes.' Ennius and Pacuvius continued to be played in Cicero's day, but there was a dearth of new plays: neither the *praetexta* nor a realistic tragedy based on daily experience supplied the want. But Frank does not mention that equally the *palliata* failed to survive after its heyday.

There is ample evidence of an awakened interest of scholarship during the last fifty years both in the fragments of Republican tragedy — now re-edited by A. Klotz (*Scaenicorum Romanorum Fragmenta*,[3] vol. I, 1953), in the extant tragedies of Seneca, and in the allegedly Senecan praetexta, *Octavia*. In a little work published in 1910 (*De Tragoedia Romana*, Göttingen) Leo considers some of the fragments and their sources, and the tragedians' use of monody and choral lyric. Later A. Rostagni wrote about the Hellenistic sources of old tragedy.[84] E. M. Stuart (AJPh 47 (1924), 272-8) argued for the possibility of direct Homeric influence on Roman tragedians — 'no mechanical imitators', she says. An American scholar, W. C. Korfmacher, has considered the philosophical aspects of early Roman tragedy (Pr.APhA 65 (1934), li). A valuable general survey of Republican tragedy is given by K. Ziegler (1937) in RE, 2 R, 6 Bd. s.v. 'Tragoedia', xxii; and an Italian monograph by O. Coppola (*Il teatro tragico in Roma Repubblicana* — Bologna, Zanichelli, 1940), which the writer has not seen, appears to survey the same ground. Of the tragic fragments, which were re-edited by E. H. Warmington, inevitably those of Ennius have called forth most comment, especially his *Iphigeneia* and his *Medea Exul*.[85] Part of an American treatise, E. S. Duckett, *Studies in Ennius* (Bryn Mawr, Penn., 1918), criticized the view of Leo that the chorus in Ennius' plays had ceased to sing as a whole, but was represented by the recitative in some stichic metre of the coryphaeus or others. A reviewer of the work (CR 32 (1918), 46) observed: 'We still feel there is much force in Leo's contention that Ennian tragedy and Plautine comedy ran upon parallel lines ... Ennius, like Plautus, seeks for variety in long trochaic and long iambic lines delivered in recitative'. And (to speak of variety) Ed. Fraenkel in his article on Naevius in RE (Suppbd. VI, 622ff) observes that Naevius turned part of the dialogue of his model (tragic or comic) into cantica, as Ennius did later on. Another article concerning Ennian technique refers to his 'contaminatio' of Greek models.[86] And the native type of *praetexta*, attempted by most of the tragedians, has been the subject of various publications.[87]

But most of what has been produced in the field of Roman

s

tragedy has concerned the only surviving tragedies, those of the younger Seneca, and the only surviving praetexta, the *Octavia*. I preface two American comments. 'Hardly has any other Latin literature experienced such remote extremes of popularity and neglect in England as the tragedies of Seneca' (AJPh 26 (1905), 343). 'The preponderantly unfavourable attitude of critics to the tragedies of Seneca may be explained, at least in part, by the almost inevitable but nevertheless erroneous practice of judging these tragedies by a gauge that is alien to them' (*ibid.*, 60 (1939), 220). And an English comment: 'In these days, the usual response evoked by an allusion to the tragedies of Seneca is a grimace with the excuse, perhaps, that the literary expression of Seneca the tragedian may be described as itself perpetually one. But it is questionable whether this modern attitude is not almost as exaggerated as Scaliger's preference of Seneca to Euripides, and Heywood's raptures about "the flower of poets"' (F. L. Lucas, CR 35 (1921), 91). And a Dutch scholar's comment: 'Senecae tragoedias nostris temporibus magis magisque legi atque emendari coeptas esse magnopere gaudeo' (Mnem.NS 46 (1918), 428).

It is instructive to note the steady flow of editions,[88] translations,[89] and criticism since the second Teubner edition of the tragedies appeared in 1902. A good deal has been published on the text-tradition and textual criticism.[90] Scholars are much indebted to the Index Verborum produced by a group of American scholars.[91] There has been discussion of the separate plays,[92] notably *Hercules Oetaeus* and the allegedly Senecan *Octavia*, which can now claim a small library for itself. The work done has been truly international, as a reference to the bibliographies will indicate. If it is not invidious to select from so wide a field of comment, one would mention Ackermann, Canter, Herrmann, Miss B. M. Marti, Moricca, Münscher, and Pease. The fullest and most documented monograph is that of L. Herrmann, *Le Théâtre de Sénèque* (Paris, Les Belles Lettres, 1924). The best general survey in English is C. W. Mendell's *Our Seneca* (New Haven, Yale U. Pr., 1941). The contribution of English scholars is modest. The ripe comments of Butler and Summers are still valuable.[93] Widely praised has been the article of O. Regenbogen, 'Schmerz und Tod in den Tragödien Senecas' (Vort. Bibl. Warburg VII (1927-28), 167-218). 'This article represents perhaps the most important attempt at profound interpretation of the plays' (P. W. Harsh). Lastly may be mentioned the discussion of Senecan influence on the Elizabethan dramatists.

An initial problem is presented by the different order of the tragedies in the recensions *E* and *A*. No chronological order of the plays yet propounded has secured general approbation.[94]

It has been a more fiercely debated problem whether the tragedies were intended for performance. (It is, of course, impossible to discover whether they were produced.) There is not space to indicate all the lines of argument which have to do with internal evidence (structure, exits and entrances, style, etc.), practical difficulties and inherent probability or improbability. Herrmann devotes a long chapter (*op. cit.*, 152-232) to the question and decides that the evidence points towards production, and that there were no insuperable difficulties. The American scholar M. Hadas agrees that the tragedies were so intended and notes that the very conditions of presentation induced a tendency to melodrama, to passionate utterance and stark contrast; and that thus the plays answered a requirement in the early Empire as they did later in the Renascence ('The Roman Stamp of Seneca's Tragedies', AJPh 60 (1939), 220ff). Miss M. Bieber also concludes in favour of production (*op. cit.*, 397). An American writer, H. L. Cleasby, after examining the practical problems ('Scenery and Stage Properties in Seneca's Tragedies', Pr.APhA 42 (1911), xix-xxi), concluded that 'the detailed consideration of the scenery and stage properties in Seneca's tragedies confirms in no small degree the belief that Seneca wrote his plays, with the exception of the *Phoenissae* and the *Hercules Oetaeus*, with the intention of having them acted'; which is the compromise solution of Butler and others. But the general view inclines to 'tragédies de cabinet' (Nisard), or even 'tragedies written for the arm-chair' (Tyrrell). Mendell (*op. cit.*, 88) claims that they were intended for recitation; Beare in an astringent paragraph scouts the idea of stage-performance: '... It is incredible that Seneca, one of the richest men in Rome and a man who openly admits his distaste for close contact with the common people or their amusements, should have composed plays intended to win the favour of the general public ... There is no evidence that Seneca (or whoever the author was) was imitating the old Latin tragedies; the Senecan tragedies are simply artificial imitations of Greek tragedy, worked up in the style of the Silver

Age, and they are meant to be read or declaimed, not to be acted' (*op. cit.*, 227).

A third problem, still debated, is the genuineness of *Hercules Oetaeus*, which appears last in both the recensions *E* and *A* (as *Hercules Furens* appears first). It has many alleged idiosyncrasies: it lacks the 'three unities', it has a double chorus, it differs in sentiment and conception from the genuine tragedies, it is too verbally imitative of them, it has peculiarities of diction, it abandons the Sophoclean myth, the latter part of the play lacks the wonted *sententiae* and antitheses. Therefore it is regarded by some as posthumous and unrevised, or a mere sketch eked out by a continuator, or an interpolated play, or even completely non-Senecan, the work of an imitator. If it is not genuine, some suspicion is cast on the list of *E*. A reviewer (CR 27 (1913), 31) of O. Edert's dissertation on the two Hercules-tragedies observed: 'This is a question which has divided the learned in recent years: F. Leo says that no one who knows Seneca's style could imagine him to be the author: Ackermann denies that there is anything in the play "a Senecae ingenio atque indole alienum" '. W. C. Summers thought that Seneca left a rough draft which was supplemented so skilfully by the amplifier that the intertexture was very difficult to detect. Edert argued it to be the work of a man well acquainted with the *Hercules Furens* but not understanding its philosophy, one who made use of Seneca without skill. Undoubtedly (as Ackermann contends) the play enshrines a panegyric of Hercules the hero, who rose above human limitations, and so is the complement of the *Hercules Furens*. A. S. Pease adduced (TAPhA 49 (1918), 1-26) many verbal and metrical echoes of the other plays which he regarded as due neither to chance nor to imitation; he accepts the play as substantially Senecan; and so do Ackermann, Herrmann, Schanz, and others.

A greater problem is posed by the praetexta *Octavia*. Its notorious difficulties are its absence from *E* MSS., its anachronisms, its allusions, its different style, and the presence among the dramatis personae of Seneca himself. The evidence is again reviewed, and all the important literature up to date cited, in L. Herrmann's monograph, *Octavie, tragédie prétexte* (Paris, Les Belles Lettres, 1924). A Dutch, an Italian, and a German edition (1909, 1917, 1923) appeared before Herrmann re-edited the play (1926). Briefly, Herrmann concludes that the *Octavia* is not genuine, but the work of a pupil of Seneca, and written in the time of Vespasian. The general verdict today agrees that it is not genuine, but prior to 1924 three champions emerged: A. Siegmund, E. Flinck (a Finnish scholar) and A. S. Pease. The latter wrote: 'In general rhetorical character the play resembles the others, save that it is somewhat less turgid and artificial ... we may plausibly conjecture that the gain in sincerity is in part due to the fact that it is the poet's own experience rather than the unreal tales of mythology which are being depicted.' (CJ 15 (1919-20), 402); but he also admits it as a posthumous apologia of Seneca. F. L. Lucas, reviewing the controversy, dismissed it as spurious. 'Its spuriousness never needed the cumbrous engines of the learned critic to prove it; no one with any literary sense could credit the author of the lurid Thyestes with this simple little piece, pale and delicate as the figures on a Wedgwood vase. But attempts to father it on any known poet are futile guesswork; and even attempts to date it have varied from Nero's reign to the Middle Ages' (CR 35 (1921), 91). K. Münscher in the course of a long article in Philologus accepted it as genuine, but in Bursian's Jahresbericht of the same year (1922) he published a palinode. An Italian critic, V. Ciaffi, noting the lack of reference to Otho, suggested it was written in his reign — by Cornutus. Since the last war two new champions have appeared, a Norwegian, S. P. Thomas, and Miss B. M. Marti, who regards it as closely related to the *Apocolocyntosis*, a pseudo-drama rather than a praetexta, in fact a diatribe against Nero.[95] Her warning that it is not a genuine praetexta was already issued by Beare. 'It is doubtful whether there is any connection between this piece and the old Republican praetextae, which celebrated the achievements of Roman consuls in battle. The *Octavia* is a purely literary and artificial treatment of recent history on the lines of Greek tragedy' (*op. cit.*, 228).

The concluding observations concern the tragedies in general. It has often been asserted[96] that the substance of the philosophical works reappears in the tragedies (the problem of chronology arises here again); on the contrary, it has been asserted that Seneca is a more orthodox Stoic in his prose than in his plays (Mendell, *op. cit.*, 153). Seneca's preoccupation with death is stressed in the article of O. Regenbogen already cited; Regenbogen finds in the Senecan tragedy a new form, partly ethical, partly psychological, stamped by the reflections on suffering and death, freedom and tyranny, to which the Neronian epoch gave rise (cf. K. Ziegler, RE suppl. VI, A2, 2007). This article is indeed symptomatic of a re-assessment of the tragedies. Their Stoic ethos has been emphasized in several studies. Perhaps the most notable is B. M. Marti's article, 'Seneca's Tragedies. A New Interpretation' (TAPhA 76 (1945), 216-45). It was noted above that recensions *E* and *A* listed the tragedies differently; Miss Marti adheres to *E*. The foreword summarizes her argument: 'Seneca's aim in the tragedies as well as in the prose works was to teach neo-Stoicism. MS. *E* has preserved the order in which he intended the tragedies to be read. They form a series, introduced and concluded by a play on Hercules; within that frame the plays, each one illustrating some Stoic idea in dramatic form, are arranged according to a deliberate order. The *Troades* and *Phoenissae*, named after the chorus, are centred upon the problems of life, death, and destiny. The *Medea* and *Phaedra*, named after the heroines, provide exemplars for a treatise of the Passions. The last group (*Agamemnon, Oedipus, Thyestes*), named after the heroes, deals with the problem of free choice in life and of sin and retribution.' So then Seneca deals with Religion, Psychology, Ethics in that order. That Hercules should appear first and last is an interesting point; 'in the first tragedy Seneca has represented the passion and in the last the apotheosis of the patron saint of Stoicism, Hercules' (*ibid.*, 221). This thesis demands the genuiness of *Hercules Oetaeus*; 'Seneca has gathered together in the Hercules Oetaeus all the threads left loose in the preceding plays, and has given us an epitome of the Stoics' creed and an abstract of their wisdom' (*ibid.*, 241). Naturally Miss Marti does not subscribe to the assumption of M. Hadas that Seneca wrote solely to entertain; this, she says, is contrary to Seneca's idea of literature (*ibid.*, 217). Obviously the theory stands or falls by the order preserved in *E* — which may be Seneca's; and criticism has been offered. 'Beyond the mechanical difficulty involved in attaching such exact significance to manuscript sequence ... there seems to be some lack of clarity in the sequence of themes which she finds in the plays' (N. T. Pratt, 'The Stoic Base of Senecan Drama', TAPhA 79 (1948), 1). And Miss Marti scarcely strengthened her position in finding prototypes in the Cynic drama of myths and the pseudo-tragedies of Varro.[97] Also, while her first paper may provide an additional argument against Seneca's authorship of the *Octavia*, in the later paper (AJPhA 73 (1952) 24-36) the *Apocolocyntosis* and it form a pair, both genuine. Finally we mention two other articles with a Stoic bearing: one is concerned with Stoic ethical concepts, the other with the Stoic interest in physiognomy.[98] So much for the neo-Stoicism of the tragedies.

There are various publications devoted to aspects of the Senecan technique in tragedy. In a long series of articles[99] U. Moricca offers an encomium of Seneca, dealing with his development of action and character, the originality of his dramatic art, the Euripidean function of his chorus, and so forth. A monograph of 1933, with the same general theme, considers Senecca's handling of his Greek sources.[100] Two dissertations investigated the choral lyric.[101] A dissertation of N. T. Pratt examined Seneca's use of dramatic suspense,[102] the fundamental and necessary distinction being made of tragedies with a human or superhuman prologue, a distinction made too in the earlier dissertation of F. Frenzel on the Senecan prologues,[103] the nature of which has been much disputed. Frenzel sought to distinguish the Senecan and Euripidean prologues not only in respect of purpose, but also of form, extent, and relation to the rest of the play.

With regard to the structure of the plays, Herrmann pointed out that they consist of episodes rather than acts — which may amount even to six (*Oedipus*) — and are of very disparate length, that MSS. and editors are at variance in the limits of scenes, and that there is no uniformity in the ratio of lyric and dramatic elements (*op. cit.*, 336ff). As to the famous 'unities' there is much dispute; A. Marek found[104] infraction of one or other in several of the plays; there is the notorious infraction of the unity of place in the *Hercules Oetaeus*. Reviewing the evidence, Herrmann rather lamely concluded that Seneca observes the unities 'avec une rigueur suffisante, sans aucune infraction grave, malgré les inconvenients qui devaient en resulter pour lui'.

In the matter of exits and entrances Seneca has long been accused of imprecision. 'Seneca did not consider it necessary to name characters. This, with the large amount of description, suggests that the plays were written for reading.'[105] The plays being drawn from Greek myths, some of the characters are superhuman and part of the action is supernatural. The author of a dissertation on the supernatural of the tragedies goes on to point out that the

Octavia differs from the tragedies in its use of allegorical dreams and apparitions in the course of the play, more conformable to Greek usage than that of Seneca.[106]

Then as to language, style, and metre. A Polish scholar's monograph on Seneca's trimeters has been warmly praised.[107] On the language and style of the tragedies a detailed and critical account is given by Herrmann (*op. cit.*, 529-51); he alleges that the language of the tragedies is more traditional, more conservative than that of the philosophical works. The outstanding feature of that style is due to the influence of rhetorical training; for a study of this the indispensable modern work is H. V. Canter's *Rhetorical Elements in the Tragedies of Seneca* (Urbana, Univ. of Illin., 1925).

It is the preponderance of rhetoric, often turgid, in the tragedies which called forth the well-known and acid comment of Mackail (*Latin Literature*, 175). A kinder estimate is found in Butler's *Post-Augustan Poetry* (49-69). Yet Butler admits that 'to Seneca more than to any other man is due the excessive predominance of exclamatory rhetoric, which has characterized the drama throughout Western Europe from the Renaissance down to the latter half of the nineteenth century'. It was just this orotund rhetorical style which captured the fancy of the Elizabethans, though it stifled the dramatic action. 'In the plays of Seneca the drama is all in the word, and the word has no further reality behind it. His characters all seem to speak with the same voice, and at the top of it; they recite in turn' (T. S. Eliot).

The influence of Senecan tragedy on Elizabethan drama lies outside the scope of classical scholarship, but mention may be made of 'Senecan Tragedy' (G. S. Gordon) in *English Literature and the Classics* (O.U.P., 1911), pp. 228-47, of F. L. Lucas's book, *Seneca and Elizabethan Tragedy* (C.U.P., 1922), and T. S. Eliot's essay, 'Seneca in Elizabethan Translation', originally printed as introduction to the Tudor Translation Series edition of the *Tenne Tragedies*.

In conclusion we refer to some publications in which the output of works on Seneca's tragedies during the last half-century may be conveniently reviewed.[108]

---

[1] 'Représente le dernier mot de la critique plautinienne' (N. I. Herescu).
[2] Cf. N. I. Herescu, *Bibliographie de la Littérature Latine* (1943), pp. 14-19.
[3] Other editions of the *Captivi* are the seventh Teubner ed. (Brix–Niemeyer–Kohler, 1930), and those of J. P. Waltzing (Paris, Champion, 1926) and Havet–Freté–

Nougaret (Paris, Budé, 1932). Among other edd. of popular plays are: *Menaechmi* (Teubner, 6th ed. Brix–Niemeyer–Conrad, 1929); N. Moseley–M. Hammond (Cambridge, Mass., Harv. U.P. 1933). *Mostellaria*, E. A. Sonnenschein, 2nd ed. (Oxford, Clarendon Press, 1907), M. Schuster–F. Schupp (Wien, Leipzig, Oesterr. Bundesverlag, 1934); *Trinummus*, Teubner, 6th ed. (Brix–Niemeyer–Conrad, 1931), J. P. Waltzing 3rd ed. (Paris, Les Belles Lettres, 1930). There is a critical ed. of the *Asinaria* (L. Havet–A. Freté, Paris, Budé, 1925).
⁴ Other editions: *Eunuchus* (G. B. Bonino, Roma-Milano, Albrighi-Segati, 1910); *Adelphi* (K. Dziatzko–R. Kauer, Teubner, 1921, 2nd ed.); *Heautontimorumenos* (F. G. Bellentine, Boston, Sanborn, 1910); *Hecyra* (S. Stella, Milano, Signorelli, 1936); *Phormio* (K. Dziatzko–E. Hauler, 4th ed., Teubner, 1913).
⁵ G. E. Duckworth, *The Nature of Roman Comedy*, 256n.
⁶ 'Although *retractatio* for a time proved a most convenient means of explaining Plautine contradictions and repetitions, the more recent tendency has been to reject it as a significant factor in Plautine criticism. As Miss Coulter says, "on the whole, the *retractatores* made no very important contributions to our text", and modern editors are far more conservative in their retention of the text as Plautine than were their nineteenth-century predecessors. The scholarly pendulum swings, and what seemed of vital significance in 1875 was hardly noticed in 1925, when scholars, working with the same or similar repetitions and discrepancies, found their answers in *contaminatio* and careless workmanship on Plautus' part rather than in the re-working of comedies in the revival period. That the newer theories were equally extreme and just as unreliable is maintained by many critics today. The importance of *retractatio* was exaggerated in the nineteenth century, but the reaction to it in the early twentieth century went too far; as a possible explanation for variant lines and dittographies, awkwardly inserted jests, and passages that lack Plautus' style and expression it still deserves consideration' (Duckworth, *op. cit.*, 68).
⁷ K. F. Weston, 'The illustrated Terence manuscripts', HSCPh 14 (1903) 37-54; Pl. 1-96.
J. C. Watson, 'Scene headings and miniatures in the MSS of Terence', *ibid.*, 55-172.
O. Engelhardt, *Die Illustrationen des Terenzhandschriften* (Jena, 1905).
These were followed by L. W. Jones–C. R. Morey, *The Miniatures of the Manuscripts of Terence prior to the thirteenth century* (Princeton, U.P. 1930-31. 2 vols.) . . . 'travail qui inaugure une ère nouvelle dans l'histoire du texte de Térence' (A. Ernout). On the folio reproduction of the famous Vatican illustrated Terence (*C*) (Leipzig, Harrasowitz 1929) see C. P. Morey, 'The Vatican Terence', ClPh 26 (1931) 374-85. And cf. Marouzeau, *Térence*, coll. Budé, I, intro. 84-5.
⁸ The references are:

NAEVIUS	1926-1930 (K. Glaser)	Bd. 242 (1934)	56-57
PLAUTUS	1895-1906 (W. M. Lindsay)	Bd. 130 (1906)	116-282
	1907-1911 (W. M. Lindsay)	Bd. 167 (1914)	1-158
	1912-1920 (O. Kohler)	Bd. 192 (1922)	1-45
	1921-1925 (O. Kohler)	Bd. 217 (1928)	57-81
	1926-1934 (F. Conrad)	Bd. 247 (1935)	63-93
TERENCE	1898-1905 (R. Kauer)	Bd. 143 (1909)	176-269
SENECA (Tragedies and *Octavia*)			
	1903-1906 (J. Tolkiehn)	Bd. 134 (1907)	197-204
	1907-1910 (J. Tolkiehn)	Bd. 158 (1912)	1-20
	1911-1914 (K. Münscher)	Bd. 171 (1915)	15-30
	1915-1921 (K. Münscher)	Bd. 192 (1922)	185-214

⁹ Yet in his review Phillimore was complimentary: 'A book which truly marks an epoch, not only in Terentian studies, but in the movement of scholarship and literary criticism . . . We shall hear more of this'. CR 39 (1925) 41. The last sentence was prophetic.
¹⁰ Reviewed by G. Norwood, Univ. Tor. Q'ly., 13 (1943-44), 235-41, and (unfavourably) by W. H. Alexander, AJPh 66 (1945), 96-100.
¹¹ Review by G. E. Duckworth, AJPh 70 (1949), 221-4.
¹² 'A convenient collection of the pertinent material' (Duckworth).

[13] Cf. L. R. Taylor: 'The Opportunities for Dramatic Performances in the Time of Plautus and Terence', TAPhA 44 (1913), 87-97.
[14] Cf. his art. 'Masks on the Roman Stage', CQ 33 (1939), 139-146.
[15] W. W. Mooney, *The Housedoor on the Ancient Stage* (Diss.) (Baltimore, Williams & Wilkins Co., 1914).
[16] 'Its special significance in drama is to denote the back-street supposed to run behind the houses which face on to the stage, connecting them by means of their backdoors and gardens with each other and also with the town, harbour and country. The angiportus is not shown and could not be shown to the eye; its use is exceptional, and requires mention; it is a device which enables the dramatist to escape at times from the general rule that a character who leaves the stage by a particular door or wing must return by the same door or wing' (*op. cit.*, 173).
[17] Cf. E. F. Rambo, 'The Significance of the Wing-entrances in Roman Comedy', ClPh 4 (1909), 355-389; P. W. Harsh, 'Angiportus, Platea, and Vicus', ClPh 32 (1937), 44-58.
[18] Cf. V. E. Hiatt, *Eavesdropping in Roman Comedy* (Chicago, 1946).
[19] Cf. W. Beare, 'Seats in Greek and Roman Theatres', CR 53 (1939), 51ff. G. E. Duckworth, *Nature of Roman Comedy*, 81.
[20] Cf. H. W. Prescott, 'Three *Puer*-Scenes in Plautus, and the Distribution of Roles'. HSCPh 21 (1910), 31-50; and cf. 'The Doubling of Roles in Roman Comedy', ClPh 18 (1923), 23-34.
[21] 'Link Monologues in Roman Comedy', ClPh 34 (1939), 1-23, 116-26; 'Exit Monologues in Roman Comedy', ClPh 36 (1942) 1-121. He refers to F. Leo, 'Der Monolog im Drama', *Abh. Ges. Gött.* X, 5 (1908), and to W. Schadewalt, 'Monolog und Selbstgesprach', AGWG. II (Berlin, 1926). In the relevant literature 'monologue' and 'soliloquy' are sometimes used interchangeably; but it is better to understand the former to mean an address to the audience, to a god and so forth, the latter as a self-communing under stress of emotion. Bickford, using the term soliloquy quite generally, attempted to classify the soliloquies of Plautus and Terence according to their context (J. D. Bickford, *Soliloquy in Ancient Comedy* (Princeton Univ. Diss. 1922)).
[22] Cf. H. Siess, 'Ueber die Charakterzeichnung in den Komödien des Terenz', *Wien. St.*, 28 (1906), 229-262; 29 (1907), 81-100, 289-320.
[23] Weissmann, *De servi currentis persona apud comoedos Romanos* (Giessen, 1911). For bibl. see G. E. Duckworth, 'Dramatic Function of the *servus currens*' in *Classical Studies presented to Ed. Capps* (Princeton Univ. Press, 1936), 93-102. Cf. Ed. Fraenkel, *Plaut. im P.* viii 'Die Vorherrschaft der Sklavenrolle'.
[24] O. Stolz, *De lenonis in comoedia figura* (Darmstadt, 1920).
[25] J. O. Lofberg, 'The Sycophant-Parasite', ClPh 15 (1920), 61-77.
[26] P. L. Dunkin, *Post-Aristophanic Comedy* (Univ. of Ill. Pr. 1946).
[27] Cf. Legrand-Loeb, *The New Greek Comedy*, 393ff; Michaut, *Plaute*, II 116ff.
[28] The work was praised by A. Freté, REL 14 (1936), 41f. See the summary account, 'Foreshadowing and Suspense', ch. 8 of Duckworth's *The Nature of Roman Comedy*.
[29] W .W. Blancke, *The Dramatic Values in Plautus* (Diss., U. of Penn. Geneva, N. York, Humphrey, 1918). A. Freté, 'Essai sur la structure dramatique de Plaute', REL 7 (1929), 282-94; 8 (1930), 36-81. J. N. Hough, 'The Development of Plautus' Art', ClPh 30 (1935), 42-57; 'The Understanding of Intrigue; a Study in Plautine Chronology', AJPh 60 (1939), 422ff.
[30] E.g. by P. Faider, *Musée Belge* 13 (1909), 33ff.
[31] 'Terence's failure to achieve the popular acclaim which had come to his predecessor, though not without other bases too, may have been due in part to a too rapid continuation of Plautus's tendency to leave more and more to the audience's understanding' (J. N. Hough, AJPh 60 (1939), 435).
[32] Cf. R. C. Flickinger, 'On the Originality of Terence', PhQ 7 (1928), 97-114.
[33] Cf. H. R. Clifford, 'Dramatic Technique and the Originality of Terence', CJ 26 (1930-31) 605-18. E. K. Rand, 'The Art of Terence's *Eunuchus*', TAPhA 63 (1932), 54-72 — 'an excellent appreciation but Rand goes too far in finding Terentian originality' (P. W. Harsh). P. J. Enk, 'Terence as an adaptor of Greek comedies', *Mnem.* (1947), 81-93. W. Beare, 'Terence, an original Dramatist in Rome', *Herm.* 71 (1948), 64-82.

[34] A. Körte, 'Contaminare', BPhW 36 (1916), 979-81. J. B. Hofmann, 'Contaminare', IF 53 (1935), 187-95. R. Waltz, '*Contaminare* chez Térence', REL 16 (1938), 269-74.

[35] 'Das vornehmste Beispiel plautinischer Kontamination stellt der *Miles* dar, deswegen weil hier die Arbeitsweise des römischen Dichter in allen wesentlichen Punkten klar erkennen ist' (*ibid.*, 162). For opinions *pro* and *con.* see Enk, *op. cit.*, II, 2, 52-4.

[36] 'I deplore', he says, 'the tendency of scholars, who, like Jachmann, in their search for arguments to bolster up their individual theories of *contaminatio*, ascribe to Plautus faults of which he is not guilty, or wrongly interpret passages to which there are other more likely explanations. It is particularly unfortunate when their criticisms deny artistic merit to such an excellent and effective comedy as the *Miles Gloriosus*' (*ib.*, 230).

[37] Cf. Michaut, *Plaute*, ii, ch. 16.

[38] Cf. 'Contaminatio in Plautus and Terence', RevPh 3rd. S. 14 (1940), 28-42; *op. cit.*, 100-4.

[39] 'The Interpretation of Roman Comedy' (ClPh XI (1916), 125-47. 'The Antecedents of Hellenistic Comedy' (*ibid.*, XII (1917), 405-25; XIII (1918), 113-37; XIV (1919), 108-135. Cf. K. M. Westaway, *The Original Element in Plautus* (C.U.P., 1917).

[40] About the same time the author of another dissertation examined the prologues of Terence with a chronological aim; W. Meyer, *Quaestiones Terentianae*, Diss. Leipzig, 1902: pp. 5-61 'ex prologis Terentianis quid de ordine fabularum chronologico discamus'.

[41] W. B. Sedgwick, 'The Cantica of Plautus', CR 39 (1925), 53-8; cf. 'The dating of Plautus' plays', CQ 24 (1930), 102-5.

[42] 'Plautine Chronology', AJPh 70 (1949), 376-84.

[43] 'The use of Greek words by Plautus', AJPh 55 (1934), 346-64. 'The Development of Plautus' Art', ClPh 30 (1935), 43-57. 'The Understanding of Intrigue. A Study in Plautine Chronology', AJPh 60 (1939), 422-35. 'Link Monologues and Plautine Chronology', TAPhA 70 (1939), 231-41. 'Miscellanea Plautina', *ibid.*, 71 (1940), 186-98. 'The Reverse Comic Foil in Plautus', *ibid.*, 73 (1942), 108-18.

[44] Cf. A. Mattingly and E. S. G. Robinson, CR 47 (1933), 52f. T. Frank, AJPh 54 (1933), 368-72; 56 (1935), 225-31. W. Beare, CR 48 (1934), 123f.

[45] CR 42 (1928), 214-15.

[46] K. H. E. Schutter, *Quibus annis Comoediae Plauti primum gestae sint quaeritur* (Groningen, Dewaal, 1951).

[47] R. C. Flickinger, 'A Study of Terence's prologues', *Philol. Q'ly.*, 1927, 235-69. N. Terzaghi, *Prolegomeni a Terenzio* (Torino, 1931). L. Gestri, 'Studi terenziani: la cronologia', *Stud. ital. fil. class.* 1936, 61-105; R. Blum, 'Studi terenziani: didascalie e prologhi', *ibid.*, 106-16; F. Arnaldi, *Da Plauto a Terenzio*, II, 109ff.

[48] A harsher rebuke has been administered: 'in metrics Lindsay is an empiricist without any comprehensive body of formal doctrine. The newer movements in metrics are away from Lindsay. He has given us an easy exposition of a simplified Plautine problem'. G. H. Taylor, reviewing *E.L.V.*, AJPh 45 (1924), 299.

[49] Cf. his 'Bemerkungen zur plautinischen Prosodie' *Rh. Mus.* 71 (1917), 527-47.

[50] 'It is scarcely possible any longer to doubt that accent was an important feature of early dramatic verse; the quantitative nature of the measures was carefully preserved, but at the same time accent was constantly taken into account ... It was no doubt expiratory and musical at the same time; which element was the stronger we have no way of determining' (ibid., 244).

[51] Reviews in AJPh 50 (1929) 95ff. (Sturtevant), 55 (1934) 86ff (Radford).

[52] So W. Beare reviewing Drexler's work: 'His (sc. Fraenkel's) fundamental doctrine was that metrical ictus coincided completely, or almost completely, with accent, the accent that is of the words as grouped together in verse, not that which they would bear if pronounced separately. The difference between the word-accent and what we may call the verse-accent he explained in various ways ... Drexler proposed to trace the shift of accent in every case to the principle of syntactical group-unity. He assumes the identity of ictus and accent and endeavours to show that his assumption is justified by results ... Briefly the theme of the work is that the Latin stress-accent was in Plautus' time a group-accent, the group being syntactical; the group-accent is faithfully reflected by the verse ictus of drama; and that there are a few general rules which

govern the accent of word-groups. In studying them we are studying the living language that was heard in third-century Rome'. 'How far-fetched Drexler's reasoning becomes at times', he complains. (CR 48 (1934) 72-74.)

[53] 'This paper argues that although the Latin accent was clearly one of stress, the evidence for stress ictus in dialogue verse is extremely weak. The high degree of harmony of ictus and accent which had principally supported belief in a stress accent may be purely accidental, while at line-closes there is no clear attempt on the part of Plautus and Terence to attain harmony' (ibid., 127) '... there is nothing in Fraenkel's work nor in any previous or subsequent work to prove the stress ictus in Latin verse' (ibid., 140).

[54] The author observes (9n) 'The final and most disputable question is this. Did "metrical stress" occur in Latin, and was it ever so strong as to modify or change the accent of a word?'

[55] Cf. W. A. Laidlaw, 'Jacobsohn's Law of Plautine Scansion', CQ 30 (1936) 33ff; *The Prosody of Terence*, 61.

[56] For other publications regarding the metre of dialogue verse see P. J. Enk, *op. cit.*, II, 2, 312-15.

[57] Cf. Enk, *op. cit.*, II, 2, 315f.

[58] 'Es ist das Singspiel der zu seiner Zeit lebendingen griechischen Bühne, deren musikalische Form Plautus der menandrischen Komödie aufgeproft hat.'

[59] *Zur Frage der plautinischen Cantica* (SHAW 1923, Abh. 7, 1-41). Cf. Sedgwick, CR 39 (1925) 57; 'taken in conjunction with Fraenkel's *Plautinisches im Plautus*, it very much restricts the influence of the Hellenistic music-hall stage'.

[60] 'Vom Bau der Plautinischen Cantica', *Philologus*, 84 (1929) 300-19, 430-63; 85 (1930) 65-84.

[61] Cf. 'Whatever the origin of the metres — whether in Greek tragedy, or in New Comedy, or in Alexandrian or Italian mime — the distinctive feature of the Latin cantica is the use of metrical variety to produce dramatic effects' (*ibid.*, 212n).

[62] Favourably reviewed CR 44 (1930) 24f.

[63] Cf. 'Ever since Ritschl brought the study of Plautus into fashion monographs of special points of Plautine syntax have been appearing with bewildering frequency and, consequently, not the least merit of W. M. Lindsay's recent book on the Syntax of Plautus (1907) is its collection in convenient summaries of the main conclusions reached by the authors of these monographs'. R. C. Flickinger, AJPh 29 (1908) 303.

[64] F. Conrad, 'Die Diminutiven in Altlatein: Die Diminutiven bei Plautus', *Glotta*, 19 (1930-31) 127-48; 20 (1931-32) 74-80.

[65] C. J. Mendelsohn, *Studies in the Word-Play in Plautus* (Philadelphia, U. of Penn. 1907). J. M. G. M. Brinkhoff, *Woordspeling bij Plautus* (Nijmegen, Diss. 1935).

[66] B. L. Ullman, 'Proper Names in Plautus and Terence and Menander', ClPh 11 (1916) 61-4. Cp. J. C. Austin, *The Significant Name In Terence* (Urbana, U. of Ill. 1922).

[67] H. Thomsen, *Pleonasmus bei Plautus und Terentius* (Uppsala, Almquist & Wiksells, 1930).

[68] L. Gurlitt 'Plautinische Studien', *Philol.* 72 (1913) 224-49. Cf. his *Erotica Plautina: eine Auswahl erotischer Szenen aus Plautus übersetzt und erklärt* (München, Müller, 1921).

[69] F. Leo, *PF²* 132-40. Ed. Fraenkel, *Pl. im Pl.* 88ff. W. B. Sedgwick, 'Parody in Plautus', CQ 21 (1927) 88-100. A. Thierfielder, 'Plautus und römische Tragödie', *Herm.* 74 (1939) 155-66.

[70] Cf. H. T. Rowell, 'Accius and the *Faeneratrix* of Plautus', AJPh 73 (1952) 268-80.

[71] P. Faider, 'Le comique de Plaute', *Musée Belge*, 31 (1927) 61-75. E. de St. Denis, 'La force comique de Plaute', *Mélanges de Philologie, de Littérature et d'Histoire ancienne offerts à Alfred Ernout* (Paris, Klincksieck, 1940) 331-44.

[72] J. N. Hough, 'The Reverse Comic Foil in Plautus', TAPhA 73 (1942) 108ff.

[73] A. Barbieri, *La Vis Comica in Terenzio* (Milan, Paideia, 1951).

[74] Cf. L. Bernard-R. Dareste, *Le droit romain et le droit grec dans le théâtre de Plaute et de Térence* (Lyon, Rey, 1900).

O. Fredershausen, *De Iure Plautino et Terentiano* (Göttingen, (Diss.) 1906); *id.*, 'Weiter Studien über das Recht bei Plautus und Terentius', *Herm.* 47 (1912) 199-249.

F. Stella-Maranca, 'I poeti di Puglia e il diritto di Roma', *Hist.* 1934, 52-63.

[75] W. Green, 'Greek and Roman Law in the *Trinummus* of Plautus', ClPh 24 (1929) 183-92.
[76] Cf. A. Schwind, *Ueber das Recht bei Terenz* (Diss., Würzburg, 1901) Ed. Cuq, 'La jurisdiction des édiles d'après Plaute, Ménechmes, v. 590-593.' REA 21 (1919) 249ff.
J. Partsch, 'Römisches und griechisches Recht in Plautus Persa', *Herm.* 45 (1910) 595-614.
F. Stella-Maranca, 'Il diritto ereditario e le commedie di Plauto' *Hist.* 6 (1932) 508-29.
J. van Kan, 'La possession dans les comédies de Plaute', *Mélanges Cornil* (Ghent, Vanderpoorten, 1926).
M. Berceanu, *La vente consensuelle dans les comédies de Plaute* (Paris, Rivière, 1907).
P. Olagnier, *Les incapacités des acteurs et le droit romain* (Paris, 1910).
[77] Cf. 'Greek Law in Roman comedy', ClPh 5 (1910) 367.
[78] 'References to Painting in Plautus and Terence', ClPh 12 (1917) 143-57. 'References in Plautus and Terence to Plays, Players, and Playwrights', *ibid.*, 14 (1919) 35-55. 'En réunissant les passages où Plaute et Térence s'adressent au public, on apprend beaucoup sur les représentations de l'antiquité' (Marouzeau).
[79] 'Travel in ancient times as seen in Plautus and Terence', ClPh 2 (1907) 1-24; 281-304.
[80] 'References to literature in Plautus and Terence', AJPh 40 (1919) 231-62.
[81] 'The use of Greek Words by Plautus', AJPh 55 (1934) 346-64. Here indeed Hough was preceded by H. M. Hopkins, TAPhA 29 (1898) xiv. Cf. J. B. Hofmann, 'Griechisches im Plautus', *Glotta*, 25 (1934) 67-71; also F. Middelmann, *Griechische Welt und Sprache in Plautus Komödien* (Bochum, Langendreer, 1935). J. N. Hough, 'Terence's use of Greek words', CW 41 (1947-48) 18-21.
[82] A long review by G. E. Duckworth, AJPh 68 (1947) 419-26. Cf. his 'Wealth and Poverty in Roman Comedy', in *Studies in Roman Economic and Social History in honor of Allen Chester Johnson* (Princeton, Pr. Univ. Pr. 1951) 36-8; 'Certainly, from the evidence of the plays, we are not justified in drawing conclusions about the attitude of either Roman playwright toward the wealthy citizens of his day' (*ibid.*, 48). Cf. CR 62 (1948) 18f.
[83] L. Robinson, *Freedom of speech in the Roman Republic* (Baltimore, 1940). Reviewed JRS 1942, 120ff.
[84] A. Rostagni, 'Equos Troianus sive de vetere Romanorum fabula ex Hellenisticis expressa', *Riv. filol.* 44 (1916).
[85] v. E. H. Warmington, *Remains of Old Latin*, II, 46-155; I. Vahlen, *Ennianae Poesis Reliquiae*[3] (Leipzig, Teubner, 1928); Bibl., v. Enk, *op. cit.*, II, i, 85-9.
F. Skutsch, 'Zu Ennius Iphigeneia', RhM 61 (1906) 608-19; N. L. Drabkin, *The Medea Exul of Ennius* (Diss.) Geneva, N. Y. Humphrey Press, 1937.
[86] N. Terzaghi, 'La tecnica tragica di Ennio', *Stud. ital. fil. class.*, 1928, 175-96.
[87] A. Silvani, *La Pretesta* (Florence, 1903); M. L. Pasculli, *Studio sulla fabula praetexta* (Palermo, 1921).
M. Lenchantin de Gubernatis, *Riv. Filol.* 40 (1912) 445ff; K. Ziegler, *RE.* 2 R, 6 Bd. (1937) s.v. 'Tragoedia', xxiii.
[88] G. Richter, *L. Annaei Senecae Tragoediae*[2] (Leipzig, Teubner, 1902); H. M. Kingery, *Three Tragedies of Seneca* (N. York, Macmillan, 1908); F. J. Miller, *Seneca's Tragedies* (Loeb ed. 1917; II[2] 1929); U. Moricca, *L. A. Senecae Thyestes Phaedra* (Torino, Paravia, 1917); L. Herrmann, *Sénèque, Tragédies* (Paris, Budé, 1924-26); M. Schmitt-Hartlieb, *L. A. Senecae, Die Troerinnen* (Tübingen, H. Laupp, 1935); U. Moricca, *Senecae Tragoediae* (Torino, Paravia, 1947).
[89] W. Bradshaw, *The Tenne Tragedies of Seneca* (London, Swan Sonnenschein, 1902); E. I. Harris, *The Tragedies of Seneca* (London, Frowde, 1904); F. J. Miller, *The Tragedies of Seneca Translated into English Verse* (Chicago, Un. of Chic. Pr., 1907); E. M. Spearing, *The Elizabethan Translations of Seneca's Tragedies* (Cambridge, Heffer, 1912); F. J. Miller, *Seneca's Tragedies* (Loeb, v.s.); T. Newton, *Seneca his Tenne Tragedies* (London & N. York, 1927, Tudor Trs. 2nd ser. 11 & 12); M. Mignon, *Sénèque, Tragédies* (Paris, Garnier, 1938); G. E. Duckworth, *The Complete Roman Drama* (N. York, Random House, 1942, vol. 2).
[90] There is general reliance (with Leo) on the recension *E*. U. Moricca thinks more highly than Leo did of the inferior interpolated *A*. Cf. G. Richter, 1902, pref. xvii;

P. Koetschau, 'Zu Senecas Tragödien' (*Philol.* 61 (1902) 133ff); T. Düring, 'Die Ueberlieferung des interpolirten Textes von Senecas Tragödien', *Herm.* 42 (1907) 113-26, 579-94; C. E. Stuart, 'Notes and emendations . . .' CQ 5 (1911) 32-41; 'The MSS of the interpolated (*A*) tradition of the Tragedies of Seneca' *ibid.*, 6 (1912) 1-20; H. W. Garrod, 'Seneca Tragoedus again' CQ 5 (1911) 209-19; T. Düring, 'Zur Ueberlieferung von Senecas Tragödien', *Herm.* 47 (1912) 183-98; W. Hoffa, 'Textkritische Untersuchungen zu Senecas Tragödien', *Herm.* 49 (1914) 464-75. A. E. Housman, 'Notes on Seneca's Tragedies', CQ 17 (1923) 163-72; L. Herrmann, Budé ed. I, viii-xiii; G. Carlsson, *Die Ueberlieferung der Senecas Tragödien. Eine textkritische Untersuchung* (Lund, Gleerup, 1926).

[91] G. A. Oldfather, A. S. Pease, H. V. Canter, *Index verborum quae in Senecae fabulis necnon in Octavia praetexta reperiuntur*, Univ. of Illin. Stud., 1918.

[92] *HERC. FUR.* — J. Mesk, 'Senecas Apocolocyntosis und Hercules Furens', *Philol.* 71 (1912) 361-75.
TROAD. — A. Balsamo, 'De Senecae fabula quae Troades inscribitur', *Stud. it. filol.*, 1902, 41-53.
PHOEN. — U. Moricca, 'Le Fenicie di Seneca', *Riv. Fil.* 45 (1917) 467-515, 46 (1918) 1-40.
MED. — C. Knapp, 'Notes on the Medea of Seneca', TAPhA 33 (1902) viii-x; F. Pasini, ' "La Medea" di Seneca e Apollonio Rodio', *Aten. e Rom.* 5 (1902) 567-75; A. Cima, 'La Medea di Seneca e la Medea di Ovidio', *Aten. e Rom.* 7 (1904) 224-9, 11 (1908) 64-8; H. L. Cleasby, 'The Medea of Seneca', HSClPh. 18 (1907) 39-71; 'the purpose of this article is to analyse Seneca's Medea with particular attention to the two chief sources, Euripides and Ovid'. Cf. *Aten. e Rom.* 10 (1907) 306-7; T. Vente, *Die Medea-Tragödie Senecas. Eine Quellenstudie* (Strassburg, 1909).
PHAEDR. — U. Moricca, 'Le fonti della Fedra di Seneca', *Stud. ital. fil. cl.* 21 (1915) 158-224.
AGAM. — C. Brakmann, 'De Senecae Agamemnone', Mn. (1914) 392-8.
THYEST. — C. Marchesi, *Il Tieste di L. Anneo Seneca* (Catania, 1908); A. Lesky, 'Die griechischen Pelopindendramen und Senecas Thyestes', *Wien. Stud.* 34 (1912) 172-98; O. Gigon, 'Bemerkungen zu Senecas Thyestes', *Philol.* 93 (1938) 176-83.
HERC. OET. — W. C. Summers, 'The Authorship of the H.O.', CR 19 (1905) 41-54; cf. E. Ackermann, 'De Senecae Hercule Oetaeo', *Philol.* Suppl. 10 (1907) 408ff; O. Edert, *Über Senecas Hercules Herakles und den Herakles auf den Oeta*, Diss. Kiel, 1909; E. Ackermann, 'Der leidende Herakles des Seneca', *Rh. Mus.* 67 (1912) 425-71; A. S. Pease, 'On the Authenticity of the Hercules Oetaeus', TAPhA 49 (1918) 3-26; L. Herrmann, *Le Théâtre de Sénèque*, 49-57, 319-26; A. Morpugo, 'Le Trachinie di Sofocle e l'Ercole Eteo di Seneca', *Aten. e Rom.* 10 (1929) 87-115; E. Caesare, *Le Tragedie di Seneca* (Palermo, pr. l'autore, 1932), 30-44; V. Jorio, 'L'autenticità della tragedia "Hercules Oetaeus" di Seneca', *Riv. Ind. Grec. Ital.* 20 (1936) 1-59; U. Moricca, *Med.* etc. (1947) intro. xxxi-xlv; B. M. Marti, 'Place de l'Hercule sur l'Oeta dans le Corpus des Tragédies de Sénèque', REL. 27 (1949) 189-210.

[93] H. E. Butler, *Post-Augustan Poetry from Seneca to Juvenal* (Oxford, Clarendon Press, 1909); W. C. Summers, *The Silver Age of Latin Literature* (London, Methuen, 1920).

[94] Cf. K. Münscher, 'Senecas Werke: Untersuchungen zur Abfassungszeit und Echtheit', *Phil.* Suppl. 16 (1923) 84-143; Herrmann, *Théâtre de Sénèque*, 78-147; O. Herzog, 'Datierung der Tragödien des Seneca', *Rh. Mus.* 77 (1928) 51-104; E. Hansen, *Die Stellung der Affektrede in den Tragödien des Seneca* (Diss., Berlin, 1934) 64-77.

[95] K. Münscher, 'Senecas Werke. Untersuchungen zur Abfassungsheit und Echtheit', *Philol. Suppl.* XVI, 1 (1923) 126-42; *id.*, JAW 192 (1922) 198-211; V. Ciaffi, 'Intorno all'Autore dell'Octavia', *Riv. filol.*, 65 (1937) 246-65; S. Pantzerhielm Thomas, 'De Octavia Praetexta', *Symb.* Oslo. 24, (1945) 48-87; B. M. Marti, 'Seneca's Apocolocyntosis and Octavia: a Diptych', AJPh 73 (1952) 24-36.

[96] See P. Schaefer, *De Philosophiae Anneanae in Senecae Tragoediis Vestigiis* (Diss., Jena, Weida, 1909); P. B. Steele, 'Some Roman elements in the tragedies of Seneca', AJPh 43 (1922) 1-32. — 'The tragedies are political essays in which Seneca assigns to Greek characters his own views in regard to Roman conditions . . . The general view of life is the same for Seneca the philosopher as for Seneca the writer of tragedies' (*ibid.*, 30). Cf. M. Hadas, 'The Roman stamp of Seneca's Tragedies', AJPh 60 (1939) 220-31.

⁹⁷ See 'The Prototypes of Seneca's Tragedies', ClPh. 42 (1947) 1-16; 'in the tragedies he borrowed Varro's and Diogenes' method of teaching through dramatized myths, the subject-matter, and the strong philosophical cast of their works, but departed drastically from the spirit of the Varronian and Cynic pseudo-tragedy, which was humorous and often coarse' (*ibid.*, 15).
⁹⁸ R. A. Pack, 'On guilt and error in Senecan Tragedy', TAPhA 71 (1940) 360-71. E. C. Evans, 'A Stoic Aspect of Senecan Drama: Portraiture', TAPhA 81 (1950) 69-184.
⁹⁹ *Riv. fil.* 46 (1918) 345-52, 411-46; 48 (1920) 74-94; 49 (1921) 161-94.
¹⁰⁰ W. H. Friedrich, *Untersuchungen zu Senecas dramatischer Technik* (Borna–Leipzig, Noska, 1933).
¹⁰¹ W. Marx, *Funktion und Form der Chorlieder in den Seneca-Tragödien*, Diss., Heidelberg-Köln, Kappes, 1932; B. Bussfeld, *Die polymetrischen Chorlieder in Sen. Oedipus und Agam.*, Diss., Münster, 1935.
¹⁰² N. T. Pratt, *Dramatic Suspense in Seneca and in his Greek Precursors* (Princeton, Pr. Un. Pr. 1939).
¹⁰³ F. Frenzel, *Die Prologe der Tragödien Senecas* (Diss., Leipzig-Weida u. Thür. 1914).
¹⁰⁴ A. Marek, *De temporis et loci unitatibus a Seneca tragico observatis* (Wratislaviae, 1909).
¹⁰⁵ Cf. E. P. Macleane, 'Methods of introducing Characters in Seneca's Tragedies', PrAPhA 61 (1930) xxxviiif.
¹⁰⁶ M. V. Braginton, *The Supernatural in Seneca's Tragedies* (Diss., Yale Un., Menasha, Banta, 1933).
¹⁰⁷ L. Strzelecki, *De Senecae Trimetro iambico quaestiones selectae* (Krakow, Gebethner i. Wolff, 1938). 'For Seneca's usage in particular the book is a treasury upon which every surveyor of Latin metre and every editor of Seneca's tragedies must largely draw' (E. Harrison, CR 54 (1940) 152).
¹⁰⁸ SENECA, Reff. Bibl.: — JAW (Bursian's J.bericht) 134 (1907) 196-204; 158 (1912) 1-20; 171 (1915) 15-30; 192 (1922) 185-214. Schanz–Hosius, *Gesch. Rom. Lit.* II (1935) 456-70, 679-82. *Real-Encycl.* 2 R, 6 Bd. (1937) s.v. 'Tragoedia', xxii-xxv. Herrmann, *Théâtre de Sénèque*, 1-30. Oldfather–Pease–Canter, *op. cit.*, 6-13, 264f. N. T. Pratt, *op. cit.*, 116-20.

APPENDIX TO CHAPTER IX

i. Comedy

BY M. M. WILLCOCK

As some of the topics which occupied the attention of scholars in the field of Roman Comedy in the first half of the century have lost their appeal, and as the recovery of a complete play of Menander has helped to concentrate attention more on the plays themselves of Plautus and Terence, it has seemed best to alter the main headings of discussion in these supplementary pages. Works will be classified as follows:[1]

(a) New evidence for the text.
(b) The recovery of Menander's *Dyscolus* and its effects on the discussion of Roman Comedy.
(c) Editions, commentaries, and discussions, of separate plays.
(d) General and special studies in the field of Roman Comedy.
(e) Metre.
(f) Photographic reprints of important works long out of print.

(a) There has been no change in the text of Plautus during these years; the editions of Leo, Lindsay, and Ernout still hold the field. In Terence, on the other hand, an unexpected accession was the discovery of large parts of over 110 lines of the *Andria* on a papyrus of the fourth of fifth century.[2] This papyrus thus becomes, with the Bembinus, the oldest direct evidence for the text of Terence, and was used by O. Skutsch in his new edition (1958) of Lindsay and Kauer's Oxford Text. Skutsch made other small changes, but did not alter the untidiness caused by Lindsay's editorial methods.[3]

(b) The recovery of the *Dyscolus* was certainly the biggest single fact in Plautine and Terentian studies in these years. Announced in *Gnomon* 1957 by V. Martin, and published by him in 1958, it caused an immediate surge of editorial activity, the tidying up of the text taking precedence over consideration of it; but after a year or two the significance of the new evidence for

Roman Comedy started to become apparent. Three aspects have predominated:

(i) The striking similarity of technique between the *Dyscolus* and the *Aulularia* of Plautus.
(ii) The division of the *Dyscolus* into five acts by the insertion of the word XOPOY in the text; and the mention of a group of 'revellers' just before the first such division.
(iii) The strangely disconcerting end of the *Dyscolus*, with the metre changing to the 'dancing' iambic tetrameters catalectic, and the rough humour of the lower-class characters.

(i) The similarities between *Dyscolus* and *Aulularia* include the following: the stage setting; the single strongly-typed main character; the divine prologue concerned to look after the interests of the daughter of the house; the attitude of the main character to his old female servant; the cook scenes; the apparent change of heart of the main character at the end of the play. This is pretty convincing evidence to support those who already believed that the *Aulularia* derives from a Menandrian original. A brilliant article on the play, covering other aspects as well as this, is that of W. Ludwig, 'Aulularia-Probleme' in Phil 105 (1961) 44-71 and 247-62.[4]
(ii) The division into five more or less equal acts provides the evidence missing when Beare wrote the words quoted on p. 303 above, 'The most careful researches of modern scholars have been unable to discover clear evidence of five-act division in any Greek play which has reached us complete'. The mention of a band of revellers adds evidence towards the interpretation of three much discussed passages in Roman Comedy – *Bacch.* 107 (106 OCT), *Pseud.* 573a, and *Heaut.* 169ff.[5]
(iii) The final scene of the *Dyscolus* has offered interesting grounds for comparison with difficulties at the end of several Plautine plays, and particularly the vulgarity of the ending of the *Stichus*; but far more significant is the parallel with the equally disconcerting ending of Terence's *Adelphoe*. Before the recovery of the *Dyscolus* opinion inclined in favour of Terentian invention in the unexpected arrangements for the marriage of Micio at the end of the *Adelphoe* (Roman morality intruding?). This was the conclusion of Otto Rieth, whose *Die Kunst Menanders in den*

Adelphen des Terenz (Hildesheim, Olms) was published in 1964, twenty years after his death in the war.[6] Since the *Dyscolus* it seems more likely that the unexpected ending is due to Menander.[7] As W. G. Arnott suggests, the 'final ironic twist' may have been a feature of Menandrian style (cf. *Bacchides*).

(c) There is a great and obvious need for new English language commentaries on the plays of Plautus. We know so much more about the text, the metre, and the relations with Greek New Comedy, than was known in 1890; but the school and university editions we have to use were in many cases composed about then. And some of the best plays — in particular the two most powerfully Plautine (*Bacchides* and *Pseudolus*) and the funniest (*Casina*) — are not available with an English commentary at all. Even the *Aulularia*, on which so much has been written in the last few years, has to be read by students in an edition now a hundred years old.[8] Thus new approaches and new knowledge have not led to new school and university editions.

The few which have appeared have regrettable limitations. Terence is less popular, but in this respect better served than Plautus. R. H. Martin's *Phormio* (Methuen, 1959) and G. P. Shipp's *Andria* (second edition, OUP, 1961) are far superior to W. B. Sedgwick's *Amphitruo* (Manchester U.P., 1960) and the *Miles* of M. Hammond, A. M. Mack and W. Moskalew (Harvard U.P., 1963).[9]

From abroad comes a welcome edition of the *Casina* by E. Paratore (Firenze, Sansoni, 1959); Paratore also edited the *Curculio* (1958), and the *Amphitruo* and *Miles* (1959) in the same series. They have a full and helpful introduction, text, and Italian translation. The *Curculio* has for some reason attracted a good deal of attention, with another edition (by J. Collart in the French Series *Érasme*, 1962), and a large-scale study of the play by G. Monaco (*Il Curculio*, Palermo, 1963).

Apart from plays already mentioned, most progress has perhaps been made with the *Pseudolus*. Appreciation of this play was much advanced by G. W. Williams' article 'Some problems in the construction of Plautus' Pseudolus', *Hermes* LXXXIV (1956) 422-55, and A. Önnerfors' 'Ein paar Probleme im Plautinischen Pseudolus', Er LVI (1958) 21-40. These, taken together with the still eminently readable 'De Plauti Pseudolo' of H. T. Karsten in Mn XXXI (1903) 130-56, bring almost to a firm conclusion the attempts to explain the complications of this plot.[10]

(d) In 1960, E. Fraenkel's *Plautinisches im Plautus* (1922) appeared in an Italian translation by F. Munari as *Elementi Plautini in Plauto* (Firenze, La Nuova Italia). This wonderful book, far the most important contribution to Plautine studies of this century, had been brought up to date by forty-five pages of addenda by the author; in particular he admitted (p. 431) that he no longer subscribed to much of what he had written in the chapter on 'Contaminierte Stücke'. Indeed this is the pattern now; no doubt to a large extent due to the influence of Fraenkel's own book, Plautine innovation has in general replaced 'contamination' as an explanation for inconsistency in the plots.[11]

E. Paratore's *Plauto*[12] gives a succinct account of Plautus' life and works, and his poetic art. Paratore is also one of many Italian scholars who have written general works on Roman Comedy.[13] The individual qualities of Terence, and the changes (and even improvements) he made in his Latin versions of Menander and Apollodorus, are most lucidly discussed by H. Haffter.[14]

For the English reader, Duckworth's *The Nature of Roman Comedy*[15] is still the best general survey. Beare's *The Roman Stage*[16] appeared in a second, revised, edition in 1955; the chapter on Terence had been completely rewritten, and the discussion of *contaminatio* relegated to an appendix. *Roman Drama* (London, Routledge and Kegan Paul, 1965), a collection of articles by various hands, is a work of some interest for the general reader, who however will be disappointed to find that there is no chapter on Terence.

Among studies of special features of Roman Comedy, pride of place goes to the very original and ingenious discussion by G. Luck of the exclamations *Hem*, *Em*, and *Ehem*.[17] Wholly convincingly he shows the distinction between these three. All are nasal sounds. *Hem* is an interrogative, exactly like the French 'hein?', pronounced with a rising inflection. *Em* is deictic — a short, unmodulated sound. *Ehem* is the long drawled sound of one who is thinking how best to begin speech. Luck's demonstration will necessarily influence future editors and readers of Plautus and Terence. K. Abel, in a Frankfurt dissertation,[18] discusses the prologues of Plautus' plays, a subject of much significance both for the question of Plautus' relationship to his Greek originals and for the early history of the plays themselves.[19]

Two hardy perennials continued to flower — the attempt to date Plautus' plays, and the attempt to explain what Terence meant by *contaminatio*. On dates, H. B. Mattingly attacked the only evidence which had seemed secure — the didascaliae of the *Stichus* and *Pseudolus*.[20] And a series of short expressions of opinion has, if not illuminated *contaminatio*, at least kept it a live issue.[21]

(e) The second edition of Crusius, *Römische Metrik*, admirably revised by H. Rubenbauer, was published in 1955 (München, Hueber). At a lower level, a useful new introduction in English has recently appeared — D. S. Raven, *Latin Metre* (London, Faber, 1965).

One of W. Beare's latest works was *Latin Verse and European Song* (London, Methuen, 1957). In this most original book, which covered of course much more than the early Roman dramatists, Beare endeavoured to go back beyond the assumptions of modern scholars, and question the first principles of our interpretation of Latin metre. He questioned particularly the existence of a stress accent in Latin, which has been a central presupposition of most English and German (though not French) writers on the subject. At the opposite pole from Beare in every way, H. Drexler has continued his accentual studies in Plautus,[22] consistently upholding his view of the coincidence of the metrical ictus with the spoken accent.

(f) A feature of this post-war period has been the increasing use of the technique of photographic reprinting. The following, in chronological order of their first publication, are now again obtainable: Ritschl's fundamental discussion of the fragmentary facts about Plautus' name, life and works;[23] Ussing's commentary, still the only complete modern commentary on the plays of Plautus;[24] Studemund's transcript of the Ambrosian palimpsest;[25] Leo's great edition of Plautus.[26] In addition, Fraenkel, by seeing to the publication of the *Ausgewählte Kleine Schriften* of Leo,[27] has made available again the remarkable articles entitled 'Analecta Plautina'.

Terence, whether deservedly or not, awakens only modest interest at this time; but circumstances are favourable for further advances in the study of Plautus. Greater knowledge of Menander, and the new availability of the works of the great scholars of the nineteenth century, provide both material and encouragement for the Plautinist of today.

[1] An outstandingly good bibliography of Terence (author: H. Marti) appeared in *Lustrum* 6 (1961) 114-238 and 8 (1963) 5-101; it covers the years 1909 to 1959. Shorter, but useful, bibliographies may be found in E. Paratore, *Plauto* (Firenze, Sansoni, 1961), 88-100, and S. Prete, 'Terence' (CW 54 (1961) 121-2). 'Early Latin Meter and Prosody' (1935-55) was dealt with by P. W. Harsh in *Lustrum* 3 (1958) 215-50. To these works of reference may be added the first half (A-O) of *Lexicon Terentianum* by P. McGlynn (London and Glasgow, Blackie, 1963).
[2] Published by Roberts and Skutsch, Ox.Pap. 24 (1957) Nr. 2401. It contains *Andria* 602-68 and 924-79a, including what may be traces of a transition to the alternative ending of the play (only found in late manuscripts, although known to Donatus). On this see O. Skutsch, RhM 100 (1957) 53-68.
[3] The reader of the Oxford Text of Terence is not allowed to follow his own taste when there is a choice between synizesis and brevis brevians, or between prosodic hiatus and elision; he is compelled by obtrusive signs in the text to accept the views of the editor.
S. Prete's edition of Terence (Heidelberg, Kerle, 1954) was not well received (Skutsch in CR 6 (1956) 129-33; Marti in *Lustrum* 6 228).
[4] See however the important correction in Phil 106 (1962) 153. Most helpful among other articles on the *Dyscolus/Aulularia* comparison are W. Kraus in *Serta Philologica Aenipontana* 1962 185-90 and W. G. Arnott, *Phoenix* XVIII (1964) 232-7.
[5] The apparently conventional mention of 'revellers' was already known from *Epitr.* 33-5 and *Perikeir.* 71-2 (Koe.), and elsewhere in the Greek fragments.
[6] On the other hand, H. Haffter, in 'Terenz und seine künstlerische Eigenart' (MH 10 (1953) 1-20 and 73-102), had believed (with a fine perception) that the Menander original had had a more lively and comic ending, and that Terence had toned it down, attempting a greater realism (p. 89).
[7] A. Thierfelder, 'Knemon, Demea, Micio' in *Menandrea, Miscellanea Philologica* (Genova, Pubbl. dell' Ist. di Fil. Class., 1960) 107-12. W. G. Arnott has a summary of the question in G and R X (1963) 140-4.
[8] Plauti Aululario ed. Wagner, 1866; second edition 1876; reprinted 1901.
[9] Sedgwick may be accused of unhelpfulness; Hammond, Mack and Moskalew of inaccuracy (see J. G. Griffith, CR 15 (1965) 44-7).
[10] On other plays, the following will be indispensable to the hoped-for editor: A. Traina, 'Plauto, Demofilo, Menandro', *La Parola del Passato* 9 (1954) 177-203 (on the *Asinaria*); C. Questa, 'Per un' edizione delle Bacchides', *Rivista di Cultura classica e medioevale* V (1963) 215-54 and 348-65; G. W. Williams, 'Evidence for Plautus' workmanship in the Miles Gloriosus', *Hermes* LXXXVI (1958) 79-105; G. L. Mueller, *Das Original des plautinischen Persa* (Diss. Frankfurt, 1957).
[11] See pp. 246-7 above. That Terence practised 'contamination' (see note 21) is undeniable on his own evidence. His apparent ascription of the same practice to Plautus (*Andria* 18) aroused the ingenuity of two generations of very able scholars.
[12] op. cit. note 1.
[13] Particularly deserving of mention are: F. Arnaldi, 'La commedia greco-latina', *Rendiconti della Accademia di Archeologia, Lettere e Belle Arti*, Napoli, N.S. 29 (1954) 39-65; E. Paratore, *Storia del teatro latino* (Milano, Vallardi, 1957); A. Traina, *Comoedia: antologia della palliata* (Padova, Cedam, 1960). There is a natural sympathy and affinity which makes the Italian a more relaxed judge of this literature (particularly Plautus) than those from the colder north.
[14] op. cit. note 6.
[15] p. 298 above.
[16] p. 297-8 above.
[17] G. Luck, *Ueber einige Interjektionen der lateinischen Umgangssprache* (Heidelberg, Winter, 1964).
[18] K. H. Able, *Die Plautusprologe* (Diss. Frankfurt, 1955).

APPENDIX

[19] Notable among other special studies are: H. Dohm, *Mageiros. Die Rolle des Kochs in der griechisch-römischen Komödie* (München, Beck, 1964) — cooks have become more interesting with the *Dyscolus/Aulularia* comparisons; D. C. Earl, 'Political terminology in Plautus', *Historia* IX (1960) 235-43; U. E. Paoli, *Comici latini e diritto attico* (Milano, Giuffrè, 1962).

[20] H. B. Mattingly, 'The Plautine didascaliae', *Ath* 35 (1957) 78-88. See however Paratore in the introduction to his *Casina* 48-50.

[21] Apart from W. Beare's comments on this subject in the various editions of his *The Roman Stage*, three brief notes in the *Classical Review* may be quoted: H. Tredennick, CR 2 (1952) 28; W. R. Chalmers, CR 7 (1957) 12-14; W. Beare, CR 9 (1959) 7-11. Beare takes the commonsense view that *contaminare* means to spoil and not to mix; Chalmers ascribes unwritten copyright conventions to the Roman dramatists.

[22] 'Neue plautinische Akzentstudien', *Maia* XI (1959) 260-314; '*Lizenzen*' am *Versanfang bei Plautus* (München, Beck, 1965).

[23] *Parerga zu Plautus und Terenz*, 1845 (Repr. Amsterdam, Hakkert, 1965).

[24] *Commentarius in Plauti Comoedias* 1886 (Rursus edendum curavit, indicibus auxit A. Thierfelder, Hildesheim, Olms; announced for 1966).

[25] *Codicis Rescripti Ambrosiani Apographum*, 1889 (Repr. Hildesheim, Olms, 1966).

[26] *Plauti Comoediae*, 1895-96 (Repr. Berlin, Weidmann, 1958).

[27] Edizioni di Storia e Letteratura, Roma, 1960.

ii. Tragedy

BY MICHAEL COFFEY

W. BEARE's *The Roman Stage*, a useful general study of the organization of the theatre, stage conventions and the dramatists of the Republic, has appeared in a third edition.[1] A comparable Italian work by E. Paratore includes Seneca and *Octavia*.[2] H. J. Mette in a *Lustrum* report on Roman Tragedy provides a bibliography and examines sources play by play; T. B. L. Webster in the last chapter of *Hellenistic Poetry and Art* discusses the rendering of Greek originals by Roman Republican dramatists and the archaeological evidence for Greek drama in the West.[3] These last two works expound the most important general problems considered in the recent study of the Roman tragedians: evidence for Greek originals and the nature of the changes made by Roman adaptations in the introduction of scenes from other plays and in the choice of metres.

Papyrus finds without offering spectacular correspondences provide welcome new knowledge of possible sources.[3a] A fragmentary hypothesis of Euripides' *Melanippe Sophe* may be added to earlier evidence from papyri and elsewhere in the elucidation of the fragments of Ennius' *Mel*.[4] Similarly new fragments of Euripides' *Telephus* together with a reassessment of other evidence add to our knowledge of the main source for the *Telephus* plays of both Ennius and Accius.[5] Papyrus evidence confirms that Ennius' *Alexander* was closely dependent on Euripides' play of the same name,[6] but other papyri raise more complex problems. It is possible that two papyri of a Hector play are part of the source of Naevius' *Hector proficiscens*;[7] it has also been suggested that Naevius' source is Astydamas' *Hector*.[8] The papyrus texts could indeed belong to Astydamas' play, but this attribution has been questioned.[9] Sometimes uncertainty is even greater. Fragments of Euripides' *Hypsipyle* give no good grounds for assuming that it was the source of Ennius' *Nemea*,[10] and the almost inevitable similarities of phrasing in descriptions of the Minotaur may explain apparent correspondences between papyrus fragments of Euripides' *Cretans* and a fragment of Accius' *Minos (Minotaurus)*.[11]

Examination of possible sources in extant plays and book fragments including those of the fourth century has continued. A few examples of these problems will suffice. The *Eumenides* of Ennius derives from the extant play of Aeschylus; departures from a close rendering may be due to the originality of the Roman adapter or to the literal translation of an actors' version of a play that was popular in S. Italy.[12] In Ennius' *Iphigenia* a chorus is introduced not from the main source, Euripides' *I.A.*, but probably from Sophocles' *Iphigeneia*; it is not known whether Ennius inherited the contamination from an actor's text or whether (perhaps more likely) he introduced it himself.[13] The text of Ennius *Med.* 259-61 V as reconstructed by O. Skutsch suggests that Ennius had before him a copy of Euripides' play with readings similar to those of L, which at this point, it has been argued, gives a sentence structure particularly congenial to an actor.[14] But Ennius' reversal of Euripides' famous *hysteron proteron* at the beginning of the same play is more likely to have been introduced by the Roman poet himself, possibly but not necessarily, under the influence of a Greek grammarian.[15]

It has been suggested that for his *Andromacha* Ennius used a fourth century original such as the *Andromache* of Antiphon.[16] Hellenistic sources have been postulated for Accius' *Medea*[17] and also for his *Nyctegresia*,[18] which is set in the Greek camp and so cannot derive from the *Rhesus*, a popular example of a similar post-classical drama of action.[19] It has also been suggested that

APPENDIX 339

Pacuvius derived some plays with vigorous action, e.g. *Atalanta* and *Armorum Iudicium*, from fourth-century originals, the latter possibly from a play by Theodectes.[20]

Roman adapters frequently changed the metre of the corresponding part of the Greek original using e.g. trochaic septenarii to render not merely iambic trimeter but also dochmiac or choral lyric metre.[21] Discussions of these changes are an important part of Mette's *Lustrum* report.[22]

The edition of the Fragments of Roman Tragedy by Klotz, though reviewed favourably in an English journal, is inaccurate and misleading and should not be used as a citing text in preference to that of Ribbeck[3] or (for Ennius) Vahlen.[23] Work has continued on the interpretation of various lines and passages. Boscherini produces good arguments for attributing *sc.* 274V to Ennius and not to Accius.[24] O. Skutsch argues from Plautus *Amph.* 42 that Neptunus spoke the prologue of Ennius' *Andromacha* and Victoria that of *Alexander* (*sc.* 51V), also that *sc.* 380V (from Ter. *Eun.* 590) is the first line of the prologue of *Alcumena*.[25]

Recent work on Seneca's tragedies has examined further the tradition of the text, the sources and other dramatic and literary problems. A *Lustrum* report by M. Coffey discusses work on Seneca's Tragedies and *Octavia* from 1922 to 1955 and Mette's report has a section on the Senecan corpus.[26]

The most important addition to our knowledge of the textual tradition has been the discovery in Exeter by C. J. Herington of a miscellaneous manuscript of mid-thirteenth century date containing *Octavia*.[27] This manuscript (G) and two other manuscripts of the whole Senecan tragic corpus (P and C) are the earliest and along with S the best witnesses to A, the so-called interpolated tradition of Seneca's tragedies,[28] a tradition that has in recent times sometimes been esteemed more highly than the E tradition as represented by the codex Etruscus.[29] G shares a hyparchetype (δ) with P, and Herington argues that G may be used to assess individual eccentricities in P and that readings common to δ and E but not found in the rest of the A tradition arose because δ had been contaminated from the E tradition.[30] The latter view has been questioned by W. Woesler in the course of an examination of the A tradition.[31] Scholars differ in their evaluation of the relative worth of the two traditions. E. Paratore argues that A is often more reliable in the *sigla* showing change of speaker,[32] but as a general judgment Woesler accords the E tradition a somewhat greater authority.[33] Both traditions have characteristic merits and defects, and neither is to be accorded an unqualified superiority.[34] Scholars nowadays have a wider knowledge of the manuscript tradition than was available to Leo for his great edition.[35] There is now at last a new critical edition by I. C. Giardina that makes use of this knowledge.[36]

The sources of Seneca's *Phaedra* have been much discussed.[37] W. S. Barrett concludes that, as Seneca uses his sources freely, it is unwise to assume that what does not derive from the extant *Hippolytus* of Euripides must have been taken from his earlier Ἱππόλυτος Καλυπτόμενος and, while allowing for Seneca's originality, cautiously suggests Sophocles' *Phaedra* as an incidental source of some importance.[38] B. Snell believes that 'a shameless Phaedra is certainly not Sophoclean' and that the notorious Ἱππ. Καλ. was Seneca's main source.[39] Phaedra's speech (Sen. *Pha.* 646-71) illustrates some difficulties in assigning sources. Phaedra's comparison of Hippolytus to the young Theseus and her belief that he inherited his rugged appearance from his Amazon mother are not found in Ov. *Her.* 4, the main immediate source for this speech. A parallel for the comparison has been sought in Heliodorus.[40] But it is probably necessary to assume in addition to the lost Euripides play a variety of Hellenistic sources and also the originality of a restless and inventive writer.[41] The dramatic background to *Hercules Oetaeus* has been enlarged by papyrus fragments of a monologue by Herakles that have been tentatively assigned to the Hellenistic period.[42]

Formal aspects of dramatic structure are studied in works by K. Anliker on prologues and act division[43] and by G. Runchina on prologues, choruses and episodes.[44] On points of relative chronology E. Paratore argues that *Hercules Oetaeus* (which he believes to be genuine), is earlier than *Hercules Furens*; he also assigns an early date to *Oedipus*.[45] Senecan metrics are treated briefly by D. S. Raven;[46] there are useful remarks on the polymetric choruses by W. Strzelecki. [47]

In contrast to the outmoded dismissal of Seneca's Tragedies as rhetorical rant without dramatic or philosophical import many scholars in recent years discuss them as works of an unusual intrinsic interest. O. Zwierlein has written an excellent study of the plays as rhetorical drama for recitation.[47a] E. Paratore[48] discusses psychological motivation and C. Garton[49] the presentation of dramatic character. D. Henry and B. Walker, applying a modern terminology of dramatic assessment to *Hercules Furens*, expound the vision of a sterile, desolate hell and the moral impotence of Hercules.[50] Seneca's plays interpreted historically are an adaptation of the Greek tragic tradition that is permeated with both Stoic theory and political experience under the Julio-Claudian tyranny and expressed in the rhetorical language of contemporary high poetry.[51]

It is generally agreed nowadays that *Octavia* was not written by Seneca. D. W. Pye[52] adds a further piece of linguistic evidence to the formidable mass already assembled by other scholars. The attempt of F. Giancotti[53] to discount such evidence will not attain ready credence. Herington[54] concludes that excess of structural symmetry together with verbal repetitiveness and metrical clumsiness suggest not the mature and accomplished Seneca but an inexperienced verse writer who admired his style. His sympathetic account of the literary qualities of *Octavia* is a just appraisal of this moving evocation of events under a near-contemporary tyranny that was written at a time when it was likely to be at least offensive to the authoritarian regime.[55]

---

[1] W. Beare, *The Roman Stage*[3], London, 1964. The second and, even more, the third editions are far superior to the first edition of 1950.
[2] E. Paratore, *Storia del Teatro Latino*, Milan 1957; see review by E. W. Handley, CR 9, 1959, 136-9.
[3] H. J. Mette, *Die Römische Tragödie* Lustrum 9, 1964, 1-211. T. B. L. Webster, *Hellenistic Poetry and Art*, London 1964, 252-92. These two works will be referred to below by author's name only. Archaeological evidence is discussed by Webster in: *Monuments illustrating Tragedy and Satyr Play*, Bull. Inst. Class. St. Suppl 14, 1962; *Griechische Bühnenaltertümer*, Göttingen 1963, 51-60; on the Dramatic Terracottas of Lipari, in Bernabò-Brea and Cavalier, *Meligunis Lipára*, II, Palermo 1965, 320-2.
[3a] For a catalogue of papyri see R. A. Pack, *The Greek and Latin Literary Texts from Greco-Roman Egypt*[2], Ann Arbor 1965.
[4] E. G. Turner, *P. Oxy.* 27, 1962, 2455, pp. 32-6 and 55 (Pack[2] 453); see also D. L. Page, *Greek Literary Papyri*, 14.
[5] E. W. Handley and J. Rea, *The Telephus of Euripides*, Bull. Inst. Class. Stud. Suppl. 5, 1957, esp. 25-7 and 40-50. See *P. Oxy.* 27, 2460, Pack[2] 448.
[6] B. Snell, Hermes Einzelschr. 5, 1937, 1-68, Pack[2] 432, J. O. de G. Hanson, Hermes 92, 1964, 171-81 and O. Skutsch, HSCPh 71, 1966, 126f. On Pacuvius' *Antiopa* and that of Euripides see B. Snell (*op. cit.* n. 39) 72-9.

⁷ Mette, 5of. The fragments are found in Page, *GLP*, 29, Pack² 169 and 170.
⁸ Webster, 260.
⁹ Page, p. 161 argues that the incident of the frightened boy (Astyd. fr. 2 N³) and the death of Hector (Page 29(b)) could not have been included in the same play, but it is possible that Astydamas truncated the events of the *Iliad*, for the death of Hector could make a tragic climax after his departure from Andromache and Astyanax: see Webster, Hermes 82, 1954, 306.
¹⁰ Mette 57, but note the scepticism of G. W. Bond, Euripides, *Hypsipyle*, Oxford 1963, 95.
¹¹ Mette 140f.; see also R. Cantarella, *Euripide, I Cretesi*, Milan 1963; Pack² 437 and 451.
¹² Mette 57; Webster 262.
¹³ O. Skutsch, RhM 96, 1953, 193-201; Webster 264; on this play see also K. Ziegler, Hermes 85, 1957, 495-501 and L. Rychlewska, Eos 49, 1957-58, 71-81.
¹⁴ O Skutsch, *Navicula Chiloniensis*, Leiden 1956, 107-13 and A. M. Dale's suggestion mentioned 110; see Webster 263, who also discusses, 286 and 290f., the texts used by Pacuvius and Accius.
¹⁵ See Page on Eur. *Med.* 1; Mette 62 n. 2; Webster 263. See Ter. *Eun.* 7-13 for discussion of another kind of inversion of a Greek original.
¹⁶ Webster 262 and Hermes 82, 1954, 299f. O. Schönberger, Hermes 84, 1956, 255f. suggests that Ennius derives the lamentation in his *Andromacha* from Eur. *Tro*. This is the traditional attribution: see O. Skutsch, HSCPh 1966, 125.
¹⁷ Webster 289f.
¹⁸ Mette 154f.; see also G. Pacitti, Maia 15, 1963, 184-98.
¹⁹ On the added prologues to *Rhesus* see W. Ritchie, *The Authenticity of the Rhesus of Euripides*, Cambridge 1964 and Webster 264. On further problems of Accius' sources see, on *Myrmidones*, G. Barabino, *Antidoron H. H. Paoli*, Genoa 1956, 57-72, and, on *Atreus*, P. J. Enk, Eos 52, 1962, 105-10.
²⁰ Mette 103-6; 79-82; Webster 282f. On Pacuvius' sources see P. Frassinetti, *Antidoron H. H. Paoli*, 96-123 and on *Arm. Iud.*, B. Bilinski, Acc. Pol. Roma Conf. Fasc. 16, 1962, 30-54; on *Bacch.* and *Pho.* I. Mariotti MH 22, 1965, 206-16. Mariotti's short general study, *Pacuvio*, Urbino 1960, has a useful treatment of Greek models.
²¹ At Enn. *Med.* 284-6V troch. sept. renders dochmiac (see O. Skutsch, RhM 96, 1953, 197), and at Enn. *Tel.* 336V (see E. W. Handley, *op. cit.* (n. 5) 40) an Aeolic system that includes glyconic and hipponactean.
²² See also Webster, esp. 262f. and 287f. For a note on a metrical point in Naevius' *Danae* see Ed. Fraenkel, *Elementi Plautini in Plauto*, Florence 1960, 436f.
²³ A. Klotz, *Tragicorum (Romanorum) Fragmenta*, Munich 1953; W. Beare, CR 5, 1955, 170f.; but see reviews by O. Skutsch, Gnomon 26, 1954, 465-70 and by W. Strzelecki, Eos 49, 1, 1957-58, 186-94. Selected Fragments of Ennius' Tragedies have been edited with short notes by J. Heurgon, Ennius II *Fragments tragiques*, Paris 1958. For a study of the fragments of Livius in the grammarians' tradition see J. Lanowski, Eos 51, 1961, 65-77.
²⁴ S. Boscherini, SIFC 30, 1958, 106-15 (Ennius sc. 274f. V = inc. inc. 172f. R).
²⁵ O. Skutsch, HSCPh 71, 1966, 125-42, who also uses the criterion of Ennius' rhetoric along with those of language and metre in the exegesis of several passages. See also, on Ennius, Sc. Mariotti, *Due note enniane*, SIFC 31, 1959, 233-5 (*Hect. Lytr.*); on Pacuvius, id. *Studi U. E. Paoli*, Florence 1955, 508f. (*Perib.*), G. d'Anna, Riv. Cult. Class. Med. 2, 1960, 173-82 (*Arm. Iud.*), B. Bilinski, *Hommages à Léon Herrmann*, Brussels-Berchem 1960, 160-70 (postulates references in *Dul.* to Sicilian slave wars); on Accius, J. Delz, MH 12, 1955, 274-6 (*Amph.*), C. J. Herington, TAPhA 92, 1961, 239-50 (argues that Cic. not Acc. translated Aesch. *Prom. Unbound* 193 N²). On a point of literary chronology G. Marconi, Mem. Class. Sc. mor. stor. filol. 8, 12, 1966, 125-213 (see also H. B. Mattingly, CQ 7, 1957, 159-63) attempts to revive the error of Accius, who made Livius Andronicus come to Rome in 209 B.C.
²⁶ M. Coffey, Lustrum 2, 1957, 113-86; H. J. Mette (see note 3 above) 160-94.
²⁷ C. J. Herington, Rh M 101, 1958, 353-77; see also ib. 103, 1960, 96. Herington calls this MS. G(randisson) after the former owner of the manuscript, a bishop of Exeter in the fourteenth century. Its contents also include short excerpts from Seneca's tragedies somewhat similar to the Brussels excerpts; see Herington 364 n. 14.

APPENDIX 343

[28] On P(arisınus), C(antabrigensis) and S(corialensis) see Th. H. Sluiter, *L. A. Senecae Oedipus*, Groningen 1941, 10-15.
[29] See Lustrum 2, 1957, 119, 127, 173.
[30] Herington, 355-8; 371-5.
[31] W. Woesler, *Senecas Tragödien. Die H Überlieferung der α-Klasse dargestellt am Beispiel der Phaedra*, Neuwied 1965, 24-42. On the A tradition see also G. Brugnoli, Atti Acc. Naz. dei Lincei, Mem. Cl. Scienze mor. stor. fil. 8, 8, 3, 1957, 201-87.
[32] E. Paratore, SIFC 27-8, 1956, 324-60.
[33] Woesler, 83. B. Axelson, *Korruptelenkult*, Lund 1967, is important for the text of *H.O.*
[34] See G. Pasquali, *Storia della tradizione e critica del testo*[2], Florence 1952, 126-9, whose judgment still holds good today.
[35] On Leo's edition see Ed. Fraenkel, F. Leo: *Ausgewählte Kleine Schriften I*, Rome 1960, intro. XVIII-XXI.
[36] The new critical text by I. C. Giardina, Bologna 1966, provides much valuable information about MSS; there is an annotated text of *Phædra* by P. Grimal, Paris 1965. Translations: E. F. Watling, *Seneca: Four Tragedies and Octavia*, Harmondsworth 1966 (*Thy., Pha. Tro. Oed.*); M. Hadas, *Seneca; Medea, Oedipus, Thyestes*, New York 1956; rev. W. S. Maguinness, CR 9, 1959, 174f; Th. Thomann, *Seneca Sämtliche Tragöden* 1 (*HF, Tro., Med. Pha. Oct.*), Zürich-Stuttgart (Artemis-Verlag) 1961, rev. W. Schetter, Gnomon 35, 1963, 627-9; E. Paratore, *Seneca Tragedie*, Rome 1956. On the exegesis of various passages: B. Axelson, SIFC 27-8, 1956, 12-22 (on *Oed.*); N. Berg. SO 33, 1957, 110-20 (on *Oed.*); A. Ker, CQ 12, 1962, 48-51; E. Paratore, *Ut pictura poesis*, Leiden 1955, 129-66, id. *Hommages à Léon Herrmann*, Brussels-Berchem 1960, 584-8 (on *Herc. Oet.*); W. Strzelecki, Riv. Cult. Class. Med. 2, 1960, 369-70 (uses Men. *Dysk.* to support the conjecture *Phyle* at *Pha.* 28).
[37] C. Zintzen's *Analytisches Hypomnema zu Senecas Phaedra*, Meisenheim 1960, is for the most part a catalogue of sources; see reviews by M. Coffey, Gnomon 35, 1963, 310-12 and P. Grimal, REA 65, 1963, 210-12.
[38] W. S. Barrett, *Euripides Hippolytos*, Oxford 1964, 10-45. P. Grimal, REL 41, 1963, 297-314, emphasizes the importance of Sophocles' *Phaedra* as a possible source; see also H. Lloyd-Jones, Gnomon 38, 1966, 14f.
[39] B. Snell, *Scenes from Greek Drama*, Berkeley and Los Angeles 1964, 24-46.
[40] R. Merkelbach, RhM 100, 1957, 99f. (Sen. *Pha.* 646f. and Heliodorus 1, 10); see also Snell 42f. But the use of a mythological parallel to illustrate a human relationship may be no more than a rhetorical commonplace (cf. e.g. Andoc. 1, 129) and need not demand a common origin in Ἱππ. Καλ.
[41] On non-dramatic parallels for this speech (e.g. *Od.* 4, 141-6; Call. *Hec.* 274) see T. B. L. Webster, *The Tragedies of Euripides*, London 1967, 67 n. 47.
[42] E. G. Turner, *P. Oxy.* 27, 1962, 2454, 27-32, Pack[2] 1711.
[43] K. Anliker, *Prologe und Akteinteilung in Senecas Tragödien*, Bern and Stuttgart 1960; M. Coffey, CR 11, 1961, 232f. and C. J. Herington, JRS 53, 1963, 248f.
[44] G. Runchina, *Tecnica drammatica e retorica nelle Tragedie di Seneca*, Univ. di Cagliari: Estr. d. Ann d. Facoltà di Lett. Fil. e Mag. 28, Rome 1960; rev. W. Barr, CR 13, 1963, 225 and M. Coffey, Gnomon 34, 1962, 625f.
[45] E. Paratore, A. Class. 1, 1958, 72-9; id. GIF 9, 1956, 97-132.
[46] D. S. Raven, *Latin Metre*, London 1965, esp. 148ff.
[47] W. Strzelecki, Gnomon 32, 1960, 747-50, reviewing R. Giomini, *De Canticis polymetris Agamemnone et Oedipode Annaeanis*, Rome 1959. On the anapaests see J. Mantke, Eos 49, 1957-58, 101-22.
[47a] O. Zwierlein, *Die Rezitationsdramen Senecas*, Meisenheim 1966.
[48] E. Paratore, Dioniso 20, 1957, 53-74.
[49] C. Garton, CPh 54, 1959, 1-9.
[50] D. Henry and B. Walker, CPh 60, 1965, 11-22; see also (on Agamemnon) CPh 58, 1963, 1-10.
[51] M. Coffey, Proc. Afr. Class. Ass. 3, 1960, 14-20. On political interpretations see also W. Strzelecki, Eos 47, 1954-55, 97-108. M. Pohlenz, *Die Stoa* I[2], Göttingen 1959, 324-7 is of great value for both literary and philosophical interpretation; see Lustrum 2, 1957, 157.
[52] D. W. Pye, Trans. Philol. Soc. 1963, 7 n. 4: compared to *Oct.* rest of Senecan corpus has a high proportion of *-re* termination in third person plural perf. ind. act.

[53] F. Giancotti, *L'Octavia attribuita a Seneca*, Turin 1954; rev. B. Axelson, Gnonom 28, 1956, 41ff.
[54] C. J. Herington, CQ 11, 1961, 18-30.
[55] See Tac. *Dial.* 2, 1; 3, 2, and W. Liebeschuetz, CQ 16, 1966, 133. These passages have led scholars to suggest that Curiatius Maternus was the author of *Oct.* (on this see Herington's sceptical remarks, 27); the name of Fabius Rusticus, on whom see Syme, *Tacitus*, Oxford 1958, 179, may be offered as another guess.

CHAPTER X

LATE REPUBLICAN POETRY

i. Lucretius

BY C. BAILEY

THE two main trends in Latin poetry at the end of the Republic were first erotic and occasional verse, culminating in Catullus, and second didactic and scientific poetry, represented by Cicero's translations of Aratus' astronomical works and reaching its zenith in Lucretius.

When one thinks of the immense growth of scientific knowledge and investigation during the nineteenth century and of the profound influence which it has exercised on thought, political, moral, and religious, it is no wonder that recent criticism should have concentrated mostly on Lucretius, who in the *De Rerum Natura* set out the atomic theory of Epicurus in verse which at times reaches a greater height of poetry than anything else written in Latin. Here, if anywhere, science and art, reason and emotion, the material and the spiritual seem to find their union and to resolve one of the most poignant conflicts of our own times. It is significant that within the last fifty years not only has there been a flood of critical literature on Lucretius, but in Europe and America there have appeared no less than five full editions with commentary and at least ten complete translations; that is an indication of no ordinary interest in an ancient poet.

1. *Editions*. Attention in these editions and in these critical writings has been focused mainly on two aspects, the technical, dealing with the text, language, style, and metre — what might be called the form of the poem — and on its matter, the philosophical and scientific thought which constitute its contents. On both sides the tendency has been to treat of the poem not as a thing by itself, standing against an alien background, but as a phenomenon taking its place in a natural series of development. In matters of form nineteenth-century criticism had for the most part set up Virgil as the standard of hexameter writing from which Lucretius 'regrettably' deviated; the new tendency was rather to see him as an innovator, who made great progress in the evolution towards

the perfection reached by Virgil. As regards the matter of the poem, it had been passed over as 'puerile' and 'erroneous'; it was left to the twentieth-century critics to study his master Epicurus and to put Lucretius into his place in the development of human thought.

Speaking roughly and generally the tendency of the last fifty years on the technical side has been to greater accuracy, showing itself in textual criticism by a more careful evaluation of the MS. evidence and less readiness to depart from it, and in the treatment of grammar, metre, vocabulary and style to a closer estimate of Lucretius' own idiosyncrasies and at the same time to an appreciation of his place in the series of Latin poets, based on his relation both to his predecessors and to his successors. Each of these topics will be dealt with separately, but it will be useful to start by some account of the complete editions with commentaries, in which of necessity all the subjects are dealt with. The foundation of twentieth-century criticism was laid in two great pioneer works of the nineteenth, for the text in Lachmann's edition of 1850, for other matters and in particular for the knowledge of Epicureanism in the work of H. A. J. Munro, ranging from the 'sixties to the 'eighties. Mention must also be made of the edition of Carlo Giussani, Professor at Milan, who was the first to examine Lucretius thoroughly in the light of Epicurus.

Of the five editions with full commentary which have been produced since the beginning of the present century two come from America, one from France, one from Germany, and one from England; there have also been editions of single Books, which have had an influence on the general tradition.

The edition of W. A. Merrill, Professor of Latin at Berkeley, California, in 1907 was a careful and diligent summary of work done in the previous thirty years or so. One can usually find there a statement of the views of his predecessors, but the editor is shy of giving his own opinion on a controversial point. He was an indefatigable student of Lucretius and published a number of brochures which must be noticed in their place. His edition of the text in 1917 (Berkeley) was, as he said himself, a 'ballon d'essai' to see how far Lucretian idiom and idiosyncrasy could be pushed, but had little permanent effect.

The next complete edition was that of Hermann Diels, the veteran editor and student of the Pre-Socratics. In 1923 he published a text, which is notable in that it has a far fuller *apparatus criticus* than any other edition, and a valuable collection of *testimonia* from later authors. His own suggestions and emendations are not as a rule very happy, and in filling up *lacunae* in the text he does not succeed in giving the impression of Lucretian diction. In the following year he put out a translation in German hexameters, which is vigorous and forceful, but the metre does not strike a foreign ear as suiting the German language any better than it suits English. Diels also wrote a full commentary; financial considerations made it impossible to publish it at the time and it was deposited in the University Library at Berlin. It is to be hoped that it will some day see the light, for one who knew the Pre-Socratics better than anyone else could give much information about the sources and meaning of Lucretius.

After Germany it was the turn of France to make its contribution. A. Ernout, Professor at the Sorbonne, had (during the First World War) published a useful edition of Book IV (Paris, Klincksieck) in 1916, and in 1920 brought out a full text and translation of the poem in the Budé series. The text is sound but exhibits no marked characteristics of its own; the translation has all the qualities of crispness and lucidity which distinguish the best French scholarship. After these first essays Ernout published a complete edition of the poem in three volumes in 1925, 1926 and 1928 (Paris, Belles Lettres). His own fine scholarship is exhibited on the technical side of the work and he was fortunate in having associated with him L. Robin, a brilliant exponent of Greek philosophy, whose notes on the subject-matter of the poem are always illuminating but often regrettably short.

The edition of Leonard and Smith (Wisconsin, 1942) is intended primarily for undergraduate students rather than advanced scholars. It has an admirable introductory essay on the MSS. by Smith, but oddly enough no *apparatus criticus*. Its notes are mostly explanatory, but contain very little comment on the philosophy or science. It opens with an enthusiastic essay by Leonard, which explains his own life-long devotion to the poem and should rouse the interest of his readers.

My own edition, published in three volumes at Oxford (Clarendon Press) in 1947, is intended to be in the main expository, an attempt to work out in detail what the poet meant. This of course involves the constitution of the text and comment on other technical points, but its prime interest is in the subject-matter, and it endeavours to put together critically the work done on Epicureanism and on Lucretius' treatment of it.

There have been many publications of individual Books with commentary, for the most part written for schoolboys or undergraduates. But two stand out above the rest, that of Book I by C. Pascal published at Rome (Paravia) in 1904 and revised for a second edition by Castiglioni in 1928; this contains valuable comment both on text and content. More important is the edition of Book III published just outside our period in 1897 at Leipzic (Teubner) by R. Heinze, whose wide-ranging knowledge of Greek philosophy throws light on many difficult phrases and makes one wish that he had been able to comment on the whole poem.

2. *Translations.* There is almost more variety in the translations of Lucretius which have appeared in this century than in the editions. Of non-English translations notice has already been made of Diels' rendering in German hexameters and Ernout's in French prose. I have also received from the author a translation into Serbian verse by A. Savie Rebac (Belgrade, 1951), but am naturally not competent to form a judgment on it.

The English versions all look back in varying degrees to the translation of H. A. J. Munro whose majestic qualities made it the standard for verse translations as well as prose. Of the nine English versions published from 1910 onwards it is perhaps significant that five are in verse and four in prose; it seems hard to decide which is the more suitable vehicle. Of the verse translations three are in blank verse, those of W. E. Leonard, Professor of English at Wisconsin (Dent, 1916), Sir R. Allison (Humphreys, 1919) and R. C. Trevelyan (Cambridge, 1937). Two versions selected the hazardous experiment of English hexameters, A. S. Way (Macmillan, 1933), who employed hexameters docked of half a foot and arranged in rhyming couplets, and W. Hannaford Brown (Rutgers Press, New Brunswick, 1950). Both these versions prove that hexameters are too heavy and too monotonous in English, and Brown's rhymes seem to point these defects by an inappropriate 'neo-Gothic' ornamentation. Mention should be made of Charles Foxley's (Heffer, 1933) unexpected attempt to render some of the great passages into Spenserian verse. They fit the form surprisingly well, but it would not have been possible to apply the attempt to the whole poem.

LATE REPUBLICAN POETRY 349

The three translations in blank verse illustrate perhaps what becomes clearer in the prose versions, that the poem of Lucretius strikes readers — and specially modern readers — very differently. At the extremes stand the impression that it is for the most part scanning prose, rising at times to great levels of poetic inspiration, and the belief that it is all high poetry, which in the more argumentative parts shows itself in extreme accuracy rather than in obvious nobility of expression. Leonard, turning away from what appeared to him to be the affected archaisms of the prose versions and seeking to represent the imagination of the whole, yet sank into a certain pedestrianism; Allison, too, bewitched by the desire to render the ideas and expressions faithfully and clearly has lost a good deal in nerve. Trevelyan to my mind, and I expect to that of most readers, if at times he sacrifices meticulous accuracy, has got nearest to the spirit of Lucretius both in general thought and in detailed expression.

The translations in English prose published during these years represented a gradually increasing tendency to move away from the 'translationese' of the end of the last century. My own translation (Clarendon Press), published first in 1910 and revised in 1921 and in the edition of 1947, was written strongly under the influence of Munro, but had two objects of its own, firstly to represent the Latin as fully and closely as possible, and secondly to show that the *De Rerum Natura*, even in its most closely argumentative parts, was still poetry. The consequences were some long and involved sentences, and the employment of archaic words and antiquated turns of phrase. Rouse's version (Loeb edition, Heinemann, 1924) is a sound and vigorous work, employing a more normal vocabulary, yet retaining much of the poetic touch. Thomas Jackson's rendering (Blackwell, 1929) is interesting for the experiment of using 'a rhythmical or measured prose', an endeavour to obtain the best of both worlds. It reads pleasantly and smoothly, but whether one would have detected its secret without being told, I am not sure. Finally in 1951 Penguin Books have published a version by R. E. Latham, which is on a par with many present-day translations of the classics, where the form of the original has been comparatively disregarded and the effort made to convey the poet's meaning in language that the ordinary man, uneducated in the classics, can comprehend. Those of an older generation may perhaps be allowed to say that they miss the spirit of the original. It will be interesting to see how much further we are to travel along this road.

3. *The Poet and the Poem.* Very little is known for certain of the provenance, life, and death of Lucretius and they have therefore been the subject of very various conjectures in which the last fifty years have fully played their part. To the two notices known to earlier editors in Jerome (Euseb., *s. ann.* 94 (?93) B.C.) and in Donatus' Life of Virgil, J. Masson (JP, xxiii, 221ff) added a document in the handwriting of Girolamo Borgia, prefixed to the *editio Veneta* of 1495, which professes to give an account of Lucretius' life and friends, but has been regarded with much suspicion by most critics. These three accounts are inconsistent with one another and have given rise to much discussion. The dates of the poet's birth and death are uncertain, but the general limits of the 'nineties and the 'fifties may be accepted (see discussion by F. H. Sandbach in CR, liv, 1940, 72ff). More important is the problem of Lucretius' social standing. The orthodox view is that he was a member of the aristocratic family of the *Lucretii Tricipitini* and took his place in the good society of his day, going as a friend with C. Memmius to Bithynia. This view was challenged by F. Marx (*Neue Jahrb.*, 1899, 535), who, on the ground of his *cognomen* — *Carus*—, held that Lucretius must have been a freedman; this assumption was refuted by Tenney Frank (*Studies in honour of Hermann Collitz*, 1930, 63). V. E. Alfieri (*Lucrezio*, 1929, 11-12) believed that Lucretius was a Roman, but a poor plebeian, and G. della Valle (*Tito Lucrezio Caro e l'Epicurismo campano*, 1933) maintained that he was a small landowner in the neighbourhood of Naples, who learned his Epicureanism from Philodemus and Siro. More recent opinion seems to be moving back to the traditional view.

The story recorded by Jerome of the love-philtre, Lucretius' insanity and ultimate suicide has been bandied to and fro. Nothing can be proved, but there is no convincing argument against the general idea of the tradition. Similarly Jerome's statement that Cicero *emendavit* the *poemata* of Lucretius has been interpreted in various ways, but the Borgia 'Life', for what it is worth, suggests that Cicero merely suggested improvements for certain phrases, and cannot be regarded as having prepared the work for publication, as previous editors supposed.

More important than biographical details are the features of Lucretius' character and mind, as they can be inferred from the poem. Almost all the editions discuss this, and an illuminating essay (*Lukrez, Seine Gestalt in seinem Gedicht*, Teubner, 1932) was published by O. Regenbogen. The points which come out in discussion are his faithfulness to the doctrine of Epicurus in all its details, and his difference from his master in his imagination, stimulated by his political experience in Rome, and his poetic mind, which worked more by visual imagination than by strict logic.

The Poem. Much work has been done in these years on Lucretius' sources. When the question was first raised at the end of the nineteenth century, it was assumed that the poem was based on the first of the *Letters* of Epicurus preserved by Diogenes Laertius. Giussani (*Studi Lucreziani*, 1-11) showed that in spite of general agreement there were also discrepancies, and suggested that Lucretius also used the Μεγάλη 'Επιτομή and probably the Περὶ Φύσεως itself. This view has been in the main accepted and supported.

A special question with regard to the sources of Books V and VI was raised by an Arabic work first noted by Bergsträsser (*Heidelberger Sitzungsbericht*, 1918, 9. Abhandlung, 12ff); on the strength of this W. Lück (*Die Quellenfrage in 5. und 6. Buch des Lukrez*, 1934) propounded the theory that Lucretius worked mainly on the writings of Epicureans who were his own contemporaries. This notion was contested by Reitzenstein (*Zur Quellenfrage bei Lukrez*, 1934) and has not found supporters. Others have worked on Lucretius' Latin diction, in particular Merrill, and have traced his debt to Ennius and to Cicero's translation of Aratus.

Another subject which has received much attention is the structure of the poem and the order of composition of the Books (see especially J. Mussehl, *De Lucretiani libri primi condicione et retractatione*, Berlin, 1912). His main conclusion is that the order of composition was i, ii, v, iv, iii, vi. This has been recently disputed by H. Diller (*Die Proömien des Lukrez*, St. It., 1951, 5ff), but the previous belief has been in the main reinstated by Karl Büchner (Classica et Mediaevalia, 13, Fasc. 2, 1952).

4. *MSS. and Text.* From Lachmann's main conclusions, that the two MSS. in the Library of the University of Leyden are our oldest and best authorities for the text and that they were derived from a French MS. of the fourth or fifth century, there has been no dissent, but Chatelain in his introductions to the facsimiles of O

and Q published by Sijthoff at Leyden in 1908 and 1913 respectively has modified them in two important respects: (1) he dated Q as well as O to the ninth century, probably not many years after O; (2) he demonstrated that though, as Lachmann held, many of the mistakes in O and Q point to an archetype in capitals, others require a MS. in minuscules. They were not therefore copied direct from the fourth- or fifth-century MS. but from an intermediate seventh-century copy, made by a British or Irish scribe. This seventh-century MS. must therefore be regarded as the archetype, and Lachmann's deductions as to pagination, etc., transferred to it, the fifth-century MS. now becoming an 'ancestor'. From the same seventh-century copy was derived the MS. which Poggio found and lost (P), which was the father or grandfather of all the *Itali*. Diels, going further than Chatelain, supposed complicated interconnections between the three MSS., which have not generally been accepted. Chatelain also showed that the Schedae Haunienses or Gottorpienses, the loose sheets now preserved at Copenhagen, have an affinity with Q and were probably copied from the same archetype in the same century.

After Lachmann's decisions the *Itali* for a while sank into the background and were looked on as little more than a possible supplement to the Leyden MSS. But Munro had collated them and Merrill, who worked at them for many years, published in 1920, 1927, 1928 and 1929 (Univ. of California Press) records of their readings. Martin too who edited the fourth edition of the Teubner text in 1934 consulted them again and made considerable use of them.

The establishment of the relation of the MSS. was the first requisite for the constitution of a sound text, but more was needed: a correct appreciation of Lucretius' accidence and syntax, of his metre and prosody, and more than all an adequate understanding of the Epicurean philosophy. The contribution of the period under consideration to all these matters will be estimated below.

Of the text in the twentieth-century commentaries of Merrill, Ernout, and Diels something has already been said. It may be added that of them Ernout's text is probably the soundest, Diels' the most venturous and interesting. Of the later Teubner texts Brieger's of 1909 showed a greater respect for tradition than his earlier editions, Martin's of 1934 exhibited the marked influence of Diels and contributed much from his own study of the *Itali*.

The general tendency has been away from emendation to a greater belief in the MSS. based on a truer understanding of the poem. This might be illustrated by my own texts. Comparing the edition of 1898 with that in the three-volume edition of 1947 I have returned to the MS. reading in almost 200 places, the text of 1921 representing nearly a half-way house. This result would not have satisfied Housman, but may, I believe, be taken as the general view of students of Lucretius at the present time.

5. *Formal Criticism. Grammar, metre, and style.* Earlier criticism of Latin literature was based on the assumption that prose style found its norm in Cicero and poetic style in Virgil, and that all that differed from these norms, even if historically it preceded them, was a failure or dereliction, or at best a deviation or licence. It was the attitude of criticism in the last fifty years to think of Latin literature as a whole and to see each author in his place in the series, based on what was past and leading up to what was to come. It follows that there is not one ideal Latin syntax or hexameter, from which there are deviations, but that every author has his own grammar or metre which are personal and individual; an idiosyncrasy in an author is far more satisfactorily explained by a parallel in his own works than in those of any other writer.

(a) *Grammar.* This has been the main line of development in the formal criticism of Lucretius in this century. There has been, as far as I know, no one book devoted to Lucretian grammar, but it is dealt with in all the commentaries, and specially in that of Ernout, whose main interest it is, and who apart from notes on individual words and passages, has given to it a short but illuminating section of his introduction (vol. I, xxii-xlii); his main contention is that Lucretius' grammatical style was even in his own day 'archaizing', which made it seem to those who looked back on it from the Virgilian standard even more archaic. In my Commentary I endeavoured to collect the evidence and, as far as possible, to account for its archaic flavour. Roughly speaking it may be said that Lucretius' idiosyncrasies of accidence are attributable partly to his midway position in Latin literature, partly to metrical convenience, still more to the sense of dignity which he felt was added to his verse by archaic forms such as the genitive in *-ai* in the first declension. In syntax more was due to the fluidity in expression in a transitional period of the language.

(b) *Metre.* Much work has been done during the last fifty years on the development of Latin metres (e.g. by W. R. Hardie, *Res Metrica* (Clarendon Press, 1920) and in articles by E. H. Sturtevant (*Trans. Am. Phil. Ass.*, 1923) and L. P. Wilkinson (CQ, xxxiv, 1940). A special study of Lucretius and his relation to other poets was made in a series of articles by W. A. Merrill, published by the University of California from 1921 to 1924, which were chiefly concerned with the facts rather than the explanation of them. The general tendency has been to consider Lucretius as standing midway between the comparatively haphazard experiments of Ennius and the polished perfection of Virgil and the Augustans, and to reveal his affinity with Cicero in his translations of Aratus. A brief summary of results may be given. The problem of Latin after the introduction of the Greek quantitative metres was to adapt them successfully to a language naturally scanned by stress-accent. By the time of Cicero and Lucretius it was realized that accent and ictus must to some extent be made to coincide, especially at the end and to a less extent at the beginning of the hexameter line, but that in the middle to avoid monotony they should clash. Lucretius, though careful to create clash, yet works for more coincidence than the Augustans, and his special idiosyncrasy is a love for constituting the fourth foot of a single spondaic word, which, as it were, stabilizes the coincidence at the end of the line.

Certain other peculiarities are dictated by the vocabulary of his subject-matter in different parts of the poem, e.g. the prevalence of the pentasyllables *materiai* and *principiorum* at the end of the line in the first two Books and of the quadrisyllable *animai* in Book III. There are archaisms, such as the suppression of the final *s*, the retention of short vowels before *sc*, *st*, etc., and the lengthening of syllables *in arsi*. K. Büchner (*Beobachtungen über Vers- und Gedankengang bei Lukrez. Hermes, Einzelschriften*, Heft I, 1936, 47-103) made a valuable study of *enjambement*, the lapping over of sense from one line to the next, in Lucretius, in which he demonstrated a distinct difference of practice in Books I, II and V on the one hand and III, IV and VI on the other, which is a strong argument in favour of their composition in that order.

(c) *Style*. Grammar and Metre constitute in themselves a large element in a poet's style. But apart from these there remain other habits and practices, turns of thought and expression, which give it a marked and individual character. The nature of Lucretius' style is dealt with in all the commentaries on the *De Rerum Natura* and in books about its author. Probably the most penetrating and sympathetic is that of E. E. Sikes (*Lucretius*, Cambridge University Press, 1936) in his opening chapters. The work of the last fifty years has been largely the collection and analysis of such features of Lucretius' style as the use of compound adjectives, diminutives, and Greek words, periphrases and synonyms. The careful criticism which has resulted has substituted a more concrete idea of the nature of the poet's style than the vague impression previously accepted. Among the ornaments of Lucretius' verse, alliteration, assonance, and repetition have always been recognized, but they have been given a new significance by Rosamund D. Deutsch (*The Pattern of Sound in Lucretius*, Bryn Mawr, 1939). Though she is occasionally over-zealous in the search for evidence, she has undoubtedly revealed a vast wealth of rhyme and repetition in the poem, which set it apart from any other poem in the Latin language. An interesting appendix to her book was provided in a paper by P. Friedländer ('The pattern of Sound and the Atomic Theory', AJPh, 1941, 16-32) who has shown that Lucretius held that words, like things, have an 'atomistic' structure, which accounts for what editors have been inclined to regard as 'feeble puns'. Another characteristic to which Büchner first drew attention (*op. cit.*, 5ff, cf. C. Bailey, 'The Mind of Lucretius', AJPh, 1941, 283ff) is his habit of 'suspension of thought', an idea or sequence being interrupted and, as it were, suspended over a digression and then resumed. Both these two theories have their bearing on textual criticism.

6. *Lucretius' Thought, Philosophy, and Natural Science.* Important as is the work just described on what might be called the externals of the poem, its grammar, metre, and style, more important is the examination of his thought in the last fifty years. To understand Lucretius it is always necessary to go back to his master, Epicurus, whom he so faithfully followed. The foundation of this must be Usener's great work, *Epicurea* (Teubner, 1887) in which he not only edited the *Letters* and the Κύριαι Δόξαι, but gathered together fragments of Epicurus and references to him throughout Greek and Latin literature. This work has been supplemented by the publication of other Epicurean documents such as the inscription of Diogenes of Oenoanda (J. William, Teubner, 1907) and later on by texts recovered from the papyri, particularly by

A. Vogliano, *Epicuri et Epicureorum Scripta* (Weidmann, Berlin, 1928) and *I Resti dell' xi Libro del* Περὶ Φύσεως, Cairo, 1940) and by Wolfgang Schmid, *Ethica Epicurea* (1939). In 1949 O. Gigon published an edition and translation of such work of Epicurus as is to be found in Usener (Artemis-Verlag, Zürich). The wealth of material, now brought together, has stimulated special studies, such as C. F. Merbach's *De Epicuri Canonica*, 1907. Giussani's essays in the first volume of his commentary on Lucretius have already been noticed, and to Italy we also owe two great works by Bignone, *Epicuro* (Florence, 1920), a valuable general study, and *Il perduto Aristote* (Florence, 1936) a learned and sometimes over-acute attempt to show the relations of Aristotle and Epicurus. From France has come a valuable study of Epicurus' religion, *Épicure et ses Dieux* by A.-J. Festugière (Paris, 1946) and an earlier and more comprehensive book *Épicure* by Joyau (Paris, 1910). There has also been general work on Epicurus in English, notably a short study by A. E. Taylor (Constable, 1911) and *Stoic and Epicurean* by R. D. Hicks (Longmans, Green, 1910), which had a less sound basis of understanding than was required. In the 'twenties I attempted in two volumes, *Epicurus, the Extant Remains* (1926) and *The Greek Atomists and Epicurus* (1928) both published at the Clarendon Press, to sum up and comment on what is now known and to present a more complete account of the philosopher than had hitherto been put together in English.

An interesting study of Lucretius' appeal to the modern man of science, 'Lucretius, the Poet of our Time', by Dr. H. St. Vertue, was published in *Greece and Rome* in June 1948. A special interpretation of the poem was given by B. Farrington in *Science and Politics in the Ancient World* (Allen & Unwin, 1939) and later articles. He believes that in the *De Rerum Natura* Lucretius, following Epicurus in Greece, was making an attack on the State Religion of Rome on behalf of the 'popular' movement of science. As it stands it goes too far, but it is a suggestive study and propounds a contemporary motive for the poem, which deserves closer consideration. Its attitude receives some support in M. Rozelaar's *Lukrez* (Amsterdam, 1942).

Lucretius himself (I, 934-7) claimed to be first a philosopher who could release men's minds from superstition and only secondarily a poet, who to attract his readers covered his work with the 'honey of the muses'. The result of all this modern criticism of the subject-matter has been, if not to weaken his claim as a poet, certainly to enhance his reputation as a thinker, not an original thinker, but one who by the prolonged and determined employment of his genius set out faithfully and convincingly the materialist creed of his Master.

ii. Catullus

BY R. G. C. LEVENS

Catullus, like Lucretius, is a poet more congenial to the taste of the twentieth century than to that of the nineteenth. A generation which has elevated Donne to the status of a major poet, which has produced and accepted Dylan Thomas, and has come to judge poetry more by the energy it transmits than by the polish of its surface, is naturally drawn to a poet whose sense of form was the servant of his urge to express emotion. The present age is all the more at home with Catullus because the feelings he expressed were those of an individualist clinging, in a disintegrating society, to the one standard which he could feel was secure, that of personal integrity.

This new understanding of Catullus must be recognized at the outset of any survey of his place in twentieth-century studies. But it is in no sense the result of scholarship applied to his poems; it is the product of a changed environment, and can be observed even in the reactions of students introduced to him for the first time. It may, indeed, be said that in appreciation of Catullus the scholar has lagged behind the general reader. To read Lucretius at all requires some study; but all that is most vital in Catullus can be read by anyone with a basic knowledge of Latin. So the common reader has been enjoying Catullus behind the scholar's back, while the latter, as he labours to extricate his subject from the rubble of nineteenth-century scholarship, is often too much encumbered for direct apprehension of the poet's mind and quality.

The study of Catullus has, of course, shared in the general release from those procrustean tendencies to which Dr. Bailey has referred in writing of Lucretius.[1] But in the sections which follow it will be apparent that a survey of work published in the last half-century yields only a very limited sense of achievement and progress. Much has been written, and many a skirmish has been fought; but of all the dust raised more seems to have settled than to have been dissipated. Particularly depressing to British scholars is the fact that no full commentary in the English language has been published for over sixty years; it is hoped that the next decade will see this deficiency repaired.

1. *Editions*. It will be convenient to follow the plan adopted for Lucretius and speak first of complete editions with commentaries.[2]

At the beginning of this century three commentaries on Catullus may be said to have held the field. These were the Latin commentary of E. Baehrens (second edition, 1885), R. Ellis, *A Commentary on Catullus* (second edition, 1889), and the French commentary begun by E. Benoist and completed by E. Thomas (1882-90). The last, which was attached to a verse translation by Eugène Rostand,[3] deserves mention as a work of undoubted scholarship,[4] but it is the first two which have continued to bulk large in the minds of scholars, not because they were of superlative merit, but simply because they have yet to be replaced by commentaries on the same ample scale. Both are storehouses of information, and the mutual antipathy of the two editors at least ensures that both sides of a question are generally represented in their second editions. Neither, however, is serviceable to modern scholars except as source-material. Both editors shared the contemporary passion for imaginative conjecture, and both were capable of manipulating the discussion of evidence so as to prepare the ground for emendations which had occurred to them. Baehrens was handicapped by a literal and prosaic mind which led him to insist that a poet should express himself in terms of standard literary usage; consequently much of his space is taken up with the manufacture of difficulties which would trouble no one nowadays, and the tendency of his solutions is towards re-writing Catullus in a manner which, if he had so written, would have been fatal to his survival as a poet. The principal weakness of Ellis' commentary is that he so frequently fails to reach the conclusion indicated by the evidence he presents, or to achieve consistency between the views he expresses on related topics. Nevertheless this remains, after sixty-five years, the only full commentary in English, and is still spoken of with respect by those who have little occasion to examine it closely. There was also an edition by E. T. Merrill[5] (Harvard U.P., 1893, re-issued 1951), which became, and still remains, the standard edition for the use of American students. Allowing for its small scale and for its date, this must be ranked as an excellent piece of work, and it is a pity that there has never been an English edition to make it available for general use in this country.

The first substantial twentieth-century edition was that of G. Friedrich, with German commentary (Leipzig, 1908). This was an eccentric work, inspired by a romantic temperament sharply contrasted with the general tone of German scholarship. Friedrich devoted much space to elaborate reconstructions of the processes of textual corruption, yet printed his text without *apparatus criticus*; he leapt from problem to problem, leaving many intervening lines uncommented, yet found time to speak of the beautiful peasant girl whom he saw on the peninsula of Sirmione, or to pour scorn on the Italians as no match for the Germans at drinking. It follows that his commentary is best used in conjunction with others; but useful it is, not only because he is the first editor to show a proper understanding of the relation of Catullus' language to popular speech, but because he is a great collector of parallel instances, whether of textual corruptions or of grammatical and stylistic usages. Many of these, especially from authors such as Silius Italicus of whom he had special knowledge, are additions to the common stock, and any grammarian studying a Latin usage of which Catullus affords an instance would do well to consult Friedrich, as his commentary may well furnish the *locus classicus* for that usage.

W. Kroll's edition with German commentary, first published in 1923 (Leipzig, Teubner) and reprinted, with a brief appendix of additional notes, in 1929, was intended to replace that of B. Schmidt (1887) as a students' text-book. For this reason, and because of the exigencies of German publishing after the First World War, its scale was severely restricted, and it may reasonably be described as a major edition compressed into a small volume. The introduction is too brief, the *apparatus criticus* inconveniently sparse, and the notes, printed in small type below the text, have a forbiddingly cramped appearance. But they show a remarkable gift for selecting what is most useful and significant from the mass of available data; in particular, Kroll is the first editor to make a proper use of the remains of Hellenistic poetry, which have an important bearing on the study of Catullus. Though somewhat heavy-handed and inclined to labour obvious points, Kroll is a thoroughly objective, level-headed, and efficient commentator, and his edition is by common consent the most reliable for consultation by scholars.

The edition by M. Lenchantin de Gubernatis, with Italian commentary, first appeared in 1928 (Turin, Loescher-Chiantore). A second edition, identical except for addenda to the introduction,[6] was issued in 1933, and a reprint in 1953 has made it readily available. This edition is similar in scale to that of Kroll, to whom it is clearly indebted, but its introduction is much fuller and its commentary less closely packed. The introduction shows a fine perspective, concentrating on the literary heritage and environment of Catullus, and adding a lucid and well-balanced survey of the textual tradition. The text is, however, printed without *apparatus criticus*. The commentary allows appropriate space for introducing each poem, and blends exposition with illustration in a just economy. Lenchantin was perhaps closer in spirit to his poet than any previous editor, and if only he were more sound on points of language his edition could be warmly recommended.

2. *Translations*. The English prose translation by F. Warre Cornish, first published in 1904 (Cambridge University Press), was chosen for incorporation in the Loeb Classical Library (London, Heinemann, 1912), and is therefore the one most widely used. The editing of the Latin text is well below the standard of this series, but the translation is accurate and, though somewhat dated, seldom objectionable in style. It is not altogether complete, though modified versions of seventeen lampoons which Cornish did not choose to translate were inserted by the general editor, W. H. D. Rouse. It may be regretted that the choice for this series did not rather fall on the excellent translation by C. Stuttaford (London, Bell, 1912); it would have furnished a far better text, and time has dealt more kindly with its idiom.

Verse translations of Catullus are so numerous that it will be possible here to mention only those which are complete or nearly complete. They are also, for the most part, ephemeral; the versions of R. Kennard Davis (London, Bell, 1913) and Sir W. Marris (Oxford, Clarendon Press, 1924), well-thought-of in their day, are by now sadly out of period, and that of J. F. Symons-Jeune (London, Heinemann, 1923), is only slightly less so. By contrast that of Hugh Macnaghten (Cambridge University Press, 1925), despite some inversions which are no longer favoured, still appears remarkably fresh and well turned; his translation of poem 17 is of a noteworthy excellence. The translation by A. S. Way, though more recent (London, Macmillan, 1936) and more complete, is less to be commended than any of these; apart from the archaism of his poetic style, the translator has paid little heed to the form of his originals, and has even added flourishes of his own to their content. The Australian poet and novelist Jack Lindsay has published two complete translations (London, Fanfrolico Press, 1929, and Sylvan Press, 1948), the second vastly superior to the first. His idiom, modern and informal, hardly captures either the tenderness or the elegance of Catullus, but he is robust and ingenious, notably in places where translators usually fear to tread. He understands Catullus well, and his introduction and notes show him to be a scholar. Readers accustomed to modern poetry may well find that this translation brings them nearer to Catullus than any of its predecessors could.

I will not presume to discuss translations into languages other than English, beyond mentioning the vivid and scholarly prose translation by G. Lafaye in the Budé series. French has certain advantages over English as a medium for the translation of Catullus, and this is a version which can be consulted with profit, especially as it is set opposite one of the best available texts (see below, §5). The text of E. d'Arbela (see below, §5) is likewise accompanied by an Italian prose translation.

3. *Biography.* This must be treated under a separate heading because it is the most controversial aspect of Catullian studies.

Apart from numerous references that associate him with Verona, there are only three external data of any significance for the life of Catullus:

(1) Suetonius (*Iul.* 73) says that Caesar, after exacting an apology from him for lampoons directed at himself and Mamurra, invited him to dinner and resumed friendly relations with his father.

(2) Apuleius (*Apol.* 10) says that the real name of his Lesbia was Clodia.

(3) Jerome says that he died in his thirtieth year, placing his birth in 87 B.C. and his death in 57 B.C. (*Chron. a. Abr.*, 1930, 1960).

Oddly enough, the one chronological fact which emerges with

absolute certainty from the internal evidence of the poems is that their author was still alive in 55 B.C.[7] So Jerome must have been wrong, and is generally held to have ante-dated both birth and death by three years.[8] The poems also tell us that Catullus served in Bithynia under Memmius, and this period of service can be dated from the spring of 57 B.C. to the spring of 56 B.C.[9] Even this is no more than a deduction, and has not always been accepted as fact.[10] But the evidence for it may reasonably be called 'conclusive'. No such term can be applied to the evidence for dating any other event in the poet's life prior to 55 B.C.

Yet writers on Catullus, in this century as in the last, have seldom hesitated to give confident accounts of his career, tracing the course of his love-life and assigning particular poems to particular dates or phases. Such biographies are too numerous to list, as they occur not merely in books about Catullus and in introductions to editions or translations, but in literary histories and works of reference. At first glance most of them appear to tell much the same story; but differences apparent on a closer inspection betray the large part played by fancy in this game of reconstruction. Catullus was rich because he owned a villa near Tibur and someone owed him 100,000 sesterces; or he was poor because his villa was mortgaged for a small sum and he told a friend that his purse was full of cobwebs. As a young man at Verona, before he met Lesbia, he had had lovers of both sexes; or Lesbia was his first love, but when she proved unfaithful to him he sought consolation with these others. Such-and-such a poem is early because it shows that Catullus is not yet fully accepted by Lesbia; or it is late because it shows that the rift between them has begun.

Such biographies generally accept without demur the hypothesis that the Lesbia of the poems is none other than Clodia the wife of Metellus Celer, and that some, though not all, of the poems mentioning a Caelius or a Rufus refer to the orator Marcus Caelius Rufus. This hypothesis is the more attractive because it links Catullus with a social circle which is well documented in other sources, notably Cicero's speech in defence of Caelius. Thus, at the cost of treating a plausible hypothesis as an established fact, it becomes possible for the imaginative biographer to set up a new framework of data for the life of Catullus, with results which are best demonstrated by illustration:

LATE REPUBLICAN POETRY

When Catullus brought his letter of introduction all the way up that steep ramp to the conspicuous palace of the proconsul it is not likely that he expected to be invited to call again, much less to find Clodia all graciousness and eager to listen to his embarrassed sentences.
(Tenney Frank, *Catullus and Horace*, Oxford, Blackwell, 1928, p. 13.)

Catullus also met Cicero, as we learn from a letter of thanks which must be discussed later. Indeed he could hardly have escaped the observant eye of the ex-consul whose splendid palace stood opposite the poet's favourite haunt. But Cicero spares Catullus in his vituperations of Clodia. He had a weakness for young literary men.
(*Ibid.*, p. 32.)

In 62 B.C. a new governor, Metellus, arrived in Cisalpine Gaul, accompanied by his wife Clodia. There was a strict ordinance forbidding wives to go abroad with their husbands when these latter held an official position, but Clodia was not a woman to whom rules were of any importance. She came to Verona and met Catullus there; and that meeting was the turning-point in the young poet's life. In the spring of the next year he followed the lady to Rome.
(F. A. Wright, *Three Roman Poets*, London, Routledge, 1938, p. 102.)

In the seventy-seventh poem again, written 58 B.C., Catullus inveighs against a Rufus, who had stolen from him his dearest possession; and it was in that year, after the death of Metellus, as we know from Cicero's speech *Pro Caelio*, that Marcus Caelius Rufus was living with Clodia in her house on the Palatine.
(*Ibid.*, p. 130.)

This last extract well illustrates the vicious circle to which this type of biography is prone. It suggests a significant coincidence between two independent facts: that poem 77 was written in 58 B.C. and that Caelius Rufus was Clodia's lover during the same year. But the first of these 'facts' is a mere inference from the second; apart from the hypothesis that Catullus and Caelius were lovers of the same Clodia there is no basis whatever for dating the poem.

This hypothesis is, however, by no means so firmly established as to be capable of supporting a superstructure of inference. Nineteenth-century scholars, after weighing the evidence for and against, generally decided in its favour. But in this century, though upheld by Pascal[11] and others, it has been hotly assailed, notably by Giri and Rothstein,[12] the latter holding that the Clodia in question was not the second but the third of the sisters of P. Clodius. This hypothesis is certainly no more plausible than the other, but discussion of it has served to expose the conjectural status of the commonly accepted view, and the downright scepticism of Giri, who concluded that Catullus' Clodia belonged to some obscure branch of the *gens*, has likewise helped to induce a more cautious treatment of the matter. Thus Kroll, though he regards the usual hypothesis as highly probable, abstains from building upon it;[13] and Lenchantin de Gubernatis, though he dissents from his fellow-countryman Giri to the extent of thinking that Lesbia must be *one* of the three sisters of P. Clodius, leaves the question wide open. The commentaries of these two scholars are thus free from the dubious inferences which have cumbered earlier editions, and demonstrate that in studying the poetry of Catullus we are at no great disadvantage in knowing as little about his Lesbia as we know about Propertius' Cynthia. Among recent writers (see below, §4) Wheeler in *Catullus and the Traditions of Ancient Poetry* (1934) showed a caution sharply contrasted with the 'sure historical touch' of Tenney Frank,[14] and Havelock in *The Lyric Genius of Catullus* (1939) exposed the conjectural type of biography in a parody less far-fetched than some of its originals. Yet in the *Oxford Classical Dictionary* (1949) we find A. M. Duff repeating the familiar circumstantial account, and as recently as 1952 it has been demonstrated that this is a subject still capable of causing confusion.[15] The whole controversy has been documented up to 1940 by M. Schuster (RE VII A coll. 2358-60); he considers that there are good grounds for accepting the traditional identification, but like Kroll abstains from basing inferences upon it. The same article deals fully and fairly (coll. 2369ff) with minor questions of prosopography in Catullus.

An even broader issue than that of Lesbia was raised by P. Maas in a brisk article published in 1942.[16] Rothstein, having discarded Caelius Rufus and his Clodia, had dated all the shorter poems after Catullus' return from Bithynia in the spring of 56 B.C. Maas went further and placed *all* the extant poems after that date, supposing that the poet's brother died as late as 54 B.C., and that he himself lived a year or two longer. This article was perhaps not intended as more than a protreptic (or anatreptic?) exercise, and it makes use of some flimsy supports,[17] but its destructive value is considerable; it both exposes and illustrates the hazards of 'biographical criticism' where Catullus is concerned.

4. *Literary History and Criticism.* During the last half-century our knowledge both of early Greek lyric poetry and of the Greek poetry of the Alexandrian and Hellenistic ages has been substantially enlarged. Discoveries of new material have focused attention on these fields, with consequential benefit to the study of Latin poets who were strongly influenced by Greek models. In the case of Catullus this benefit first became apparent in 1923 in the edition by W. Kroll (see above, §1), and about the same time Wilamowitz devoted a chapter of his *Hellenistische Dichtung*[18] to a study of the more formal poetry of Catullus in relation to Greek models. This lead was followed by A. L. Wheeler in *Catullus and the Traditions of Ancient Poetry* (Berkeley, U. of California Press, 1934); what was chiefly interesting about this book was that, while demonstrating how closely Catullus in his set pieces followed in the steps of his predecessors, it yet vigorously asserted his independence and originality.

Surprisingly little general criticism of the poetry of Catullus has appeared in book form in this century, compared with the large amount of periodical literature devoted to particular aspects of his work or to particular poems. D. A. Slater's *The Poetry of Catullus* (Manchester, 1912) was only a single lecture, but it contained many shrewd observations and is still worth reading when obtainable. Tenney Frank's *Catullus and Horace* (Oxford, Blackwell, 1928) was directed mainly to placing Catullus in the context of his times, and lavish use of the author's wide knowledge of the first-century background makes it attractive reading; but its historical and critical methods invite considerable reserve (see above, §3). S. Gaetani's *La Poesia di Catullo* (Rome, Formiggini, 1934) is of interest mainly for its study of Catullus in relation to Lucretius, Horace, and Virgil. F. A. Wright's *Three Roman Poets*

(London, Routledge, 1938) is not, so far as Catullus is concerned, a work of any durable value. But in 1939 E. A. Havelock's *The Lyric Genius of Catullus* (Oxford, Blackwell) swept like a gust of fresh air through the stuffy corridors of Catullian criticism. Unfortunately its publication coincided with the outbreak of war, and the not very distinguished English 'imitations' of twenty-six lyrics of Catullus, with which the volume opens, may also have served to distract attention from the excellence and importance of the essays which follow; hence, despite two laudatory notices,[19] it does not appear to have received adequate recognition. Havelock's especial contribution lies in viewing Catullus as a whole, not as two or more poets writing in different styles,[20] and in observing the impact of the Transpadane circle of poets on Roman society and literature, and its bearing on those elements in the Italian heritage which cannot be explained in terms of Roman *gravitas*. His essays act as a powerful corrective to the weaknesses of a critical tradition too closely centred on the Augustan age, a tradition which seems at times to be regarding Catullus as a deviationist because he did not model himself on poets who at the time of his death had not begun to write. Such a challenge to familiar views, even if too provocative for general acceptance, at least earns the credit due to those who refresh the mind by suggesting new answers to old questions. Certainly no teacher could wish for a more stimulating book to put into the hands of present-day students, and a revised edition would be most welcome.

H. Bardon in *L'Art de la Composition chez Catulle* (Paris, Belles Lettres, 1943) develops by stylistic analysis a view which supports both Wheeler and Havelock. He sees Catullus as a poet too profoundly Italian to be significantly affected by foreign influences; metrical tests do not show him following formal Alexandrian patterns, and his debt to Callimachus is negligible. Bardon especially notes Catullus' habit of expressing his emotional mood in the opening line of a poem, and returning to it at the end, as evidence that with him passion prevails over form.

The influence of Catullus on English poetry has been the subject of special studies by three American scholars, E. S. Duckett, J. B. Emperor, and J. A. S. McPeek.[21] His influence on later ages in general has been cursorily traced in a small volume by K. P. Harrington.[22] The material assembled by these writers is sufficient to suggest that G. A. Highet in *The Classical Tradition*

(Oxford, Clarendon Press, 1948) might reasonably have allocated more space to Catullus.

5. *MSS. and Text.* Apart from the codex Thuaneus (T) containing poem 62 only, all the surviving MSS. of Catullus, some 120 in number,[23] are believed to stem from a codex known to have existed at Verona in the fourteenth century,[24] and generally denoted by the symbol V. The only extant MSS. believed to have been copied within the same century are the Oxoniensis (O),[25] the Sangermanensis (G),[26] and the Romanus (R). None of these was known to Lachmann,[27] whose pioneer edition (1829) was founded on two fifteenth-century MSS., the Datanus (D) and the Santenianus (L). G was first brought into the foreground by Schwabe, O by Baehrens;[28] the latter, following Lachmann's principle of concentrating on the best MSS. available, based his text exclusively on OG, as did Merrill in his edition of 1893 (see above, §1). The reaction against this principle was led by Ellis, who recognized the superiority of OG but thought it worth while to cite a great many other MSS., some for no better reason than that their aberrations afforded a basis for conjecture. K. P. Schulze, re-editing Baehrens's text in 1893, claimed that a Venetian MS., which he called M,[29] was the parent of most of the *deteriores*, and associated it with OG in his *apparatus criticus*; but he made a breach in this otherwise closed system by giving credit to the variants of Lachmann's D. This MS., though copied as late as A.D. 1463, only a few years before the first printed edition,[30] is distinguished by archaic orthography often coinciding with that of O, and contains many readings which differ sharply from those of OG. Some of these are obvious interpolations, but others have been regarded by many scholars as beyond the inventive powers of fifteenth-century humanists; yet it is difficult to envisage a process by which one late MS. could, in a period of active copying and cross-checking,[31] become the sole repository of an independent tradition. Difference of opinion concerning the value of D may be said to constitute the principal line of division between two schools of twentieth-century criticism.

It was not till 1896 that R was discovered by the American scholar W. G. Hale.[32] It proved to be so closely akin to G that it added little to our knowledge of the tradition, since almost all its readings were duplicated either in G or its correcting hand or in M, which Hale, much to Schulze's disgust, declared to be a direct copy of *R*. Consequently the interest aroused by its discovery soon gave place to disappointment and, in certain quarters, to a quite irrational hostility provoked by Hale's habit of announcing the results of his research in advance and then failing to produce them. After promising a full collation and a fascimile, Hale published nothing except a series of articles spread over twenty-seven years,[33] during which he and his research assistants collated 115 MSS. with a view to proving that *R* was an elder brother of *G* and the parent of all the *deteriores*. Had this been established, the textual criticism of Catullus would at least have been greatly simplified, even if no substantial improvement of the text had resulted. As it was, the only effect was to divert European palaeographers to other fields, and this frustrating episode helps to explain why most twentieth-century editions are characterized by fog-bound ambivalence and by a tendency to rest content with citations available in printed sources.

The only systematic attempt at rationalization of the MS. tradition since the discovery of *R* has been that of A. Morgenthaler in his dissertation *De Catulli Codicibus* (Strasbourg, 1909). Morgenthaler's conclusion was that *O* and *G* were transcribed from separate copies of *V*, and that *G* had a brother from which three copies were made, *R*, *M*, and a third which became the parent of the *deteriores*.[34] He thus provided a by-pass route which was a boon to the partisans of *D*, though he himself considered this MS. worthless. Morgenthaler, who was twenty-three years of age when he completed his dissertation, relied on the published facsimiles of *G* and *M*[35] and on photographs of *R*, which at that date are unlikely to have enabled a beginner to distinguish accurately between original readings and corrections *in rasura*; and not being well versed in the habits of the fifteenth century he made too little allowance for the likelihood of crossing between families and sub-families. Nor was he free of the thesis-writer's tendency to pick his objective in advance and brush aside evidence pointing elsewhere. Nevertheless his analysis has had great influence, if only because it is so conveniently simple; like Hale's hypothesis, it has been neither verified nor superseded.

If little progress towards a reconstruction of the archetype can be reported, at least much has been gained by a recoil from the *prurigo coniciendi* which vitiated nineteenth-century criticism. Recognition that Augustan canons of language and metre do not apply to Catullus has led to the restoration of MS. readings in many passages formerly molested by editors. Here Schulze set a fine example, and the prevailing twentieth-century tendency has been to resort to emendation only in desperate cases, and even then to prefer conjectures which have stood the test of time. This development can be simply illustrated by reference to hiatus, of which the MSS. exhibit eleven clear instances,[36] excluding those following *o* or *io*, or where there is correption of a long syllable. Not one of these instances survived the attentions of such scholars as Lachmann, Haupt, and Baehrens, to whom hiatus was 'intolerable' or 'inadmissible'. Schulze restored the received text in all eleven places, while Ellis and Merrill accepted it in only three; only one subsequent editor has departed from the MS. reading in as many as three of these passages.

It remains to show briefly how the more important twentieth-century texts[37] compare with one another in regard to the matters discussed above.

To mention Robinson Ellis among editors of this century seems anachronistic, since he first edited Catullus in 1867, but his volume in the Oxford Classical Text series did not appear till 1904, and is still current. Ellis had himself twice collated R,[38] and rated it highly, though out of deference to Hale he cited only a limited number of readings from it; some of these were later repudiated by Hale.[39] Apart from this his new edition showed no great advance on that of 1878, and was retrograde compared with such nineteenth-century recensions as those of Riese, Schulze, and Merrill. Many unwarrantable emendations were printed in the text, and still more crowded the critical apparatus, in which as many as twenty-three MSS. were cited, some of them for reasons which did little credit to the editor's judgment.[40]

It will be convenient, and almost in accordance with chronological sequence, to take next a group of editors who reverted to Lachmann's principle. Friedrich (see above, §1) was an unorthodox member of this group: he based his text and critical observations principally on OG, but opened the door to D alone among the later MSS.;[41] he had inspected R, but dismissed it as worthless. Kroll (see above, §1) was a firmer adherent of Lachmann and Baehrens, and his skeleton *apparatus criticus* cited no MS. other than OG (and, for poem 62, T) except by a general symbol denoting *deteriores*. His text shows every mark of caution, with free use of the obelus, yet contains several dubious emendations. In the same year (1923) Merrill edited a Teubner text based on *OGR*. Since he had access to Hale's collation, this should have been the edition to give a true conspectus of the three oldest complete MSS.; but the opportunity was sadly missed. The house of Teubner was working under conditions of austerity, and Merrill's *apparatus criticus* was too sparse to give a clear picture,[42] or even to add greatly to our knowledge of *R*. His text, incorporating numerous conjectures derived from Ellis, was quite out of line with modern trends.[43]

The editors of the remaining group were all to some degree influenced by Morgenthaler. G. Lafaye prepared for the Budé series (Paris, Belles Lettres, 1922) a soundly conservative text, with an *apparatus criticus* in which *OGMD* predominated but sundry other MSS. were cited from time to time, the editor having no very firm view concerning the *deteriores*. *R* was cited only where its readings were already on record, but this is equally true of later editions. The clarity of the *apparatus criticus*, from which rejected emendations are excluded, combines with the soundness of the text and the excellence of the translation (see above, §2) to make this a singularly useful volume. Lenchantin de Gubernatis (see above, §1) showed good judgment in the constitution of his text, but printed it without *apparatus criticus*. Doubtful readings are discussed in his commentary, but his principal contribution to textual criticism is the second section of his introduction. This is far and away the most lucidly condensed account of the MS. tradition yet written, but it amounts to little more[44] than an abstract of Morgenthaler's thesis, from which the supporting evidence appears to be taken on trust.[45] A similar account, less skilfully presented and somewhat inaccurately printed, forms the Prolegomena to an edition by E. d'Arbela (Milan, Istituto Editoriale Italiano, 1947), and is worth mentioning if only because it is in Latin, whereas Lenchantin's is in Italian. This edition resembles that of Ellis more than any other, but is a great improvement on it, having a less interpolated text and a more concise critical apparatus; d'Arbela cites even more MSS. than Ellis did, but saves space by using symbols to denote a consensus, and records the better-known conjectures merely, as he says, to demonstrate the industry of critics. The most recent text is that of Mauriz Schuster, issued in the Teubner series in 1949 to replace that of Merrill. This is a fine specimen of modern editing in that it separates *testimonia* from MS. readings, and by a neat system of abbreviation gives a wide range of bibliographical reference with the minimum expenditure of space. As it includes, besides a documented *Index nominum*, an *Index metricus* and an *Index verborum et locutionum*, it serves many of the purposes for which recourse to a commentary is normally required. From a critical standpoint it is less satisfying. An uneasily written preface leaves no clear impression except that Schuster has contributed no fresh work on the problems confronting an editor. Having been led to the view that other MSS. besides *OG* may sometimes be of assistance in recovering the reading of *V*, he might be commended for his plan of singling out *RMD* and citing them only when the reading is in doubt; but this plan is not consistently followed in the *apparatus criticus*.[46] In constituting his text Schuster is generally so conservative that when he does discard a defensible MS. reading it comes as a shock;[47] it is in poem 66 that his judgment is most seriously at fault. Had Schuster's edition come up to expectations, little need have been said of the text prepared by E. Cazzaniga and revised by L. Castiglioni for the Paravia series (Turin, 1945), since its editor did not attempt to grapple with the problems discussed above. As it is, this unpretentious work is not merely the most inoffensive, but for general purposes the most serviceable, of modern texts. Cazzaniga was consistently level-headed in his choice of readings, and his *apparatus criticus*, firmly based on *OG* with selective reference to *R* (which he inspected in facsimile), is fully adequate for readers who are not concerned with the difference between one fifteenth-century MS. and another; *testimonia* are printed separately, and appendices assemble useful data on metre, language, and orthography.

It is clear that what has chiefly been lacking in recent editions of Catullus, and what must chiefly be looked for from future editors, is independence of judgment based on first-hand study of the MSS.;[48] in particular, the status of *R* needs clarifying by a full collation employing expert diagnosis to identify the readings of its first hand.[49] For the later MSS. the existing American collations might reasonably suffice, especially as most of them were made by B. L. Ullman,[50] whose name now stands high among palaeographers and textual critics; examination of these collations, if only by a post-graduate student, might at least have the effect of consigning all but a few of the fifteenth-century MSS. to oblivion, which was precisely the intention with which they were collated.

Finally, separate mention must be made of the *Coma Berenices*, since it is the only poem of Catullus directly affected by recent discoveries.[51] Its setting belongs to a period of history about which much has been learnt from papyri, and the life-story of Ptolemy III and Berenice II is now much better documented than it was when Ellis wrote his commentary. Further, two papyri[52] containing substantial portions of the Πλόκαμος of Callimachus have shed new light on the text of Catullus' translation. The first of these, published by G. Vitelli in 1929, corresponded to ll. 44-64 of Catullus 66, and its appearance occasioned a fresh outbreak of the *prurigo coniciendi* which extended even beyond the passage directly concerned.[53] Most of the resulting conjectures, and many others of earlier date, were made to look very foolish when within twenty years a second papyrus came to light, overlapping with the first and corresponding to ll. 43-55, 65-78, 89-94, with marginal scholia which helped to supplement the defective text. It was reconstructed by E. Lobel, who has since edited it, but R. Pfeiffer was allowed to publish it in the first volume of his edition of Callimachus (Oxford, Clarendon Press, 1949), and rendered a great service to students of Catullus by printing opposite the Greek fragments (pp. 112-23) a complete text of the Latin translation with its own *apparatus criticus*, and a commentary which takes account of both versions. The general impression resulting from the juxtaposition of these two texts is that Catullus was a less free translator than was formerly believed,[54] closely following the structure and rhythm of his original even where he was unable to reproduce its elaborate conceits. His text was affected in several interesting ways: the two papyri were found to have different readings where the Catullus MSS. exhibit a fusion of these two readings;[55] a winged horse which editors had long striven to expel with a pitchfork was re-installed by the second papyrus;[56] and a couplet which had been exposed to all manner of ingenious reconstructions was found to need a change of only one letter, and that in a word which had never been suspected.[57] This last discovery pointed at least two morals: that corruption does not necessarily reside where the difficulty appears greatest, and that conjectures requiring only a slight adjustment are more likely to be right than those which involve re-writing a whole passage.

6. *Language, Metre, and Style.* As far as concerns these branches of criticism, the early decades of this century are notable only for the process of liberation to which Dr. Bailey has referred in the corresponding section of his chapter on Lucretius.[58] On the completion of this process the scholar and critic no doubt hoped to enjoy the liberated territory on his own terms. But such is not the way of this fast-moving century, and infiltration by the agents of two upstart neighbours, psychology and semantics, has forced him to acquire new techniques and to wrestle with a new critical language which is still in its formative stage. Consequently work published in the 'thirties and 'forties[59] on the language, metre, and style of Catullus is best regarded as transitional, to be superseded when the critical revolution enters upon a more stable phase.

Much of the recent literature consists of articles devoted to the analysis of particular poems.[60] But there have been some more substantial contributions, the best of them forming an intelligible link between the analytical criticism which infers a poet's state of mind from his vowel-patterns and the more general type of modern criticism which is seen at its best in E. A. Havelock's book described in §4 above. The thesis of H. Bardon, mentioned in the same section, is a link of this type.

What is perhaps one of the most enlightening works in the new critical tradition is also one of the earliest, J. van Gelder's *De Woordherhaling bij Catullus* (The Hague, 1933). The author, a disciple on the one hand of de Saussure, on the other of Husserl, here isolates a phenomenon which must be obvious to every reader of Catullus (word-repetition), and after close analysis defines it not as some mechanical neoteric device but as denoting 'linguistic exuberance, created on the basis of the obsessed oscillation of the attention between some conceptions or experiences'. Though the book is written in Dutch, and even the English summary at the end is, as this excerpt shows, rather oddly expressed, it well repays study as illustrating, on a conveniently narrow front, the legitimate uses of a critical method which has since increasingly come to the fore.

A more forbidding side of this method is seen in Ilse Schnelle's *Untersuchungen zu Catulls dichterischer Form* (Philologus Suppl. 25,

1933), a work justly criticized by an Italian scholar for its *eccessiva cerebralità*. Here vowel-patterns and psychology join hands in the most suspect manner, and the authoress herself is in danger of being overwhelmed by her own jargon. It is evident, however, from the minor literature of subsequent years that this work has had considerable influence.

A reminder that the poet's choice of vowels and of words is not entirely a matter of psychology was administered by T. Cutt in a matter-of-fact thesis entitled *Meter and Diction in Catullus' Hendecasyllabics* (University of Chicago Libraries, 1936). Laborious statistics are here used to show how the metre forces on the poet a preference for certain types of word and certain inflexions.

An Italian scholar, A. Ronconi, who uses the modern approach with discretion, has usefully covered several aspects of Catullus' language and style in a series of articles published in 1938-40.[61]

The relation of Catullus' metre and diction to those of his Latin predecessors has received very scanty treatment. R. Avallone's *Catullo e i suoi Modelli Romani* (Salerno, 1944) is limited to Ennius and Plautus, and what useful data it contains are diluted and obscured by the inclusion of such coincidences as no two writers in the same language could well avoid. This work needs to be done again, and continued through the rest of Republican poetry.

M. N. Wetmore's *Index Verborum Catullianus* (Yale University Press, 1912) is a useful instrument for workers in this field.

[1] See above, p. 280.
[2] The scope of this chapter is taken to exclude selections edited for use in schools, and commentaries appended to translations for the enlightenment of the general reader, such as the second volume of V. Errante's *La Poesia di Catullo* (Milan, Hoepli, 1945), which is frankly derivative and popular. The edition by C. Stuttaford (London, Bell, 1909) was very slight and has long been out of print.
[3] Not to be confused with the dramatist Edmond Rostand.
[4] French reviewers still complain (RPh 1950, 223, REL 1950, 384) if this commentary is neglected, but it is none too easily come by; there is not even a complete copy in the Bodleian Library.
[5] Not to be confused with W. A. Merrill, the editor of Lucretius.
[6] These addenda were occasioned mainly by the Vitelli papyrus of Callimachus, which outdated the commentary on poem 66. Since the addenda have themselves been outdated by the discovery of a new papyrus and by Pfeiffer's *Callimachus*, it is a pity that the edition was not revised before reprinting in 1953. See §5, *MSS. and Text*, ad fin.
[7] Catul. 55.6, 113.2; cf. also allusions to Britain at 11.12, 29 passim, 45.22.
[8] The notion, said to have been first advanced by Gibbon at the age of nineteen, that C. must have been alive in 47 B.C. because he refers to Vatinius as swearing by his consulship (52.3) has long since been exploded; Cicero made a similar jest at V.'s expense (*in Vat.* 11), alleging that as early as 62 B.C. he was talking about his *second* consulship; and anyway there were no curule aediles in 47 B.C. (52.3, cf. Dio. xlii. 20.4,

27.2, 55.4). Yet it was recently revived, in complete innocence of its previous history, by two Belgian scholars (P. Gilbert and M. Renard in AC 1942, 93-6).

[9] Catul. 10 and 28. Memmius was praetor in 58 B.C., and is likely to have governed a province the following year, while L. Calpurnius Piso Caesoninus, cos. 58, was governing Macedonia (a chilly province, cf. 28.5).

[10] See Ellis, *A Commentary on Catullus*, pp. lvff.

[11] C. Pascal, *Poeti e Personaggi Catulliani*, Catania, 1916.

[12] G. Giri, *Riv. Indo-greco-ital.* 1922, 161ff, *Athenaeum* 1928, 183ff, 215ff; M. Rothstein, *Philologus* 1923, 1-34, cf. 1926, 472f.

[13] Surprisingly, Kroll (p. 253) refuses to identify the Lesbius of Catul. 79 with P. Clodius, though this is usually the trump card of those who wish to identify Lesbia with a sister of this Clodius.

[14] K. P. Harrington in AJPh 1935, 182 points this contrast, evidently intending it to the disadvantage of Wheeler.

[15] Cicero, *pro Caelio*, ed.² R. G. Austin (Oxford, Clarendon Press, 1952), App. III, pp. 148ff. Austin appears to regard the identification of Lesbia with the Clodia of the speech as established fact, that of the Rufus of the poems with Caelius Rufus as conjecture. But the first identification can hardly stand unless supported by the second; cf. n13 above. Possibly Austin shared the delusion of H. J. Rose (*Handbook of Latin Literature*, p. 140, n. 64) that Apuleius specified the Clodia who was concealed by the name Lesbia.

[16] CQ 1942, 79-82.

[17] Maas finds it easier to believe that C. made a second journey to Asia Minor than that Veranius and Fabullus twice went on foreign service together; and he represents C. as saying, in effect (68.15ff): 'I used to compose love poetry as a lad, but that was over ten years ago, and since my brother's recent death I have written nothing'; yet Maas attributes most of the extant poems to the two years preceding the brother's death. For a criticism of Maas by a supporter of the traditional chronology see R. J. M. Lindsay in CPh 1948, 42-4.

[18] U. v. Wilamowitz-Moellendorff, *Hellenistische Dichtung in der Zeit des Kallimachos* (Berlin, Weidmannsche Buchhandlung, 1924), vol. II, pp. 277-310.

[19] By M. B. Ogle (CPh 1940, 440-2); and by C. J. Fordyce (CR 1941, 36-7), who described it as 'a book of extraordinary freshness and vitality' and 'one of the most interesting and stimulating studies in Latin literature which have appeared in this country for a long time'.

[20] For a further study along similar lines see J. P. Elder in HSPh 1951, 101-36.

[21] E. S. Duckett, *Catullus in English Poetry* (Northampton, Mass., Smith College Classical Studies No. 6, 1925); J. B. Emperor, *The Catullian Influence in English Lyric Poetry ca. 1600-1650* (New York, Columbia U.P., 1928); J. A. S. McPeek, *Catullus in Strange and Distant Britain* (Harvard U.P., 1939).

[22] *Catullus and his Influence* (London, Harrap, 1923).

[23] See the list given by W. G. Hale, CPh 1908, 236ff.

[24] See R. Ellis, *Catullus in the Fourteenth Century* (Oxford U.P., 1905); W. G. Hale, 'Benzo of Alexandria and Catullus', CPh 1910, 56-65; B. L. Ullman, 'Hieremias de Montagnone and his citations from Catullus', CPh 1910, 66-82.

[25] *O* is now generally held to be older than *G*. It used to be vaguely assigned to the latter end of the century; Hale at one time thought it might be up to fifty years earlier (CR 1906, 164), but withdrew this estimate on the ground that the ornamentation of the first initial could not be much earlier than A.D. 1400 (CPh 1908, 243). But the illumination may be of later date than the MS.

[26] An adscript at the end of this MS. gives A.D. 1375 as the date of copying; but an 'etc.' at the end of this adscript has led some scholars to believe that the scribe of *G* copied out part of a longer adscript which he found in his exemplar, and that it was the latter which was transcribed in 1375. See E. Châtelain, *Paléographie des Classiques Latins*, vol. I (1884-92), p. 4, and Hale in CR 1906, 162, where Lindsay is said to support this view.

[27] Attention had been called to *O* in 1822 by A. J. Valpy in an appendix to his London edition of Doering's *Catullus* (vol. II, p. 837), but this can hardly have come to Lachmann's notice. *G* was first mentioned by Sillig a year after the publication of Lachmann's edition.

376 LATE REPUBLICAN POETRY

²⁸ Ellis made use of it in his edition of 1867, but without realizing its importance.
²⁹ *Ven.* in the *app. crit.* of Ellis's O.C.T.
³⁰ The earliest dated edition is that of 1472, but there is an undated one which may be earlier; see Ellis, *Catulli Veronensis Liber* (Oxford, 1878²), p. lix.
³¹ As early as A.D. 1375 the scribe of *G* (or of its parent MS., see n26 above) had apologized for being unable to check his copy against a second exemplar, implying that this was already customary.
³² It had been concealed in the Vatican Library by faulty cataloguing.
³³ CR 1896, 314; TAPhA 1897, liii-v; CR 1898 447-9; H. 1899 133-4; CR 1906, 160-4; CPh 1908, 233-56; TAPhA 1922, 103-12. See also B. L. Ullman in AJPh 1917, 98-9. One of Hale's most significant claims was that the second hand in *R* was that of Coluccio Salutati, whose ownership of the MS. was attested by a legend on its first page. This is confirmed, in a private letter, by Professor Ullman, who has examined over 100 MSS. owned by Coluccio.
³⁴ His *stemma codicum* is reproduced by M. Schuster on p. vii of his Teubner text and in RE VII A col. 2400.
³⁵ *G* was published in facsimile by E. Châtelain (Paris, 1890), *M* by C. Nigra (Venice, 1893).
³⁶ 11.11; 38.2; 66.11; 66.48; 67.44; 68.158; 76.10; 97.2; 99.8; 107.1; 114.6.
³⁷ I have not had access to the editions of F. Ramorino (Florence, 1912), E. Stampini (Turin 1921), on which see Hale, TAPhA 1922, 103ff, W. B. MacDaniel (New York, 1931), and G. Bonazzi (Rome, 1936). Nor have I thought it necessary to mention texts devoid of both *apparatus criticus* and commentary. For the Loeb text see §2, *Translations*.
³⁸ In 1897 and again in 1901. He noted the variants of *R* in his copy of Schulze's text, which is now in my possession.
³⁹ CR 1906, 160. Five readings attributed to *R* by Ellis were described by Hale as corrections made a century after the MS. was copied. Hale may have been overanxious to protect his beloved *R* from the charge of harbouring 'good' (i.e. deviationist) readings; but Ellis's skill in distinguishing between original and correcting hands has more than once been called in question (see below, n48).
⁴⁰ E.g. at 38.4, where a line longer than its neighbours was split in two by one late copyist, Ellis comments: 'quo indicio mancum declaratur poema'. At 66.15-16 he claims support for a conjecture not even from an aberrant MS. of Catullus, but from an aberrant MS. of a work written A.D. 1329 by Hieremias de Montagnone, in which Catullus is quoted.
⁴¹ Friedrich might perhaps have pleaded, as Ellis had done, that he valued *D* out of respect for Lachmann, since it was one of the latter's two MSS. But A. E. Housman (CR 1905, 21-3) had made short work of this plea: 'Parisians ate rats in the siege, when they had nothing better to eat: must admirers of Parisian cookery eat rats for ever?'
⁴² The best source of information about *O* and *G* is still the critical appendix to Merrill's edition of 1893 (Harvard U.P., re-issued 1951), which gives a full and accurate account of the readings of these MSS., marginal notations, ligatures and all.
⁴³ See A. E. Housman in CR 1924, 25-7.
⁴⁴ Lenchantin differs from Morgenthaler in suggesting that the common ancestor of *O* and *G* must ante-date *T*, because *T* and *O* both omit 62.43-4. But since ll. 42 and 44 both end with the words *optavere puellae*, nothing would be easier than for ll. 43-4 to be omitted independently by copyists several centuries apart.
⁴⁵ Lenchantin's impressive array of citations is wholly derived from Morgenthaler. On p. xlviii, n2, he says that *M* has *multos* for *multis* at 64.263, where in fact the MSS. generally, including *M*, have *multi* for *multis*. This error is traceable to the following consecutive entries in Morgenthaler, p. 51: '64, 262 *aere*] M *era*; 66, 9 *multis*] M *multos*'.
⁴⁶ Schuster, in his list of sigla, commits himself to the view that the reading of *V* is reconstituted by the consensus of *OG*. If this is so, it should follow that where such consensus exists there is no occasion to cite the other MSS.; yet he frequently does so, thus giving the false impression that he considers them independent of *V*. Where the *V* reading is not established by *OG*, it would be logical to cite the readings of all the other three, but this is seldom done. Consequently the *app. crit.* affords no basis for assessing the characteristics and value of *RMD*. Is this merely because full collations are not available in print?

LATE REPUBLICAN POETRY 377

⁴⁷ It is surprising to find him reviving Haupt's oxymoronic suggestion *horribile aequor* at 11.11 (where the English Channel is sufficiently described by the graphic hiatus), and printing *ebria acina* at 27.4 on the strength of a text of Gellius incorporating five conjectures by Haupt, four of which are unwarrantable; see Hosius' *app. crit.* to Gellius VI. 20. 6 (Teubner 1903, vol. I, p. 279), and Ellis, *Catulli Veronensis Liber* (1878²), pp. 316-19.

⁴⁸ The only recent instance of close study of a Catullus MS., under the improved conditions which palaeographers now enjoy, is the editing by G. B. Pighi (Bologna, Zanichelli, 1950) of the codex Bononiensis (*B*), written in 1412, collated by Ellis, and also cited by Lafaye and d'Arbela. It is disconcerting to note how many of the 'good' readings ascribed to this MS. by Ellis have been found by Pighi to be corrections in a late hand. See his article 'Codex Catulli Bononiensis 2621 cum apparatu Ellisiano minore collatus', RhM 1950, 24-6. This, taken in conjunction with Hale's obiter dicta (see above, n39), suggests that recent editors have been working on data which are overdue for verification.

⁴⁹ Another MS. which might well repay careful examination is Parisinus 7989, famed as the sole source of the *Cena Trimalchionis*; though comparatively early (A.D. 1423), it has been strangely neglected since Rossbach's edition of 1860. Hale (TAPhA 1922, 103ff) hinted that it was of greater value than others of which much had been made.

⁵⁰ Ullman wrote a doctoral thesis on *The Identification of the MSS. of Catullus cited in Statius' Edition of 1566* (Chicago U.P., 1908). For his later work as a research assistant of Hale see AJPh 1917, 98-9 and CPh 1929, 294-7, where he wrote that he had collated a hundred MSS. of Catullus and that the collations from Hale's collection had passed into his possession.

⁵¹ It would be a pity, however, to ignore the only Soviet contribution to Catullian studies which has come to my notice. This was the publication by A. I. Malein and A. A. Trukhanov (*Comptes Rendus de l'Académie des Sciences de l'USSR*, 1928, 293-7) of a 'sixth-century palimpsest' containing three epigrams of Catullus numbered CIV, CV, CVI, written in uncials and overlaid by a German lyric in a fifteenth-century script. O. A. Dobiash-Rozhdestvenskaya promptly denounced it on palaeographical grounds (*ibid.*, 1929, 59-61), even though it had not struck her as odd that the numeration coincided with that first occurring in printed editions well after 1600 and allowing for three Priapea (nos. 18-20 in old editions) which do not occur in any MS. This was pointed out by E. H. Minns and E. Harrison (CR 1929, 123-4) and by B. L. Ullman (CPh 1929, 294-7); the latter went to the trouble of identifying the text as that printed opposite a German translation in Heyse's *Lyra* (1855). The good faith of the Russian scholars was not in question; but it was evident that the former owner of the palimpsest, the late Fedor Plushkin of Pskov, had been hoaxed by an enterprising German.

⁵² *PSI* ix (1929), No. 1092, ed. G. Vitelli; *POxy* xx (1953), No. 2258, ed. E. Lobel.

⁵³ In these circumstances Lenchantin (in the 1933 additions to his introduction), Cazzaniga, and d'Arbela kept their heads well enough, but Schuster, elsewhere by no means partial to flights of fancy, was betrayed into printing several conjectures of prodigious demerit; for examples see below, nn 56 and 57.

⁵⁴ The second papyrus, as reconstructed by E. Lobel, indicates that there was nothing in the Greek to correspond to ll. 79-88 of Catullus; and there are traces of an additional couplet at the end. But Pfeiffer thinks it more likely that the papyrus represents an early version of the poem, later superseded by the version which Catullus translated, than that Catullus departed so far from his original.

⁵⁵ Corresponding to 66.54, where *OG* have *elocridicos*, *PSI* 1092 has λοκρικος, *POxy* 2258 λοκ[ρ]ιδος. This is hard on Kroll, whose only change in the text of his second edition (1929) was from *Locridos* to *Locricos* on the evidence of the former papyrus.

⁵⁶ In the same line, for *OG alis equos*, generally read as *ales equus*, many scholars including Housman had favoured Achilles Statius' *alisequus*; and Schuster had printed Bickel's outrageous suggestion *alitebos* (supposed to represent *halitibus*). But *POxy* 2258 establishes ἵππος.

⁵⁷ 66.77-8, *quicum ego, dum virgo quondam fuit omnibus expers | unguentis, una milia multa bibi*. The end of the hexameter had been much assailed, and Schuster printed . . .

Hymenis expers, | *unguenti cuatum* (i.e. *cyathorum*) . . . But when the new papyrus showed πολλά πέπωκα | λιτά, Lobel was quick to see that *milia* was a corruption of *vilia*.

⁵⁸ Above, p. 280. See also the remarks on hiatus in §5 of the present chapter (p. 296).
⁵⁹ For bibliography up to the late 'thirties see M. Schuster's sections on 'Sprache' and 'Versmasse und Verstechnik' in RE VII A (1948), coll. 2383-98.
⁶⁰ See, for a good example, J. P. Elder, 'Catullus' *Attis*', AJPh 1947, 394-403.
⁶¹ 'Stile e Lingua di Catullo', A & R 1938, 139-56 (see also A & R 1940, 141-58); 'Alliterazione e Stile in Catullo', *Studi Urbinati* 1939, 1-77; 'Quae Catullus ex graeco ascita usurpaverit', AIV 1939/40 717-55.

APPENDIX TO CHAPTER X

i. Lucretius

BY D. E. W. WORMELL

THE special appeal of the *De Rerum Natura* to the modern reader is reflected in the steady stream of publications devoted to the poem and its author. Interest in Lucretius manifests itself in places as far apart geographically as Finland and Argentina, and as far separated ideologically as Spain and the U.S.S.R. (Russia appears to have been the only country to celebrate the bimillennial anniversary of the poet's death.)[1]

V. d'Agostino, 'Avviamento bibliografico allo studio di Lucrezio' (*Rivista di Studi Classici* iv (1956), pp. 41-59), gives a brisk survey of recent literature. C. A. Gordon, *A Bibliography of Lucretius* (London, Hart Davis, 1962), provides full particulars of printed editions of the poet in a most attractively written book. He divides his material into: 1) plain texts, 2) annotated editions, 3) pocket editions, 4) translations, 5) illustrated editions, 6) selections, and 7) ghosts. He raises the interesting question why the *De Rerum Natura* has been printed far less often than any other Latin classic of comparable importance, and finds the explanation in Lucretius' materialist philosophy and denial of the immortality of the human soul, and in the fact that Epicureanism counselled non-participation in politics.

1. *Editions*. Lucretius has been fortunate in his editors. Lachmann's and Munro's editions were amongst the greatest achievements of nineteenth century classical scholarship. C. Bailey's three-volume edition (Oxford, Clarendon Press, 1947) shows the maturity of judgment resultant on a lifetime's study of Lucretius and Epicureanism. Though he is extremely cautious in formulating his own conclusions, Bailey's careful weighing of the evidence and sympathetic understanding of Lucretius as poet and thinker, together with his full presentation of his predecessors' researches, make his book an outstanding contribution to the interpretation of the *De Rerum Natura*, which can rank with the distinguished editions of the past. Leonard and Smith's useful edition has been reissued (Wisconsin, 1961). J. Martin's valuable if over-conservative Teubner text has reached a fifth

edition (Leipzig, 1963). The most recent edition is by Karl
Büchner (Wiesbaden, Steiner, 1966). The introduction provides
a fresh and convincing analysis of the place to be accorded to
the *Itali* in the manuscript tradition, and discusses their relationship with each other. The text reflects long familiarity with
Lucretius, and wide reading in the learned literature, but Büchner's own contributions to the interpretation and emendation
of the poem are not in general particularly cogent or persuasive.

2. *Translations*. R. C. Trevelyan's version (Cambridge, 1937)
has established itself as the best verse translation in English.
A. D. Winspear has turned the *De Rerum Natura* into irregular
English verse (New York, Russell, 1956), which is lively but
perhaps too close to rhythmical prose. L. L. Johnson, *Lucretius
On the Nature of Things, a translation in the metre of the original*
(London, Centaur Press, 1963) wrestles valiantly, but like his
predecessors not too successfully, with the problems of English
hexameters. Most recently R. M. Geer has provided a straightforward if uninspired prose version (Indianapolis, Bobbs-Merrill,
1965). R. Waltz has published a crisp and lucid French prose
translation (Paris, Les Belles Lettres, 1954); his introduction
contains some excellent criticism.

3. *The Poet and the Poem*. Bailey's view that 'there is no convincing argument against the general idea of the tradition'
preserved in Jerome is almost impossible to sustain in the light of
K. Ziegler's brilliant and incisive paper 'Der Tod des Lucretius'
(*Hermes* lxxi (1931) pp. 420 ff.). From Ziegler's scrutiny of the
evidence it emerges that the story of the love philtre, of Lucretius'
insanity and suicide, and of the Ciceronian editing of the poem
reflects Christian propaganda dating from the fourth century
A.D., and is as unreliable as most propaganda. In fact the only
valid approach to the understanding of Lucretius' personality
is through his poem (*seine Gestalt in seinem Gedicht*, as Regenbogen
put it). Here the tension between Lucretius the philosopher and
Lucretius the poet, of which he himself was acutely aware, may
help to explain his impact on the modern world. But tension is
not the same as madness. Critics should bear in mind Sir William
Osler's remark (*Brit. Med. Journal*, July 5 (1919) p. 5a) cited by
H. J. Rose, *A handbook of Latin literature*[3] (London, Methuen,
1954): 'of insanity of any type that leaves a mind capable in
lucid intervals of writing such verse as *De Rerum Natura* we

(physicians) know nothing...' It is not surprising that most recent work on the poet has tended to disregard such suspect evidence. One may instance the essays assembled by D. R. Dudley, *Studies in Latin Literature and its Influence Lucretius* (London, Routledge and Kegan Paul, 1965). I have attempted in 'Lucretius: the personality of the poet' (*G and R* vii (1960) pp. 54 ff.) and in 'The personal World of Lucretius' (in D. R. Dudley, *op. cit.* pp. 35 ff.), to glimpse the man behind the poem, though such an attempt, based as it is on impressions and inferences, is necessarily subjective. What Bailey describes as 'the orthodox view', that Lucretius 'was a member of the aristocratic family of the *Lucretii Tricipitini* and took his place in the good society of his day, going as a friend with C. Memmius to Bithynia', is a triple hypothesis, of which the first two parts are rather more securely based than the third, but of which no part can be regarded as proved or provable.

The Poem. Since on analysis nothing remains of the biographical tradition concerning Lucretius beyond his date in the first half of the first century B.C., and the fact that he died before his work was finished (both of which could have been demonstrated from the poem itself) it is natural that scholars should have increasingly concentrated their attention on the *De Rerum Natura*. Controversy continues to rage around the problems of the structure of the poem and the order of composition of the six books, as also around the related question of whether one can trace an evolving design corresponding to an evolving consciousness of his mission by Lucretius. The evidence is to be found in cross-references, doublets, the proems of the six books (especially iv and i), transitional passages linking the proems with the main argument, and in significant variations in metrical and stylistic practice. The wider question of Lucretius' attitude to philosophy, to poetry, and indeed to life, is also involved. K. Büchner has reissued his long essay 'Die Proömien des Lukrez' (first published in *Classica et Mediaevalia* xiii (1952) pp. 159 ff.) together with his lesser Lucretian writings (some hitherto unpublished) and has added *Schlußbemerkungen* in *Studien zur Römischen Literatur, Band* i, *Lukrez und Vorklassik* (Wiesbaden, Steiner, 1964). The debate opened by J. Mussehl and J. Mehwaldt and continued by W. Schmid, H. Diller, and K. Büchner, has been energetically prosecuted by F. Giancotti, *Il preludio di Lucrezio* (Florence, 1959),

U. Pizzani, *Il problema del testo e della composizione del De rerum natura di Lucrezio* (Rome, 1959), and with widening ramifications by F. Giancotti, *L'ottimismo relativo nel 'De rerum natura' di Lucrezio* (Turin, 1960), *Lucreti de rerum natura locos praecipue notabiles collegit et illustravit H. Paratore, commentariolo instruxit H. Pizzani* (Rome, 1960), F. Giancotti, *Lucrezio poeta Epicureo, Rettificazioni* (Rome, 1961), and F. Giancotti, 'Postilla metodologica sull' exegesi di Lucrezio' (*Athenaeum* xli (1963) pp. 86 ff.). Although there has been some enlargement in our understanding of Lucretius, it remains true that this controversy has engendered more heat than light; perhaps in the future scholars will concentrate on the poem as it is rather than as they would like it to be. Clearly the *De Rerum Natura* has suffered in transmission; yet it seems unlikely that very much has been lost (and still more unlikely that there has been extensive interpolation) and it is well to bear constantly in mind that we know nothing of Lucretius' technique of composition. Even if he had a prose 'blue print' of his poem, as tradition tells us Virgil had of the Aeneid, he would be most unlikely to begin at the beginning and work through to the end; and at any stage in the progress of his task he could have turned back to a passage with which he was dissatisfied in order to modify and improve his earlier draft. There may well have been extensive recasting, but it is most unlikely that we can determine how and when it was done. G. Müller, 'Die Problematik des Lukreztextes seit Lachmann' (*Phil.* cii (1958) pp. 247 ff., and ciii (1959) pp. 53 ff.) and 'Die Darstellung der Kinetik bei Lukrez' (*Deutsche Akademie der Wissenschaften zu Berlin* vii (1959)) argues with much force and ability that if we pare away what he regards as interpolated lines and passages, a close-knit argument and a carefully articulated poem emerge. One may perhaps query whether the 'interpolations' are not rather Lucretian *tibicines* indicating that the poet was revising or hoped to revise the passages concerned at the time of his death. Similarly when lines used before are needlessly reintroduced it is at least possible that this was meant as a note of cross-reference pending the final revision of the poem. One cannot but agree, however, with Müller's emphatic statement that we do not know whether Lucretius wrote a book at a time or was working simultaneously on all six books.

The fullest and most balanced recent study is P. Boyancé, *Lucrèce et l'Épicurisme* (Paris, 1963), which touches on most aspects of the poet and his poem, and is especially good on the philosophical background. The same author's *Lucrèce, sa vie, son œuvre, avec un exposé de sa philosophie* (Paris, 1964) is slighter but still authoritative. E. Bignone's *Storia della letteratura latina* ii (Florence, 1945) contains a very valuable assessment of Lucretius and makes an interesting contribution to the vexed question of how he planned to end book vi. The poet's treatment of his material in this, the least finished and least integrated part of his work, has been studied by H. S. Commager, 'Lucretius' Interpretation of the Plague' (HSCPh lxii (1957) pp. 105 ff.) and by M. Bollack, 'La Chaîne aimantine' (REL xl (1962) pp. 38 ff., and xli (1963) pp. 165 ff.). D. R. Dudley's *Studies in Latin Literature and its Influence, Lucretius*, includes essays by O. E. Lowenstein 'The Pre-Socratics, Lucretius and Modern Science'; by B. Farrington, 'Form and Purpose in the *De Rerum Natura*'; by Gavin Townend, 'Imagery in Lucretius'; by D. R. Dudley, 'The Satiric Element in Lucretius'; and by T. J. B. Spencer, 'Lucretius and the Scientific Poem in English'. R. Waltz has published two valuable studies: 'Lucrèce satirique' and 'Lucrèce dans Lucrèce' (Paris, Lettres d'Humanité, 1949 and 1953). B. Farrington, *Science and Politics in the Ancient World* has been reissued in a paperback edition (London, Allen and Unwin, 1966). His series of lively and original articles continues: 'Lucretius and Manilius on friendship' (*Hermathena* lxxxiii (1954) pp. 10 ff.), 'The meaning of *persona* in De Rerum Natura iii' (*ibid.* lxxxv (1955) pp. 3 ff.), 'Vergil and Lucretius' (*Acta Classica* i (1958) pp. 45 ff.). Farrington has also explored Lucretius' relationship with Memmius in *Anales de Filología Clásica* vii (1959) pp. 13 ff. New light has been thrown on the wider audience to which the poet addresses himself by H. M. Howe, 'Amafinius, Lucretius, and Cicero' (AJP lxxii (1957) pp. 57 ff.).

4. *MSS and Text.* A. Dalzell, 'Some recent work on the text of Lucretius' (*Phoenix* xiv (1960) pp. 96 ff.) gives a balanced and useful survey. Although Bailey (*De Rerum Natura* vol i p. 44) expresses himself in full agreement with Merrill's view that 'the famous archetype survives merely as an example of Lachmann's ingenuity and clear vision, and is now hardly more than an intellectual curiosity', and states categorically that 'Lachmann's calculations and their application cannot be regarded as trustworthy', G. P. Goold, 'A lost manuscript of Lucretius' (*Acta Classica* i (1958) pp. 21 ff.) has shown that a page by page re-

construction of the archetype can in fact be made by using the evidence which Lachmann assembled. Goold further points out the similarity between the manuscript tradition of Lucretius and Manilius, and tentatively suggests that the same scholar may have studied and transcribed the text of both poets. K. Büchner's very different treatment of the archetype in 'Präludien zu einer Lukrezausgabe' (*Hermes* lxxxiv (1956) pp. 198 ff., reprinted in *Studien zur Römischen Literatur* i, *Lukrez und Vorklassik*, pp. 121 ff.) appears to be misguided (Goold describes Büchner as going 'wildly astray'). F. Brunhölzl, 'Zur Überlieferung des Lukrez' (*Hermes* xc (1962) pp. 97 ff.) detects six receding stages in the tradition by which our earliest manuscripts have come down to us. The archetype, two removes away, was written in minuscule. Behind it can be glimpsed a minuscule source, and behind this again three stages of transmission in capitals. The latest of these was the manuscript which Lachmann rightly postulated as written in rustic capitals in the fourth or fifth century (though he erred in regarding this as the archetype). Prior to this there is evidence for two earlier stages of cursive majuscule dating back to the second or third centuries and to the second half of the first century respectively. This takes us back to the age of M. Valerius Probus, who is known to have edited Lucretius. It is then possible, but no more, that our text ultimately derives from his edition (as Leonard and Smith had previously conjectured). While Bailey could speak of a general tendency away from emendation to a greater belief in the MSS, and could illustrate this tendency from his own editorial practice, most scholars would probably agree that as a textual critic Bailey was excessively cautious, and that a somewhat more radical approach will be adopted by future editors. This does not mean that they will necessarily follow the lead of G. Müller (*op. cit.*), though he presents his case well, in deleting up to four per cent of the lines in the poem as interpolated.

5. *Formal criticism. Grammar, metre, and style.* There is a succinct and illuminating assessment in L. R. Palmer, *The Latin Language* (London, Faber, 1954) pp. 106 ff. He concludes '... it is especially in his use of such conventional devices of traditional poetic diction (genitives in -*ai* and in -*um*, infinitives in -*ier*, simple verbs for compound, and the rest) that Lucretius reveals the poet of genius. When his fire bursts through the

superincumbent material of natural philosophy, the archaism and the gloss blaze with a light not of this world.' W. S. Maguinness' chapter on 'The Language of Lucretius' (in D. R. Dudley's *Studies in Latin Literature and its Influence, Lucretius*, pp. 69 ff.) explores the shaping of the poet's usage by the metrical medium and the epic tradition. His appendixes contain valuable lists of new coinages and of archaisms in Lucretius' vocabulary. V. P. Naughtin, 'Metrical patterns in Lucretius' hexameters' (CQ xlvi, 1952, pp. 152 ff.) substantiates many of Bailey's findings (*De Rerum Natura* Vol i pp. 109 ff.) particularly with regard to Lucretius' careful treatment of the fourth foot of the hexameter. It is becoming increasingly evident that Lucretius was breaking new ground in many directions, and that in the process he remoulded Latin to his purpose forging a disciplined yet impassioned and intensely personal style.

6. *Lucretius' Thought, Philosophy, and Natural Science.* P. de Lacy surveys recent literature on Epicurus and Epicureans in CW xlviii (1955) pp. 169 ff. H. Usener's indispensable *Epicurea*, long out of print and unobtainable, has been reissued (Rome, L'Erma (1963)). A. Grilli has edited Diogenes of Oenoanda (Milan (1960)). A new Teubner edition is promised. G. Arrighetti, *Epicuro, Opere. Introduzione, testo critico, traduzione e note* (Turin, Einaudi (1960)) is a complete edition of Epicurus' work, including all the new passages recovered in recent times. C. W. Chilton's English translation of A. J. Festugière's book, *Epicurus and his gods* (Oxford, Blackwell (1955)) has corrections and additions made by the author, especially in the notes and bibliography. N. W. DeWitt, *Epicurus and his philosophy* (Minneapolis, 1954) is learned and challenging. The same author's *St Paul and Epicurus* (Minneapolis, 1954) is slighter and more speculative. E. Paratore, *L'epicureismo e la sua diffusione nel mondo latino* (Rome, 1960, but written several years earlier) is a semi-popular treatment yet balanced and scholarly. The publication of B. Farrington's new book *The Faith of Epicurus* will be awaited with interest.

In an entertaining preface to R. C. Trevelyan's verse translation of the *De Rerum Natura*, H. S. Davies, writing on Macaulay's marginalia, reminds us of the need to keep a sense of historical perspective when reading Lucretius. Much of Epicurus' physics, and especially his astronomy, is of course outdated and seems ingenuous in the light of modern scientific advances. It is, however, salutary to be reminded (by O. E. Lowenstein *op. cit.*) that 'our understanding of the basic nature of visual perception differs from that of the ancients only in precision of analytical detail'. And modern physicists (E. N. da C. Andrade in the preface to a reissue of Munro's commentary (London, Bell, 1928) and E. R. J. A. Schrödinger, *Nature and the Greeks* (Cambridge, 1954)) have paid their tribute to the power and penetration of Democritus' and Epicurus' thought and insight. It should not be forgotten, however, that for Epicurus science is a means to an end, not an end in itself; that he regards himself as a man with a mission — to free humanity from the fear of death and the fear of the supernatural.

It seems certain that Lucretius had read widely and with discrimination in the very voluminous works of Epicurus. If so, it is probable that the *De Rerum Natura* owes to Lucretius, rather than Epicurus, the coherent logical forward march of its argument, no less than the constant sequence of apposite illustrations, just as it owes to him its unity of form and style, its profusion of metaphor, and the richness of its imagery.

A. D. Winspear, *Lucretius and scientific thought* (Montreal, Harvest House, 1963) gives a readable but rather superficial assessment. F. Klingner 'Lucrez' in *Römische Geisteswelt*[3] (Munich, Ellermann, 1956) pp. 173 ff. probes deeper, but shortage of space prevents the full development of his ideas. It is part of Lucretius' appeal that he is wrestling with the intractable problem of reconciling science, ethics, and philosophy with poetry, of writing a didactic poem whose theme embraces varied and conflicting attitudes towards the material world and the living creatures that inhabit it. He succeeds because he combines a profound intellectual grasp of frequently abstruse argument with a never failing response to the beauty and wonder of the universe, and because he is intensely in sympathy with animate, and indeed with inanimate nature. His view of life is essentially religious, the *De Rerum Natura* paradoxically in the final analysis a religious poem. G. Santayana's fine appreciation of *Three philosophical poets* (*Harvard Studies in Comparative Literature* i (1910); reissued by Doubleday Anchor Books, New York, 1953) places Lucretius firmly where be belongs in the company of Dante and Goethe.

[1] I regret that I am not competent to report on the Russian contribution to Lucretian studies.

CHAPTER XI

THE AUGUSTAN POETS

BY T. E. WRIGHT

THE Augustan poets of Rome — and particularly Virgil and Horace — have been studied for so long and in so many countries that in this twentieth century a radically new approach could hardly be expected. Our modern scholars have sought rather to deepen and enrich our appreciation of the poets' genius by analysing their structural, linguistic, and metrical art; by interpreting their meaning and their 'message'; and by examining their influence upon later centuries. This predominantly literary approach is one which naturally commends itself to the general public, and already it appears to have done much to keep alive the popular interest. In this country a Virgil Society was founded in 1943, and a Horatian Society some ten years earlier; while the bimillenaries of Virgil (1930) and Horace (1935) were enthusiastically celebrated by many lectures and publications both in the Old World and the New.

Meanwhile the work of 'professional' scholarship has by no means languished. Numerous new critical editions have appeared but few are revolutionary; for by the turn of the century the texts of the chief Augustan poets (Propertius excepted) had been in large measure settled. Questions of doubtful authenticity (e.g. the authorship of the poems in the *Virgilian Appendix*) have continued to be keenly debated, but the results have, on the whole, been inconclusive. In three specific directions, however, a definite advance seems to have been achieved — in our interpretation of Virgil's *Eclogues*, our grasp of the relation of Horace's *Satires* and *Ars Poetica* to their Greek sources, and our recognition of the originality of the Roman personal love-elegy.

VIRGIL

As the greatest of the Latin poets and one of the chief formative influences of our Western civilization, Virgil has occupied a unique place among all the Classical authors, having been held in affection alike by Pagan and Christian, alike by the ancient, medieval, and modern worlds. Yet during the last fifty years the study of Virgil has, if anything, been intensified, and much fresh light has been thrown upon many aspects of his poetry. In this movement English scholarship has played a notable part: the names of J. W. Mackail, R. S. Conway and W. Warde Fowler are known to Virgilians all over the world, while the series of 'Virgilian Studies' published by B. H. Blackwell, Oxford, provides a contribution of singular range and value.

'The study of Virgil', said Warde Fowler, 'is for me one of the things that make life worth living'; and something of the same feeling seems to have inspired the numerous general appreciations of the poet which have been a feature of our period. Such, for example, was T. R. Glover's *Virgil* (London, Methuen, 1904) which is intended for those whose interest is primarily in 'the human value of what they are reading'. Accordingly, after first examining various elements in Virgil's environment — domestic, literary, and national — Glover devotes the second half of his book to Virgil's 'interpretation of life' — to his thoughts on human character, on the gods, and on the after-life. This is a fresh and eminently readable presentation of the subject, and is particularly suitable for the young student. Similar in aim and treatment is *Virgil and his Meaning to the World of Today* by J. W. Mackail (London, Harrap, 1923) — later embodied, with some modifications, in the introduction to his edition of the *Aeneid* (313 *infra*). Here, as we should expect from the author's name, we have a sympathetic and masterly analysis of Virgil's art, universality, and significance for our age as well as his own. Another interesting study of Virgil's universality is *Vergil in the Experience of South Africa* by T. J. Haarhoff (Oxford, Blackwell, 1931) — republished in slightly revised form in 1949 under the title of *Vergil the Universal*. By comparing Calvinism with ancient Stoicism, the Boer Voortrekker with the Italian farmer, the political and economic problems of modern South Africa with those of Augustan Rome, Haarhoff shows that Virgil has a living message even for a new country like his own, and seeks thereby to establish Virgil's universality in his treatment of man, nature and the spiritual world. Much more provocative and esoteric are the books of W. F. J. Knight of which *Roman Vergil* (London, Faber, 1944) may be taken as typical. Knight is a sensitive and enthusiastic Virgilian scholar, and he has some good and suggestive comments to make; but few readers are likely to feel entirely happy about his psychological approach (e.g. his statement that the *Georgics* are Virgil's 'least erotic poem'); about certain of his judgments (e.g. that Virgil moulded Augustus' policy); or about his emphasis upon his supposed rhythmical patterns — a topic also treated in his *Accentual Symmetry in Vergil* (Oxford, Blackwell, 1939). French Virgilianism[1] is well represented by A. Bellesort's *Virgile, son œuvre et son temps* (Paris, Perrin, 1920); while from America we have *The Magical Art of Virgil* by E. K. Rand (Harvard University Press, 1931), and from Germany *Vergil, Vater des Abendlandes* by T. Haecker (Bonn, Buchgemeinde, 1933).

Some of the most valuable studies of Virgil were originally delivered as lectures. In this category H. W. Garrod's 'Vergil' in *English Literature and the Classics* (Oxford, Clarendon Press, 1912) is particularly stimulating; in it he discusses the 'spiritual conflict' in Virgil's poetry, and especially his sense of failure in the *Aeneid* — a failure which 'is of the order which sanctifies'. Among the lectures given in this country to celebrate Virgil's bimillenary may be mentioned in particular 'Virgil and Roman Civilisation' by R. M. Henry (*Proceedings of the Classical Association*, 1930); 'Virgil in English Poetry' by G. S. Gordon; 'Vergil's Creative Art' by R. S. Conway; and 'Virgil as a "Master Mind" ' by J. W. Mackail (all in the *Proceedings of the British Academy*, 1931): the titles illustrate significantly the various aspects of the humanistic approach which has been so marked in recent English scholarship. Discussions of more specialized Virgilian topics (e.g. 'The Growth of the Underworld') will be found in the two volumes of collected lectures by R. S. Conway — *New Studies of a Great Inheritance* (London, Murray, 1921) and *Harvard Lectures on the Vergilian Age* (Harvard University Press, 1928).

In any general study of Virgil much attention is inevitably given to his religious outlook. This particular topic is exhaustively treated by C. Bailey in *Religion in Virgil* (Oxford, Clarendon Press, 1935). The author resolves Virgil's religious background into four elements — magic, animism, Graeco-Roman anthropomorphism, and philosophy; collects his references to each; and seeks to reconstruct from these abundant data a balanced picture of his religious views on the divine government of the world, the relation of determinism and free-will, the duty of man, and the destiny of the soul after death. A much briefer, but excellent, account of Virgil as a religious poet is contained in W. Warde Fowler's *Religious Experience of the Roman People* (London, Macmillan, 1911), chapter 18.

The details of Virgil's biography — at least of his earlier years — have provided the subject of considerable discussion. The dates of his birth and death are not disputed, and all the ancient evidence has been collected by J. K. Fotheringham (CR 44, 1930). His racial affinities, on the other hand, are much less certain. For a time there was a tendency to emphasize the Keltic strain in him, and to this was attributed the peculiarly Virgilian tenderness and pity (e.g. H. W. Garrod *op. cit.* and Introduction to the *Oxford Book of Latin Verse*, xvii-xxv). The whole question was examined on philological grounds by G. E. K. Braunholtz in 'The nationality of Vergil' (CR, 29, 1915). He concludes that Virgil had probably a blend of Etruscan and Keltic blood: the names *Vergilius* and *Maro* appear to be Etruscan or Etruscan-Latin, while that of Virgil's mother *Magia* seems to be Keltic. Another controversial topic has been the exact site of the farm on which Virgil was brought up and from which he was later evicted. R. S. Conway (*Harvard Lectures* and elsewhere) argued strongly against the ancient tradition, known to Dante, which placed it at Pietole, three miles to the S.E. of Mantua; and he supported instead the claims of Calvisano, thirty miles to the N.W. The traditional location, on the other hand, was vigorously defended by E. K. Rand, *In Quest of Virgil's Birthplace* (Harvard Univ. Pr., 1930): see also B. Nardi, *The Youth of Virgil*, translated by B. P. Rand (Harvard University Press, 1930). The attempt to reconstruct a continuous biography of Virgil was made almost simultaneously by two transatlantic scholars — by Tenney Frank in *Vergil: a Biography* (Oxford, Blackwell, 1922) and by N. W. de Witt in *Virgil's Biographia Litteraria* (Oxford University Press, 1923). Assuming the authenticity of the *Appendix* almost in its entirety and employing great freedom of inference, they proceed to recreate the details of Virgil's life and poetic development, but their conclusions, however novel and interesting, must obviously be accepted with caution.

America also provided Virgilian scholars with a most useful concordance in M. N. Wetmore's *Index verborum Vergilianus* (New Haven, Yale University Press, 1911).

The whole of Virgil was translated into tasteful English prose by

J. Jackson (Oxford, Clarendon Press, 1908); but no exegetical edition has yet appeared to supersede the great work of J. Conington, or the smaller, but extremely serviceable, volumes of T. E. Page.

The Eclogues

A new era in the interpretation of the *Eclogues* was introduced by the publication by F. Skutsch of *Aus Vergils Frühzeit* and *Gallus und Vergil* (Leipzig, Teubner, 1901 and 1906 respectively). The *Eclogues* of Virgil — to quote the opening words of the former — 'look out at us with dark, enigmatical eyes'. Of Virgil's authentic works they are by far the most puzzling — puzzling in their origin and puzzling in their contents. Their true significance must lie beneath the surface if only we could find the key. That key Skutsch endeavours to discover.

Skutsch concentrates especially on two of the more enigmatic Eclogues — the sixth and the tenth. In the former the problem lies in the strange miscellany of subjects in the Song of Silenus (31ff); in the latter in the apparently disconnected vicissitudes which Gallus seems to undergo. Skutsch claims to provide the solution by showing that in each case Virgil is giving us a synopsis of Gallus' poetry — of his *epyllia* (including the *Ciris*) in 6, and of his amatory elegies in 10. If therefore we had the fuller knowledge possessed by Virgil's contemporaries the difficulties that we find in the poems would disappear.

Whether or not we agree with Skutsch's detailed exposition — and he has had doughty opponents, notably F. Leo (*Hermes*, 37, 1902) — there is no doubt that he has provided a new and fruitful clue to the understanding of the *Eclogues*. This clue was followed up by J. S. Phillimore in *Pastoral and Allegory: a re-reading of the Bucolics of Virgil* (Oxford, Clarendon Press, 1925). In this racy and suggestive pamphlet Phillimore maintains that the *Eclogues* are 'the book of a circle'; that Virgil saw here 'a scheme for glorifying, under some humorous mystifications of form and diplomatic equivoques of allegory, his distinguished poetical friends'; and that 'in the difficult discrimination of what is Allegory and what is not we shall be ready to allow to Allegory a larger part'. It is this emphasis on the allegorical element in the *Eclogues* that gives Phillimore's study its chief interest. We know that Menalcas in Eclogue 9 is Virgil himself; and other real persons doubtless also masquerade under the fictitious names of Daphnis, Mopsus, etc.[2] The key to the interpretation is therefore to be sought in 'personality and association': for example, just as Skutsch had shown that the sixth Eclogue is 'alive with Gallus', so the fourth Eclogue is 'alive with Pollio'.

The fourth (or 'Messianic') Eclogue is, of course, the most puzzling of all the poems in the collection. What Virgil's purpose was in writing it and addressing it to Pollio in his consulship; who was the wonder child destined to usher in a new Golden Age; and from what source Virgil drew his apparently unclassical imagery — all these questions have been the subject of lively controversy. Among the many studies of the problem the most notable are perhaps *Virgil's Messianic Eclogue* by J. B. Mayor, W. Warde Fowler, and R. S. Conway (London, Murray, 1907); *Die Geburt des Kindes* by E. Norden (Leipzig, Teubner, 1924); and *Virgile et le Mystère de la IVe Églogue* by J. Carcopino (Paris, L'Artisan du Livre, 1930). The generally accepted view is that the poem is an Epithalamium, and that it may well owe some of its unusual colouring to the Hebrew scriptures,[3] perhaps directly, but more probably indirectly through Sibylline literature: see T. F. Royds, *Virgil and Isaiah* (Oxford, Blackwell, 1918). Most scholars agree further (although Norden argues to the contrary) that Virgil had in mind the birth of a real child. The child is commonly identified with the expected child of Octavian and Scribonia (who turned out to be Julia); but there is a strong case for the expected child of Antony and Octavia whose marriage sealed the Peace of Brundisium in 40 B.C. This is the view of W. W. Tarn (JRS, 22, 1932) who gives us the salutary caution that we must envisage the historical situation as it was in 40 B.C. and must not argue backwards from the later careers of Antony and Augustus.

The fourth Eclogue is only one, though the greatest, of the problems of the *Bucolics*; and the relevant literature is both voluminous and widely scattered. Fortunately, however, we can now gain a synoptic view of the whole discussion in a single volume — *The Eclogues of Vergil* by H. J. Rose (Berkeley and Los Angeles, University of California Press, 1942). This is a masterly survey of all the points at issue, and, whether or not we accept the author's own conclusions, we find the evidence and the arguments fully and lucidly set out.

The Georgics

In contrast to the complex problems of the *Eclogues* the comparative simplicity of the *Georgics* has but little need of interpreters; and no major work on the poem has been produced during the last fifty years. There have, however, been several specialized studies which are virtually indispensable for a full understanding of it. Such are *The Beasts, Birds, and Bees of Virgil* by T. F. Royds and *The Trees, Shrubs, and Plants of Virgil* by J. Sargeaunt (Oxford, Blackwell, 1914 and 1920 respectively). These delightful volumes provide a naturalist's handbook to the *Georgics* and carry on worthily the tradition of John Martyn, the Cambridge Professor of Botany who edited the poem in the eighteenth century. To these we have a French counterpart in *L'agriculture dans l'antiquité d'après les Géorgiques de Virgile* by R. Billiard (Paris, Boccard, 1928); and the technical aspects of the *Georgics* generally are discussed in P. d'Hérouville's *A la campagne avec Virgile* and *Géorgiques, 1 et 2* (Paris, Les Belles Lettres, 1930 and 1942 respectively).

Perhaps the most famous passage in the *Georgics* is the *Aristaei fabula* (4. 315-558), which, according to Servius, was substituted for the *laudes Galli*, on Augustus' instructions, after the disgrace and death of Gallus in 26 B.C. This curious statement of Servius is convincingly refuted by W. B. Anderson in 'Gallus and the Fourth Georgic', CQ, 27 (1933).[4] Assuming that the praise of Gallus would have been suggested by the reference to Egypt (287-314), he argues (*a*) that Gallus' prefecture of Egypt did not begin until August or September 30 B.C. by which time the *Georgics* were virtually completed; (*b*) that it would have been a *bêtise* on Virgil's part to devote half a book to the praise of a mere prefect and to say nothing of Augustus, the recent conqueror and true hero of Egypt (and we must remember that Virgil read the *Georgics* to Augustus in 29 B.C.); and (*c*) that it is incredible that not a single line of the alleged original ending has survived despite some four years of circulation. The artistry of the *Aristaei fabula*, as 'the most beautiful of the Latin epyllia', is finely analysed by M. M. Crump, *The Epyllion from Theocritus to Ovid* (Oxford, Blackwell, 1931), chapter 9: there she shows how within the narrow limits of the genre, with its formal conventions of main theme and digression, Virgil succeeds in creating a great poem.

The *Georgics* have a peculiar appeal in this country, perhaps because we share with Virgil in especial measure the love of the soil, the tastes of the naturalist, and an almost mystical feeling towards nature. This may account for the numerous attempts to render the *Georgics* into our own language. Within little more than the last decade alone three notable verse translations have appeared — *The Georgics of Virgil* by C. Day Lewis (London, Cape, 1940); *The Eclogues and Georgics* by R. C. Trevelyan (Cambridge University Press, 1944); and *The Singing Farmer* by L. A. S. Jermyn (Oxford, Blackwell, 1947). The first of these is the most original: the verse consists of unrhymed lines of six stresses, occasionally interspersed with shorter lines of three stresses, while the diction attempts to 'steer between the twin vulgarities of flashy colloquialism and perfunctory grandiloquence'. Of the two latter, which are in blank verse, Jermyn's spirited translation perhaps deserves special mention because it was made amid the squalor and discomfort of a Japanese prison camp at Singapore. Among the other translations of our period *The Georgics in English Hexameters* by C. W. Brodribb (London, Benn, 1928) is interesting because of its comparative success with the quantitative system — a system which became fashionable for a time after the experiment of R. Bridges, the then poet-laureate, in *Ibant Obscuri* (Oxford, Clarendon Press, 1916).

Aeneid

In our study of the *Aeneid* we are still compelled to rely mainly on the standard commentaries of the last century. R. S. Conway indeed planned to revise radically the great edition of Conington–Nettleship–Haverfield, but the work was cut short by his death and has not been resumed; only Book 1 has been published (Cambridge University Press, 1935). To celebrate the bimillenary, however, J. W. Mackail produced an interesting edition of the whole poem — *The Aeneid* (Oxford, Clarendon Press, 1930). Its interest lies in its essentially literary approach. 'It is designed', he states, 'not so much for professional scholars ... as for readers and lovers of great poetry.' A great part of his labour as editor 'has consisted in discarding accumulated material in order that the work of art may not be encumbered by masses of scaffolding'; for 'the work of commenting on commentators is endless, and except for the specialist, is profitless'. The commentary is therefore briefer than the text and is concerned not only to supply the necessary minimum of explanatory and critical matter but also to analyse the beauties and subtleties of Virgil's art.

There have been several important editions of single Books. Of these[5] pride of place must be given to E. Norden's *Aeneis Buch VI* (Leipzig, Teubner, 1903). This outstanding work of modern scholarship (which reached its third edition in 1927) consists of introduction on Virgil's eschatology and its sources; text and verse translation; commentary of nearly 250 pages; and appendices dealing chiefly with stylistic and metrical matters. It is not only indispensable for those who wish to understand the philosophical and popular ideas out of which Virgil has created his poetical picture of the Underworld; it is also a major contribution to the study of ancient eschatology in general. Norden finds Virgil's main sources in Posidonius and in an Orphic-Pythagorean poem of the sixth century B.C.; and concludes that Virgil took an apocalyptic treatise of Posidonius as his groundwork and dressed it out in the conventional style of the Revelation-poetry.

A development of particular note in English Virgilian scholarship was provided by W. Warde Fowler's three volumes of text and commentary published at Oxford by Blackwell — *Virgil's Gathering of the Clans (Aeneid 7, 601-817)*, 1916; *Aeneas at the Site of Rome (Aeneid 8)*, 1917; and *The Death of Turnus (Aeneid 12)*, 1919. These have a freshness and individuality which put them in a class by themselves. The author avoids commenting on passages which, in his view, have already been fully explained elsewhere. Instead he gives us the original fruits of his own lifelong love of Virgil, his imaginative insight into the poet's mind, and his profound knowledge of Italy, and of Roman history, legend, and religion. 'It may be doubted', wrote Conway, reviewing the first of the three books, 'whether anything else has been written in the last forty years — save the discoveries of Skutsch *Aus Vergils Frühzeit* and Norden's massive commentary on Book 6 — which has added so much to our understanding of the greatest poet of the ancient world.'

The geography and *Realien* which lie behind the last six books of the *Aeneid* have been made the subject of more exhaustive study by several other scholars. In his important work *Virgile et les Origines d'Ostie* (Paris, Boccard, 1919), J. Carcopino argued that there was no city of Laurentum, that Aeneas founded Lavinium a second time, and that his New Troy was a primitive Ostia on a different site from the city of historic times. Though his conclusions are highly controversial, his book is of great value for the Virgilian lore which it contains and for the fresh light which it throws on many Virgilian problems. The same ground is covered again by Catharine Saunders in *Vergil's Primitive Italy* (New York, O.U.P., 1930) — a useful study which seeks 'to test the accuracy of Vergil's picture of primitive Italy by the results of archaeological exploration and by the testimony of ancient literature'. *Vergil's Latium* by Bertha Tilley (Oxford, Blackwell, 1947) is primarily valuable because of the author's first-hand investigation of the ancient sites in the coastal area of the Campagna.

The poetic art of the *Aeneid* is another subject which has engaged the attention of scholars. On this the classic work is *Vergils Epische Technik* by R. Heinze (Leipzig, Teubner, 1903). This important treatise falls into two parts. In the first Heinze analyses the various sections of the poem — the fall of Troy, the Voyage, Dido, etc. In the second he reconstructs in fullest detail the artistic principles which Virgil followed, discussing, for example, his handling of character (like Warde Fowler he sees a development in Aeneas' character with Book 6 as the turning point); his fondness for the dramatic style in narrative; the influence of rhetoric; and the aims of Virgil's poetry. Much of Heinze's material was later embodied in a popular study for the Latinless reader — *The Development of Virgil's Art* by H. W. Prescott (Chicago, University of Chicago Press, 1927).[6]

However much we may ourselves admire Virgil's epic technique we know that Virgil himself was dissatisfied — that he required another three years for the revision of the *Aeneid* and that on his deathbed he ordered it to be burned. This dissatisfaction is often traced to Virgil's piecemeal methods of composition[7] which naturally left inconsistencies; and attempts have been made to reconstruct the stages of the poem's growth and so to reveal the deficiencies which Virgil would have removed had he lived longer. Thus A. Gercke, *Die Entstehung der Aeneis* (Berlin, Weidmann, 1913), supposed that Virgil's original intention was to celebrate the wars of Aeneas; accordingly 7-12 were composed first; and then, as a more mature conception of Aeneas' character and destiny grew in his mind, the earlier Books were added. This thesis, however, is contradicted by Suetonius' explicit statement that the *Aeneid* was first sketched out in prose in *twelve* books. A more fruitful approach is that of M. M. Crump, *The Growth of the Aeneid* (Oxford, Blackwell, 1920). She assumes three stages: (1) The original prose sketch in which the order of Books was 3, 5, 1, 2, 4, 6-12; (2) Composition of the poem, and subsequent revisions in which the order of Books was changed, for artistic reasons, to that which we now have (Book 3 being altered from the third to the first person); (3) The — still unfinished — text as published by Varius and Tucca after Virgil's death. (At that date some revision was required in each of the first six Books, chiefly in 3, to bring the poem into harmony with itself, and there were also minor weaknesses to remove.) In this able study due weight is given both to the aesthetic probabilities and to the scanty external evidence; and though the arguments are complicated and the conclusions necessarily tentative, the book is both readable and interesting. Among other signs of the unfinished state of the *Aeneid* are the fairly numerous half lines and repetitions: a careful and scholarly examination of these was made by J. Sparrow in *Half lines and Repetitions in Virgil* (Oxford, Clarendon Press, 1931.)

Among verse translations of the *Aeneid* may be mentioned those of C. J. Billson (London, Arnold, 1906) and of C. Day Lewis (O.U.P., 1952): the latter was originally written for the purpose of broadcasting.

The Virgilian Appendix

The authenticity of the miscellaneous poems contained in the *Virgilian Appendix* has provoked much discussion; and while this is primarily the concern of professional scholars, it is obviously not without relevance for those whose interest in Virgil is mainly literary. The finished mastery of the *Eclogues* can only have been achieved after a prolonged period of youthful experimentation; and if we can prove that the poems of the *Appendix* are in fact Virgil's youthful experiments we shall learn something of the influences which moulded his early years and at the same time see the rudimentary first-beginnings out of which developed the superb artistry of his maturer poetry.

There are four tests which can be applied: (1) the external evidence (the lists of Suetonius-Donatus and Servius, and, in the case of the *Culex*, miscellaneous references elsewhere); (2) general probability (how far these alleged early poems are compatible in treatment and subject-matter with Virgil's authentic works);

(3) parallel passages (whether the authentic Virgil borrowed from the *Appendix* or *vice versa*); (4) significant similarities and differences in vocabulary and metrical practice. According to the importance which they assign to these several tests the views of scholars differ widely, and range from complete rejection to complete acceptance.

An excellent general introduction to the whole subject will be found in 'Virgil and Virgilianism: a study of the minor poems attributed to Virgil' by J. W. Mackail (CR, 22, 1908). After eliminating three poems (*Est et non*, *Vir bonus*, and *Maecenas*) as obviously post-Virgilian, he concludes that the remainder were written in Virgil's lifetime, roughly between Catullus' death and the publication of the *Georgics*, and emanated from the poetic circle to which Virgil belonged in his youth. He accepts *Culex*, some of the poems of the *Catalepton*, and (probably) the *Moretum* as genuine.

Another helpful study is *The Youth of Vergil* by R. S. Conway (*New Studies*, see p. 308 *supra*). After reminding us that youth has its privileges of free experiment, and cautioning us not to judge the work of early years by the work of an artist's maturity, he discusses *Ciris*, *Culex*, *Ite hinc*, and *Copa*, accepting a Virgilian authorship for all except *Ciris*.

The *Appendix* has aroused considerable interest among American scholars. While some of his compatriots support the claims of Ovid, E. K. Rand in 'Young Virgil's Poetry' (*Harvard Studies*, 30, 1919) defends the authenticity of all the poems listed in Suetonius' *Life*, not excluding the *Aetna* about which there was doubt even in antiquity. In this well-documented survey Rand examines the several poems in detail and concludes that there is 'nothing that cannot be reconciled with the testimony of the ancient life of the poet' and that the *Appendix* is 'the record, not of a series of impeccable masterpieces, but of the essays of a slowly flowering genius'.

The many studies of detailed problems cannot be recorded here, but something should perhaps be added about the two longest and most important poems — the *Culex* and the *Ciris*. The *Culex* has on the whole been accepted as Virgil's.[8] Not only is the external evidence strong but the poem is thought to contain the germs of his later work in its account of country life and the underworld. This verdict was also reached by D. L. Drew in *Culex: Sources and their bearing on the problem of authorship* (Oxford, Blackwell, 1925). Through a series of difficult and complicated arguments Drew concludes that there is no proof that *Culex* drew from (i.e. came after) the authentic Virgil; that it was a youthful experiment not published or intended for publication; and that it is just the sort of poem that we should expect from Virgil in his early years.

The *Ciris*, on the other hand, is generally thought not to be Virgil's; and many scholars, including Mackail and Conway, have been persuaded by F. Skutsch (*Aus Vergils Frühzeit*, 310 *supra*) that it is the work of Gallus.[9] He bases his argument on *Ecl.* 6, 74ff (*quid loquar aut Scyllam Nisi*, etc.) which he regards as a résumé of Gallus' poetry; and he explains the parallelisms between *Ciris* and the authentic Virgil by the hypothesis that Virgil borrowed — and improved — phrases from the *epyllion* of his former friend and collaborator. His thesis gains a certain support from stylistic and metrical tests which favour a Virgilian authorship of *Culex* but not of *Ciris*.[10]

HORACE

'To attempt to say anything new about Horace may seem absurd', wrote Henry Nettleship in 1883. Of all the Latin poets — not excluding Virgil — he has probably been the most consistently popular since the Renaissance. He has been edited by a long succession of able scholars; he has been studied continuously in our schools and universities; and he has been the delight in later life both of men of letters and of men of affairs.

Yet, despite Nettleship's misgivings, there has been no dearth of fresh contributions to Horatian study and literature during the present century. New texts and new commentaries — some of which will be mentioned later — have been produced both in England and the Continent; there has been a steady stream of translations, particularly of the *Odes*; and there have been numerous general appreciations of Horace's poetic art and influence.

To begin with these more general works, we have a useful and well-documented survey of Horace's times[11] in *Horace and his Age: a Study in Historical Background* by J. F. D'Alton (London, Longmans, 1917). Reminding us that 'writers are in most things children of their age' he endeavours 'to recapture the atmosphere in which Horace moved, to estimate a portion at least of the influences under which many of his thoughts were bodied forth'.

The main topics which he treats are politics; philosophy and religion, particularly the Augustan revival; social problems; popular beliefs; and contemporary literary criticism. A few years later G. Showerman published a study of the poet himself in *Horace and his Influence* (London, Harrap, 1922). In this essentially popular work, the author seeks to interpret Horace as poet and philosopher by copious references to his writings; to analyse his influence on literature through the ages; and to show what he has contributed to literary standards and the art of living. Much more scholarly and stimulating is *Horace: A new Interpretation* by A. Y. Campbell (London, Methuen, 1924). It is regrettable that he has seen fit to include in it a highly personal theory of 'literary cycles' and to claim that this is indispensable for his thesis; for he has a real love and understanding of Horace, and he gives us what is perhaps the most interesting and illuminating literary criticism of him in English since the days of Sellar.[12] Particularly noteworthy are his opening chapter ('A Classic as seen by Romantics'), his analyses of some of the Odes, and his final summing up of Horace as poet. A much slighter, but pleasant and skilful, appreciation — originally delivered as two lectures at Bristol — is T. R. Glover's *Horace: A Return to Allegiance* (Cambridge University Press, 1932). And finally, to conclude our list,[13] we may add the graceful tribute by one who is not, like the above, a professed scholar, but a man of letters who writes 'primarily from the point of view of poetry' — *Portrait of Horace* by Alfred Noyes (London, Sheed and Ward, 1947).

The literary influence of Horace is naturally touched upon in the general surveys which have been already mentioned. It is, however, made a subject of more specialized study in two books by E. Stemplinger — *Das Fortleben der horazischen Lyrik seit der Renaissance* (Leipzig, Teubner, 1906) and *Horaz im Urteil der Jahrhunderte* (Leipzig, Dieterich, 1921). These volumes, especially the latter, deal mainly with Horace's influence in France and Germany. A wider treatment which covers the literature of thirteen countries will be found in the bimillenary volume *Orazio nella letteratura mondiale* (Rome, Istituto di Studi Romani, 1936).

The facts of Horace's life are much less controversial than those of Virgil; indeed the only topic of serious discussion has been the site of his Sabine farm in the valley of the Licenza. All doubts on this point now seem to have been removed, thanks to the work of

G. H. Hallam, *Horace at Tibur and the Sabine Farm* (Harrow, Harrow School Bookshop, 1923) and G. Lugli, *La Villa d'Orazio nella valle del Licenza* (Rome, Morpurgo, 1930). Hallam, relying on Suetonius' *Vita*, also claimed that Horace had a second country house at Tibur (on the site of S. Antonio); but his view was attacked by R. L. Dunbabin in 'Horace's villa at Tivoli' (CR 47, 1933), and Suetonius' allusion to his *rus Tiburtinum* is now largely discredited.

Among translations of all Horace's works may be mentioned the useful prose version of E. C. Wickham, *Horace for English Readers* (O.U.P., 1903).

Odes and Epodes

The editions of the *Odes* and *Epodes* by Lucian Mueller (St. Petersburg and Leipzig, Ricker, 1900) and by V. Ussani (Turin, Loescher, 1900-01) mark the end of a notable succession of commentaries. The previous few decades had been a period of great activity in Horatian scholarship, and produced, both in England and on the Continent, the editions on which we still mainly rely. Since the turn of the century new commentaries on the *Odes* — and indeed on Horace as a whole — have been rare. In England we have had H. Darnley Naylor's *Odes and Epodes: a study in poetic word order* (Cambridge University Press, 1922) and the two critical editions by A. Y. Campbell — *Horati Carmina* and *Horace, Odes and Epodes* (Liverpool University Press, 1945 and 1953 respectively). The first of these, as the title indicates, is almost wholly concerned with Horace's verbal artistry, and particularly with his placing of noun and adjective; but the principles enunciated seem too rigid and make insufficient allowance for the exigencies of the lyric metres. In the two latter, the text is assumed to be much more corrupt than most editors are prepared to admit, and there are numerous transpositions and many violent emendations. In France the *Odes* and *Epodes* were edited by F. Plessis (Paris, Hachette, 1924) with full introduction and notes, mainly exegetical; but the result is disappointing in view of Plessis' high reputation as a literary critic. Much more important and valuable was the German edition of the *Odes* and *Epodes* by R. Heinze (Berlin, Weidmann, 1930) — actually it is the seventh edition of Kiessling's commentary, but it has been so altered that Kiessling's name may well be dropped. As we should expect from the author of *Vergils Epische Technik*, this edition shows the thoroughness which characterizes the best German scholarship (the volume runs to 568 pages) and concentrates chiefly on the interpretation of Horace's full meaning, the analysis of his art, and the discussion of the literary, historical, and philosophical background. There is no general introduction; and Heinze's revolutionary theory that Horace's strict metrical practice was merely the regularization of a tendency already present in Hellenistic lyric is not mentioned.[14]

General studies of the *Odes* include *Orazio Lirico* by G. Pasquali (Florence, Felice le Monnier, 1920). This is a pleasant book, but contains little fresh in its 800 pages apart from a full and interesting discussion of Horace's relationship to the Hellenistic poets. Of much briefer compass is L. P. Wilkinson's *Horace and his Lyric Poetry* (Cambridge University Press, 1945). This is an admirable and scholarly study which is yet — to quote the author — 'within the scope of anyone who can read Latin or could once read it'. The central chapter is that on 'The Horatian Ode' with its suggestive comments on nature symbolism, the element of surprise, and Horace's verbal and metrical art; but the author also discusses more general topics such as Horace's attitude to poetry, with particular reference to the *Ars Poetica*.

Wilkinson devotes one of his chapters to the difficulty — or rather impossibility — of translating the unique qualities of the *Odes* into another language. Yet the very difficulty of the task seems to possess an irresistible attraction, and a new version appears almost every other year. The attempts in English alone during this century are too numerous to record.[15] In prose A. D. Godley's *Odes and Epodes* (London, Methuen, 1898) has not yet been surpassed. In verse, which is naturally a far more popular medium, the two most successful translations are probably those of W. S. Marris (O.U.P., 1912) and E. Marsh (London, Macmillan, 1941): the former combines grace and simplicity with remarkable fidelity to the Latin; the latter seeks rather to catch the tone and spirit, and gives us what are in some respects original poems. Two excellent anthologies of verse renderings have also been published — that of S. A. Courtauld (London, Bickers, 1908) and that of H. E. Butler (London, Bell, 1929).

The *Epodes* are the least popular of Horace's works and have attracted little attention. A general discussion of their form and spirit will be found in *Das Iambenbuch des Horaz* by T. Plüss

(Leipzig, Teubner, 1904). The dispute whether the Sixteenth Epode is answered by Virgil's fourth Eclogue or *vice versa* has continued without conclusive result; the balance of opinion favours the priority of Horace's poem. The problem of the ninth Epode — where and when it was written — has likewise not yet received a wholly convincing solution. One ingenious suggestion has been that Horace, writing at Rome after Actium, portrayed in it dramatically the feelings of one of the combatants — feelings that passed from despair through hopeful suspense to final triumph. For this see W. W. Tarn, 'The Battle of Actium' in JRS, 21 (1931) and L. P. Wilkinson, 'Horace *Epode* 9' in CR, 47 (1933).

Finally, we should also record *Q. Horati Flacci Carminum Liber Quintus* (Oxford, Blackwell, 1920) edited with Latin preface and *apparatus criticus* by A. D. Godley, and translated into English verse by Rudyard Kipling and Charles Graves. This witty *tour de force* is in the best traditions of the lighter vein of English Classical scholarship.

Satires, Epistles and Ars Poetica

Among the few editions of the Satires published this century one stands out pre-eminent — that by P. Lejay (Paris, Hachette, 1911). This monumental work, intended for 'des esprits mûrs et déjà préparés', contains text, full commentary, and detailed introductions to the individual satires (that on 2.3 covers 34 pages). Perhaps the most valuable feature, however, is the massive general introduction in which Lejay vindicates the originality of Roman Satire, but shows at the same time that its roots are deep in the past. Satire may be, as Quintilian claims, *tota nostra*,[16] but it owes much to Bion and the Cynic diatribe; to Mime, Atellan, and New Comedy; and, as Horace himself states (*Sat.* 1.4.1ff), to Old Comedy which it resembles both in spirit and structure. In general, considerable new light has been thrown on the literary antecedents of Horatian Satire by twentieth-century scholarship, aided as it has been by the discovery of new fragments of the Cynic writers such as Cercidas. Among other studies of the subject may be mentioned *Lucilius and Horace* by G. C. Fiske (Madison, University of Wisconsin Studies, 1920); *Les origines de la diatribe romaine* by A. Oltramare (Lausanne, Payot, 1926); and *Per la storia della satira* by N. Terzaghi (Turin, Erma, 1932). Those who desire a short survey of the whole question should consult A. Y.

Campbell, *Horace* (319 *supra*), 147-60; or J. Wight Duff, *Roman Satire* (Cambridge University Press, 1937) ch. 2.

So far as the *Epistles* are concerned, interest has been almost wholly concentrated on the *Epistula ad Pisones* or *Ars Poetica*. This work had long been a puzzle alike in its structure and selection of topics, and we had no clue to guide us except a cryptic remark of the commentator Porphyrion that Horace embodied in it the *praecepta* of Neoptolemus of Parium, *non quidem omnia sed eminentissima*. The beginning of a new chapter in the interpretation of the poem was marked by the publication of some papyrus fragments of Philodemus which had been discovered at Herculaneum (C. Jensen, *Philodemus über die Gedichte, fünftes Buch*, Berlin, Weidmann, 1923). In part of this papyrus Philodemus appears to be attacking the poetic theories of Neoptolemus which can in consequence be reconstructed with some degree of accuracy. For the first time, therefore, we could claim to have some direct knowledge of the Greek sources of the *Ars Poetica*.

Jensen's book naturally raised in acute form the question of Horace's originality and of the relevance of his literary precepts to his own time. In their enthusiasm for the new discovery scholars at first tended to over-emphasize Horace's dependence on his Hellenistic model. Jensen himself claimed that Horace was indebted to Neoptolemus both for his form and substance; and A. Rostagni (*Arte Poetica di Orazio*, Turin, Chiantore, 1930) finds in him merely the 'Classicist' exponent of Hellenistic theory and ultimately of Aristotle himself. This explains the surprising prominence given to drama and the satyr drama. Two years later a reaction set in with the important edition by O. Immisch, *Horazens Epistel über die Dichtkunst* (Leipzig, Dieterich, 1932). While accepting from Rostagni a threefold division of the poem into *poesis*, *poema* and *poeta*, Immisch insists that Horace introduced Roman and Horatian elements into this traditional Hellenistic framework, and that in his choice of subjects for treatment he had in mind the literary requirements of his own age.[17] He claims, moreover, that Horace's knowledge of Neoptolemus was not obtained directly but through the eclectic literary criticism of the New Academy. The discussion was carried further by F. Klingner, *Horazens Brief an die Pisonen* (Leipzig, Hirzel, 1937) and by W. Steidle, *Studien zur Ars Poetica* (Wurzburg-Aumühle, Triltsch, 1939). Klingner holds that even the plan is not Hellenistic and that the poem is an essay on the single theme of 'Amateur poets and the art of poetry'; Steidle abandons the division based on *poesis* and *poema*, and concludes that we must begin with Horace's own text, not with Hellenistic theories; the latter are helpful only in so far as they throw light on Horace's meaning.

The true solution seems to lie somewhere between the two extremes. It is improbable that Horace is throughout mechanically transcribing traditional material, but at the same time some at least of his topics are anachronistic and irrelevant to Roman poetry. A full and balanced survey of the whole problem is given by W. K. Smith in 'Horace's Debt to Greek Literature' (CR 49, 1935). He also discusses the reasons for dating the poem to about 20 B.C.

TIBULLUS

Although, in the judgment of Quintilian, Tibullus was the best of the Latin elegiac poets, he has during the last fifty years been a comparatively neglected author. The slender bulk of his writings, the perspicuity of his Latin, and his simple themes of love and country life present no strong challenge to scholarship and offer but little scope for a new assessment.

The chief champion of Tibullus in England during our period was J. P. Postgate. His *Selections from Tibullus* (London, Macmillan, 1903) is still the standard edition in this country. It provides a judicious and representative anthology of the poems; a succinct introduction on Tibullus and the authors of the *Corpus Tibullianum*; a commentary of reasonable proportions; and useful appendices on certain specialist topics. Postgate also edited Tibullus for the Oxford Classical Texts (1905), and translated him for the Loeb volume entitled *Catullus, Tibullus, and the Pervigilium Veneris* (London, Heinemann, 1912). In America a useful edition was published by K. F. Smith (New York, American Book Co., 1913): this contains introduction, full text, and commentary on all the poems except 3.1-7 ('Lygdamus' and the *Panegyricus Messallae*). In Hungary G. Némethy produced a complete edition with Latin commentary in two parts: (1) Tibullus and Sulpicia; (2) Lygdamus and *Pan. Mess.* (Budapest, Mag. Tudom., 1905-06).

The energies of Tibullan scholars, particularly on the Continent, have been chiefly devoted to the complex problems of the *Corpus Tibullianum* which is the name given to Book 3 (or Books 3 and 4 into which the Italians of the Renaissance divided it). Although the Book goes under Tibullus' name, it obviously contains the work of more than one author, and the following parts can be clearly distinguished: (*a*) the poems of 'Lygdamus' (1-6); (*b*) the *Pan. Mess.* in hexameters (7); (*c*) the 'Garland of Sulpicia', i.e. poems about Sulpicia and her lover Cerinthus (8-12); (*d*) the elegies of Sulpicia herself (13-18); and (*e*) two poems of which the first is ostensibly Tibullus' work (19-20). To determine the authorship of these various groups is the task to which scholars have addressed themselves.

The most notable contributions to the problem since 1900, apart from the editions already mentioned, have been: A. Cartault, *A propos du Corpus Tibullianum* (Paris, Alcan, 1906) and *Tibulle et les auteurs du Corpus Tibullianum* (Paris, Colin, 1909); N. Salanitro, *Tibullo* (Naples, Loffredo, 1938); L. Pepe, *Tibullo Minore* (Naples, Armanni, 1948); and E. Bréguet, *Le Roman de Sulpicia* (Geneva, Georg, 1946).

It is common ground that the *Corpus* gains a certain unity through its special connection with Messalla the friend and patron of Tibullus; and there is no dispute about the elegies of Sulpicia who was Messalla's ward and probably his niece. On all other points agreement has not been reached, and here we can merely indicate some of the solutions proposed to the several problems.

(1) *Lygdamus*. It is disputed whether this is his real name or a pseudonym. On the former assumption, he is generally held to have been a freedman (Postgate): on the latter he has been identified with the youthful Tibullus writing under a *nom de plume* (Pepe) or with Ovid (Salanitro). Salanitro's view, which had been held by many before him, gains plausibility from the fact that Lygdamus and Ovid were both born in the year 43 B.C. which they describe in identical words. ([Tib.] 3.5.18; Ov. *Tr.* 4.10.6.) Chronological considerations appear to make Pepe's thesis untenable.

(2) *The 'Garland of Sulpicia'*. This is variously attributed to Tibullus (Cartault, Némethy), to 'Lygdamus' (Smith), or to Ovid (Bréguet).

(3) *Panegyricus Messallae*. This inferior poem is almost certainly not Tibullus' work, but attempts to discover the author have been unavailing: see J. Hammer, *Prolegomena to an edition of the Pan. Mess.* (New York, Columbia University Press, 1925).

(4) *The genesis of the Corpus.* How these miscellaneous poems were gathered together in a single collection which came to be attributed to Tibullus is obscure, except that they all seem to have emanated from the circle of Messalla. Suggestions are that it was published after Tibullus' death by Ovid and Sulpicia (Salanitro) or by Lygdamus, 'a freedman who had some connexion with the Messalla family' (Postgate).

Among the tests applied to the above questions of authorship are those of metrical technique. This is discussed by A. Cartault, *Le distique élégiaque chez Tibulle, Sulpicia, Lygdamus* (Paris, Alcan, 1911). A more general, and most useful, survey of the metrical practice of all the surviving Augustan elegists is contained in *Latin Elegiac Verse* by M. Platnauer (Cambridge University Press, 1951).

A volume concerned rather with the literary appreciation than with the critical problems of Tibullus is M. Schuster's *Tibullstudien* (Vienna, Hölder, 1930). In it he defends Tibullus against the charge of formlessness, and adds a balanced survey of his life and character.

PROPERTIUS

Of the three surviving Roman elegiac poets, Propertius seems to appeal most to the present age. Uneven and obscure though he sometimes is, he has in him a depth of passion, an originality of language, and a capacity for greatness which set him above the gentler Tibullus, and the more polished, but shallower, Ovid. At the same time the many problems of reading, of arrangement, and of interpretation make strong demands upon the ingenuity and resources of professional scholarship.

For half a century the standard edition in this country was that of Paley with its Latin commentary (1853) — a work which Haupt described as *liber vulgaris ac futilis*. The gap was indeed partially filled by J. P. Postgate's *Select Elegies of Propertius* (1881) — an anthology with full introduction and notes which has passed through six editions and is still used in our schools and universities; but no complete critical and exegetical edition was available for English readers until the publication of H. E. Butler's *Sexti Properti opera omnia* (London, Constable, 1905). This has now been superseded by *The Elegies of Propertius* produced jointly by H. E. Butler and E. A. Barber (Oxford, Clarendon Press, 1933). This full and authoritative edition is, as the authors emphasize, essentially a new work, embodying the fruits of Propertian scholarship during the intervening years, and particularly the critical contributions of K. Hosius in his Teubner editions of 1911 and 1922. The introduction of some eighty pages discusses in detail the biographical, literary, and critical problems of Propertius, and the text is furnished with an ample commentary. More recently an important edition of Book 1 with prolegomena, text, and commentary has been published in Holland — *Sexti Properti Elegiarum liber I* by P. J. Enk (Leiden, Brill, 1946). Enk had long been a student of Propertius — in 1911 he had produced *Ad Properti Carmina Commentarius Criticus* (Zutphen, Thieme) — and his prolegomena would be suitable for a complete edition.

One of the notorious features of Propertius is the abruptness of his transitions and the apparent inconsequence of his thought. One school of critics has ascribed this to the imperfection of the MS. tradition and has sought to remedy it by the wholesale transposition of passages. The chief example[18] of this line of approach is *Sexti Properti quae supersunt omnia* by O. L. Richmond (Cambridge University Press, 1928). Richmond assumes that our existing MSS. are derived from a lost uncial archetype containing 16 verses per page, and that the pages of this MS. became loose and were then wrongly replaced or even lost. On this basis he proceeds to reconstruct the text by means of a few deletions, 120 transpositions, and lacunae of some 1000 lines; blank pages in his edition represent the supposedly lost leaves of the archetype. It seems pretty certain that there are some dislocations in the MSS., but Richmond's remedies are founded on an unproven hypothesis. At least some of Propertius' sudden transitions of thought may be due to his own confused emotions — a topic discussed by E. Reitzenstein, *Wirklichkeitsbild und Gefühlsentwicklung bei Properz* (Leipzig, Dieterich, 1936) and A. la Penna, *Properzio* (Florence, La Nuova Italia, 1951). Recent textual criticism has tended to be more conservative.

A minor problem that has engaged the attention of editors since Lachmann first raised it has been the division into Books. In 2.13.25 Propertius mentions his *tres libelli*. Lachmann accordingly proposed — and Richmond agrees — that Book 2 should be divided into Books 2 and 3. Among the other current solutions (e.g. that Propertius was anticipating the future, or that Books 2 and 3 were published simultaneously), Butler and Barber (*op. cit.*, xxviii-xxxv) tentatively made the novel suggestion that *tres libelli* means 'three rolls', and that whereas the short Book 1 (the *Cynthia Monobiblos*) required one roll only, Book 2, which is extremely long, required two.

Several translations have been published in English prose and verse. Of these the most notable are the prose translations by J. S. Phillimore (Oxford, Clarendon Press, 1906) and H. E. Butler in the Loeb series (London, Heinemann, 1912). While Butler's version is sound and skilful, if conventional, Phillimore employs modern and colloquial expressions, producing an effect which is certainly lively even if somewhat bizarre. Phillimore also published an *Index Verborum Propertianus* (Oxford, Clarendon Press, 1905), and had previously edited Propertius for the Oxford Classical Texts (1901).

The study of Propertius during the present century has stimulated the discussion of one question of major literary importance — the originality or otherwise of the personal love-elegy which was written by the Romans. Previously it had been held as axiomatic that the Roman elegists imitated those of Alexandria and that their subjective love-elegies were modelled upon similar Greek poems, now lost. This assumption appeared to gain support from the statements of grammarians and from the language of the Roman elegists themselves (cf. Prop. 3.1.1.: *Callimachi manes et Coi sacra Philitae*). Further evidence was thought to be discovered in the numerous coincidences between Roman Elegy and other types of Greek and Latin literature, and it was claimed that these could only be explained by the existence of an Alexandrian subjective love-elegy as a common source.

This view was first called in question by F. Jacoby[19] who pointed out that Greek elegy was objective and mythological, and argued that the subjective Roman type was first invented by Gallus in his four lost books of elegies in honour of Lycoris. His revolutionary thesis has been the subject of keen and protracted controversy, but his view has steadily gained ground and may now be said to have won wide acceptance. An admirable discussion of the evidence and the arguments will be found in Butler and Barber, *op. cit.*, pp. xxxv-lxii; and a special survey of the whole problem was made by A. A. Day, *The Origins of Latin Love-Elegy* (Oxford, Blackwell, 1938). Day agrees with Butler and Barber that there is no evidence for a personal Love-Elegy among the Alexandrians, and, like Legrand,[20] he finds no need to postulate the existence of such a *genre* to account for certain similarities between Roman Elegy and other literary types.

But if Roman erotic elegy, like Roman Satire, had no immediate Greek models it nevertheless owed much to earlier Greek literature — to New Comedy (e.g. the role of *praeceptor amoris*), the Narrative Elegy, the Pastoral, the Lyric Paignion, and, in particular, the Erotic Epigram. The originality of the Roman Elegists was therefore displayed within the tradition and embodies the principle of *contaminatio* which is so characteristic of Roman poetry as a whole.

OVID

Since the Romantic Revival Ovid has been in eclipse. In contrast to Virgil and Horace, the third great Augustan poet has been little studied except in our schools where his lucid and graceful verse — in selections — provides the ideal introduction to Latin poetry. The worship of Virgil has depressed Ovid in an age which demands that poetry shall be *utile* as well as *dulce*; and the poet who was the delight of the Middle Ages and Renaissance, of Chaucer and Shakespeare, and the French Pleiade, is despised as the idle and barely respectable singer of the smart set in Augustan Rome.

In this general climate of opinion it is hardly surprising that there are few achievements of scholarship to record. New texts have indeed been published and there have been annotated editions of parts of Ovid's poetry, but of these only three — all in English — are on the grand scale. The first appeared at the very end of the nineteenth century — A. Palmer's *Heroides* (Oxford, Clarendon Press, 1898). This valuable work (which was completed by L. C. Purser after Palmer's death) contains introduction, text, Planudes' translation, and copious notes. The introduction (which is Purser's) discusses, among other things, the originality of Ovid in the *Heroides*, his literary antecedents (drama and the *suasoriae*), and his skill in portraying feminine character. In the commentary Purser reviews at length the arguments for and against the authenticity of 15 (Sappho to Phaon), and — following Palmer — defends the Ovidian authorship, despite the defective MS. tradition. On the other hand Palmer rejects 'the double Epistles'

(16-21), chiefly on metrical and stylistic grounds, while admitting their descriptive brilliance, and attributes them to the Silver Age. To this verdict Purser demurs (Introd. xxxi-xxxii) and expresses the reasonable view that Ovid probably added them as a separate volume at a later date by which time his style and metrical practice had slightly altered. The second notable edition is S. G. Owen's *Tristium Liber Secundus* (Oxford, Clarendon Press, 1924) with introduction, text, prose translation and commentary. The chief interest of this Book of the *Tristia* is that it contains Ovid's apologia to Augustus in which he defends his *Ars Amatoria* and seeks to extenuate his misconduct. The real cause of Ovid's banishment to Tomis in A.D. 8 is one of the puzzles of antiquity; and though he himself describes it as *carmen et error* (*Tr.* 2, 207) the *error* appears to have been a graver offence than the *carmen* (which was, of course, the *Ars*). As Ovid never divulges the nature of this *error*, there has naturally been an ample field for speculation. The various conjectures of scholars, along with the relevant texts, are fully and judiciously examined in Owen's introduction; and while he does not commit himself he is inclined to conclude that Ovid's offence was not amatory intrigue but political indiscretion — that he had incurred the enmity of Tiberius and Livia because he had appeared to interfere with their dynastic aims; this (he argues) would account for Tiberius' refusal to recall him after Augustus' death. Finally there is J. G. Frazer's *Fastorum Libri Sex* (London, Macmillan, 1929) — a sumptuous work in five volumes which was described by a reviewer as 'the most important full edition of a Latin classic published in England since the war'. The text is furnished with a prose translation, and it is to the translation rather than to the original Latin that the massive commentary (vols. 2-4) is attached. This monumental edition is primarily designed for the anthropologist and illustrates Ovid's subject matter with all the wealth of learning and freshness of outlook which we associate with the author of *The Golden Bough*. In it the reader will find a rich storehouse of history and folklore, archaeology and art, religion and anthropology, drawing its material not merely from Greece and Rome but from all over the world. Similar in purpose but very much briefer in scope is C. Bailey's *Fastorum Liber III* (Oxford, Clarendon Press, 1921). Here, too, the notes are primarily concerned with the subject matter, and there is a short and useful introduction on the beginning and subsequent development of Roman religion, the Roman Calendar, and the origin and functions of Mars.

The *Ars Amatoria*, though eschewed by English editors, has nevertheless been thrice translated into English verse within two decades — by F. A. Wright, *Ovid, the Lover's Handbook* (London, Routledge, 1920); by E. P. Barker, *The Lover's Manual* (Oxford, Blackwell, 1931); and by B. P. Moore, *The Art of Love* (London and Glasgow, Blackie, 1935). Mention may also be made of F. Munari's excellent critical edition of the *Amores* with an Italian translation (Florence, La Nuova Italia, 1951).

The comparative paucity of scholarly works on Ovid, despite the great bulk of his writings, is eloquent testimony to the general neglect into which he has fallen in the twentieth century. Yet from time to time there is a protest against the current verdict, an attempt to restore to him some measure of that popularity which, at certain periods of the past, he enjoyed in no less measure than Virgil himself. In this sense alone is it possible to speak of a new approach.

The first powerful plea for justice to Ovid was made by a Frenchman of letters, E. Ripert in *Ovide, poète de l'amour, des dieux, et de l'exil* (Paris, Colin, 1921). In this charming and refreshing study Ripert reviews Ovid's life and poems, traces his great influence on French literature, and rebukes the academic criticism which transfers its contempt for Ovid the man into contempt for Ovid the poet. Shortly afterwards came a similar appeal from America in E. K. Rand's *Ovid and his Influence* (London, Harrap, 1926). Rand emphasizes the essential modernity and marvellous versatility of Ovid's poetry. His modernity springs from his universal qualities — 'his wit, his art, his creative fancy, the mastery of his own moods and of his plastic world'. His versatility manifests itself in his range of tone: now he writes epic and now elegy, now comedy or tragedy, now didactic or oratory or panegyric. In this respect he is like Shakespeare, for 'Ovid's spirit eludes us. If we call him this or that, he quickly performs a metamorphosis and shows another face'. Confirmation of Ovid's great poetic gifts is to be found by tracing his influence through the centuries — on the Goliards and Romances of the Middle Ages, on Dante and Chaucer, Petrarch and Boccaccio, and on post-Renaissance poetry; this Rand does in an interesting and scholarly survey. A less sympathetic attitude was displayed in E. Martini's *Einleitung zu Ovid* (Prague, Brünn-Rohrer, 1933). He has more of the moralist's outlook and complains of Ovid's shallowness and his indifference to the deeper things of life. At the same time he acknowledges Ovid's rich poetic talent, and recognizes his originality in perceiving the further possibilities of elegy and in creating a new type of narrative poetry by employing the resources of rhetoric. The least successful of the attempts to rehabilitate Ovid was that of H. Fränkel in his Sather Lectures — *Ovid: a poet between Two Worlds* (Berkeley and Los Angeles, University of California Press, 1945). Fränkel's treatment is largely psychological. To him Ovid was one of those who help to prepare the passage from Antiquity to Christianity and his poetry therefore possesses some 'deeper significance'. The whole study is vitiated by this preconception: e.g. the *Ars* merely enjoins 'loving care and patient humble devotion' while the *Metamorphoses* give 'ample scope for displaying the phenomena of insecure and fleeting identity'.

In this country the campaign for Ovid has been desultory. S. G. Owen examined the debt of English poetry to Ovid in a lecture entitled 'Ovid and Romance' (*English Literature and the Classics*: see p. 308 *supra*). D. A. Slater in *Ovid in the Metamorphoses*[21] analysed both the spirit and the structure of the poem: the spirit was influenced by the Pythagorean doctrine of the kinship of all living creatures; while the vast structure is harmonious through all its parts because it is dominated by a single idea — 'the interchange and interplay of all life in the world'. Some of the finest criticism of Ovid is given incidentally in Gilbert Murray's 'Poesis and Mimesis' (*Essays and Addresses*: London, Allen and Unwin, 1921). There he rebukes the present generation for its blindness to Ovid. Ovid was 'a poet utterly in love with poetry, not perhaps with the soul of poetry . . . but with the real face and voice and body'. He was 'a man who seems hardly to have lived at all except in the world of the imagination', and 'among all the poets who take rank merely as story-tellers and creators of mimic worlds, Ovid still stands supreme'. A particularly valuable contribution to a just appraisal of Ovid is 'Ovid: some aspects of his character and aims' by T. F. Higham (CR, 48, 1934). Ovid (he maintains) was not the child of his age. He was a born poet whose sole ambition was to create and through his creations to live for ever. In the literary controversies of his time he had to decide between the school of Horace with its insistence on instruction as well as charm, and the Callimachean school, or 'water-drinkers', whose aims were primarily aesthetic. He gave his verdict against the former on grounds of literary, not moral, principle; the *genres* had their *descriptae vices*, and elegy, which Ovid knew by instinct to be his *métier*, was traditionally *levis*. Ovid and his opponents therefore 'lived on different planes and had no common ground for argument. His standards were aesthetic, not moral'.

Whether the pleas of these apologists will avail to restore Ovid to favour cannot yet be known; perhaps in 1957, Ovid's bimillenary year, we shall have at least a partial answer.

MANILIUS

The obscure astronomical poet Manilius is not a general favourite. Apart from his difficult and technical subject-matter, his text has long been in an unsatisfactory condition, and such scholarly work as has been done on him has mostly been devoted to improving it. H. W. Garrod produced a useful edition of Book 2 with translation and commentary (Oxford, Clarendon Press, 1911); but the supreme glory of Manilian — one might almost say of Latin — scholarship in the present century is the five volumes of the great critical edition (with Latin commentary) by A. E. Housman (London, Richards, 1903-30). Of particular interest are the prefaces — in English — to Books 1 and 5 which give a brilliant exposition of the principles of textual criticism and contain many pungent remarks on other scholars in the style which Housman has made peculiarly his own. Although Housman's superb achievement will naturally appeal but little to the literary student of the Classics, it is nevertheless a happy circumstance that we can end this review of the Augustan poets by adducing such striking evidence that the spirit of Scaliger and Bentley has survived into our present age.

---

[1] More recent French studies are A. M. Guillemin, *Virgile: poète, artiste, et penseur* (Paris, Michel, 1951), and J. Perret, *Virgile, l'homme et l'œuvre* (Paris, Boivin, 1952.)

[2] L. Hermann, *Les Masques et les Visages dans les Bucoliques* (Brussels, Rev. de l'Univ., 1930) goes so far as to claim that the same fictitious name always denotes the same real person, and that no real person had more than one fictitious name. If, therefore, Menalcas is Virgil, Tityrus is not.

[3] It has even been conjectured that Virgil introduced Biblical imagery out of compliment to Pollio who had Jewish connections. See H. W. Garrod, CR 19 (1905), p. 37, and T. F. Royds, *Virgil and Isaiah*, Appendix B.

⁴ Also by E. Norden 'Orpheus und Eurydike', *Sitzungsber. der preuss. Akad. der Wissenschaft* 1934, pp. 626-83. For a defence of Servius see 'The Fall of Cornelius Gallus' in R. S. Conway's *New Studies* (p. 308 *supra*); also E. Galletier, *Bull. Ass. Budé* 12 (1926), pp. 11-29.
⁵ Others are *Il Libro di Didone* by C. Buscaroli (Milan, Albrighi, 1932): Book 4 by A. S. Pease (Harvard, University Press, 1935): Book 6 by H. E. Butler (Oxford, Blackwell, 1920).
⁶ Other interesting studies of Virgil's art are A. Cartault, *L'art de Virgile dans l'Enéide* (Paris, University Press, 1926) and V. Pöschl, *Die Dichtkunst Virgils: Bild und Symbol in der Aeneis* (Innsbruck-Vienna, Rohrer, 1950); the latter discusses the unity of feeling in the *Aeneid*, and the part played by Virgil's imagery in creating it.
⁷ According to Suetonius *Vita* 23 Virgil composed his first verse-draft *prout liberet quidque et nihil in ordinem arripiens*.
⁸ But C. Plésent, *Le Culex, poème pseudo-Virgilien* and *Le Culex, Étude sur l'Alexandrinisme Latine* (Paris, Fontemoing, 1910) regards it as a forgery in the latter part of Augustus' principate. E. Fraenkel, 'The Culex' (JRS 42, 1952), strongly supports his general thesis, but places the date a little later, probably in the reign of Tiberius.
⁹ Others, however, consider it a neoteric survival composed after Virgil's death, e.g. R. Helm, *Ein Epilog zur Cirisfrage* (*Hermes* 72, 1937) who dates it between Ovid and Persius. In general, recent criticism tends to be sceptical of the Virgilian authorship of the *Appendix*: see J. Perret, *op. cit.*, pp. 147-8 and 182-3.
¹⁰ See W. Warde Fowler 'A Metrical Peculiarity in the *Culex*' CR 33 (1919): R. B. Steele 'The Authorship of the *Ciris*', AJP 51 (1930): M. M. Crump, *The Epyllion* (p. 312 *supra*), pp. 263-70.
¹¹ For a similar work in French see T. Zielinski, *Horace et la Société romaine du Temps d'Auguste* (Paris, Les Belles Lettres, 1938).
¹² The standard English works of literary criticism on the Augustan poets are still W. Y. Sellar's *Virgil* (1876) and *Horace and the Elegiac Poets* (1891).
¹³ During our period several Italian scholars also published useful general studies, e.g. E. Turolla, *Orazio* (Florence, Le Monnier, 1931) and A. Rostagni, *Orazio* (Rome, 'Res Romanae', 1937).
¹⁴ For this see R. Heinze, 'Die lyrischen Verse des Horaz', *Berichte der sächsischen Gesellschaft der Wissenschaften*, Bd. 70, Heft 4 (1918). Previously the current view had been that Horace's strict rules about long syllables and *caesurae* were based upon a recently published Handbook of metrical theory, and that his lyric measures were derived from the dactylic hexameter and from the iambic and trochaic metres.
¹⁵ In his lecture on *Ad Pyrrham* to the Horatian Society (1953) Sir Ronald Storrs stated that he had discovered 183 translations of Odes 1. 5 into English verse from the seventeenth century onwards.
¹⁶ This may be interpreted as 'wholly ours' or 'altogether in our favour': see W. Rennie, C.R. 36 (1922), p. 21.
¹⁷ The similarity between Horace's *Ars Poetica* and Cicero's *Orator* and *De Oratore* as topical works is discussed by G. C. Fiske and M. A. Grant in *Harvard Studies* 35 (1924) and *University of Wisconsin Studies* 27 (1929) respectively.
¹⁸ Another example is *The Elegies of Propertius in a reconditioned text* by S. G. Tremenheere with verse translation and commentary (London, Simpkin, Marshall, 1931).
¹⁹ 'Zur Entstehung der römischen Elegie', *RM* 60 (1905).
²⁰ *Revue des Études anciennes* 13 (1911), pp. 1-32.
²¹ *Occasional Publications of the Classical Association* No. 1 (Cambridge, University Press, undated). For a criticism of Slater's philosophical interpretation and for a good literary appreciation of the *Metamorphoses* see M. M. Crump, *The Epyllion* (p. 312 *supra*), chapters 10 and 11.

CHAPTER XII

ROMAN ORATORY

BY S. F. BONNER

ANCIENT rhetorical theory, particularly in its treatment of the subject of style, has a considerable intrinsic interest; for certain branches of classical studies, notably education, literature, and literary criticism, it is an important basic discipline; for the proper understanding and appreciation of Roman oratory it is quite indispensable. Learned opinion does not, to be sure, consider the cultivation of the seeds of rhetoric to be directly responsible for all the finest flowers of Ciceronian oratory; but neither does it consider that oratory to be due to a kind of spontaneous generation. During the past fifty years, scholars who have investigated questions as diverse as Cicero's invention of arguments, his application of philosophical and historical knowledge, his use of emotional appeal, wit, word-play, irony, digression, and variety of style, have not only shown themselves conversant with the art of rhetoric, but have often made it the starting-point for their researches. Those who have studied the problem of Cicero's oratorical rhythm have made themselves familiar with his own exposition in the *Orator*, but it may be noticed that some theorists have incurred criticism on the ground that the treatise did not provide evidence to justify the particular methods which they employed. Finally, in the most recent account of Roman oratory, by M. L. Clarke,[1] in which the relation of theory to practice is considered, rhetoric plays a prominent part. The present chapter will be divided into four sections, the pre-Ciceronian orators, Cicero, Cicero's contemporaries, and the orators of the period of decline. The section on Cicero will, naturally, be by far the longest; but who would have more cordially approved of that than Cicero himself?

I. PRE-CICERONIAN ORATORY

One of the main difficulties, which prevents the modern student of Roman oratory from seeing the subject in a true and clear perspective, is the heavy loss which time has inflicted on the speeches of the pre-Ciceronian orators. Much was done to repair its ravages by the patient work, over a century ago, of H. Meyer,[2] who assembled and annotated the fragments not only of the Republican orators but of those of the Empire as well. For the whole of the Republican period, his work has now been superseded by the collection of E. Malcovati,[3] who in her valuable Prolegomena incorporated the results of modern research, and included numerous criticisms of earlier scholars in detailed interpretations. These could not possibly be summarized here, but her edition will remain of basic importance to all students of the subject. A substantial critical study of the whole of the pre-Ciceronian era was published in 1903 by A. Cima,[4] who mainly concerned himself with the historical background of the fragments, but also made some observations on the style of individual orators and the influence of Greek studies. During our period, the historical and political setting has been re-examined, but although Malcovati has published a short essay on Roman eloquence,[5] and M. L. Clarke has devoted a chapter to the influence of rhetoric on Roman oratory before Cicero, there has been no full literary account.

For all practical purposes, Roman oratory begins with the elder Cato. Here the development of knowledge in our period begins with the useful dissertation of M. O. Baumgart,[6] who sought to date the earliest edited collection of Cato's speeches. He argued that, for at least a century, the speeches, even those which Cato had included in his *Origines* (Gell. 6.3.7; 13.25.15), were forgotten. He contrasted the extreme paucity of references in writers before Cicero with the much greater knowledge shown of them under the Empire, and particularly the very general remarks in Cicero's *De Oratore* (55 B.C.) with the much greater interest shown in the *Brutus* (46 B.C.), where (65) Cicero says he had discovered and read over 150 of them. Developing Soltau's[7] view that Plutarch's *Life of Cato* contained much material drawn from the special biography composed by Nepos (not the extant *Life* — cf. Nep., *Cat.* 3.5), Baumgart deduced that the edition must have appeared before 36 B.C. In view of the fact that the special biography was composed at Atticus' request, and that Cicero was very interested in Cato and dedicated his *Cato major* to Atticus, he conjectured that the edition came from the latter's publishing-house between

46 and 36 B.C. The view of Soltau and Baumgart on the importance of Nepos' special biography was subsequently accepted by P. Fraccaro, and, recently, by F. della Corte,[8] who has covered more thoroughly the ground traversed by Baumgart, in a study of Cato's life, and subsequent repute, as evidenced by his contemporaries, by the Roman Annalists, by Cicero, Nepos, Sallust, Livy, the elder Pliny, Quintilian, Plutarch, Fronto, Gellius, and Aurelius Victor.

A series of important contributions to our knowledge of the speeches was made by P. Fraccaro, whose findings were, with a few exceptions, approved by Malcovati. Fraccaro reconstructed the historical background and interrelation of the fragments with great skill, and made several improvements on the dating and interpretation of earlier writers. He discussed in detail the consular speeches,[9] the censorship speeches,[10] and several of later date.[11] As an example of a clear improvement of knowledge, we may take his placing of the speech *De Sumptu Suo* in 164 B.C.; previous scholars had taken the charge of extravagance to refer to Cato's consulship in 195, but, by an elucidation of Gellius 13.24.1 and Plutarch, *Cato*, 4.4, Fraccaro showed that it must have been much later, probably in a *iudicium de moribus* (the censor censured!), when Cato in old age had somewhat relaxed his Spartan strictness.[12] Further historical interpretations were made by B. Janzer, who used the fragments to illustrate Cato's political principles.[13]

A study of Cato's language and style, including numerous illustrations from the speeches, was made by R. Till,[14] who expressed his intention (apparently unfulfilled) of editing the fragments. He set out the evidence for the archaic element, as shown in orthography, word-meanings, syntax, and sentence-structure, and then proceeded to illustrate the colloquial element, and the poetical element, in which the influence of Ennius was noted. He further listed many Greek loan-words, and devoted special attention to words which made their first appearance in Cato. But his work was not merely linguistic; he also observed such stylistic features as alliteration, asyndeton, anaphora, and pleonasm. Much earlier, E. Norden[15] had regarded some of these features as indicative of the influence of Greek studies. Others regarded them as, in the main, characteristic of Cato's own sturdy personality, and typical of the Latin language itself.[16] Till was also inclined to the latter view, which seems to

z

have gained some currency. The question cannot be said to be finally settled; Fronto and later rhetoricians sometimes *discovered* in Cato such figures, and Cicero (*Brut.* 65) said that there could be found in his speeches 'all the oratorical virtues'. It is too early to say for certain whence those virtues were derived. Nor are we yet sure of the significance of Cicero's use of Cato in the Asianist-Atticist controversy, though some suggestions were put forward by Charles Knapp[17] in an article on the development of Latin prose style.

It was again Fraccaro who made, in 1912-13, a historical investigation into the surviving fragments of the speeches of Cato's successors, whose lives extended into the Gracchan era, and of the Gracchi themselves.[18] A little later, the fragments of the orations of C. Gracchus, and the testimonia concerning them, were separately edited in the dissertation of Natalie Häpke, who began by examining the reliability of the writers who preserved them.[19] She argued that Cicero and Gellius must have possessed copies of the speeches and that their wording of the fragments could be trusted. Proceeding then to compare the evidence of Cicero and Gellius with that of Plutarch, she found that the latter did not differ in essentials, though he may not have worked from the originals, any more than the late grammarians and glossographers, the origins of whose citations she endeavoured to trace. Basing her collection on these sources, she annotated the fragments of 24 speeches, of which she placed 8 before the period of Gaius' tribunate, 13 during his tenure of that office, and 3 subsequent to it. The work of Fraccaro and Häpke was taken into account and further discussed in Malcovati's Prolegomena.

From a rhetorical and stylistic viewpoint, Norden (I, 169-74) made some comments on the fragments of the Gracchan orators. It may also be noted that R. Reitzenstein's brochure,[20] in which he observed indications of Stoic rhetorical theory in the few fragments of Scipio Aemilianus, was a predecessor of several works in our period, in which the importance of the Stoic theory of style and its contemporary and subsequent influence was stressed. M. Bonnet[21] collected interesting parallels for the well-known dilemma-fragment of C. Gracchus, quoted and more than once imitated by Cicero (cf. *De Orat.* 3.56.214; *Mur.* 88) and others: 'Quo me miser conferam? Quo vortam? In Capitoliumne? At fratris sanguine madet. An domum? Matremne ut miseram lamentantem videam et abiectam?' But imitators, he well observed, made of it merely a rhetorical figure; no one ever matched the depth of its original pathos. Finally, a few illuminating pages were devoted by J. Marouzeau to the analysis of fragments of Cato and C. Gracchus in the light of remarks of the Auctor ad Herennium and Aulus Gellius.[22]

The eminence of Antonius and Crassus, and the amount known about them (in general, not as much as we should like in detail) entitled them to the special consideration which they were given in the neat and systematic work of M. Krüger,[23] who unfortunately did not fulfil his intention of editing all the pre-Ciceronian fragments. In the introduction to his edition, Krüger argued that Cicero is a first-rate authority for our knowledge of these orators, in whom he placed the ἀκμή of Roman eloquence (*Brut.* 138). True, he may have tended, in the *De Oratore*, to exaggerate their achievements and to over-stress the distinction between the great natural talent of Antonius, the born forensic orator, largely independent of rhetorical theory and philosophical study, and Crassus, the fully-developed πολιτικὸς ῥήτωρ, so deeply imbued with Greek culture; but in essence the distinction was true. Krüger found few direct citations from Antonius in the fragments of ten speeches (dated 113-90 B.C.), which he collected and annotated; the shrewd Antonius, Cicero tells us (*Clu.* 140), did not publish them, in order to leave himself free to contradict anything he might subsequently be alleged to have said. But in the fragments of 13 orations of Crassus (dated 119-91 B.C.), Krüger found considerably more direct citation, for Crassus did publish some at least of his speeches, and left sections of others (*Brut.* 160ff). Krüger and Malcovati have given us a clearer picture of the background and characteristics of Antonius and Crassus by their systematic regrouping of the information given mainly by Cicero, and Clarke has compared and contrasted their methods and style.

Here we must leave the pre-Ciceronian orators. The literature on them is very limited, and, we must admit, by far the most has been done by Italian and German scholars. Italy, particularly, had quite a tradition in this field.[24] Elsewhere, this interesting period seems to have been unduly neglected; at any rate, in the words of Dionysius, himself a searcher after works on ancient orators, ἐγὼ γοῦν οὐδεμιᾷ τοιαύτῃ περιτυχὼν οἶδα γραφῇ, πολλὴν ζήτησιν αὐτῶν ποιησάμενος. οὐ μέντοι διαβεβαιοῦμαί γε ὡς καὶ σαφῶς εἰδώς. τάχα γὰρ ἂν εἶέν τινες αἱ ἐμὲ διαλανθάνουσαι τοιαῦται γραφαί (*De ant. orat., Praef.* c. 4).

2. CICERO

In nineteenth-century scholarly researches on Cicero's speeches, a not inconsiderable part was played by investigations into questions of authenticity, and the genuineness of, for instance, the two speeches *Post Reditum*, the *De Domo*, the *De Haruspicum Responso*, even the *Catilinarians* and other well-known speeches, was at various times challenged or upheld. In the present century, only very occasional echoes have been heard of these old controversies.[25] But in their place there gradually arose another problem, much more difficult to resolve, namely, that of the exact relationship between the speeches as they were actually delivered, and the speeches as Cicero subsequently saw fit to publish them. Already in 1907, although no extensive study had yet been made, the idea that some, at least, of the published speeches, though Ciceronian, were artistic productions which did not faithfully represent the spoken word, was sufficiently in the air for L. Laurand to make it the subject of the opening chapter of his celebrated studies on Cicero's style.[26] Laurand realized that there was sufficient evidence to justify an inquiry, but was convinced that only a very limited amount of modification of the originals had taken place. True, there was the undoubted fact that the extant *Pro Milone* is not the speech which Cicero originally so unsuccessfully delivered — a failure to which Milo owed his opportunity of sampling the delicious mullets of Marseilles (Dio Cassius, 40.54). But on the occasion of that speech the circumstances were exceptional. Speculation, however, seemed to be invited by Cicero's statement (*Brut.* 91) that speeches were frequently written after delivery, and Quintilian's remark (10.7.30) that Cicero himself merely wrote out beforehand the most important sections, especially the *exordia*, and otherwise relied largely on careful premeditation, and improvization. The opinion of the younger Pliny (1.20.7ff), that Cicero shortened some of his speeches for publication was partly based on the fact that in the *Pro Murena* (57), for instance, omitted topics are indicated simply by headings. On the other hand, later additions might be traceable in certain passages of the

Catilinarians, and, finally, some stylistic revision might have taken place. All this Laurand was willing to admit, but beyond it he was not prepared to go. Against the belief in wide modifications, he set the fact that the *Post Reditum in Senatu* was described by Cicero himself as 'dicta de scripto' (*Planc.* 74); that Nepos (*ap.* Hieron., *Patr. Lat.* 23, col. 419) said that the *Pro Cornelio* had been published in the very words actually used; that the argument of the *prima Miloniana* was the same as that of the extant speech (Ascon. 37, Stangl); that evidence from the *Letters* proved that, in several instances, Cicero did not wait long before publishing, and therefore, presumably, his audience, at least, would have been able to detect any tampering with the original.

But Laurand's reasoned objections failed to stem the flow of conjecture. In 1914, T. Opperskalski brought out a study of the delivery and publication of six judicial speeches (*Rosc. Am., Clu., Mur., Sest., Planc., Cael.*).[27] Summarizing the ancient evidence, he decided that Cicero based his revised versions on his original *commentarii*, together with his impromptu passages (either recollected or supplied from the stenographer's copy), but omitted some passages that seemed superfluous, and added others which he had neither written out nor improvised. He urged that, in the speeches mentioned, certain passages which seemed to disturb the flow of argument, or to be for various reasons inappropriate, were additions made in subsequent revision. But there was in this view one fatal flaw: it was clear that, by detecting these 'irregularities', he was admitting imperfections, and he could not satisfactorily explain why Cicero should have taken the trouble to insert passages which, by Opperskalski's own admission, merely succeeded in spoiling the general effect of the finished literary product. He was evidently conscious of this difficulty (pp. 82-3), but fell back on the rather lame explanation (though not unsupported by some general evidence) that Cicero did his revision carelessly and in haste. An interesting test of subsequent opinion on Opperskalski's theory of additions has been made with the *Pro Caelio*, for which Norden, in the previous year, had also published an elaborate but rather different theory of improvisations made during the speech and later incorporated in the revised version.[28] R. G. Austin's discussion, in his second edition of that speech, shows that opinion has gradually moved away from belief in the explanations of both of these scholars.[29] It may be, then, that the comparatively simple theory of passages added in revision will, in general, go the same way as the *Echtheitskritik* of the nineteenth century; but there is a much more serious rival in the field.

In 1925, there appeared the important study of J. Humbert, who strongly rejected the methods of his predecessors as subjective and revealing ignorance of the real conditions of legal procedure.[30] He was a pupil of Jules Martha, one of whose great merits was that he strove to see Cicero in the surroundings in which he actually worked.[31] Confining himself to the judicial speeches, Humbert began with an examination of Roman legal procedure. He reconstructed the order of proceedings within the *actio*, and argued that the interrogation of witnesses invariably followed the speeches for prosecution and defence. The advocate, then, would make further observations during the interrogation, which he was not in a position to make before. Moreover, adjournments had an important effect, since they would also necessitate further addresses and interrogations. Under such conditions, Cicero's published speeches rarely represented a single original address. The revised version would not be composed from a single stenogram, as had been previously assumed, but from a number of stenograms, and represented a sort of *contaminatio* of what had actually been spoken on various distinct occasions during the entire hearing of the case. But the problem was to decide which stages were represented and at which points, in individual speeches, and this problem he proceeded to examine.

As a whole, Humbert's thesis has remained uncontroverted. W. Kroll, after a few criticisms, remarked of it: 'Im übrigen ist was Humbert über die Redaktion der ciceronischen Reden sagt, sehr bedeutsam und beherzigenswert'.[32] But a true balance of judgment can only be reached when Humbert's arguments have been carefully weighed for all the speeches individually. As an example of dissent may be quoted T. B. L. Webster, who, in his edition of the *Pro Flacco*, disagrees with Humbert's conclusion that the speech is not a unity.[33] But, in the history of the whole question, the significance of this work was in its method of approach.

The name of Kroll is intimately associated with the study of Cicero's *Rhetorica*. His revision of Jahn's *Brutus*,[34] during our period, and particularly his edition of the *Orator*[35] (though it does not displace that of Sir John Sandys[36]) added not a little to the understanding of those treatises, and his article, 'Rhetorik',[37] is an admirable historical guide to the whole subject and the ramifications of its literature. The most systematic study of Cicero's rhetorical sources has been that of Laurand,[38] in which his indebtedness to Plato, Isocrates, Aristotle, Hermagoras, the Stoics, the Academics, and others, his original contributions to doctrine, and his changes of opinion, are assessed with excellent judgment. One of the merits of Laurand's work, apart from numerous contributions to detail, was his correction of the tendency to regard some of Cicero's rhetorical treatises, or large parts of them, as mere transcripts of a single Greek original. Notable as one of the few studies of Cicero's life which included a proper account of his *Rhetorica* was the biography of T. Petersson.[39] A useful point, not always fully appreciated, was made in Weidner's dissertation on the relationship of Cicero's theory to contemporary 'school-rhetoric'.[40] He showed that, although Cicero (*De Orat.* 1.5) disparaged his youthful *De Inventione* (of which the formal, stereotyped system has so much in common with the treatise *Ad Herennium*), and developed in his *De Oratore* and *Orator* a much more mature conception of oratory, he never entirely abandoned that system even in his major works on rhetoric, and it reappeared in his *Partitiones Oratoriae*, and, partly, in the *Topica*.[41] Cicero protested against its misuse, and the supposition that it was, *per se*, an adequate training for an orator. These are works covering a wide field of Cicero's theory; a few contributions dealing with particular problems will be mentioned in due course. Meanwhile, we may consider publications of the period which deal with Cicero's application of that theory to practice.

At the beginning of the century, there was nothing new in the idea of rhetorical analysis of Cicero's speeches. But a useful detailed examination of the correspondence of Cicero's practice with theory was that made in the dissertation of F. Rohde,[42] published in 1903. Rohde confined himself to the judicial speeches; but, instead of analysing them individually, he gathered cumulative evidence from them, according to the rhetorical rules for the main speech-divisions. He found that, in many *exordia*, Cicero rendered the members of jury *benivolos, attentos, dociles*, by the prescribed methods, for instance, by modestly recounting his services, by stressing his difficulties, by flattery, by exposing the evil motives of his adversaries, by emphasizing the importance of the case, by alluding briefly to the facts. His *narratio* was often, as theory required, *brevis, aperta, probabilis*; in fact, there was increasing brevity, for in the *Pro Quinctio* the narrative took up a fifth of the speech, whereas in some of the later speeches it had shrunk to a fifteenth or a twentieth. But in some it had disappeared altogether, especially where Cicero's fellow-advocates had already addressed the court, and occasional omission had some support in theory (*De Inv.* I. 21. 30). In the *partitio*, the orator did not often follow the theory that he should state the points of agreement with his adversary, but did often clarify the issue before the court, and outline the arguments he intended to make. In the *argumenta*, he utilized the innumerable *loci* concerning the tangible evidence and the various inherent probabilities. Finally, in the *peroratio*, he only occasionally used *enumeratio*, but more often, especially in accusation, *indignatio*, and nearly always, in defence, *conquestio*. In the main, Cicero followed his own rules.

Two years later, Rohde's work was supplemented by the study of R. Preiswerk, whose approach showed important differences.[43] He, too, collected cumulative evidence according to the speech-divisions, but he included the non-judicial speeches; he noted not only *loci* which were in the handbooks but many which were not, and he was as ready to stress the characteristics which reflected Roman practice as those which suggested the influence of Hellenistic theory. In the *exordia*, for instance, he found several *loci* which Rohde had neglected because they were not in the handbooks, such as the orator's frequent explanations why he had taken up the case, and his emphasis on his personal connections with his client. Here he emphasized the difference between the Greek practice of defending oneself, and the Roman practice of employing a *patronus*. In the *argumenta*, he showed that Cicero often supplemented or developed the current *loci*. For instance, in the handbooks, defence of a man's previous career served a minor purpose as one of many ways of proving that he was not likely to have committed the misdeeds with which he was charged (*probabile ex vita*); in the speeches its use was extended at many points. Preiswerk's study as a whole, though marred by a habit of regarding two or three parallels as a *locus*, and a curious idea (p. 73) that Cicero had all his commonplaces ticketed and docketed in his library (!), was a necessary corrective to Rohde's work.

Meanwhile, in a series of published lectures, Jules Martha[44] was taking a line of argument even farther from Rohde's view. In his eyes, Cicero the advocate had to be a realist, not tied to the apron-strings of theory. He had, above all, to direct his attention to the points most menaced by opposing counsel; if necessary, he took his narrative back to a point beyond that at which it was strictly relevant, or used it as a weapon of offence by anticipating his arguments. He adapted his arguments to demolish the allegations of the prosecution by satire or invective. But he followed rhetorical precept in enlarging special questions to general issues and in making adroit use of historical *exempla*. It was characteristic of Martha that he illustrated Cicero's practice not from the *De Inventione*, but from the precepts of Antonius in the *De Oratore*.

We must now see how these three views have been substantiated by the work of some subsequent scholars concerned with individual speeches, for the subject has not been fully treated since. For the *Pro Milone*, F. P. Donnelly's refreshing commentary,[45] written by that *rara avis* among Ciceronian editors, a Professor of Rhetoric, has much relevant information — in fact, it might almost be taken as a demonstration of the amount of truth there is in a broad statement of J. S. Reid, who, in his own brief analysis, remarked: 'It contains indeed hardly a clause which has not been consciously framed with the precepts of the art rhetorical in view.'[46] The *Pro Archia* was rhetorically analysed by W. Sternkopf, who was concerned to show, by a careful study of its argument according to the prescribed rhetorical divisions, that it was much more logically constructed than had been previously thought, and that the long *extra causam* section in praise of poetry and of Archias as poet (12-30) was an integral part of the development of Cicero's case.[47] In an analysis of the *Pro Flacco*, T. B. L. Webster found that the system could be successfully applied, apart from the lack of a narrative. In the *Pro Caelio*, analysed by van Wageningen[48] and discussed by Heinze,[49] the model *exordium*, the long *praemunitio*, necessitated in defence of Caelius' earlier career, the inclusion of προσωποποιίαι, the lack of a clearly-defined *narratio*, and the appeal for sympathy in the *peroratio*, have all been noted. The general position has been shown to be one of modification of rhetorical structure to suit the circumstances, and Preiswerk's view seems most applicable.[50] As to the *Pro Cluentio*, Kroll found very little correspondence with the rules; the introduction has no *insinuatio*, the narrative is fused, the case is complicated by a previous trial, and practical considerations predominate.[51] Kroll, again,[52] for the *Pro Plancio*, argued that the circumstances of the case, particularly Cicero's friendship for both accuser and accused, made it difficult for him to follow the prescribed rules, though some rhetorical influence appeared. Even the *Pro Roscio Amerino*, for which Landgraf's monumental work[53] provided so much rhetorical analysis, has been challenged; F. Solmsen has, in a thoughtful article, shown that the political situation had much influence, and that, in devoting so much attention to emotional appeal in his extended attack on Chrysogonus, Cicero went beyond the standard Hellenistic theory, and approached the ideals of his *De Oratore*.[54] These are all judicial speeches; in the non-judicial speeches, it is natural to expect less conformity to doctrine, as A. Yon has shown in a study of the second *Catilinarian*.[55] To sum up from these examples, we may say that scholars are fully aware of considerable agreement with theory, although rhetorical gems like the *Pro Milone* are rare. They are also increasingly aware of the practical needs of the orator, and provided it is not over-stressed, this is an important counterbalancing factor.

The methods of training so fully expounded in the *De Inventione* take in the *De Oratore* a subordinate position. There Crassus, Antonius, and other renowned orators of the generation before Cicero discuss the importance of an encyclopaedic education, the value of an ability to stir the emotions and to charm with wit, and the characteristics of an attractive and effective style. The orator must not only instruct (*docere*), he must delight (*delectare*), and move (*movere*). The question of the origins of this development in Cicero's ideas is a complex and far-reaching one, and has been much discussed. It is not certain how far it represents a return to the doctrines of Isocrates and Aristotle, and how far it is the result of more recent and contemporary teaching. It was urged by H. M. Hubbell that Cicero's programme of wide culture had much in common with Isocrates.[56] On the other hand, much of the actual doctrine of the *De Oratore* may be paralleled from Peripatetic sources; the influence of Aristotle's *Rhetoric*, often recognized, whether or not Cicero had read the original, has been further examined by F. Solmsen.[57] He argues that, whereas, in the Hellenistic handbooks, the treatment of τὰ πάθη was mainly confined to the epilogue, in Aristotle it was a major subject affecting the λόγος as a whole. This is, he observes, the position in the *De Oratore*. These scholars can also point to the strong evidence of Cicero himself on the three books of this treatise (*Fam.* 1.9.23, 'omnem antiquorum, et Aristoteliam et Isocratiam, rationem oratoriam complectuntur'). But, earlier, H. von Arnim[58] and Kroll[59] regarded the immediate source as the New Academy, von Arnim referring much of the third book (especially on the subject of θέσεις) to Philo of Larisa, and Kroll that and more to the Stoic-influenced Antiochus of Ascalon. These arguments have met with some criticism, but H. K. Schulte,[60] in the latest full discussion of the whole history of Cicero's educational ideal, also finds a contemporary source in Poseidonius.

We must next consider some of the main modern studies which have illustrated the application of the theory of the *De Oratore* (and *Orator*), in that they are concerned with Cicero's knowledge of philosophy, history and law, his skill in emotional appeal, and the ways in which he delighted and held his audience. Philosophy, Cicero declared in the introduction to his *De Natura Deorum*, had always been one of his favourite studies; he had, in his youth, been instructed by Diodotus, Philo, Antiochus, and Poseidonius, and his own speeches were, he claimed, 'refertae philosophorum sententiis'. Just before our period, Cicero's theory on the use of philosophy for the embellishment of oratory was set forth by A. Lieby, who found the application of this theory mainly in the expansion of *loci communes* and *theses*.[61] It was not difficult to find plenty of examples, e.g. on such subjects as gratitude and revenge (*Planc.* 80-1. *Post. Red. ad. Quir.* 22-3). The anti-Stoic banter of the *Pro Murena* and the anti-Epicurean invective of the *In Pisonem* illustrated Cicero's use of opportunities to show his familiarity with philosophical doctrine. The subsequent dissertation of Ranft added some useful analysis.[62] He went more closely than Lieby into the *thesis* and its application to oratory and took (rightly) a wider view of its character — that is, not merely as a general proposition *per se*, but also as a general proposition arising out of a particular issue (ὑπόθεσις). Ranft also illustrated the influence of dialectical training on the argument of a few of the speeches.

Just as Cicero was aware of the value of the philosophical *thesis*, and *locus*, so he was aware of the use of the historical *exemplum* (cf. *Orat.* 120; *Verr.* 2.3.209); and just as the improvement in knowledge in the former was due to a closer investigation of methods of use, so it has been in the latter. The task of collecting historical allusions in the speeches was not neglected in the nineteenth century, and has since been performed with great thoroughness by F. Sauer[63] and R. Schütz.[64] Laurand also contributed his collection.[65] These scholars agreed that although the evidence did not show Cicero to be a historian in the specialist sense, it did reveal wide historical knowledge. More interesting was H. Schoenberger's work on the form of these historical allusions, and the ways in which they were brought into the service of oratory.[66] Like Laurand, he noticed that there was a recurrent use of certain famous names from Roman history, but he distinguished between those which he regarded as the stock examples of the rhetorical schools and those which Cicero drew from his own experience, and found more of the stock examples in the earlier speeches than in the later. He observed that, generally, though not invariably, Cicero followed chronological sequence, that when he used foreign examples as well, he usually placed the Roman examples first, and that the foreign examples were often disparaging, or given limited recognition, or were contrasted with Rome, or served to heighten the iniquity of a Roman evil-doer. Studying the occurrence of *exempla* in the various parts of the speech, he found a heavy preponderance in the *argumenta*. He illustrated Cicero's modest disclaimers in his introduction of historical knowledge, and noted a certain fondness for placing examples in triads. Stylistically, he found that they frequently appeared in the form of a rhetorical figure, such as anaphora, asyndeton, *praeteritio*, and rhetorical question.

Compared with the historical *exempla*, the number of literary references in the speeches is very small. The mythological allusions and literary citations were collected and briefly analysed by M. Radin,[67] in an article which may be used in conjunction with the substantial dissertation of W. Zillinger.[68] In the latter, all the works of Cicero are examined, and his quotations from the early Roman poets are fully set out and discussed. With regard to the speeches, Zillinger observes that Cicero carefully adapts his quotations to the taste of his listeners by drawing especially upon the tragedies and comedies which they could see on the stage. Both Radin and Zillinger observed that the literary references were particularly noticeable in the speeches delivered about the time of the *De Oratore* (esp. *Sest.* and *Cael.*), and neither was disposed to regard this as merely fortuitous.

But far more important for the study of Roman oratory than any of these subjects is the question of Cicero's knowledge of law — a question which has interested scholars for a few centuries. Here our period has produced a work of quite fundamental value, the detailed and learned study of Emilio Costa, the result of many years of devotion to the subject.[69] Costa collected from all the writings of Cicero the passages bearing upon the law, and reconstructed and set out systematically his evidence on the principles of public and private law, and compared that evidence with what was otherwise known of their development. The amount of information thus shaped into an organic whole might naturally seem to justify the granting of the title 'iurisconsultus' to Cicero.[70] But here there are objections from some of the authorities on Roman Law.[71] Cicero, it is observed, was not a member of that select body of men who performed the function of giving advice (in later times, official advice) upon the law, and, it is declared, he has not such authority in the *Digest*, even though he was sufficiently advanced in the subject to compose a work *De iure civili in artem redigendo* (Gell. 1.22.7; cf. *De Orat.* 1.42.190 and Quint. 12.3.10). But, whether or not he be granted the title, the important question which legal scholars are still discussing is: 'How much had Cicero in common with the jurists, and to what extent did the general ideas which he (together with earlier and later orators and rhetoricians) is known to have held, and to have put into practice, influence the thought of the *iurisconsulti*?'

A work of Johannes Stroux, originally published in 1926 and fairly recently reissued, has attracted wide attention.[72] Entitled 'Summum Ius Summa Iniuria', it concerns the interpretation of the law, and is based on the evidence of Cicero for the sharp distinction drawn between rigid adherence to the letter (*verba*), and consideration of the intention of the lawgiver (*voluntas*), between strict legal interpretation (*ius*) and the basic principles of fairness and morality (*aequitas*). This distinction, ultimately traceable back to Aristotle, and furthered by subsequent philosophical and grammatical studies,[73] comes right out of the heart of the most technical part of the often-despised Hellenistic manuals of rhetoric, the doctrine of *constitutiones causae*, and was illustrated by Stroux from the *De Inventione* of Cicero. He further cited the account of the famous *causa Curiana* (a case of testament) in which Crassus successfully upheld the wish of the testator against Scaevola's adherence to the wording of the will (*Brut.* 194-8; *De Orat.* 1.180). Moreover, he observed that Cicero's own *Pro Caecina* is very largely concerned with the idea of *ius* as opposed to *aequitas*. But these very ideas of *aequitas* and *voluntas* existed in the *Digest* — and the *Digest*, said many legal scholars, was mainly post-classical, and *voluntas*-texts were Byzantine. So this study had repercussions at the time on the vexed question of the sources of the *Digest*. Salvatore Riccobono, in a foreword to the Italian edition of Stroux's work,[74] declared: 'This monograph is of more importance for the understanding of the development of Roman law than the combined works of criticism of the last thirty years.' This was, indeed, an enthusiastic tribute to Rhetoric from a deeply-respected legal scholar. Considerable discussion followed. Stroux and Riccobono received some further support from the dissertation of J. Himmelschein, who argued that not all, by any means, of the *voluntas*-texts in the *Digest* could possibly be regarded as interpolated, and that the rhetoricians did have some influence on the jurists.[75] At present, we are speaking of the use of the evidence of Cicero. But the question is also of great importance for the assessment of the legal value of the declamations, which are quite permeated with the *ius*)(*aequitas* arguments.

It would, however, be quite wrong to give the impression that the Stroux-Riccobono view is commonly accepted in legal circles. It is the considered verdict of so learned an authority as F. Schulz[76] that such philosophical-rhetorical ideas as *ius*)(*aequitas* would merely have been misleading in the solution of a given case, and he is not disposed to attach importance to the evidence of orators and rhetoricians in matters of law. Similar opinions appear to be quite widely held; the ideas of men like Cicero, it is felt, did not exercise any lasting effect on Roman jurisprudence.[77]

On the other hand, a few legal scholars have continued to see some significance in the fact that important developments in both rhetoric and law were taking place at much the same time, that is, from about the middle of the second century B.C.; Greek rhetorical studies were then coming into prominence at Rome, Hermagoras formulated the detailed theory of *constitutiones causae*, and by the *Lex Aebutia* (between 149 and 126 B.C.) the old system of procedure by *legis actio* became superseded by the formulary system. An important article has been published by A. Steinwenter,[78] discussing the explanation of the fact that there exist rather remarkable coincidences of terminology in the rhetorical theory of *constitutiones* and certain clauses of that system. The essential clause in the latter was *intentio*, which contained the plaintiff's statement of claim. Another clause (earlier in the formula, it seems) was *praescriptio*, inserted, when necessary, to safeguard the plaintiff or defendant (e.g. if the decision would prejudice another important issue). But these (and also the term *translatio*) are rhetorical technical terms of the doctrine above-mentioned. Steinwenter does not claim that rhetoric had a direct influence on the development of the formulary system,[79] but relates it rather to the *usus fori*, which gave general guidance to the judge. But he does urge strongly that the doctrine of *constitutiones* had an immediate influence upon the civil procedure by *libellus conventionis* in the time of Justinian. Much of Steinwenter's argument has quite recently been accepted and further developed by Ernst Meyer.[80]

But, to return to the theory of the *De Oratore*, even supposing that a man were an adept in the art of discovering and presenting arguments, of basing those arguments on a sure legal knowledge, and of reinforcing them with illustrations drawn from a wide range of culture, he would still lack the master-key to great oratory unless he possessed the power to arouse the emotions. In an American thesis by E. A. Lussky, Cicero's theories have been collected and applied in detail to the study of twenty-five of Cicero's speeches.[81] So he, too, began with rhetoric, and enquired, both in theory and in practice, what was the relative importance of the appeal to the emotions and the appeal to the understanding, what were the methods by which the various emotions were aroused, and in which parts of the speeches were these appeals particularly used. In theory, he observed (*De Orat.* 2.185-216), emotional appeal was strongly stressed (cf. 215 'in quo sunt omnia'), provided it was tactfully used. In practice, he argued, the preponderant stress was on the appeal to the understanding in most speeches (exclusively so in the civil cases); emotion was only aroused when the ground had been carefully prepared. Practice was here superior to theory. Both in theory and in practice the methods of arousing the emotions, both direct (grieving relatives, etc.) and indirect (appeal to *odium, misericordia*, etc.), were much the same. The theory of powerful appeal for sympathy in the peroration was frequently followed, but there was often diffused emotion. In Lussky's work there are some debatable points. For instance, by classing ἦθος and πάθος together he gave so wide a connotation to the word 'emotion' that a good deal of material was included which is of dubious relevance. The borderline between ἦθος and πάθος is not always easy to draw, but quiet and skilful *captatio benevolentiae* is a different thing from the *saeva indignatio* of more vehement passages. Also, Lussky seemed to regard emotion as something which could be turned on *ad lib.*; Cicero said that the orator had to feel the emotions before he could convey them (*Orat.* 132), just as Horace said later of the poet. How far this was true of Cicero in practice is an interesting question. But Lussky's thesis seems to be the only one of its kind in our period.

But from τὸ πάθος it is sometimes but a short step to τὸ γελοῖον. Contemporaries of Cicero who flattered his inordinate vanity by making collections of his witticisms, genuine and spurious, have had few successors in modern times. Brugnola[82] and Kelsey[83] made their contributions, but for a proper appreciation of Ciceronian humour in theory and practice, we must consult a German dissertation, that of Paul Faulmüller.[84]

In theory, in the long discussion of the *De Oratore* (2.216-89, cf. *Orat.* 87-90), observes Faulmüller, important points are that the orator must use discretion in selecting the time and object of his witticism; not seek to mock signal wickedness or genuine distress, but consider the feelings of those who are regarded with affection; not use wit too frequently like the *scurra*, but direct it to some purpose and preserve *gravitas*. Moral delinquencies and intellectual shortcomings are legitimate material, and physical ugliness may be satirized. As to the type of wit, it may take the form of brief, clever sayings (*dicacitas*) or be diffused in continuous satire (*cavillatio*). In the former type, stylistic devices, such as double-entendre and other forms of word-play, are useful; in the latter, though style is not excluded, the subject-matter requires more attention, and it takes the form of satiric narrative or anecdote. Faulmüller's summary of theory here has since been taken very much further by Mary Grant in her study of the history of τὸ γελοῖον. She has not only examined Cicero's sources and his indebtedness to Aristotle and the Stoics, but has also studied the terminology involved.[85]

As to Cicero's practice, Faulmüller's opinion was that this was fairly in accord with detailed theory, but that Cicero was, in general, by no means as restrained in his use of wit as he recommended in the less exuberant moments of his theorizing. It was not difficult to illustrate Cicero's derision of physical abnormalities or personal appearance, as, for instance, Vatinius' goitre (or whatever excrescence it was), Piso's swarthy complexion, Gabinius' addiction to beauty-culture; or the enjoyment he takes in casting suspicion on a man's parentage, family, and ancestors; or his extended satiric descriptions and word-play, especially in the *Verrines*. Perhaps more attention will be given to these, now that R. G. C. Levens has done so much for the fifth.[86] L. H. G. Greenwood's translation, as those who have used it will agree, deserves especial mention.[87]

For Cicero's use of word-play, and, also, irony, anecdote, and digression, we have expert guidance. For word-play, there is the detailed monograph of H. Holst:[88] he started with an exposition of rhetorical theory on the subject, and carefully analysed the various types in the speeches. They are frequently, of course, not examples of humour but simply tricks of style. He classified them according to the exact nature of the *immutatio*, whether they exemplified a *double-entendre* of nouns or of verbs, an active and passive form of the same verb, the same verb compounded with different prepositions, or the simple verb with the compounded verb, words with alliteration, assonance, and so on. His statistics and register of words make this monograph a useful work of reference.

As examples of modern studies of Cicero's use of irony, we may take the contributions of two very different scholars, L. Laurand[89] and H. V. Canter[90] — Laurand the stylist and Canter the statistician — who have both, in a few pages, done a good deal to advance our knowledge and appreciation. Both remarked on the varying shades of irony in the speeches — 'tantôt mordante et terrible, tantôt fine et légère', as Laurand says, and none but a French critic could say it so well. An interesting point which he argued was that Cicero progressed from a certain rather obvious sarcasm in his earliest speeches to the more delicate and refined irony of, for instance, the *Pro Murena* and the *Pro Ligario*. The stylist naturally looks for development, and to this subject we shall

AA

ROMAN ORATORY 435

recur. But the fullest evidence, so far, is in Canter's paper. Once again, the investigation started with rhetoric, and Canter classified the various types under their headings in the rhetorical doctrine of figures (including the evidence of the lesser Latin rhetoricians). He then considered the length of the many passages which he had examined, and noted that, although in more than a half of them the irony was restricted to a sentence or two, in over fifty passages it was sustained to much greater length. He observed that resort to irony was most common in the judicial speeches, that it generally accompanied the use of the plain rather than the elevated style, and that it was most prominent in the *argumentatio*. It is obviously impossible to carry out a study like this without a certain subjective element; but more use might be made of this paper; it is packed with information, and is clearly the starting-point for a full investigation.

Out of the discussion of humour arose the mention of anecdote, and extended anecdote can become one of the forms of digression. Here again, Canter has a condensed article,[91] and here again, Canter started from rhetoric. Cicero was well aware that for delighting or stirring his audience, nothing succeeded better than a *digressio* (*Brut.* 322 'delectandi causa'; *De Orat.* 2.311 'permovendorum animorum causa'). After illustrating the point from theory, Canter sought to assess the extent of the employment of *digressio*, to consider the details of its usage, and to compare that usage with rhetorical theory. For the last-mentioned point, the evidence of Quintilian and later rhetoricians had to be brought in to supplement that of Cicero, and the traditional speech-divisions were not always easy to establish; most of the digressions could be found in the *argumentatio*, but theory itself was not altogether consistent, and it seemed that Cicero digressed whenever it seemed to him to suit the interests of the case. Canter collected over fifty examples (many of them extended), and observed that, although this was an average of less than one per speech, the proportion was much smaller in the non-forensic than in the forensic speeches. He outlined the contents of the digressions, studied their purpose, and noted the skill with which they were introduced and the apologetic formulae with which they were concluded. He thought them more relevant to the main theme than was commonly believed, particularly in arousing the emotions of the listeners. The latter point finds some support in a chapter in Elizabeth Haight's book on the Roman use of anecdotes.[92]

With these latter studies, we have entered the province of style, the subject of the third book of the *De Oratore* and much of the *Orator*. Far and away the most outstanding contribution to the study of Cicero's style was the major work of Laurand, already mentioned (see note 26). It ran through four editions, and was supplemented by its author in several smaller publications. Among the many things which Laurand has helped us to appreciate is the fact that there is not merely one Ciceronian style even in the speeches, but a marked variety in various speeches, and sometimes within the same speech. He began (in vol. 3 — there is a sort of *crescendo* of interest in Laurand's book — at least, the writer found this volume the most stimulating) by illustrating features of the familiar style, such as the various pleasantries mentioned above, and the miniature dialogues in which Cicero, often in staccato fashion, answers his own rhetorical questions or refutes imaginary objections. Laurand was particularly interested in the varied and subtle nuances of diminutives and the various compounds of *per*. We must note here, however, that his opinions on the relation of *per*-compounds to the familiar style are not altogether approved by J. André, who has recently re-examined the whole question of their use and significance over a wide field.[93] But, to return to Laurand, he next had the happy idea of illustrating Cicero's command of the three types of style from three speeches which Cicero himself had declared to be characteristic (*Orat.* 101-2), namely, the *Pro Caecina* for the plain style, the *De Imperio Cn. Pompei* for the middle, and the *Pro Rabirio perduellionis reo* for the grand. In the first he found colloquial expressions, and less careful use of rhythm than in the other two. In the second he found more use of metaphor, frequent anaphora, and above all a finely modulated rhythm and periodic structure. In the third, he noted such features as gravity, imagery, antithesis, exceptionally sustained anaphora, and a more spirited rhythm. Laurand then proceeded to show how varied the style might be within individual speeches or a group of speeches, particularly by studying it according to the various rhetorical divisions in each case. These valuable studies, for which Cicero himself had supplied the idea to Laurand, were taken further in a dissertation by P. Gotzes, who worked out the idea, as far as it would go, by a more detailed comparison of the style of these speeches with these precepts of rhetoric, particularly as supplied by the *Orator*.[94] A somewhat similar idea, though extended as much to subject-matter as to style, was that of D. Mack, who investigated Cicero's two speeches *Post Reditum*, and his 3rd and 4th *Philippic* (to the senate, and to the people), that is the adaptation of treatment and style to the audience and the situation.[95] Here, too, the rhetorical doctrine of τὸ πρέπον is in evidence.

But, if there is this variety of style in the speeches, the question naturally arises whether there is any development, any increasing maturity noticeable in a comparison of earlier and later speeches. The *iuvenilis redundantia* of the early speeches, alluded to by Cicero himself (*Orat.* 107-8), had been carefully studied by Landgraf[96] long before our period begins (cf. Norden, I, 225-31). A good comparison was made by Laurand between the early *Pro Quinctio* and the last *Philippic*; he observed that many of the inelegant word-combinations and repetitions, and an occasional ill-constructed period, had disappeared in the mature style.[97] Very recently, F. Klingner has contributed an important study,[98] containing much original thought, of the *Pro Roscio Comoedo*, which he dates 77 or 76 B.C., just after Cicero's return from Rhodes. Norden (I, 227) had been puzzled to account for the 'Asianism' in this speech, since Cicero had said (*Brut.* 316) that Molon checked his *iuvenilis licentia*. Klingner well shows that Cicero found in Rhodes no new stylistic ideal, but learnt the art of moderation in both delivery and style. Molon was a pupil of Menecles of Alabanda, whose style was Asianist, but of a type (*Brut.* 325) which aimed at 'crebrae venustaeque sententiae' — a neater, more concise form of parallelisms, antitheses, and other figures. These Klingner (well contrasting the two examples in *Orat.* 107-8) illustrates from the speech.

Considerable detailed evidence of Ciceronian usage was collected in the two parts of P. Parzinger's dissertation on the development of his style.[99] This contribution was based not only on the speeches, but on the whole of the works, and was equipped with statistics. At many points this dissertation belongs to the study of language rather than to that of oratory in the broad sense, but naturally contains the kind of information which an editor would need to consider and check by more recent linguistic studies of a wider scope. Parzinger classified his evidence for the speeches into four periods, the first to 66 B.C., the second to 59, the third to 50, and the last to 43. Some of the aspects which he considered were the favourite form of antithesis in which a negatived phrase precedes and emphasizes the contrast ('non opinari, sed scire': 'neque in uno sed in omnibus', etc.), the kind of *adnominatio* in which the same verb is repeated in a different tense ('aut est aut fuit'; 'et esse et fuisse'; 'fecisse et facere', etc.), parataxis of nouns (e.g. 'civibus civem'), adjectives ('omnes omnia', etc.), pronouns and verbs, and also the use of *conduplicatio* and parallelism of phrase. Much of his second part deals with individual word-usage and is beyond the scope of this chapter. It may be said, on the whole, that his statistics, though they may have their uses, are not particularly exciting to the student of oratorical style in the wider sense.

Ciceronian diction has also been illustrated, particularly by Laurand, in his first volume, by a comparison of the diction of the speeches with that of his other works. Laurand drew up lists of words which occur in poetical citations made by Cicero and words which are used in Cicero's own poetry, and argued that as they did not occur in the speeches but recurred in less particular writers, they were evidence of careful avoidance of archaic and poetic diction. The method was not altogether convincing, for the question of subject-matter naturally enters into any such comparison — many of the words Cicero probably never needed to use in a speech, so the fact that he did not use them does not prove very much. Laurand's comparison of the vocabulary of the *Letters* was more to the point, and here it was not difficult to illustrate the difference; his information at this point on the use of Greek words may be compared with the full list subsequently made by H. J. Rose.[100] A small work on Cicero's diction was produced by L. Delaruelle, who listed and discussed words which occur in Cicero's other writings, particularly the philosophical works, but are rarely, if ever, found in the speeches.[101] In some observations on Cicero's use of metaphor, C. Morawski likewise noted that Cicero permitted himself greater freedom in the philosophical works than in the speeches, but that, although the tendency to metaphorical expression was occasionally marked, as in the *Pro Rabirio*, Cicero never exhibited the licence shown by the declaimers.[102] A special dissertation on Cicero's use of metaphor was that of Wiegandt, in which material was drawn from the

ROMAN ORATORY 439

Rhetorica as well as the speeches, and which contained, *inter alia*, some examples of metaphors drawn from military and gladiatorial sources.[103] On the subject of Cicero's vocabulary of abuse, S. Hammer wrote a dissertation in which the orator's achievements in this respect were compared with those of Plautus.[104] These are merely a few contributions especially concerned with Cicero, but there is a wealth of information on Cicero's language and style in works on 'stylistic', such as those of Nägelsbach[105] and J. Marouzeau,[106] and the bibliography of the subject has been brought up to date in a recent important work by Jean Cousin.[107] But, to use Cicero's own words (*De Orat.* 3.48), 'praetereamus igitur praecepta Latine loquendi'; something must be said on the subject of rhythm.

There are numerous indications in ancient rhetorical literature, especially the *Orator* of Cicero and the *De Compositione Verborum* of Dionysius, that the ancients were far more sensitive than we are ourselves in matters of prose rhythm. Their ears were much more keenly attuned to the harmony of words, especially at the close of the sentence. Interest in the Ciceronian *clausulae* goes back to the time of the Humanists, and systematic study was well under way before the end of the nineteenth century. But it was not until 1904 that T. Zielinski, after some ten years' research, produced his most remarkable work, based on a study of all the *clausulae* in the speeches (17,902 of them), and startled the learned world by speaking not of favourite forms, but of a law of *clausulae* (*Clauselgesetz*).[108] Though familiar to most readers, it must be briefly summarized. In its original purity, it was a masterpiece of simplicity. The *clausula* consisted of a cretic 'basis' followed by a trochaic 'cadence'. The minimum cadence was a single trochee (or spondee, for the last syllable was doubtful, as in verse). The 'genuine' *clausulae* (V, verae) were then as follows: V.1 $-\cup-|-\overset{\smile}{-}$; V.2: $-\cup-|-\cup|\overset{\smile}{-}$; V.3: $-\cup-|-\cup|-\overset{\smile}{-}$. In V.2 and V.3, the basic cretic could be 'strengthened' to a molossus, giving: $---|-\cup|\overset{\smile}{-}$ and $---|-\cup|-\overset{\smile}{-}$. On this formula, Zielinski claimed to account for 60 per cent of all the *clausulae* in the speeches. To establish his second major group (L, licitae), he resorted to resolutions of long syllables into two shorts, and metrical substitutions. A resolved cretic might produce $-\cup\cup\cup$ (as in 'esse videatur'), or $\cup\cup\cup-$ or even $\cup\cup\cup\cup\cup$. The trochee in the cadence might become a tribrach. The basic cretic might be replaced by a choriambic ($-\cup\cup-$), and the basic molossus by an epitrite (– ᴗ – –). V and L forms together accounted for 86 per cent of the *clausulae*. Other forms (S, selectae, M, malae, and P, pessimae) accounted for very nearly all of the remainder. Zielinski was not primarily concerned with word-division, but did classify the major form (Grundform) into types according to *caesura* (Hauptform). From these illustrations of his main law, he proceeded to deduce numerous other laws, as for instance that concerning coincidence of metrical ictus with word-accent. The chief criticisms directed against him were, first, that his metrical interpretations (which also included 'transposed' and 'unrestricted' cretics) were too free; secondly, that his method of sentence-division (which lay at the base of his statistics) was arbitrary (he punctuated according to what he called his 'Gefühl', applied in a private declamation of his own Russian translation of many of the speeches!): thirdly, that the *Orator* did not justify the basis-cadence distinction, or the assumption of a ubiquitous cretic, however disguised. But his work was regarded as of great importance, not least in the field of textual criticism.[109]

Zielinski's subsequent application of his theory to the internal rhythms was similarly criticized and won much less support than his original study of the *clausulae*.[110] Nor did the contemporary theories of F. Blass,[111] Johannes May,[112] or C. Zander[113] have any lasting influence. Their 'theory of responsions' was based on the belief that Cicero's rhythm was due to the metrical correspondence of *word-groups* between the *clausula* and earlier sections, or within the sentence as a whole. It would be agreed that there is some general evidence in Cicero's theory and practice of interest in the *concinnitas* characteristic of Isocrates; there are passages in which close, and even exact numerical correspondence of syllables occurs;[114] but it has generally been felt that metrical correspondence could not be proved without considerable licence and disregard of grammatical structure.

More lasting in its influence was the work of Bornecque,[115] who applied his method over a wide field, including sections of the speeches. For him, the observance of *word-division* was of primary importance, and he classified the occurrence of various feet before final words of two syllables (types 'ferant', 'ferrent'), three syllables (types 'videar', 'ferantur', 'differant', 'ferrentur'), and four syllables (eight types). He argued that the form of the final word influenced and limited the choice of the immediately preceding metrical form. He was not, however, satisfied with the absolute frequency of types in a given author, as he did not regard this as a proper criterion of intentional use. He therefore applied his system to 'non-metrical' texts, which he believed indicated the inherent possibilities of the language, and by comparison established the 'relative frequency'. This 'comparative method' had considerable influence on subsequent theorists, particularly Novotny and De Groot, though they applied it in quite different ways. The chief criticisms of Bornecque were that his method was extremely complicated, that the selected 'non-metrical' texts were not necessarily devoid of metrical application, and that the *Orator* did not justify the use of word-division in establishing *clausulae*, even though later writings did.

In the same year that Bornecque produced his large work on metrical *clausulae*, Laurand went into the question (vol. 2), but his views are best taken from later revised editions. He refused to admit any method of analysing *clausulae* which could not show a firm basis in the *Orator*, and it was on this ground that he could not accept either the resolutions, metrical substitutions, and ubiquitous cretic of Zielinski, or the 'responsions' theory of Blass and May, or the procedure by word-division of Bornecque. After illustrating from the *Orator* Cicero's general principles, and from the speeches his general practice, regarding harmonious word-choice, hiatus, symmetry, assonance, alternation of periods and short sentences, and avoidance of verse-form, he analysed the *clausulae* of the sixth *Philippic*, and then compared Cicero's theory with his practice regarding the use of the double trochee, the cretic, the paeon, the spondee, and their various combinations. He also analysed the concluding *clausula* of each of the speeches. He further gave clear illustrations (as for instance from word-order) of the care bestowed upon the *clausula* by Cicero. Laurand did not attempt detailed statistics, but he remarked in his general conclusions on the frequency of the double-trochee, the cretic-spondee and the double-cretic, though he insisted that combinations such as the double-spondee, the spondee-cretic, and various forms compounded with the paeon, were also common. Elsewhere,[116] Laurand tabulated the occurrence of the *clausula heroica*, of which he found only seventy-one examples in the speeches; and it may be added that F. W. Shipley[117] sought to reconcile an apparent discrepancy between Cicero's rare use of this form in practice and his apparent admission of it in a passage of the *Orator* (217).

This, then, was the general position before 1914. There was great disagreement on method, and consequently little progress in achieving agreed results. The most that can be said is that three combinations seemed to be emerging as particularly favoured by Cicero in the *clausula*, namely, those which Norden called the 'original' forms,[118] the double-trochee (which Zielinski did not admit as a *clausula* in itself, but frequently found preceded by a cretic), the cretic-spondee (or cretic-trochee, the last syllable being doubtful), and the double-cretic (or cretic-dactyl). Since 1914, there has been further diversity of method, and useful statistical work has been done, but it does not seem to the present writer that, from the point of view of agreed results, matters have proceeded much further than the point already indicated.

Important subsequent theorists were Novotný, Broadhead, and De Groot. All three were as much concerned with the internal rhythms as with the *clausula*. More is generally known of Novotný's method[119] than of his detailed results, as his major work was written in Czech.[120] He applied the comparative method internally, by comparing the frequency of recurrent rhythms at the end of the sentence with their frequency within the sentence itself, and giving the value of a *clausula* to those forms which recurred more frequently at the end than elsewhere. H. D. Broadhead and A. W. De Groot published, with much other material, statistics for the *clausula* in Cicero's speeches, and these are of more direct concern. Broadhead[121] introduced a new method (though Novotný claimed some priority),[122] in that he used the *word-accent* as his guide in establishing *clausulae*, which he measured from the accented syllable of the penultimate word. He undertook the unenviable task of reclassifying Zielinski's *Clauselgesetz* statistics on this new principle, but strongly disagreed with the idea of a ubiquitous cretic, and classified the occurrence of many types of combination. De Groot also gave statistics,[123] but used a quite different method, and measured purely by the succession of long and short syllables, without dividing into feet; he, like Bornecque, compared absolute with relative frequency, but with texts which were so remote that they could not reasonably be claimed to be in any way 'metrical'. Both Broadhead and De Groot seem to substantiate the prevalence of the three forms already mentioned.

Broadhead's table gave the double-trochee as the most prevalent combination at the end of a period. His next highest frequency was the cretic-trochee (or cretic spondee), his third the double cretic (or cretic-dactyl). De Groot marked the most favoured form as $-\cup--\cup\overset{\smile}{-}$, which he found to have a high absolute frequency and to be nearly three times as common in Cicero as in the compared texts: he also found that the form $-\cup--\overset{\smile}{-}$ had the highest absolute frequency, and was over twice as common in Cicero as in the compared texts. Later, M. T. Baley, in a brief but clear and well-reasoned article,[124] partly based on Laurand, also took the view that the double-trochee was most common, and that cretic combinations made a good second; for the latter he considered the *Pro Caelio* a characteristic oration.

Space does not permit a discussion of the contributions of P. Wuilleumier, who made a further exposition of Cicero's theory;[125] of L. Bayard, who argued that Cicero chose particularly those *clausulae* in which the ictus corresponded with the accent (in his view, pitch),[126] of W. De Moulin,[127] who considered how far the principles of ictus and accent (in his view, stress) evolved in E. Fraenkel's well-known work could be applied to the *clausulae*; or of the many studies in which the relationship of Zielinski's three main forms to the three forms of the mediaeval *cursus* (planus, tardus, velox) was upheld or challenged.[128]

To conclude, although the history of the subject and the problems involved was systematically set out by Novotný[129] half way through our period, there is no proper synthesis of results known to the writer. Interest in the subject seems to have waned in the latter half of the period, and the diversity of methods employed has naturally caused some perplexity. Many scholars will no doubt feel that it is important in these matters to pay particular regard to ancient rhetorical theory on the subject. This was fully set out from the main Latin sources by Bornecque in his above-mentioned major work, and it may be added that a very useful collection of *testimonia*, both Greek and Latin, together with some interesting exemplary passages (unfortunately, not including Cicero), was published in a handy form by A. C. Clark.[130] Whether or not the evidence of the *Orator* is in itself a sufficient guide for the speeches remains a debatable question. Neither Bornecque nor Clark (who followed Zielinski) felt that it was; but Laurand would not have agreed.

A brief mention may be made here of the question of the *clausula* and word-emphasis. H. J. Rose used the work of Zielinski (which he thought substantially correct) to compare the frequency of occurrence of emphatic words within the closing cadences with their frequency elsewhere in the sentence or phrase,[131] in the *Pro Caecina* and *Pro Ligario*. He deduced that the logically emphatic words tended to avoid the end of the sentence or phrase; but with rhetorical emphasis he found the position somewhat different, in that rhetorical balance and antithesis could necessitate a division of emphasis which might bring emphatic words within the closing cadences. Much valuable information on Cicero's word-order, from a different point of view, and a particularly detailed treatment of his *isocola* and *tricola*, was included in E. Lindholm's stylistic studies.[132]

In so short a survey as this, it would be impossible to give due credit to all the scholars who have, by their work on individual speeches, advanced our detailed knowledge of Cicero, or those who in biographies, historical studies, and accounts of social life, have provided so much of the necessary background. In the present circumstances, the most that can be done is to add at this point in the notes[133] references to some of the studies and appreciations (mainly in English) of Ciceronian oratory. Suffice it to say that there are nowadays no eminent *obtrectatores Ciceronis*, such as Mommsen, and many scholars would surely echo the tribute of Arellius Fuscus: 'quoad humanum genus incolume manserit, quamdiu suus litteris honor, suum eloquentiae pretium erit, quamdiu reipublicae nostrae aut fortuna steterit aut memoria duraverit, admirabile posteris vigebit ingenium tuum' (*ap.* Sen. rhet., *Suas.* 7.9).

3. CICERO'S CONTEMPORARIES

When Cicero produced his *De Oratore* in 55 B.C., he gave little (if any) indication that there existed any important divergence of opinion between himself and his contemporaries on the subject of oratorical style. But when he wrote the *Brutus* and *Orator* nine years later, his tone was at many points markedly polemical, and he made it clear that there was a very definite cleavage of opinion between himself and those who liked to describe themselves as 'Atticists', but who used the term in a very narrow sense. At the turn of the nineteenth century, the questions of the significance of the term 'Asianism', the rise and development of the type of oratory described as 'Asiatic', and the origins of the 'Atticist' reaction, were very much in the air. Three important scholars made contributions to the subject at that time, E. Norden, L. Radermacher and U. von Wilamowitz-Möllendorff. Norden, in the course of his classic work on ancient prose style,[134] followed Cicero's indication in the *Brutus* (325) that there were two types of Asiatic style. The one, characterized by epigrammatic brevity, short, symmetrically-balanced clauses, and effeminate rhythms, he illustrated from fragments of Hegesias. The other, characterized by florid diction, bombastic expression, and bold metaphor, he illustrated from an inscription of Antiochus of Commagene, which he described as 'a dithyramb in prose'. Asianism was for Norden, as for most scholars, synonymous with corrupt standards in eloquence, as typified later in the style of the declamations and the Second Sophistic, the reverse of Attic purity and restraint. Its origin lay in the *levitas* of the Asiatic character, and the origin of the reaction (soon after 200 B.C.) lay in the wider culture of such centres as Alexandria and Pergamum, where the Attic orators were still studied. Other scholars had previously much favoured Pergamum, and connected the origins of Atticism with the grammatical studies of the Stoics. Radermacher[135] did not agree with this latter opinion, arguing that such linguistic studies were only one facet of Atticism, and that Atticism as a stylistic ideal owed its development to the reading and imitation of the Attic orators, particularly Demosthenes, in Athens and, to some extent, Rhodes, in the Alexandrian era; that is, it was originally a continuation of classicism, rather than the development of purism. It was transmitted particularly through Peripatetic channels. Wilamowitz had begun by regarding Pergamum as the source of Atticism, but by 1900 had abandoned that view, and, although still emphasizing the important influence of grammatical studies, now gave equal weight to the stylistic teaching of the New Academy and later Peripatetics, but considered that the centre of the reaction was Rome itself,[136] and that it began with Greek teachers in the capital in the first century B.C. He was particularly opposed to Norden's view that Asianism was an old-established term for corrupt oratorical style, and argued that, until the polemic in the *Orator*, Cicero used the term 'Asiatic' to describe a type of oratory mainly, but not exclusively, cultivated in Asia, and one which he did not by any means regard as entirely reprehensible. In Wilamowitz' opinion, the term 'Asianism' only came to be commonly used as a term of condemnation for a very short period at the close of the Republic and early in the Empire.

Modern scholarship has done very little more to clarify the development and connotation of the term 'Asianism', and this is a question which still requires attention. On the other hand, the study of the origins of Atticism and the influences which affected the Roman Atticists has been more fully discussed. There has been a marked tendency to connect the Roman ultra-Atticist movement with Stoic theories of style current in Rome from the days of the Scipionic circle onwards. Hendrickson was firmly of the opinion that the ideals of Calidius, Calvus, Brutus, and others were merely a reappearance under new leadership of the ideals of Diogenes of Babylon, in that both he and they stressed the importance of correctness and purity of diction.[137] In a useful dissertation, H. Heck,[138] whilst agreeing with the view that Athenian teaching prepared the way by its re-establishment of classicism, stood closely with Hendrickson in his emphasis on Stoic influence on the Roman strict Atticists, but took more account of the Stoic virtues of style as a whole, rather than insisting on the grammatical element. That is to say, he looked not only to diction, but also to lucidity, brevity, and propriety. A valuable feature of Heck's work was that he assembled Cicero's criticisms of nine Roman orators, who are described as practising a plain style, such as C. Aurelius Cotta (his best example), and showed that Cicero's accounts of the shortcomings of such a style, and indeed his very terminology, was remarkably similar to his general attitude and terminology when criticizing Calidius, Brutus and Calvus. He therefore regarded the tradition from the second-century Stoics to the strict Roman Atticists as an unbroken one, and was fairly close to Hendrickson's position. The position, however, is not impregnable.

But if the views which Cicero so strongly combats had already been in existence so long both in theory and in practice, what suddenly precipitated the quarrel? Here Hendrickson and Heck took a fairly similar view. Hendrickson refused to accept the common opinion that there are no indications of the polemic in the *De Oratore*, but saw in Cicero's rather cursory treatment of *Latinitas* in that work (3.37ff and 52) a veiled attack on the Atticist position. This, he argued, together with the praise accorded in that treatise to an ornamented style which was so obviously a reflection of Cicero's own, provoked Caesar's work *De Analogia* (for which Hendrickson posited the earliest possible date, 54 B.C.); this, he argued, was polemic in tone, and helped to knit the issue which became so prominent in the *Brutus* and *Orator*. Heck did not press this conjecture; but he, too, considered that the stress laid in the *De Oratore* on the *copia* and *ornatus* so characteristic of Cicero's own style, provoked the open opposition of the strict 'Atticists'. He emphasized this by arguing that it was precisely in the years immediately following the publication of the *De Oratore* that Calvus was rising to eminence, whilst Cicero's own star was, for various reasons, on the wane. But by 46 B.C. Calvus was dead, and it only remained to convince Brutus.

The correspondence between Cicero, Calvus, and Brutus on oratorical style (mentioned by Tacitus and Quintilian) has also been brought into the picture in the consideration of this problem. The opinions of Wölfflin[139] and Gudeman[140] that this correspondence was spurious have not been upheld. Harnecker[141] had discussed the importance of a letter from Cicero to Calvus mentioned in *Ad Fam.* 15.21 (47 B.C.), but considered that this was the first of its kind, and that it must have been sent shortly before Calvus' death in 48. Heck, in an appendix, attacked this view, showed that there was a considerable collection of letters concerning oratorical style, which had passed between Cicero and Calvus and Cicero and Brutus (both ways, that is), and argued that the correspondence had been going on for some years before 48. Hendrickson later followed up the question of the significance of the correspondence in a further article,[142] in which he examined several references in Quintilian (12.1.22; 12.10.12; 9.4.1; 9.4.63, etc.), argued that the objections of Cicero's detractors must have related largely to his cultivation of rhythm, and used the evidence of the correspondence-fragments to illuminate the problem of the origins of the *Brutus* and *Orator*. He argued that the limited praise given to Calvus in the *Brutus*, and the general depreciation of the type of oratory which he represented, dissatisfied Brutus, and led to a further interchange of letters which, in turn, brought Cicero still more into the open in the *Orator*. To conclude this brief survey of works on the Asianist-Atticist controversy, we may add that the whole subject has been handled in a balanced account by

J. F. D'Alton, which presents a synthesis of the various views (except Hendrickson's second article), and develops them at several points.[143]

Special works on Calvus and Brutus have been few, but they have raised difficulties. M. Krüger published a scholarly little work on Calvus[144] (better than that of Plessis-Poirot),[145] in which a clear picture of the personality and career of that orator emerges, his energy, industry, and self-confidence, his rise to become very nearly the equal of men like Cicero and Hortensius (all three took part in the Sestius case in 56), his vigorous denunciations of Vatinius (which K. dated 58, 56 and 54), his leadership of the Atticist group, and his early death at the age of thirty-five. In a useful account of the Atticist movement, Krüger made good distinctions between the styles of the various contemporary orators, such as Caesar, Curio, and Caelius, as well as Brutus, Calvus, and Cornificius. He regarded Calidius as the forerunner of the movement, and noted that, as a pupil of Apollodorus of Pergamum, he might well have imbibed Stoic linguistic ideas. Like Harnecker, he placed the flourishing-period of Atticism in 51-50, during Cicero's absence abroad, and the literary-letter skirmish only in 48-47. Finally, in a sketch of the oratorical personality of Calvus, he made the important point, often overlooked, that some of the characteristics ascribed to Calvus by later critics (Sen. rhet., *Contr.* 7.4.6ff; Quint. 10.1.115; Pliny *Epp.* 1.2.2; Fronto, p. 114 N.) are very hard to reconcile with the picture given by Cicero, and show us an orator whose delight was not in the quiet logical argument of the Stoic stylist, but who sought to move quite as much as to instruct. This is a problem which must still be faced in assessing the true features of Roman Atticism. E. Castorina, in a pleasing account of Calvus as orator and poet,[146] also noted this discrepancy, and attributed it to deliberate falsification on Cicero's part. But Castorina differed from his predecessors in that he attached no importance to the private correspondence in the study of the development of Atticism, and he also dated the speeches against Vatinius differently from Krüger and others.

Nor are scholars quite clear in their ideas of the oratory of Brutus. E. J. Filbey[147] collected the evidence on this in two categories, the evidence of sources other than Cicero, and the evidence of Cicero himself. Here the discrepancy is the other way round.

He established that the common verdict was that the oratory of Brutus was serious, plain, brief, and rather monotonous. But he showed that in several passages of the *Brutus* a different picture emerged; Brutus was represented as having been taught richness and sweetness of speech (120), as admiring the style of C. Gracchus (125), as regarding fire and wit as the chief requirements of an orator (204), as likely to have approved of the ornateness of Hortensius (327), even as criticizing Stoic oratory as dull and meagre (118). Filbey thought Cicero guilty of too much latitude in ascribing these ideas to Brutus, and of misrepresenting his views. But, in the same year as Filbey, C. Morawski also argued that Brutus did not avoid the *lumina dicendi* and was quite addicted to metaphorical expression.[148]

It appears from these general and special studies that the Asianist-Atticist controversy still needs further clarification. The two most recent contributions confirm this opinion.[149] A. Desmouliez, in an original article, has widened the field of investigation into the sources by bringing the Atticist reaction into relation with that against the Hellenistic style in art, and uses in support the frequent parallels in rhetorical writings between literary style and sculpture or painting. E. Castorina, in a separate study of the development of Cicero's views on the subject of Atticism, puts forward the thesis that Cicero in his youth had strong Atticist (!) tendencies, that after 76 B.C. he turned to Asianism, and finally, in his closing years, supported a moderate Atticism against the extremist set. But, in the present writer's opinion, an early addiction to Atticism could not be demonstrated even by vastly exaggerating the significance of allusions to *brevitas* in the *De Inv.* and *Pro Quinct.*

In leaving the Ciceronian period, mention must be made of the Invective (and Letters), ascribed to Sallust, on the authenticity of which there is a literature in itself; scholars may now be referred to the very recent bibliography of A. D. Leeman on this subject.[150] As we turn to the Empire, it may be noted that J. André has included a chapter on Pollio's oratory in his account of that versatile statesman and scholar;[151] that P. Lunderstedt made a full collection of the fragments of the work of Maecenas, and illustrated his oratorical style, and particularly his rhythms;[152] and that E. Malcovati has collected what is known of the speeches of Augustus.[153]

4. THE PERIOD OF DECLINE

There has been no survey devoted exclusively to the oratory of the Empire since that of V. Cucheval,[154] published in 1893, but considerable attention has been paid both to the declamations and to Quintilian. It is still generally agreed that political conditions under the Empire were largely responsible for the decline of oratory and the increased popularity of declamation, although it is realized that this practice was well established in the late Republic, chiefly as a method of training. The common view has, however, been challenged by E. P. Parks,[155] who maintained that there was plenty of scope for legal eloquence under the Empire, and that the declamatory schools, for all their strange fantasies, were in fact providing a training for advocates, for whose activities there must have been some outlet in public life. But, although one may strongly believe in the underlying legal value of the declamations, it is not necessary to support the opinion that there was equal opportunity for public oratory under the Empire. The most recent writer, M. L. Clarke, reverts to the traditional view.

Both the *Controversiae* and the *Suasoriae* of the elder Seneca have been edited, with French translation and brief but valuable notes, by H. Bornecque.[156] The *Suasoriae* have been edited with English translation and commentary by W. A. Edward.[157] Bornecque also produced a study of the Senecan declamations, in which he discussed their historical background, style and characteristics, subject-matter and legal value, and gave much useful information on the declaimers themselves.[158] Our knowledge of individual declaimers was also advanced by the dissertation of W. Hoffa,[159] and by a series of articles by H. de la Ville de Mirmont.[160] The present writer has re-examined the origins and development of declamation before Seneca, its procedure and rhetorical characteristics under the Empire, the relation of the laws in the Senecan *Controversiae* to genuine legislation, the criticisms made of declamation and the literary criticism recorded by Seneca, and declamatory influence on some of the contemporary literature.[161] A lexicon of Seneca's terminology, with discussion, was produced by H. Bardon.[162]

German scholarship has done much during our period to advance knowledge of the rhetorical exercises which must be examined by those who seek the origins of the declamations; the history of the doctrine of στάσεις (*constitutiones causae*) has been traced by W. Jaeneke,[163] that of θέσεις (*infinitae quaestiones*) by H. Throm,[164] that of deliberative themes by J. Klek,[165] and that of certain quasi-forensic themes by W. Hofrichter.[166] The present writer has sought to illustrate the influence of the στάσις-doctrine in the development of the *controversiae*, and of the θέσις on both these and the *suasoriae*, particularly the latter. M. L. Clarke, however, has argued that *theses* were not much used in the Republican rhetoric schools, except by a few teachers who stood 'outside the main tradition'.[167]

Considerable work has been done on the subjects used in the *Controversiae* and *Suasoriae* of the elder Seneca, many of which recur, or appear in similar form, in the declamations ascribed to Quintilian. The Senecan themes were collected and discussed before our period by T. S. Simonds.[168] During it, R. Kohl assembled from all rhetorical sources, Greek and Latin, those exercises which had a historical background; his chronological tabulation of this material made his study a useful work of reference.[169] Parallels, both from history and from legend, were produced by M. Schamberger,[170] but rather significant of a changing attitude were the short articles of S. Rossi[171] and N. Deratani,[172] who began to see in the declamations indications not merely of past history or of the influence of New Comedy, but of Roman life. C. Morawski had, long before,[173] observed a few parallels between the poisoning-cases of the exercises and those recorded by Tacitus; Deratani supported this and noted also that several Senecan exercises dealt with situations created by the Civil Wars, and Rossi even claimed for Roman experience features of the pirate themes, which it had always been usual to compare with New Comedy. The present writer has argued that there are numerous points in the declamations which may be held to reflect Roman life under the Empire, such as the adultery-cases, and the frequent references to extravagant living, large estates, sumptuous villas, and effeminacy in dress and behaviour.

It is, in fact, in this stress on Roman parallels as a counterbalance to that which may be compared with Greece, that a marked trend in the whole study of declamation has developed. Of nothing is this more true than of the laws and legal background of the exercises. At the head of most of the *Controversiae* of the elder Seneca we find quoted a law or, sometimes, two or three laws. On the application of these laws to the particular set of circumstances given in the subject of the exercise, the recorded discussion is based. In the discussion, the essence is nearly always a question of interpretation — should the law be strictly applied, or should considerations of fairness prevail over a literal application? We saw that this *ius*)(*aequitas* conflict in Cicero's *De Inventione* and elsewhere had been related to the question of early Roman jurisprudence. In the study of declamation the same question has arisen of the relationship of the general argumentation of the Senecan exercises to Roman legal thinking. But it has gone farther, and affected the question of the relationship of the actual laws quoted to Roman legislation. If the *ius*)(*aequitas* idea has genuine legal connections (and a number of scholars now believe it has), there is at least a *prima facie* case for supposing that the laws may not be as fictitious as they have commonly been declared to be.

Just before our period begins, Boissier declared that the legislation invoked in the declamations was everywhere imaginary,[174] Pichon likewise asserted that the declamatory laws would make quite a fantastic Digest.[175] Other scholars, such as Lecrivain[176] and Bornecque, constantly looked to Greece for parallels (that is, where they did not consider the laws imaginary), and claimed comparatively little for Rome. This attitude has had a marked effect, and has been taken by many scholars who have had occasion to write generally on the subject. It was not until 1911 that a fairly thorough examination of the question was made by J. Sprenger, who, although he ascribed a good deal to declamatory invention or adaptation from Greek sources, did find further Roman evidence for some of the laws invoked.[177] But it was the influence of the Stroux-Riccobono view regarding the legal value of the *constitutiones causae* which led F. Lanfranchi in 1938 to make a very extensive study of the legal connections of all the declamations.[178] He not only showed that the *ius*)(*aequitas* arguments of the declaimers faithfully represented Roman legal thinking (a view which was also taken afterwards by E. P. Parks), but also stressed the Roman connections, wherever possible, of individual laws. Subsequently, R. Düll, one of the very few legal scholars who have fairly recently paid attention to the declamations, showed that the frequent cases of *abdicatio* could not represent the Greek ἀποκήρυξις, as had so often been stated, and gave valuable evidence of the character of the Roman procedure from other sources besides the declamations.[179] It may be added that H. F. Jolowicz and D. Daube have compared such cases with the *querela inofficiosi testamenti*.[180] The present writer may perhaps be permitted to record some of his own conclusions. They are as follows: (1) that we must not dismiss laws as fictitious because their form may, especially in the use of the term 'sit actio', be modified for purposes of debate, (2) that very few lack any kind of supporting legal evidence whatever, (3) that although for some the balance of evidence suggests Greek influence, there are several for which Roman evidence is as good as the Greek, (4) that nearly a half have strong Roman parallels, some previously unrecognized, (5) that two of the laws may reasonably be claimed as having been taken from the Twelve Tables (*Contr.* 3.8 'qui coetum et concursum fecerit, capital sit'; *Contr.* 6.3 'maior frater dividat patrimonium, minor eligat') — especially as we know that in the exercises of the *Ad Herennium* the Tables were sometimes used (1.13.23), (6) that a few laws may reflect contemporary Augustan legislation, (7) that there is strong evidence in Quintilian of the close relationship between declamatory *ius)(aequitas* arguments and Roman legal thinking (cf. the comparisons with jurisconsults in 7.6.1 and 12.3.7), and that, in general, for young students, nicely-flavoured themes were a sort of coating of the legal pill. But it is not claimed that the declaimers are to be regarded as jurists.

With Quintilian we return once more to the theory of oratory, and find the influence of Cicero emerging strongly again, but supplemented by wide rhetorical studies, and by long experience in court and schoolroom. It is gratifying that within our period two British scholars, F. H. Colson[181] and R. G. Austin,[182] have provided valuable editions of the first and last books of the *Institutio Oratoria*. Much remains to be done for the other books, except the tenth, for which W. Peterson's edition is still standard.[183] For a wider public H. E. Butler's text and translation was a welcome addition to the Loeb Library,[184] and, recently, a book of selections has been produced by D. M. Gaunt.[185] It is not possible here to make mention of the numerous publications which have been devoted to, or connected with, Quintilian's rhetorical sources; they touch almost every point of learned literature on ancient rhetorical theory. But special mention should be made of W. Kroll's investigation[186] of the sources of Quintilian's doctrine on composition, propriety, and delivery, and of the important contribution of Jean Cousin,[187] which is a mine of information on the whole subject, and contains a praiseworthy bibliography. Cousin's second volume is devoted to Greek rhetorical terminology in Quintilian. But it is on account of his humane and sensible views on education rather than his technical knowledge that Quintilian has always been most widely appreciated, and considerable attention has been paid to this, particularly by B. Appel,[188] A. Gwynn,[189] W. M. Smail,[190] and H. I. Marrou.[191] M. L. Clarke has devoted two chapters to Quintilian's rhetorical theory and rhetorical teaching. Quintilian's philosophical alignments have been much discussed, particularly his indebtedness to Stoic doctrine[192] (which some scholars think has been exaggerated), but his juridical connections have received much less attention. It is possibly significant, in view of what has been said above regarding declamation, that Cousin has given considerable prominence to the legal connections of Quintilian; for it is to his 'orientation juridique' that the first of Cousin's three final summarizing chapters is devoted. This was quite a new departure, and Quintilian's long experience of the Roman courts well entitled him to special consideration in this respect. It may be added at this point that modern opinion is much inclined to regard the *Declamationes Minores*, attributed to Quintilian, as representing the teaching of the master,[193] and that Lanfranchi has argued that they contain much evidence of correspondence with legal thinking and some evidence of correspondence with legislation. Lanfranchi also used the *Declamationes Maiores* to establish his view, but here scholars are less inclined to accept the attribution to Quintilian, and there has been some support (on the evidence of *clausulae*[194] and detailed linguistic usage) for the view of Ritter[195] that they were written by several hands, but fall into definite groups.

The long-debated question of the relationship of the *Institutio Oratoria* to the *Dialogus de Oratoribus* is still by no means settled; although the *Dialogus* (of which Gudeman's important second edition[196] appeared in our period) is now widely believed to be by Tacitus, and scholars are aware that there are rather remarkable similarities of phraseology and ideas in the two treatises (though some stress the differences), the inferences drawn from such evidence differ. There is no general agreement whether the *Institutio* preceded the *Dialogus*, or vice versa, whether the coincidences indicate the influence on Tacitus of the *Institutio* or not, or whether the differences of opinion indicate that one is criticizing the other, or, indeed, whether some coincidences and differences merely reflect current literary thought and controversy, or, finally, which of the interlocutors in the *Dialogue* really represents Tacitus' own views. But there has been in our period a fairly strong case made for the belief that the *Dialogus* was written shortly after the *Institutio*. J. Cousin[197] dates the completion of the latter in 96, and G. Wormser[198] and H. Bardon[199] date the *Dialogus* in 96 or 97 (though a wide variety of dates has been suggested by others), and both believe that Quintilian exercised a marked influence on Tacitus. R. Dienel,[200] on the other hand, was firmly of the opinion that Tacitus was criticizing and refuting the doctrines of the *Institutio*, and is not alone in that opinion. It would not, however, be possible, within the narrow confines of the present section, to give an adequate summary of the diverse views expressed on the dating and purpose of the *Dialogus*, and the works concerned with its sources and connections. The writer must therefore be content to refer here to those who have already listed and discussed the extensive literature of the treatise.[201]

But, even though Quintilian provides us with a full-scale theory of oratory at the end of the first century A.D., we lack the evidence of practice with which to compare it. Pliny the younger was a keen student of Demosthenes, Cicero, and Calvus, and undoubtedly a distinguished speaker in his day. But Fate has presented us with his Panegyric of Trajan, and denied us his speeches to the Centumviral Court, which would have enabled us once more to trace the relationship of oratory with rhetoric on the one hand and law on the other. Some interesting general information on Pliny's cases, on the fees of advocates, and on the length of court-speeches, has been put together from the *Letters* by W. Menzies in an article on Pliny and the Roman Bar.[202] Nor does the age of Hadrian and of the Antonines yield us much oratory, though it gives us the theories of Fronto on oratorical style.[203]

There is, however, one branch of oratory, not hitherto discussed, which has survived in some bulk — the oratory of the panegyrists, in whose adulation of the Emperors we see epideictic at its worst — how different from the simple sincerity of that tribute of praise which survives from the age of Augustus, the *Laudatio Turiae*, which languished so long amid the texts of the Roman law,[204] and has now been edited, with a worthy introduction and commentary, by M. Durry.[205] Pliny's *Panegyricus* had also been edited, several years before, by Durry,[206] and the *Collection Budé* has now also included an edition of the *Panegyrici Latini* by E. Galletier.[207]

In epideictic oratory, too, the question of rhetorical influence has arisen. But whereas M. Durry does not consider that rhetoric had any appreciable influence on the *laudatio funebris*,[208] both he and, earlier, J. Mesk have found among the many commonplaces of Pliny's *Panegyricus* some derived from rhetoric.[209] With the later panegyrists, who were devotees of the art, it is agreed that the influence is very clearly marked. Several of their orations are anonymous; the opinion is now very strongly held that they are by several hands, and not a unity, as was once argued. In helping to establish this, A. Klotz[210] studied the literary connections (particularly with Cicero) of the various writers, but J. Mesk[211] used the degree of addiction to the precepts of Menander rhetor as a criterion. W. A. Maguinness, who had previously discussed the methods of Pliny and the later panegyrists, and pointed out several examples of adaptation and development of Ciceronian passages,[212] also gave interesting examples, among their locutions, of rhetorical figures.[213]

Here we must conclude, and, looking back over the work of fifty years, attempt a very brief summary of the general position. Oratory has not proved an independent study; it has involved both Rhetoric and Law. So it was in antiquity, for it was in the schools of rhetoric that the would-be orator was trained, and it was mainly in the courts of law that he hoped to achieve his reputation. Modern scholarship has done much to illustrate the relationship between rhetorical theory and practical oratory; it was the obvious procedure, and it has produced useful results. Among the comparatively few scholars who have attempted the task of relating oratory and rhetoric to law, Costa and Stroux must take pride of place. Roman Law is a highly specialized study, with a vast literature of its own, and it is gratifying to observe that, during the latter part of our period, some legal scholars have been disposed to pay rather more attention to oratory and, particularly, to rhetoric, in their endeavours to throw further light upon their own subject. This interest might well be reciprocated; closer

ROMAN ORATORY 457

collaboration between classical and legal scholars might prove beneficial to both and much aid the progress of knowledge.

[1] M. L. Clarke, *Rhetoric at Rome, A Historical Survey* (London, Cohen and West, 1953).
[2] H. Meyer, *Oratorum Romanorum Fragmenta ab Appio inde Caeco et M. Catone usque ad Q. Aurelium Symmachum* (Zurich, 2nd edn., 1842).
[3] E. Malcovati, *Oratorum Romanorum Fragmenta* (Turin, 1930) (3 vols.).
[4] A. Cima, *L'eloquenza latina prima di Cicerone. Saggio storico-critico* (Rome, 1903).
[5] E. Malcovati, 'L'eloquenza romana' (AFLC 11 (1941), pp. 137-61).
[6] M. O. Baumgart, *Untersuchungen zu den Reden des M. Porcius Cato Censorius* (Diss., Breslau, 1905).
[7] W. Soltau, 'Nepos und Plutarchos' (NJA 153 (1896), pp. 123-31).
[8] F. della Corte, *Catone Censore, La Vita e la Fortuna* (Torino, Rosenberg & Sellier, 1949).
[9] P. Fraccaro, 'Le fonti per il consolato di M. Porcio Catone' (*Studi Storici* 3 (1910), pp. 129-202).
[10] P. Fraccaro, 'Ricerche storiche e letterarie sulla censura del 184/183' (SS 4 (1911), pp. 30-70).
[11] P. Fraccaro, 'Catoniana' (SS 3 (1910), pp. 241-85).
[12] P. Fraccaro, 'L'orazione di Catone *de sumptu suo*' (SS 3 (1910) pp. 378-86).
[13] B. Janzer, *Historische Untersuchungen zu den Redenfragmenten des M. Porcius Cato. Beiträge zur Lebensgeschichte und Politik Catos* (Diss. Wurzburg, 1937). See also H. H. Scullard, *Roman Politics, 220-150 B.C.* (Oxford, Clarendon Press, 1951), pp. 256-72.
[14] R. Till, 'Die Sprache Catos' (Philologus, Supplementband 28, 2 (1935) pp. 1-102).
[15] E. Norden, *Die antike Kunstprosa* (Leipzig, 1898), I, pp. 164-9).
[16] E.g. Malcovati, I, pp. 89-90; cf. now Clarke, *op. cit.*, pp. 41-2.
[17] C. Knapp, 'A phase of the development of prose writing among the Romans', (CPh 13 (1918), pp. 138-54).
[18] P. Fraccaro, 'Studi sull'età dei Gracchi' (SS 5 (1912), pp. 317-448; 6 (1913), pp. 42ff).
[19] N. Häpke, *C. Semproni Gracchi Oratoris Romani Fragmenta Collecta et Illustrata* (Diss., Munich, 1915).
[20] R. Reitzenstein, *Scipio Aemilianus und die stoische Rhetorik* (Strassburger Festschrift, Strassburg, 1901). (Sonderabdruck.)
[21] M. Bonnet, 'Le dilemme de C. Gracchus' (REA 8 (1906), pp. 40-6).
[22] J. Marouzeau, 'Pour mieux comprendre les textes latins' (RP 45 (1921), pp. 165-73).
[23] M. Krüger, *M. Antonii et L. Licinii Crassi Oratorum Romanorum Fragmenta* (Diss., Breslau, 1909).
[24] Started by A. Tartara, 'I precursori di Cicerone' (ASNP 18 (1888) pp. 291-528) (praised); continued by J. Cortese, *Oratorum Romanorum reliquiae* (Turin, 1892) (considered less reliable); A. G. Amatucci, *L'eloquenza latina nei primi cinque secoli di Roma* (Benevento, 1893); A. G. Amatucci, *L'eloquenza giudiziaria a Roma prima di Catone* (Naples, 1904); C. Marchesi, 'I primordii dell' eloquenza agraria e popolare di Roma' (Riv. Stor. Ant. N.S.9. (1905), pp. 359ff); L. Illuminati, *L'eloquenza romana prima di Cicerone* (Messina, 1948). (The non-periodical publications appear quite inaccessible in Britain.)
[25] E.g. G. A. Harrer, 'The genuineness of Cicero's *Pro Murena*' (CPh 9 (1914) pp. 83-4), refuting a German attempt to prove it was written by Poggio! On other speeches mentioned, see W. Peterson's preface to his recension in O.C.T. vol. 5.
[26] L. Laurand, *Études sur le style des discours de Cicéron*, 3 vols. (Paris, Les Belles Lettres, 4th edn. 1938-40), vol. I init.
[27] T. Opperskalski, *De M. Tulli Ciceronis orationum retractatione quaestiones selectae* (Diss., Greifswald, 1914).
[28] E. Norden, 'Aus Ciceros Werkstatt' (SPA 1913, pp. 2-34, esp. 12ff).
[29] R. G. Austin, *M. T. Ciceronis Pro M. Caelio Oratio*, 2nd edn. (Oxford, Clarendon Press, 1952), Appendix 8.

[30] J. Humbert, *Les plaidoyers écrits et les plaidoiries réelles de Cicéron* (Paris, Les Presses Universitaires, N. D. (1925)).
[31] J. Martha, 'Les discours judiciaires de Cicéron' (RCC 1904-05, pp. 299-305, 404-10, 631-8, 777-82; 1905, pp. 56-63, 296-302, 359-69, 500-8).
[32] W. Kroll, 'Ciceros Rede für Plancius' (RhM 86 (1937), pp. 127-39, p. 137, n37. cf. Klotz in PhW 1926, col. 1267-1270.
[33] T. B. L. Webster, *M. T. Ciceronis Pro L. Flacco Oratio* (Oxford, Clarendon Press, 1931), Appendix A.
[34] O. Jahn, *Ciceros Brutus* (5th edn., revised by Kroll, Berlin, 1908).
[35] W. Kroll, *M. T. Ciceronis Orator* (Berlin, 1913). For an analysis of the treatise see also R. Sabbadini, 'La composizione dell' *Orator* ciceroniano' (RF 44 (1916) pp. 1-22).
[36] J. E. Sandys, *M. T. Ciceronis ad M. Brutum Orator* (Cambridge, University Press, 1885).
[37] W. Kroll, 'Rhetorik' (RE, Supplementband 7; Sonderabdruck, Stuttgart, 1937).
[38] L. Laurand, *De M. Tulli Ciceronis studiis rhetoricis* (Paris, Picard, 1907).
[39] T. Petersson, *Cicero, a biography* (University of California Press, Berkeley, 1920), pp. 366-442; cf. H. Taylor, *Cicero, a sketch of his life and works* (2nd edn., Chicago, 1918), pp. 320-53.
[40] R. Weidner, *Ciceros Verhältnis zur griechisch-römischen Schulrhetorik seiner Zeit* (Diss., Erlangen, 1925.)
[41] On the last-named, see now the detailed work of B. Riposati, *Studi sui 'Topica' di Cicerone* (Milan, 1947). On *Part. Or.*, P. Sternkopf, *De M. T. Ciceronis partitionibus oratoriis* (Diss., Münster, 1914).
[42] F. Rohde, *Cicero, quae de inventione praeceperit, quatenus secutus sit in orationibus generis iudicialis* (Diss., Königsberg, 1903).
[43] R. Preiswerk, *De inventione orationum Ciceronianarum* (Basel, 1905). I have not seen his article 'Griechische Gemeinplätze in Ciceros Reden' (*Juvenes Dum Sumus*, Basel, 1907, pp. 27ff).
[44] J. Martha, 'Les discours judiciaires de Cicéron' cont'd (RCC 1905, pp. 537-46, 593-602, 634-43, 791-800).
[45] F. P. Donnelly, *Cicero's Milo, a rhetorical commentary* (New York, Bruce Publishing Company, 1935).
[46] J. S. Reid, *M. T. Ciceronis pro T. Annio Milone ad iudices oratio* (Cambridge, University Press, 1894), Appendix B. A good analysis in A. C. Clark's edition (Oxford, Clarendon Press, 1895).
[47] W. Sternkopf, 'Die Oekonomie der Rede Ciceros für den Dichter Archias' (Hermes 42 (1907), pp. 337-73). (He had previously analysed the *Div. in Caec.* in a Dortmund programme, 1905.)
[48] J. van Wageningen, *M. T. Ciceronis Oratio pro M. Caelio* (Groningen, 1908), pp. xxiv-xxix; cf. R. G. Austin (s.v. 29), pp. 41, 45, 90, 94, 102, 112, 133, 140.
[49] R. Heinze, 'Ciceros Rede Pro Caelio' (Hermes 60 (1925), pp. 193-258).
[50] Cf. W. Kroll, *Rhetorik* (s.v. 37), col. 1103.
[51] W. Kroll, 'Ciceros Rede für Cluentius' (NJA 53 (1924), pp. 174-84).
[52] *Op. cit.*, s.v. 32.
[53] G. Landgraf, *Kommentar zu Ciceros Rede Pro Sex. Roscio Amerino* (Leipzig, 2nd edn., 1914).
[54] F. Solmsen, 'Cicero's first speeches; a rhetorical analysis' (TAPhA 69 (1938), pp. 542-56).
[55] A. Yon, 'A propos de la composition chez les anciens; le plan d'un discours de Cicéron (la IIe Catilinaire)' (REL 14 (1936), pp. 310-26); cf. H. Bornecque, *Les Catilinaires de Cicéron* (Paris, Mellottée, 1936), for further analyses.
[56] H. M. Hubbell, *The influence of Isocrates on Cicero, Dionysius, and Aristides* (Yale University Press, 1913), pp. 16-40.
[57] F. Solmsen, 'Aristotle and Cicero on the orator's playing upon the feelings' (CPh 33 (1938), pp. 390-404), cf. his further articles on 'The Aristotelian tradition in ancient rhetoric' (AJPh 62 (1941), pp. 35-50 and 169-90).
[58] H. von Arnim, *Leben und Werke des Dio von Prusa* (Berlin, 1898), pp. 93-114.
[59] W. Kroll, 'Studien über Ciceros Schrift *De Oratore*' (RhM 58 (1903), pp. 552-97), and 'Cicero und die Rhetorik' (NJKlP 11 (1903), pp. 681-9). But see C. Prumm, *Quaestionum Tullianarum ad dialogi De Oratore partes philosophicas quae dicuntur spectantium specimen* (Diss. Munster, 1927).

ROMAN ORATORY

[60] H. K. Schulte, *Orator; Untersuchungen über das ciceronianische Bildungsideal* (Frankfürter Studien zur Religion und Kultur der Antike, Frankfürt, Klostermann, 1935).

[61] A. Lieby, *Quantum philosophiae studio ad augendam dicendi facultatem Cicero tribuerit* (Paris, thesis, 1901).

[62] H. Ranft, *Quaestiones philosophicae ad orationes Ciceronis pertinentes* (Diss., Leipzig, 1912).

[63] F. Sauer, *Über die Verwendung der Geschichte und Altertumskunde in Ciceros Reden* (Progr., Ludwigshafen a. Rhein, 1909-10).

[64] R. Schütz, *Ciceros historische Kenntnisse* (Diss., Berlin, 1913).

[65] L. Laurand, 'L'histoire dans les discours de Cicéron' (MB 15 (1911), pp. 5-34).

[66] H. Schoenberger, *Beispiele aus der Geschichte, ein rhetorisches Kunstmittel in Ciceros Reden* (Diss., Augsburg, 1910).

[67] M. Radin, 'Literary references in Cicero's orations' (CJ 6 (1911), pp. 209-17).

[68] W. Zillinger, *Cicero und die altrömischen Dichter* (Erlangen Diss., Würzburg, 1911).

[69] E. Costa, *Cicerone Giureconsulto* (2 vols. Bologna, Zanicelli, 1927).

[70] The title was also used by A. Gasquy, *Cicéron jurisconsulte* (Paris, Thorin, 1887), R. Sabbadini, 'Cicerone giureconsulto' Ath. 4 (1916), pp. 342ff, and E. Cocchia, 'Cicerone oratore e giureconsulto' (AAN 9 (1926), pp. 423-59).

[71] E.g. V. A. Georgesco, 'Nihil hoc ad ius, ad Ciceronem!' (*Mélanges Marouzeau*, (Paris, Les Belles Lettres, 1948), pp. 189-206).

[72] J. Stroux, *Summum Ius Summa Iniuria* (Festschrift Paul Speiser-Sarasin, Leipzig, 1926), reprinted in his *Römische Rechtswissenschaft und Rhetorik* (Potsdam, Stichnote, 1949).

[73] J. Stroux, 'Die griechischen Einflüsse auf die Entwicklung der römischen Rechtswissenschaft' (Originally delivered to the 'Congresso internazionale di diritto Romano' in Rome, 1933, and included in *Römische Rechtswissenschaft*, pp. 83-107).

[74] In Stroux, R. R., pp. 69-80; cf. Riccobono's review in Gnomon 5 (1929), pp. 65-87.

[75] J. Himmelschein, *Studien zu der antiken Hermeneutica Iuris* (Leipzig, 1935).

[76] F. Schulz, *History of Roman Legal Science* (Oxford, 1946), pp. 71-80.

[77] Cf. U. von Lübtow, 'Cicero und die Methode der römischen Jurisprudenz', *Festschrift Wenger*, I (Munich, 1944, pp. 224-35).

[78] A. Steinwenter, 'Rhetorik und römische Zivilprozess' (ZRG 65 (1947), pp. 69-120).

[79] As did la Pira, *La genesi del sistema nella giurisprudenza Romana* (Siena, 1934), criticized by Steinwenter.

[80] E. Meyer, 'Die Quaestionen der Rhetorik und die Anfänge juristische Methodenlehre' (ZRG 68 (1951), pp. 30-73).

[81] E. A. Lussky, *The appeal to the emotions in the judicial speeches of Cicero as compared with the theories set forth on the subject in the De Oratore* (University of Minnesota thesis, 1928).

[82] V. Brugnola, *Le facezie di Cicerone* (Città di Castello, 1896); further in A & R 10 (1907) pp. 11-12 (from the Letters).

[83] F. W. Kelsey, 'Cicero as a Wit' (CJ 3 (1907-08), pp. 3-10).

[84] P. Faulmüller, *Über die rednerische Verwendung des Witzes und der Satire bei Cicero* (Diss., Erlangen, 1906).

[85] Mary Grant, *Ancient Rhetorical Theories of the Laughable* (University of Wisconsin Studies 21, Madison, 1924).

[86] R. G. C. Levens, *Cicero, the fifth Verrine oration* (London, Methuen 1946).

[87] L. H. G. Greenwood, *Cicero, the Verrine orations* (London, Heinemann, 1928, Loeb Library, 2 vols.).

[88] H. Holst, *Die Wortspiele in Ciceros Reden* (Oslo, 1925, Symbolae Osloenses, Supp. I).

[89] *Op. cit.*, s.v. 26, vol. 3, pp. 248-55.

[90] H. V. Canter, 'Irony in the orations of Cicero' (AJPh 57 (1936), pp. 457-64).

[91] H. V. Canter, '*Digressio* in the orations of Cicero' (AJPh 52 (1931), pp. 351-61).

[92] E. H. Haight, *The Roman use of anecdotes in Cicero, Livy, and the Satirists* (New York, Longmans, 1940).

[93] J. André, 'Les adjectifs et adverbes à valeur intensive en *per-* et *prae-*' (REL 29 (1951), pp. 121-54).

[94] P. Gotzes, *De Ciceronis tribus generibus dicendi in orationibus pro A. Caecina, De Imperio Cn. Pompei, pro Rabirio perd. reo adhibitis* (Diss., Rostock, 1914).

⁹⁵ Dietrich Mack, *Senatsreden und Volksreden bei Cicero* (Kieler Arbeiten zur klassischen Philologie, Würzburg, Triltsch, 1937).
⁹⁶ G. Landgraf, *De Ciceronis eloquentia in orationibus pro P. Quinctio et pro S. Roscio Amerino conspicua* (Diss., Würzburg, 1878).
⁹⁷ L. Laurand, 'Sur l'évolution de la langue et du style de Cicéron' (RPh 59 (1933), pp. 62-72); cf. his charmingly informal brochure, *Cicéron est intéressant* (Paris, Les Belles Lettres, 3rd edn. 1937), pp. 42-9, on reading the speeches chronologically.
⁹⁸ F. Klingner, 'Ciceros Rede für den Schauspieler Roscius. Eine Episode der Entwicklung seiner Kunstprosa' (SBA 1953). See now Schmid's review in Gnomon, 1954, pp. 317-22.
⁹⁹ P. Parzinger, *Beiträge zur Kenntnis der Entwicklung des Ciceronischen Stils* (I. Diss., Landshut, 1910; II, Programm, Landshut, 1912).
¹⁰⁰ H. J. Rose, 'The Greek of Cicero' (JRS 41 (1921), pp. 93-114).
¹⁰¹ L. Delaruelle, *Études sur le choix des mots dans les discours de Cicéron* (Toulouse, 1911).
¹⁰² C. Morawski, 'De metaphoris Tullianis observationes' (Eos 16 (1910), pp. 1-5).
¹⁰³ M. Wiegandt, *De metaphorarum usu quodam Ciceroniano* (Diss., Rostock, 1910).
¹⁰⁴ S. Hammer, *Contumeliae quae in Ciceronis invectivis et epistulis occurrunt quatenus Plautinum redoleant sermonem* (Diss., Cracow, 1905).
¹⁰⁵ K. F. Nägelsbach, *Lateinische Stilistik* (9th edn. Nürnberg, 1905).
¹⁰⁶ J. Marouzeau, *Traité de stylistique appliquée au Latin* (Paris, Les Belles Lettres, 1935). See also Stolz–Schmalz, *Lateinische Grammatik* 5th edn. by Leumann and Hofmann (Munich, 1928), pp. 789-850 ('Lateinische Stilistik'). An important work is J. Lebreton, *Études sur la langue et la grammaire de Cicéron* (Paris, Hachette, 1901).
¹⁰⁷ J. Cousin, *Bibliographie de la Langue Latine* (Paris, Les Belles Lettres, 1951).
¹⁰⁸ T. Zielinski, *Das Clauselgesetz in Ciceros Reden* (Leipzig, 1904).
¹⁰⁹ T. Zielinski, 'Textkritik und Rhythmusgesetz in Ciceros Reden' (Philologus Suppbd. 1906, pp. 604-29). Opinions will differ on the degree of validity of the *clausula*-criterion in textual criticism. See Laurand, *Études*, vol. 2, pp. 215-28; he admits its value, if applied with care, in certain cases of doubtful reading, and in the weighing of conjectural restorations.
¹¹⁰ T. Zielinski, *Der constructive Rhythmus in Ciceros Reden* (Leipzig, 1914). Contrast A. C. Clark's enthusiastic reception of the *Clauselgesetz* in CR 19 (1905), pp. 164-72, with his rather more sceptical acceptance of the above-mentioned work in CR 30 (1916), pp. 22-6.
¹¹¹ F. Blass, *Die Rhythmen der asianischen und römischen Kunstprosa* (Leipzig, 1905).
¹¹² J. May, *Rhythmische Analyse der Rede Ciceros Pro S. Roscio Amerino* (Leipzig, 1905); *Rhythmen in Ciceros katilinarischen Reden* (Durlach, 1909); *Rhythmische Formen nachgewiesen durch Beispiele aus Cicero und Demosthenes* (Leipzig, 1909); *Rhythmen in Ciceros Reden* (Durlach, 1912). These are inaccessible to me, but May's reports in Bursian 134 and 153 are full of his own theory.
¹¹³ C. Zander, *Eurythmia* (sic) 3 vols. (Leipzig, 1914), vol. 3, *Eurythmia Ciceronis*. See further A. C. Clark's review in CR 30 (1916), pp. 53-5; Novotný in Eos, Supplement 5 (1929), sections 27-9 (both unfavourable).
¹¹⁴ Cf. *Rosc. Com.* 14 (his ego ... iudicari debeat); this is analysed by Parzinger, I, p. 71, into 12+12, 10+10, 14+14).
¹¹⁵ H. Bornecque, *Les Clausules métriques latines* (Lille, 1907); cf. his article 'Wie soll man die metrischen Klauseln studieren?' (RhM 58 (1903), pp. 371-81).
¹¹⁶ L. Laurand, 'Les fins d'hexamètre dans les discours de Cicéron' (RPh 35 (1911), pp. 75-88).
¹¹⁷ F. W. Shipley, 'The heroic clausula in Cicero and Quintilian' (CPh 6 (1911), pp. 410-18); see further his article 'The treatment of dactylic words in the rhythmic prose of Cicero, with special reference to the sense pauses' (TAPhA 41 (1910), pp. 139-56).
¹¹⁸ E. Norden, *op. cit.*, s.v. 15, vol. 2, pp. 930-9.
¹¹⁹ F. Novotný, 'Eine neue Methode der Klauselforschung' (BPhW 37 (1917), col. 217-22); 'Le problème des clausules dans la prose latine' (REL 4 (1926), pp. 221-9). The latter is a reply to De Groot.
¹²⁰ F. Novotný, *Eurhythmie recké a latinské prósy* (Prague, 1921).
¹²¹ H. D. Broadhead, *Latin Prose Rhythm. A New Method of Investigation* (Cambridge, Deighton Bell, 1922).

ROMAN ORATORY 461

[122] See his review of Broadhead in Philologica (Journal of Comparative Philology), 2 (1923-24), pp. 115-19.
[123] A. W. De Groot, *Handbook of antique prose-rhythm* (Groningen, 1918); *De numero oratorio latino* (Groningen, 1919); 'La prose métrique latine: état actuel de nos connaissances' (REL 3 (1925), pp. 190-204; 4 (1926), pp. 36-50). My summary is based on the last-mentioned. See also W. C. Shewring, 'Prose Rhythm and the Comparative Method' (CQ 24 (1930), pp. 164-73; 25 (1931), pp. 12-22).
[124] M. T. Baley, 'Ciceronian metrics and clausulae' (CJ 33 (1938), pp. 336-50).
[125] P. Wuilleumier, 'La théorie cicéronienne de la prose métrique' (REL 7 (1929), pp. 170-80).
[126] L. Bayard, 'La clausule cicéronienne' (RPh 58 (1932), pp. 37-55).
[127] W. de Moulin, *De Clausulis Ciceronianis Quaestiones Epicriticae* (Freiburg, 1931).
[128] Laurand published a bibliography of the *cursus* in REL 6 (1928), pp. 73-90, including, of course, A. C. Clark's *Fontes prosae numerosae* (Oxford, Clarendon Press, 1909) and *The cursus in mediaeval and vulgar Latin* (Oxford, Clarendon Press, 1910). See also M. G. Nicolau, *L'origine du cursus rhythmique* (Paris, Les Belles Lettres, 1930) (cf. REL 6 (1928), pp. 319-29, and 7 (1929), pp. 47-74).
[129] F. Novotný, 'État actuel des études sur le rhythme de la prose latine' (Eos, Supplement 5 (1929)).
[130] A. C. Clark, *Fontes prosae numerosae* (Oxford, Clarendon Press, 1909).
[131] H. J. Rose, 'Logical and rhetorical emphasis in the Ciceronian sentence' (Philologica (Journal of Comparative Philology) 1 (1921-22), pp. 54-77).
[132] E. Lindholm, *Stilistische Studien* (Lund, 1931), pp. 117-73. On assonance, K. Polheim, *Die lateinische Reimprosa* (Berlin, 1925), pp. 183ff.
[133] The following is merely a select list.
(a) Biographies: E. G. Sihler, *Cicero of Arpinum* (New Haven, 1914); works of H. Taylor and T. Petersson (see n39); E. Ciaceri, *Cicerone e i suoi tempi* (2 vols. Milan-Rome-Naples, 1926-30); R. N. Wilkin, *Eternal Lawyer. A Legal Biography of Cicero* (London and N.Y. (Macmillan) 1947).
(b) Studies and Appreciations: V. Cucheval, *Cicéron orateur* (2 vols. Paris, 1901); A. C. Clark, 'Ciceronianism' (in *English Literature and the Classics*, Oxford, 1912) (an essay based on Zielinski's *Cicero im Wandel der Jahrhunderte*, Leipzig-Berlin, 3rd edn., 1912); J. E. Granrud, 'Was Cicero successful in the art oratorical?' (CJ 8 (1913), pp. 234-43); Grant Showerman, 'Cicero the stylist; an appreciation' (CJ 8 (1913), pp. 180-92); A. P. McKinlay, 'Cicero's conception of literary art' (CJ 21 (1926), pp. 244-259; W. A. Oldfather, 'Cicero, a sketch' (CJ 23 (1928), pp. 404-27; J. C. Rolfe, *Cicero and his Influence* ('Our Debt to Greece and Rome', London, Harrap, N.D.); Tenney Frank, *Cicero* (repd. from Proc. Brit. Acad. 18, London, 1932); L. Laurand, 'L'art oratoire de Cicéron, théorie et pratique' (LEC 1 (1932), pp. 381-7); id., *Cicéron est intéressant* (Paris, 1937); id., *Cicéron* (Paris, 1938); id., *Cicéron*, volume complémentaire (Paris, 1938); W. L. Grant, 'Cicero on the moral character of the orator' (CJ 38 (1943), pp. 472-8); P. MacKendrick, 'Cicero's ideal orator' (CJ 43 (1948), pp. 339-47 ('reactionary propaganda'); A. Guillemin, 'Cicéron et la culture latine', (REL 25 (1947), pp. 148-57; M. L. Clarke, 'Ciceronian oratory' (G & R 14 (1945), pp. 72-81); id., *Rhetoric at Rome* (London, 1953), pp. 62-84; E. Laughton, *Rhetoric and the Roman Heritage* ((inaugural lecture, Sheffield Univ. Press, 1953).
(c) Editions (in English only): Many late nineteenth-century editions are still valued (e.g. by J. S. Reid, A. C. Clark, W. Peterson, W. Y. Fausset, J. R. King, W. E. Heitland, H. A. Holden, A. B. Poynton and others). Important editions in our period are those mentioned in notes 29, 33, 45, 86; add: *De Domo*, ed. R. G. Nisbet (Oxford, 1939); *In Vatinium*, ed. L. G. Pocock (London Univ. Press, 1926); *De Prov. Cons.*, ed. H. E. Butler and M. Cary (Oxford, 1924); *Phil.* 1 and 2, ed. J. D. Denniston (Oxford, 1926).
(d) Background: (1) Legal. A. H. J. Greenidge, *The legal procedure of Cicero's time* (Oxford, 1901); N. W. de Witt, 'Litigation in the Forum in Cicero's time' (CPh 21 (1926), pp. 218-24); R. N. Wilkin, in (a). (2) Social. W. Warde Fowler, *Social life at Rome in the age of Cicero* (London, 1908); W. Kroll, *Kultur der ciceronianischen Zeit* (2 vols., Breslau, 1933). (3) Historical: F. H. Cowles, *Gaius Verres—an historical study* (Cornell Univ. Stud. 1917); E. G. Hardy, *The Catilinarian conspiracy in its*

context; a re-study of the evidence (Oxford, 1924); H. Frisch, *Cicero's fight for the Republic*; the historical background of the Philippics (Copenhagen, 1946). Numerous useful articles on individual speeches in CJ and CW, and some first-rate Introductions in the Budé series.

[134] *Op. cit.*, s.v. 15, vol. I, pp. 131-55.

[135] L. Radermacher, 'Über die Anfänge des Atticismus' (RhM 54 (1899), pp. 351ff).

[136] U. v. Wilamowitz-Möllendorff, 'Asianismus und Atticismus' (Hermes 35 (1900), pp. 1-52.)

[137] G. L. Hendrickson, 'The *De Analogia* of Julius Caesar; its occasion, nature and date, with additional fragments' (CPh 1 (1906), pp. 97-120). On Stoic stylistic theory, see also S. Striller, 'De Stoicorum studiis rhetoricis' in Breslauer Philologische Abhandlungen I (1887); C. N. Smiley, *Latinitas and* Ἑλληνισμός (Univ. of Wisconsin thesis, 1906); G. C. Fiske, 'The Plain Style in the Scipionic Circle' (Univ. of Wisconsin Studies 3, 1919) and his *Lucilius and Horace* (Univ. of Wisconsin Studies 7, 1920), *passim.*, cf. W. Kroll, *Studien zum Verständnis der römischen Literatur* (Stuttgart, 1924), pp. 87-116.

[138] H. Heck, *Zur Entstehung des rhetorischen Attizismus* (Diss., Munich, 1917).

[139] E. Wölfflin, '*Enervis* und der Redner Calvus' (Archiv. f. Lat. Lex. 13 (1904), p. 438.)

[140] A. Gudeman, in his 2nd edn. of the *Dialogus* (see n196), p. 317.

[141] O. Harnecker, 'Cicero und die Attiker' (NJA 125 (1882), pp. 610ff).

[142] G. L. Hendrickson, 'Cicero's correspondence with Brutus and Calvus on oratorical style' (AJPh 47 (1926), pp. 234-58).

[143] J. F. D'Alton, *Roman literary theory and criticism* (London, Longmans, 1931), pp. 208-65).

[144] M. Krüger, *C. Licinius Calvus. Ein Beitrag zur Geschichte der römischen Beredsamkeit* (Breslau, 1913).

[145] F. Plessis, *Calvus, édition complète des fragments et des temoignages ... avec un essai ... par J. Poirot* (Paris, 1896). Quite important, but inaccessible to me, was G. Curcio, *De Ciceronis et Calvi reliquorumque Atticorum arte dicendi quaestiones* (Acide prope Catinam, 1899).

[146] E. Castorina, *Licinio Calvo* (Catania (Crisafulli), 1946).

[147] E. J. Filbey, 'Concerning the oratory of Brutus' (CPh 6 (1911), pp. 325-33).

[148] C. Morawski, 'De M. Iunii Bruti genere dicendi et Philippica decima Ciceronis' (Eos, 17 (1911), pp. 1-6).

[149] E. Castorina, *L'Atticismo nel evoluzione del pensiere di Cicerone* (Catania (Gianotta), 1952). A. Desmouliez, 'Sur la polémique de Cicéron et des Atticistes' (REL 30 (1952), pp. 168-85).

[150] A. D. Leeman, *A Systematical Bibliography of Sallust* (Leyden (Brill), 1952, pp. 44ff).

[151] J. André, *La vie et l'œuvre d'Asinius Pollion* (Paris (Klincksieck), 1949, pp. 67ff).

[152] P. Lunderstedt, *De C. Maecenatis Fragmentis* (Comm. Phil. Ien. 9 (Leipzig), 1911).

[153] E. Malcovati, *Imperatoris Caesaris Augusti Operum Fragmenta* (3rd. edn., Torino (Paravia), 1948).

[154] V. Cucheval, *Histoire de l'éloquence romaine depuis la mort de Cicéron* (43 B.C.-117 A.D.) (Paris, Hachette, 1893, 2 vols.).

[155] E. P. Parks, *The Roman rhetorical schools as a preparation for the courts under the early Empire* (Johns Hopkins University Studies in Historical and Political Science, Series 63, no. 2, Baltimore, 1945) (cf. my review in JRS 40 (1950), pp. 157-8).

[156] H. Bornecque, *Sénèque le Rhéteur, Controverses et Suasoires* (2nd. edn., Paris, Garnier, 1932, 2 vols.).

[157] W. A. Edward, *The Suasoriae of Seneca the Elder* (Cambridge, University Press, 1928).

[158] H. Bornecque, *Les déclamations et les déclamateurs d'après Sénèque le Père* (Lille, 1902).

[159] W. Hoffa, *De Seneca patre quaestiones selectae* (Göttingen, 1909).

[160] H. de la Ville de Mirmont, 'Les déclamateurs espagnols aux temps d'Auguste et de Tibère' (Bull. Hisp. 12 (1910), pp. 1ff; 14 (1912), pp. 11ff, 229ff, 341ff; 15 (1913), pp. 154ff, 237ff, 384ff).

[161] S. F. Bonner, *Roman Declamation in the late Republic and early Empire* (Liverpool, University Press, 1949).

ROMAN ORATORY

[162] H. Bardon, *Le vocabulaire de la critique littéraire chez Sénèque le Rhéteur* (Paris, Les Belles Lettres, 1940).
[163] W. Jaeneke, *De statuum doctrina ab Hermogene tradita* (Diss., Leipzig, 1904).
[164] H. Throm, *Die Thesis — ein Beitrag zu ihrer Entstehung und Geschichte* (Paderborn, 1932) (Rhetorische Studien 17).
[165] J. Klek, *Symbuleutici qui dicitur sermonis historia critica* (Paderborn, 1919) (Rhet. Stud. 8).
[166] W. Hofrichter, *Studien zur Entwicklungsgeschichte der Deklamation von der griech. Sophistik bis z. römischen Kaiserzeit* (Diss., Ohlau, 1935).
[167] M. L. Clarke, 'The thesis in the Roman rhetorical schools of the Republic' (CQ NS 1 (1951), pp. 159-66).
[168] T. S. Simonds, *The themes treated by the elder Seneca* (Diss., Baltimore, 1896).
[169] R. Kohl, *De scholasticarum declamationum argumentis ex historia petitis* (Paderborn, 1915) (Rhet. Stud. 4).
[170] M. Schamberger, *De declamationum Romanorum argumentis* (Diss., Halle, 1917).
[171] S. Rossi, '*Vita e realta nelle Controversie di Seneca il retore*' (RIGI 2 (1918), pp. 203ff; 3 (1919), pp. 13-28).
[172] N. Deratani, 'Le réalisme dans les Declamationes' (RPh 55 (1929), pp. 184-9).
[173] C. Morawski, 'Zu lateinischen Schriftstellern' (WS 4 (1882), pp. 166-8).
[174] G. Boissier, 'The schools of declamation at Rome', in *Tacitus and other Roman studies* (trans. Hutchinson) (London, 1906).
[175] R. Pichon, '*L'éducation romaine au premier siècle*' (Revue Universitaire 4 (1895), p. 160).
[176] C. Lécrivain, 'Le droit grec et le droit romain dans les Controverses de Sénèque le Père et dans les Déclamations de Quintilien et de Calpurnius Flaccus' (NRH 15 (1891), pp. 680-91).
[177] J. Sprenger, *Quaestiones in rhetorum Romanorum declamationes iuridicae* (Diss., Halle, 1911).
[178] F. Lanfranchi, *Il diritto nei retori Romani* (Milan, 1938) (cf. P. W. Duff's review in JRS 40 (1950), pp. 154-6).
[179] R. Düll, 'Iudicium domesticum, abdicatio und apokeruxis' (ZRG 63 (1943), pp. 54-116).
[180] Cf. *Roman Declamation*, p. 102.
[181] F. H. Colson, *M. Fabii Quintiliani Institutionis Oratoriae Liber I* (Cambridge, University Press, 1924).
[182] R. G. Austin, *Quintiliani Institutionis Oratoriae Liber XII* (Oxford, Clarendon Press, 1948; revised edn. 1953).
[183] W. Peterson, *M. Fabi Quintiliani Institutionis Oratoriae Liber Decimus* (Oxford, Clarendon Press, 1891).
[184] H. E. Butler, *The Institutio Oratoria of Quintilian, with an English translation* (London, Heinemann, 1921 (rpd.), 4 vols.).
[185] D. M. Gaunt, *Selections from Quintilian* (London, Heinemann, 1952).
[186] W. Kroll, '*Quintilianstudien*' (RhM 73 (1924), pp. 243-72).
[187] J. Cousin, *Études sur Quintilien* (Paris, Boivin, 1936, 2 vols.).
[188] B. Appel, *Das Bildungs-und Erziehungsideal Quintilians* (Diss., Donauwörth, 1914).
[189] A. Gwynn, *Roman education from Cicero to Quintilian* (Oxford, Clarendon Press, 1926).
[190] W. M. Smail, *Quintilian on Education* (Oxford, 1938).
[191] H. I. Marrou, *Histoire de l'éducation dans l'antiquité* (Paris, 1948).
[192] E.g. by H. Raubenheimer, *Quintilianus quae debere videatur Stoicis popularibusque qui dicuntur philosophis* (Diss., Würzburg, 1911).
[193] F. Leo, 'Quintilians kleine Deklamationen' (NGG 1912, pp. 109ff); N. Deratani 'De rhetorum Romanorum declamationibus; I De minorum declamationum auctore' (RPh 49 (1925), pp. 101-17).
[194] G. Golz, *Die rhythmische Satzschluss in den grösseren pseudo-Quint. Deklamationen* (Diss., Kiel, 1913).
[195] C. Ritter, *Die quintilianischen Deklamationen* (Freiburg, 1881); N. Deratani, 'Quaestiones ad originem maiorum quae sub nomine Quintiliani feruntur declamationum pertinentes' (RPh 53 (1927), pp. 289ff).

[196] A. Gudeman, *P. Cornelii Taciti Dialogus de Oratoribus* (2nd edn. Leipzig, Berlin, 1914).
[197] J. Cousin, 'Problèmes biographiques et littéraires relatifs à Quintilien' (REL 9 (1931), pp. 64-76).
[198] G. Wormser, 'Le dialogue des orateurs et l'institut oratoire de Quintilien' (RPh 36 (1912), pp. 179-89).
[199] H. Bardon, '*Dialogue des Orateurs* et *Institution Oratoire*' (REL 19 (1941), pp. 113-31). See also R. Güngerich, in CPh 46 (1951), pp. 159-164.
[200] R. Dienel, 'Quintilian und der Rednerdialog des Tacitus' (WS 37 (1915), pp. 239-71).
[201] JAW 167 (1914), pp. 242ff (Remme); 224 (1929), pp. 258ff (Drexler); 247 (1935), pp. 24ff (Marx); 282 (1943), pp. 8off (Koestermann). Most recent contribution: Karl Barwick, 'Der *Dialogus de Oratoribus* des Tacitus. Motive und Zeit seiner Entstehung' (S. Leipz. Ak. 1954).
[202] W. Menzies, 'Pliny and the Roman Bar' (Juridical Review 36 (1924), pp. 197-217).
[203] M. Dorothy Brock, *Studies in Fronto and his Age* (Cambridge, University Press, 1911), pp. 97-124.
[204] P. F. Girard, *Textes de Droit Romain* (6th edn., Paris, 1937), pp. 817-21; also in F. Vollmer, 'Laudationum funebrium Romanorum historia et reliquiarum editio' (NJA, Suppbd. 18 (1892), pp. 445-528).
[205] M. Durry, *Éloge funèbre d'une matrone romaine* (*éloge dit de Turia*) (Paris, Les Belles Lettres, 1950). See also A. E. Gordon, 'A new fragment of the *Laudatio Turiana*' (AJA 54 (1950), pp. 223-6.
[206] M. Durry, *Pline le jeune, Panégyrique de Trajan* (Paris, Les Belles Lettres, 1938).
[207] E. Galletier, *Panégyriques latins* (2 vols., Paris, Les Belles Lettres, 1949, 1952; vol. 3 awaited).
[208] M. Durry, 'Laudatio funebris et rhétorique' (RPh (1942), pp. 105-14).
[209] *Op. cit.*, s.v. 206, Introduction; cf. J. Mesk, 'Zur Quellenanalyse des plinianischen Panegyricus' (WS 33 (1911), pp. 71ff).
[210] A. Klotz, 'Studien zu den Panegyrici Latini' (RhM 66 (1911), pp. 513-72).
[211] J. Mesk, 'Zur Technik der lateinischen Panegyriker' (RhM 67 (1912), pp. 569-90.
[212] W. S. Maguinness, 'Some methods of the Latin Panegyrists' (Hermathena 47 (1932), pp. 42-61).
[213] W. S. Maguinness, 'Locutions and formulae of the Latin Panegyrists' (Hermathena, 48 (1933), pp. 117-38).

The writer desires to express his deep sense of gratitude to the Staff of the National Central Library for their valuable assistance in locating and forwarding copies of many of the above-mentioned works; to the Staff of the Harold Cohen Library of the University of Liverpool, particularly for excellent liaison with N.C.L.; and last, but not least, to the Librarian of the Bodleian, for facilities graciously accorded to a Reader.

ADDENDUM: On the elder Cato see now D. Kienast, *Cato der Zensor: seine Persönlichkeit und seine Zeit* (Heidelberg, Quelle und Meyer, 1954).

'What is important is not that I should correct and explain Juvenal but that Juvenal should be corrected and explained.'[148] To Leo's 1910 edition is devoted a great part of Housman's 1931 Preface. An excellent book on the satirist's style, entitled *Juvenalis declamans*[149] and written by Josue de Decker, was published in 1913. Knoche's *Die Überlieferung Juvenals* (mentioned in the discussion of the Bodleian Fragment) was regarded by Housman as 'marking a stage in the slow improvement of Juvenalian criticism since the early years of the century'.[150] The year 1931 brought, as stated above, a corrected reprint of Housman's *Juvenal*.

Knoche, while admiring the merits of this work, observed that the setting-forth of manuscript readings called for basic revision and completion.[151] P. Wessner's *Scholia in Iuvenalem vetustiora*[152] was published in the same year. This collection of the ancient scholia, prepared with great industry and helpfully set out, is invaluable for research in Juvenal. The latest Italian text of the satirist, that of Natalis Vianello in the *Corpus Paravianum*,[153] is one of the four texts which form the basis of the Kelling–Suskin *Index*. Of the numerous writings on the satires in the last twenty years the most important would be said by many to be U. Knoche's *Handschriftliche Grundlagen des Juvenaltextes*,[154] judged by S. Prete to be 'l'ultimo e il piu importante lavoro preparatorio alla edizione critica'.[155] The German scholar's edition of Juvenal published three years ago and mentioned above[156] (it is the second volume in the series 'Das Wort der Antike') presents the most modern text and the richest *apparatus criticus* we yet possess. The words written by Housman on the completion of 'an enterprise undertaken in haste and in human concern for the relief of a people sitting in darkness'[157] have not been written in the sand.

[1] Ov. Met. 2. 107-8.
[2] *A Literary History of Rome in the Silver Age* (London, Fisher Unwin, 1927), p. 8.
[3] A. E. Housman in CR 14 (1900).
[4] *op. cit.*
[5] JRS 18 (1928), pp. 124-6.
[6] Oxford, The Clarendon Press, 1909.
[7] CR 23 (1910), pp. 193-6.
[8] London, Methuen, 1920.
[9] *A Study of the Argonautica of Valerius Flaccus* (Cambridge, Deighton Bell, and London, Bell, 1894).
[10] CR 35 (1921), pp. 169-70.
[11] Leipzig, Hirzel, 1886.
[12] Leipzig, Hirzel, 1895.
[13] RPh 26 (1952), p. 253.
[14] In the series 'Studies in Language and Literature'.

[15] JRS 9 (1919), p. 105.
[16] Dublin, Hodges, Figgis & Co., 1927.
[17] CR 42 (1928), pp. 84-5.
[18] YWCS, 1927, p. 20.
[19] Washington, Catholic University of America, 1940.
[20] *Index Verborum Valerianus* by W. H. Schulte (Scottdale, Pennsylvania, Mennonite Press, 1935).
[21] *Index Verborum Silianus* by Norma D. Young (obtainable from the author — 2845, Seventh Ave., Rock Island, Illinois, 1940).
[22] *A Concordance of Statius* by R. J. Deferrari and M. C. Eagan (R. J. Deferrari, Brookland, D.C., 1943).
[23] *Index Verborum Juvenalis* by Lucile Kelling and Albert Suskin (Chapel Hill, University of North Carolina Press, 1951).
[24] *Petronius* (London, Heinemann, 1913).
[25] New York, Columbia University Press, and London, Frowde.
[26] *Die Verseinlagen im Petron* (Leipzig, Dieterich, 1933).
[27] Gnomon 12 (1936), pp. 649-51 'Alles in allem; eine tüchtige Leistung'.
[28] *L. Iuni Moderati Columellae Opera Quae Exstant* (Upsala, Lundequist Library, 1902).
[29] Bari, Fratelli d'Ecclesia, 1946. H. B. Ash's *L. Iuni Moderati Columellae Rei Rusticae Liber Decimus: De Cultu Hortorum* (Philadelphia, obtainable from the author, 1930) contains a fair prose translation and a reliable exegesis.
[30] *Silver Age*, p. 166.
[31] *Aetna* erklärt von Siegfried Sudhaus (Leipzig, Teubner, 1898).
[32] CR 13 (1899), pp. 130-4.
[33] *Aetna* (Oxford, The Clarendon Press, 1901).
[34] R. Y. Tyrrell in CR 16 (1902), pp. 128-30.
[35] Paris, Fontemoing, 1905. See also his *Le Poème de l'Etna* (Paris, Les Belles Lettres, 1923).
[36] London, Heinemann, 1934.
[37] London, Bell, 1890.
[38] Quoted by E. D. A. Morshead in CR 5 (1891), p. 327.
[39] *Calpurnii et Nemesiani Bucolica* (Naples, Detken & Rocholl, 1910).
[40] CR 40 (1926), p. 42.
[41] *The Silver Age*, p. 91.
[42] *Post-Augustan Poetry*, p. 156.
[43] Paris, Imprimerie Nationale, 1894.
[44] Paris, Hachette, 1895.
[45] The phrase is J. Gow's, CR 15 (1901), p. 57.
[46] CR 14 (1900), p. 467.
[47] Oxford, The Clarendon Press, 1920.
[48] CR 34 (1920), pp. 121-4.
[49] *Phèdre* (Paris, Les Belles Lettres, 1924).
[50] *Phèdre et ses Fables* (Leiden, Brill, 1950).
[51] André Labhardt in Gnomon 24 (1952), p. 92; for a blunter estimate see C. J. Fordyce in CR, NS 1, p. 182.
[52] *Lucan* (Oxford, Blackwell, 1926), p. vi.
[53] Leipzig, Teubner, 1898.
[54] Leipzig, Teubner, 1900.
[55] London, Bell, 1904.
[56] *Silvae:* J. S. Phillimore (Oxford, The Clarendon Press, 1905).
[57] CR 20 (1906), pp. 317-24.
[58] Oxford, The Clarendon Press, 1908.
[59] YWCS, 1910, p. 111.
[60] *Statius* by J. H. Mozley (London, Heinemann, 1928).
[61] *Stace, Silves* (Paris, Les Belles Lettres, 1946).
[62] See the distinction drawn by Housman on page xxxiii of his *Lucan*.
[63] Leipzig, Teubner, 1892, 1905 and 1913.
[64] W. E. Heitland in CR 8 (1894), pp. 34-8.
[65] Paris, Klincksieck, 1894.
[66] Leyden, Brill, 1896-97.

⁶⁷ Housman, *op. cit.*, pp. xxxiv-v.
⁶⁸ *De Bello Civili VII* (Cambridge, Pitt Press, 1896).
⁶⁹ *De Bello Civili VIII* (Cambridge, Pitt Press, 1917).
⁷⁰ *De Bello Civili I* (Cambridge, Pitt Press, 1940).
⁷¹ *pace* A. Ernout (RPh 15 (1941), 190-1) who says it is 'tout à fait digne' of Postgate's edition.
⁷² *Les Sources de Lucain* (Paris, Leroux, 1912).
⁷³ Housman, *op. cit.* p.v.
⁷⁴ YWCS, 1926, p. 13.
⁷⁵ JRS 15 (1926), p. 291.
⁷⁶ *Lucan: The Civil War* (London, Heinemann, 1928).
⁷⁷ *Lucain: La Guerre Civile* by A. Bourgery (Paris, Les Belles Lettres, vol. I, 1927; vol. II, 1929).
⁷⁸ CR 41 (1927), 189-91, CR 44 (1930), p. 136.
⁷⁹ *op. cit.*, note 9.
⁸⁰ Berlin, S. Calvary & Co., 1896-97.
⁸¹ Housman in CR 14 (1900), p. 468.
⁸² London, Bell, 1900.
⁸³ Milan, Sandron, 1904.
⁸⁴ Leipzig, Teubner, 1913.
⁸⁵ *The Argonautica of Gaius Valerius Flaccus Setinus Balbus, Book One* (Oxford, Blackwell, 1916).
⁸⁶ London, Heinemann.
⁸⁷ Gnomon 13 (1937), p. 221.
⁸⁸ Aberdeen, The University Press, 1934.
⁸⁹ *De P. Papinii Statii Thebaide* (Berlin, Mayer & Muller).
⁹⁰ *P. Papinius Statius*, vol. III, by R. Jahnke (Leipzig, Teubner, 1899).
⁹¹ Fasc., iv, 1904.
⁹² Paris, Société nouvelle de Libraire et d'Édition, 1905.
⁹³ Same publisher and date.
⁹⁴ By H. W. Garrod in CR 20 (1906), p. 274-8.
⁹⁵ *P. Papini Stati Thebais* (Leipzig, Teubner, 1910).
⁹⁶ *Statius* by J. H. Mozley (two volumes).
⁹⁷ Zutphen, Nauta, 1934.
⁹⁸ *P. Papini Stati de Opheltes funere carmen epicum.*
⁹⁹ Leipzig, Teubner, 1902.
¹⁰⁰ Oxford, The Clarendon Press, 1906.
¹⁰¹ *P, Papinio Stazio, l'Achilleide* (Firenze, Barbera, 1950). O. A. W. Dilke's *Statius: Achilleid* (Cambridge, The University Press, 1954), though furnished with notes which are sometimes pedantic and unimaginative, is a most welcome addition to Statian studies. The introduction is good and there is a most copious *apparatus*.
Recent work on Statius includes a series of sensible and penetrating notes on the *Silvae, Achilleid*, and *Thebaid* by A. Ker. These are mainly concerned with punctuation and choice of lections, and are to be found in CQ NS 3 pp. 1-10 and 175-82.
¹⁰² By M. Durry in REL 28 (1950), 401-2.
¹⁰³ Leipzig, Teubner, 1890 (two volumes).
¹⁰⁴ Journal of Philology 24 (1896), p. 188-211.
¹⁰⁵ Fasc. iv, 1904.
¹⁰⁶ London, Heinemann (two volumes).
¹⁰⁷ CR 49 (1935), pp. 216-17.
¹⁰⁸ CR 50 (1936), p. 56.
¹⁰⁹ Oxford, Blackwell, 1936.
¹¹⁰ Duff gives strong support to this view (*Silius*, vol. I, pp. xii-xiii).
¹¹¹ Oxford, The Clarendon Press.
¹¹² Fasc. iii, 1900.
¹¹³ Oxford, The Clarendon Press, 1903 (2nd ed. 1908).
¹¹⁴ CR 17 (1903), pp. 389-94.
¹¹⁵ Berlin, Weidmann, 1910.
¹¹⁶ Paris, Les Belles Lettres, 1918.
¹¹⁷ Paris, Les Belles Lettres, 1921.

[118] Dublin, Hodges, Figgis & Co., 1901.
[119] London, Heinemann, 1918.
[120] Oxford, Blackwell, 1930.
[121] Paris, Les Belles Lettres, 1920.
[122] Munich, Heimeran, 1950.
[123] Naples, Armanni, 1950.
[124] Oxford, The Clarendon Press, 1903.
[125] CR 39 (1925), p. 199.
[126] Fasc. v, 1905.
[127] Leipzig, Teubner, 1925.
[128] CR 39 (1925), p. 199.
[129] London, Heinemann, 1919-20 (two volumes).
[130] CR 34 (1920), pp. 176-7.
[131] Paris, Les Belles Lettres, 1931-33 (two volumes).
[132] Cambridge, The University Press, 1924.
[133] Stuttgart, Kohlhammer, 1928.
[134] Palermo, Trimarchi, 1938.
[135] Stuttgart-Berlin, Kohlhammer, 1934.
[136] H. J. Wilson in AJPh 19 (1898), pp. 193-209.
[137] *D. Iunii Iuuenalis Saturae XIV* (Cambridge, The University Press, 1898).
[138] *D. Iunii Iuuenalis saturarum libri V* (New York, The Johns Hopkins University Publishing Co., 1903).
[139] CR 17 (1903), pp. 465-8.
[140] *D. Iunii Iuuenalis Saturae* (London, Grant Richards, 1905), p. xxix.
[141] *op. cit.*, note 115.
[142] *Iuuenalis*, p. xxix.
[143] CR 50 (1936) Notes and News, p. 50.
[144] Berlin, Ebering, 1926.
[145] *D. Junius Juvenalis: Saturae* (München, Hueber, 1950).
[146] Lund, Ohlsson, 1939.
[147] *op. cit.*, p. xii.
[148] *Ibid.*, p. xxx. See also the Preface (p. xxxvii) of the 1931 edition: 'Its actual contribution to learning is of less interest than its character as the memorial of an epoch.'
[149] Ghent, Van Goethem, 1913.
[150] CR 40 (1926), pp. 170-1.
[151] Gnomon 9 (1933), pp. 242-52, esp. 247.
[152] Leipzig, Teubner, 1931.
[153] *D. Iunii Iuvenalis satirae* (Turin, Paravia, 1935).
[154] Philologus, Suppbd., 33 (1940), p. 1ff.
[155] Gnomon 24 (1952), p. 328.
[156] See note 145.
[157] *op. cit.*, p. xxxvi.

It is gratifying to be able to report that in the Jubilee Year of the Classical Association there has appeared a large-scale work of scholarship devoted to the greatest of the Silver Latin poets. I refer to Professor Gilbert Highet's study entitled *Juvenal The Satirist* (Oxford, The University Press, 1954). This book I have not as yet seen myself, but the lively erudition of its energetic author is a guarantee that though its conclusions may not win universal approval, it is a book to provoke serious thought. And let us hope its auspicious appearance may stimulate the production of further studies on the poets of the Silver Age.

APPENDIX TO CHAPTER XIV

THE past twelve years have seen much activity by scholars working in the field of Silver Latin poetry, and there is no lack of evidence that this interest will continue. The published lists of work in progress for higher degrees show clearly that there exists a useful reserve-force of younger Latinists, though the cynic is probably right in suspecting that greater co-ordination between researchers would bring faster and better results. Two men who did much to promote Silver Latin studies and whose loss many of us felt personally have died since *Fifty Years* appeared; Robert Getty was a man of great kindness and immense industry; the *uiridis senecta* of the ebullient Petrus Enk seemed incapable of destruction. The number of relevant periodicals has grown and casualties have been few. From Texas came *Arion* to shatter our complaisance and to suggest that we deny ourselves the scholarly luxury of multilingual footnotes; to the *succés de scandale* it achieved I shall refer later. The appearance of the first volume of *Lustrum* in 1956 was an event of major importance. Published in Göttingen with support from UNESCO, it contained a most valuable account by Rudolf Helm of work done on post-Augustan secular poets (with named exceptions) between the years 1925 and 1942. The second volume (1957) concluded this massive survey. An international team of specialists will keep classicists abreast of important developments in various aspects of classical antiquity. In the series entitled *Studies in Latin Literature and Its Influence* two fresh volumes are in active preparation; the first, *Silver Latin of the Neronian Age*, is edited by D. R. Dudley; T. A. Dorey, his colleague, will be responsible for *Silver Latin II*, in which different authors will write *inter alia* on post-Neronian epic. There is still in my opinion a great need for a major work in English on Silver Latin epic from the pen of a scholar who treads as surely in the well-mapped but difficult terrain of the *Aeneid* and the *Metamorphoses* as in the obscure and treacherous paths of the *Thebaid* and the *Argonautica*. And many university teachers of Latin literature would express their gratitude if the good work done by O. A. W. Dilke on Lucan and Statius could be matched by corresponding editions of Valerius and Silius. One requires the selfless co-operation of a generous scholar and an altruistic publisher; for such a volume promises neither glory to the editor nor profit to the press.

In the observations which follow, my intention has been to give some idea to the non-specialist of the kind of work which has been done on the authors of our period. The expert can negotiate the labyrinth without my modest clue. Severe limitations of time and space have forced me to be selective. If the selection by its sins of omission or commission gives offence, let the injured party ascribe it to my carelessness, obtuseness or ignorance, but not to animus. I have quoted in the main articles in English, since this seemed the most sensible way of limiting the vast subject. Moreover I have occasionally referred to more general articles, for the pullulation of scholarly annotations is no automatic guarantee that an original mind is here at work.

The final volume of the Loeb Columella appeared in 1955, recension and translation being the work of E. M. Forster and E. H. Heffner; this completes the *De Re Rustica*, and concerns us only because the tenth book discusses gardens in didactic hexameters.[1] The translation gains little by being in blank verse; there are short explanatory notes. In 1961 F. R. D. Goodyear published some textual 'Notes on the "Aetna" ';[2] in 1965 his full edition of the poem[3] became the second volume in the new series 'Cambridge Classical Texts and Commentaries'. It is a work of good judgment and sound scholarship.

Petronius continues to attract attention. Books by H. Schmeck[4] and G. Bagnani[5] came out in 1954 and were shrewdly reviewed by R. Browning.[6] A. F. Sochatoff has written on 'Stephanus and the text of Petronius' *Bellum Civile*'.[7] He has also considered afresh the purpose of the *Bellum Civile* and decided that Petronius chose to attack the conditions which he believed partly responsible for the literary decline he lamented and for the prominence of the rhetorical theories to which he was strongly opposed.[8] The well-known hexameters beginning *Somnia quae mentes ludunt volitantibus umbris* (Petronius, Fr. 30(31) = 121 *P.L.M.*) are investigated for their symbolical content by H. Musurillo.[9] W. Arrowsmith's translation of *The Satyricon of Petronius*[10] I have not read; but I have read the versions of Fr. 28 (= 101 *P.L.M.*), *Foeda est in coitu et brevis voluptas*, by eight hands (including Ben Jonson, Helen Waddell, Jack Lindsay and J. P. Sullivan) in

Arion, and cannot fault the editors in awarding the palm to the worthy Ben.[11]

Persius is a forbidding author, whose crabbed and enigmatic thoughts daunt even the boldest researcher. N. Scivoletto and W. V. Clausen offer us new editions of the *Satires*.[12] The latter's Oxford Classical Text (1959), containing Persius and Juvenal, replaces that of S. G. Owen.[13] More views on the famous Choliambi are expressed by E. Paratore[14] and E. C. Witke.[15] D. Henss in 'Die Imitationstechnik des Persius'[16] cites Horace, Virgil and Ovid. W. H. Semple offers a graceful tribute to the Stoic satirist.[17] H. Hommel's article 'Die Frühwerke des Persius'[18] tackles the notorious crux †*vescio et opericon*† in the *Vita*, and suggests it conceals a reference to a *liber* ἀποριῶν, giving examples of this rhetorical figure (ἀπορία = διαπόρησις = *dubitatio*) from Persius. The indefatigable Clausen looks again at Sabinus' MS.[19]

Turning now to the Silver Latin epic poets I shall view them not in chronological sequence but in ascending order of the amount of scholarly incense burning on their shrines. Silius' temple is not thronged, but some of the offerings are good. I enjoyed E. L. Bassett's 'Regulus and the Serpent in the *Punica*'.[20] D. R. Shackleton Bailey in 'Siliana'[21] presents with his unique blend of learning and forthrightness several conjectures. F. Tietze examines the description of the Rhone in *Punica* 3, 444-65 and compares the use of *extrahit* (448) with the Greek ἐκτείνειν.[22] M. V. T. Wallace's 'The Architecture of the *Punica*: a hypothesis'[23] describes the work as 'a diptych of two parallel panels of epic proportions'. Silius, he contends, either wrote or intended an epic of 18 books, perhaps to match Ennius' *Annals*.

It is surprising that comparatively few Latinists rise to the attractive bait of Valerius Flaccus. When they do, it is mostly to approach closer to a satisfactory text — a laudable goal. W. M. Edwards[24] and J. D. P. Bolton[25] offer short textual notes. K. Stiewe's contribution, '*invideo* (Val. Fl. 5, 507)',[26] suggests that *invidere* in this passage means 'neidisch unterbrechen'. Mary Smallwood believes that the invocation to Vespasian (I, 5-21) is a grossly exaggerated picture of the part played by Vespasian in Claudius' campaigns in Britain.[27] E. Courtney has written three important and persuasive articles on the text of the *Argonautica*, giving us some very interesting emendations.[28] R. W. Garson's examination of the episodic structure in Valerius, his use of sources, his characterization, and his appeals to the emotions of his readers, is a useful and attractive contribution.[29] E. Merone's 'Sulla Lingua di Valerio Flacco'[30] I cannot admit to having read.

It will be convenient to consider Statius' *Silvae* before moving to his epics. In 1961 appeared the new Teubner *Silvae* edited by A. Marastoni[31] which A. J. Gossage in his review[32] praises for the real attempt made to recover the MS tradition. Among those contributing notes on the *Silvae* are J. H. Bishop[33] and D. F. S. Thomson.[34] The latter's *cocunt* for *colunt* in the hendecasyllables to Plotius Grypus (IV. ix. 13 – where Heinsius had offered *olent*) is exceptionally neat. A. Wasserstein in 'The Manuscript Tradition of Statius' *Silvae*'[35] makes a strong reply to P. Thielscher. Articles on the subject-matter of the *Silvae* include E. Erkell's 'Statius' "Silvae" und das Templum gentis Flaviae',[36] V. Buchheit's 'Statius' Geburtstagsgedicht zu Ehren Lucans'[37] (*Silvae* II. vii is an irresistible magnet), and P. R. C. Weaver's 'The Father of Claudius Etruscus: Statius, *Silvae* 3.3'[38] (a careful study of his career). Cornelia C. Coulter's 'Statius, *Silvae* V. 4 and Fiammetta's Prayer to Sleep'[39] traces the resemblances between the Latin poem 'Somnus' and Boccaccio's *Elegia di Madonna Fiammetta*.

O. A. W. Dilke's edition of the *Achilleis* (1953) has been favourably and intelligently reviewed by R. J. Getty,[40] R. T. Bruère[41] and R. Browning.[42] Dilke has also written on 'The Value of the *Puteaneus* of Statius'[43] (the 9th Century MS containing the *Thebaid* and the *Achilleid*) and, in '*Magnus Achilles* and Statian Baroque',[44] on the means employed by the poet to render more impressive the somewhat girlish Achilles.

H. M. Mulder, a pupil of P. J. Enk, has put readers of the *Thebaid* (Enk always insisted on *Thebais*!) in his debt by his Latin commentary on Book 2,[45] lucid, learned and packed with sensible observations. The reviews by R. J. Getty[46] and J. H. Bishop[47] are most helpful. Miscellaneous notes on the *Thebaid* have been contributed by — *inter alios* — J. B. Poynton[48] (on ten passages), G. G. Betts[49] (on I. 72), E. W. Bower[50] (on I. 138), A. J. Gossage[51] (on V. 593) and H. H. Huxley[52] (on X. 935-9). W. Schetter, in 'Die Einheit des Thebais prooemium von Statius',[53] has written learnedly on the unity of that incredible epic prelude which the critic who said *quid dignum tanto feret hic promissor*

APPENDIX 519

hiatu?[54] was born too early to savour. In the Festschrift for P. J. Enk, *Ut Pictura Poesis*,[55] H. M. Mulder considers the relations between gods, men and the fates in the *Achilleid*; the same volume contains contributions on the *Silvae* from J. F. Lockwood and H. Wagenvoort.[56]

Lucan undoubtedly is the most popular post-Augustan epicist among scholars. New editions have appeared, Book I having been competently handled by P. Wuilleumier and H. Le Bonniec,[57] while J. P. Postgate's familiar *Lucan VII* has been given an attractive new look by O. A. W. Dilke,[58] with the notes brought up to date and two fine maps drawn by Mrs. Dilke. So the seeds I hopefully planted in *Fifty Years* (p. 421) did not all fall on stony ground. From what I have already seen I look forward to reading the full text of Mark P. O. Morford's forthcoming *The Poet Lucan: Studies in Rhetorical Epic* (Basil Blackwell, Oxford). In H. P. Syndikos' 'Lucans Gedicht vom Bürgerkrieg',[59] a doctoral thesis printed privately, we have a sound if not very inspiring piece of work. Jacqueline Brisset's *Les Idées politiques de Lucain*[60] is less successful, a pudding with far too many plums. Robert Graves' Penguin *Lucan*[61] contains a disappointing translation and a — to me — infuriating introduction. O. A. W. Dilke's inaugural lecture at Grahamstown was, predictably, on *Lucan, Poet of Freedom*.[62] Of the utmost importance is W. Rutz's survey in *Lustrum*, Vol. 9 (243-334) of research on Lucan between 1943 and 1963. The items listed by me constitute a tiny sample personally selected. Efforts to improve and explain the text by emendation, transposition, positing of anacoloutha and other means continue unabated. In this vineyard labour many doughty workers, among them A. Ernout, M. Erren, A. Hudson-Williams, L. A. MacKay and C. W. Whitaker.[63] R. T. Bruère has written three articles most usefully connecting Lucan with Virgil (the Helen episode), with Claudian (*In Rufinum, In Eutropium* and *De Bello Gildonico*) and with Petrarch (major Lucanian reminiscences in the *Africa*).[64] Space precludes the mention of more than a few general items; R. J. Getty has applied — *utinam ne fecisset* — the Golden Mean ratio to Lucan;[65] S. J. Bonner's 'Lucan and the Declamation Schools' is a mine of information and acute comment;[65a] W. Rutz discusses Pompey's dreams,[66] O. Schönberger Lucan's leitmotivs,[67] V. Buchheit the first-hand testimony of *Silvae* II. vii. for the non-completion of the epic,[68] M. Rambaud the defence of Pompey in Book 7,[69] and P. Grimal the praise of Nero in Book I.[70]

Work done on Martial has not been excessive. L. Herrmann's article, 'Le "livre des spectacles" de Martial',[71] sets out interpretations and conjectures. A. Hudson-Williams cleverly suggests *togulis* for the corrupt *Getulis* in *Spect.* IV. I. 4.[72] H. H. Huxley re-interprets Martial, IV. iv, an aeschrological poem.[73] A. Nordh writes soundly on 'Historical exempla in Martial'.[74] Martial's relations to earlier poets are considered by G. Donini (in 'Martial I. 69: Horatius in Martiale')[75] and J. Ferguson (in 'Catullus and Martial').[76] W. H. Semple addresses the general reader in a printed lecture, 'The Poet Martial'.[77] Two curious numbers of *Arion*[78] provide verse-translations of some of the epigrams; the poets are R. A. Swanson, P. Murray, M. W. M. Pope and J. P. Sullivan. Here is one example, Martial III, 35 by P. Murray — 'These fish were carved by Phidias; / Add water and they will swim'. As Housman said of a luckless conjecture, 'Better one than two!'.

Finally — Juvenal. *Quando uberior librorum copia?* Satire 17 on 'The Cult of Myself' will contain far better lines than *Quae scribas quaerit nemo, sed scribere oportet.* Several books call for notice. Wendell Clausen, the first U.S. citizen to edit an Oxford Classical Text, has done a noble service to Latinists through his edition of Juvenal and Persius;[79] A. Serafini, the author of *Studio sulla satira di Giovenale*,[80] scarcely so much, for his critical faculty is not always sure. W. S. Anderson's *Anger in Juvenal and Seneca*[81] labels Juvenal as 'a Democritean satirist' and overstresses the influence on him of such works as Seneca's *De Ira*. A modest 7/6 will buy an Oxford Paperback of G. Highet's controversial study, *Juvenal The Satirist*.[82] Even if we call it, as one reviewer did, 'a disappointingly uncritical handbook', it is still, for the general reader at least, a great bargain. Certainly it has proved no mean catalyst. Rolfe Humphries has done a verse translation of Juvenal[83] which has provoked the epithets 'Brechtian and undignified'.[84] W. S. Anderson's study, 'Juvenal and Quintilian'[85] runs to 91 pages. Interesting articles which take in more than a single satire include E. J. Kenney's 'Juvenal: Satirist or Rhetorician',[86] Sister Stella Marie's 'Prudentius and Juvenal',[87] W. S. Anderson's 'Studies in Book I of Juvenal',[88] his 'Imagery in the Satires of Horace and Juvenal'[89] and his article 'The

APPENDIX 521

Programs of Juvenal's later books',[90] and D. Wiesen's 'Juvenal's moral character'.[91] Meanwhile there is no lack of enthusiasm for textual criticism; fresh salves are continually applied to old wounds or the apparent illness may be declared to be imaginary. Here I mention the treatment given by W. Clausen[92] (though I prefer A. T. von S. Bradshaw's explanation of *glacie aspersus maculis Tiberinus*, Juv. V. 104),[93] E. W. Bower[94] (*erectas* in IV. 128 refers to the turbot's dorsal fins which 'proceed in an upwards direction'), J. G. Griffith[95] (retain *a grandi* in XII. 14) and L. A. MacKay.[96] Though many other scholars have shed light on dark places in the *Satires*, space permits only a brief reference to a group of articles treating in the main the form and structure of single poems. W. C. Helmbold and E. N. O'Neil have examined 'The structure of Juvenal IV'[97] and 'The form and purpose of Juvenal's Seventh *Satire*',[98] Helmbold has reconsidered 'Juvenal's Twelfth *Satire*'[99] and O'Neil 'The structure of Juvenal's Fourteenth *Satire*',[100] finding the key to it in the double meaning of *avaritia* (as a passive vice (miserliness) and an active vice (greediness)). W. S. Anderson's 'Juvenal 6: a problem in structure'[101] has been countered by E. C. Courtney's 'Vivat ludatque cinaedus',[102] while J. G. Griffith in 'The Survival of the longer of the so-called "Oxford" Fragments of Juvenal's Sixth Satire',[103] has intrigued us with 'an excursion into the less savoury side of Roman Imperial society'. G. Lawall has looked into '*Exempla* and theme in Juvenal's Tenth Satire',[104] and D. E. Eichholz has revealed 'The Art of Juvenal in his Tenth Satire'.[105]

In the twelve years since *Fifty Years* first appeared much good work has been done in the elucidation of Silver Latin poetry, though perhaps too much attention has been paid to too few authors. One wishes that more scholars could echo Lucretius' boast:

> *avia Pieridum peragro loca nullius ante*
> *trita solo.*

---

[1] *Columella III: De Re Rustica X-XII* (London, Heinemann, 1955); see C. J. Fordyce's review in CR NS 7 (1957), 130-2.
[2] Proceedings of the Cambridge Philological Society, NS 7 (1961), 18-20.
[3] *Aetna*, edited with an Introduction and Commentary, F. R. D. Goodyear (CUP, 1965).
[4] Helmut Schmeck, Petronii *Cena Trimalchionis* (Heidelberg, 1954).
[5] G. Bagnani, *Arbiter of Elegance: A Study of the Life and Works of C. Petronius* (Toronto & London, 1954).
[6] CR NS 6 (1956), 44 and 45-7.
[7] TAPA 94 (1963), 281-92.

[8] TAPA 93 (1962), 449-58.
[9] CPh (1958), 108-10.
[10] Mentor Paperbacks, M493D.
[11] *Arion* 2 (1963), 82-4.
[12] Nino Scivoletto, *Auli Persi Flacci Saturae* (Florence, 1956); W. V. Clausen, *A. Persi Flacci, Saturarum liber* (OUP, 1956).
[13] W. V. Clausen, *A. Persi Flacci et D. Iuni Iuuenalis saturae* (OUP 1959).
[14] Latomus 23 (1964), 685-712 'L'ultimo verso dei "choliambi" di Persio'.
[15] Mn Series IV 15 (1962), 153-8, 'The Function of Persius' Choliambics'.
[16] Phil 99 (1955), 277-94.
[17] BRL 44 (1962).
[18] Phil 99 (1955), 266-76.
[19] Hermes 91 (1963), 252-6.
[20] CPh 50 (1955), 1-20.
[21] CQ NS 9 (1959), 173-80.
[22] MH II (1954), 41-43, 'Zur Rhone-Schilderung bei Silius'.
[23] CPh 53 (1958), 99-102.
[24] CR NS 4 (1954), 9-10, 'Valerius Flaccus VI 239-42'.
[25] CR NS 7 (1957), 104-6, 'Notes on Valerius Flaccus'.
[26] MH 13 (1956), 169-72.
[27] Mn Series IV 15 (1962), 170-2, 'Valerius Flaccus, *Argonautica* I.5-21: a problem raised by the invocation to Vespasian'.
[28] CR NS 11 (1961), 106 ff.; CR NS 12 (1962), 115-18; CR NS 15 (1965), 151-5.
[29] CQ NS 14 (1964), 267-79 and CQ NS 15 (1965), 104-20.
[30] Published by Armanni, Naples, 1957.
[31] *P. Papini Stati Silvae* (Leipzig, Teubner, 1961).
[32] CR NS 12 (1962), 214-16.
[33] CR NS 4 (1954), 95-7, 'Two notes on Statius, *Silvae*, IV. 1.'
[34] Phoenix 18 (1964), 'A Note on Statius, *Silvae*, 4.9.13', 37-8.
[35] CQ NS 8 (1958), 111-12 answering P. Thielscher in CQ NS 7 (1957), 47-52.
[36] Er 56 (1958), 173-82.
[37] Hermes 88 (1960), 231-49.
[38] CQ NS 15 (1965), 145-54.
[39] AJP 80 (1959), 390-5.
[40] AJP 78 (1957), 97-101.
[41] CPh 51 (1956), 206-7.
[42] CR NS 5 (1955), 281-3.
[43] Acta Classica 5 (1962), 58-63.
[44] Latomus 22 (1963), 498-503.
[45] *Publii Papinii Statii Thebaidos Liber Secundus* (Groningen, 1954). Mention should also be made of R. Ten Kate's useful book, *Quomodo Heroes In Statii Thebaide Describantur Quaeritur* (Groningen, Wolters, 1955). He too is Enk's pupil.
[46] AJP 78 (1957).
[47] CR NS 5 (1955), 283-5.
[48] CR NS 13 (1963), 259-61.
[49] Mn Series IV 15, 44.
[50] CR NS 8 (1958), 9-11.
[51] CR NS 12 (1962), 114-5.
[52] CPh (1961), 253-4.
[53] MH 19 (1962), 204-17.
[54] Hor., *Ars Poet.* 138.
[55] E. J. Brill, Leiden, 1955.
[56] 'Fata Vetant', 119-28; J. F. Lockwood, 'Note on Statius, *Silvae* 4.4', 107-11; H. Wagenvoort, 'Ad Stati *Silv. I. i.* adnotationes', 195-203.
[57] *Bellum Ciuile, Liber Primus* (Presses Universitaires de France, Paris, 1962).
[58] *De Bello Civili VII* (CUP, 1960); see Bruère in CPh 56 (1961), 69-70.
[59] Munich, 1958; see E. J. Kenney in CR NS 10 (1960), 139-40.
[60] Paris, 1964.
[61] *Lucan: Pharsalia: Dramatic Episodes of the Civil Wars* (Penguin Classics, Harmondsworth, 1956).

APPENDIX 523

[62] Grahamstown, Rhodes University, 1961.
[63] A. Ernout, 'Lucain: *Bellum Civile*, I, 8-12' (RPh 37 (1963), 186-8); M. Erren, Hermes, 91 (1963), 74-103, 'Elf Lukanverse' (vii. 510-20); A. Hudson-Williams, 'Notes on Lucan, Book 7' (CQ NS 4 1954, 187-93); L. A. MacKay, 'Lucan I. 280-5' (AJP 79 (1958), 183-7); C. W. Whitaker, 'Lucan and the Loire' (Mn Series IV 9 (1956), 320-4.
[64] CPh 59 (1964), 267-8, 'The Helen Episode in *Aeneid* 2 and Lucan'; ibid. 223-56, 'Lucan and Claudian: the Invectives; CPh 56 (1961), 83-99, 'Lucan and Petrarch's *Africa*'.
[65] TAPA 91 (1960), 310-23, 'Neopythagoreanism and Mathematical Symmetry in Lucan, *De bello civili I*'.
[65a] AJP 87 (1966), 257-89.
[66] Hermes, 91 (1963), 334-45, 'Die Träume des Pompeius in Lucans *Pharsalia*'.
[67] RhM NF 103 (1960), 81-90, 'Leitmotivisch wiederholte Bilder bei Lucan'.
[68] RhM NF 104 (1961), 362 ff. 'Lucans *Pharsalia* und die Frage der Nichtvollendung'.
[69] REL 33 (1955), 258-96, 'L'Apologie de Pompée par Lucain au Livre VII de la *Pharsale*.'
[70] REL 38 (1960), 296-305, 'L'éloge de Néron au debut de la *Pharsale* est-il ironique?'
[71] Latomus 21 (1962), 494-504.
[72] CQ NS 4 (1954), 170.
[73] Latomus 24 (1965), 647-8.
[74] Er 52 (1954), 224-38.
[75] AJP 85 (1964), 56-60.
[76] Proc. Afr. Class. Assoc. 6 (1963), 3-15.
[77] BRL 42 (1960), 432-52.
[78] Arion 2 (1963), No. 2, 54, 122, 75-9 (= 'Fourteen from Martial'); ibid. No. 4, 61.
[79] *A. Persi Flacci et D. Iuni Iuuenalis saturae edidit W. V. Clausen* (OUP, 1959); see W. C. Helmbold in CP 56 (1961).
[80] Florence, 1957; see E. J. Kenney in CR NS 8 (1958), 254-6.
[81] Berkeley, 1964; see M. Coffey in CR NS 15 (1965), 299-301.
[82] Oxford Paperbacks, No. 40; First Edition (hard covers), OUP 1954.
[83] *The Satires of Juvenal* (Bloomington, Indiana, 1958).
[84] W. Frost in CPh 55 (1960), 144-6.
[85] YClS 17 (1961), 3-93.
[86] Latomus 22 (1963), 704-20.
[87] Phoenix 16 (1962), 41-52.
[88] YClS 15 (1957), 33-90.
[89] AJP 81 (1960), 225-60.
[90] CPh 57 (1962), 145-60.
[91] Latomus 22 (1963), 440-71.
[92] AJP 76 (1955), 47-62; in Juv. V. 104 Clausen reads *aut glaucis sparsus maculis*. *Silva Coniecturarum* discusses also II. 133 and XI. 106-7.
[93] CQ NS 15 (1965), 121-5. 'Glacie aspersus maculis: Juv. 5. 104'; the fish suffered from a fungus disease, saprolegnia or 'scab', possibly contracted while wintering in the Tiber near a sewage outfall. Retain the text.
[94] CR NS 8 (1958), 9-11, 'Notes on Juvenal and Statius'.
[95] CR NS 10 (1960), 189-92 'A Gerundive in Juvenal'.
[96] CPh 53 (1958), 236-40, 'Notes on Juvenal'.
[97] AJP 77 (1956), 68-73.
[98] CPh 54 (1959), 100-8.
[99] CPh 51 (1956), 14-23.
[100] CPh 55 (1960), 251-3.
[101] CPh 51 (1956), 73-94.
[102] Mn Series IV 15 (1962), 262-6.
[103] Hermes 91 (1963), 104-14.
[104] TAPA 89 (1958), 25-31.
[105] G & R 2nd Series 3 (1956), 61-9.

CHAPTER XIII

THE ROMAN HISTORIANS

BY A. H. MCDONALD

IN the study of the Roman historians during the last fifty years we may distinguish three major trends. First, historical analysis has developed the methods of Mommsen in treating their subject-matter; secondly, literary criticism has applied the conventions of Roman rhetoric and Hellenistic historiography to examination of their style; and thirdly, increasing interest in Roman ideas has led to discussion of their standards of historical judgment. We shall describe these trends in general terms and then survey the research on the individual historians; finally, since scholars on one side have tended to ignore those on another, we may consider how best to combine the results of their work.[1]

At the beginning of our period the figure of Theodor Mommsen, as he himself said of Polybius, shone like a sun in the field of Roman studies. In history and law, in language and texts, in numismatics and epigraphy he illuminated everything he touched, and his work shed its influence over the critical study of the Roman historians. We may place it in the perspective of the great developments in historical technique that mark the nineteenth century. Not to judge the past nor to instruct ourselves for the future, but to reconstruct the history of a period as it specifically occurred — this, Ranke argued, was the function of the historian. It involved the analysis of traditions, the sifting of evidence, and the correction of tendentiousness, after which one set aside what was demonstrably false — and those guilty of the falsification — and built upon what remained. This procedure had already been taken up by critics of early Roman history starting with Niebuhr; Mommsen established it fully with accurate methods of scholarship and broad scope in knowledge and interpretation.[2]

It is important to appreciate the contribution which Mommsen and his disciples have made to the study of the Roman historians. Who can criticize a historical narrative without independent knowledge of its subject-matter? We dare not discuss historical ideas or literary motives unless we have control of the material to which they were applied. Mommsen may have done his work with other ends in view, but his results throw light upon his historical authorities. Indeed, every major history and much of the detailed historical research carried out during our period must be regarded as indispensable to proper understanding of the Roman historical tradition and its literary representatives. And when in the course of their reconstruction of events the practising historians have to analyse the narrative of their Roman authorities, they bring a full command of the material to the task.

The historical approach did not exclude literary treatment. In textual matters — for a historian is worth little unless we have an authoritative text — a sound apparatus of scholarship was set up last century, and the work has continued to the present. We need only mention the Teubner, Oxford, Budé, Paravian, and Loeb texts, H. Peter's edition of the fragments, and the numerous commentaries which have gathered up the fruits of research. Here and in separate studies of language and grammar we find abundant material for stylistic examination of the Roman historians.[3]

Yet Mommsen's influence limited the study of the Roman historians. They emerged from the strict historical analysis with tarnished reputations, and lost standing as subjects for serious appreciation. Great scholars like Eduard Meyer, J. B. Bury and G. De Sanctis might take up the problems of historiography; but for the most part historical critics kept to factual discussion, literary critics applied narrow stylistic standards, and the Roman historians suffered from the fatal specialization. Perhaps Mommsen's personal prejudices also affected scholarly opinion; for his devastating attack on Cicero brought a fine Roman humanist into contempt and may have discouraged treatment of the historians as representatives of Roman thought. In any event, we have to look beyond Mommsen and the historical school for light on the character of Roman historiography.[4]

Coming to the literary criticism of our period we may begin with rhetoric, which in theory and in practice dominated Roman writing. Among the Roman historians, as we shall see, H. Taine found Livy's chief excellence in his rhetorical composition, and R. Ullmann examined the structure of the speeches in Sallust, Livy and Tacitus.[5] This work is valuable, as far as it goes; yet it touches only part of the problem. Rhetoric in Roman historiography covered the entire process of arranging and presenting material, nor was rhetoric the only literary influence. We are now able to consider a fresh development that is of great importance for the understanding of the Roman historians.

When F. Susemihl compiled his handbook of Alexandrian literature in 1890/1, there was little appreciation of Hellenistic civilization, and few saw the significance of Hellenistic influence on Roman literature. Since then, thanks to the help of epigraphy and papyrology, the situation has changed completely. Some of the best modern historians have devoted themselves to Hellenistic history, and on the literary side U. von Wilamowitz-Möllendorff exercised an influence comparable with that of Mommsen. Among the literary critics we may note especially E. Schwartz, R. Reitzenstein, and F. Jacoby, whose work is indispensable to the study of Hellenistic historiography.[6] From the Hellenistic historians the Romans learned literary techniques which they proceeded to employ independently in their own work, and we have to outline the character of the three main influences.

First, the rhetorical methods, deriving their inspiration from the teaching of Isocrates and later associated with the style of Timaeus, became popular in Rome during the Gracchan period, and Cicero accepted the 'Isocratean' canons in his judgment of historical writing. History was an *opus oratorium*, in which the historian should apply rhetorical rules to the presentation of his subject-matter. The material would normally be collected for him — in the form of memoirs — and his professional duty was to interpret the facts and describe them in formal literary fashion so as to make them easily intelligible to his reader. He must set out clearly the time and place of events. In treating memorable actions he must discuss the plans, recount their execution, and explain the results. Where prominent men appeared, he must depict their character and might enliven his account with 'characterizing' speeches. His narrative must be circumstantial, clear and concise, moving in smooth periodic style. Among the later historians Dionysius of Halicarnassus and Livy belong to this school.[7]

We find in the second place the influence of dramatic history, now (confusingly) called 'Peripatetic', because it appears to adapt Aristotle's theory of tragedy to historical exposition. If one justifies tragic drama by reference to 'catharsis' of the emotions, might this not be true for history, where the subject-matter is tragic? The historian might take his material — already prepared for him — and set it out according to dramatic conventions. Within the framework of his narrative he would develop episodes as dramatic scenes, balanced and complete, and depict the actions and feelings of his characters with vivid, affecting detail, making the reader, as it were, a spectator. The aim should be to inspire directly the emotions of pity and horror. In presentation of this kind the historian would refrain from discussion of causes and results; for objective comment spoils the illusion of the scene. Among the Greeks Duris and Phylarchus practised dramatic methods; Cicero refers to this technique as a standard form of historiography; and recent research has found evidence for its influence partly on Livy and especially on Tacitus.[8]

Two points may be noted. First, the effect of 'Isocratean' circumstantiality and 'Peripatetic' vividness may sometimes be the same, if the subject-matter is in itself tragic, e.g. an episode of brutality and passion, moving the emotions. The difference will lie in the former's analysis of motives and reactions, which the latter leaves to be felt directly. Secondly, we must not press the significance of the terms too far. There is no reason why a historian should not adapt both techniques for his own purpose. In particular, a historian who preferred the greater scope of the 'Isocratean' treatment might well refine his methods of detailed description under 'Peripatetic' influence.[9] Finally, we may ask what these professional historians would do if the material available to them did not provide the full details they needed. A memoir prepared for the use of an 'Isocratean' historian, for instance, would attempt to provide factual circumstantiality, and to this extent memoirs come under rhetorical rules for composition. But if material were lacking, the historian might press the implications of what evidence he possessed and thus achieve 'verisimilitude' in the eyes of his reader in place of factual circumstantiality. He could build up set pieces of description, e.g. for battles, meetings, and incidents of a common type, and adorn them with freely composed speeches. This technique, which appears in Livy, is found at its most banal in Dionysius of Halicarnassus. At the best it was an 'armchair' product; at the worst it seriously misrepresented the facts.

Both trends were open to more fundamental criticism. Neither the 'Isocratean' historian — for his interest in discussion was purely superficial — nor the 'Peripatetic' was concerned with the analysis of underlying causes. Here we may turn to the third main Hellenistic influence, which derived from Thucydides and was later represented by Polybius. Polybius not only stressed the need for checking facts and limiting exposition to what was soundly established; he went on to claim that only the practical man was competent to interpret history, and he set as its highest aim the analysis of events in terms that would permit valid historical generalization. The historian's scope would vary with the subject. Events that were restricted in time or place provided less evidence than did a long period or extensive action. Yet, whether one wrote a monograph or a 'universal history', the task would be the same, viz. to present a serious political treatment without concessions to purely literary effect. In Rome, after the first senatorial histories in Greek, Polybius introduced the systematic analysis of history and influenced Sempronius Asellio, while Sallust looked back to Thucydides himself.[10] Of course, strict historical method does not prevent good writing, and a training in the rhetorical or dramatic style would assist even a sober historian like Polybius in setting out his material to the best advantage. But the language of political analysis and historical generalization will rise directly out of the thought of the man who is using it, and he will be the master of his models. This introduces a personal factor into the development of style, as we find, for instance, in Sallust and Tacitus. Though the impact of Hellenistic historiography upon the Roman historians must be carefully examined, we have also to study the character of the men themselves in their own tradition.

In their historical ideas the Romans are more difficult to treat sympathetically than the Greeks. Although Thucydides and Polybius, for instance, reflect the thought of their day, they still discuss history with a dispassionate air of analysis that makes an immediate appeal. But how do we take up the harsh judgment of Sallust on the Roman Republic, the Augustan idealism of Livy, or the bitter hostility of Tacitus to the Principate? These men stand firmly on their own ground. They are Roman in tradition and attitude, lacking the wider intellectuality of the Greeks, and we may regard them as unduly preoccupied with morality, dogmatic and prejudiced. Yet we must know their standards if we are to appreciate their work. Here Cicero is important. His political thought continues the attempt of the circle of Scipio Aemilianus, including Polybius and Panaetius, to define the problems of the Roman state, and we may compare his conclusions with those of Sallust. From this angle a number of distinguished scholars have made a fresh approach to the Roman historians. After exploring the Hellenistic world R. Reitzenstein and R. Heinze returned to study the Roman way of life; J. Vogt and V. Pöschl have treated the Roman aspect of Cicero's political ideas; and F. Klingner has set Roman historiography against its background of tradition. We may note the new methods of research into the major Roman conceptions, e.g. *imperium* and *auctoritas*, *dignitas* and *libertas*, *mos maiorum* and *virtus*, *fides* and *humanitas*. One may handle these topics broadly, as H. Wagenvoort did for *imperium*, or more strictly, using the *Thesaurus Linguae Latinae*; particularly instructive is the work of R. Heinze, U. Knoche, and C. Wirzsubski. It is important to develop this technique, which moves between philology and history. After clarifying the essential meaning of the terms, we have to distinguish their special significance at different times and their application by different men, with allowance — as R. Syme and Lily Ross Taylor have shown — for their debasement in political propaganda. Then we may resume discussion of Sallust, Livy, and Tacitus with more precise understanding of the context and point of their historical ideas.[11]

The strength of tradition in Roman historiography is most conspicuous in the Annalists, whose work takes us from the second century B.C. through the Sullan period to a climax in the Augustan history of Livy. We must attempt to reconstruct the original character of the documentary material upon which they built their narrative. Presumably the Roman archives provided the basis, but the records underwent considerable editing before they reached literary form. What is the validity of the earliest information? In discussing this question, which will affect our judgment of the Annalistic tradition, we have to turn to the modern historians, especially E. Pais and K. J. Beloch, G. De Sanctis and P. Fraccaro, H. Stuart Jones and H. Last. The roll is long and distinguished, and the results, even where they differ most radically, must be carefully studied. The evidence for lists of magistrates has been conveniently collected by T. R. S. Broughton.[12]

It is also necessary to examine the rise of the literary Annalistic form and the development of its character as we find it in Livy. His narrative, it will be recalled, turns on yearly sections containing formal notices about the election of magistrates, their entry on office, the allotment of commands, and the other official business in Rome, together with news of the priestly colleges, after which we come to the accounts of events in the provinces. When Fabius Pictor wrote the first Roman history, the Pontifex Maximus was keeping records in a yearly arrangement, as *Annales*, with some day-by-day publication. Had this material already emerged as a pontifical chronicle? Did Fabius Pictor, following such a chronicle or merely referring to the records, compose his history in the same priestly form? Until recently this was the common view, represented, for instance, by W. Soltau and F. Leo, on the basis of what was taken to be evidence from Cicero. M. Gelzer, however, has argued that, if we interpret Cicero in the light of his 'Isocratean' theory, this evidence does not refer to the form of arrangement but to the lack of rhetorical elaboration. In writing to influence the Hellenistic world, Fabius Pictor and his senatorial successors composed their material freely, as Cato did when he presented his *Origines* to the Roman and Italian public, and we may refer to H. H. Scullard's treatment of the political setting.[13]

In any event the Gracchan period is important, and we have to study not only the fragments of men like Cassius Hemina and Calpurnius Piso but the signs of constitutional, legal, and antiquarian research at that time. When people are interested in their history, they demand ready information; so P. Mucius Scaevola published the pontifical records as the *Annales Maximi*. If the Annalistic form did not appear in earlier histories, we may attribute its characteristic features, official and sacral, to the arrangement of material in the *Annales Maximi*. With such weighty authority behind it, one can understand why the Annalistic subject-matter never suffered radical criticism. But one point must be borne in mind. At this time the 'Isocratean' technique of literary elaboration reached Rome, and the Annalists seem to have applied it to their material. Undoubtedly they expanded special episodes according to the rhetorical rules and added freely composed speeches. According to M. Gelzer again, they also touched up the basic Annalistic form to make it a conventional literary frame-work, adorned with the regular phraseology of constitutional and priestly formulae.[14]

Political motives played a part in the Annalistic development during the Gracchan and Sullan periods. In particular, the disputes arising from Gracchan policy coloured the description of earlier agrarian conditions; and the strife between Optimates and Populares gave point, anachronistically, to the 'struggle of the orders'. Since Sulla claimed to be refounding Rome, his historians looked for precedents as well as inspiration in the past, which they then depicted in the light of the present. Romulus, Servius Tullius, the Decemvirate, Camillus and Scipio Africanus received special attention, and constitutional matters became the object of antiquarian research. What we read in Livy may be attributed in many places to his Sullan authorities. Despite their tendentiousness we owe much of our knowledge of the Roman constitutional tradition — as set out in Mommsen's *Römisches Staatsrecht* — to their systematic accounts. The evidence for the Gracchan and Sullan Annalists is discussed by W. Soltau, U. Kahrstedt, A. Klotz and M. Gelzer. Their results may vary in value, but they have contributed to an important line of research in Roman historiography.[15]

The Annalistic tradition represents the main line of Republican history, stretching from the distant past to contemporary events. Meanwhile, the interest in contemporary history as a subject in itself had increased. Under the influence of Polybius and in opposition to the Annalists, Sempronius Asellio attacked the problems of the Gracchan and Marian periods, and Cornelius Sisenna continued his work for the Sullan period, under the influence of Cleitarchus. Coelius Antipater in describing the Second Punic War established the historical monograph as a literary genre in Rome.[16] A man who took up the interpretation of a special period could now develop his technique under the full influence of Hellenistic historiography as far as he chose to follow it — whether in the rhetorical or dramatic manner, or in the school of serious political history. It was in this literary setting that Sallust began his work.

In his *Histories* Sallust carried on the writing of contemporary history after Sisenna, while in his *Bellum Catilinae* and *Bellum Jugurthinum* he adopted the fashion of monographs. Among the schools of history his inclination was towards analysis and generalization, though he lacked neither rhetorical skill nor dramatic imagination. But was he, in fact, anything more than a brilliant propagandist? This is the prime question with which recent research on Sallust has been concerned. The case for regarding his work as direct propaganda in favour of the Populares was ably stated by E. Schwartz in analysing the *Bellum Catilinae*. At the other extreme, W. Schur made him a philosophical historian, all political passion spent, under the Stoic influence of Posidonius. In the form in which these views are argued, there appears little hope of reconciliation. F. Klingner, however, finds in Sallust's thought a broad conception of moral and political degeneration, concerned with the loss of Roman *virtus*, which could be illustrated in the episodes of Catiline and Jugurtha. It has been argued that Sallust's prologues merely served up philosophical or rhetorical commonplaces, with tendentious emphasis, and that they have no integral relationship with the narrative; but most critics agree that his generalizations have direct political relevance and dominate his full account. In fact, Sallust's chief fault is to apply too closely his impression of the underlying causes. At this point we may call in G. De Sanctis, who shows how strictly in the *Bellum Jugurthinum* Sallust imposed his generalized view upon his selection and treatment of detail. He was, in fact, a man of great strength and clarity of mind — not unfairly, in this respect, to be compared with Thucydides — and certainly, at the worst, he was no ordinary propagandist.[17] In judging Sallust's historical standpoint, it should be noted, we must pay attention equally to the current opinion among the Populares and to his personal conception of Roman society. In this connection we have to decide how far it is permissible to use the two *Epistulae ad Caesarem* and the *Invectiva in Ciceronem* as evidence for the development of his thought.[18]

The study of Sallust's style raises questions of peculiar interest not only for its literary quality but for the light it may throw upon his mind and temperament. Anyone writing with a dominant conception of a period and visualizing strongly the men and events in it will tend to dramatize his narrative. Sallust's procedure is dramatic — it has even been (falsely) called 'Peripatetic' — but his motives were more than literary. He composed in clear episodes so as to project his view of the underlying causes upon his account, and he wrote in a severe style to intensify the effect. Most significant is the influence upon him of Thucydides and Cato — both men close to Sallust's way of thought — and he consciously developed an aggressiveness of phraseology and syntax which produces a striking individual effect. We may turn to W. Kroll and K. Latte for an appreciation of Sallust's style as the man.[19]

We have so far been concerned — in the Annalists and Sallust — with the literary presentation and political interpretation of history in a fully developed narrative. Where does the preliminary preparation of material fit in the historiographical scheme? Memoirs are important, and even Cicero with his rhetorical standards of judgment recognized the literary excellence of Caesar's *Commentarii*. A. Klotz regarded personal *commentarii* as an adaptation of Hellenistic ὑπομνήματα, which 'Isocratean' theory treated as the raw material of history. H. Oppermann, however, has shown that the question is more complex. Primary information about Roman events could come from two sources: first, the official records of legislation and the reports from governors and generals which, after being read to the Senate, were placed in the archives; secondly, the personal accounts which the same men might draft in order to influence a wider circle. The official documents, indeed, were the raw material of history. The memoirs, on the other hand, as Lucian explains, might enlarge upon and discuss the official data, providing their subject-matter in a more advanced state of preparation for the professional historian to elaborate in full literary style — and they might be published immediately for a special purpose. F. Bömer has recently stressed the Roman character of both official and personal *commentarii*; but we must not underestimate the influence of the ὑπομνήματα on the literary composition of the latter. From the second century B.C. we have 'letters' of Scipio Africanus and Scipio Nasica Corculum. Aemilius Scaurus, Rutilius Rufus, Catulus, and Sulla himself published full-dress memoirs; and Cicero worked up material on his consulship. When Caesar wrote his *Commentarii* he was following a recognized political and literary convention.[20]

Reading Caesar's *Commentarii* simply as the memoirs of a soldier, we may refer in particular to the work of T. Rice Holmes. Yet we immediately encounter wider questions. Caesar was not only a general but a politician who had a past and desired a future. If the *Gallic War* aimed at defending his Gallic proconsulship against the attacks of Cato, if the *Civil War* opened as a justification of his move against Pompey and the Senate, or even if he wrote with no more than a sensitive feeling for the political implication of his account, how far would such tendentiousness affect the historical truth of his work? The question is treated in the general histories of the period and in the biographies of Caesar. We shall mention only the detailed studies, which range from the scepticism of P. Huber and C. E. Stevens to the more sympathetic criticism of T. Rice Holmes, H. Oppermann and N. J. De Witt.[21] In the end, however, we must apply to Caesar's narrative an analysis as subtle as Caesar's composition, and this will involve close literary examination.

Did Caesar write the *Gallic War* as a whole work in 51 B.C., as Mommsen and Rice Holmes believed? There are certain signs of piecemeal composition. May we attribute these merely to original drafting in the field, or do they support the argument, now presented afresh by K. Barwick, that Caesar let the *Gallic War* appear serially in yearly parts, after which he also began to publish the *Civil War* in parts? The difficulty is to decide how far evidence for *composition* may be referred to the question of *publication*. In scrutinizing the narrative and style we come upon another problem that must be treated at the same time. The geographical excursuses in the *Gallic War* have fallen under suspicion on the grounds that they contain more information than Caesar could have obtained from personal observation, that they sometimes fit awkwardly into the narrative, and that their style is not that of Caesar. A. Klotz wished to make them interpolations based on Greek material (e.g. in Timagenes). If we discount the argument from style — and the idiom is less un-Caesarian than has been supposed — we may join F. Beckmann and H. Oppermann in attributing the excursuses to Caesar himself, who presumably had them compiled for his purpose. But the evidence of later insertion will indicate at least piecemeal composition, whatever we may think about the publication of the work.[22]

The study of Caesar's composition leads into examination of his literary achievement. We have discussed the character of *commentarii*, and it is known that Caesar was interested in the theory of Latin usage. Above all, we have to appreciate the *facultas atque elegantia summa scribendi* which gave Caesar's pure Latinity its unique quality and made his memoirs a true work of literary art in their own right. It may seem tasteless to compare with Caesar's elegance the work of Hirtius and the other men who completed the *Commentarii*. Yet their books have historical value and, apart from the problems of authorship, are interesting for the light they throw upon ordinary writing and Vulgar Latin.[23]

Contemporary history continued in the Caesarian period with the work of Asinius Pollio and Tanusius Geminus, the former an outstanding figure whose stature can be measured although his work is lost. Apart from the study by E. Pierce, most of the research on Pollio lies in detailed articles; but we have a recent survey of his life and work by J. André.[24] The period of the struggle between Octavian and Antony was marked by an outburst of pamphleteering, which K. Scott and R. Syme have examined in its political setting. Against the background of the early Principate we may set the writings of Augustus himself — the fragments conveniently edited by E. Malcovati — above all, the *Index rerum gestarum* (*Monumentum Ancyranum*). It would take us too far from the historians if we were to discuss this remarkable document and the models which influenced its form in celebrating the position and actions of the Princeps; we shall only note its significance as raw material of history dressed for popular effect.[25]

More relevant to Roman historiography at this time is the rise of biography, which we may study in Cornelius Nepos. F. Leo and D. R. Stuart have described the nature of Greek biography and discussed its influence in Rome. By Hellenistic times Greek biography had evolved a conventional arrangement of material according to topics — birth, youth and character, achievements, death, all with illustrative anecdotes — and this literary fashion is found in Roman biography. Leo believed that the Romans merely imitated Hellenistic models. Yet they had the roots of biography in their aristocratic tradition of celebrating the dead in *laudationes funebres* and *elogia*, and Stuart has stressed the importance of this custom not only as an inspiration to literary biography but in providing a pattern for the summing up of the significant features of a man's life and character. We may study the background in F. Münzer's work. If Hellenistic influence added precision and polish, it was to a genuine Roman form.[26]

When Octavian set about establishing the Principate by an appeal to the Roman tradition, he encouraged a revival of interest in the origins and early history of the Roman people. He himself felt the fascination of the name of Romulus, not as king but as founder of the city destined to rule the world. Horace gave poetic expression to this sentiment in his Roman Odes, while Virgil advanced from his Italian patriotism to the full theme of Aeneas and his descendants. The Capitoline *Fasti* were now (if not a little later) published in monumental form, and Livy began to write history with a profound conception of the greatness and responsibilities of imperial Rome.[27]

The developments in research on Livy cast a clear light on the trends of study during the last fifty years. At first the historical critics held the field, and Livy was for them the last of the Annalists. He had accepted both the form and the material of the Annalistic tradition, which had already been elaborated by the Sullan historians. The weight of authority in this tradition, as we have recognized, limited his criticism of his subject-matter to superficialities. Further, since his main Annalistic authorities appear to have shared the traditional form, he was able to incorporate their material fairly mechanically. This at least is the most likely explanation of the frequent discrepancies in his narrative. Livy, in short, provided ample evidence for source-criticism. After W. Soltau we have A. Klotz, while among the historians U. Kahrstedt and G. De Sanctis have carried out valuable analysis; and W. Hoffmann has returned to the question of Livy's use of his authorities.[28]

To discount Livy's critical methods is not to deny the power of his historical conception, and recent advances in the study of the Augustan period have influenced the attitude of scholarship towards his intellectual position. It is now possible to appreciate Livy more fully in his historical 'milieu'. One point is worth making. We may distinguish between the first years of the Principate, when peace brought a renaissance in Roman thought, and the later years of Augustus, when men might feel that order had cost them their political freedom. Idealism could make an appeal when Livy began writing, and even if Augustus exploited his work, Livy himself wrote it in a spirit of Roman patriotism. He took pride in the march of Roman history, with its great men and its tremendous events. He was a humanist, interested in the motives and reactions of men under the stress of necessity, and his Roman dignity did not exclude wider sympathy. At the same time, although we may appreciate his conception of Roman history, we still have to apply strict criticism to Livy's material, against its Annalistic background, before we take up the higher interpretation of his Augustan sentiment.[29]

Livy's genius lay in visualizing human action and in conveying his impression by description and comment, and he developed his natural gifts under the influence of Hellenistic historiographical theory and Roman rhetoric. To the Annalistic histories he aimed at adding finer literary style. If Cicero had prayed for a history worthy of Rome by rhetorical 'Isocratean' standards, Livy's work was to be the answer. In this perspective we may examine the literary study of Livy's work. H. Taine showed the rhetorical excellence of his writing, above all in his speeches, and R. Ullmann has refined upon Taine's results. It was also necessary to analyse the composition of his narrative. K. Witte opened up an important line of research in the Fourth and Fifth Decades, when he showed by comparison with the original text of Polybius how Livy selected and elaborated his account in well-balanced episodes within the Annalistic framework. In the more difficult First Decade E. Burck and others have shown the dramatic power of Livy's descriptions, mainly in terms of the 'Peripatetic' technique. Undoubtedly he knew and practised dramatic methods; yet we should resist the temptation to make him primarily a 'Peripatetic' historian. Livy generally explains his narrative, and this marks the 'Isocratean' historian. In fact, he controlled both methods — the contrast with Dionysius of Halicarnassus, where the two historians handle similar material, is striking — and he combined them in his own literary mode. Livy was the master, the techniques his servants; and our best guide to his work is W. Kroll. Further, we have to study the literary effect of the Annalistic form. Livy enjoyed the traditional atmosphere of its sacral notices, especially the records of prodigies, and he made the most of the varied impression of his subject-matter upon his readers.[30]

In the light of the wider discussion we may now turn to Livy's style, not only in the passages of fine writing but in the regular Annalistic sections about formal business. We normally speak of his style as 'periodic', but this approach is too narrow; for we find an infinite variety of sentence construction. As regards vocabulary, S. G. Stacey discerned a steady development from the poetical in the First Decade to more regular prose usage later on; but K. Gries has challenged his definition of poetical vocabulary. We have to study both style and language throughout the surviving books with attention to the sources, the content, and the impression which Livy aimed at creating in each part. The evidence of syntax and grammar is available in O. Riemann, and E. Löfstedt has pronounced on the problems. How serious was Asinius Pollio's charge of 'Patavinitas'? If we maintain Quintilian's interpretation, we have K. Latte's discussion in terms of literary wit and J. Marouzeau's treatment of *urbanitas*; but R. Syme has argued acutely that the word originally reflected Pollio's view of Livy's 'moral and romantic' history.[31]

Alongside the Augustan appeal to Roman tradition, Roman history was also conceived in Hellenistic perspective, critical rather than loyal, and we may turn to H. Fuchs for light on the anti-Roman sentiment of the period. Livy, like Horace and Virgil, had to insist upon the primacy of the city of Rome in his great 'Camillus speech'. It was against *levissimi ex Graecis*, we may recall, that he directed his excursus about Alexander the Great. The broader treatment of history is found after Timagenes in Pompeius Trogus, whom we know through his epitomator Justin. How deeply was Trogus in debt to Timagenes? After nearly a century of debate the question is still open. On the other hand, still in the Hellenistic fashion, Curtius Rufus received material on Alexander already composed in rhetorical and dramatic style, and he presented it with clarity and elegance. In the midst of our work on the 'classical' authors we should not neglect the historians who represent the cosmopolitan development of the early Roman Empire.[32]

In the systematic study of Roman historiography we miss sadly two groups of authors whose work laid the foundations of the major histories. The first, as we have noted, comprised the Gracchan and Sullan Annalists, upon whose material Livy built his narrative. The second, which we must now consider, included the various historical writers under the Principate before Tacitus. Fenestella's antiquarian interests, it is true, might add little to Livy, and those who, like Valerius Maximus, collected historical *exempla* may be connected rather with the rhetorical schools. Yet memoirs and biography continued to flourish. What would we not give for Tiberius' *Commentarius de vita sua* or the younger Agrippina's memoirs? It is fortunate that Velleius Paterculus has survived — and that not only for his account of Tiberius, which we may set against the dark picture from the hand of Tacitus. His subject-matter has been carefully analysed, and most students of the early Principate make their estimate of his authority. Velleius combines a practical view of military problems with wider cultural interests, and applies biographical methods in his account of historical figures; his style follows the rhetorical conventions of the day.[33]

The other historians of this period are little more than names; but Cremutius Cordus and Aufidius Bassus will command respect, and the Elder Pliny's collection of historical material must have been formidable. Both Aufidius Bassus and Pliny, it may be noted with later reference to Tacitus, wrote about the Roman wars in Germany. We know the names but not the work of Cluvius Rufus and Fabius Rusticus, and we may recognize the work but not the name of an Annalist who, according to E. Schwartz, gave Tacitus and Dio Cassius their impression of Tiberius; another authority, possibly the Elder Pliny, provided the common material in Tacitus, Suetonius, and Plutarch about the events of A.D. 69-70. The direct evidence for these historians is fragmentary, and most of the research on them has arisen out of the source-criticism of Tacitus.[34]

Ever since Voltaire questioned Tacitus' account of Tiberius, modern critics have admired but feared the great Roman historian. Ranke, for instance, stressed the need to separate his expression of opinion from his factual narrative, and this principle has been regularly followed, most recently by B. Walker. We find the earlier source-criticism of Tacitus set out by Ph. Fabia, whose conclusions have now been modified by F. Münzer, F. B. Marsh, and F. A. Marx, not to mention the historians who have treated the periods covered by his extant work. Expert analysis of his military narrative has enlarged on Mommsen's view of Tacitus as an unmilitary historian — unmilitary, that is, in his disregard of systematic details of strategy, for he appreciated the importance of the armies as a factor in Roman politics. Finally, the vast increase in epigraphic and archaeological information has broadened the perspective in which we may set Tacitus' account of conditions and events and his conception of the Principate. Who could ignore British archaeology in reading the *Agricola*, German archaeology in studying the *Germania*, or the general contribution of archaeology to study of the *Annals*? On the social and economic aspects of Imperial policy we have M. Rostovtzeff, whose material may be expanded with the aid of Tenney Frank and his collaborators. For these reasons no historian has greater need than Tacitus of good commentaries, and few have been served better during our period.[35]

When all this is said, however, Tacitus remains a major authority himself. Source-criticism and the examination of supplementary evidence will not meet the chief problems arising from his narrative. He was in command of his material, arranging it according to his historical and literary purposes, as G. Boissier showed, and we have to study him in his own right. R. von Pöhlmann's survey of Tacitus' 'Weltanschauung', with reference to fate, fortune, and the gods, led him to conclude that the historian was inconsistent in his beliefs. But this is to treat him as a theologian or philosopher, whose use of terms in detail will correspond to his essential doctrine, whereas a historian, even if he propounds a main thesis, may make conventional remarks in the course of his account. More relevant, indeed, is C. Wirszubski's analysis of *libertas* in Tacitus, which aims at clarifying his dominating conception; yet the problem is complex, and we must consider Tacitus' work as a whole.[36]

In the *Dialogus de oratoribus* Tacitus follows the model of Cicero in discussing the decline of oratory in his day, as Quintilian did in his *De causis corruptae eloquentiae*; but he interprets the question in his own political terms. R. Reitzenstein took the criticism of Republican disorder and the appreciation of the Imperial peace by Maternus to reflect Tacitus' first support of the Principate, which the historian decided afterwards had been fatal to the Roman state. F. Klingner, however, has found in the *Dialogus* the same intellectual conflict that marks the historical writings, and we may associate this work with the *Agricola* and the *Germania*.[37]

Tacitus falls among the biographers in the *Agricola*, yet his position is not simply defined. If the work seems more than a memorial biography, should we, like A. Gudeman, connect it with the imperial panegyric of the rhetoricians? The large amount of space devoted to history and geography is significant, and most critics emphasize the effect of Tacitus' historical flair, which exploited even a pious tribute to his father-in-law. G. L. Hendrickson hardly goes far enough in explaining the historical parts as indirect eulogy of Agricola, but F. Leo perhaps exaggerates in declaring that Tacitus made a biography into a historical monograph in the style of Sallust. D. R. Stuart insists on the biographical character of the work. The problem will best be considered in the judicial summing-up of J. G. C. Anderson.[38]

The *Germania* clearly belongs to the class of geographical and ethnographical literature, the terms of which are set out by K. Trüdinger, and its place has been studied by E. Norden. It is generally assumed that Tacitus published this work in order to prepare the ground for his histories, since its material was too bulky for an excursus. Yet, even if he did so, he took the trouble to compose it artistically, perhaps under the influence of Seneca's *De situ Indiae*, and we cannot ignore its literary form. Its overtones of historical feeling have tempted scholars to look for ulterior motives in its publication. Should we accept an immediate political purpose associated with Trajan's presence on the Rhine — to influence or justify his policy by showing the formidable character of German society — or, if we believe that it idealizes certain aspects of German *virtus*, may we point to the moral condemnation of degeneracy in Rome? The issues again are ably discussed by J. G. C. Anderson, and we now have a comprehensive treatment of Tacitus' attitude towards the frontier peoples by G. Walser.[39]

The rhetorician, the biographer, and the ethnographer in Tacitus, then, cannot repress the historian, while the historian has control of the necessary techniques for handling his material. With this in mind we may take up his full-dress historical writing. In the *Histories* Tacitus covered the events from A.D. 69 to the close of Domitian's reign, after which he seems originally to have intended to proceed to the period of Trajan. In the *Annals*, however, he went back to the period of the Julio-Claudian dynasty, when Rome first found the Principate irreconcilable with civic liberty and the heirs of the Republic surrendered to the force of Imperial despotism. Here is history composed in the traditional Annalistic form, and we may apply our modern methods of criticism to it. Yet the work enshrines the historical ideas of Tacitus himself, expressed with passionate conviction. What were his principles of judgment? That the historian hated the Principate is clear; but he recognized its rule as necessary for law and order, and — according to J. Vogt and E. Ciaceri — he accepted imperialism in the hands of men like Agricola and Corbulo. Although he rated the government of the Senate most highly, he was no Republican idealist, and at the outset — as R. Reitzenstein marked — he criticized the lawlessness under the Republic. E. Fraenkel and C. Wirszubski have emphasized that he was less concerned with constitutional forms than with their political and moral implications for the freedom and dignity of man. Power tends to corrupt, while subjection leads to degeneracy; and Tacitus condemned both the Emperors' progress in despotism and the servility of their subjects. F. Klingner has stressed that his central theme is the decline of Roman *virtus*. This view can be elaborated with the aid of H. Drexler, who analyses the clash of ideas in the historical situation, and we may recall our discussion of Sallust.[40]

But we must not allow the issue to be confused. Tacitus did not write history *in order to* illustrate the crisis of Roman *virtus*. Rather, *in the course of* describing Roman history, he made his conception of Roman *virtus* the standard by which he judged the men and their actions. We, too, must treat the question in concrete historical terms, as Tacitus felt it, by visualizing the course of events. Through the vivid portrayal of the impact of despotism upon virtue in the minds of men, his history takes on its 'psychological' character; and the picture of men in moral defeat casts the 'Tacitean' gloom over his later work. This is the tragedy of the Principate and the drama of Tacitus.

On the literary side we may refer again to the schools of historiography. The *Dialogus* reflects Tacitus' knowledge of rhetorical theory, and his own practical oratory sharpened his application of it. To one trained in composition the Annalistic form, as W. Kroll pointed out, not only recalled tradition but provided a framework within which to vary the subject-matter. The direct speeches, which we may study in R. Ullmann's analysis, increased the scope of characterization and enlivened the narrative. Tacitus' experience in ethnography helped his descriptions, while his biographical technique lent precision to his commemorative epilogues. Even more important, as E. Norden emphasized, the influence of the 'Peripatetic' school heightened the effect of his dramatic presentation. There is art as well as power in his brilliant episodes, where he aims at inspiring feelings of pity and horror; we may consult C. W. Mendell on his dramatic construction. This is the explanation of his 'unmilitary' narrative, viz. to compress detail at the beginning and end of a scene, however necessary it may be in systematic reporting, in order to 'spotlight' the action.[41]

For all his artistry Tacitus cannot be labelled merely rhetorical or dramatic. He aimed seriously at authoritative generalization, as Sallust had done, with stronger reference to the underlying causes in human behaviour. His rhetoric helps in formulating his thought; his dramatic presentation gives it visual directness; and he explains and persuades through his narration, with irony and innuendo. Yet his appeal is intellectual as well as emotional, and he insists upon interpreting and judging history in his own terms. His historical purpose raises his style in the grand manner, intensified by distinctive and poetical diction, from which his pronouncements issue in epigrammatic form. From the prose of his day Tacitus evolved his own style, which has been studied by many scholars from E. Wölfflin to E. Löfstedt. In its ruthless concentration and asymmetry it gives dynamic expression to the tension of his thought, above all in the early books of the *Annals*, where his historical imagination focused upon what he believed to be the fatal point of Roman history under the Principate.[42]

Historical biography was resumed by Suetonius, whose work survives chiefly in the *De vita Caesarum*. After A. Macé we may refer once more to F. Leo and D. R. Stuart, and to the commentaries on single Lives. The historian will turn to Suetonius for his widely gathered material, and the main task is to establish its sources of origin. Here, on account of the conventional arrangement of biographical subject-matter according to topics, source-criticism must include systematic analysis of the literary composition. The same methods are also necessary in studying Plutarch, where his Roman Lives provide evidence for Roman biography.[43]

During the first two centuries of the Empire the peaceful development of the provinces had challenged the primacy of Italy, and Greek influence spread throughout Roman civilization. We might with good reason include Nicolaus of Damascus and Diodorus, Appian, and later Dio Cassius and Herodian among the Roman historians. The Imperial crisis of the third century A.D., which broke the Italian tradition of the Principate, also saw the increase of Oriental ideas, until Diocletian could alter the balance of the Roman Empire and Constantine confirm the change by his acceptance of Christianity and his foundation of Constantinople. Yet in the fourth century, if new emperors rose and ruled outside

Rome, they felt themselves the heirs of Roman imperialism; Christians, under the guidance of Damasus, glorified the place of Rome in the history of the Church; and the senatorial class, especially those members of it who, like Symmachus, maintained paganism, kept their faith in the Roman cultural tradition. T. R. Glover, F. Klingner and C. N. Cochrane have treated the cultural aspects, and A. Alföldi is now stressing the intellectual tension of the period.[44] It is in the light of these conditions that we may take up the last works of Roman historiography.

Imperial biography had continued as a fashion after Suetonius, following his pattern; but little of it remains. We need cite only Marius Maximus and Aurelius Victor before we come to the *Historia Augusta*. This work is of peculiar interest both for the character of the problems it presents and for the controversy which they have aroused. It comprises the Lives of the emperors from Hadrian to Numerian (A.D. 284), with a small gap (244-53); six authors are named, and the dedications would date its publication to the reigns of Diocletian and Constantine. Although some distinguished scholars, including G. De Sanctis, have accepted this evidence, it is generally assumed at present that the *Historia Augusta* contains later material. Should we, with Mommsen, keep the original dating and assume revisions? H. Dessau attributed the work to the Theodosian period (c. 380-95), and this view has won wide support. We need scarcely set the date later, with A. von Domaszewski and O. Seeck. On the other hand N. H. Baynes makes the *Historia Augusta* a propaganda piece of the time of Julian the Apostate (362-3), and he has a strong following. H. Mattingly would set it a decade earlier. Especially where the later Lives (after that of Caracalla) indulge in tendentious invention, we must examine the process; and this involves treating not only the signs of direct propaganda but the evidence for a general conception of the Roman tradition, in pagan senatorial terms opposed to Christianity. We have also to study the literary character of the work, with special reference to the reading public. The problem of the *Historia Augusta* calls for a combination of detailed analysis and further study of the politics and thought of the third and fourth centuries A.D.[45]

Alongside the biographical writing we find the production of epitome and chronicle, owing much to the material in Livy. It is sufficient to mention Florus and Eutropius, who led on the one hand to Nicomachus Flavianus in the pagan senatorial circle and on the other to the Christian historians, Hieronymus (St. Jerome) and Orosius. The trend has been described by M. Galdi. We may note the importance of Nicomachus as an authority for the history of his own period, possibly influencing Ammianus Marcellinus. The new development of Christian historiography, however, lies outside our scope; so, remembering that St. Augustine would soon publish the *City of God*, we may return to the pagan tradition of Eternal Rome.[46]

Amidst the triviality of the compendious history the work of Ammianus Marcellinus must command our respect. A Greek, who had fought in the Roman armies, he felt himself so much the Roman that on retirement he settled in Rome to write a history, not in Greek but in Latin, that should continue the *Histories* of Tacitus, i.e. from Nerva to the death of Valens (378). It was serious history treated by a practical man, who in the last part of it could use his first-hand knowledge. We have only Books 14-31, covering A.D. 353-78, but they preserve information of inestimable value for this period. How far was Ammianus master of the earlier source-material? The Annalistic form, centred on Rome, had to be modified to cover adequately the various theatres of Imperial policy. If he followed an Annalist — whether or not this was Nicomachus Flavianus — he also incorporated material more broadly composed. Here we meet the problems of source-criticism, which E. A. Thompson has reopened by denying that Ammianus was closely dependent on his authorities. Then, despite the competence of his account, did his strong historical conception affect his political judgment? A. Alföldi is now applying more aggressive criticism to Ammianus' work.[47] Not only his source-material and his interests influenced his composition; he also used the regular techniques of Roman historiography. We may note the rhetoric in his speeches, the ethnographical style in his excursuses, and the biographical conventions in his commemorative character-sketches; also his fondness for literary allusion. Above all, he wrote with dramatic power in conscious imitation of Tacitus. How far might his literary tricks give a false historical impression, especially where his material was defective? The problem calls for combined research along historical and literary lines. On his Latinity, in the context of contemporary usage, we have the authoritative work of E. Löfstedt.[48]

THE ROMAN HISTORIANS

Our survey of the comprehensive study which has been devoted to the Roman historians during the last fifty years is now finished, and it is time to sum up. Sound historical method and the wider interests of scholarship on the literary and cultural side have led to important advances in knowledge and understanding. Yet on the whole our work needs co-ordination. If the historical critics, following the aims and technique of Mommsen, have often treated the Roman historians merely as purveyors of source-material, the scholars taking up their historical ideas and literary principles have tended, in reaction against Mommsen, to ignore the necessity for analysing their factual subject-matter and political interpretation. We have made play with the historiographical influences, since it is useful to distinguish the methods in which the Roman historians were trained; but we should not apply the labels — and this has been a common fault — indiscriminately. In handling their material, in formulating their interpretation, and in presenting their results, the major Roman writers expressed their personal conception of their theme, and we have to estimate the quality of their work as a whole.

What is the nature of historical evidence and its transmission? Historical critics will be prone to error if they argue from their Roman authorities without keeping this question in mind. One dare not dismiss a historian summarily after factual analysis. This is to treat our relationship with the past too simply. Historical reconstruction does not mean drafting a sketch, as it were, in two dimensions, regardless of our own position in the present or the problems of historical knowledge. Our impression of history is three-dimensional. We look back from a distance, down a long historical vista obscured by time and tradition, towards an unfamiliar scene, which we dimly perceive and which we interpret as best we can. By analysis we may reduce the distortion, by study we may clarify the picture, but we cannot remove the intermediate effects. We must try to understand how the historical evidence took shape and how it has been transmitted to us.

While we test the subject-matter of the Roman historians, we have also to consider the writers themselves in their 'milieu'; and the historical critic can assist by treating not only the period which they described but also, if it was not contemporary history, that in which they lived and worked. Sallust and Livy, Tacitus and Ammianus Marcellinus, however drastically we revise their judgments, still throw light upon the tradition in which they stood. Then, since the historians were men of independent opinion, we must examine their particular historical ideas. Here it is important to remember that a historian is not primarily a philosopher or moralist. He is usually driven by his own impulse to describe and interpret human action, and in the course of his narration, consciously or unconsciously, he applies his principles of judgment. There is no reason to separate the discussion of historical ideas from criticism of the account of events. Finally, when great writers practise a mature literary technique, they make it serve their intellectual and artistic ends. Beginning with the canons of their day, their style rises with their conception of their subject-matter and in turn lends precision to their individual manner of presenting it. Modern scholarship has been able to develop refined methods of literary analysis. Our task, following on the research of the last fifty years, is to employ these methods in closer conjunction with the procedure of historical criticism.

[1] For a survey of Roman historiography in terms of historical material, see A. Rosenberg, *Einleitung und Quellenkunde zur römischen Geschichte*, Berlin, Weidmann, 1921; in terms of historiographical theory, A. H. McDonald, 'Historiography, Roman', *Oxford Classical Dictionary*, Oxford, The Clarendon Press, 1949; in terms of Roman thought, F. Klingner, *Römische Geisteswelt*, Leipzig, Dieterich, 1943; and for a recent appreciation of the problems, M. L. W. Laistner, *The Greater Roman Historians*, Berkeley, University of California Press, 1947.
[2] Sir J. E. Sandys, *A History of Classical Scholarship*, vol. III, Cambridge, The University Press, 1908; J. W. Thompson, *A History of Historical Writing*, vol. II, New York, Macmillan, 1942; G. P. Gooch, *History and Historians in the nineteenth century*, 2nd edition, revised, London, Longmans, 1952.
[3] H. Peter, *Historicorum Romanorum Reliquiae*, 2 vols. (vol. I, 2nd edition), Leipzig, Teubner, 1906-14; E. Norden, *Die antike Kunstprosa*, 3rd edition, 2 vols., Leipzig, Teubner, 1915-18; E. Löfstedt, *Syntactica*, vol. II, Lund, Gleerup, 1933.
[4] Eduard Meyer, *Kleine Schriften*, 2 vols. (vol. I, 2nd edition), Halle, Niemeyer, 1924; J. B. Bury, *The Ancient Greek Historians*, London, Macmillan, 1909; G. De Sanctis, *Problemi di storia antica*, Bari, Laterza, 1932. On Mommsen's attitude towards Cicero in terms of 'anti-humanism', see W. Rüegg, *Cicero und der Humanismus*, Zürich, Rhein-Verlag, 1946.
[5] See p. 409, n19; cf. J. F. D'Alton, *Roman Literary Theory and Criticism*, London, Longmans, 1931; H.-I. Marrou, *L'Histoire de l'éducation dans l'antiquité*, Paris, Du Seuil, 1948.
[6] W. W. Tarn and G. T. Griffith, *Hellenistic Civilisation*, 3rd edition, revised, London, Arnold, 1952; note F. Susemihl, *Geschichte der griechischen Litteratur in der Alexandrinerzeit*, 2 vols., Leipzig, Teubner, 1891-92; E. Schwartz in Pauly-Wissowa, *Real-Encyclopädie*, s.v. 'Diodorus', 'Dionysius'; R. Reitzenstein, *Hellenistische Wundererzählungen*, Leipzig, Teubner, 1906; for F. Jacoby's work, see above, p. 151; and in general, P. Scheller, *De hellenistica historiae conscribendae arte*, Diss., Leipzig, 1911; H. Peter, *Wahrheit und Kunst*, Leipzig, Teubner, 1911.
[7] On the 'Isocratean' methods and especially Timaeus see Polybius, Bk. 12, and Cicero, *de Orat.* 2. 51-64; H. M. Hubbell, *The Influence of Isocrates on Cicero, Dionysius, and Aristides*, New Haven, Yale University Press, 1913; B. L. Ullman, 'History and Tragedy', TAPhA 73 (1942), 25; cf. M. Gelzer, H 70 (1935), 269.

⁸ On Phylarchus see Polybius in Bk. 2. 56-63; on 'Peripatetic' methods, Cicero's letter to Lucceius (*Fam.* 5. 12); with R. Reitzenstein and B. L. Ullman, as cited; cf. F. W. Walbank, JHS 58 (1938), 55.
⁹ These points may be set against B. L. Ullman's argument (*op. cit.*, 33sq.) that a 'Peripatetic' school would hardly have departed from Aristotle's views on history, and that what appears to be 'Peripatetic' stems rather from Isocrates' use of tragic elements. The 'Peripatetic' school must be considered Hellenistic, not Aristotelian, and a rhetorical description may produce a dramatic effect without being 'tragic' in conception. Polybius certainly distinguishes between Timaeus on the one hand and Phylarchus on the other.
¹⁰ Polybius stresses these principles especially in his criticism of Timaeus and Phylarchus.
¹¹ Consult Ed. Meyer, *Caesars Monarchie und das Principat des Pompejus*, 2nd edition, Stuttgart, Cotta, 1919; R. Reitzenstein, *Das Römische in Cicero und Horaz* (*Neue Wege zur Antike*, 2) Leipzig, Teubner, 1925; J. Vogt, *Ciceros Glaube an Rom*, Stuttgart, Kohlhammer, 1935; V. Pöschl, *Römischer Staat und griechisches Staatsdenken bei Cicero*, Berlin, Junker, 1936; R. Heinze, *Vom Geist des Römertums*, Leipzig, Teubner, 1938; R. Syme, *The Roman Revolution*, Oxford, The Clarendon Press, 1939; Lily Ross Taylor, *Party Politics in the Age of Caesar*, Berkeley, University of California Press, 1949; and in particular e.g. U. Knoche, 'Magnitudo animi', Ph Supplementband, 27, 3, 1935; H. Wagenvoort, *Roman Dynamism*, Oxford, Blackwell, 1947; C. Wirszubski, *Libertas*, Cambridge, The University Press, 1950; cf. K. Büchner and J. B. Hofmann, *Lateinische Literatur und Sprache in der Forschung seit 1937*, Berne, Francke, 1951, 64 sq.; M. Rambaud, *Cicéron et l'histoire romaine*, Paris, 'Les Belles Lettres', 1953.
¹² E. Pais, *Storia critica di Roma durante i primi cinque secoli*, 4 vols., Rome, Loescher, 1913-20; K. J. Beloch, *Römische Geschichte bis zum Beginn der punischen Kriege*, Berlin, De Gruyter, 1926; G. De Sanctis, *Storia dei Romani*, vols. I-IV, Turin, Bocca, 1907-23; P. Fraccaro, *La storia romana arcaica*, Milan, Hoepli, 1952; H. Stuart Jones and H. Last in *Cambridge Ancient History*, vol. VII, Cambridge, The University Press, 1928; T. R. S. Broughton, *The Magistrates of the Roman Republic*, 2 vols., New York, American Philological Association, 1951-52; cf. De Sanctis, vol. IV, 2 (1), Florence, 1953.
¹³ Cicero, *de Orat.*, 2. 52; *Leg.*, 1. 6; W. Soltau, *Die Anfänge der römischen Geschichtschreibung*, Leipzig, Haessel, 1909; F. Leo, *Geschichte der römischen Literatur*, vol. I, Berlin, Weidmann, 1913; M. Gelzer, H 69 (1934), 46 (cf. F. W. Walbank, CQ 39 (1945), 15 sq.). On Fabius Pictor note M. Gelzer, H 68 (1933), 129; P. Bung, *Q. Fabius Pictor*, Diss., Cologne, 1950; on Cato, F. della Corte, *Catone Censore*, Turin, Rosenberg, 1949; and on the general background, H. H. Scullard, *Roman Politics*, 220-150 B.C., Oxford, The Clarendon Press, 1951.
¹⁴ Tenney Frank, *Life and Literature in the Roman Republic*, Berkeley, University of California Press, 1930; H. Bardon, *La Littérature latine inconnue*, vol. I, Paris, Klincksieck, 1952. On the *Annales Maximi*, see now J. E. A. Crake, CPh 35 (1940), 375; on elaboration of the records, M. Gelzer, above, note 7.
¹⁵ W. Soltau, *Livius' Geschichtswerk*, Leipzig, Dieterich, 1897; U. Kahrstedt in O. Melzer-U. Kahrstedt, *Geschichte der Karthager*, Berlin, Weidmann, vol. III, 1913, and *Die Annalistik von Livius, B. 31-45*, Berlin, Weidmann, 1913; A. Klotz, *Livius und seine Vorgänger* (*Neue Wege zur Antike*, 2 Reihe, 10-11), Leipzig, Teubner, 1941; M. Zimmerer, *Der Annalist Qu. Claudius Quadrigarius*, Diss., Munich, 1937; K. Petzold, *Die Eröffnung des zweiten römisch-makedonischen Krieges*, Berlin, Junker, 1940.
¹⁶ See the works cited above, notes 12-15.
¹⁷ E. Schwartz, H 32 (1897), 554; W. A. Baehrens, *Sallust als Historiker, Politiker und Tendenzschriftsteller* (*Neue Wege zur Antike*, 4, 2), Leipzig, Teubner, 1927; G. De Sanctis, *Problemi di storia antica*, c. 8; W. Schur, *Sallust als Historiker*, Stuttgart, Kohlhammer, 1934; K. Latte, *Sallust* (*Neue Wege zur Antike*, 2 Reihe, 4, 2), Leipzig, Teubner, 1935; V. Pöschl, *Grundwerte römischer Staatsgesinnung in den Geschichtswerken des Sallust*, Berlin, De Gruyter, 1940. Note on the prologues F. Egermann, *Die Proömien zu den Werken des Sallust*, Vienna, Hölder, 1932; cf. E. Bolaffi, *Athenaeum* N.S. 16 (1938), 128; M. Rambaud, REL 24 (1946), 115; and K. Bauhofer, *Die Komposition der Historien Sallusts*, Diss., Munich, 1935. Cf. P. Perrochat, *Mémorial des Études latines*, Paris, 'Les Belles Lettres', 1943, 197 sq.; also K. Büchner, *Der Aufbau von Sallusts* Bellum Jugurthinum, H Einzelschrift 9, 1953.

[18] W. Kroll, H 62 (1927), 373; O. Seel, *Sallust von den Briefen ad Caesarem zur Coniuratio Catilinae*, Leipzig, Teubner, 1930; W. Steidle, H 78 (1943), 80; E. H. Clift, *Latin Pseudepigrapha*, Baltimore, 1945, 107 (cf. R. Syme, JRS 37 (1947), 198 sq.) 11. On the *Invectiva* see O. Seel, Kl Beiheft 47 (1943), 150; F. Oertel, RhM 94 (1951), 46. On the *Epistulae*, for their authenticity, note Ed. Meyer, *op. cit.*, 563; H. Dahlmann, H 69 (1934), 380; G. Carlsson, *Eine Denkschrift an Caesar über den Staat*, Lund, Gleerup, 1936; M. Chouet, *Les Lettres de Salluste à César*, Paris, 'Les Belles Lettres', 1950; against their authenticity, in whole or part, H. Last, CQ 17 (1923), 87, 151; 18 (1924), 83; *Mélanges offerts à J. Marouzeau*, Paris, 'Les Belles Lettres', 1948, 357; cf. B. Edmar, *Studien zu den Epistulae ad Caesarem*, Lund, Ohlsson, 1931; K. Latte, JRS 27 (1937), 301; E. Fraenkel, *ibid.*, 41 (1951), 192 sq.

[19] W. Kroll, 'Die Sprache des Sallust', Gl 15 (1927), 280; K. Latte, *Sallust*, c. 1; cf. R. Ullmann, *La technique des discours dans Salluste, Tite Live, et Tacite*, Oslo, Dybwad, 1927; E. Skard, SO 10 (1932), 61; *ibid.*, Supplet. 11 (1942), 141; P. Perrochat, *Les Modèles grecs de Salluste*, Paris, 'Les Belles Lettres', 1949.

[20] Cicero, *Att.* 2. 1. 1; Lucian, *Hist. conscr.*, 48; A. Klotz, *Caesarstudien*, Leipzig, Teubner, 1910; RhM 83 (1934), 66; H. Oppermann, *Caesar, der Schriftsteller und sein Werk* (*Neue Wege zur Antike*, 2 Reihe, 2, 2), Leipzig, Teubner, 1933; F. Bömer, 'Der Commentarius', H 81 (1953), 210; and in general G. Misch, *Geschichte der Autobiographie*, 3rd edition, Berne, Francke, vol. I, 1949-50; English translation by E. W. Dickes, London, Routledge, 1950, 2 vols.

[21] T. Rice Holmes, *Caesar's Conquest of Gaul*, 2nd edition, reprinted, 1931; *Ancient Britain and the Invasions of Julius Caesar*, 2nd edition, 1935; *The Roman Republic*, 3 vols., 1923, vol. 2; all three works, Oxford, The Clarendon Press. Note P. Huber, *Die Glaubwürdigkeit Cäsars in seinem Bericht über den gallischen Krieg*, 2nd edition, Bamberg, Buchner, 1931; C. E. Stevens, *Latomus* 11 (1952), 3, 165; N. J. De Witt, TAPhA 73 (1942), 341; M. Rambaud, *L'Art de la déformation historique dans les* Commentaires *de César*, Paris, 'Les Belles Lettres', 1953.

[22] Consult T. Rice Holmes and H. Oppermann, as cited; K. Barwick, 'Caesars Commentarii und das Corpus Caesarianum', Ph Supplementband 31, 2, 1938, and 'Caesars Bellum Civile', BSG 99, 1, 1951. On the geographical excursuses see A. Klotz, *Caesarstudien* (above, note 20); F. Beckmann, *Geographie und Ethnographie in Caesars Bellum Gallicum*, Dortmund, Ruhfus, 1930; H. Oppermann, H 68 (1933), 182.

[23] See above, note 20, especially H. Oppermann; H. Fraenkel, NJW 9 (1933), 26; J. J. Schlicher, CPh 31 (1936), 212. On the 'Caesarian Corpus' note K. Barwick, as cited; H. Pötter, *Untersuchungen zum Bellum Alexandrinum und Bellum Africum, Stil und Verfasserfrage*, Leipzig, Noske, 1932; O. Seel, 'Hirtius', Kl Beiheft 22, 1935; on B. Hisp., H. Drexler, H 70 (1935), 203.

[24] E. Pierce, *A Roman Man of Letters: C. Asinius Pollio*, Diss., Columbia University, New York, 1922; J. André, *La vie et l'œuvre d'Asinius Pollion*, Paris, Klincksieck, 1949.

[25] K. Scott, 'The Political Propaganda of 44-30 B.C.', *Memoirs of the American Academy in Rome* 11 (1933), 1; R. Syme, *op. cit.*, cc. 18-19; cf. above, note 18. On Augustus note H. Malcovati, *Imperatoris Caesaris Augusti operum fragmenta*, 3rd edition, Turin, Paravia, 1947 (with bibliography); cf. J. Gagé, *Res gestae divi Augusti*, Paris, 'Les Belles Lettres', 1935; M. A. Levi, *Suetoni Divus Augustus*, Florence, 'La Nuova Italia', 1951 (appendix).

[26] F. Leo, *Die griechisch-römische Biographie*, Leipzig, Teubner, 1901; D. R. Stuart, *Epochs of Greek and Roman Biography*, Berkeley, University of California Press, 1928; cf. F. Münzer, *Römische Adelsparteien und Adelsfamilien*, Stuttgart, Metzler, 1920.

[27] Note R. Heinze, *Virgils Epische Technik*, 3rd edition, reprinted, Leipzig, Teubner, 1928, and *Die Augusteische Kultur*, 2nd edition, Leipzig, Teubner, 1933; A. von Premerstein, 'Vom Werden und Wesen des Prinzipats', ABAW N. F. 15, 1937; F. Klingner, *op. cit.*, 91 sq.; R. Syme, *op. cit.*, 464 sq.; on the Capitoline *Fasti*, A. Degrassi, *Fasti Consulares et Triumphales* (*Inscriptiones Italiae* 13, 1), and T. R. S. Broughton, *op. cit.*, I, xii-xiii; on Livy's preface, H. Dessau, *Festschrift O. Hirschfeld*, Berlin, Weidmann, 1903, 461.

[28] G. De Sanctis, *Problemi di storia antica*, c. 10; H. Bornecque, *Tite-Live*, Paris, Boivin, 1933; for the works on source-criticism, above, note 15; A. A. Howard, HSPh 17 (1906), 161; W. Hoffmann, H Einzelschriften 8, 1942.

[29] On Livy's relations with Augustus see H. Dessau, H 41 (1906), 142; on his

'Augustan idealism', R. Heinze, F. Klingner and W. Hoffmann, as cited; E. Burck, WG 1 (1935), 446; Paolo Zancan, *Tito Livio*, Milan, Mondadori, 1940; H. Hoch, *Die Darstellung der politischen Sendung Roms bei Livius*, Frankfurt, Klostermann, 1951; cf. G. Stübler, *Die Religiosität des Livius*, Stuttgart, Kohlhammer, 1941; F. Calderaro, *Nuovi Discorsi sulla prima Deca di Tito Livio*, Padua, Cedam, 1952. Against exaggeration in this treatment of Livy note R. Syme, JRS 35 (1945), 104 sq., and A. Momigliano, *ibid.*, 142 sq.

[30] H. Taine, *Essai sur Tite-Live*, 7th edition, Paris, Hachette, 1904; W. Kroll, *Studien zum Verständnis der römischen Literatur*, Stuttgart, Metzler, 1924, 351 sq.; E. Burck, *Die Erzählungskunst des T. Livius*, Berlin, Weidmann, 1934; cf. R. Jumeau, REA 38 (1936), 63; on his composition, above, notes 15, 28; K. Witte, RhM 65 (1910), 270, 359; L. Declaruelle, RPh 37 (1913), 145; R. Jumeau, RPh 65 (1939), 21; F. Hellmann, *Livius-Interpretationen*, Berlin, De Gruyter, 1939; on the speeches, H. V. Canter, AJPh 38 (1917), 125; 39 (1918), 44; R. Ullmann, as cited above, note 19; A. Lambert, *Die indirekte Rede als künstlerisches Stilmittel des Livius*, Diss., Zürich, 1946; K. Gries, AJPh 70 (1949), 118.

[31] O. Riemann, *Études sur la langue et la grammaire de Tite-Live*, 2nd edition, Paris, Thorin, 1885; S. G. Stacey, ALL 10 (1898), 17; K. Gries, *Constancy in Livy's Latinity*, New York, 1947; cf. R. Ullmann, *Étude sur le style des discours de Tite-Live*, Oslo, Dybwad, 1929. On 'Patavinitas' note K. Latte, CPh 35 (1940), 56; cf. J. Marouzeau, *Traité de stylistique latine*, 2nd edition, Paris, 'Les Belles Lettres', 1946; R. Syme, *op. cit.*, 485.

[32] Horace, *carm.* 3.3; Virgil, *A* 12.828; Livy 5.51 sq. H. Fuchs, *Der geistige Widerstand gegen Rom in der antiken Welt*, Berlin, De Gruyter, 1938; cf. A. N. Sherwin-White, *The Roman Citizenship*, Oxford, The Clarendon Press, 1939, c. 12. On the historians in general consult W. W. Tarn, *Alexander the Great*, Cambridge, The University Press, 1948, vol. II; P. Treves, *Il mito di Alessandro e la Roma d'Augusto*, Milan, Ricciardi, 1953; on Pompeius Trogus, E. Schneider, *De Trogi historiarum consilio et arte*, Leipzig, 1913; A. Momigliano, *Athenaeum*, N.S. 12 (1934), 45; on Justin, M. Galdi, *L'epitome nella letteratura latina*, Naples, Federico & Ardia, 1922; on Curtius Rufus, W. Kroll, *op. cit.*, 331 sq.; H. Bardon, *Études classiques* 15 (1947), 3, 120, 193.

[33] F. Leo, *op. cit.*, 240; F. Münzer, 'Zur Komposition des Velleius', *Festschrift 49 Versammlung Deutscher Philologen*, Basel, 1907, 247; W. Schaefer, *Tiberius und seine Zeit im Lichte der Tradition des Velleius Paterculus*, Halle, John, 1912; I. Lana, *Velleio Patercolo o della propaganda* (Pubbl. Fac. Lett. Univ. Torino, 4, 2), Turin, 1952.

[34] H. Peter, *Die geschichtliche Literatur über die römische Kaiserzeit bis Theodosius I und ihre Quellen*, 2 vols., Leipzig, Teubner, 1897. Note on Aufidius Bassus and Pliny, F. Münzer, RhM 62 (1907), 161; F. A. Marx, Kl 26 (1933), 323; 29 (1936), 94, 202; and below, note 39; on the 'Tiberius Annalist', E. Schwartz, Pauly-Wissowa, *Real-Encyclopädie*, s.v. 'Cassius Dio'; on the source for the events of A.D. 69, N. Feliciani, RSA 11 (1909), 3, 378; P. Zancan, *La crisi del principato*, Padua, Cedam, 1939; F. Klingner, 'Die Geschichte Kaiser Ottos bei Tacitus', BSG 92, 1, 1940.

[35] Ph. Fabia, *Les sources de Tacite dans les Histoires et les Annales*, Paris, Imprimerie Nationale, 1893; F. Münzer, *Bonner Jahrbücher*, 104 (1899), 66; Kl 1 (1901), 300; F. A. Marx, H 60 (1925), 74; Ph 92 (1937), 83; F. Graf, *Untersuchungen über die Komposition der Annalen des Tacitus*, Diss. Berne, Thun, 1931; F. B. Marsh, *The Reign of Tiberius*, London, Milford, 1931; J. Martin in *Studien zu Tacitus* (Würzburger Studien zur Altertumswissenschaft 9), Stuttgart, Kohlhammer, 1936, 21; D. M. Pippidi, *Autour de Tibère*, Bucharest, Inst. de Istorie universală, 1944.

On the distinction of 'factual' and 'non-factual' see B. Walker, *The Annals of Tacitus*, Manchester, University Press, 1952; cf. I. S. Ryberg, TAPhA 73 (1942), 383; R. S. Rogers, *ibid.*, 83 (1952), 279; on the military narrative, E. G. Hardy, JPh 31 (1910), 123; B. W. Henderson, *Civil War and Rebellion in the Roman Empire*, London, Macmillan, 1908; and finally M. Rostovtzeff, *The Social and Economic History of the Roman Empire*, Oxford, The Clarendon Press, 1926; Tenney Frank (editor), *An Economic Survey of Ancient Rome*, vols. II-V, Baltimore, Johns Hopkins Univ. Press, 1936-40.

[36] G. Boissier, *Tacite*, Paris, Hachette, 1903 (translated by W. G. Hutchinson, *Tacitus and other Roman studies*, London, Constable, 1906); R. von Pöhlmann, 'Die Weltanschauung des Tacitus', 2nd edition, SBA, 1913; C. Brakmann, Mn 1928, 70; N. Eriksson, *Religiositet och irreligiositet hos Tacitus*, Lund, Gleerup, 1935; W. Theiler, 'Tacitus und die antike Schicksalslehre', *Phyllobolia P. von der Muhll*, Schwabe, 1946, 35; C. Wirszubski, *op. cit.*, 160 sq.; cf. below, note 40.

[37] On the *Dialogus*, see above, pp. 373-4; for its historical implications, R. Reitzenstein, *Tacitus und sein Werk (Neue Wege zur Antike,* 4), Leipzig, Teubner, 1927; F. Klingner, *Römische Geisteswelt,* 329-30.

[38] F. Leo, *op. cit.,* 224 sq.; D. R. Stuart, *op. cit.,* 237; J. G. C. Anderson, revising Furneaux's edition, Oxford, The Clarendon Press, 1922; cf. A. Gudeman's edition, Boston, Allyn and Bacon, 1928; G. L. Hendrickson, *The Proconsulate of Julius Agricola in relation to history and to encomium,* Chicago, University Publications, 1902; J. Cousin, REL 14 (1936), 326. Note I. A. Richmond, 'Gnaeus Julius Agricola', JRS 34 (1944), 34; E. Birley, *Roman Britain and the Roman Army,* Kendal, Wilson, 1953.

[39] K. Trüdinger, *Studien zur Geschichte der griechisch-römischen Ethnographie,* Diss., Basel, 1918, 146 sq.; E. Norden, *Die germanische Urgeschichte in Tacitus' Germania,* 3rd edition, Leipzig, Teubner, 1923; E. Wolff, H 69 (1934), 121; F. Pfister in *Studien zu Tacitus* (above, note 35), 59; and in general, J. G. C. Anderson's edition of the *Germania,* Oxford, The Clarendon Press, 1938; G. Walser, *Rom, das Reich und die fremden Völker in der Geschichtschreibung der frühen Kaiserzeit,* Baden-Baden, Kunst und Wissenschaft, 1951.

[40] See above, notes 35-36; J. Vogt, *Tacitus als Politiker,* Stuttgart, Kohlhammer, 1924, and in *Studien zu Tacitus* (above, note 35), 1; E. Fraenkel, 'Tacitus', NJW 8 (1932), 218; H. Drexler, *Tacitus, Grundzüge einer politischen Pathologie,* Frankfurt, Diesterweg, 1939; E. Ciaceri, *Tacito,* Turin, Unione tipografica torinese, 1941; E. Kornemann, *Tacitus,* Wiesbaden, Dieterich, 1946; R. Feger, 'Virtus bei Tacitus', WJA 3, 1948, 301; E. Paratore, *Tacito,* Milan, Istituto editoriale cisalpino, 1952.

[41] F. Leo, *Tacitus,* Festrede, Göttingen, 1896; on the Annalistic form, F. G. Moore, TAPhA 54 (1923), 5; W. Kroll, *op. cit.,* 369; on literary presentation, E. Courbaud, *Les procédés d'art de Tacite dans les Histoires,* Paris, Hachette, 1918; P. S. Everts, *De Tacitea historiae conscribendae ratione,* Diss., Utrecht, Kerkrade, 1926; R. Ullmann, as cited above, note 19; C. W. Mendell, Y Cl S 5 (1935), 1; H. Hommel in *Studien zu Tacitus* (above, note 35), 116; E. Norden, *Römische Literatur,* 4th edition, Leipzig, Teubner, 1952, 93.

[42] E. Löfstedt, *Syntactica* II, 276 sq. and JRS 38 (1948), 1. Note J. Gantrelle, *Grammaire et style de Tacite,* 3rd edition, Paris, Garnier, 1908; N. Eriksson, *Studien zu den Annalen des Tacitus,* Lund, Gleerup, 1934; G. Sörbom, *Variatio sermonis Tacitei,* Uppsala, Almqvist-Wiksell, 1935; cf. A. Bourgery, *Sénèque prosateur,* Paris, 'Les Belles Lettres', 1922.

[43] See above, note 26; A. Macé, *Essai sur Suétone,* Paris, Fontemoing, 1900; G. Funaioli, 'I Cesari di Suetonio', *Miscellenea per F. Ramorino,* Milan, Vita e Pensiero, 1927, 1; W. Steidle, *Sueton und die antike Biographie,* Munich, Beck, 1951; M. A. Levi, as cited above, note 25. On Plutarch's *Roman Lives* see R. E. Smith, CQ 34 (1940), 1.

[44] T. R. Glover, *Life and Letters in the Fourth Century,* Cambridge, The University Press, 1901; F. Klingner, *op. cit.,* 338 sq.; C. N. Cochrane, *Christianity and Classical Culture,* Oxford, The Clarendon Press, 1940; cf. F. Altheim, *Literatur und Gesellschaft im ausgehenden Altertum,* 2 vols., Halle, Niemeyer, 1948-50. Note on the 'pagan revival' D. M. Robinson, TAPhA 46 (1915), 87; P. de Labriolle, *La réaction païenne,* Paris, L'Artisan du libre, 1934; J. A. McGeachy, *Q. Aurelius Symmachus and the Senatorial Aristocracy of the West,* Diss., University of Chicago, 1942; cf. J. Straub, *Historia* 1 (1950), 52; A. Alföldi, *A Conflict of Ideas in the Late Roman Empire,* Oxford, The Clarendon Press, 1952.

[45] In general see W. Hartke, *De saeculi quarti exeuntis historiarum scriptoribus quaestiones,* Diss., Berlin, 1932, and 'Geschichte und Politik im spätantiken Rom', Kl Beiheft 45, 1940. On the *Historia Augusta,* for the traditional dating, note E. Klebs, HZ 61 (1889), 213; G. De Sanctis, RSA 1 (1896), 90; C. Lécrivain, *Études sur l'Histoire Auguste,* Paris, Fontemoing, 1904; for revisions, Th. Mommsen, H 25 (1890), 228 (*Ges. Schr.* 7, 302); for the Julian date, N. H. Baynes, *The Historia Augusta, its Date and Purpose,* Oxford, The Clarendon Press, 1926 (cf. CQ 22 (1928), 166); E. Hohl, Kl 27 (1934), 149; W. Ensslin, *ibid.,* 32 (1939), 90; W. Seston, REA 44 (1942), 224; 45 (1943), 49; *Dioclétien et la Tetrarchie,* vol. I, Paris, Boccard, 1946, 19 sq.; cf. H. Mattingly, HThR 39 (1946), 213, proposing a date c. 350; H. Stern, *Date et destinataire de 'l'Histoire Auguste',* Paris, 'Les Belles Lettres', 1953, dating to 352-4; for a Theodosian date, H. Dessau, H 24 (1889), 337; 27 (1892), 561; 29 (1894), 393; A. Alföldi, *Die Kontoriaten,* Budapest, Magyar Numismatikai Tarsulat, 1943; W. Hartke, as above; for a later date, A. von

Domaszewski, SHA Abh. 13, 1918; O. Seeck, RhM 67 (1912), 591. J. Straub, *Studien zur Historia Augusta*, Berne, Francke, 1952; Cf. A. Momigliano, JWI 17(1954).

[46] M. Galdi, as cited above, note 32. On the epitome of Livy see E. Kornemann, Kl Beiheft 12, 1904; A. Klotz, H 48 (1913), 542; Ph 91 (1936), 67; on Florus, S. Lilliedahl, *Florusstudien*, Diss., Lund, Gleerup, 1928; P. Zancan, *Floro e Livio*, Padua, Cedam, 1942; on Eutropius and Hieronymus, R. Helm, RhM 76 (1927), 138, 254; Ph Supplementband 21, 2, 1929; on Orosius, H. Svennung, *Orosiana*, Diss., Uppsala, 1922; and with reference to St. Augustine, H.-I. Marrou, *Saint Augustin et la fin de la culture antique*, 1938, 'Retractatio', 1949, Paris, de Boccard.

[47] Consult E. Stein, *Geschichte des spätrömischen Reiches*, vol. I, *284-476 n. Chr.*, Vienna, Seidel, 1928; A. Piganiol, *L'Empire chrétien, 325-395* (*Histoire ancienne*, ed. G. Glotz, Pt. 3, 4, 2), Paris, Presses universitaires de France, 1947; cf. above, notes 44-45. Note E. von Borries, H 17 (1892), 170; O. Seeck, *ibid.*, 41 (1906), 481; W. Klein, Kl Beiheft 13, 1914; A. Klotz, RhM 71 (1916), 461; W. Ensslin, Kl Beiheft 17, 1923; G. B. Pighi, *Nuovi studi Ammiani*, Milan, Vita e Pensiero, 1936; M. Schuster, WS 58 (1940), 119; E. A. Thompson, *The Historical Work of Ammianus Marcellinus*, Cambridge, The University Press, 1947.

[48] J. W. Mackail, 'The Last Great Roman Historian', *Classical Studies*, London, Murray, 1925, 159. On literary associations note F. Leo, *op. cit.*, 236 sq.; G. B. A. Fletcher, RPh 11 (1937), 377; on language, E. Löfstedt, Er 7 (1907), 131, and *Beiträge zur Kenntnis der späteren Latinität*, Diss. Uppsala, 1907; H. Hagendahl, *Studia Ammianea*, Uppsala Univ. Arsskrift, 1921; Er 22 (1924), 161; R. B. Steele, CW 16 (1922), 18, 27; J. B. Pighi, *Studia Ammianea*, 1935, and *I discorsi nelle storie d'Ammiano Marcellino*, 1936, both works Milan, Vita e Pensiero.

APPENDIX TO CHAPTER XIII

WHEN I wrote this chapter I was preoccupied with the need to study the Roman historians in systematic reference to their own firm tradition of thought and style, as I had written in literary terms about Roman historiography for the *Oxford Classical Dictionary*, that is, to show the authors in their place before indicating their special distinction. The method is basic, I think, if only to control our subjective impressions, and I am glad that it will remain on record both here and in the revised *O.C.D.*; but it covers only half the task of good criticism, for great historians have chosen their own position. We still have the duty of individual appreciation. What was the man's personal experience, as far as it is reflected in his work? How far can one test his judgment of the events he is describing? We are concerned here with history as well as historiography. Then we may well pay him the compliment of applying wider standards than his own to the quality of his work. This is a matter of historical technique and imagination. We now turn to Sir Ronald Syme in two books, viz. *Tacitus* (Oxford, 1958) and *Sallust* (Sather Classical Lectures, California, 1964), for the method and its results; he has also used it on Livy, with reference to the later books, in 'Livy and Augustus', *Harvard Studies in Classical Philology* LXIV (1959), p. 27. I believe that this combination of historical and literary study offers most promise for the future. For the Republican background see my survey of studies in *Journal of Roman Studies* L (1960), p. 135, and my description of social and cultural conditions in *Republican Rome* (Thames and Hudson, 1966). One can go further. For a fresh treatment of Roman historiography and the historians we now have *Latin Historians* (ed. T. A. Dorey, Routledge, 1966), a book which adds liberally to the present chapter.

With regard to the Roman Annals we may recall what fifteen years have made the modern *Annales Maximi*, indispensable to historical studies: T. R. S. Broughton's *Magistrates of the Roman Republic* (2 vols., 1951-52, vol. 2 reprinted with a supplement in 1960; above, n. 12). On Fabius Pictor and the senatorial historians, as well as Polybius himself, consult F. W. Walbank, *Historical Commentary on Polybius*, Vol. 1, Bks. 1-6 (Oxford, 1957).

APPENDIX

Likewise on the Annalists, as well as Livy himself, see R. M. Ogilvie, *Commentary on Livy, Bks. 1-5* (Oxford, 1965). D. C. Earl has treated *The Political Thought of Sallust* (Cambridge, 1961), and P. G. Walsh has described *Livy, his Historical Aims and Methods* (Cambridge, 1961), both with an eye on the historian's position. Fergus Millar moves in *Cassius Dio* (Oxford, 1964) from Imperial interpretation to the earlier Roman sources. Finally, for later Roman historiography, we should study A. D. Momigliano (ed.), *The Conflict between Paganism and Christianity in the Fourth Century* (Warburg Studies, Oxford, 1963). These books will bring the reader up to date in the bibliography of the last twelve years.

CHAPTER XIV

SILVER LATIN POETRY

BY H. H. HUXLEY

Subiit argentea proles,
  auro deterior.

As in the myth of the Four Ages the silver race of men succeeded the golden and marked a falling-off from its purity and simplicity, so in the literary history of Rome the golden era of the late republic and the Augustan principate was followed by a period of great and varied literary activity, a period which, possessing no champion of the strength and stature of Lucretius or Virgil, is fittingly described by the name of the less precious metal. Ovid's story holds more than one lesson for readers of ancient literature who are too apt to seize upon the pejorative phrase *auro deterior* and to ignore all that follows. The poet stresses the difficulties under which life was lived in these later times and points to material progress attained by industrious effort and the acquisition of techniques. Again it is both ungracious and unprofitable to find fault with silver because its properties are not those of gold; rather should we discover and appreciate the peculiar excellencies of the former. The chariot of Phoebus Apollo, patron of song, was made by Vulcan the master-craftsman; though its wheels had golden rims, the spokes were of silver.[1] J. Wight Duff in his excellent handbook of the Silver Age reminds us that we discover, in an adventure among its masterpieces, artistic production of high quality, thought commensurate with the achievement of the times, and engrossing portrayal of life.[2] Small indeed is the number of those scholars who in the past half-century have addressed themselves seriously and primarily to the elucidation of the four post-Augustan epics; though many more have *bis terve* hazarded a cautious foot into what must have seemed to them *loca senta situ* and, extricating themselves with difficulty, modestly awaited the approbation due to those who have 'set back the frontier of darkness'. Furthermore it is broadly true to say the text of a Silver Latin poet is most often approached as a complex of intellectual problems capable of solution by the pure light of reason. Much more rare is the attitude of W. C. Summers who undoubtedly enjoyed the *Argonautica*. But the eye which can discern the worth of Valerius Flaccus may fail to focus itself properly upon Statius and so may produce a distorted image. Another hindrance to clarity of perception and soundness of judgment is a preoccupation with *loci similes* and alleged *imitationes*. Such a preoccupation may lead to results which are far from negligible but must be considered as a flank attack, since, if a late writer is deserving of study, it is the original quality of his work which chiefly compels our attention. The establishment of a text as correct as human industry and ingenuity can achieve is, need it be said, the first essential. But after this must come a commentary in which the stress is laid rather on exegesis than on textual problems. How few of the poets under our consideration have yet been furnished with a satisfactory modern commentary! The sky, however, is not enveloped in darkness, and there are signs, welcome though few, that scholars, *pedetemptim progredientes* after their fashion, are striving to supply the need.

Before the task of assessing progress in the several fields is approached, a word of apology and explanation is called for. In so short a survey it will not be possible always to give praise where praise is due. The laborious collation and recension of manuscripts, the flashes of illumination which render intelligible a *locus desperatissimus*, the restoration of the true order of lines in a perplexing passage, the identification of strange names and places — these and similar achievements are the foundation stones on which an enduring edifice must rest. But they are lost sight of as the eye surveys the proportions of the whole. If such contributions seem here to receive inadequate notice, it is not because the present writer underrates them but that by their intrinsic nature they are bound to stand out no more than single threads correctly placed in a complex piece of weaving. *Sic vos non vobis mellificatis apes!*

The period of scholarship under review will for most of our authors begin with the last decade of the nineteenth century. Those ten years and the ten which followed them are peculiarly rich in contributions to our knowledge and understanding of Silver Latin poetry. And it is pleasurable to record the splendid achievements of British scholars in this field — Robinson Ellis, W. M. Lindsay, J. P. Postgate, J. S. Phillimore and A. E. Housman (to name only a few). The fifth and final fascicule of Postgate's *Corpus Poetarum Latinorum* saw the light of day in 1905; the completion of this work 'so long required and so signally useful'[3] by a team of experts, most of whom were British, placed in the hands of Latinists convenient and reliable texts of the Post-Augustan poets. In the last half-century such learned studies have twice been interrupted by World Wars, the second bringing in its train an economic crisis so severe that the flow of scholarly publications (on this side of the Atlantic) has been very seriously retarded. Furthermore it is a truism that, since the privileged position of the Humanities began to be undermined by the rapid growth of the physical, economic, and social sciences, an increasingly high proportion of the country's ablest intellects was diverted into non-classical channels. And in the narrower field of classical literature Greek subjects exercised a wider appeal than Latin; while of Latin authors those of the republican era and the age of Augustus rightly and understandably were preferred to imperial writers. This apologia is intended to offer a partial explanation of the fact that of recent years progress in the study of the later poets cannot hope to match the brilliance with which the century opened. But much useful work has been completed, large tracts have been levelled and cleared, and tools forged to facilitate the labours of research. There are for the guidance of the non-specialist reader who has neither time nor inclination to consult literary histories and *Jahresberichte* three attractive books in English, each of which, with a difference of stress, discusses the poets of the Silver Age. Of these the fullest and, in my view, the least biased is J. Wight Duff's *A Literary History of Rome in the Silver Age*.[4] W. B. Anderson, no mean judge of the literature of this period, gave this book an enthusiastic welcome, his only major criticism being that Lucan seemed to receive less than justice.[5] H. E. Butler's *Post-Augustan Poetry from Seneca to Juvenal*[6] is slighter, less sympathetic and covers a shorter period. However, its appearance in 1909 was interpreted by J. W. Mackail as 'one of several signs pointing to a reaction against the contempt into which Latin poetry of the Silver Age had fallen'.[7] *The Silver Age of Latin Literature — from Tiberius to Trajan*[8] — was published ten years after Butler's book — and seven years before Wight Duff's. The author, W. C. Summers, had as early as 1894 written an able and interesting monograph on the epic of Valerius

Flaccus.[9] It is not therefore surprising that a reviewer in the *Classical Review*[10] should note his particular success in dealing with this poet; but in view of Anderson's strictures on the reviewer, Wight Duff himself, one reads with a smile that 'Lucan hardly seems to get his due in comparison'.

Mention has been made of tools designed to facilitate the study of ancient authors. The most useful of these is the word-index or concordance. In the last century scholars had for the most part either to use indexes appended to useful but inferior texts or laboriously to note each separate occurrence of an important word. Honourable exceptions must be made of the excellent editions of Martial[11] and Juvenal[12] by Ludwig Friedlaender; the former contains an indispensable *Wörterverzeichnis* and a *Namenverzeichnis* by Carl Frobeen; the word-index in the latter was compiled by Franz Atorf. The twentieth century is remarkable for the refinement and extensive practice of a form of self-inflicted torture which vies in monotony with the task of the Danaids — I refer to the preparation of a complete index of a classical author. America has provided most of the victims; their sacrifice has lightened the labours of all students of Silver Latin. A. Ernout, reviewing the latest of these works, spoke of it as a happy addition 'aux index que les philologues des États-Unis composent avec autant de patience que d'abnégation'.[13] In 1918 an *Index Verborum* to the plays of Seneca and the *Octavia* was published by the University of Illinois.[14] It represented the joint work of W. A. Oldfather, A. S. Pease and H. V. Canter and was praised for its accuracy by J. Wight Duff.[15] George W. Mooney's *Index to the Pharsalia of Lucan*[16] appeared eight years later as the first supplementary volume of *Hermathena* and was warmly recommended to Latin scholars by W. B. Anderson[17] and A. D. Nock.[18] Three American scholars, R. J. Deferrari, M. W. Fanning and A. S. Sullivan, produced during the late war a complete *Concordance of Lucan*;[19] excellent though this is, many will prefer Mooney's book for their private use, since it is cheap, attractively-printed and of a convenient size. The years 1935, 1940, 1943 and 1951 brought us indexes of Valerius Flaccus,[20] Silius Italicus,[21] Statius,[22] and Juvenal.[23] Though such monuments of human endurance and academic self-denial are by no means free from imperfections (for, where manuscripts are many and emendations legion, not all permutations can be recorded), their utility for literary, semantic, and lexicographical research can scarcely be overestimated. Operations which seemed as unlikely to see fulfilment as the theoretical onslaught of seven maids with seven mops on the sandy shore have been completed, and a path is cleared for all kinds of necessary investigations. One would welcome a comparative study of the language of the four Post-Augustan epics, a study which would carefully analyse their relations to each other, and their varying degrees of indebtedness to earlier Roman poets.

Though the minor poetry of the Silver Age is of considerably greater interest to the literary historian and the antiquarian than to the classically-minded reader who innocently prefers the *dulce* to the *utile*, there are some poems which deserve to be more widely known and which the industry of scholars in the last half-century has elucidated and placed before us in a convenient and acceptable form. Those whose acquaintance with Petronius' *Satyricon* is limited to the separately-edited *Cena Trimalchionis* could do worse than glance at two poems (or, more precisely, two fragments) found at sections 89 and 119-24. The first, *Troiae Halosis*, consists of 65 senarii on the episodes of the wooden horse and the death of Laocoon; the second, *Bellum Civile*, an implied criticism of Lucan's epic style, runs to a little less than 300 hexameters. The prose translation by Michael Heseltine[24] is convenient but undistinguished and occasionally inaccurate. Florence T. Baldwin efficiently edited the *Bellum Civile* in 1911,[25] providing a good commentary. More recently both fragments were edited by Heinz Stubbe[26] to the satisfaction of Wilhelm Heraeus.[27] The versified tenth book (*de cultu hortorum*) of Columella's *Res Rustica* was published separately as the sixth fascicule of V. Lundström's fine critical edition[28] and also equipped with an Italian translation and commentary by A. Santoro.[29] Wight Duff thus drily sums up this didactic *tour de force* — 'Columella succeeds, as Martial did after him, in making some at least of his vegetables poetic'.[30] Another didactic poem, falsely ascribed to Virgil, deserves mention here, though there are some scholars who argue for a very early date. Sudhaus produced at the end of the nineteenth century an edition of the *Aetna*[31] which amazed Robinson Ellis because of 'the extravagant self-confidence' with which the editor defended the 'obvious corruption of the manuscript tradition'.[32] The British scholar crowned a series of penetrating articles in the *Journal of Philology* by publishing a text and commentary on the poem[33] which contains 'much to charm those who are still capable of being delighted by an ingenious and scholarly emendation'.[34] Five years later J. Vessereau, who believed that Virgil wrote the *Aetna*, produced a useful French edition.[35] J. Wight Duff and A. M. Duff were responsible for the *Minor Latin Poets*[36] in the Loeb Classical Library, a volume which conveniently assembles a number of the less well-known writers. It includes the *Aetna* and the *Eclogues* of Calpurnius. These pastorals of the Neronian age were put into verse by E. J. L. Scott[37] 'at the urgent request of Robinson Ellis'.[38] Together with the pastorals of a later poet Nemesianus, who lies outside our purview, they were printed in a valuable critical edition by Caesar Giarratano.[39] His second edition contained also the Einsiedeln Fragments and was considered by J. S. Phillimore 'a useful, convenient, and in every way meritorious book'.[40] Compared with other writers of the Silver Age Calpurnius has attracted very little attention in the world of scholarship. Perhaps this is as it should be. Virgil is below his best in the *Bucolics* and Calpurnius is no Virgil. Wight Duff withholds blame where he cannot praise. Summers suggests 'one could hardly look for a better example of the verse that Persius pilloried',[41] while Butler makes no attempt to conceal his contempt — 'these poems lack what is often the one saving grace of Silver Latin poetry, its extreme cleverness'.[42]

The fabulist Phaedrus is more interesting and therefore more popular. We notice first Ulysse Robert's *Les Fables de Phèdre*[43] (a book consisting in the main of two copies of the *Codex Pithoeanus*), not because the volume advances the study of the author but because it provides an excellent example of a book produced rather for its *species* than for its *res*, and also since it makes a splendid foil to a notable work published in the same city in the following year, Louis Havet's *Phaedri Augusti liberti fabulae Aesopiae*.[44] The 'cross-nibbed pen'[45] of Housman delivered the following judgment on its learned author — 'the most vigilant critic he (Phaedrus) has ever had and the most egotistical he can ever possibly have'.[46] This volume contains (as one would expect from Havet) a long and careful essay on metric. The Oxford Text of Phaedrus appeared a quarter of a century later and was edited by J. P. Postgate,[47] whose ear for the Latin iambic seemed to the merciless editor of Manilius to fall short of perfection.[48] After another four years was published a text and prose translation (in French) by Alice Brenot,[49] who with minor adaptations and additions reproduced the version by Chauvin. Recently there has appeared a large and sumptuous edition of the *Fables* by L. Herrmann,[50] a volume the usefulness of which is scarcely in direct proportion to its size. The author, noted for his vast erudition and surprising originality, has been described as possessing 'une faculté étonnante de combiner les faits en d'audacieuses hypothèses conduisant aux résultats les plus inattendus'.[51] The White Queen, it will be remembered, managed to believe as many as six impossible things before breakfast. Her amiable eccentricities (or a diluted form of them) are, though uncommon, not without parallel in the academic world. Hence Housman's statement, 'the art of understanding Lucan makes no steady and continuous progress and relapse accompanies advance',[52] may be extended from Lucan to Latin literature in general.

In our brief survey of miscellaneous verse we touch finally on the *Silvae* of Statius, a collection of poems on which many of the acutest minds of our generation have striven to throw light. Our starting point is the richly-documented edition of Friedrich Vollmer,[53] furnished with a learned commentary, critical apparatus, *auctores*, *imitationes*, *testimonia*, prosodiacal and metrical appendix, and thorough analyses of each poem. Vollmer's text, in the main conservative, was by no means acceptable to all scholars. But new editions speedily followed. Alfred Klotz, to whom readers of Statius owe no small obligation, considerably improved upon Vollmer's text in his edition of 1900.[54] Fasc. iv of the *Corpus Poetarum Latinorum*[55] included a good text of the *Silvae* by J. P. Postgate, the general editor. The following year saw the first edition (the second followed in 1920) of the Oxford Text of the *Silvae*.[56] Postgate himself urged the need of a thorough revision of this work but allowed that it gives 'the best modern text of the *Silvae* which has been *separately* published'[57] (the italics are mine). D. A. Slater's prose translation of the *Silvae*[58] (the first English version ever made of this work) is a courageous and largely successful effort. In a brief mention of this book J. F. Dobson remarked 'an English commentary is still badly needed'.[59] The need remains. The first volume of the Loeb Statius contains the *Silvae*.[60] The rendering though sometimes jerky and unduly literal is in the main accurate. The corresponding volume in the 'Budé' Series,[61] representing the joint work of H. J. Izaac (who died in 1938) and Henri Frère, is amply annotated and contains a reliable translation. The limits of this summary exclude the mention of much valuable work on the manuscript tradition and of numerous important discussions of the relations between the poet and his contemporaries.

Statius' fame in European literary tradition rests rather on his epics than on his minor poems, and to epics we now turn, though first to Lucan who has chronological priority. For Lucan and for the study of Lucan[62] much has been done since the last decade of the nineteenth century. The story begins with Carl Hosius' excellent critical text of Lucan (the first of three notable editions)[63] which, appearing in 1892, 'marked an important epoch in the critical study of Lucan'.[64] Two years later came P. Lejay's scholarly edition of the first book of Lucan,[65] equipped with commentary and an excellent introduction. C. M. Francken's edition of the *Pharsalia*[66] which appeared in two volumes was so disfigured by gross errors that its good qualities were at first unrecognized. Housman has weighed his merits and demerits in a masterly paragraph of abusive prose with a neat 'surprise ending'.[67] J. P. Postgate's commentary on the seventh book was published in 1896 and revised in 1913.[68] In 1917 he edited the eighth book for the same series;[69] this, at the time of writing, is regrettably out of print. Over twenty years later the Pitt Press published an edition of the first book by R. J. Getty,[70] which, though marred by certain errors and inferior to the work of Postgate,[71] nevertheless contains much that is helpful to the student of Lucan. These three companion volumes have been mentioned together to show how much has been done to encourage the study of Lucan at school and university. Lucan's historical sources and kindred problems such as the order in which the books were composed were considered in an important volume by René Pichon.[72] Pichon upheld the view that Livy was practically the sole historical source behind the *Bellum Civile*, and believed that the three books alleged in Vacca's life of the poet to have been written first were II, VII and VIII. Housman's celebrated edition 'for the behoof of editors'[73] saw the light in 1926 and justly elicited superlatives from the reviewers. A. D. Nock regarded it as 'the event of the year, both for what it does for its author and as a model of sincere investigation and masterly condensation',[74] while by Alexander Souter it was judged 'one of the greatest events of the present century for the Latin scholar'.[75] The introduction contains a shrewd exposition of the peculiar difficulties of Lucan's text and a pungent summary of previous scholarship written as only Housman could write. The astronomical appendix is, as one would expect from the editor of Manilius, of particular value. I shall close by mentioning the translations of the *Bellum Civile* in the Loeb[76] and Budé[77] series. The Loeb volume by J. D. Duff reprints, with insignificant deviations, the text of Housman; Duff attended Housman's lectures on Lucan at Cambridge and acknowledges his debt in the preface. This is one of the best volumes in an excellent, if uneven, series. Both volumes of the Budé Lucan were reviewed by Housman[78] and pronounced unsatisfactory. A long procession of detected errors was headed by the remark (mild for its author) — 'This translation is not quite all that a translation should be.' The study of Lucan does not stand still; conjectures and elucidations regularly appear; but one would give much for a new commentary on the whole epic, or, if that is too much to hope for, a revision of Postgate's editions, particularly the unobtainable Book VIII.

Considerably less has been done in the last half-century for the text and exegesis of Valerius Flaccus than for Lucan. W. C. Summers, who regarded Valerius as the second in merit of the Roman epic poets, wrote an excellent introduction to this neglected poet, entitled *A Study of the Argonautica of Valerius Flaccus*.[79] Three years later came P. Langen's 'diligent, intelligent, honest, and unpretentious commentary',[80] words of praise indeed considering who wrote them.[81] J. B. Bury was responsible for the text of the *Argonautica* which appeared in Fasc. III of Postgate's *Corpus*.[82] An extremely conservative text was published by Caesar Giarratano[83] in 1904 and Otto Kramer's Teubner edition[84] appeared nine years later. The first book of the epic was later translated by H. G. Blomfield[85] in a prose version which combined biblical English with modern colloquialisms. J. H. Mozley translated the whole epic for the Loeb Classical Library[86] in 1934. Unfortunately this is the only text of the *Argonautica* which can be easily obtained by British students. Neither text nor translation reaches the general level of the Loeb series. Of the text H. Haffter (referring to the editions used by Schulte in his *Index Verborum Valerianus*) remarked 'Mozley liess er mit Recht beiseite'.[87] A fairly recent monograph on the manuscript tradition deserving of mention is

R. J. Getty's *The Lost St. Gall MS. of Valerius Flaccus*,[88] which is both learned and lucid. Modern scholars are generally of the opinion that the *Argonautica* was composed wholly in the reign of Domitian, and some good work has been done on the interrelation of the poets writing under that emperor. There are signs that a new text is in preparation; when this comes it will be very welcome.

The epics of Statius have (throughout our period) attracted considerable attention from scholars, some of whom after making themselves familiar with the poems have discovered in them much that is pleasing, while others have regarded them as a field of combat, in which victories might be gained after strenuous grappling with textual problems, metrical puzzles and unparalleled obscurities of language. In 1892 Rudolph Helm[89] attempted to assess the obligations of Statius in the *Thebaid* to earlier poets; the book is diffuse but contains useful material which was to be developed by later writers. At the close of the nineteenth century was issued the third volume of the Teubner Statius,[90] left unfinished by the death of Kohlmann. This contains the late *commentarii* of Lactantius Placidus on the *Achilleid* and the *Thebaid*, and is far more accurate than earlier versions. The text of the two Statian epics in Postgate's *Corpus* is the work of A. S. Wilkins.[91] It was closely followed by three excellent works from the pen of Léon Legras. The smallest of these — *Les Puniques et la Thébaïde* — is an offprint from REA 7 (1905); the title explains itself. *Les Légendes thébaïnes dans l'Épopée et la Tragédie grecques*[92] gives the background of the Theban story and serves as a valuable introduction to Statius' version. But it is for his notable *Étude sur la Thébaïde de Stace*[93] that Silver Latin scholars owe the deepest obligation to Legras. It covers literary sources, epic treatment, imitations of earlier authors, style, language, and prosody, and makes excellent reading. It has been compared to Heinze's *Epische Technik*.[94] Writing in 1953 I should say it stands midway between Heinze and Pierre Fargue's *Claudien*, a book written nearly thirty years after Legras. A new Teubner *Thebaid* appeared in 1910; this edition by Alfred Klotz[95] provides the basis of modern textual study. It is marked everywhere (except in the realm of prosody) by great learning and balanced judgments. The Loeb text and translation was made available in 1928.[96] Though better than the Valerius Flaccus, it is by no means outstanding.

Yet for all that it is very welcome since there is no other prose translation in English. Two Dutch editions published in 1934 by the same press help to fill a large vacuum. H. Heuvel's *P. Papinii Statii Thebaidos liber primus*[97] contains a Dutch translation and copious exegesis in Latin. H. W. Fortgen in a companion volume[98] has treated the elaborate funeral rites celebrated for Opheltes, the babe of Hypsipyle and victim of a monstrous serpent. The epics of Statius bristle with such formidable difficulties that one fears the gestatory period of a new commentary will resemble that of an elephant. There is comfort in the knowledge that competent scholars in Britain and elsewhere are striving to meet this need.

For Statius' unfinished *Achilleid* not so much has been done. A. S. Wilkins' text in the *Corpus Poetarum Latinorum* has been mentioned above. Alfred Klotz's edition[99] contains a valuable description of the late ninth-century *Codex Puteanus*. H. W. Garrod edited the *Achilleid* (with the *Thebaid*) not with complete success for the Oxford Classical Texts.[100] From Italy has come recently a critical text and commentary on the poem by Silvia Jannaconne.[101] This has not yet been seen by the present writer who records, however, that it has been favourably reviewed.[102]

It is much more fashionable to vie with others in seeking pejorative epithets sufficiently strong to describe the longest epic poem in Classical Latin than to read the *Punica* with a mind emptied of the prejudice born of the lecture room and the histories of literature. Abuse of Silius — the Aunt Sally of Roman literature — often appears to serve as a kind of compensation for an attempt to push too far the claims of some other writer not in the first class. The last twenty years of the nineteenth century and the first decade of the twentieth saw the publication of numerous useful monographs on this author embracing historical sources, similes, epithets and syntactical peculiarities. Our starting point for a modern text is the edition of Ludwig Bauer,[103] an industrious and astute scholar. W. E. Heitland in an important paper published a few years later discussed the 81 verses (*Punica* 8. 145-225) found in the Aldine edition of 1523 and nowhere else and declared them genuine.[104] Bauer's work was revised and corrected by W. C. Summers, the editor of the *Punica* in Postgate's *Corpus*.[105] In the next thirty years no major work of general interest was produced, though Silian studies were far from stagnation. The Loeb translation of Silius undertaken by J. D. Duff and published in 1934[106] is a superlative performance; for accuracy and lucidity it has few rivals in the series. The introduction, necessarily short, is scrupulously fair, the notes are brief and apposite, and there is a useful index of proper names. In 1935 W. M. Calder found in Caria the top of an inscribed marble basis giving the name of the poet — Tiberius Catius Asconius Silius Italicus — who was proconsul of Asia ca. A.D. 77.[107] D. J. Campbell argued from the cognomen Asconius that the poet was born in Patavium.[108] In the same year (1936) J. Nicol's book *The Historical and Geographical Sources used by Silius Italicus*[109] was published; this embodies an admirable account of the researches of continental scholars on the poet's sources and a synthesis of their results, and is the first book published in English on this subject. I am loath to dismiss Silius without hazarding the observation that the time is ripe for a revaluation of his poetic gifts. While admitting that the grain is hidden beneath much chaff I submit that the better passages of the *Punica* compare favourably in respect of strength, simplicity, and sentiment with much that a student accepts without question and reads without initial bias derived from prejudiced and sometimes misinformed sources.[110]

It remains to discuss satire and epigram. The third and last edition of *The Satires of A. Persius Flaccus* (J. Conington's work edited by H. Nettleship) appeared in 1893.[111] This text, translation, and commentary on the Stoic homilist is still a valuable work. W. C. Summers edited Persius for the *Corpus Poetarum Latinorum*,[112] and three years later came the Oxford text of Persius and Juvenal prepared by S. G. Owen.[113] Housman flatly rejected Owen's observation (*correpto* rogas *more Plautino*) on the prosody of 5.134 (*rogas? en saperdas advehe Ponto*), affirming that, if the reading were correct, the shortening was due not to Plautine but to colloquial influence.[114] F. Leo's *Persii Iuuenalis Sulpiciae Saturae*[115] is notable rather for the editor's arguments in favour of a double recension of Juvenal than for any outstanding novelties in the text of Persius. The amplest treatment of the young Stoic's poems is that of F. Villeneuve, whose two volumes *Essai sur Perse*[116] and *Les Satires de Perse*[117] exhaustively discuss all aspects of the poet's work. At times, especially in the search for Stoic terminology in the satires, the author seems to push his theories further than the facts warrant. Translations of Persius made in the twentieth century include those of S. Hemphill,[118] G. G. Ramsay[119] and J. Tate[120] (the last-named a neat version in rhymed couplets), A. Cartault[121] — in French — and, very recently, Otto Seel[122] (in German). Numerous articles and essays have dealt with his criticism of literature, his Stoicism, his indebtedness to earlier writers (to Lucilius and Horace in particular), and the sincerity of his austere but friendly disposition.

Persius and Martial are as different as two poets of the Silver Age could possibly be. Martial is rarely read from cover to cover, and few could claim (or would care to admit) they have understood all he wrote. And yet from time to time attempts are made to whitewash Martial, attempts which carry little conviction. Luigi Pepe, for example, in his attractive little book *Marziale*[123] suggests that 'malgrado ogni apparenza Marziale e moralmento sano'. To embrace the opposite error and judge him peculiarly fitted to make mud pies is just as uncritical. Advanced study of Martial (irrespective of textual criticism and examination of metre and prosody) seeks to discover how Martial influenced and was influenced by contemporary writers, what were his obligations to Greek epigrammatists and earlier Roman poets, by what stylistic devices he introduced variety into common themes, and within what limits his epigrams can be used as source-material for social life and for such manifestations as emperor-worship. The magnificent edition of Martial by Friedlaender mentioned earlier, together with his indispensable *Sittengeschichte Roms* (the seventh enlarged and revised edition of which is available in a useful but not wholly reliable English translation), go a long way towards answering these and similar questions. But though tribute is justly due to the *Wissenschaft* of the German, the first great modern text is that of W. M. Lindsay.[124] 'Students of Martial', wrote Housman, 'now live in an age which was begun by Professor Lindsay's edition of 1903, one of those works which are such boons to mankind that their shortcomings must be forgiven them.'[125] J. D. Duff's text in the *Corpus Poetarum Latinorum*[126] owes much to Lindsay's devoted services on behalf of Martial. Twenty years later W. Heraeus' *M. Valerii Martialis epigrammaton libri*[127] signalized a further textual advance. The Teubner editor supplied the *testimonia* which Lindsay had for the most part ignored. In praising Heraeus Housman gently alludes to his own 'insufferable arrogance' — 'Mr. Heraeus makes choice among the lections of the MSS. with a judgment which I am bound to regard as good because it so often coincides with my own'.[128]

From texts to translations, two of which are versions of the complete works: Walter Ker surmounted with credit the unenviable task of putting Martial into English dress. Those familiar with the Loeb *Martial*[129] will readily approve Wight Duff's commendation of Ker's adroitness in 'translating the maximum possible of a writer who can be ineffably coarse'.[130] The Budé *Martial*[131] was entrusted to the capable hands of H. J. Izaac, who executed an admirably accurate version in lucid French. Many scholars have tried their hand at translating single poems or selections. Readers of *The Silver Age* will know Wight Duff's own verse-renderings. Perhaps the best-known selection in English is *Martial's Epigrams: Translations and Imitations*[132] by A. L. Francis and H. F. Tatum. Otto Weinreich in *Studien zu Martial*[133] has discussed the poet's relation to the later Greek epigrammatists; he has written well on the way in which common themes are varied, and has investigated the usage of mythology in adulation of the emperor. Part of the same ground is, as the title promises, trodden by Orsola Autore in *Marziale e l'Epigramma greco*.[134] Eulogistic language applied to Domitian is treated at length in the excellent monograph of Franz Sauter, *Der römische Kaiserkult bei Martial und Statius*.[135] As studies of the interrelation of contemporary writers necessarily have much common ground, I shall mention only one, 'The literary influence of Martial upon Juvenal,'[136] written at the beginning of the period under review by a capable editor of the satirist. The studies referred to above make up, it need hardly be said, only a very small fraction of the total contribution to the text and exegesis of a poet who, whatever his shortcomings, is unlikely to suffer neglect.

We turn finally to Juvenal, without question the greatest of the Silver Latin poets. The interpretation of the Roman satirist — like the writing of verse at Rome — has been undertaken with zeal, if not always with discretion, both by the *docti* and the *indocti*. From such an *embarras de choix* must be chosen a few significant items, lest the general outline be obscured by a profusion of detail. Three years after the publication of Friedlaender's Juvenal (mentioned above) the first edition of an excellent commentary, that of J. D. Duff,[137] was placed on the market. Duff generously acknowledges (on page v) his debt to the learned edition of

J. E. B. Mayor, a work lying outside our scope. Generations of students and teachers have profited and will long continue to profit from Duff's sensitive and sensible annotations. When Housman, in a review of an American commentary by H. L. Wilson,[138] wished to indicate his satisfaction, he placed it in the same category as Duff's book, which 'unpretending school edition'[139] is cited in his own *Juvenal* as a model of 'candour and clear perception'.[140] In 1899 E. O. Winstedt unearthed in the Bodleian Library and published in the CR of the same year a fragment (34 lines) of the sixth satire coming after line 365 and found nowhere else. A full account of the varying fortunes of *codex Canonicianus class. Lat. 41 Bodleianus* would require a separate chapter, so extensive and so complicated is the 'literature' it has provoked. Here it must suffice to say that for many years most Latinists (it had its enemies) accepted it as authentic; hence it was incorporated in new texts as they were issued. In Leo's revision of Bücheler's Juvenal[141] published two years after the latter's death the newly-recovered verses formed the base on which was erected a fresh argument for the double recension of the satires. As the years passed fresh doubts were cast upon the authenticity of the lost portion, which Housman amusingly describes as having been brought out by Nemesis 'from the arsenals of divine vengeance'[142] (i.e. the Bodleian Library) to punish Friedlaender for his groundless confidence in the completeness of Juvenal's text. In 1936 the hard-worked pen of the inimitable scholar-poet was laid down for the last time and 'classical scholarship lost its fine edge'.[143] Since his death Ulrich Knoche, the greatest living authority on the manuscripts of Juvenal, who had suggested in *Die Überlieferung Juvenals*[144] that the Bodleian Fragment may have been given in the early scholia at the very beginning of the text, has excluded these verses from his own edition.[145] B. Axelson condemned them also in Δρᾶγμα *Martino P. Nilsson*.[146] So, unless a stout champion comes speedily to the aid of Winstedt's manuscript, it seems that some well-known histories of literature will cry for correction.

Housman's *D. Iunii Iuuenalis Saturae* incorporated and defended the suspected verses. Of the brilliance of this book much has been said elsewhere. The reader should, however, be reminded that Housman, who considered his task (like Madvig's before him) to be that of 'maintaining reason against superstition',[147] wrote